PROVIDIN GLOBAL PUBLIC GOODS

MANAGING GLOBALIZATION

Global public goods are an often ignored but enormously important aspect of multilateralism. Whether we are talking about preserving biodiversity, preventing climate change, fighting the spread of communicable diseases, establishing rules for trade and aviation, or setting global standards of human rights, it is impossible for any single state to secure such goods on its own. Quite the contrary, global public goods can only be attained if countries work together, and globalization has only increased this fundamental interdependence. This book offers practical suggestions for improving the way in which the community of nations addresses common vulnerabilities and seizes common opportunities, and it highlights a basic truth about our times: global problems require global action.

Kofi A. Annan
Secretary-General
United Nations
July 2002

PROVIDING GLOBAL PUBLIC GOODS

MANAGING GLOBALIZATION

EDITED BY
INGE KAUL
PEDRO CONCEIÇÃO
KATELL LE GOULVEN
RONALD U. MENDOZA

Published for
The United Nations Development Programme

New York   Oxford
Oxford University Press
2003

Oxford University Press

Oxford   New York

Auckland   Bangkok   Buenos Aires   Cape Town   Chennai
Dar es Salaam   Delhi   Hong Kong   Istanbul   Karachi   Kolkata
Kuala Lumpur   Madrid   Melbourne   Mexico City   Mumbai   Nairobi
São Paulo   Shangai   Singapore   Taipei   Tokyo   Toronto

and an associated company in Berlin

Published by Oxford University Press, Inc.
198 Madison Avenue, New York, New York, 10016

Oxford is a registered trademark of Oxford University Press

Library of Congress Cataloging-in-Publication Data

Providing global public goods: managing globalization/ edited by Inge Kaul, Pedro
    Conceição, Katell Le Goulven, Ronald U. Mendoza
    p. cm.
    Includes bibliographical references and index.
    ISBN 0-19-515740-0 (cloth). — ISBN 0-19-515741-9 (paper)
1. Public goods. 2. Globalization. 3.International economic relations. I. Kaul, Inge. II.
    Conceição, Pedro. III. Le Goulven, Katell. IV. Mendoza, Ronald U.

HB846.5 .P76 2002
363—dc21

                                                                    2002074902

Cover and design: Gerald Quinn, Quinn Information Design, Cabin John, Maryland

Editing and production management: Communication Development Incorporated, Washington, DC

Printed in the United States of America
on acid-free paper

"This book fills a critical gap. It helps the business sector understand the provision of global public goods and provides a platform for dialogue between private and public actors."

MARSHALL N. CARTER
Chairman and Chief Executive Officer (Retired)
State Street Bank and Trust Company

"The collection of essays and studies in *Providing Global Public Goods* is a welcome addition to the literature. They fill a gap in the development and economic discourse and bring up issues that are mostly neglected. The very concept of public goods, both national and global, necessarily means that 'globalization' is a process of political economy—and nothing is inevitable or irreversible."

CHAKRAVARTHI RAGHAVAN
South North Development Monitor/
Third World Network

"This volume constructively advances the theory and assessment of global public goods. It offers innovative approaches to address the deep inadequacies of many existing global institutional arrangements. It will undoubtedly be an important reference for academics, researchers, and policymakers interested in fresh approaches to global institutional reform."

BARBARA STOCKING
Director, Oxfam

"Africa has reason to be skeptical about globalization. But the strength of the case presented in this book gives encouragement to all who seek just and sustainable development."

AKILAGPA SAWYERR
Association of African Universities

"UNDP has done the world a great service by contributing a global public goods perspective to discussions of globalization."

"Global public goods such as international financial stability, environmental sustainability, and infectious disease control are underprovided, often dramatically. *Providing Global Public Goods: Managing Globalization* is a must read for those interested in guideposts toward a prosperous, sustainable, and equitable 21st century."

"I found this book extremely interesting. It significantly advances our knowledge about a critical challenge faced by the international community: the provision of global public goods. Both students and practitioners of international relations will find this volume an indispensable guide."

"If sustainable development is to become a reality, the debate on global public goods needs to be vigorously pursued. This comprehensive volume opens up the discussion on managed globalization."

"Providing global public goods is exactly what the doctor ordered for a global public either worried about or discontented with globalization. This book is indispensable for those who need to understand globalization—as well as those who think they know enough about the subject."

SOLITA C. MONSOD
Minister of Socio-Economic Planning,
Philippines (1986–1989)
University of the Philippines

"Financial stability, the environment, the fight against major pandemics, and everyday security are no longer only national goals but global public goods. We need to think afresh about how to provide and finance them."

DOMINIQUE DE VILLEPIN
Minister of Foreign Affairs, France

"Protests against globalization have arisen from a sense of frustration among people who feel that the private sphere is growing without rules and regulations, at a cost to be borne by the rest of the society. Civil society organizations therefore demand equitable access for all, without arbitrariness, based on the right to development and protection of human rights. This book is a timely reminder of the issues at stake, and it offers an analytical framework to create a more equitable international order."

IRENE KHAN
Secretary-General, Amnesty International

"In today's global economy the production of private goods has taken precedence over the provision of public goods. Correcting this imbalance is a major policy challenge to which this book makes an important contribution."

GEORGE SOROS
President and Chairman,
Soros Fund Management LLC

CONTENTS

PROLOGUE

RICHARD A. MUSGRAVE AND PEGGY B. MUSGRAVE

The distinction between public and private goods was first made in the late 18th century, when Adam Smith (1994 [1776] p. 779) noted the existence of certain products "which though they may be in the highest degree advantageous to a great society are, however, of such a nature that the profits could never repay the expenses to any individual or small number of individuals, and which it therefore cannot be expected that any individual or small number of individuals should erect." Thus Smith, though an ardent advocate of the market, recognized that it does not solve all problems. Moreover, he concluded that because the market fails to provide public goods, government must do so.

Ever since, public goods have been an intriguing issue in economic theory. In addition, debates on what should be provided and who should pay have been central to the political economy of public finance. This is not surprising given that such debates involve issues related to distribution and the balance between states and markets.

Public goods create challenges because their benefits are not limited to a single consumer or group of consumers—as with private goods—but are available to all. Consumption of private goods is rival, while consumption of public goods (at least pure public goods) is nonrival. This distinction initially guided two types of analysis of public goods. First, conditions for their efficient provision were shown to differ from those for private goods. In the 1880s marginal utility theory asserted that provision of both public and private goods should equate costs and benefits at the margin.

But as Samuelson (1954) showed 70 years later, that relationship differs for the two types of goods. Efficient provision of private goods calls for their marginal rate of transformation in production to equal their marginal rate of substitution in consumption. But efficient provision of public goods calls for their marginal rate of transformation in production to equal the sum of their marginal rates of substitution in consumption. This distinction has been of primary interest to economic theorists—but it is only half the story.

Determining the efficient level of public goods requires knowing consumer preferences. That knowledge is often assumed as given in theoretical models of optimal provision, but obtaining it is a major challenge when it comes to actual policy. Thus a second distinction is made between public and private goods. To obtain the benefits of private goods, individual consumers must bid and pay for their share of them. These activities, in turn, tell the market what to supply and what consumers will pay—enabling the market to act as an efficient provider.

But with public goods benefits are nonrival: benefits available to an individual consumer are also available to all other members of the group. If many people are affected and exclusion from benefits is impractical (as with policies to improve air quality), individual consumers will not reveal their preferences and will not bid. Instead they will free ride, relying on others to pay. But market failures occur in the absence of consumer bidding. Thus an alternative mechanism, involving public budgets and taxes, is needed to pay for and provide such goods. Wicksell (1882) was the first to focus on this failure of preference revelation, suggesting that it could be overcome in democratic societies, where voters can support politicians whose tax and spending policies meet their wishes. With mandatory acceptance of political outcomes, consumers have an incentive to reveal their preferences, suggesting an efficient provision of public goods. Securing preference revelation through the political process opens a second dimension of public goods analysis, pursued now as an issue in public choice.

While the core of the public goods problem rests with nonrival consumption and nonexcludable benefits, in practice goods may have aspects of both privateness and publicness. Exclusion may be possible—for example, by charging a toll to cross a bridge. But the charge will be inefficient if the bridge is underused, because in that case the bridge's benefits are nonrival. Charging becomes efficient only when a facility is crowded, because entry of additional users reduces each user's benefits. Where crowding occurs, user clubs may serve as a market-like mechanism to secure efficient provision without requiring the state to step in. The potential for such "club goods" (Buchanan 1965) has been of major interest in local finance, as shown by the widely used example of swimming pools. But it appears to be of limited significance in the global context.

Nonrival availability of benefits to all members of the benefiting group is the essential characteristic of public goods, but the group has to be defined. Groups can be defined along various dimensions. Public concerts provide benefits to people who like music but are of no value to the deaf. Many groups can be considered. But among them the area over which benefits extend is of particular concern to this volume, with its linkage of public and global in the role of global public goods.

The benefits from some public goods—such as legal institutions, defense systems, and nationwide highways—extend over the entire nation-state in which they are provided. The benefits from others, such as local roads or traffic lights, cover a limited area. Using a voting process to reveal preferences implies that public goods should be chosen and paid for by those who benefit from them. This suggests that goods with a narrow range of benefits be voted on and paid for locally, those with a nationwide range of benefits be provided centrally, and those with a global range of benefits be provided globally.

Because benefiting regions may not coincide with political boundaries, arranging for the provision of public goods may require determining and designing jurisdictional boundaries. Moreover, the benefits of public goods provided by one state may spill over into others. As a result provision becomes an international and, with unlimited benefit space, global issue. Truly global public goods stand at the end of a chain stretching from local street cleaning to national defense and environmental protection to global warming. The more global is the region over which benefits extend, the greater is the need for global policy instruments.

The discussion so far has addressed the nonrival nature of the benefits and provision of public goods. A parallel problem exists in the prevention of public bads. Externalities generated by country A's production or consumption may be harmful to countries B and C. Again, because the market does not restrain the generation of external costs, a public policy instrument—fiscal or regulatory—is needed to account for them. Thus the points made about the provision of public goods, including the role of spatial incidence, also apply to the reduction of public bads. Reducing the social bad of pollution supports the social good of clean air, and the cost of cleaner air may be reflected in a higher cost of driving polluting vehicles. Externalities can be harmful as well as beneficial, and corrective policies are needed in either case.

As suggested by this brief prologue and as clearly shown by the far-reaching analyses in this volume, moving public goods and bads to the global level poses many challenges. Their provision also raises some broader concerns, including the role of global public goods in equitable global distribution. When provision of public goods (or prevention of bads) is handled through interjurisdictional agreements, the relatively small number of actors means that agreements can generally be reached through bargaining. As the Coase theorem (1960) shows, such agreements might yield efficient outcomes whether country A is entitled to pollute and disturb B or whether country B is entitled not to be disturbed by A. But who benefits and who is harmed will differ according to how entitlements are assigned. If A is entitled to pollute, B must pay A to desist. But if B is entitled to protection, A must pay to disturb B. Both outcomes may be efficient, but the transaction does not resolve the need for an equitable result. For this, entitlements must be chosen.

More generally, the equitable provision of global public goods can be viewed as part of the challenge of achieving global equity—an all-encompassing public good. Thus provision of some goods and prevention of some bads must take into account equity considerations. But problems arise depending on the public good or bad in question. Reducing an activity with harmful externalities may be cheaper in a low-income country than in a high-income country, posing a conflict between efficiency and equity considerations. Compensating transfers can be used to resolve this conflict—including, if there is political will to provide them, transfers that can be used to acquire private goods. For many social goods, however, concern with global equity is not an issue.

The United Nations Development Programme and its Office of Development Studies are to be congratulated for having placed these vital issues at the center of their research. No sponsors are better suited to carry out this work. This volume extends the analysis and findings of its precursor (Kaul, Grunberg, and Stern 1999), with an emphasis on crucial issues of implementation. It broadens the concept of public goods in their many forms, examines the political process and instruments needed to deal with them efficiently and equitably, and provides an insightful set of case studies. As with its predecessor, no one concerned with the role of public goods in the global setting should miss this book.

REFERENCES

Buchanan, James. 1965. "An Economic Theory of Clubs." *Economica* 32 (125): 1–14.

Coase, Ronald. 1960. "The Problem of Social Cost." *Journal of Law and Economics* 3 (1): 1–44.

Kaul, Inge, Isabelle Grunberg, and Marc A. Stern, eds. 1999. *Global Public Goods: International Cooperation in the 21st Century.* New York: Oxford University Press.

Samuelson, Paul A. 1954. "The Pure Theory of Public Expenditure." *Review of Economics and Statistics* 36 (4): 387–89.

Smith, Adam. 1994 [1776]. *The Wealth of Nations: An Inquiry into the Nature and Causes.* New York, NY: Modern Library.

Wicksell, Knut. 1958 [1894]. "A New Principle of Just Taxation." In Richard A. Musgrave and Alan Peacock, eds., *Classics in the Theory of Public Finance.* London: Macmillan.

FOREWORD

The concept of global public goods is still new and somewhat unfamiliar. But it has huge implications not just for development but also for multilateral approaches to a wide range of pressing global problems. That is why we at the United Nations Development Programme (UNDP) have been enthusiastic supporters of research into a concept that we believe adds real value to efforts to address today's huge challenges.

Essentially, the concept of global public goods—or bads—tells us that we are not facing myriad problems and that disparate crises are not erupting for different reasons in nearly every sphere. Rather, we are facing just one major challenge: how to rethink and reorient public policymaking to catch up with today's new realities of interdependence and globalization.

Many of the world's main crises—from climate change to terrorism—have characteristics of global public bads. They affect all of us indiscriminately but hit those with the fewest assets more severely than those with private or national means to protect themselves against crises, risks, and human insecurity.

At a recent meeting of heads of UN system agencies, we went around the table and exchanged information on our work areas. News abounded on the ill effects of worsening global public bads: the International Civil Aviation Organization raised the issue of terrorism control, the World Health Organization cited global health crises, the International Monetary Fund pointed to international financial instability, the UN Environment Programme and others identified global environmental challenges, including the challenge of averting a global water crisis, and so on.

The time has come for all of us to remind ourselves that nationally we benefit from such public goods as traffic lights, public health care, libraries, and judicial systems. And that reminder highlights the pressing need to ask—and open a fully participatory debate on how to answer—the question of which global public goods we need to produce jointly in this age of open borders and increasingly intertwined national public domains.

We have made progress in forging international agreements and adopting resolutions stating political intentions to cooperate in key areas. But words need to be matched by actions, and actions often require financing—notably, financial incentives so that cooperation becomes economically worthwhile for all.

The global public goods agenda should be seen as a crucial but separate complement to development assistance efforts. The two must not be confused. Our view at UNDP is that addressing the global public goods agenda more effectively will enhance aid effectiveness. We need to meet both challenges together, in a determined and fully funded way.

Mark Malloch Brown
Administrator, United Nations Development Programme

ACKNOWLEDGMENTS

Experts, practitioners, and academics around the world contributed to this volume. Based on its antecedent, *Global Public Goods: International Cooperation in the 21st Century* (Oxford University Press, 1999), this book explores the provision of global public goods. Responses to the first volume in large part shaped the theme and focus of the present volume. We are most grateful to our interlocutors for their valuable comments and suggestions.

Special thanks are due to Mark Malloch Brown, the Administrator of the United Nations Development Programme (UNDP) for his support, personal interest, and dynamic leadership throughout this project. And we thank Zéphirin Diabré, Associate Administrator of UNDP, for his encouragement of our focus on the challenges of developing countries and the operationalization of the concept of global public goods.

We would also like to thank those who were kind enough to devote time and effort to peer reviewing and commenting on parts of the manuscript: Arnab Acharya, Nicola Acocella, Denis Aitken, Manuel Agosin, Yilmaz Akyüz, Diana Alarcón, George A. O. Alleyne, Jens Christopher Andvig, Daniel G. Arce M., Malik Amin Aslam, Scott Barrett, Robert Beaglehole, Keith Bezanson, Odile Blanchard, Kwesi Botchwey, Henk-Jan Brinkman, Thora Broughton, James M. Buchanan, the Canadian International Development Agency Global Public Goods Working Group, Richard Carson Jr., Margaret Catley-Carlson, William Cline, Anthony Clunies-Ross, Damien Conaré, Richard Cooper, John Cullis, Dana Dalrymple, Aleta Domdom, Michael Doyle, Nick Drager, Björn Ekman, Guzin Erlat, Andreas Ershammar, Tim Evans, Hazem Fahmy, Jean-Claude Faure, Marco Ferroni, Cary Fowler, Irene Freudenschuss-Reichl, Eduardo Galvez, José Goldemberg, Leo Goldstone, Isabelle Grunberg, Joyeeta Gupta, Catherine Gwin, Peter Haas, David Hall, Paul Harris, Pamela Hartigan, Virginia Haufler, Geoffrey Heal, Eric Helleiner, Peter Heller, Carlsten Helm, Heather Hudson, Dean Jamison, Raghbendra Jha, Michael Johnston, Philip Jones, Ahmad Kamal, Geoffrey Lamb, John Langmore, Kelley Lee, François Lerin, Edward Luck, Carlos Massad, Jorg Mayer, Rohinton Medhora, Andrea Mogni, Ashoka Mody, Susanna Moorehead, Françoise Moreau, Ramón Moreno, Benito Müller, Peggy B. Musgrave, Richard A. Musgrave, Jane Nelson, Alan Nicol, Carin Norberg, Kwabena Osei-Danquah, Sheila Page, Charles Perrings, P. G. Ponnapa, John Quiggin, Jacques Martin, J. Mohan Rao, Sanjay Reddy, Carmen Revenga, Dani Rodrik, Bruce Russett, Francisco Sagasti, Todd Sandler, Serdar Sayan, Roger Sedjo, Alfredo Sfeir-Younis, Jason F. Shogren, Udo Simonis, Richard Smith, Eugene Smolensky, Paul Bernd

Spahn, Janet Stotsky, Paul Streeten, Hannumappa Reddy Sudarshan, Lawrence Susskind, M.S. Swaminathan, Alexandre Taithe, Koy Thompson, Laurence Tubiana, Victor Venida, Ellen Wiegandt, John Williamson, Klaus Winkel, Ben White, Ngaire Woods, David Woodward, Oran Young, Christina Zarowsky, and Ian William Zartman.

Thanks also to our UNDP colleagues whose queries raised incisive issues and whose comments improved the analysis: Ali Al-Zatari, Ingvar Andersson, Francis Blain, Chandrika Bahadur, Tim Boyle, Moez Doraid, Michele Falavigna, Sakiko Fukuda-Parr, Andrew Hudson, Selim Jahan, Bruce Jenks, Thomas B. Johansson, Mumtaz Keklik, Kamal Malhotra, Brenda McSweeney, Saraswathi Menon, John Ohiorhenuan, Maxine Olson, Seeta Prabhu, Ramaswamy Sudarshan, Mark Suzman, Emma Torres, Håkan Tropp, Antonio Vigilante, and Mourad Wahba. We also thank Anne-Birgitte Albrectsen (Office of the Administrator), Normand Lauzon (United Nations Capital Development Fund), and the heads of UNDP's regional bureaus and their teams: Abdoullie Janneh (Africa), Rima Khalaf Hunaidi (Arab States), Elena Martínez (Latin America and the Caribbean), Kalman Mizsei (Europe and the Commonwealth of Independent States), and Hafiz Pasha (Asia and the Pacific).

We are grateful to the members of our Advisory Board for their guidance and advice during the two years of shaping and compiling this publication. We also thank delegates of the Permanent Missions to the United Nations for their support throughout this endeavor.

We benefited from the generous financial support of the Governments of Austria, Canada (through the International Development Research Center), France, Sweden, Switzerland, The Netherlands, and the United Kingdom. Additional support was provided by the MacArthur Foundation and the Rockefeller Foundation.

Nonetheless, the views expressed in this volume are those of the authors and do not necessarily reflect those of UNDP or of other institutions with which they are affiliated.

We are indebted to Masha Beliaeva, Vikas Nath, Grace Ryu (who also managed the book production process), and Mirjam Schnupf for valuable research assistance. We also acknowledge former Office of Development Studies team members Thorsten Benner, Kevin Morrison, Marc A. Stern, and Jan Martin Witte for their dedicated work on the project during its inception. Furthermore, we thank our interns Fiorella Aller, Edda Costarelli, Dan Bennett, Erik Eldhagen, Michael Faust, Yonita Grigovova, Maki Kobayashi, Asli Kubilay, Sarah Mulley, Kirsten Neumann, Frederic Nikiema, Daria Oziashvili, Maria Elena Pérez, Jonathan Rose, Klaus Stubkjaer Andersen, Achille Toto Same, and Mizuho Yokoi.

Our appreciation also goes out to Paul Donnelly and Stephen McGroarty of Oxford University Press for their help, Gerald Quinn for design, and Bruce Ross-

Larson, Meta de Coquereaumont, Paul Holtz, Alison Strong, and Kim Bieler of Communications Development Incorporated for editing and production of the volume.

Finally, we are grateful to Flora Aller, Rocio Kattis, and Zipora Vainberg-Rogg for their valuable administrative support.

Your comments on this publication are not only welcome but very much solicited. Please send your observations and inquiries about the book to the Office of Development Studies, UNDP, Uganda House, 336 East 45th Street, 4th floor, New York, NY 10017, USA. Fax: (212) 906 3676. Email: ods@undp.org. http:// www.globalpublicgoods.org.

CONTRIBUTORS

CECILIA ALBIN
University of Reading

DYNA ARHIN-TENKORANG
London School of Hygiene and Tropical
Medicine

SCOTT BARRETT
Johns Hopkins University

ODILE BLANCHARD
University of Grenoble

ARIEL BUIRA
Oxford University

RENÉ CASTRO
Central-American Business
Administration Institute

PAMELA CHASEK
International Institute for Sustainable
Development

PEDRO CONCEIÇÃO
United Nations Development
Programme

SARAH CORDERO
Central-American Business
Administration Institute

CARLOS M. CORREA
University of Buenos Aires

PATRICK CRIQUI
Institute of Energy Policy and Economics

MEGHNAD DESAI
London School of Economics and
Political Science

MICHAEL EDWARDS
Ford Foundation

PETER EIGEN
Transparency International

CHRISTIAN EIGEN-ZUCCHI
World Bank

MADHAV GADGIL
Indian Institute of Science

STEPHANY GRIFFITH-JONES
University of Sussex

DAVID HELD
London School of Economics and
Political Science

INGE KAUL
United Nations Development
Programme

ALBAN KITOUS
Institute of Energy Policy and Economics

MICHAEL KREMER
Harvard University

KATELL LE GOULVEN
United Nations Development
Programme

ANTHONY MCGREW
University of Southampton

LYLA MEHTA
University of Sussex

RONALD U. MENDOZA
United Nations Development
Programme

CHARLES PERRINGS
University of York

LAVANYA RAJAMANI
Oxford University

TODD SANDLER
University of Southern California

AGNAR SANDMO
Norwegian School of Economics and
Business Administration

LAURENT VIGUIER
University of Geneva

SIMON ZADEK
Institute of Social and Ethical
AccountAbility

OVERVIEW

WHY DO GLOBAL PUBLIC GOODS MATTER TODAY?
Inge Kaul, Pedro Conceição, Katell Le Goulven, and Ronald U. Mendoza

HOW TO IMPROVE THE PROVISION OF GLOBAL PUBLIC GOODS
Inge Kaul, Pedro Conceição, Katell Le Goulven, and Ronald U. Mendoza

WHY DO
GLOBAL PUBLIC GOODS
MATTER TODAY?

INGE KAUL, PEDRO CONCEIÇÃO, KATELL LE GOULVEN, AND RONALD U. MENDOZA

Globalization is often associated with increased privateness—with liberalizing the economy, moving more goods and services into markets, fostering integration of international markets, and encouraging such private cross-border economic activity as trade, investment, transport, travel, migration, and communication. These are certainly accompaniments of globalization.

But globalization is also—perhaps even quintessentially—about increased publicness—about people's lives becoming more interdependent. Events in one area of the globe often unleash repercussions that are felt around the world. And a growing collection of international policy principles, norms, treaties, laws, and standards is defining common rules for an ever-wider range of activities.

Just consider the elaborate rules governing "free trade." International markets are far from unfettered. Or think of the many international agreements on such global concerns as advancing peace and security, controlling terrorism and drug trafficking, averting the risk of global climate change, combating the spread of communicable diseases, or constructing global communication and transportation networks. All concern in some way the provision of public goods whose benefits—or, in the case of public "bads," costs—cut across borders. They prove that many national public goods have gone global. Globalization and global public goods are inextricably linked. In fact, whether—and how—global public goods are provided determines whether globalization is an opportunity or a threat. Not surprisingly, such provision issues are what multilateral negotiations—and civil society protests against them—are typically about.

Managing globalization requires understanding and shaping the provision of global public goods so that all parts of the global public benefit—a daunting challenge considering the world's diversity and complexity. Yet an inescapable one. The world today seems caught in an ever-widening spiral of global turmoil and crises. Breaking out of this precarious spiral requires a clear, decisive approach to providing global public goods. Open borders and the free flow of private economic activity are one side of globalization. Concerted cross-border public policy action must be the other side if globalization is to serve as a means of improving people's lives rather than wreaking havoc on them.

But how precisely are globalization and global public goods linked?

GLOBAL PUBLIC GOODS: A KEY INGREDIENT OF GLOBALIZATION

Public goods are best understood by contrasting them with private goods.[1] Private goods can be made excludable and exclusive in consumption. They are associated with clear property rights. And it is up to their owners to determine how to use them—to consume, lease, or trade them. Public goods, by contrast, are goods in the public domain: available for all to consume and so potentially affecting all people. Global public goods are public goods with benefits—or costs, in the case of such "bads" as crime and violence—that extend across countries and regions, across rich and poor population groups, and even across generations.

In part, global public goods—and bads—are the result of globalization. As financial markets become integrated, for example, what would once have been only a national financial crisis can become an international one, if not carefully managed from the start. Witness Mexico's "tequila" crisis in 1994–95, East Asia's financial crisis in 1997–98, the Russian Federation's debt default in 1998, and more recently, the Argentine financial crisis. But global public goods are also important drivers of globalization. Consider the international civil aviation system. Airplanes could not travel around the globe as swiftly and safely as they do without carefully harmonized national civil administration services and infrastructure. Managing globalization depends largely on providing global public goods.

While the link between globalization and public goods has rarely been explored,[2] globalization is being contested precisely where people feel overwhelmed and even attacked by goods—or, more often, bads—in the public domain, including contagious diseases, financial meltdowns, ecological calamities, and computer hacking. These bads tend to affect people indiscriminately. As Held and McGrew (in this volume, p. 186) argue, "contemporary globalization has several distinctive features. It is creating a world where the extensive reach of cross-country relations and networks is matched by their high intensity, velocity, and impact propensity across many facets of life. . . ." Under these conditions individual, including national, policy responses are often ineffective.

As a result many people around the world feel a pervasive uncertainty and sometimes even a loss of personal security. Looking at industrial countries, analysts see a "fearful North" (Bhagwati 1997), "timid prosperity" (Taylor-Gooby 2000), and the paradox of even the most powerful countries being unable to "go it alone" (Nye 2002). In developing countries globalization is said to generate an ever-growing feeling of "loss of autonomy" (Mahbubani 2001). And for people everywhere, globalization increasingly means a "runaway world" (Giddens 2000).

Some analysts wonder whether globalization has gone too far (Khor 2000; Rodrik 1997, 2001). They urge revisiting global public goods, such as the multilateral trade regime, to assess what has been lost (in national policy sovereignty) and what has been gained (in increased income and wealth). But others think globalization has not gone far enough. This group includes theorists such as Ohmae (1995), who foresee the end of nation-states and a trend toward region-states. It also includes civil society advocates. As Sen (1999) notes, the concerns of civil society often transcend affiliations of nationality, citizenship, and income group. Some feminists may want enhanced human rights worldwide to promote equity as a global norm, available for all to enjoy. Environmentalists may favor stricter international regimes to contain carbon dioxide emissions and avert global climate change. Perceptions of globalization vary across population groups—but they also vary by global public good.

Thus it is possible to pin down more precisely the reasons for discontent about globalization. Discontent often arises from the ways that global public goods are—or are not—provided.

The provision of public goods, including global public goods, can suffer from many problems. Sometimes a good may be lacking. Instead of peace, conflict and war may prevail, ravaging people's lives. And sometimes a good may exist but be shaped in such a way that it entails costs for some people or countries while benefiting others. For example, procedures for managing international financial crises have at times placed a heavier burden on borrowers than on lenders. So it is not only the *level* at which goods are provided that may affect people's lives; the *way* in which they are provided matters too.

There are growing expectations among countries and the general public that public goods—because they affect all—should be provided in a participatory and fair manner. Indeed, the clamor against globalization could be interpreted as a call for better provision of global public goods. The protests can be seen as the general public voicing its demand for a more effective say in global public matters—so that globalization can one day deliver on its promise as an opportunity for enriching the lives of all people.

Thus the "how to" of managing globalization is moving more and more to the political center stage. In fact, it is becoming a hotly debated issue. While some parties favor a "go it alone" approach, others call for deeper cross-border cooperation. Finding practical answers to the "how to" of managing globalization is an urgent challenge, because lack of consensus on process issues often holds back policy consensus and action. As a result global crises are proliferating, and the world is becoming entangled in an ever-denser net of political turmoil and disaster.

Inaction has a high price. Even for a small group of global public goods, the costs of underprovision amount to billions of dollars a year (see Conceição in this volume). Moreover, the costs of inaction—of failing to address problems of underprovision—dwarf those of corrective actions. More important, the costs of corrective actions would be incurred only until problems are solved, while the costs of inaction are continuous—and mounting.

WHAT THIS BOOK IS ABOUT

Given the critical link between globalization and global public goods, this volume presents a series of analyses aimed at contributing to a fuller understanding of the provision of global public goods. The analyses reveal that the provision of global public goods occurs largely without the benefit of relevant, up-to-date theory. Public goods theory often lags behind the rapidly evolving political and economic realities—marked by a state-centric and national focus and, consequently, providing poor support for advice on the provision of global public goods in today's multiactor world. Moreover, political decisionmaking is often poorly suited to the wide range of spillovers for many global public goods, with few sometimes deciding the fate of many. In addition, financing for global public goods is often perceived as aid—distorting the value of the goods, sending misleading policy signals, and confusing investment decisions. And in many cases the production of global public goods is impeded or defeated by organizational divides between economic sectors, between "domestic" and "foreign," and even between markets and states.

The result is a serious mismatch between the inclusive, multifaceted nature of many global challenges and the exclusive, fractured way in which public policy is often made. Despite an ever-growing volume of international conferencing and decisionmaking, global public bads linger on and cross-border spillovers continue.

The provision of public goods today—nationally and internationally—resembles the provision of public goods in the Middle Ages. It involves multiple authorities and actors of varying power at different jurisdictional levels, reacting to crises in ways that are moved more by "political compulsion than concern for all" (Keane 2001, p. 4).

Although the analyses in this volume point to many weaknesses, they also provide encouraging and constructive policy messages. They suggest that it is desirable and feasible to correct many current problems. In particular, they propose four main ways of improving the provision of global public goods and making globalization more manageable:

- *Refurbishing the analytical toolkit*—to better reflect current realities in public goods provision.
- *Matching circles of stakeholders and decisionmakers*—to create opportunities for all to have a say about global public goods that affect their lives.
- *Systematizing the financing of global public goods*—to get incentives right and secure adequate private and public resources for these goods.

- *Spanning borders, sectors, and groups of actors*—to foster institutional interaction and create space for policy entrepreneurship and strategic issue management.

The analyses confirm that reforming the *process* of public policymaking is key to managing globalization better. As the contributions to this volume demonstrate, in many global issue areas countries from the most advanced to the least developed increasingly find cooperation necessary to achieve national goals. Indeed, the fate of many nations has become increasingly intertwined, transforming what were once national policy issues into regional issues—and regional issues into global ones. Thus as issues such as HIV/AIDS, financial stability, and peace and security bring nations into a shared fate, so too should they bring them together as partners in appropriately reformed public policymaking. What this volume proposes is that examining today's major policy challenges through the *lens of global public goods* is key in guiding the reform of public policymaking.

The authors of this volume recognize, of course, the basic differences in interests that mark globalization and international cooperation today. These differences are difficult to resolve, and care must be taken not to complicate them further. But the analyses here show that many such differences occur for conceptual and technical reasons, not political ones. Therefore, it is important to focus on understanding the nature of global public goods and explaining precisely how their provision works—and could work better. Managing globalization requires vision as well as attention to detail.

CHARTING THE WAY: WHAT THE BOOK IS BASED ON

This book is a sequel to *Global Public Goods: International Cooperation in the 21st Century* (Kaul, Grunberg, and Stern 1999). That volume examined a series of global issues through the analytical lens of global public goods. It was an attempt to explain to a wider audience the concept of public goods and to make it a more common instrument of policy analysis and policymaking, particularly for global public goods. Indeed, many readers found the concept to be a powerful tool for understanding global challenges. Follow-up discussions were dominated by three questions involving the meaning of the three words that make up the term *global public good*.

- The most frequent question was, Who decides whether to make a good public or private? As the literature on public goods points out, publicness and privateness often are not innate properties. Goods can be—and in the course of history repeatedly have been—shifted from one side of the public-private continuum to the other.
- Many penetrating questions were asked about the globalness of goods, which, as will be seen, can be understood as a dimension of publicness. Readers pointed out that many global public goods are familiar to people

worldwide as local and national public goods. Take intellectual property rights regimes, which not long ago were firmly in the realm of sovereign national policymaking. Some local communities even had institutions for keeping critical knowledge (about the medicinal effects of plants, for example) in the public domain and enabling all to benefit from collective wisdom and experience. As intellectual property rights regimes go global, national policy choices are narrowing. The question thus is, Who decides what to make global?

- For the word *good* (or service), commentators noted that the challenges to which the notion of global public goods applies have long been on national and international policy agendas. To date they have been called "global challenges" or "global concerns." What is the added advantage of looking at them through the lens of global public goods?

In preparing this volume, these three key words—*public, global,* and *good*[3]—were reexamined to help shape the analyses and recommendations in the various chapters. To situate readers and help explain the volume's perspective, it is important to describe at the outset how the notions of public, global, and good are now viewed.

Bringing the public back in: remembering and reenvisioning publicness

Public and private are used in many different, often puzzling ways. For example, is a firm part of the private or the public sphere? When a private company enters the stock market, it is said to be going public, rather than being privately held by a few people or owned by the state. Yet the market is also where bargains are struck for private, self-interested gains. The caring, loving relations in a family or household are also called private—yet laws exist to protect the rights of children in keeping with the public interest. Often, the state is labeled as the public sector. But there is also the general public—people at large—who mostly find mention when public opinion polls are discussed.

To clarify the meanings of public and private, it may be best to consider how these terms have evolved. This analysis reveals that publicness and privateness are in most cases social—human-made—constructs. It also shows that public goods are most appropriately described as goods in the public domain—not as state-provided goods—and that state agencies and markets can be viewed as public goods.

Publicness is in many ways a natural state of affairs. In the early days of humankind there were no property rights. Privateness—taking matters out of the public domain—is a human invention and institution. Certainly, many animal species also display territorial behavior, so privateness also has natural roots. But as Miller and Hashmi (2001, p. 3) emphasize, "humans are also rational and reflective creatures, and as such, we must ask ethical questions about what justifies the boundaries we have drawn between us."

If not for ethical reasons, the same questions can be asked for reasons of economic efficiency: does making certain goods private and others public help or hinder the achievement of desired ends, such as higher income or improved well-being? As Polanyi's (1957 [1944]) analysis of the recurrent oscillation between laissez-faire and state intervention, and Hirschman's (2002 [1982]) notion of "shifting involvements between private interest and public action," indicate, societies have repeatedly raised, reexamined, and reanswered these questions. Publicness and privateness are highly variable and malleable social norms. The public character of some goods tends to be persistent. For example, it would be extremely difficult—if not impossible—to prevent someone from enjoying sunlight. But privateness is intrinsically different because it is a human creation, a social institution.

The public domain is the collection of things available for all people to access and consume freely—including natural commons such as the high seas and the geostationary orbit. Over time natural commons (which exist regardless of human activity) have been supplemented by human-made public goods such as roads, irrigation systems, and armies—as well as public bads like air pollution and financial contagion. In addition, human-made public conditions have been created. Examples include social cohesion and its opposite, conflict and war.

During the Roman Empire all these elements were referred to as *res publica*, or public things.[4] For Julius Caesar the public domain was the realm of things that concerned and affected everyone, including the agencies that the public authorized to perform certain public tasks (Geuss 2000). These public agencies, or magistrates as they were called, received their authority and mandates from the public, constituting its "visible hand"—in contrast to Adam Smith's later notion of the market's invisible hand. The public, "however imperfectly, symbolized and represented the sovereignty of the Roman people" (Millar 2002, p. 142).

The relationship between the public and its visible hand, the state, was often perceived as being close and mutually supportive (Swanson 1992; Mehta and Thakkar 1980). Some cultures still see the relationship between the public and the state in this way (Miller and Hashmi 2001; Rosenblum and Post 2002). As Elias (2001) notes, the ancient Greek word for *individuals* is *idiotes*, which means people who do not take part in public affairs—indicating how closely connected private and public destinies were understood to be. Similarly, Arendt (1998 [1958], p. 158) defines private as "a privation of relations with others." But as John Stuart Mill (1991, pp. 127–28) pointed out in his 1859 essay *On Liberty*:

> *Mischief begins when, instead of calling forth the activity and powers of individuals and bodies, [the government] substitutes its own activity for theirs; when, instead of informing, advising, and, upon occasion, denouncing, it makes them work in fetters, or bids them stand aside and does their work instead of them.*

For much of human history governments controlled rather than served the public. Or they engaged in ventures that, even if well intentioned, failed miserably (Scott 1998). Some peoples and societies have fresh memories of such conditions, with the term *public* conjuring up images of human rights violations and stifled private initiative. Yet in many parts of the world layer after layer of oppression has been shaken off. Especially fast strides toward political freedom have been made in recent years, notably since the end of the cold war.

In addition, much progress has been achieved in human development, even in countries where political freedom and economic growth and development have sometimes been out of step (UNDP, various years). Wide disparities remain. But on average, people enjoy greater political, economic, and social freedoms today than ever before, as well as enhanced capabilities to function and to play an active role in matters that affect their lives (Dasgupta 1992 [1989]; Sen 1987). As Eigen and Eigen-Zucchi (in this volume) show, the fight against corruption is also making headway, gradually but persistently, through combined national and international efforts to remove "the unblushing confusion of the business of government with the promotion of private fortune" (Jenks 1963 [1927], quoted in Hirschman 2002 [1982], p. 124).

But what is the public? Civil society is an important part of it. Many studies have analyzed the growth and strength of civil society at the national, transnational, and international levels.[5] Civil society is sometimes defined as the sphere through which people, individually or collectively, in groups or partnerships, influence, pressure, and resist the state and, increasingly, corporations (Anheier, Glasius, and Kaldor 2001). But definitions vary. The public is wider than civil society organizations, the nonprofit, nonstate actors that tend to take center stage in these discussions. It also includes individuals, households, and families when they act in public on matters of shared concern.

Moreover, the public, as perceived here, includes business. Although firms mostly act as market participants, they sometimes assume public roles when acting as corporate citizens. (And when listed on stock exchanges, they are often owned by the public.) Corporations, like households and civil society organizations, might find it in their interest to discuss issues related to public goods. They may share preferences for public goods—say, maintaining a healthy labor force or an independent judiciary—with other parts of the public (Hopkins 1999).

So, a number of diverse actors define the public and contribute to the provision of public goods. These goods are public not only in their consumption but also in their production, and they are no longer what they are often depicted as being in theory—state-provided goods. The state continues to hold the main coercive and legislative powers. And through its regulatory, fiscal, and other functions, it complements and encourages private activities. Thus the state still plays a crucial role in the provision of public goods, especially pure public goods. But the state is also expected to be what it was in ancient times: the public's visible hand.

The state is a public good, as are markets. Markets can also be seen as public institutions. In fact, markets have always been open institutions and events. Tremendous efforts have been made through various interventions of the visible hand to promote their openness and competitiveness in the interests of all (Lindblom 2001).

Because this volume focuses on global public goods, it is important to define the *global public.* The global public includes national populations and transnational nonstate, nonprofit actors. But just as important, it also includes states. The inclusion of states seems justified because, as international relations theory points out, states are another set of actors at the international level (Keohane 1984; Krasner 1983; Martin 1999). They come together in international arenas to influence markets, civil society, or one another—and to be informed or pressured by nonstate actors.

Reenvisioning the term *public* in this way—remembering *the public,* viewing the state as the public's hand, and seeing the provision of public goods as a multiactor process—opens the door to more clearly recognizing public goods as such. Public goods become more visible, as does the public domain, which includes the natural commons and the human-made environment that all people live in and encounter outside their private spheres.

Bringing the local and national back in: tracing globalness
Like publicness, globalness is sometimes a natural, persistent property and sometimes a social construct. Indeed, globalness can be seen as a dimension of publicness. It transcends national borders. Thus global public goods are public in two ways: public rather than private, and public rather than national.

Some goods, such as the atmosphere or the ozone shield, are naturally global. But many other goods have undergone, or are undergoing, a process of globalization. Such globalization can occur spontaneously, with all countries following national strategies but moving in a similar direction. For example, countries may prefer rule-based interactions and so end up with similar systems of property rights. But in many cases the globalization of public goods is intentional. When looked at from the production side, global public goods can be seen as globalized national public goods or as the sum of national public goods plus international cooperation.[6]

Some of the main forms of international cooperation are shown in table 1. For example, all countries and most communities have health care services and seek to improve public health conditions—efforts that are in their interests. Yet to prevent the spread of disease and enjoy the good of disease control, they often must cooperate with other countries. So cooperation on health, especially to control communicable disease, is an example of outward-oriented cooperation.

Outward-oriented cooperation by some countries is experienced by others as a demand for national policy change—and thus as inward-oriented cooperation

TABLE 1

Forms of international cooperation—seen from the national level

Type of cooperation	Motivation	Illustration
Outward-oriented cooperation	Cooperation with others perceived as necessary to enjoy a good domestically	Country A · Rest of the world
Inward-oriented cooperation	Global exigencies or regimes requiring national policy adjustments	Country A · Rest of the world
Joint intergovernmental production	Production of a good assigned to an international organization	GPG · IO · Country A · Country B · Country I
Networked cooperation	National policy adjustments to meet the access requirements of joining a network, to capture its benefits	Country A · Rest of the world

Source: Based on Kaul and Le Goulven (chapter on financing in this volume, table 1).

and perhaps as top-down globalization. International financial codes and standards are an example. Although formulated by a limited number of countries, they are expected to be applied in countries that did not participate in defining them. (For more detail on this point, see Griffith-Jones in this volume.)

Joint intergovernmental production is a form of international cooperation that occurs when international organizations such as the United Nations, International Monetary Fund, or World Bank are assigned to produce services that their member countries value. International organizations are often given such responsibilities to exploit economies of scale or scope. For example, all countries are better off when sharing the costs of a single institution like the United Nations.

Countries sometimes support international agreements because they want others to internalize cross-border spillovers such as air pollution. But sooner or later they too are expected to comply with these agreements. Thus inward- and outward-oriented cooperation can become intertwined, generating a "boomerang effect." Such mutually binding agreements may be similar to the networked cooperation depicted in table 1. Global communication and transportation systems, for example, follow this horizontal, chain-building approach to globalization.

Differentiating the various forms of cooperation—and thus the various styles of globalization—is politically important and analytically useful. Doing so makes it possible to identify the (net) initiators and (net) recipients of international cooperation efforts. In follow-up discussions on the 1999 volume, this issue led to a frequently posed question: Why and how does globalization of public goods occur? Globalization is often perceived as the world thrusting itself on communities and countries—the result of uncontrolled spillovers or international decisionmaking by a few with impact on all. The terms used to describe this situation are telling—bioinvasion, financial contagion, and trade wars, to name a few. They reveal a sense of being under siege and attack. And they reveal a sense of not being heard, not counting, and being marginalized (De Rivero 2001).

There is growing concern about the direction of globalization. Calls are being made for a new concept of responsible sovereignty, suggesting that policy sovereignty should include countries' duty to act responsibly toward their citizens (to the inside) and toward the international community (to the outside; see Deng and others 1996 and ICISS 2001). But the concept also implies that countries must be empowered to act in this way—and if they face constraints, that the international community is obligated to extend support to avert human tragedy and, if all fails, to intervene. Responsible national development is the starting point and cornerstone of sustainable globalness. International cooperation starts at home, internalizing cross-border spillovers as much as desirable and feasible.[7]

The corollary of the responsible sovereignty concept is to promote globalization with domestic autonomy (Rodrik 1997), or globalness managed to mutual advantage. What might this entail in practical terms? It could mean viewing global public goods, wherever possible, as national public goods that cannot be provided adequately through domestic policy action alone but require international cooperation to be available locally. This approach would keep global public goods rooted in people's lives, as inputs to the well-being of local communities. It would also remind policymakers to assess the desirability of international cooperation in terms of its local and national impact—and in line with the well-established subsidiarity principle, placing the onus of proof on those who propose globalizing. In this way the international cooperation component of global public goods would remain linked to the national public goods component—rather than the national public goods component disappearing from the concept and global public goods assuming an existence of their own and becoming an end rather than a means of people's well-being.

So globalness, like publicness, must be seen as largely a social—human-made—construct. If globalization is a strategy for enhancing the well-being of all people, public goods slated for globalization must be examined carefully from the viewpoint of "*quo vadis* globalization?" Consensus is needed on whether, in the long run, it would be better for all to have globalization proceed bottom up, top down, or horizontally. As discussed throughout this volume, answering this question may involve complex balancing acts between the interests of different countries and population groups, as well as between the long and short terms.

Bringing the good out: translating policy concern into results
People's concerns can find individual or collective expression, and the expression of their concerns can help generate a political climate that facilitates action on certain issues. But concerns translate into change, into a new reality, only when action has led to the desired result—a concrete product or policy outcome.

In many cases cooperation on public goods entails only an agreement among parties expressing their common concern and stating their intention to move toward concerted action on a matter. International relations and regime theorists have given considerable thought to the challenge of making agreements more self-enforcing and fostering compliance (see Chayes and Chayes 1998 [1995] and Barrett in this volume). But between stated objectives and final outcomes lies a highly complex process—the production of global public goods. Probably because public goods are often seen primarily as national in scope and as state-provided, their production is usually depicted only in its broad overall contours.

Hirshleifer's (1983) analysis of the social aggregation functions of public goods introduced three basic production technologies: summation, weakest link, and best shot. His article spawned a rich literature (see Sandler in this volume for a more detailed discussion). Many studies view public goods as being made up of unitary elements that various actors need to combine for the goods to emerge. Yet in real life the building blocks of global public goods are highly diverse. In addition to national building blocks, global public goods may require international inputs such as pooled research or common surveillance.

The chapters in part 3 and the case studies in part 4 of this volume show how complex the production path of a global public good can be.[8] Griffith-Jones, for example, identifies missing elements needed for an efficient, effective international financial architecture. In recent years progress has been made in preventing and managing financial crises. But important measures are still lacking on financing for long-term economic growth and development. Griffith-Jones also shows that having a design for a good is only the beginning of the production process. Achieving a particular policy reform or outcome requires carefully considering the incentives and interests of different groups of actors.

Consider again the description of global public goods from the production side—as the sum of national public goods plus international cooperation—and it becomes clear that what is required is a multicountry, multilevel, and often multisector and multiactor process. It is not enough to be concerned about global climate change or a worsening HIV/AIDS pandemic. To achieve climate stability or control HIV/AIDS, a complex production process must be launched and completed.

In a world of open borders and extensive cross-border activity, the underprovision of public goods anywhere is felt around the world. As a result there is growing political resolve in the international community to move from merely expressing shared concern and relying on decentralized follow-up by individual nation-states to making commitments more binding—specifying the results to be achieved and setting definite target dates. This resolve is nourished by the fact that the world is fast approaching many critical thresholds. Without question, the atmosphere is being overloaded with polluting gases. And mounting international crime and violence expose a dangerously frayed global social fabric.

It is urgent to move from international debate to concerted action—to clearly define, set targets, and assign responsibilities for the goods to be produced. For that, effective implementation strategies are needed. Such strategies require understanding the nature and composition of the goods to be produced to ensure that action leads to desired results. Of course, designs for public policy action often differ from final outcomes. As Dixit (1996, p. xv) notes, " the political process should be viewed as indeed a process—taking place in real time, governed and constrained by history, and containing surprises for all parties." Because the provision of global public goods is a highly political process, many surprises should be expected. This is all the more reason for strategic management—having in

TABLE 2

This volume's notions of public, global, and good

Public	Refers to *the public* (general population, civil society organizations, corporate citizens), with *the global public* also including states.
	Accordingly, public goods are seen as the public's goods—goods that are in the public domain and may concern all people. What is made public—and what private—is often a matter of choice; the character of a good can change over time. Public goods can be but need not be produced by the state.
Global	Means spanning all divides—whether borders, sectors, or groups of actors.
	Global thus includes the local, national, regional, and international levels. It does not necessarily imply centralization or top-down globalization.
Good	Means "thing" (such as a legal framework) or "condition" (such as environmental sustainability).
	Many goods are complex elements made up of multiple building blocks. Understanding their architecture and production path is critical to ensuring adequate provision.

mind clear results, bringing all stakeholders on board, monitoring continuously, and adapting quickly to changed conditions.

Being mindful of the composite nature of public goods is especially important today because more of these goods are assuming less tangible forms. Conventional public goods such as roads and utilities are essentially private goods that for various reasons (natural monopolies, incomplete or lacking markets) the state sometimes chooses or is called on to provide. Many of these public goods have been privatized. A number of newer public goods, by contrast, are intangible. They concern matters such as environmental sustainability or food safety—more conditions than concrete things. Their provision is thus difficult to monitor and verify, and so especially prone to running off course.

To conclude this reenvisioning of the three terms that constitute global public good, table 2 summarizes each.

HOW THIS BOOK IS STRUCTURED

Global public goods matter today because their adequate provision is crucial for better managing globalization. It is therefore important to get the provision of global public goods right and, ideally, for theory to help guide policy practice. So, an important starting point for better provision of global public goods is ensuring that the theory of public goods better reflects current realities and encompasses global public goods. Thus part 1 of this volume revisits some of the concepts and theories associated with public goods.

Providing global public goods involves two closely related processes—political decisionmaking and production (table 3). Part 2 addresses the political process; part 3 explores production, including financing issues. The emphasis is on understanding the overall institutional framework in which the provision of global public goods occurs.

TABLE 3

The process for providing global public goods

1. Political decisionmaking	Concerned stakeholders decide which goods to produce, how to shape them, how much of each to produce, and how to distribute their net benefits.
2. Production	Policy decisions on the production of goods are implemented. This process has two parts: financing and management.
Financing	Efforts are made to foster an adequate allocation of resources—private and public—to global public goods.
Management	Strategic management actions assemble goods so that they are delivered in a frictionless, efficient, effective manner.

Part 4 comprises case studies that examine provision issues for specific goods—such as international financial stability and market efficiency, the multilateral trade regime, communicable disease control and public health, climate stability, biodiversity conservation, access to water, and corruption-free government.

Global public goods are multifaceted—and so require equally multifaceted analysis. This volume is multidisciplinary in terms of both its contributors and the literature consulted. In addition to the literature on economics, the authors draw on other social sciences, including anthropology, sociology, and political science; international relations theory; and public management theory. Furthermore, insights have been gleaned from studies in international law and development and from issue-specific disciplines, notably those related to the case studies in part 4. Adequate treatment of global public goods also requires drawing on literature pertaining to private goods and to markets, including issues of property rights and theories of the firm. This literature shows that governments are still essential in providing public goods, nationally and internationally. But private actors, whether for-profit (firms) or not-for-profit (foundations, civil society organizations, households, and individuals), also come into play.

The need for and possible confluence of these diverse strands of literature reflect a narrowing of the differences between various groups of actors and their growing involvement in both the public and the private sphere, the domestic and the international realm—a trend that will be a recurrent theme throughout this volume.

NOTES

1. In this volume *good* is often used to denote both goods and services. The term refers to a product, thing, or condition. It usually does not entail a judgment on whether the good has benefits (positive utility) or costs (negative utility). But where there is global consensus on the economic or social undesirability of a certain public good, the term *bad* is sometimes used. Yet the valuation of a good is a matter for individual actors—a person, community, nation, or any other group—to decide based on preferences and priorities. From here on, while the text may refer to the benefits of public goods, in all cases the objective is to derive positive net benefits from their consumption.

2. Notable exceptions include Ferroni and Mody (2002); Sandler (1997, 1998); ECLAC (2002); and Sweden, Ministry for Foreign Affairs (2001).

3. The discussion on "public" precedes the discussion on "global" because, as noted, publicness includes globalness as a special dimension. Therefore, it is important to address the issue of publicness first.

4. Public goods are not the only elements in the public domain. Among other things, relations among people and between groups of people also determine the character of the public sphere. But this volume's focus is public goods, including material products (such as roads and judicial systems), nonmaterial products (such

as knowledge), and policy outcomes or conditions (such as environmental sustain-ability and peace). For a more detailed discussion on notions of the public domain, see Drache (2001). For a discussion on the classification of public goods, see Kaul and Mendoza (in this volume).

5. There is a vast and proliferating literature on the history and current status of civil society. For overviews of this topic, see Anheier, Glasius, and Kaldor (2001); Keck and Sikkink (1998); Scholte and Schnabel (2001); and Rosenblum and Post (2002). Anheier (2001) is also of particular interest because it presents a first effort at quan-tifying the strength of civil society.

6. When looked at from the consumption side, global public goods can be under-stood as goods with benefits that cut across people, regions, and countries.

7. The notion that cooperation starts at home is a traditional one, familiar to many cultures. See Rosenblum and Post (2002).

8. In this context readers might find it helpful to refer to the chapter on institu-tions by Kaul and Le Goulven (in this volume)—particularly figures 2 and 3, which show the building blocks and production paths of climate stability and food safety. The figures illustrate, among other things, the links that often exist between the national building blocks of global public goods and their international components.

REFERENCES

Anheier, Helmut. 2001. "Measuring Global Civil Society." In Helmut Anheier, Marlies Glasius, and Mary Kaldor, eds., *Global Civil Society 2001.* Oxford: Oxford University Press.

Anheier, Helmut, Marlies Glasius, and Mary Kaldor, eds. 2001. *Global Civil Society 2001.* Oxford: Oxford University Press.

Arendt, Hannah. 1998 [1958]. *The Human Condition.* Chicago: University of Chicago Press.

Bhagwati, Jagdish. 1997. "The Global Age: From a Skeptical South to a Fearful North." *World Economy* 20 (3): 259–83.

Chayes, Abram, and Antonia Handler Chayes. 1998 [1995]. *The New Sovereignty: Compliance with International Regulatory Agreements.* Cambridge, Mass.: Harvard University Press.

Dasgupta, Partha. 1992 [1989]. "Positive Freedom, Markets, and the Welfare State." In Dieter Helm, ed., *The Economic Borders of the State.* Oxford: Oxford University Press.

Deng, Francis M., Sadikiel Kimaro, Terrence Lyons, I. William Zartman, and Donald Rothchild. 1996. *Sovereignty as Responsibility: Conflict Management in Africa.* Washington, D.C.: Brookings Institution.

De Rivero, Oswaldo. 2001. *The Myth of Development: The Non-Viable Economies of the 21st Century.* London: Zed Books.

Dixit, Avinash K. 1996. *The Making of Economic Policy: A Transaction-Cost Politics Perspective.* Cambridge, Mass.: MIT Press.

Drache, Daniel, ed. 2001. *The Market or the Public Domain: Global Governance and the Asymmetry of Power.* London: Routledge.

ECLAC (Economic Commission for Latin America and the Caribbean). 2002. *Globalization and Development.* Santiago, Chile.

Elias, Norbert. 2001. *The Society of Individuals.* New York: Continuum.

Ferroni, Marco, and Ashoka Mody, eds. 2002. *International Public Goods: Incentives, Measurement, and Financing.* Boston, Mass.: Kluwer Academic Publishers.

Geuss, Raymond. 2000. *Public Goods, Private Goods.* Princeton, N.J.: Princeton University Press.

Giddens, Anthony. 2000. *Runaway World: How Globalization Is Reshaping Our Lives.* New York: Routledge.

Hirschman, Albert O. 2002 [1982]. *Shifting Involvements: Private Interest and Public Action.* Princeton, N.J.: Princeton University Press.

Hirshleifer, Jack. 1983. "From Weakest-Link to Best-Shot: The Voluntary Provision of Public Goods." *Public Choice* 41: 371–86.

Hopkins, Michael. 1999. *The Planetary Bargain: Corporate Social Responsibility Comes of Age.* New York: St. Martin's Press.

ICISS (International Commission on Intervention and State Sovereignty). 2001. *The Responsibility to Protect.* Ottawa: International Development Research Centre.

Jenks, Leland Hamilton. 1963 [1927]. *The Migration of British Capital to 1875.* London: Jonathan Cape.

Kaul, Inge, Isabelle Grunberg, and Marc A. Stern, eds. 1999. *Global Public Goods: International Cooperation in the 21st Century.* New York: Oxford University Press.

Keane, John. 2001. "Global Civil Society?" In Helmut Anheier, Marlies Glasius, and Mary Kaldor, eds., *Global Civil Society 2001.* New York: Oxford University Press.

Keck, Margaret E., and Kathryn Sikkink. 1998. *Activists beyond Borders: Advocacy Networks in International Politics.* Ithaca, N.Y.: Cornell University.

Keohane, Robert O. 1984. *After Hegemony: Cooperation and Discord in the World Political Economy.* Princeton, N.J.: Princeton University Press.

Khor, Martin. 2000. "Globalization and the South: Some Critical Issues." Discussion Paper 147. United Nations Conference on Trade and Development, Geneva.

Krasner, Stephen D. 1983. *International Regimes.* Ithaca, N.Y.: Cornell University Press.

Lindblom, Charles E. 2001. *The Market System: What It Is, How It Works, and What To Make of It.* New Haven, Conn.: Yale University Press.

Mahbubani, Kishore. 2001. *Can Asians Think?* Toronto: Key Porter Books.

Martin, Lisa L. 1999. "The Political Economy of International Cooperation." In Inge Kaul, Isabelle Grunberg, and Marc A. Stern, eds., *Global Public Goods: International Cooperation in the 21st Century.* New York: Oxford University Press.

Mehta, Usha, and Usha Thakkar. 1980. *Kautilya and His Arthashastra.* New Delhi: S. Chand and Company.

Mill, John Stuart. 1991. *On Liberty and Other Essays.* Collected by John Gray. Oxford: Oxford University Press.

Millar, Fergus. 2002. *Rome, the Greek World, and the East.* Vol. 1. Chapel Hill: University of North Carolina Press.

Miller, David, and Sohail H. Hashmi, eds. 2001. *Boundaries and Justice: Diverse Ethical Perspectives.* Princeton, N.J.: Princeton University Press.

Nye, Joseph S., Jr. 2002. *The Paradox of American Power: Why the World's Only Superpower Can't Go It Alone.* New York: Oxford University Press.

Ohmae, Kenichi. 1995. "Putting Global Logic First." In Kenichi Ohmae, ed., *The Evolving Global Economy: Making Sense of the New World Order.* Cambridge, Mass.: Harvard Business Review.

Polanyi, Karl. 1957 [1944]. *The Great Transformation: The Political and Economic Origins of Our Time.* Boston, Mass.: Beacon Press.

Rodrik, Dani. 1997. *Has Globalization Gone Too Far?* Washington, D.C.: Institute for International Economics.

———. 2001. "The Global Governance of Trade: As If Development Really Mattered." Background paper to the United Nations Development Programme Project on Trade and Sustainable Human Development, Bureau for Development Policy, New York.

Rosenblum, Nancy L., and Robert C. Post. 2002. *Civil Society and Government.* Princeton, N.J.: Princeton University Press.

Sandler, Todd. 1997. *Global Challenges: An Approach to Environmental, Political, and Economic Problems.* Cambridge: Cambridge University Press.

———. 1998. "Global and Regional Public Goods: A Prognosis for Collective Action." *Fiscal Studies* 19 (3): 221–47.

Scholte, Jan Aart, and Albrecht Schnabel, eds. 2001. *Civil Society and Global Finance.* Tokyo: United Nations University.

Scott, James C. 1998. *Seeing Like a State: How Certain Schemes to Improve the Human Condition Have Failed.* New Haven, Conn.: Yale University Press.

Sen, Amartya K. 1987. *On Ethics and Economics.* Oxford: Basil Blackwell.

———. 1999. "Global Justice: Beyond International Equity." In Inge Kaul, Isabelle Grunberg, and Marc A. Stern, eds., *Global Public Goods: International Cooperation in the 21st Century.* New York: Oxford University Press.

Swanson, Judith A. 1992. *The Public and the Private in Aristotle's Political Philosophy.* Ithaca, N.Y.: Cornell University Press.

Sweden, Ministry for Foreign Affairs. 2001. *Financing and Providing Global Public Goods: Expectations and Prospects.* Study 2001:2. Prepared by Francisco Sagasti and Keith Bezanson on behalf of the Institute of Development Studies, Sussex, U.K. Stockholm. [http://www.utrikes.regeringen.se/inenglish/policy/devcoop/financing.htm].

Taylor-Gooby, Peter. 2000. "Risk and Welfare." In Peter Taylor-Gooby, ed., *Risk, Trust and Welfare.* New York: Macmillan.

UNDP (United Nations Development Programme). Various years. *Human Development Report.* New York: Oxford University Press.

How to Improve the Provision of Global Public Goods

Inge Kaul, Pedro Conceição, Katell Le Goulven, and Ronald U. Mendoza

The studies in this volume suggest that the world is at a turning point in the provision of global public goods. There are many signs of adaptive inefficiency, with institutional change lagging far behind rapidly evolving realities.[1] So, even the best-intentioned policies often lead to limited or distorted results. But incipient institutional reforms are discernible: existing molds are becoming brittle, and policymaking and public management patterns are being reconfigured. There is a clear window of opportunity for further change. Based on the analyses in this volume, addressing the following problems seems especially urgent:

- Standard concepts and theories on public goods are inadequate for understanding current realities, capturing the growing phenomenon of global public goods, and providing effective policy guidance.
- Decisionmaking systematically excludes some of those affected by global public goods.
- Financing often comes out of international development assistance.
- The organization of production is compartmentalized and scattered.

Most of the chapters' suggestions on how these problems could be solved build on current reforms and are aimed at nudging forward ongoing change—toward a more adequate provision of global public goods. The policy recommendations emanating from the analyses can be summarized in four parts: refurbishing the analytical toolkit, matching circles of stakeholders and decisionmakers, systematizing the financing of global public goods, and spanning borders, sectors, and groups of actors.

Refurbishing the Analytical Toolkit

Public goods are usually defined as goods with nonexcludable benefits and nonrival consumption. Nonexcludability means that it is technically, politically, or economically infeasible to exclude someone from consuming the good. Nonrivalry means that one person's consumption of the good does not detract from its availability to others. If a good is nonrival, it can be made available to additional users at zero—or close to zero—cost. It need not be reproduced for each new consumer. So, the only costs involved in making it more widely available would be those that its further distribution might entail.

Knowledge is an example. Think of the many generations that have benefited—and continue to benefit—from indigenously developed medicines in developing countries. Or consider the incalculable increase in human welfare due to the diffusion of mathematical and scientific knowledge—such as the Pythagorean theorem—since ancient times. It is usually inefficient to exclude someone from the consumption of nonrival goods.

Knowledge is also a useful example for illustrating the issue at the center of the chapters by Desai and by Kaul and Mendoza (in this volume): differentiation between a good's potential and actual properties. Some types of knowledge, notably knowledge with potential commercial value, are not in the public domain but instead are made exclusive through instruments such as intellectual property rights.[2] At the same time, essentially private goods such as basic education are made public by design. They are often publicly provided in such plentiful measure that there is no need for rivalry among potential consumers.[3] As brought to light by the previous chapter's reexamination of the notion of publicness and analyzed in detail by Desai in his historical review of the concept of public goods and public provision, the properties of goods are variable and subject to change—over time and across regions, cultures, and population groups. And as Desai adds, the issue of what goods to make public or private continues to generate fierce debate.

These insights, in conjunction with the challenges posed by current political realities, inspired the formulation of four analytical tools that could improve the understanding of public goods and support decisionmaking on issues of privateness and publicness. The four tools, which no doubt require further research and debate, are an expanded definition of public goods and global public goods, the triangle of publicness, the inherent connection between equity and efficiency in the provision of global public goods, and the concept of adequate provision (as opposed to optimal supply) of public goods.

An expanded definition of public goods and global public goods
Kaul and Mendoza (in this volume) propose expanding the standard definition of public goods on two levels. On one level they build on the standard definition of public goods, adding that any goods characterized by nonrival or nonexcludable properties are potential candidates for actually being public and available for all to consume. On the next level they expand the definition to identify goods that are de facto public or inclusive. The revised, two-level definition is as follows:

- *Definition 1:* Goods have a special potential for being public if they have nonexcludable benefits, nonrival benefits, or both.

- *Definition 2:* Goods are de facto public if they are nonexclusive and available for all to consume.

The difference between the two definitions is based on the distinction between a good's potential for being inclusive (a potential shared by all goods that are nonexcludable, nonrival, or both) and its actually being inclusive (which may mean that the good is rival or excludable but has been made nonexclusive). Taken together, the definitions clarify how the inclusiveness and publicness of goods may change even though the goods do not. Whether goods become de facto public often depends on technology and on policy choice.

By analogy, de facto global public goods are defined as follows:

- *Definition 3:* Global public goods are goods with benefits that extend to all countries, people, and generations.

Just as goods can be potentially public, they can be potentially global. And public goods can be made global. For example, national postal systems have been harmonized and linked to form a global postal system. Definition 3 refers to a good that is actually global in its publicness. It is a demanding definition. Some goods may be universal, but many others are not. As suggested in the 1999 predecessor to this volume (Kaul, Grunberg, and Stern 1999), a less strict definition could be that a good is globally public when it benefits more than one group of countries and does not discriminate against any population group or generation.

The expanded definition avoids the normative element that often marks discussions of public goods. Many textbooks conclude, based on the standard definition, that a good with potentially rival and excludable properties is—or ought to be—private and that its provision ought to be left to the market. This means that the decision about which goods to make private and which public is seen largely as a technical rather than a political matter. The state's role becomes one of providing "market rejects"—nonrival and nonexcludable goods that do not fit the conditions of market transactions. Partly because of this standard definition, there is a widespread misconception that public goods are state-provided.

The expanded definition proposed by Kaul and Mendoza proceeds in a positive way and defines public goods as what they are: goods in the public domain, available for all to consume and affecting all. A wide range of things occur in the public domain, including potentially excludable public bads such as crime, noise, violence, pollution, and computer viruses. Looking through the lens of the expanded definition at the issues discussed in the case studies in part 4 brings out the socially determined character of many public goods, including global public goods. The chapter by Mehta (in this volume), for example, shows how water is being pulled along the public-private continuum by different societal forces and interests. Recognizing the social mantle of goods also makes it possible (as seen below) to better understand why some of these goods are engulfed in controversy.

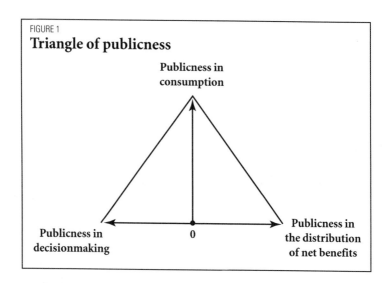

FIGURE 1
Triangle of publicness

Publicness in
consumption

Publicness in
decisionmaking

0

Publicness in
the distribution
of net benefits

The triangle of publicness
Placing public goods back in the public domain and reintroducing a notion of policy choice raises the question of how well publicness in consumption is matched by publicness in decisionmaking and in the distribution of net benefits across various parts of the global public. Publicness in decisionmaking and distribution does not form part of the definition of a public good. The intention here is to examine goods identified as public in greater detail across these dimensions.

Kaul and Mendoza (in this volume) offer a simple framework for such an analysis: the triangle of publicness (figure 1). The vertical axis measures publicness in consumption, the left side of the base publicness in decisionmaking, and the right side publicness (or equity) in the distribution of a good's benefits. The triangle makes it possible to examine how various public goods fare along these three dimensions.

The triangle of publicness raises a host of conceptual and methodological issues. Yet its potential usefulness is clear even at this early stage. It could eventually be used to draw attention to one of the key imbalances considered in this volume: the discrepancy between the full publicness in consumption that typically marks global public goods and the limited publicness of the decisionmaking through which these goods are selected and placed in the global public domain. The triangle could help policymakers and the public identify issues that require review of current institutions and ways of managing globalization.

The connection between equity and efficiency in the provision
of global public goods
Another conceptual issue related to the provision of public goods involves the tradeoff between equity and efficiency. This issue is controversial enough at the

national level—but what about in the international context? Sandmo (in this volume) extends Samuelson's (1954) treatment of optimal public spending to the international level. Sandmo's two-country (rich and poor), two-good (public and private) model introduces the concept of varying cost efficiency across countries in the production of a pure public good, implying the possibility of efficiency gains from comparative cost advantages in its production.

Suppose that there is a certain level of total output of private goods in the world today. Now suppose that a global public good (such as climate stability) needs to be produced and that its production requires private goods as inputs. If it is cheaper (that is, more cost efficient) to produce the good in a poor than in a rich country, it would make sense for a poor country to produce more of it. But in the absence of international income transfers, contributing more to the provision of the global public good would require the poor country to reduce its consumption of private goods, of which it has fewer than the rich country to begin with. Thus the pursuit of more efficient production of the global public good could generate an inequitable outcome: the poor country could be made worse off.[4] Without international income transfers, it is difficult to achieve efficient and equitable provision of global public goods. This provides theoretical support for the assertion that the criterion of cost efficiency alone cannot guide international cooperation. If no country is to be made worse off as a result of cooperation, equity considerations have to be borne in mind.

From optimal supply to adequate provision

Policymakers have made good use of the "Samuelson condition" on the optimal provision of public goods (Samuelson 1954). This condition states that a public good is optimally provided when the cost to society of an additional unit of the good equals the amount that society is willing to pay for that unit. Sandler (in this volume) discusses the many conceptual and methodological problems that arise when attempting to empirically assess this notion of optimality. Because of these measurement problems, Sandler proposes an interesting innovation: an index of optimality based on the insight that club-provided public goods (goods that are relatively nonrival and excludable) tend to be provided efficiently. In simplified terms, the index suggests that the larger is the number of club-provided goods—relative to the total number of public goods—the smaller is the risk of underprovision.

Samuelson's optimality condition was formulated in the context of the theory of public finance and thus as a tool for determining the balance between public preferences and public expenditures. But today public goods are not necessarily state-produced and are often multiactor products. They depend on public and private spending. So, a balance between public preferences and public expenditures could coincide either with overprovision, if private spending is adequate, or with abject underprovision of many public goods, if private resource allocations

---

BOX 1

NEW ANALYTICAL TOOLS FOR UNDERSTANDING PUBLIC GOODS

- Expanding the definition of public goods and global public goods.
- Assessing goods using the triangle of publicness.
- Recognizing the link between efficiency and equity in the provision of global public goods.
- Complementing the concept of optimal supply with that of adequate provision.

---

are insufficient. Taking a good—partly or fully—out of the fold of government requires rethinking the notion of adequate provision.

Conceição (in this volume) focuses on this issue. He suggests a definition of deficient provision that differentiates among provision problems—underuse, underprovision, undersupply, malprovision, overuse, and various access problems. Based on this definition, he offers profiles of the provision of selected global public goods. The profiles start with technical assessments of the goods' provision status, attempting to answer such questions as these: How close has the world come to controlling polio? And do all countries benefit from the multilateral trade regime? The consequences of provision problems are then translated into economic terms and, in some cases, human development terms.

Though preliminary, the profiles illustrate the usefulness of this approach. Such profiles could be helpful when searching for opportunities where additional investment in global public goods offers high social—and global—returns. The profiles are intended to encourage further analysis, yet even in their present state they convey a sense of urgency. In many cases the data show that the costs of deficient provision are extremely large—and growing—and clearly outweigh the costs of corrective actions.

Box 1 recaptures the main suggestions of this section. It shows that from the suggested expanded definition of public goods flow a number of possibilities for the development of analytical tools that could help generate new policy insights and support decisionmaking on issues of privateness and publicness.

MATCHING CIRCLES OF STAKEHOLDERS AND DECISIONMAKERS

Because the provision and even the public and global properties of global public goods are often contested and a matter of choice, this volume devotes considerable attention to analyzing the structures and processes of political decisionmaking on global public goods. These decisionmaking structures and processes correspond to the political side of the provision process (as opposed to the production side). Ideally, an examination of the political process should start from the national level. But such an approach requires detailed country studies that are beyond the scope of this volume, though certainly desirable as follow-on research. Thus the analyses in this volume focus on how decisionmaking on global public goods works internationally.

According to Desai (in this volume), political decisionmaking on the provision of global public goods has two important aspects:

- *Preference revelation*—what goods the public wants in the public domain and what it is willing to pay for them.

- *Political bargaining*—how decisions are made on which goods to include in the public domain, how much of these goods to include, and how to make them accessible to all (including through such means as logrolling, "pork barreling," free riding, and other strategies that negotiating parties may pursue).

In addition, other chapters discuss another, more problematic aspect of decisionmaking:

- *Political participation*—of different groups of actors and stakeholders.

Broad representation in political decisionmaking is not yet a reality at the international level. Inadequacies in the political process result from a mismatch between the decisionmaking circles represented in international arenas and the range of spillovers associated with specific global public goods. The decisionmaking circles for some globally *inclusive* public goods are *exclusive* in the sense that not all the people affected by a good's spillovers are included or, if they are, the decisionmaking process does not ensure their fair participation in the decisions made.

The forgotten principle of equivalence
Given the mismatch in decisionmaking, it is not surprising that protesters have been marching outside the conference halls of the Group of Eight (G-8)[5] and Bretton Woods institutions (World Bank and International Monetary Fund). Inside these halls issues are being negotiated that are likely to affect the protesters' lives and those of future generations.

By the same token, it is appropriate that representatives of emerging and yet-to-emerge market economies be included in some of the (so far highly exclusive) meetings dealing with international financial issues, such as the Financial Stability Forum (http://www.fsforum.org). Regardless of whether they are engaged in international financial markets, all countries are affected by international financial instability: the ripple effects of these markets' boom and bust cycles reach into every corner of the world.[6] Moreover, it is not by chance that women's groups seek to add a gender-sensitive perspective to all major policy debates, particularly since men and women are often affected differently by various aspects of globalization—as with international trade.[7]

These developments at the international level are somewhat surprising, since at the country level this mismatch has been solved—at least in theory, if not always in practice—through the well-established principle of fiscal equivalence or subsidiarity. This principle, based on important work by Breton (1965), Olson (1971 [1965]), and Oates (1972), suggests in simplified form that those affected by a good should have a say in its provision. So, it is desirable to align as much as possible the structure of political decisionmaking (particularly different levels of geographic jurisdiction) with the range and type of a good's spillover effects. This implies that a local public good would best be provided at the local level and that a good with benefits extending throughout a region would best be provided at the regional level.[8] When it comes to global public goods, these principles often seem to be forgotten.

In many cases issues that concern all people are discussed by only a few decisionmakers, operating as "clubs" of technically specialized negotiators (Keohane and Nye 2000). And decisions on dimensions—or building blocks—of global public goods that would best be dealt with at lower levels are often made internationally, through an approach that is overly standardized and oblivious to local realities (for examples, see Castro and Cordero, Correa, Griffith-Jones, Mehta, Mendoza, and Perrings and Gadgil in this volume). This approach is disconcerting because it curtails the role of political decisionmaking as a means of revealing the demand for global public goods. The lack of effective representation may translate into a lack of political pluralism. And this lack of political pluralism may limit competition between alternative goods in assigning spending priorities or between alternative ideas about policy and strategy (see Breton 1996 for a discussion on this point in reference to the national level).

This is not just a theoretical risk. It is real, as Buira (in this volume) demonstrates. The lack of publicness in decisionmaking can weaken the technical soundness of policy choices, undermine the legitimacy and credibility of organizations, and erode the sense of policy ownership so essential for effective follow-up to international agreements. Once implementation begins, it may take years or decades to correct wrong policy choices, as the bitter and costly experiences with first-generation structural adjustment programs showed.

The right of all people to have a say in matters that affect their lives is a widely recognized basic principle of democracy and equity. So, for both equity and efficiency reasons it is important to search for ways of making political decisionmaking on global public goods more inclusive and more public. The challenge is to align the circles of those to be consulted (or to take part in the decisionmaking) with the spillover range of the good under negotiation.

New sources of political power

But where do those who seek fairer, more effective representation turn? As Held and McGrew (in this volume) argue, the world has entered a new era of politics characterized by overlapping networks and constellations of power and an increasingly dense web of international regimes and organizations—all a response to the growing cross-border policy challenges. The characteristics of today's world, Held and McGrew suggest, are markedly different from the Westphalian principle of sovereign state rule over a bounded territory. Power is now apportioned and bartered by various entities—including governments, civil society organizations, and corporations—at the national, transnational, regional, and international levels. Groups of actors and stakeholders are reaching out and linking up, creating circles of interests—whether to control corruption, improve accounting standards, promote gender issues, protect the environment, or formulate norms and standards for the construction of dams—and partnerships of all kinds (Reinicke and Deng 2000).

Nation-states—individually or collectively, as intergovernmental bodies—are no longer the sole locus of power. Summits and informal gatherings outside the multilateral system are the main and perhaps only decisionmaking bodies on global affairs. As Edwards and Zadek (in this volume) point out, civil society organizations and corporations are key players on the global stage. They have created international arenas for consultation and formation of political consensus. The World Economic Forum (http://www.weforum.org) has developed tremendous convening power. And Porto Alegre (http://www.portoalegre2002.org) and other summits of civil society have become well-established events (Pianta 2001). Moreover, business is increasingly setting norms and standards, as is civil society. Human rights are just one of many examples. This trend has led some to ask what this expansion of nonstate public policymaking means for public life (Cutler, Haufler, and Porter 1999, p. 22).

Where do these trends leave governments and intergovernmental, notably multilateral, decisionmaking bodies? It is occasionally useful to summarize what is emerging as a possible societal consensus from the manifold processes of political networking, debate, partnering, and alliance building. Drawing from tacit concerns and translating these into firmer, or even binding, agreements helps create a common, updated set of rules that can serve all as reference points for some time. This summing up, and the preference aggregation that often goes with it, are better accomplished by the conventional governmental and intergovernmental bodies.

Only governments have the power to turn decisions into firm and binding agreements. And only through governments can voting power temper the influence of private purchasing power. This is one reason that democracy has been promoted and spread worldwide. Balanced, sustainable development needs both the invisible hand of the market and the visible one of the state. And the visible one must be the public's hand, not a hand severed from the public.

But thinking and acting globally is not a natural strength of governments, precisely because nation-states are territorially bound. Transnational nonstate actors, such as business or civil society organizations, sometimes have a more genuinely global perspective—say, on environmental issues. That explains why intergovernmental meetings, such as the UN Earth Summit in Rio de Janeiro in 1992, attract such huge interest from business and civil society organizations. But for the relationships between state and nonstate actors to be effective, two conditions must be met: multilateral bodies must be fully representative, and arrangements must be in place for systematic dialogue and consultation between state and nonstate actors. Today's multilateral decisionmaking bodies meet these conditions only partially.

Persistent imbalances in decisionmaking: missing voices, failing rules
The current problems with multilateral decisionmaking affect both state and nonstate actors. Among state actors, developing countries are the main concern. The imbalances among states as well as those between state and nonstate actors are not always easy to detect, because in many cases the problem is not merely a quantitative issue—whether all parties have a seat at the negotiating table. The main problem is often qualitative—how well various stakeholders are represented.

For developing countries, Buira (in this volume) shows that in some instances matters not only have failed to improve but have actually worsened. The divide among member countries in the International Monetary Fund (IMF)—in decisionmaking and in access to its resources (Special Drawing Rights, or SDRs)—has widened since the IMF was created in the mid-1940s. The IMF's membership comprises a small group of creditor industrial countries with a majority vote and a large group of mostly debtor developing countries with a minority vote and limited influence over the IMF's policies. For example, on the IMF's executive board 24 industrial countries hold 10–11 seats—while 42 African countries hold only 2. As Buira (p. 235) points out,

> *Only with transparency, accountability, and legitimacy can international institutions like the IMF hope to reconcile each country's political and economic objectives with the international community's wider interests, including the provision of global public goods like financial stability and market efficiency.*

Even in multilateral arenas where all countries have a seat, some countries clearly form the inner circle of decisionmaking, leaving others in the outer circle, as Chasek and Rajamani (in this volume) point out. There is a vast gap in negotiating capacity between industrial and developing countries. Industrial countries generally have large delegations equipped with various kinds of negotiating and technical expertise, while developing countries often depend on one-person delegations. Moreover, a one-person delegation today does not necessarily have the same negotiating strength as a one-person delegation several years ago. The negotiating load has increased: the international policy agenda is lengthening, issues are becoming increasingly complex, organizations are multiplying, conference venues are being shifted from continent to continent, meetings are being held in parallel sessions, and "informal informals" are becoming a common negotiating tool.[9] All this stretches small delegations to the limit.

In addition, developing countries have become a highly diversified group. As a result relying on traditional alliances such as the G-77 may not be the best coping strategy for small delegations to pursue.[10] So, they are losing an important support mechanism. A further constraint is that developing countries often cannot depend on briefings from their capitals. They are, as Chasek and Rajamani put it, "negotiating on hollow mandates." Thus many have come to rely on civil society organizations for technical inputs. All this means that while many developing countries are doing their best to cover multilateral negotiations, they are hardly in a position to set agendas. Most are agenda-takers and even policy-takers.

Thus having a seat at the negotiating table does not ensure effective representation. Matters become even more complicated when one examines the structure of multilateral bargaining, as Mendoza (in this volume) does. To bargain successfully, each party should have some chips to put on the table. Developing countries have fewer things to give than industrial countries and so fewer possibilities to strike a good deal. They may have to settle for the "least bad" compromise, as many developing countries did when "trading" for enhanced access to industrial countries' agricultural and textiles markets against the World Trade Organization agreement on Trade-Related Aspects of Intellectual Property Rights (TRIPS). Furthermore, Eigen and Eigen-Zucchi (in this volume) depart from the standard definition of corruption—the misuse of public office for private gain—and refer to a case of cross-national pressure as a possible example of corruption in the international context. While practices such as cross-bargaining and quid pro quo are quite commonplace in many international arenas, the discussion in Eigen and Eigen-Zucchi suggests that the international community needs to further elaborate what is, or is not, a corrupt practice in certain contexts—and determine how to respond to such practices.

But the developing countries' bargaining strength may vary by issue. As the chapters by Perrings and Gadgil and by Castro and Cordero (in this volume) show, in the environmental area developing countries often hold the key to solving critical global problems—and could potentially improve their negotiating position.

The structure and functioning of many multilateral bodies thus remain controversial and unsettled. It is not surprising that these bodies' interactions with nonstate actors are often similarly unsettled—stumbling along from meeting to meeting but, as Edwards and Zadek (in this volume) point out, far from following clear rules of the road. The reasons lie on both sides.

On the side of nonstate actors, coordination among themselves is often a major challenge for a host of reasons, including the large number of actors, the diversity of interests, and the lack of resources and meeting facilities. The result is a cacophony of voices, making it difficult for government representatives to discern a coherent, actionable message.

On the side of intergovernmental bodies and organizations, a major constraint is lingering concern about the legitimacy and accountability of nonstate actors—a concern that nonstate actors at times fail to allay satisfactorily. According to Edwards and Zadek, part of the legitimacy and accountability problem is that the international advocacy efforts of civil society organizations are often weakly rooted in local and national politics. As they say (p. 210), "There is always a temptation to leapfrog over the national arena and go directly to Washington or Brussels, where it is often easier to gain access to senior officials and achieve a response."

For business actors the legitimacy issue is doubly difficult. It requires gaining trust among both civil society and governmental partners. Yet as Edwards and Zadek stress (p. 214),

[B]oth enthusiasts and skeptics must be clear about how legitimacy is claimed and avoid conflating the requirements of different criteria, because doing so confuses the debate, makes solutions harder to find, and increases the likelihood that criticisms of legitimacy will be used to exclude rather than structure the involvement of dissenting voices. Any nonstate actor is entitled to voice an opinion.

For the time being, confusion continues to reign, and there is no systematic interaction between the different groups of actors. It is easy to see how G-8 decisions filter into multilateral negotiations but more difficult to determine whether organizations such as Oxfam, Greenpeace, Amnesty International, Médecins Sans Frontières (Doctors Without Borders), and the Self-Employed Women's Association (India) are heard.

Compared with just 10 or 20 years ago, today the world is much more democratic, pluralistic, and participatory. But compared with the publicness and globalness of the policy challenges it faces, decisionmaking is still too exclusive and nontransparent. And for global public goods to emerge, many actors worldwide have to contribute their share. Too little is done to enable all to have a sense of ownership of international policy agreements. Many stakeholders have a stake only in the global problems that affect them—not in the strategies to resolve them.

Moving the circles closer together

The principle of fiscal equivalence and the related notions of subsidiarity and decentralization were formulated with hard-nosed efficiency considerations in mind. Several chapters in this volume reconfirm the validity of these principles, pointing to costly policy mistakes that have occurred because the voices of key stakeholders are not being heard.

So why not apply, appropriately adjusted, the equivalence principle of public finance internationally? Recall that the principle suggests a simple formula: matching the span of jurisdictions (decisionmaking bodies) with that of taxpayers (stakeholders). Yet people can be taxed in many ways—by paying money to the state, by bearing the brunt of financial crises, by paying with one's health for, say, an inflexible intellectual property rights regime. Thus it would be appropriate to broaden the principle of fiscal equivalence into a more general principle of decisionmaker-stakeholder equivalence.

Albin (in this volume) arrives at a similar conclusion despite approaching the issue from quite a different angle and discipline. She examines what participants in multilateral negotiations perceive as just and fair in practice and concludes that "negotiators clearly believe that justice and fairness entail representing, protecting, and promoting the needs and concerns of all parties. . . . In practice, then, justice and fairness mean a balanced settlement of conflicting claims" (p. 269). As she suggests, this perception highlights the importance of the structure and process of multilateral negotiations. According to her analysis, a fair process:

- Ensures as much as possible that all parties have an effective voice in representing their interests and concerns.
- Ensures that all claims are considered fully in the negotiation process.

How can a fair process be achieved? Several recommendations flow from the analyses in this volume. For example, Albin offers a set of criteria for reviewing the fairness and inclusiveness of current decisionmaking structures and processes. But many processes are complex and context-specific. In such cases, adjusting decisionmaking patterns would require the type of in-depth analysis provided by Buira. Moreover, decisionmaking patterns must allow constitutional and procedural issues to be raised and to be addressed transparently. There may be a need for an independent—perhaps civil society—actor to bring to light some of the current imbalances in participation and representation.

When considering enhanced participation by developing countries, it is also important to focus on capacity building, which Chasek and Rajamani (in this volume) highlight. For many developing countries a lack of national institutional capacity means a lack of negotiating strength in international negotiations. So, longer-term capacity building is important. But if global inequity is to be ended, shorter-term measures are also needed. As Chasek and Rajamani emphasize, providing financial support to enable delegates from developing countries to attend international conferences is important, but it does little to improve their countries' negotiating positions. What could be more effective is to support networking arrangements among developing country delegations. Another option would be to create issue-specific participation funds, following the example of the Intergovernmental Group of 24 (G-24).[11] The purpose would be to improve developing countries' capacity to define their policy positions on global issues and play a more active role in shaping the international policy agenda.

Edwards and Zadek (in this volume) present two sets of rules of the road to guide the interaction between state and nonstate actors. One, for nonstate actors, suggests ways in which they can enhance their legitimacy and strengthen their role in global governance, including improving transparency, demonstrating value added, and forming umbrella groups. The other, for international organizations, proposes steps for engaging more systematically with nonstate actors, such as adopting clear and impartial rules and supporting the participation of civil society organizations from developing countries. In addition, Edwards and Zadek recommend that international organizations consider establishing more joint bodies to facilitate open debate—for example, a world financial forum linked to the work of the IMF or a world trade forum linked to the work of the World Trade Organization.

Blanchard and others (in this volume) illustrate a potential role for the epistemic community in multilateral negotiations. They show, as Albin (in this volume) does, that concepts of justice and fairness are highly contested when applied to policy outcomes and can give rise to long and sometimes inconclusive debates. Modeling exercises could assist negotiators in trying to define what is just and fair when drafting a particular agreement. Mendoza (in this volume) also refers to modeling results, to assess whether and to what extent some reforms in the multilateral trade regime are fair. If such modeling capacity were regularly available at multilateral negotiations—on all sides of the negotiating table—debate could be made more productive and better informed, and decisionmaking considerably more transparent.

The work of the Intergovernmental Panel on Climate Change (http://www.ipcc.ch) has clearly demonstrated this, playing an important role in increasing certainty and generating policy consensus on global warming. Perhaps similar advisory panels should be formed for all key global issues. Such bodies would assess the current provision of goods and identify the costs of inaction and the costs of corrective actions, as suggested by Conceição (in this volume). This approach would allow the international community to see where investing in the global public domain could yield high social returns for all.

Besides the need to make existing decisionmaking arenas more public, contributors to this volume also sometimes see a need to form new bodies. In considering the growing scarcity of water, Mehta proposes the creation of a world water parliament, backed by regional parliaments, to help realize social and economic rights to water. She also sees a need for a mechanism to redress grievances, such as a world water court. Similarly, Mendoza proposes a trade and development review council, to allow members of the World Trade Organization, notably developing countries, to make a case for modifications in or exceptions to existing trade rules.

Many global public goods are not intrinsically beneficial. Their provision should be enhanced only if they are cost effective. At the same time, public goods are not distribution-neutral. A good may provide more utility to some actors than to others. And global public goods, probably more so than others, suffer from free riding (Keohane 1984; Martin 1999) because internationally there exists no equivalent to the institution of the state, which sometimes enforces or encourages cooperation nationally. It would thus be desirable for the international community to have a forum in which the provision status of global public goods could be reviewed and decisions made on how to avoid trapping the world in a prisoner's dilemma—a situation in which individual actors try to maximize their welfare by choosing not to cooperate, but end up worse off than if they had cooperated. The need to create such a body has long been recognized, and various proposals have been made to that end. Chief among them is the suggestion to transform the UN Economic and Social Council into an economic security council.[12] But the Economic and Social Council is a subsidiary body of the UN General Assembly. For a global policy forum to be effective, it would need to be a true apex body.

A forum that might perform such a role could be constituted by the countries that are members of the General Committee of the UN General Assembly. The committee has 28 members: 1 president, the chairs of the 6 main committees of the General Assembly,[13] and 21 vice presidents. Among the 21 vice presidents, 5 are the permanent members of the UN Security Council (China, France, the Russian Federation, the United Kingdom, and the United States). The other vice

---

BOX 2

NEW TOOLS TO FOSTER PUBLICNESS IN DECISIONMAKING

- Promoting the principle of stakeholder-decisionmaker equivalence.
- Developing criteria for fair negotiations.
- Strengthening the negotiating capacity of developing countries.
- Developing rules for interactions between state and nonstate actors.
- Creating advisory scientific panels for all major global issues, following the example of the Intergovernmental Panel on Climate Change.
- Creating negotiating arenas for new priority issues (such as the right of access to water for all people) together with appropriate grievance panels (such as a world water court).
- Creating demand-driven review and response facilities to promote flexible implementation of policy regimes, such as a trade and development review council within the World Trade Organization.
- Creating a G-29 based on the membership of the General Committee of the UN General Assembly.

presidents and the chairs are nominated annually by each group of UN member states: Africa, Asia, Eastern Europe, Latin America and the Caribbean, and Western Europe and other states. For the purposes here, the president of the Economic and Social Council could probably also be invited to join. Thus a group of 29 members, a G-29, would emerge. If this group were to convene annually at the level of heads of state, say, for a day at the beginning of each year's General Assembly meetings, the world would have a representative, manageable intergovernmental forum to provide global vision and policy guidance.

Box 2 summarizes the main recommendations for fostering publicness in decisionmaking.

Systematizing the financing of global public goods

The financing of public goods involves the use of policy tools—financial and non-financial—to facilitate an adequate flow of public and private resources to these goods. It is about resource allocation rather than resource mobilization. Sometimes adequate provision of global public goods may call for increasing overall spending, public or private, at least temporarily. But this is a different issue than determining what constitutes an adequate allocation of resources to particular goods. One good may require additional resources in order to be adequately supplied, while another could be overfinanced and, as a result, possibly generate a public bad. A case in point is defense spending in the context of an arms race. National defense is a public good. But if countries are locked in a nuclear arms race, overfinancing—in zealous pursuit of a national public good—can generate a global public bad.

As noted, when viewed from the production side, global public goods can be seen as the sum of national public goods plus international cooperation. Not surprisingly, the largest part of global public goods financing is national. Kaul and Le Goulven (in their chapter on financing in this volume) estimate that national public spending on global public goods is 200 times international spending.

National financing of public goods can draw on a well-established body of theoretical literature and practical experience in national public finance. That does not mean that it is a settled issue. There are competing theories, and different experts interpret experiences differently.

Still, national financing of public goods is a recognized, debated issue. That is not the case for international financing of global public goods, which is largely unrecognized and hidden. To the extent that public finance theory addresses international dimensions, it deals primarily with revenue issues rather than the much broader allocation issues of interest here. Although studies have been emerging on the international dimensions of public finance, they tend to focus on instruments, addressing a tool or set of tools for a certain global issue.[14] But a coherent analytical framework is still missing. In addition, the financing of global public goods often remains hidden because it is presented as—and drawn from—official development assistance. Both facts contribute to the underprovision of global public goods, according to Kaul and Le Goulven (financing chapter). That is why the discussion in this volume focuses on the international financing of global public goods, particularly on the public financing side of it—as an incentive and complement to private financing.

The invisible international component of global public goods financing
To recognize the financing measures for global public goods at the international level, it is useful to consider the tools used to finance national public goods. Most of the public finance tools used domestically to steer resource allocations also exist internationally:

- *Subsidies.* A multitude of international subsidy schemes can be found, as Arhin-Tenkorang and Conceição (in this volume) show. In health, for example, such subsidies are intended to encourage research and development related to global health concerns. This research and development has special relevance to developing countries and would not happen without these subsidies. Other such subsidies are the various payments, usually in the form of aid, to developing countries for purposes related to global public goods—such as controlling corruption, harmonizing legal frameworks, promoting human rights and democracy, and implementing internationally recommended financial codes and standards. Many of these initiatives are vital to integrating markets across borders.
- *Compensation.* Examples of compensation include the incremental cost payments by the Global Environment Facility for purposes such as biodiversity conservation, mentioned by Perrings and Gadgil (in this volume), and carbon sequestration, mentioned by Castro and Cordero (in this volume). These payments are meant to reimburse developing countries for the extra costs they incur in providing global environmental services that they would not produce if guided solely by national self-interest.
- *User fees and charges.* User fees and charges are levied in a wide variety of situations. Examples are overflight charges for aircraft (as a user fee for the civil aviation infrastructure on the ground), sharing of postage revenue to finance delivery services provided by sending and recipient countries, and the charges (or even royalties) that signatories to the International Treaty on Plant Genetic Resources for Food and Agriculture must pay when obtaining genetic materials from the multilateral system. Even the interest that debtor countries incur on loans from the International Monetary Fund falls into this category, particularly when one views the IMF as a "credit cooperative" (see Buira in this volume).
- *Direct payments.* Direct payments include contributions by countries to the regular budgets of the main multilateral organizations, such as those of the UN system. These payments are for the core functions of these agencies—notably their role as arenas for discussions and negotiations among

governments and other actors—and are among the few international financing arrangements that are obligatory.

- *New property rights and markets.* Castro and Cordero (in this volume) describe Costa Rica's experience in creating a market for emissions trading. They show how important—and difficult—it is to define new commodities, create and assign new property rights, and establish an efficient and fair price for a new commodity such as carbon dioxide reductions.

- *Regulation.* As is evident from some of the other chapters, "soft" regulation is probably the tool used most often to encourage enhanced resource allocations for public goods. Soft regulation is usually based on nonbinding international agreements urging governments to pursue concerted policies of public finance nationally, mainly with a view to reducing negative cross-border spillovers. According to Barrett (in this volume), however, such agreements are often ineffective because they lack credible incentives. Yet there are exceptions. An important example is discussed by Correa (in this volume): the TRIPS agreement. In the trade regime there is a clear trend toward what international relations scholars call a "legalization" of commitments. Intellectual property rights are a powerful tool for channeling resources into research and development of new technology. Yet as argued by Correa and by Arhin-Tenkorang and Conceição (in this volume), these rights could price medicines out of the reach of poor people.

The financing of some global public goods works fairly well. These "self-running" global public goods include network-based goods such as the international communication and transportation systems. Their public finance requirements are usually part of the budgets of the relevant national agencies. And they are able to attract considerable private financing, mainly because providers can levy user fees and charges. But many other global public goods are dependent on aid and financed out of official development assistance. Most goods linked to international subsidy or compensatory payment schemes fall into this category.

Kaul and Le Goulven (financing chapter) present estimates showing that 30 percent of official development assistance—about $16 billion a year—flows to global public goods. Moreover, this share is rising. Under such conditions it is doubtful that more efficient resource allocations to global public goods or a fairer distribution of net benefits can be achieved. Financing for global public goods thus faces a double jeopardy of either not being recognized or being considered a form of aid. Neither is a good starting point for managing globalization better.

Differentiating between distribution and allocation
Why should official development assistance not be used to finance global public goods? Public finance theory provides the answer. This theory draws a distinction between the allocation and distribution branches of public finance. The role of

the allocation branch is to foster efficient financing of public goods, while the role of the distribution branch is to help society achieve its objectives for equity through various transfer programs. An appropriate recognition of both concerns—efficiency and equity—implies recognition of both branches. As Musgrave and Musgrave (1989, p. 11) write,

> *While redistribution inevitably involves an efficiency cost, this consequence by itself establishes no conclusive case against such policies. It merely tells us that any given distributional change should be accomplished at the least efficiency cost and a need exists for balancing conflicting equity and efficiency objectives. An optimally conducted policy must allow for both concerns.*

While Musgrave and Musgrave refer to the national context, there is no reason to expect the international scene to be different

Official development assistance, or aid, constitutes the international component of the distribution branch of public finance. Its stated purpose is to help developing countries because they are poor. By analogy, the financing of international cooperation on global public goods constitutes the international component of the allocation branch of public finance. The task of this international allocation branch, combined with appropriate national public finance measures, is to enhance the provision of particular goods because their provision level is deficient.

Confounding aid and financing for global public goods has serious implications for developing and industrial countries—and for the world. First, aid resources are redirected from the national priorities of developing countries to international—often donor country–driven—priorities. As a result development may suffer, and poverty may even increase. Second, aid does not bring out the proper scarcity value of such critically important global services as biodiversity conservation or carbon sequestration. As a result developing countries providing these services might be underpaid. Third, because of this undervaluation, wrong policy signals are sent to industrial countries, and important policy reforms in these countries, such as in energy, may be delayed. In addition, developing countries are not always the most pivotal countries for providing global public goods. So, there is a risk that aid resources will be diverted away from these countries.

Industrial countries show many signs of aid fatigue. But world poverty is too deep and too extensive to allow cutting back aid and reorienting the international component of the distribution branch toward global concerns. Yet global challenges must also be addressed, and many require a more decisive and determined policy response. So, for reasons of both effective aid and adequate provision of global public goods, there is an urgent need to create a separate, complementary international component of the allocation branch.

Setting up the international component of the allocation branch
Creating an international component of the allocation branch involves a number of activities—some oriented toward institutional reform, others focused on policy. Some of the institutional issues are outlined below.

Adopting an integrated approach to budgeting. One purpose in separating the distribution and allocation branches is to return to the official development assistance account the resources being channeled to global public goods. By implication, a priority task in setting up the international allocation component is to identify new and additional sources for the financing of global public goods.

This can be achieved, for example, by anchoring spending on international cooperation in the budgets of the national government agencies in charge of financing the national components of a good. These agencies would thus absorb the costs of the international cooperation necessary to enjoy the global public good domestically. Self-running global public goods follow this financing pattern. Similarly, national contributions to the regular budgets of multilateral organizations often come from the budgets of the organizations' national counterpart ministries.

Integrating the financing of the national and international components of a good would have the added advantage of drawing attention to spending inconsistencies. A glaring example is the large volume of "perverse subsidies." These subsidies support activities that generate public bads, which then require corrective measures and additional spending. Maintaining fossil fuel subsidies while investing to avert global warming is an example of possible policy incoherence.

Creating national matching grant funds for international cooperation. As emphasized throughout this volume, every public good is different. Thus the incentive structures underpinning each good also tend to differ. For self-running global public goods the advantages of cooperating—and in some cases even making private payments for some dimensions of the goods—are much clearer to individual actors than they are for other global public goods. For example, most people probably favor effective international crime control. But the benefits of this good are so diffuse that it is difficult to levy charges and generate revenue for the agency managing the issue. Matters are different when it comes to airport security, for which airport taxes could be increased to help finance added control measures. So, by agreeing to finance the international cooperation part of a global public good, different government agencies would accept different responsibilities—and would probably do so with different levels of commitment, depending on the added financial burden or the new revenue sources that this might entail.

To reduce the risk that spending on international cooperation will be neglected, national funds for international cooperation could be created. These funds could be attached to the ministry of foreign affairs or to the office of the head of government. In many countries central or federal government entities provide matching grants to lower levels of government to support the provision of goods with national spillovers. Similarly, national funds for international cooperation could, where necessary, provide matching grants to government entities for pursuing the interests of the country in international cooperation.

Establishing international accounts for global issues. The creation of an international component of the allocation branch must start at the national level. National public finance needs to be reformed so that it can link up with corresponding international measures. Yet international reforms are also required. For example, Kaul and Le Goulven (financing chapter) recommend establishing accounts for international issues identified by national and international political processes as needing action. Efforts have already been made in this direction: many accounts or trust funds have sprung up in recent years, including the Global Environment Facility and the Global Fund for HIV/AIDS, Malaria, and Tuberculosis.

Defining policy principles
Creating—and shaping—an international component of the allocation branch also involves policy issues. Various chapters highlight four issues that deserve consideration.

Embedding fairness in allocation decisions. As noted, Sandmo (in this volume) examines a theoretical case in which income transfers are required to bring about a win-win scenario for both a rich country and a poor country in producing a global public good. This brings to light a key issue in the provision of global public goods: achieving a Pareto-efficient multilateral agreement often requires making transfers to countries that would otherwise be made worse off by the agreement. These transfers are therefore an integral part of the allocation decision. They can, in fact, be considered payments for services related to the provision of global public goods. An example is an agreement to trade carbon emission reductions, allowing a country to buy part of another country's pollution quota, ideally at competitive market rates. The aim is to move toward a Pareto-efficient outcome—to achieve a reallocation of resources that makes at least one actor better off and none worse off.

Transfers aimed at achieving such Pareto improvements can occur between actors regardless of whether they are poor or rich. Yet poor countries may in some cases be able to provide inputs to a global public good—say, biodiversity preservation—more cheaply than rich countries. So, transfers aimed at Pareto improvements may often occur between industrial and developing countries—but for efficiency reasons, not to substitute for the distribution branch.

In fact, international relations and negotiation theories arrive at similar conclusions. They usually emphasize that for international cooperation to succeed, all participating parties—whether rich or poor—need to perceive it as generating clear net benefits for them. So, facilitating a fair negotiation outcome is different from transferring resources to developing countries because they are poor. Achieving a fair negotiation outcome is an integral function of global public goods financing—and is thus a matter for the allocation branch. This holds true regardless of the income or development status of the negotiating parties. But helping countries overcome poverty is clearly a task for the distribution branch.

Building private-public finance partnerships. Just as at the national level, at the international level financing public goods often involves multiple funding sources and financing arrangements. Arhin-Tenkorang and Conceição (in this volume) and other authors point to the growing role of global public policy (and financing) partnerships, such as the Global Alliance for Vaccines and Immunization, International AIDS Vaccine Initiative, Medicines for Malaria Venture, and Global Water Partnership. Private philanthropic foundations often take a lead in these partnerships, acting as social venture capitalists by investing in emerging concerns or in new ways of doing things to advance urgent but politically stagnating public concerns. So, besides representing a new form of cooperation, these partnerships have experimented with innovative financing instruments. One example is the provision of pooled incentives for pharmaceutical companies to engage in research and development focused on diseases of poor people.

Ideas for ways in which governments could enable private actors to enhance their contributions to global public goods abound throughout this volume. Kremer (box 2 in the chapter by Arhin-Tenkorang and Conceição) proposes the creation of an international vaccine purchasing fund to promote research and development on vaccines, a measure that could also be applied in other issue areas. Mehta discusses how to combine marketizing water with guaranteeing access for all. Castro and Cordero examine the process of creating new commodities (carbon sequestration services) and new markets (emissions trading). From these examples it is evident that, often, all that governments may have to do is to set a new policy framework—new property rights, new standards, and perhaps some incentive funds. They may not have to spend public revenue directly on global public goods, instead using it to enable private actors to contribute to solutions to global social concerns.

Moving beyond controlling bads to providing goods. Fair net benefits for all are an important ingredient of successful cooperation. But it is one thing to share net costs fairly and another to share net benefits fairly. As Desai (in this volume) emphasizes, the provision of public goods has often been driven by crises, both nationally and internationally. As a result a major preoccupation of policymaking has been controlling bads and sharing the costs of crises. Just think of the recurrent debates on sharing the costs of peacekeeping among UN member states, providing disaster relief, preventing and managing financial crises, and, even more recently, controlling international terrorism. Preventing and managing crises often generates no net gains. It just helps avert reversals of development.

Yet what makes self-running global public goods more successful than others is that besides offering a fair bargain, they provide net benefits for all. They enrich the public domain and people's lives. Crises will continue to erupt—and they need to be controlled. The lesson from experience is that policy strategies should first be enabling and then move beyond merely controlling the bad to creating the corresponding good.

Do possibilities exist for a shift in policy focus from controlling bads to producing goods? The case studies in this volume seem to say yes. With a change of mindset and a deliberate search for win-win scenarios, it appears possible to identify cooperation initiatives that would yield benefits for all. Castro and Cordero show how providing clean electricity to off-grid communities in Costa Rica could contribute to climate stability. Griffith-Jones explains how a more development-oriented international financial architecture could be in the interests of developing and industrial countries as well as private actors. And Barrett holds the view that a global climate treaty should, among other things, promote cooperative research and development on clean technologies and encourage the transfer of such technologies to enable countries to comply with the treaty.

Where cooperation is not only fair but also provides positive utility and improves people's lives in tangible ways, compliance with international agreements will be much easier to achieve. As both Correa and Mendoza (in this volume) conclude, in the long run more equitable cooperation strategies will also be more efficient and enduring.[15]

Striking a balance between subsidiarity and globalness. Several authors of chapters in this volume agree that to realize the policy goals outlined above, local communities, nations, and other actors need room for policy maneuver and for contributing to global goals through context-specific strategies. As Mehta suggests, the principle of fiscal equivalence or the notion of subsidiarity has to be balanced with the imperative of cooperating to achieve common objectives and pursuing concerted policy strategies. Correa, Griffith-Jones, and Mendoza underscore the same message in their chapters. This call for policy pluralism pertains to policy design in general but also to the financing strategies that different communities may choose for various policy purposes. Realizing these policy principles will be easier if policymaking on global public goods becomes more open and participatory.

Exploring investment options

It is often said that public economics and finance are about which goods to produce, how much of each to produce, and at what net benefit to whom. But international debates on global public goods often address only the question of which goods to produce. As a result the global public domain is strewn with under-funded and incompletely implemented resolutions and agreements on a host of public bads to be corrected and goods to be produced. The UN Secretary-General's *Road Map* report on the implementation of the UN Millennium Declaration reveals this problem (UN 2001).

The report also shows that the international community's vision of the global public domain focuses on 10 global public goods:

- Basic human dignity for all people, including universal access to basic education and health care.
- Respect for national sovereignty.
- Global public health, particularly communicable disease control.
- Global security or, put differently, a global public domain free from crime and violence.
- Global peace.
- Communication and transportation systems harmonized across borders.
- Institutional infrastructure harmonized across borders to foster such goals as market efficiency, universal human rights, transparent and accountable governance, and harmonization of technical standards.
- Concerted management of knowledge, including worldwide respect for intellectual property rights.
- Concerted management of the global natural commons to promote their sustainable use.
- Availability of international arenas for multilateral negotiations between states as well as between state and nonstate actors.

Many of these concerns are reflected in the chapters in this volume. If the Millennium Declaration, the *Road Map* report, and the chapter analyses are taken as reference points, four areas appear to deserve priority consideration when exploring options for investment in global public goods—because progress on other issues depends at least in part on progress in these areas.

Fostering the signature, ratification, and implementation of existing agreements. Most if not all of the 10 global public goods listed above rest on multilateral agreements. Yet many of these agreements lack even the first steps toward implementation: signature and ratification by all concerned nation-states. There seems to be widespread recognition of the need to provide support so that each nation-state can analyze agreements and determine their likely effects on the country and on various population groups. Support is also needed for follow-up initiatives so that countries can comply with the commitments they want to make. Such support is needed in areas ranging from control of terrorism, drug trafficking, weapons smuggling, money laundering, and smuggling of human beings to enhanced water management, disaster preparedness, human rights promotion, and implementation of multilateral trade rules, environmental norms, and health and food safety standards.

Under the proposal for an international component of the allocation branch of public finance, providing such support would be the responsibility of technical and sector agencies, including ministries or departments of defense, justice, the interior, homeland security, natural resources, health, trade, and the environment. The public goods at stake are those that these agencies are mandated to provide to national constituencies.[16]

The UN Secretary-General could play a role in moving agreements forward by urging multilateral decisionmaking bodies to review all major agreements to see whether an additional operational facility is needed to advance their implementation.

Promoting efficient management of global knowledge. The provision of many global public goods—such as climate stability and communicable disease control—involves establishing balanced access to the relevant knowledge. As suggested by Correa and by Arhin-Tenkorang and Conceição (in this volume), effective and efficient knowledge management is a crucial input to the provision of global public goods.

Knowledge is the most public of all public goods: it is strongly nonrival, and its benefits cut across many issues of public concern. The challenge is to strike a balance between promoting the broader use of knowledge (enhancing static efficiency) and providing incentives to generate more knowledge (fostering dynamic efficiency). Mechanisms to protect intellectual property rights already exist, in the form of the World Trade Organization agreement on TRIPS and the World Intellectual Property Organization.[17] But complementary arrangements are needed to generate knowledge that reduces poverty and to disseminate existing knowledge as widely as possible. Priority can be given to allocating additional resources to basic research and product development focused on diseases of poor people, creating a global clean energy access fund, and strengthening agricultural research.[18]

Making basic education and health care globally public by design. A robust public domain requires a strong public—one with the capabilities to be discerning and active. And that requires basic education and health care for all. These two goods generate negative spillovers when underprovided and positive spillovers when adequately provided. Moreover, education and health care are essential to the successful provision of almost every other public good—and to the enjoyment of private goods.

Therefore, both education and health care are—in the terminology of Sandler (in this volume)—joint products. The incentives for their consumption and thus their provision are in part private. People pursue education to better themselves. Analogously, at the national level, countries prefer to have better-educated populations because human capital contributes to economic growth and development. Yet education also has positive spillovers internationally: higher education levels can lead to slower population growth, better disease control, more stable governments, and even more peace and security. Perhaps more important, providing these goods contributes to a more healthy polity—the foundation of stable and more robust political systems, both nationally and internationally. If the public is to have a greater say in the provision of global public goods and the management of globalization, access to basic education and health care must not depend on people's income. The international community as a whole benefits from any one nation's strong human development through education and health. Hence, these goods must be available for all to enjoy. They must be made public by design.

In addition, these national public goods could be elevated to global public goods on the basis of the growing sense of commodity egalitarianism shared by many nations (Tobin 1970). Yet another rationale is that in the national context, across diverse political traditions and regimes, the critical importance of basic education and health care to society has led to their being considered key merit goods. In a globalizing world this policy principle could be extended worldwide. Hence, any international provision of these goods would no longer rely exclusively on foreign aid, but also involve global public good financing.[19]

Strengthening international policymaking arenas. Flowing from part 2 of this volume, one of the key issues in—and perhaps the most appropriate starting point for—providing and financing global public goods involves the lack of opportunities and means for the public to voice its concerns and preferences. As noted, not all those concerned are included in the process, and many who are lack the capacity for effective decisionmaking. Thus, after a strong and healthy public, fair and well-functioning international arenas for consultation and decisionmaking could be considered the second basic element of the global public domain. Without these two elements, other global public goods are at risk of underprovision or malprovision.

Although all parties are likely to gain from enhanced international cooperation, developing countries stand to gain the most. Thus they may have to take the lead on this issue, including mobilizing the required funds on their own.[20] Doing so could be considered a high-return investment, because it would help developing countries build much-needed capacity for international negotiations and allow them to achieve significant net benefits in the form of better outcomes from such negotiations.

Who will take the first steps? The UN Secretary-General has an important leadership role to play in bringing about these reforms, in his capacity as custodian and manager of the implementation of policy commitments such as the Millennium Declaration. But all parts of the global public have a role to play. As Held and

BOX 3

**POSSIBLE TOOLS AND MECHANISMS FOR FINANCING
GLOBAL PUBLIC GOODS**

- Creating an international component of the allocation branch of public finance.
- Restoring official development assistance spent on global public goods to its purpose of providing aid.
- Including the costs of international cooperation for global public goods in the budgets of line agencies or ministries.
- Creating national matching grant funds for international cooperation.
- Establishing international accounts or trust funds for global issues.
- Identifying priority investment opportunities.
- Establishing a broadly representative technical body to facilitate cooperation on global public goods.

McGrew (in this volume) suggest, governance of today's policy challenges calls for global, multilayered issue communities. Such communities or partnerships would probably be best suited to developing concrete ideas and suggestions on how to advance "their" global public goods. A special responsibility falls on the epistemic communities, which could show where and when investing in the global public domain yields relatively high social returns. If established, the G-29 could also provide crucial political impetus in moving the global public goods agenda forward, especially when supported in its work by rigorous policy and financing studies.

In addition, there might be a need to create a forum that would do for global public goods what the Organisation for Economic Co-operation and Development's Development Assistance Committee does for official development assistance—help the international community devise tools and mechanisms for international cooperation across issues and help monitor and report on resource flows, commitments, and spending. Since its aim would be the provision of global public goods, the new body should include representatives of all major groups of actors and stakeholders and would probably be most appropriate as a tripartite—state, civil society, and business—organization.

Some of the tools and mechanisms discussed in this section are summarized in box 3.

SPANNING BORDERS, SECTORS, AND GROUPS OF ACTORS

An important part of the political process for providing global public goods is to channel national interests upward, to the international level, so that they can enter and become reflected in multilateral negotiations. Once an agreement is reached, implementation starts. Crucial to this process is that the commitments by country delegations in international meetings filter back into national policymaking. In many cases national action is complemented by cooperative international arrangements, even if only to monitor compliance with the agreement reached. But international action can also entail producing the inputs to global public goods with production paths that involve economies of scale and scope. For example, some of the new partnerships in health are aimed at encouraging research and development that no country would be inclined to sponsor on its own.

As noted, when seen from a production perspective, global public goods can be described as the sum of national public goods plus international cooperation. Many elements, including many private goods and activities, enter the production paths of national public goods. Similarly, many elements make up the international cooperation component. Kaul and Le Goulven (in their chapter on institutions in this volume) illustrate the complex production paths of global public goods through two production trees, one for climate stability and one for food safety. These production trees show that producing global public goods requires reaching across many of the lines that humankind has established to order and systematize human activity—notably national borders, sectors, and groups of actors.

Held and McGrew (in this volume) characterize contemporary globalization as being of high intensity, velocity, and impact across many facets of life. Indeed, globalization has resulted in deep, far-reaching transformations. Yet many conventional organizational forms persist and should probably continue to exist. National borders (however porous), economic sectors, and differences (as well as complementarities) between various groups of actors are important and in many ways desirable.

Yet from the viewpoint of producing global public goods, such dividing lines present risks. They could stymie the production process. To avoid breakpoints and friction, national and international public management structures may have to be amended in two ways, as the analyses in this volume suggest. One challenge is to bridge divides that impede interaction and exchange. Bridging the foreign-domestic divide in national policymaking is especially important. The other challenge is to bundle efforts and resources to bring together various (now isolated) parts and allow the desired good to emerge. This calls for global, issue-specific public policy partnerships—and especially strategic management.

Overcoming the foreign-domestic divide
Effective provision of global public goods is often impeded by the division of policymaking into domestic and foreign affairs. But important changes are under way. National sector ministries and other government entities are putting more emphasis on international relations and transgovernmental networking

(Slaughter 2002). And ministries of foreign affairs, including their embassy staff abroad, are focusing more on topics that go beyond traditional notions of foreign affairs and diplomacy. The foreign affairs and diplomacy concerns of industrial countries now include such issues as health, poverty, and the environment—and those of developing countries, trade and finance.

In light of these reforms, Kaul and Le Goulven (institutions chapter) recommend reinforcing the increasing interaction between foreign affairs and technical ministries—to make exceptional practices routine. One step along this path could be for countries to appoint more issue ambassadors for global public goods of particular importance to them. Another step might be to establish a system of matrix management to link knowledge of countries and regions with knowledge of issues and sectors. The experience with successful self-running global public goods—notably communication and transportation networks—suggests that assigning each good to a national lead agency, and making that agency substantively as well as financially responsible for the good, is also effective. This would anchor the provision process in national efforts and systematically connect the domestic and international cooperation components of global public goods—fostering a more integrated and coherent approach to public policymaking and management. If in addition countries were to create, as discussed earlier, a national fund for international cooperation (to encourage government agencies to engage in international cooperation in the national interest), policymaking on the executive side of government would be much better equipped to manage interdependence and shape globalization than it is today.

But to avoid a growing democratic deficit, national legislatures must also become more involved in international cooperation activities as more and more policy is made internationally. This is important not only to ensure that the concerns of national electorates are adequately reflected in international negotiations, but also to facilitate the implementation of agreements. Martin (2000), for example, finds evidence that follow-up to international agreements tends to be more effective when legislators are involved from the outset. Legislators ultimately translate international agreements into national and local law—and authorize funding when and where required. Without their support—and their ownership of local policy—national compliance with international agreements is not likely to go far.

A practical reform measure placing no additional demands on legislators would be to review parliamentary committee structures so as to ensure that the interface between "domestic" and "foreign" works. An issue raised by Edwards and Zadek (in this volume) is relevant here: the interaction between national policy constituencies, including legislators, country negotiating teams, and civil society organizations. More systematic consultations between these groups could smooth the interaction between domestic and international policymaking.

After all these reforms, perhaps the final step would be for each ministry of foreign affairs to consider changing its name—to the ministry of foreign affairs and international cooperation.

Managing issues strategically
Even when the foreign-domestic divide is bridged, the question remains of how to bring together all the national and international inputs into a global public good. Theories of the firm and of public management can help answer this question, having long recognized the special coordination problems posed by production involving multiple agents.

Firms are highly organized structures functioning under the visible hand of entrepreneurs and management boards. Following Coase's (1990 [1937]) path-breaking article on the theory of the firm, various analyses and studies have shown that when transaction costs are high, firms can organize production processes more efficiently than markets can (see Chandler 1977 and Williamson 1985). In fact, many goods could not come together if their production were left to individual, specialized input providers.

The same holds true for the production of global public goods. Yet international cooperation on global public goods often resembles a market without firms. Scattered initiatives are undertaken in many countries and by many international agencies, but they do not necessarily yield coherent products. To enhance the effectiveness of international cooperation and the likelihood that decisions will lead to intended results, Kaul and Le Goulven (institutions chapter) therefore suggest the establishment of an implementation council for multilateral agreements ready to be translated into policy action. This council could function as an advisory board to the multilateral agency that backstops the agreement and help draw up an integrated implementation strategy.

Should the present multilateral organizations strengthen their coordination activities and try to produce some of the currently underprovided global public goods? The answer is certainly yes. But the production of these goods requires more than just better coordination between the present organizations—typically large-scale entities guided by multiple mandates and principles. It calls for strategic horizontal management—in addition to the functions performed by existing agents, nationally and internationally. In particular, what is needed is more systematic use of flexible, issue-specific, multilayered, time-bound, and outcome-oriented global public policy partnerships, complementing the existing set of multilateral agencies.

According to Sproule-Jones (2000), such partnerships and the horizontal management role they would perform are required when several agents (countries, governmental or intergovernmental organizations, private actors) provide different inputs and are functionally interdependent, multiple levels of activity have to be integrated, and consensual (rather than vertical, command-based) decisionmaking is essential. Horizontal management requires combining vision and leadership with actions to facilitate interaction, broker between parties, and bring all on board.

Steps are already being taken toward this new approach to public policy management. The growing number of global public policy partnerships signals that outcome-oriented, time-bound management arrangements are probably better suited to tackling some of today's global challenges than are the much larger, more bureaucratic agencies. As noted, Arhin-Tenkorang and Conceição (in this volume) identify several such partnerships in health, while Mehta (in this volume) refers to the Global Water Partnership. More examples include the International Organization for Standardization and the Global Reporting Initiative.

These and similar networks and partnerships span borders, sectors, and groups of actors, overcoming much of the compartmentalization that characterizes current public policymaking and management. But many of them have emerged only recently. These first-generation public policy partnerships, not surprisingly, have weaknesses, primarily concerning legitimacy and accountability (Slaughter 2002). A model for second-generation global public policy partnerships should, therefore, have two distinguishing features:

- A *clear legislative mandate*—forming the basis for the partnership's activities. This mandate could take the form of a multilateral agreement. But agreements would also need to change, becoming more concrete and focusing on a policy outcome that can be delivered.

- A *clear contractual arrangement*—between the multilateral organization backstopping the agreement and the partnership. The contract would specify, among other things, requirements for accountability, transparency, and publicness that the partnership would be expected to meet. But it would also allow room for the partnership to exercise policy entrepreneurship.

The last point is important, because many of today's partnerships—notably those focusing on policy implementation rather than policy advocacy—have succeeded as a result of entrepreneurial leadership. To build on this experience, Kaul and Le Goulven (institutions chapter) propose that multilateral agencies consider creating more opportunities for strategic issue management—for example, by creating clear policies for second-generation partnerships and for issue-focused chief executive officers (CEOs) to lead these partnerships. If policy conditions are conducive—for example, if consensus exists on a well-defined issue, the objectives are clearly feasible, and the agreement on the issue is backed by political support and requisite funding—issue-focused CEOs might emerge spontaneously. They might even compete to get the job done. Alternatively, they could be invited to undertake a particular task by the UN Secretary-General in consultation with the relevant technical agencies of the UN system and other stakeholders. The CEOs' role would be to carry out a time-bound task—

BOX 4

NEW TOOLS FOR MANAGING THE PRODUCTION OF PUBLIC GOODS

- Appointing national issue ambassadors for key global public goods.
- Designating a national lead agency, such as a technical ministry, for each key global public good.
- Linking foreign and domestic affairs through matrix management and integrated budgets.
- Renaming foreign affairs ministries as ministries for foreign affairs and international cooperation.
- Establishing implementation councils for multilateral agreements.
- Creating second-generation global public policy partnerships.
- Inviting high-level, issue-focused CEOs to lead and strategically manage public policy partnerships.

---

encouraging the world to break out of a bad policy equilibrium and enter a new and better one.

The goal would be to bring in entrepreneurial and managerial skills to accomplish more effectively the complex and often unfamiliar tasks involved in producing global public goods. Entrepreneurs are innovators. In Schumpeter's (1962 [1934], p. 88) words, "it is this 'doing the thing,' without which possibilities are dead, of which the leader's function consists." Many of today's crises have become too serious to allow possibilities for change to slip by.

Historically, eminent private actors have shown strong leadership on public issues. The Rockefeller and Ford Foundations, for example, were involved in some of the first global public policy partnerships in agricultural research—leading to such initiatives as the Consultative Group for International Agricultural Research (Baum 1985). Paul G. Hoffman, the former president of Studebaker Corporation, served as the administrator of the Marshall Plan and so helped lay the foundations for the reconstruction of war-torn Europe. More recent examples include Ted Turner and Bill and Melinda Gates. Eminent CEOs the world over have from time to time entered national politics, moving from the private domain into the public.

Of course, different issues require different responses. Partnerships are especially appropriate when the challenge is to correct an acute crisis. In other cases more permanent organizations are preferable—say, for functions such as those entrusted to the International Criminal Court or for those that a possible future world financial authority or world water court would assume.

To sum up, management of global public goods provision could be enhanced through both innovative reforms and adjustments to existing institutions. Some of the main policy options for reform are summarized in box 4.

LOOKING TO THE FUTURE: RESOLVING
THE PARADOX OF GLOBALIZATION

The beginning of the 21st century has ushered in many opportunities: new technologies to cure diseases, new economic and political arrangements to integrate national and regional markets, and new political alliances where animosity and uncertainty once prevailed. But behind this façade of technological, economic, and political openness and integration are sharp divides, tensions, and conflicts—cutting across countries, regions, population groups, and current and future generations. Globalization has created conditions that could produce massive wealth but also wreak havoc on people's lives. The paradox of globalization is that never before has the future appeared so promising and yet so threatening—for all.

Making sense of globalization is a daunting task. But mounting global challenges demand deep analysis of globalization's causes and processes. This volume is intended to shed new light on these issues and to encourage further research and policy debate on how to manage globalization.

At the end of the day, common concerns bind all people. Everyone wants to participate in a fair, stable global market economy. Everyone seeks an end to diseases such as HIV/AIDS and tuberculosis. Everyone hopes to benefit from nature. And everyone desires peace. Such issues also bind nations. They are concerns that have been echoed not just in the hallowed meeting halls of the United Nations, International Monetary Fund, World Bank, and G-8, but also—perhaps more so—on the streets. And they constitute global public goods.

The unifying message of this volume is that we have a choice—often a much wider choice than is implied by international political processes. Although globalization in its broadest sense may be irreversible, the publicness—and globalness—of particular goods are not. They reflect past policy decisions and in most cases can be adjusted to fit new realities, expectations, and preferences. As the analyses in this volume show, managing globalization is an art, requiring policy vision, innovation, and leadership. But it is also a craft, requiring new tools for new policy challenges. It is to this second dimension of globalization—providing new tools—that this volume speaks. Like its predecessor, this volume is intended to open the debate on a new set of issues—a debate that its contributors hope will be global and public.

NOTES

1. The term *institution* refers to the rules and norms of behavior that structure the incentives of economic and social agents, in the sense proposed by North (1990). As North (1998 [1995], p. 26) notes, "allocative efficiency is a static concept with a given set of institutions; the key to continuing good economic performance is a flexible institutional matrix that will adjust in the context of evolving technological and

demographic changes as well as shocks to the system"—that is, adaptive or dynamic efficiency.

2. Knowledge is often made exclusive for good reason. As Correa (in this volume) discusses, there is a tradeoff between static efficiency (the gains from sharing existing knowledge as widely as possible) and dynamic efficiency (providing incentives for innovators to generate more knowledge). The objective is to strike the proper balance so that welfare gains are maximized within the current generation and across different generations.

3. Beyond ethical and moral reasons, this may occur with education because consumption of this private good generates such large and important positive externalities (an example of "joint products" in the public goods literature) that a decision is made to make it not only free of charge but often compulsory. Most countries have public systems that make education accessible to the general public. International efforts to enhance the provision of basic education may elevate this national public good to the status of a global public good. See the Millennium Development Goals at http://www.un.org/millennium/.

4. Furthermore, since income transfers could make everyone better off, the situation is not Pareto optimal.

5. Since 1975 the heads of state or government of the major industrial democracies have met annually to deal with the major economic and political issues facing their societies and the international community. The six countries at the first summit, held in Rambouillet, France, in November 1975, were France, Germany, Italy, Japan, the United States, and the United Kingdom. They were joined by Canada at the San Juan, Puerto Rico, summit of 1976 and by the European Community at the London summit of 1977. Starting with the 1994 Naples summit, the G-7 and the Russian Federation have met as the "Political Eight" (P-8) following each G-7 summit. The 1998 Birmingham summit saw full Russian participation, giving birth to the G-8, although the G-7 continues to function alongside the formal summits (http://www.g7.utoronto.ca/g7/what_is_g7.html).

6. Moreover, economic policies in industrial countries, made individually or in concert (such as through the G-8), often have a substantial impact on developing countries. For example, Esquivel and Larrain (2002) find that a 1 percentage point increase in exchange rate volatility in the G-3 (Germany, Japan, and the United States) reduces real exports from developing countries by 2 percent.

7. See Cagatay (2001) for a discussion on the impact of trade liberalization on gender inequality and on the impact of gender inequality on trade performance. For a broader discussion of global issues and gender, see the Web site of Development Alternatives with Women for a New Era at http://www.dawn.org.fj.

8. For a more detailed discussion on these principles, see the financing chapter by Kaul and Le Goulven (in this volume), especially box 1. That chapter also discusses conditions that may override the principles discussed here. Those conditions involve situations where the production of a good entails economies of scope or scale. But

even then it would be important to match the circle of potential consumers with that of decisionmakers.

9. "Informal informals" are consultations among parties outside the formal negotiating process aimed at exploring the scope for consensus or possible bargains.

10. The Group of 77 (G-77) was established on 15 June 1964 by 77 developing countries, signatories to the Joint Declaration of the Seventy-Seven Countries issued at the end of the first session of the United Nations Conference on Trade and Development (UNCTAD) in Geneva. Beginning with the first ministerial meeting of the G-77 in Algiers in 1967, which adopted the Charter of Algiers, a permanent institutional structure gradually developed, leading to the creation of G-77 chapters in Rome (Food and Agriculture Organization of the United Nations), Vienna (United Nations Industrial Development Organization), Paris (United Nations Educational, Scientific, and Cultural Organization), and Nairobi (United Nations Environment Programme) and the Intergovernmental Group of 24 in Washington, D.C. (IMF and World Bank). Although the membership of the G-77 has increased to 133 countries, the original name has been retained because of its historical significance (http://www.g77.org/).

11. The main objective of the G-24 is to harmonize the positions of developing countries on monetary and development finance issues. To this end, the group runs a studies program and organizes meetings and seminars, among other things (see http://www.g24.org/about.htm).

12. Suggestions along these lines emanated in particular from global commissions convened in the late 1980s and early 1990s to reflect on the future of world development. See Commission on Global Governance (1995); Independent Working Group on the Future of the United Nations (1995); South Commission (1990); Stockholm Initiative on Global Security and Governance (1991); and World Commission on Environment and Development (1987).

13. The six main committees are the Disarmament and International Security Committee, Economic and Financial Committee, Humanitarian and Cultural Committee, Special Political and Decolonization Committee, Administrative and Budgetary Committee, and Legal Committee. The chairs of the committees are nominated each year based on their qualifications.

14. For references to some of the literature on financing global public goods, see the financing chapter by Kaul and Le Goulven (in this volume).

15. But widening the focus from correcting global public bads to providing global public goods might mean added expenditures, at least until the goods exist. Given this, and the large resources that developing countries need to set aside as financial reserves, it would thus be desirable for the IMF to undertake a new allocation of Special Drawing Rights (as also suggested by both Buira and Griffith-Jones in this volume) as new and additional resources.

16. The suggested support would best be linked to individual agreements. The costs of support for developing nations to assess country-specific implications of mul-

tilateral agreements over the next few years could be in the range of $40–50 million annually (see the institutions chapter by Kaul and Le Goulven).

17. One of the 16 specialized UN agencies, the World Intellectual Property Organization administers 23 international treaties on intellectual property protection. The organization has 179 member nations (http://www.wipo.org).

18. The estimated overall annual spending would be $10.5 billion (see Kaul and Le Goulven, financing chapter).

19. According to Delamonica, Mehrota, and Vandermoortele (2001), financing basic education for all would require an additional $9 billion a year. Financing basic health care would require an additional $15 billion a year until 2015 (estimate based on CMH 2001; UNDP and others 1998; and Devarajan, Miller, and Swanson 2002).

20. Once again the G-24 is an example. Member countries contribute to the financing of the group's research program through a fund administered by the United Nations Conference on Trade and Development (http://www.g24.org). But the governments of Canada, Denmark, and the Netherlands also contribute to this fund. This practice can be interpreted as an investment in a more robust system of international discussion and debate—an objective that clearly transcends narrow national self-interest. Assuming that a similar arrangement could be created in another three to four issue areas, the additional cost would amount to about $5 million a year.

REFERENCES

Baum, Warren C. 1985. *CGIAR—How It All Began.* Washington, D.C.: Consultative Group for International Agricultural Research.

Breton, Albert. 1965. "A Theory of Government Grants." *Canadian Journal of Economics and Political Science* 31 (2): 175–87.

———. 1996. *Competitive Governments: An Economic Theory of Politics and Public Finance.* Cambridge: Cambridge University Press.

Cagatay, Nilufer. 2001. "Trade, Gender and Poverty." Background paper to the United Nations Development Programme Project on Trade and Sustainable Human Development, Bureau for Development Policy, New York.

Chandler, Alfred D. 1977. *The Visible Hand: The Managerial Revolution in American Business.* Cambridge, Mass.: Belknap Press of Harvard University Press.

CMH (Commission on Macroeconomics and Health). 2001. *Macroeconomics and Health: Investing in Health for Economic Development.* Geneva: World Health Organization.

Coase, Ronald H. 1990 [1937]. "The Nature of the Firm." In Ronald H. Coase, *The Firm, the Market, and the Law.* Chicago: University of Chicago Press. Reprinted from *Economica* 4: 386–405.

Commission on Global Governance. 1995. *Our Global Neighborhood.* New York: Oxford University Press.

Cutler, A. Claire, Virginia Haufler, and Tony Porter, eds. 1999. *Private Authority and International Affairs.* Albany: State University of New York Press.

Delamonica, Enrique, Santosh Mehrota, and Jan Vandermoortele. 2001. "Education for All Is Affordable: A Minimum Cost Global Estimate." UNICEF Staff Working Paper. United Nations Children's Fund, New York.

Devarajan, Shantayanan, Margaret J. Miller, and Eric V. Swanson. 2002. "Goals for Development: History, Prospects, and Costs." Policy Research Working Paper 2819. World Bank, Washington, D.C. [http://econ.worldbank.org/files/13269_wps2819.pdf].

Esquivel, Gerardo, and Felipe Larrain. 2002. "The Impact of G-3 Exchange Rate Volatility on Developing Countries." G-24 Discussion Paper 16. United Nations Conference on Trade and Development, Geneva.

Independent Working Group on the Future of the United Nations. 1995. "The United Nations in Its Second Half-Century." Ford Foundation, New York.

Kaul, Inge, Isabelle Grunberg, and Marc A. Stern, eds. 1999. *Global Public Goods: International Cooperation in the 21st Century.* New York: Oxford University Press.

Keohane, Robert O. 1984. *After Hegemony: Cooperation and Discord in the World Political Economy.* Princeton, N.J.: Princeton University Press.

Keohane, Robert O., and Joseph S. Nye Jr. 2000. "Introduction." In Joseph S. Nye Jr. and John D. Donahue, eds., *Governance in a Globalizing World.* Washington, D.C.: Brookings Institution Press.

Martin, Lisa L. 1999. "The Political Economy of International Cooperation." In Inge Kaul, Isabelle Grunberg, and Marc A. Stern, eds., *Global Public Goods: International Cooperation in the 21st Century.* New York: Oxford University Press.

———. 2000. *Democratic Commitments: Legislatures and International Cooperation.* Princeton, N.J.: Princeton University Press.

Musgrave, Richard, and Peggy Musgrave. 1989. *Public Finance in Theory and Practice.* 5th ed. New York: McGraw Hill.

North, Douglass C. 1990. *Institutions, Institutional Changes and Economic Performance.* Cambridge: Cambridge University Press.

———. 1998 [1995]. "The New Institutional Economics and Third World Development." In John Harris, Janet Hunter, and Colin M. Lewis, eds., *The New Institutional Economics and Third World Development.* London: Routledge.

Oates, Wallace E. 1972. *Fiscal Federalism.* New York: Harcourt, Brace, Jovanovich.

Olson, Mancur. 1971 [1965]. *The Logic of Collective Action: Public Goods and the Theory of Groups.* Cambridge, Mass.: Harvard University Press.

Pianta, Mario. 2001. "Parallel Summits of Global Civil Society." In Helmut Anheier, Marlies Glasius, and Mary Kaldor, eds., *Global Civil Society 2001.* Oxford: Oxford University Press.

Reinicke, Wolfgang, and Francis Deng. 2000. *Critical Choices: The United Nations Networks and the Future of Global Governance.* Ottawa: International Development Research Centre.

Samuelson, Paul A. 1954. "The Pure Theory of Public Expenditure." *Review of Economics and Statistics* 36: 387–89.

Schumpeter, Joseph A. 1962 [1934]. *The Theory of Economic Development: An Inquiry into Profit, Capital, Credit, Interest, and the Business Cycle.* Cambridge, Mass.: Harvard University Press.

Slaughter, Anne-Marie. 2002. "Global Government Networks, Global Information Agencies, and Disaggregated Democracy." Working Paper 18. Harvard Law School, Public Law, Cambridge, Mass.

South Commission. 1990. *The Challenges to the South: Report of the South Commission.* New York: Oxford University Press.

Sproule-Jones, Mark. 2000. "Horizontal Management: Implementing Programs across Interdependent Organizations." *Canadian Public Administration* 43 (1): 92–109.

Stockholm Initiative on Global Security and Governance. 1991. "Common Responsibility in the 1990s." Stockholm, Sweden: Prime Minister's Office.

Tobin, James. 1970. "On Limiting the Domain of Inequality." *Journal of Law and Economics* 13: 263–77.

UN (United Nations). 2001. *Road Map towards the Implementation of the United Nations Millennium Declaration.* Report of the Secretary-General. 6 September. A/56/326. New York. [http://www.un.org/documents/ga/docs/56/a56326.pdf].

UNDP (United Nations Development Programme), UNESCO (United Nations Educational, Scientific, and Cultural Organization), UNFPA (United Nations Population Fund), UNICEF (United Nations Children's Fund), WHO (World Health Organization), and World Bank. 1998. *Implementing the 20/20 Initiative: Achieving Universal Access to Basic Social Services.* New York: UNICEF.

Williamson, Oliver E. 1985. *The Economic Institutions of Capitalism.* New York: Free Press.

World Commission on Environment and Development. 1987. *Our Common Future.* Oxford: Oxford University Press.

1

CONCEPTS: RETHINKING *PUBLIC*, *GLOBAL*, AND *GOOD*

Many problems related to globalization involve the provision of global public goods. When farmers in developing countries protest unfair trade, they demand reforms in the multilateral trade regime—a global public good. When protesters in Genoa (Italy) and Washington, D.C., advocate reforms in the international financial architecture, they are pursuing the global public good of international financial stability, which affects all countries. And when environmentalists call for the easing of pollution pressures on the atmosphere, they are asking that a social choice be made not to overconsume this global common.

Underpinning all these policy challenges are basic questions on how to structure the global public domain: Which goods should be made public, and which private? And which should be globalized, and which left in the national domain? Making informed policy decisions on these questions requires a clear concept of global public goods—indeed, a clear concept of public goods. Clarifying concepts is not just an academic exercise. Concepts influence how the world is viewed. They shape human expectations and actions. Conceptualizing public goods goes to the root of how globalization is perceived—and of whether it is seen as manageable or unmanageable. Thus this volume begins with five chapters that explore and expand the concept of public goods.

Meghnad Desai starts with a discussion on the history of the theory of public goods as well as the history of state provision of private as well as public goods. He notes that the theory of public goods is of fairly recent origin. Paul A. Samuelson laid its analytical foundation in the mid-1950s. At that time the world favored a strong role for the state. This approach continues to be reflected in public goods theory and has encouraged a frequent equation of public goods with state-provided goods. Yet Desai observes that public goods have been provided since the Middle Ages. In a way they predate the nation-state. And just as throughout history, over the past 50 years notions of public and private and of the role of the state have changed—and been contested and embattled. The statist notion of public goods belongs to a particular historical era, one that is about to end or that is already over. Thus the debate on global public goods cannot presume that public goods are a settled issue and that all that is required is to extend existing concepts from the national to the international level. The theory of public goods needs to be revisited and updated in light of current political realities.

Building on Desai's analysis, Inge Kaul and Ronald U. Mendoza discuss the concept of public goods, then consider global public goods. Their starting point is that the privateness and publicness of goods are social constructs. Departing from conventional practice, they propose an expanded two-tier definition of public goods that distinguishes between a good's potential for publicness and its being de facto nonexclusive and available for all people to consume. Anchored on this definition, but not part of it, Kaul and Mendoza offer a novel tool for analyzing public goods: the triangle of publicness. The triangle suggests capturing and comparing three dimensions of publicness. The first is publicness in consumption: is the good consumed by all? The second is publicness in net benefits: are the net benefits of the good equitably distributed? The third is publicness in decisionmaking: who decided to place the good in the public domain? Turning to global public goods, the authors state that a public good is global if its benefits (or costs) cut across countries in several regions and across current and future generations, and do not discriminate against any population group. To help make the concept of global public goods operational, Kaul and Mendoza also propose typologies of these goods.

Agnar Sandmo takes a further step toward extending public goods theory to the international level. Based on Samuelson's "The Pure Theory of Public Expenditure" (Review of Economics and Statistics, 1954), he shows how the theory of pure public goods can be generalized to an international setting. The analysis reveals that pursuing global production efficiency may result in inequity. Global production efficiency may call for developing countries to contribute more to a global public good—such as preservation of rain forests or biodiversity—and for industrial countries to contribute less. In the absence of income transfers, developing countries could suffer welfare losses. If this is considered undesirable, equity and efficiency considerations should go hand in hand internationally.

This balance between equity and efficiency is at the heart of many debates on globalization and global public goods. But in many cases there is also concern about the adequacy—or inadequacy—of a good's provision. In his chapter Todd Sandler explains that searching for a measure of optimal provision is like searching for the Holy Grail. Considering the nature of a good's benefits and the aggregation technology of its provision, it is possible to identify public goods at risk of being underprovided. But it is extremely difficult to measure optimal provision—that is, whether a community's demand for an additional unit of a public good is equal to the amount it is willing to pay for that unit. Thus Sandler proposes an alternative: an index of optimality that assesses the extent to which public goods are provided by clubs, based on the assumption that club goods tend to be optimally provided. Yet even the measurements required for this index are difficult to generate.

Finally, the chapter by Pedro Conceição approaches the provision issue in a different way. He points out that the current notion of optimal provision is based on aligning state spending with aggregated voter and taxpayer preferences. But a public good that is optimally provided from this perspective can be underprovided, at high cost to society. For example, underprovision can occur if voters or taxpayers lack information about a good and demand that the state underinvest in its provision. Thus Conceição recommends using technical assessments to determine the provision status of global public goods—and if a good's provision is deficient, exploring the costs of underprovision and of corrective actions. The message, based on assessments of selected global public goods, is that the costs of underprovision are generally many times the costs of corrective actions. Moreover, the costs of corrective actions decline over time and eventually disappear once a global public good is adequately provided—while the costs of underprovision persist and may even increase.

PUBLIC GOODS:
A HISTORICAL PERSPECTIVE

MEGHNAD DESAI

The current debate on global public goods relies largely on the theory of—and political experience with—the provision of national public goods (see Cornes and Sandler 1996; Kaul, Grunberg, and Stern 1999b; and Sandler 1997).[1] This approach creates two problems. First, the current theory of national public goods is statist: it assigns state institutions an important role in making decisions about public goods and in financing and producing them. In fact, public goods are often defined as being provided by the state, and the provision of these goods is seen as one of the main rationales for the existence of the state. Internationally, however, there is no equivalent to the institution of the state.

Second, while the theory of public goods assumes this role for the state, state functions have changed considerably over the past three decades—as have the goods (and services) provided by the state. Questions about state functions started with critiques of Keynesian policies and spread to a general critique of the role of the state (see Buchanan and Musgrave 1999 for a discussion of the many issues involved). As a result notions of public and private have been rethought, though in many cases they have only been queried and not yet recast. So politicians and the public at present may have clearer ideas about what should be private and "in the market" than about what is meant by the notion of public goods. This poses a second dilemma for the debate on global public goods: for the debate on such goods to advance, it must continue to occur at the national level rather than be presumed to be settled there.

Nationally, the responsibility for providing public goods is often decentralized to subnational government entities. Internationally, a similar plurality of unilateral and bilateral agencies are engaged in international cooperation and global public goods provision. And both nationally and internationally, nonstate actors are increasingly involved in these activities. Private and voluntary provision of public goods is also becoming more common, as are public-private partnerships. Thus today's polity and public goods provision have a neomedieval character (Keane 2001). Multiple authorities of varying power are involved at different levels of jurisdiction. And internationally, the United Nations plays an overarching but not sovereign role not unlike that performed by religious institutions—such as the Catholic Church—in earlier centuries.

Thus this chapter opens the debate and examines public goods from a historical perspective, exploring the history of the theory of public goods as well as the broader history of their provision by the state. The analytical history involves classical writings in public finance since the late 19th century, when the issues were crystallized in a discussion on the proper role of the state (Musgrave and Peacock 1958). Along the way the chapter also examines the actual history of how the provision of public goods grew within the broader framework of an expanding role for the state in making public provision for private as well as public goods. This broader framework concerns three main issues:

- *Preference revelation*—what goods the public wants in the public domain and what it is willing to pay for them.
- *Political bargaining*—how decisions are made on which goods to include in the public domain, how much of these goods to include, and how to make them accessible to all.
- *Production* of these goods by public or private agents.

In what follows, these three processes are referred to as the three Ps of public goods provision.

A BRIEF HISTORY OF THE THEORY OF PUBLIC GOODS

The theory of public goods has fairly recent origins. Its analytical foundations were laid by Paul A. Samuelson in his 1954 article, "The Pure Theory of Public Expenditure." But the literature Samuelson could have drawn on was produced no earlier than the late 19th century in Austria, Italy, and Sweden. Though lean and elegant, Samuelson's contribution and others that followed it beg serious political questions.

For example, the discussion assumes that the community of consumers has a well-functioning, formal state structure. Like a benevolent dictator, this state somehow guesses the preferences that people have for public goods. Another common assumption is that public goods are financed by the public treasury. It is also assumed that the state can produce public goods or find efficient private agents to do so. Moreover, public goods are analyzed in close analogy with private goods. Hence the notion of excludability emerges as a crucial differentiating element. This setup presumes well-defined property rights for private goods and, by extension, for access to and use of public goods.

These statist aspects of the public goods notion are rooted in the Austrian-German and Italian political economy tradition of the late 19th century, when the main concern was the crown's obligation to ensure the welfare of its subjects. It then quickly developed into a discussion of how a democratic polity would decide on the same question. Adolph Wagner started the debate but was soon followed by Erik Lindahl, Knut Wicksell, and others (see the articles by Lindahl, Mazzola,

Sax, Wicksell, and Wieser in Musgrave and Peacock 1958). Richard A. Musgrave, in his Ph.D. thesis and subsequent article in the *Quarterly Journal of Economics* (Musgrave 1939), drew attention to this problem of collective (as he called them) goods.

When Samuelson took up the concept in the 1950s, economists and the world at large favored an active role for the state in the economy (Samuelson 1954, 1955, and 1958, all reprinted in Samuelson 1966). Keynesian macroeconomics and Pigouvian welfare economics were basic to the paradigm, and many countries practiced planning and state control of the economy. Thus it was in a way natural to presume a large role for the state in the provision of public goods. Such a role was a response to a presumed preference on the part of the public for public goods.

But many things have happened in the nearly 50 years since Samuelson wrote his seminal piece. First, our analytical understanding of public goods has deepened. We now recognize a larger array of goods as public goods and differentiate among, for example, pure, impure, and club goods and joint products as well as between public goods and externalities (Cornes and Sandler 1996). In addition, the notion of public goods has been extended to the global level (see Kaul, Grunberg, and Stern 1999a and Sandler 1997).

At the same time, we have learned from the theory of public choice and new political economy as well as from bitter political experience that the provision of public goods does not take place in a neutral, politics-free public space. The issue of public or private goods is contested, as is the larger issue of the role of the state. Instead of public-minded altruistic citizens, we have logrolling, "pork barreling," free riding, overgrazing of the commons, and Coasian theorems, which suggest that clear property rights will provide the incentives needed for mutually beneficial exchanges and relations among individual actors.

Public goods and the three Ps noted above constitute an embattled area (for an early warning shot in this battle, see Buchanan 1960). Instead of elastic financing of public goods, there is political bargaining. There is also the perennial problem of the revelation of public preferences for public goods and of people's willingness to pay. These issues have been ignored in some approaches, particularly Samuelson's. But the difficult issues they raise cannot be ignored.

Although the notion of public goods has a strong analytical tradition, its contested nature in the national domain carries over into the international realm. Thus to improve the provision of global public goods, we need to find a different way of discussing the issues summed up by the three Ps. A historical look at public provision is helpful in this regard.

A HISTORICAL ACCOUNT OF PUBLIC PROVISION

Let us perform a mental experiment. Consider the world before states became the efficient fiscal machines they are today. In the late 18th century—Adam Smith's days—the British state spent almost all its money waging war or servicing debt incurred in previous wars. The French state—the *ancien régime*—could not even raise enough funds to cover defense expenses. "Premodern" states produced few public goods; their primary concern was national security. The question is, how were citizens' needs for the other kinds of things now grouped into the category of public goods met in those days, before the state did so?

The 13th through 17th centuries

Many things now taken for granted as public goods or even publicly provided private (that is, excludable) goods were in earlier days either not provided (as with public sanitation) or provided through voluntary or private action. For example, in the 13th and 14th centuries hospitals were run and funded privately by churches or charities. But such hospitals were often motivated not just by compassion but also by fear of infection and death (see Cipolla 1973). Similarly, poorhouses were born not merely out of charitable considerations but also out of concerns about public health and protection against crime and social unrest (Mollat 1986, pp. 119–57). During that time towns were often invaded by rural poor people, notably during famines (Braudel 1992; Walter and Schofield 1989).

Similarly, today people are used to thinking at the national level, where there is some uniformity in the quality of public goods provided. That is not how goods were provided in the medieval polity. The amount and quality of provided goods varied widely depending on a town's economic situation or, even more frequently, on the relationship between a lord and vassal or tenant or on kinship ties (Walter and Schofield 1989). In a city such as Avignon (France) in the 14th century, Tuscan merchants, for example, lived close together and were responsible for one another's debts. This is because they were foreigners in France.

But serious epidemics—notably the 1348 Black Plague in Europe—set in motion initiatives with characteristics of public goods, initially often at the level of a town but also increasingly reaching beyond. These included such public health efforts as sanitation (Walter and Schofield 1989, p. 64), quarantine (Herlihy 1997, p. 71), and the introduction of health certificates, as in Germany and Spain (Braudel 1992, p. 85).

The growth of capitalism gave further impetus to the emergence of a modern state. In its early phases mercantile capitalism and the mercantilist kingdom went hand in hand. Notably, in the 16th century states often sponsored or owned trading companies and invested in nautical training, shipbuilding, and arms manufacturing. The challenge in such cases was finding the needed resources. Taxation powers sometimes became more centralized, as in England. In addition, surpluses were mobilized through trading with or looting of (for Europeans at least) far-flung parts of Africa, Asia, and the Americas. Yet there was no strict separation between a king's treasure and a state's revenues. As feudalism declined in Western Europe in the late 18th century, kings became increasingly responsible for financing armies, and war was a major cause of spending. Yet war was also one way of enhancing territory and so a king's treasure (Anderson 1976; Cameron 1997).

Thus during this period the role of the state and public goods initiatives emerged primarily in response to the interests of rich, powerful population groups. To the extent that such initiatives reached poor people, it was the result more of political compulsion than of concern for all. Society was still too fractured for that.

The 18th and 19th centuries

The industrial revolution of the late 18th century, in parallel with twin political revolutions in France and North America, changed the nature of the state. Industrial capitalism created mass working populations concentrated in urban agglomerations where steam power was harnessed to produce textiles and other products. The French and American Revolutions created the notion of the citizen as a source of political power whose approval was vital for the legitimacy of any rule. Wealth was created that surpassed that of kings, and many European kings saw their possessions "privatized" by political upheavals. Far from being sources of wealth, kings and states became supplicants for revenues (Goldscheid 1958 [1889]).

During the 19th century Europe's population tripled and urban concentrations rose everywhere. The externalities, or public bads, caused by crowded populations became too costly for church institutions, private capitalists, and other rich population groups to bear. In England a series of famines and food riots led to demands for a central Poor Law (Randall and Charlesworth 2000). Here and elsewhere in Europe there were growing demands for popular elections to the legislature whether a country was a republic or a monarchy (Rude 2000). It was during this era that governments increasingly entered into international cooperation agreements on transport and communication as well as health issues such as quarantine (Cooper 1989, pp. 193–203).

These types of states began to provide merit goods through the public treasury. Adam Smith (1937 [1776]) had made a powerful plea for the state to provide education and training to overcome the debilitating effects of the division of labor in modern factories. To the plea for education were added calls for urgently needed urban infrastructure—roads, water, sanitation, housing, transport. The state started by being minimalist, providing water and sanitation but not housing and transport.

But this provision was not automatic. It had to be fought for by reformers, political movements, trade unions, and health and sanitation experts. Private charities often exposed the poverty and ill health prevailing amid vast wealth. As the franchise spread, the pressure to deliver such facilities also grew. The 1832 Reform Act in Britain was followed by further extension of the franchise in 1867 and 1884. Urban areas increased their representation in parliaments. The 1830 and 1848 revolutions in France were also effective in putting popular demands on the state's agenda. Fear of the urban proletariat led enlightened politicians like Germany's Bismarck to preempt agitation by creating a welfare state while denying democratic rule. A mix of public and merit goods was provided across these polities.

These goods were public in only one sense. They were not always nonexcludable or nonrivalrous in the sense that those terms are understood today. Their nonprovision had externalities that were largely negative. In addition, they affected large groups of people in small areas. Thus they were public in the sense that they were almost universally beneficial or at least beneficial for a large group. The first such goods in modern times were oriented toward urban, working class citizens. Fear of the mob—of fast-growing urban populations—made European states provide such goods even while they preached the doctrine of laissez-faire and balanced budgets. Thus it was a question not so much of gauging the preferences of consumers as of guessing what was needed to keep them from revolting—an elite response to democratic but extraparliamentary pressure.

The 20th century

The decisive breakthrough in public provision came in the 20th century with the advent of universal franchise in industrial countries. As a result the state's share in GDP rose from about 10 percent in 1870 to its current 30 percent in the United States and southern Europe, 40–50 percent in France, Germany, and the United Kingdom, and even higher in Scandinavian countries (Tanzi and Schuknecht 2000).

The state's growth was most marked during the "golden age" of Keynesianism, from 1945 to 1975. Higher incomes and higher public revenues were matched by growing populations with higher expectations of public provision. Public provision changed on three fronts:

- Goods and services already publicly provided, such as roads and education, were provided more generously and more widely.
- Public provision was extended to new areas, such as health, housing, higher education, and social services.
- Transfer payments were made to new claimants, and enhanced payments to old claimants, through pensions, social security, and poverty-related benefits.[2]

The theory of public goods—indeed, of public economics—matured during this period.

But this period was exceptional, not normal. Inflation was low for the first half or two-thirds of this period. There was growing demand for unskilled and semiskilled (blue collar) workers. Women were not major participants in the labor market. The growth in industrial workers led to growth in their unions and in their influence on national politics across OECD countries. But beginning in the late 1960s, inflationary pressures hit OECD countries almost simultaneously. The prices of public goods began to rise faster than the prices of private goods.[3] There was a fiscal crisis.

This crisis was exacerbated by the rise in oil prices in 1973. Because income tax thresholds were not indexed, far more people were caught by the direct tax net—leading to tax revolts across OECD countries. There began a questioning first of the need for transfer payments and then of the need for public provisioning of public goods. Thus the three-pronged process was reversed in the 1970s and 1980s. Privatization and outsourcing shrank the goods and services provided in the public domain. Moreover, the goods provided were less generously funded: payments were not indexed, and quality was not maintained. For transfers, the conditions of entitlement were tightened. In many countries pensions became less generous and fell relative to average income and sometimes even in absolute terms. (For an overview of the events of this era and the response to them by economists, see Galbraith 1987.)

All these events occurred through a democratic political process. In some complex way the preferences of the public—taxpayers and voters—were gauged by political parties to have changed. Electoral success was gained by lowering the provision of public goods. So while the theory of public goods was being developed in analytically challenging ways, the practical side of public goods was changing because of political considerations. The reason is that, far from being a neutral technical process of summing up preferences and locating the optimal solution through a social welfare function, as in Samuelson's characterization, the provision of public goods is a political process—one influenced by elections and mediated by political parties.

A FURTHER EXAMINATION OF THE THEORY OF PUBLIC GOODS

Neoclassical economics is notoriously ahistorical. Thus the theory of public goods starts with Samuelson, and while he provides many citations in his three seminal articles of the mid-1950s, not many economists bother to examine them. So let us now take another look at the literature before Samuelson's contribution.

The volume *Classics in Public Finance,* edited by Richard A. Musgrave and Alan Peacock in 1958, can be our reference. It sets out the evolution of the concept of modern public finance in the works of Wagner, Panteleoni, Sax, Weiser, Mazzola, Wicksell, and Lindahl. There is also a "sociological" discussion of public finance by Goldscheid and Ritschl. These articles treat the state and public finance not as hard and settled notions but as contingent and problematic, which is precisely the approach needed in any discussion of global public goods. But it is also worth looking at modern, post-Samuelson literature about public choice and constitutionalism, about preference revelation and agenda limitation. (For a recent "*duo*logue" between two giants of public economics on these issues, see Buchanan and Musgrave 1999.)

After the medieval era of feudalism in Western Europe, there was a rise of absolutist monarchies in some areas—England, France, the Hapsburg Empire in the 16th century (Ertman 1997). This is when the king's need for resources to fight wars became a serious concern of economists. Mercantilism, for example, wished to harness a monopoly of foreign trade to the king's treasure. As Goldscheid (1958 [1889], p. 203) notes: "The earliest form of the science of public finance was chrematistics, which [sought] to enrich the prince's treasury. If those early financial experts occasionally tried to identify the wealth of the prince with the well-being of the people, they did so in a purely incidental manner."

The rich prince with many possessions gave way to a world in which his properties were appropriated by private capital. This coincided with the rise of early capitalism. Once the prince's wealth had been transferred to private hands, what emerged was the state, which was poor in terms of wealth. The state had to use taxation to pay for its demands or the demands made on it by the people.

But then there arose the question of the basis on which the state was to tax. By the time Wagner was writing in the late 19th century, democratization was spreading across Europe. So the question was of the principles the state should follow in spending its revenue. It was in searching for these principles that economists began to use the twin principles of methodological individualism and utility maximization. In this view the state is not a compulsory association but a voluntary coming together of self-interested individuals. Thus the same theory that explained the determination of demand and supply in the private economy should apply to the public economy.

These assumptions are now taken to be axiomatic. But not everyone agreed in these early debates. In a spirit some distance from methodological individualism, Stein (1958 [1885], p. 29) wrote:

> The strength of the community resides in what each individual surrenders to it from his personal life—material, spiritual and social matters. It is thus . . . impossible that the community should offer the individuals the conditions of economic accomplishment, unless the individuals return to it part of their earnings made possible by the very existence of the community. As long as human beings and nations exist, this reciprocal process will continue, even though the individual may neither want it nor even be aware of it. This is the economic principle of human society.

But if this special reciprocal relationship between the individual and the state and its associated doctrine of the dual (communal and individual) nature of human personality is rejected, then justification of public spending has to be based on marginalist principles. Mazzola began to develop this notion in his 1890 article, and Wicksell improved on it in his 1896 article. Wicksell saw that using the individualist marginal calculus, as in the private goods exchange, may produce "meaningless" results. As he states (1958 [1896], pp. 81–82):

> *If the individual is to spend his money for private and public uses so that his satisfaction is maximized, he will obviously pay nothing whatsoever for public purposes. . . . Of course, if everyone were to do the same, the State will soon cease to function. The utility and the marginal utility of public services (Mazzola's public goods) for the individual thus depend in the highest degree on how much the others contribute, but hardly on how much he himself contributes. . . . Equality between the marginal utility of public goods and their price cannot, therefore, be established by the single individual, but must be secured by consultation between him and all other individuals or their delegates.*

Note that Wicksell's formulation differs from the one that Samuelson established as the authoritative one. First, Wicksell's individuals may have interdependent utilities, where each person's benefit depends on what everyone else consumes. Second, the equality between marginal utilities and price has to be established by consultation among individuals or "their delegates." This political economy is very different from that which Samuelson assumes.

Samuelson has independent utilities: "I assume no mystical collective mind that enjoys collective consumption goods" (1954, p. 387). But Samuelson posits a social welfare function of the Bergson-Samuelson type. This allows him to aggregate marginal utilities or marginal rates of substitution across individuals. Samuelson called his crucial aggregation condition, his equation 2, "the new element . . . which constitutes a pure theory of government expenditure on collective consumption goods" (1954, p. 388; see also Musgrave 1983, 1986). The most important point is that Samuelson is able to bypass what has come to be known as the revelation of preferences problem. This is because, contrary to his assertions, there is a collective mind, an ethical observer to whom preferences are somehow known (Samuelson 1954, p. 388). Thus the revelation issue is bypassed. All that would be needed in his scenario is for taxes and transfers to "be varied until society is swung to the ethical observer's optimum" (Samuelson 1954, p. 388).

Thus while Samuelson is technically on safe ground in his solution of the public goods problem, the assumptions required make the solution useless for policy purposes. But a reliance on aggregation through consultation, as Wicksell wants, offers a guarantee neither of theoretical efficacy nor of practical usefulness. Some of the debates and doubts about the state's role in the economy that erupted in the 1960s and 1970s arose from these twin problems.

The central problem is of revelation of preferences. How can we make the public reveal its preferences between public and private goods and among public goods? The Samuelson fiction of pure nonexcludable goods is just that. There are few goods like that, and the allocation of public funds for them is often the least difficult problem. Most public goods are excludable and have externalities but are genuinely beneficial to many people. They are also rivalrous in the sense that one has to choose among them as well as determine the quantity and quality of the provision of those chosen. There is a choice problem and a budget problem. Even for goods such as national security, there can be differences among citizens and their representatives about the optimal level of provision.

This is why the domain of public spending can expand or shrink. At the beginning of the democratic revolution poor people formed a majority in every country. When universal franchise came, the majority expressed a preference for a basic supply of public goods by voting for parties that gave them that. As countries prospered and citizens became richer, their preferences became more sophisticated. They were also able to express their multiple identities in a political way. So instead of a homogeneous electorate with single peaked preferences, there are citizens groups organized along age, gender, and ethnic lines. Their demands for public goods are fragmented by the quality and variety of goods they want. They can afford to opt out of some publicly provided merit goods—such as schooling—because public provision does not satisfy them.

The state supplies many goods. Some are pure public goods of the Samuelson type, such as a judicial system. Some are private goods that have universal benefits and are consumed by specific age groups, such as basic education by children. And some goods are demanded at different intensities by different groups, such as uncongested roads or a pollution-free environment. Consumers calculate over the entire range of available public goods—some for which they have zero demand and others for which they have varying positive demand—whether the taxes they pay are worth the utility they enjoy from the public goods. If consumers determine that the taxes are not worth it, most do not exit from the system. Rather, they agitate and form coalitions. Because their wants are increasingly differentiated, they choose private or club-based rather than collective provision for some goods, then resent paying taxes to finance the provision of goods they are never likely to consume.

As these trends reveal themselves, political parties change their promises so as to build majority coalitions. If once there were large, homogeneous class or occupation blocks of votes that stood behind certain parties, there suddenly appear to be small, fragmented blocks defined by particular loyalties. To build a winning coalition, political parties have to cater to a variety of views, some of them conflicting. Parties describe this as a nonideological approach to politics. The reason is that the parties must accommodate the fragmented demands of many small groups for public goods.

Thus the provision of public goods and citizens' access to them are determined by a much more robust political process than Samuelson's social welfare function or Wicksell's delegates. Democratic polities have political parties that, acting as imperfect aggregators of citizen preferences, decide budget allocations in a robust—but far from neutral—legislative process. This is where pork barreling, logrolling, and coalition forming come into play. There are no stable, permanent majorities with fixed demands for public goods. This cyclicity of the majority is not a defect, as social choice theorists often conclude. It is the only guarantee that each portion of the public has a chance of getting its turn at the public largesse.

Hence a dual process is now under way. As people become more prosperous, they want a wider and better quality range of goods, some of which can be collectively supplied. They want cleaner air, better human and legal rights, and healthier lifestyles, avoiding the negative externalities of, say, other people's smoking. They do not like to see massacres in faraway lands on their televisions if their government can do anything to help. They want better education for their children and themselves—not just primary and secondary education but tertiary education and lifetime learning. They want safer, less congested roads and safe food and medicine.

But they also want these goods to be supplied at low cost. When surveyed, people often say that they are willing to pay more for their desired public goods, but they vote for anyone promising a tax cut. Politicians promise more efficient delivery of public goods, which means private production and a combination of some free delivery with prices for extra quality or quantity. Thus the three Ps are dealt with in the political process rather than through any technical economic optimizing exercise. The result is suboptimal from a purely economic angle but is sustained by citizens' commitment to the political process and willingness to live within it. (Economists continue to search for the holy grail of the perfect polity, which is one that will follow their notions and rules; for a recent attempt, see Bailey 2001.)

CONCLUSION

This review of the analytical history of public goods and the history of public provision leads to five main conclusions. First, we need to rethink and reconceptualize—in light of today's socioeconomic and political realities—the notion of national public goods, including the three Ps of public goods provision identified at the outset.

Second, considering how public provision has changed over history, we must reckon with the fact that countries at different levels of development have different preferences for national public goods as well as global public goods. Poor countries still have to provide many national public goods. Intuitively, such countries may attach higher priority to national than to global public goods. We need to explore whether, in today's interdependent world, this is a feasible strategy—or whether poor countries have to simultaneously enhance the provision of national and global public goods that matter to them.

Third, in the provision of global public goods we are in the middle ages or, perhaps more appropriately, in a neomedieval age. Demands for global public goods come from scattered groups around the world. The intensity of their preferences for these goods differs. And to the extent that past experience can serve as a guide to the future, we must expect that action on global public goods will happen only to the extent that the international community faces a crisis and must respond.

Fourth, political parties help people deprived of national public goods press for their concerns more effectively. Internationally, of course, there are no political parties. But civil society organizations could perform internationally some of the tasks that political parties perform nationally, by acting as aggregators of preferences (Anheier, Glasius, and Kaldor 2001).

Fifth, international organizations have little or no coercive power. Thus there are no global taxes as yet. So the financing of global public goods has to be done with the cooperation of nation-states. Citizens and taxpayers in these states will have to realize that these goods constitute national public goods "gone global" as well as traditionally external goods (such as the atmosphere) "gone national"—that is, requiring concerted national-level action for their sustainable management. Citizens and taxpayers will have to lobby their countries to contribute more to the financing of global public goods to which they attach top priority. The United Nations and its agencies have a role to play in this regard. They not only can foster coordination and cooperation—that is, the *production* of global public goods—they also could help on decisions about the other two of the three Ps of global public goods: understanding and expressing *preferences* and ensuring fair and just *political bargaining* about which goods to provide, how much, and with what burden-sharing formula. These are, in short, the issues that the following chapters seek to clarify.

Today it is clear that the statist notion of public goods belongs to a particular historical era—one that we are about to leave or have even already left. Yet during the middle ages private and voluntary provision by the better-off was not a satisfactory solution. It was often a defensive type of doing good. Future efforts to provide public goods and tackle the three Ps can rely in a growing number of countries on an increasingly active and engaged civil society, including more socially concerned businesses and governments aspiring to transparency and accountability. It seems the time has come for the public to be much more directly involved in formulating *preferences*, promoting just *political bargaining*, and contributing to the *production* of national and global public goods, nationally and internationally.

NOTES

1. In this chapter national public goods are public goods provided at the national (as well as local) level.

2. Between 1870 and 1995 government spending on subsidies and transfers rose from an average of 1 percent of GDP to about 23 percent, thus accounting for about half of average spending in 1995 (Tanzi and Schuknecht 2000, pp. 6, 31).

3. The price index of publicly provided goods rose faster than privately provided goods. This was called the "wedge." The reasons originally advanced were that publicly provided goods were more labor intensive and the public sector workforce was more strongly unionized. Many governments were not willing to resist wage inflation in the public sector.

REFERENCES

Anderson, Perry. 1976. *Lineages of the Absolutist State.* London: New Left Books.

Anheier, Helmut, Marlies Glasius, and Mary Kaldor, eds. 2001. *Global Civil Society 2001.* New York: Oxford University Press.

Bailey, Martin. 2001. *Constitution for a Future Country.* New York: Palgrave.

Braudel, Fernand. 1992. *The Structures of Everyday Life: Limits of the Possible.* Berkeley and Los Angeles: University of California Press.

Buchanan, James. 1954. "Social Choice, Democracy and Free Markets." *Journal of Political Economy* 62: 114–23. Reprinted in Buchanan (1960).

————. 1960. *Fiscal Theory and Political Economy.* Chapel Hill: University of North Carolina Press.

Buchanan, James, and Richard A. Musgrave. 1999. *Public Finance and Public Choice: Two Contrasting Visions of the State.* Cambridge, Mass.: MIT Press.

Cameron, Rondo. 1997. *A Concise Economic History of the World: From Paleolithic Times to the Present.* New York: Oxford University Press.

Cipolla, Carlo. 1973. *Christofano's Plague: A Study of the History of Public Health in the Age of Galileo.* London: Collins.

Cooper, Richard N. 1989. "International Cooperation in Public Health as a Prologue to Macroeconomic Cooperation." In Richard N. Cooper, Barry Eichengreen, Gerald Holtham, Robert Putnam, and Randall Henning, eds., *Can Nations Agree? Issues in International Economic Cooperation.* Washington, D.C.: Brookings Institution.

Cornes, Richard, and Todd Sandler. 1996. *The Theory of Externalities, Public Goods, and Club Goods.* 2nd ed. Cambridge: Cambridge University Press.

Ertman, Thomas. 1997. *Birth of the Leviathan: Building States and Regimes in Medieval and Early Modern Europe.* Cambridge: Cambridge University Press.

Galbraith, John Kenneth. 1987. *Economics in Perspective: A Critical History.* Boston, Mass.: Houghton Mifflin.

Goldscheid, Rudolf. 1958 [1889]. "A Sociological Approach to Problems of Public Finance." In Richard A. Musgrave and Alan Peacock, eds., *Classics in the Theory of Public Finance.* London: Macmillan.

Herlihy, David. 1997. *The Black Death and the Transformations of the West.* Cambridge, Mass.: Harvard University Press.

Kaul, Inge, Isabelle Grunberg, and Marc A. Stern. 1999a. "Defining Global Public Goods." In Inge Kaul, Isabelle Grunberg, and Marc A. Stern, eds., *Global Public Goods: International Cooperation in the 21st Century.* New York: Oxford University Press.

————, eds. 1999b. *Global Public Goods: International Cooperation in the 21st Century.* New York: Oxford University Press.

Keane, John. 2001. "Global Civil Society?" In Helmut Anheier, Marlies Glasius, and Mary Kaldor, eds., *Global Civil Society 2001.* New York: Oxford University Press.

Mazzola, Ugo. 1958 [1890]. "The Formation of the Prices of Public Goods." In Richard A. Musgrave and Alan Peacock, eds., *Classics in the Theory of Public Finance.* London: Macmillan.

Mollat, Michel. 1986. *The Poor in the Middle Ages: An Essay in Social History.* New Haven, Conn.: Yale University Press.

Musgrave, Richard A. 1939. "The Voluntary Exchange Theory of Public Economy." *Quarterly Journal of Economics* 53 (February): 213–37. Reprinted in Musgrave (1986, vol. 1).

————. 1983. "Samuelson on Public Goods." Reprinted in Musgrave (1986, vol. 2).

————. 1986. *Public Finance in a Democratic Society: Collected Papers.* Vol. 1, *Social Goods, Taxation and Fiscal Policy;* Vol. 2, *Fiscal Doctrine, Growth and Institutions.* Brighton, Sussex: Wheatsheaf.

Musgrave, Richard A., and Alan Peacock, eds. 1958. *Classics in the Theory of Public Finance.* London: Macmillan.

Randall, Adrian, and Andrew Charlesworth, eds. 2000. *Moral Economy and Popular Protest: Crowds, Conflict and Authority.* New York: St. Martin's.

Ritschl, Hans. 1958 [1931]. "Communal Economy and Market Economy." In Richard A. Musgrave and Alan Peacock, eds., *Classics in the Theory of Public Finance.* London: Macmillan.

Rude, George. 2000. *Revolutionary Europe, 1783–1815.* Oxford: Blackwell.

Samuelson, Paul A. 1954. "The Pure Theory of Public Expenditure." *Review of Economics and Statistics* 36 (4): 387–89. Reprinted in Samuelson (1966).

————. 1955. "Diagrammatic Exposition of a Theory of Public Expenditure." *Review of Economics and Statistics* 37 (4): 350–56. Reprinted in Samuelson (1966).

————. 1958. "Aspects of Public Expenditure Theories." *Review of Economics and Statistics* 40 (4): 332–38. Reprinted in Samuelson (1966).

————. 1966. *The Collected Scientific Papers of Paul Samuelson.* Vol 2. Cambridge, Mass.: MIT Press.

Sandler, Todd. 1997. *Global Challenges: An Approach to Environmental, Political, and Economic Problems.* Ann Arbor: University of Michigan Press.

————. 1999. "Intergenerational Public Goods: Strategies, Efficiency and Institutions." In Inge Kaul, Isabelle Grunberg, and Marc A. Stern, eds., *Global Public Goods: International Cooperation in the 21st Century*. New York: Oxford University Press.

Smith, Adam. 1937 [1776]. *The Wealth of Nations*. New York: Modern Library.

Stein, Lorenz von. 1958 [1885]. "On Taxation." In Richard A. Musgrave and Alan Peacock, eds., *Classics in the Theory of Public Finance*. London: Macmillan.

Tanzi, Vito, and Ludger Schuknecht. 2000. *Public Spending in the 20th Century: A Global Perspective*. Cambridge: Cambridge University Press.

Wagner, Adolph. 1958 [1888]. "Three Extracts on Public Finance." In Richard A. Musgrave and Alan Peacock, eds., *Classics in the Theory of Public Finance*. London: Macmillan.

Walter, John, and Roger Schofield. 1989. "Famine, Disease and Crisis Mortality in Early Modern Society." In John Walter and Roger Schofield, eds., *Famine, Disease and Social Order in Early Modern Society*. Cambridge: Cambridge University Press.

Wicksell, Knut. 1958 [1896]. "A New Principle of Just Taxation." In Richard A. Musgrave and Alan Peacock, eds., *Classics in the Theory of Public Finance*. London: Macmillan.

ADVANCING THE CONCEPT OF PUBLIC GOODS

INGE KAUL AND RONALD U. MENDOZA

Recent decades have seen major shifts in what is considered and treated as private and as public. Economic liberalization, technological advances, and privatization have allowed markets to expand into new product areas and be integrated across national borders. In addition, ever-increasing numbers of private corporations have gone public, floating shares on stock markets.

As a result the public—people in general and shareholders in particular—want to know much more about companies' production and marketing principles. Consumers insist on product labeling. Labor and environmental policies can no longer be hidden behind boardroom doors. Public norms define expected standards. And civil society organizations assess and publicize corporate citizenship (Keane 2001; UNRISD 2000). Moreover, private businesses engage in self-regulation, in setting norms and standards, and in arbitrating conflicts—functions usually associated with the state (Cutler, Haufler, and Porter 1999).

Meanwhile, government programs increasingly follow market principles, outsourcing service delivery to private providers and recovering costs through user fees and other charges. There are also calls, from businesses and civil society organizations, for governments to operate more transparently and accountably. As the growing literature on good governance signals, the public sector often lacks publicness.

Yet as Edwards and Zadek (in this volume) show, businesses and states are also shining the spotlight of publicness on civil society organizations—on their representativeness and legitimacy. The shifts between private and public thus reflect greater shared concern for the public domain among all the main actors—the state, businesses, civil society organizations, and households—and for what others expect of them and how their private activities affect others (figure 1). A wider arena, and probably a new era, of publicness have emerged.

Assessments of these trends vary widely. Some analysts applaud the greater freedom granted to Adam Smith's "invisible hand" (Micklethwait and Wooldridge

The authors are grateful to Isabelle Grunberg, Todd Sandler, Victor Venida, and Oran Young for helpful comments.

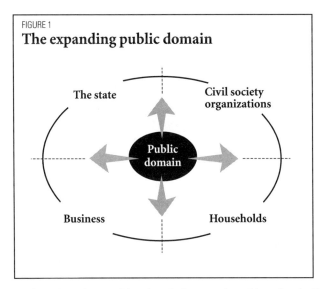

FIGURE 1
The expanding public domain

The state

Civil society organizations

Public domain

Business

Households

2000). Others fear that the world is headed toward ruthless "turbo" capitalism, driven by shareholders and property owners (Luttwak 1999). Still others waver, recognizing both risks and opportunities. As Giddens and Hutton (2000) point out, optimists and pessimists write with equal fervor because they share the same preoccupation: trying to strike the right balance between markets and states.

Markets and states are two of society's mechanisms for coordinating economic activity.[1] Each plays a role in providing private as well as public goods. Sometimes one mechanism works better, sometimes the other. It all depends on the good (or service) to be provided.[2] Curious, then, that there is hardly any debate on how to strike the right balance between private and public goods. Yet that is essentially the balance on which people's well-being depends.

Even the lives of the richest people depend on this balance. Enjoying wealth is difficult in the midst of crime, violence, political turmoil, virulent disease, or excessive financial volatility. Thus public goods complement private goods. Similarly, escaping poverty is difficult if there is no public consensus on respect for all people's lives—on people's need to drink unpolluted water, eat safe food, have a limited working day, enjoy the security of lawfulness, and be protected against ill health. A decent life depends on having such goods in the public domain, available for all people to consume.

But what are private goods? And what are public? Economics textbooks define private goods as those that are rival in consumption and that have excludable benefits (or costs).[3] That is, consumption of a private good by one person or group diminishes its availability for others—and one person or group can exclude others from consuming it. Private goods meet the requirement for market transactions. Their ownership can be transferred or denied conditional on exchange—that is, paying their price.

Public goods are defined as having the opposite characteristics: as being non-rival in consumption and having nonexcludable benefits. The market cannot price these goods efficiently. Accordingly, they are often classified as market failures and as justified cases for government intervention. Thus the textbook definitions return to the market-state issue: the provision of private goods is assigned to the market, and public goods to the state. The public domain appears as a residual category, with states performing tasks that markets cannot. But as noted, "private" can no longer simply be equated with markets, and "public" with states. Both contribute, among others, to the public and private domains. Moreover, the properties of goods can change from being public to private and from private to public.

This chapter revisits the standard definition of public goods, suggesting that a distinction be made between these goods' basic or original properties (such as being nonrival or nonexcludable) and their actual characteristics—those that society has assigned to them. For some goods the basic and the actual qualities may be the same. But for many, perhaps even most, they are not. According to this expanded definition, public goods are those that are nonexclusive—that is, de facto public in consumption.

The next section shows how this definition may require reconsidering some aspects of the theory of public goods. The discussion then turns to global public goods, the public goods of interest in this volume. The analysis covers the definition and typology of these goods, the politics of their provision, and the dimensions of their production—highlighting issues clarified in subsequent chapters.

The discussion shows that to better understand global public goods, it is important to advance the concept of public goods in general, including that of national public goods.[4] This is especially important because most global public goods are national public goods that, in the wake of globalization, have gone global. Viewed from the production side, they can be seen as national public goods plus international cooperation (see also the chapter on institutions by Kaul and Le Goulven in this volume). So, understanding global public goods requires understanding national public goods, and under current conditions the theory of public goods would be incomplete without a full discussion of global public goods. This chapter identifies some aspects of the theory of public goods that may need to be reconsidered and subjected to further study and policy debate.

RETHINKING THE DEFINITION OF PUBLIC GOODS

Although the literature on public goods is extensive and diverse, there is a standard definition of public goods anchored on nonrivalry and nonexcludability.[5] But the properties of goods do not always correspond to this standard definition. The main reason is that society can modify the (non)rivalry and (non)excludability of a good's benefits. Goods often become private or public as a result of deliberate policy choices. That is why consideration should be given to expanding the definition—to recognize that in many if not most cases, goods exist not in their original forms but as social constructs, largely determined by policies and other collective human actions. According to this revised definition, public goods are nonexclusive or, put differently, de facto public in consumption.

Public and private as social constructs

The conventional approach to defining private and public goods is to identify a good's (non)rival and (non)excludable properties (figure 2), then define the good as private or public based on those properties. As noted, rival benefits mean that one person's consumption of a good diminishes its availability for others. For example, if one person consumes a glass of milk, it is no longer available for others. Although the link between rivalry in consumption and excludability of benefits is not always automatic, the example of the glass of milk shows that by consuming a rival good, a person can exclude others from its enjoyment. In this sense milk is both a rival and an excludable good, and so falls into quadrant 1 of figure 2. It is a private good.

Another example, land, is also both rival and excludable in its original state. As a result land has been a source of conflict throughout history. Many struggles over land continue, but many societies have introduced property rights regimes that regulate land ownership, minimize uncertainty, and reduce the need for constant vigilance to defend territories against potential claimants. Thus property rights make excludable goods, such as land, a private good of recognized and reliable stature. Private goods usually have clear property rights specifying who has the exclusive right to determine how they can be used, including the ability to trade them in the market.

Even though land is a rival and excludable good, many traditional societies maintain open, nonexclusive grazing and hunting grounds. And some communities still manage as commons such natural resources as land, forests, water, and plant and animal species (Barzel 1997; Bromley 1990; Demsetz 1967; Ostrom 1990). These approaches reconfirm that excludable resources do not necessarily have to be made private or exclusive. Doing so is a policy choice, and often a societal choice to ensure the sustainable use of certain goods.

Compare the standard classifications in figure 2 with those in figure 3, which groups goods primarily according to their socially constructed status. The main difference between the two sets of classifications lies in where in terms of "private" and "public" goods fall when assessed according to their basic properties and their socially determined status.

Consider the atmosphere. In figure 2 it is in quadrant 4 as a rival, nonexcludable, open-access good. Figure 3 also lists the atmosphere in quadrant 4, but with a difference. In quadrant 4B, which is part of the public domain, the atmosphere is listed in its familiar form, as a common pool resource. But today the atmosphere's status is contested. Because of policy debates on global environmental issues, the

FIGURE 2
The basic properties of goods: a conventional approach to public goods

	RIVAL	NONRIVAL
EXCLUDABLE	**QUADRANT 1**[a] Examples: • Milk • Land • Education	**QUADRANT 2** Examples: • Research and development • Noncommercial knowledge (such as the Pythagorean theorem) • Norms and standards • Property rights regimes • Respect for human rights • Television signals
NONEXCLUDABLE	**QUADRANT 4** Examples: • Atmosphere • Wildlife	**QUADRANT 3**[b] Examples: • Moonlight • Peace and security/conflict • Law and order/anarchy • Financial stability/excessive financial volatility • Economic stability/flagging growth • Growth and development potential (such as an educated workforce) • Efficient/inefficient markets • Communicable diseases spreading/controlled or eradicated

Note: These properties are basic in that they have not been altered by public policies or other human actions.

a. In the literature, goods that fall into this quadrant—those with rival and excludable benefits—are often automatically deemed private goods. But as argued in this chapter, the properties of (non)rivalry and (non)excludability only signal a good's potential for being (public) private—not its de facto provision status.

b. Goods that fall into this quadrant are often called pure public goods—nonrival and nonexcludable in consumption. Most of these can exist in variable quantities, ranging from adequately supplied (as with peace) to inadequately supplied (as with open conflict). But the available "amount" of the good is the same for all consumers.

FIGURE 3

The socially determined status of goods: an expanded concept of public goods

RIVAL	NONRIVAL
QUADRANT 1	**QUADRANT 2**
PRIVATE GOODS	2A NONRIVAL GOODS MADE EXCLUSIVE
• Milk	• Patented knowledge of manufacturing
• Land	processes
• Education	• Cable and satellite television

EXCLUSIVE / **NONEXCLUSIVE**

PRIVATE DOMAIN / **PUBLIC DOMAIN**

2B NONRIVAL GOODS KEPT OR MADE NONEXCLUSIVE
- Public television
- Property rights regimes
- Norms and standards
- Noncommercial knowledge (such as the Pythagorean theorem)
- Respect for human rights
- As yet unknown "bads" (such as undiscovered pollutants)

QUADRANT 4

4A RIVAL GOODS MADE (PARTIALLY) EXCLUSIVE
- Atmosphere: air pollution permits
- Fish stocks: fishing quotas
- Toll roads

4B RIVAL GOODS KEPT OR MADE NONEXCLUSIVE[a]
- Atmosphere
- Wildlife such as fish stocks
- Public parks and nature reserves
- Basic education and health care for all

QUADRANT 3

PURE PUBLIC GOODS
- Moonlight
- Peace and security/conflict
- Law and order/anarchy
- Financial stability/excessive financial volatility
- Economic stability/flagging growth
- Growth and development potential (such as an educated workforce)
- Efficient/inefficient markets
- Communicable diseases spreading/controlled or eradicated
- Knowledge embodied in pharmaceutical drugs

a. There are two main types of goods in this category. The first are rival and nonexclusive, often referred to as common pool resources. Because these goods are innately rival, intensive use can threaten their sustainability. The solution is often to make such goods more exclusive, though not entirely so. New counterpart private goods such as pollution permits (see quadrant 4A) are often invented to manage the use of these resources. In countries with air pollution controls, for example, the atmosphere is still available for the general public to enjoy. But it can no longer be used excessively as a pollution sink by firms, which must now buy privately held and tradable pollution permits. The second type of goods in this category includes basic education and health care—public goods that can be made fully private but that are often made nonexclusive by policy choice.

atmosphere is increasingly linked to new, humanmade private products—namely, permits (allowances) for pollution (especially carbon dioxide) emissions.[6] Such permits do not turn the atmosphere into a private good, but they limit some actors' use of it in a particular way. If an international agreement such as the Kyoto Protocol were to enter into force (see http://unfccc.int/resource/convkp.html), what would become a private (national) entitlement is a specific aspect of this resource: the right to use the atmosphere as a "pollution sink" or, more precisely, to emit certain types and amounts of gases into it. Limiting its use in this way would preserve the atmosphere so that all actors could enjoy it more broadly.

Hence the atmosphere appears twice in figure 3: in quadrant 4A because of national and international arrangements to preserve it and in quadrant 4B because—clean or not—it is available to be consumed by all people. Other natural commons, such as lakes, rivers, and various species of wildlife, have also developed dual status. Hunting permits and fishing quotas are widely used policy instruments for natural resource management. So are norms and standards limiting or banning the release of hazardous effluents into public waters.[7] Thus the earlier finding for originally rival and excludable goods also holds for originally rival and nonexcludable ones, but in the opposite way: they can be public and there for all to consume in unlimited measure, but they need not be. (There are exceptions, however, discussed below.)

Nonrival goods have experienced similar policy-induced shifts. Some scholars have expanded the standard definition of nonrival goods to include those that can be made available to additional users at minimal or no cost (Nicholson 1998; Rosen 1999; Stiglitz 2000). For example, a new chemical formula could be shared with the concerned professional community simply through an email.

Yet many knowledge elements are made exclusive and private through property rights. In the form in which society often likes to see them, they fall into quadrant 2A of figure 3—in the private domain, as nonrival but exclusive goods. An example is manufacturing procedures protected by process patents. Yet scientific knowledge applied to and embodied in physical products, such as pharmaceuticals, tends to be subject to reverse engineering and authorized use.[8] Judged on its natural properties, such knowledge is probably more of a nonrival, nonexclusive good and belongs in quadrant 3 of figure 3.

Society can also choose to make nonrival goods more public (nonexclusive) by design; see quadrant 2B of figure 3. In some cases it may even be compulsory to consume such goods. For example, people are usually required to respect property rights. Similarly, growing policy attention is being paid to encouraging respect for human rights, including gender equality.[9] Most countries still have some way to go in making respect for human rights fully nonexclusive, ensured for all groups. Progress on universalizing more technical norms and standards—weights and measures, common currencies and languages, certain traffic rules—has been much easier to achieve.

Rival goods can also be kept or made nonexclusive; see quadrant 4B of figure 3. As noted for land, one policy option for doing so is to create a management regime that maintains broad public access. Public parks and nature reserves are examples. Another is to make rival goods available in such plentiful quantities that there need not be any competition over who gets to use them. Many societies have chosen this policy route for basic education and health services.

This approach is usually taken for two reasons. First, goods such as education and health are often seen as human rights and as having intrinsic value. Societal notions of fairness might require that education be made available to all in the spirit of commodity egalitarianism (Tobin 1970). Second, an educated and healthy population generates important private and public benefits. Educated people tend to be more productive and to contribute more to economic growth and development. Thus many countries have made basic education not just free and universal but compulsory as well.

If basic education is assessed only in terms of its natural properties, it falls into quadrant 1. But when judged on its actual form, as in figure 3, it must appear three times. In quadrant 1 it figures as a private good of educated individuals. In quadrant 4B it appears as a universally available, nonexclusive service. And in quadrant 3 it shows up as having added to a country's overall productivity and economic growth potential. Two of its dimensions (in quadrants 4B and 3) are in the public domain. As social institutions evolve, many goods—private and public—develop into "mixed" cases, displaying both exclusive and nonexclusive properties.

The goods in quadrant 3 in figures 2 and 3 are technically nonexcludable and so also exist de facto in nonexclusive form. An example is moonlight. With current technology, policymakers have no choice but to leave moonlight in quadrant 3. Its nonexcludability—and hence its nonexclusiveness—appears to be an innate quality. Obviously such goods are not socially determined and so constitute a possible exception to the notion of mixed or evolving properties.

But goods can change their positions if new technology develops. Take television signals. There was no question of public or private television before it became possible to scramble television waves and to restrict transmission through cables. Now some channels can be viewed only for a fee. As a result television falls partly in the private domain (quadrant 2A in figure 3) and partly in the public (quadrant 2B).

Returning to quadrant 3, the main goods are policy outcomes or overall conditions such as peace, law and order, financial stability, efficient markets, and communicable disease control and eradication. Once these conditions exist, all people can—and sometimes must—consume them. The goods' benefits are indivisible, so they exist for all in the same amount and with the same characteristics.

These goods are often more evident when undersupplied. For example, conflict is more noticeable than peace, which is often taken for granted. Similarly, people realize that they are "part of the market" much more when a stock market crashes and the value of their investments tumbles. Or they recognize the close links between general health conditions when a flu epidemic strikes. The corresponding public bads are also listed in quadrant 3.

Hence figure 3 illustrates that in most if not all cases, publicness and privateness are social constructs. It often takes a long time and repeated efforts to anchor a good firmly in the public domain, as with equity or respect for human rights. Similarly, it often takes a policy decision to make a good private. And in the follow-up, it takes an elaborate institutional and organizational framework to define, assign, and monitor private property rights, update and revise them as needed, enforce them, and settle disputes.

Societal norms and decisions of what is and is not private and in the realm of discretion of individual actors often reach deeply into what many perceive as the private sphere of people's lives—such as matters of matrimony and inheritance of private property. Most societies recognize that people should not be abused, even in the privacy of their homes and not even by their relatives. Children also enjoy this right, along with broader freedom from violence. On a much broader level, state borders can no longer be used as shields behind which to curtail human rights, practice corruption, spew air pollution, or pursue publicly frowned-on policies.

The standard definition of public goods has illuminated many important issues in the provision of such goods, including free riding and the prisoner's dilemma. But that definition does not fully capture the policy approach needed when dealing with the novel nature of many of these goods. As a result many public goods are still analyzed in an almost passive manner. Too often it is assumed that a nonrival and nonexcludable good must be public, or that a rival and excludable good must be private and is best left to the market.

That approach misses a basic point. Before goods appear in the market or in the portfolio of state agents, policy choices have been made or norms established to make the goods private in the sense of being exclusive or public in the sense of being nonexclusive. And even if these decisions have already been made in the past, that does not preclude rethinking them in light of new realities. "The public will operates constantly, not only before and/or after. If it operated 'before', that is tantamount to admitting that it operates afterward and at all times in between" (Wildavsky 1994, p. 388).

The excludability or nonexcludability of goods often facilitates or hampers such public policy choices. But it usually does not obviate the need to make them. In any event, the defining characteristics of many public goods are not inherent and are often socially endogenous. This issue has been noted in the literature on public goods (Cornes and Sandler 1994, 1996; Malkin and Wildavsky 1991; Marmolo 1999; Wildavsky 1994). Yet its recognition has not led to the formulation of a definition to complement the standard one and help policymakers distinguish between goods' original properties of (non)excludability and (non)rivalry and their de facto status as public or private.

Expanding the definition of public goods

The challenge is to define public goods in a way that does not leave the task of identifying "public" and "private" solely to the market but that also involves the general public and the political process. One way forward would be to develop a definition that encompasses all the goods in the public domain (see figure 3). These goods typically fall into three groups: technically nonexcludable, public by policy design, and inadvertently public.[10]

Technically nonexcludable—and so nonexclusive—goods have already been discussed. So have goods made or left public by policy design. It is worth adding that goods in this category can include those commonly perceived as having benefits (such as communicable disease control) as well as those generally referred to as public bads (crime, violence, air pollution). Bads left in the public domain may primarily affect voiceless future generations or politically weak groups, or may be perceived as being too costly to correct or secondary to other concerns. Uncertainty about the exact nature of a problem or its solution can also contribute to bads being left knowingly in the public domain. Such uncertainty is still evoked in discussions of how to respond to now certain global climate change.

The public domain has often contained for long periods public bads and goods not recognized as such. These may have become inadvertently public because of unanticipated or unforeseen circumstances. The first reports on the thinning of the ozone layer emerged only in the 1970s.[11] Even today the public domain may contain elements that tomorrow's scientists could recognize as having negative public effects and that tomorrow's policymakers might decide to ban from the public domain.

Bads also show that goods do not only migrate from the public domain into the private, or the other way around. They can also be eradicated, as with several communicable diseases (such as smallpox). Or they can move from the open public sphere into tight state control. For example, weapons of mass destruction are usually kept under close guard. Some governments also try to recapture small arms, such as guns, through special weapon surrender programs. Moreover, there is growing concern about how to reduce the risks of germ warfare as well as a host of new security threats against which present defense systems cannot protect the public.

The standard definition of public goods could be interpreted to indicate a good's potential of being public. It could be restated as:

Definition 1: Goods have a special potential for being public if they have nonexcludable benefits, nonrival benefits, or both.

This definition does not differ much from the current textbook definition except that it does not automatically categorize public or private goods based merely on (non)rivalry and (non)excludability—properties clearly malleable and subject to change by policy choice. This serves as a reminder to explore whether and to what extent all goods with the potential for publicness are public in practice. If a good is found not to be public, it is worth asking whether this is desirable from various viewpoints, including considerations of efficiency and equity.

The complementary definition, referring to the actual properties of public goods, would be:

Definition 2: Goods are de facto public if they are nonexclusive and available for all to consume.

This definition underscores the often temporary properties of goods. Some goods may be in the public domain today but not tomorrow. They may not have been in the public domain before—or even existed—but have slipped into it, perhaps due to new technologies. Examples include the recent phenomenons of computer viruses and Internet-based crime. Thus this definition stresses the need for society to be vigilant—to constantly scan the development horizon to assess whether a policy choice that seemed preferable at one time still holds. Moreover, it clarifies that the main determinant of publicness is inclusivity: the goods' being there de facto for all to consume. Public goods are not just market failures, and they are not merely state-produced goods. The public and private domains exist on their own, beyond states and markets.

It can even be argued that the state and the market are part of the public domain: they are both public goods. In its original and present form the market is an institution that is largely public. All can participate, and the more actors there are in the market, the more competitive and (potentially) more efficient it will be. Of course, to participate in the market, a person needs to have something to exchange. That many people lack means of exchange does not speak against the market as a public good. Instead it signals a problem with the distribution of income.

Similarly, a well-functioning state is a public good.[12] The more people who accept and use the state apparatus, the greater is its legitimacy. So, a state that builds its strength not on coercion but on legitimacy needs to be inclusive. As the market and the state show, being nonrival in consumption facilitates a good's inclusivity or publicness. But by itself this property does not create publicness. Nonrival goods, including knowledge, are merely goods that by design lend themselves to being made public. As noted, additional users do not reduce the goods' availability, and allowing wider consumption often enhances efficiency.

Although some goods have significant characteristics of publicness, some potential consumers may find it impossible to acquire them. Take the Internet. To use it, individuals usually need to have command over private means—to be able to afford a computer, telephone line, and related costs. So, the Internet is not fully in the public domain. Similarly, illiterate people remain excluded from large parts of the world's knowledge because they cannot absorb knowledge that exists in written form. Only goods that are truly available for all people to consume qualify as de facto or fully public. The consumption of a public good can be voluntary: some people may want to enjoy a beautiful sunset, others may not. Or it can be mandatory: it is usually a requirement to respect traffic rules.

The case of access barriers must be distinguished from that of some individuals being able to afford a private exit strategy (up to a point) from a public condition. For example, people can protect themselves against crime and violence by increasing the number of locks on their doors. But crime and violence remain in the public domain. Making greater use of private goods to compensate for degraded public goods—such as a public domain filled with negative externalities and threats to human security and well-being—is what Cropper and Oates (1992) call averting behavior. It may allow some individuals to avoid harm to their well-being, often at high cost. But it does not change the character of the public domain.

In sum, public goods are those that are in the public domain because they are technically nonexcludable, because they are placed or left there by policy choice, or because they are allowed to be there inadvertently. To the extent that access barriers limit their consumption, they are only partly public. Public goods thus form important components of the public domain, but the public domain is more than the ensemble of public goods.

More than the notion of public goods, the concept of the public domain is actively and often heatedly debated. In some societies a public sphere remains a rather unfamiliar concept.[13] Yet as markets and states have expanded and become more differentiated, they have moved out of and away from individual households, creating the private domain and the public. The actors in the public space are primarily civil society organizations and the general public. But they are also firms pursuing profits within publicly defined parameters and in the public spotlight. The suggestion here is to refer to the various goods in the public sphere—tangible and intangible—as public goods.

EXPANDING THE THEORY OF PUBLIC GOODS

A more active, policy-driven approach to identifying public goods opens the door for an equivalent expansion of other aspects of public goods theory and research. The proposed expansion of the definition of public goods could thus be accompanied by further analyses of various provision-related policy issues. Here four such issues are discussed: public choices, the difference between publicness in consumption and publicness in utility, aggregation technologies and strategies, and the adequacy of provision.

Re-envisioning public choices

The literature on public economics and finance usually emphasizes that the provision of public goods involves both a political process and a production process. The political process is usually seen as being concerned with fiscal decisions. Voters and taxpayers are seen as having to decide how to allocate their resources between private and public spending—and for public spending, expressing their preferences for certain public goods. The question of whether and to what extent to make certain goods public (or private) is usually not considered.

Considerable attention is devoted to how politicians and government agents could encourage individuals to reveal their preferences for public goods. The reason is that public goods, being available for all to consume once they are produced, are predicted to suffer from free riding. Put differently, individuals are likely to understate their preferences for these goods to avoid being taxed and to make others pay so that they can enjoy the goods free of charge.[14]

Some public economics scholars see government as a solution to free riding, however difficult it might be to make individuals reveal their preferences. But others add to this challenge a host of problems stemming from the fact that politicians and government agents tend to act in "rational," welfare-maximizing ways. They are likely to pursue not only the mandates and tasks entrusted to them by voters but also their own agendas. For politicians that could involve a desire to be reelected; for bureaucrats, an interest in advancing their careers.[15]

Much public choice theory was formulated before the 1980s, so its focus on the formal political process and on state agents is not surprising. The worldwide swing toward markets took off only in the 1990s (Held and others 1999), as did the tremendous growth in civil society (Anheier, Glasius, and Kaldor 2001). Yet even newer contributions to the topic, such as principal-agent and transaction cost theory (Dixit 1996), stay within the context of the state.

As noted, policymaking happens in a variety of ways. Because of its legislative and coercive powers, the state still plays a special role. But decisions on issues related to public goods are also driven by financial and other public pressures on businesses, by interactions within civil society, and by demands from civil society organizations to be consulted by governments and to influence how governments and politicians implement their mandates from voters. The public wants to be closely involved in selecting, designing, and even producing public goods—and in watching out for possible undesirable public effects that could accompany private goods or result from private consumption and production (negative externalities).[16] Sometimes it even seems like the public is not hiding or understating its preferences at all. In such cases the problem is getting the attention of policymakers.

Given this altered state of policymaking, it is important to widen the focus of public choice theory and to initiate theoretical and empirical research on how political decisionmaking on public goods actually functions. A principle to be reconsidered in this context is fiscal equivalence, first formulated by Breton (1965) and Olson (1971 [1965]). The principle suggests that the scope of a good's benefits be matched with jurisdictional borders. Doing so ensures that those affected by a good can participate in decisions about its provision and that the good reflects local preferences and conditions. Put differently, local public goods should be provided locally, national public goods at the level of the central government, and global public goods at the international level.[17]

Because the provision of public goods is not just a state-centered process, it is important to broaden the fiscal equivalence principle. Perhaps it could be reformulated as an "equivalence of publicness" principle calling for the matching of the circle of stakeholders in a particular public good with the circle of participants in negotiations on its provision, either with a consultative or a decisionmaking voice. To achieve such equivalence—particularly in the international context—decisionmaking would need to expand across fiscal or political jurisdictions to encompass all the stakeholders for the good in question.

Differentiating between publicness in consumption and publicness in utility
As also underscored by Breton (1965, p. 176), that a good's benefits are public in consumption "is independent of the subjective evaluation which individuals attach to the objective benefits derived from the good." Consider financial stability. In many countries the provision of this good requires the central bank to maintain adequate reserves—often at high cost. Although poor people benefit from financial stability, they may not consider this public good a top priority. So while financial stability is public in consumption, poor people probably do not gain as much from it as do richer people.

To determine whether and to what extent publicness in consumption and utility overlap, one could determine whether consuming a particular public good adds in similar measure to what people can and want to do (Sen 1982). Not every public good can be expected to provide similar satisfaction to all population groups. Yet there is a widely shared view that the public sphere should be fair and just—a sphere of civility and decency. Indeed, it often seems that promoting a fair and just public domain is precisely why the public wants to be more involved in decisionmaking on public goods.

It can be argued that the arena—and era—of publicness has emerged to better ensure that goods public in form (in consumption) are also public in substance (with benefits distributed equitably across population groups). For example, traditional judicial systems assign women a small fraction of the voice of men but are often highly public in consumption—there to judge both men and women. As a result, in some cases they are advantageous to men and disadvantageous to women. Until recently women were often not part of public decisionmaking and so traditionally have observed the public domain with concern—and often sharp critique.[18]

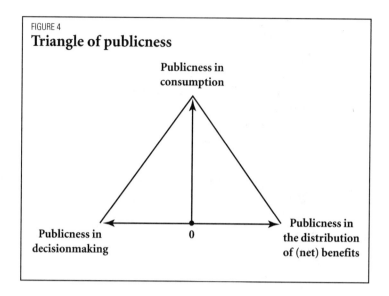

FIGURE 4
Triangle of publicness

Other disempowered groups hold similar views. Thus civil society, with its strengthened engagement in public policymaking, is seeking to change the "not so public" nature of the public sphere. Perhaps precisely because of these efforts, methodologies should be developed to systematically assess individual public goods and the public domain as a whole against two criteria:

- *The publicness—or participatory nature—of decisionmaking* on which goods to place in the public domain, how much of them to produce, how to shape them, and how to distribute their benefits among all concerned.
- *The publicness—or equity—of the distribution of benefits;* that is, the extent to which various groups (consumers of public goods) derive benefits.

These two criteria can be combined with the main, distinguishing criterion of public goods:

- *The publicness of consumption*—the nonexclusiveness of the consumption of public goods across individuals and groups.[19]

Combining these three criteria (or dimensions) of publicness results, as suggested by Kaul (2001), in an ideal "triangle of publicness" (figure 4). This triangle shows a good that is public in consumption, based on decisionmaking that fully meets the condition of the generalized equivalence principle, and with net benefits evenly distributed across diverse population groups.

Refining the concept of aggregation technologies and strategies
Public goods are often still equated with state-provided goods—for a reason. From the 1940s to the 1970s the state played a prominent role in their provision. In particular, the state provided many essentially private goods such as fertilizer, steel, and communication systems. In most countries these goods have been moved into

the private domain and into markets. Yet while the state was often taken out of the production of tangible, excludable goods, it was expected to become more active in the provision of more intangible but equally real and important goods, such as respect for law or the creation of incentives for private activity.

It is probably because of the long-standing equation of public goods with state-provided goods that only in 1983 did Hirshleifer draw attention to the fact that "standard models have assumed…that there is nothing at all special on the supply side, in the social technology for the *production* of public goods" (p. 372). He proposed examining alternatives such as "*social composition functions*, i.e. as different possible ways of amalgamating individual productions into social availabilities of a public good" (p. 372, italics in the original). Since then a debate has emerged on the aggregation technologies for various types of public goods. The three main technologies are summation, weakest link, and best shot.[20]

Public goods can require various inputs from different aggregation technologies. Climate stability is often mentioned as an example of a summation process because it requires all countries to limit carbon dioxide emissions to certain levels. Yet some of the building blocks of this good show that other aggregation technologies are also used, such as the required technological advances in cleaner energy that may be achieved through a best shot strategy (see figure 2 in the chapter on institutions by Kaul and Le Goulven in this volume). Furthermore, enabling all countries to stay within certain emission limits could call for a weakest link strategy of providing development assistance.

Moreover, different building blocks could be based on different production or public policy partnerships, each following different incentives and requiring different types of financing. The question of how the production of public goods works has found limited attention because for many years public goods were often financed and produced by the state. But since the 1980s government has become less involved in the production of essentially private goods such as telecommunication services. Meanwhile, it has played a larger role in creating an enabling framework for private and voluntary activities.

Yet few studies have followed particular goods to study how these changes have affected the goods' public-private properties and production processes. There has often been an outcry about the marketization of goods. But an important dimension is whether and to what extent marketization has been—or failed to be—accompanied by public incentives to enable private actors to internalize externalities. This information is important for understanding why goods may or may not have been underprovided in certain instances.

In today's multiactor world it is thus critical to think beyond the main types of social aggregation technologies. It is important to examine in more detail the various building blocks of public goods, exploring especially the types of incentives that different groups, notably private actors, might require to be motivated and able to deliver their expected contributions to a particular public good.

Moving from optimal public spending to adequate provision

The provision of public goods is usually considered optimal when the "Samuelson condition" is met. This condition, formulated by Paul A. Samuelson (1954), requires that the sum of all individuals' marginal willingness to pay for an additional unit of a particular public good equal the marginal cost of producing that unit. The main issue here is not that it could be difficult to ascertain and aggregate societal preferences. It is that the Samuelson condition does only what it was intended to do—provide guidance on how to adapt government revenue and spending to the preferences of the consumers of state-provided services. But a balanced pattern of spending and preferences does not necessarily indicate that a public good is adequately provided.

Assume, for example, that effective global control of HIV/AIDS would cost $10 billion a year in additional international funding, but that voters—taxpayers, and hence governments—are willing to spend only $2 billion more a year. The good—control of HIV/AIDS—could be considered optimally provided from a budget viewpoint. But its provision would be suboptimal or inadequate from a technical viewpoint. Moreover, not all required spending would have to come from government sources. For HIV/AIDS, all actor groups contribute.

It is thus desirable to expand the discussion of the provision of public goods in two ways. First, technical criteria for adequate provision should be formulated for each public good. These technical assessments could then form the basis for economic (cost-benefit) assessments of each good. The main question for technically underprovided goods is whether enhancing their provision promises high social returns. Most public goods are nothing "good" in themselves. They should be promoted only if they enhance economic growth and people's well-being. But to know their value to the economy and society, they have to be assessed in a development context, not just a budget framework.[21]

The well-established theory of public goods carries the marks of bygone eras. The first era—from the late 1940s to the late 1970s—saw the state playing a leading role in the economy, even in market economies. The second—starting in the late 1970s and early 1980s—was marked by a rebalancing between markets and states. Today's theory of public goods defines public goods as market failures but leaves the rest of the debate within the framework of the state and the theories of the first era. Now that a new multiactor era has emerged, and with it new concerns about the balance between public and private goods, the theory of public goods requires further expansion. The basic challenge is to regain a timely notion of public goods in general. But there is an additional challenge: to begin to understand global public goods.

THE SPECIAL CASE OF GLOBAL PUBLIC GOODS

So far, public goods have been discussed without specifying the geographic or jurisdictional reach of their benefits—local, national, regional, or global.[22] This section focuses on global public goods. It starts by identifying which public goods have global benefits. An interesting issue is the extent to which some goods are global naturally and others have become global by policy choice. The analysis then considers whether any aspects of the provision of global public goods are specific to their political decisionmaking and production. This second question sets the stage for some of the points examined further in subsequent chapters.

Two main findings emerge. First, globalized national public goods are an important class of global public goods. Second, the expansion of public goods theory suggested earlier becomes even more important when considering global public goods—because such goods require and create commonality in a world of extreme disparities.

Understanding global public goods: definitions and typologies
The discussion here builds on the definition of global public goods proposed by Kaul, Grunberg, and Stern (1999):

> *Definition 3: Global public goods are goods whose benefits extend to all countries, people, and generations.*

Goods can be potentially public as well as potentially global. That is, many goods can be made public or global (or both) through human actions or public policies (or both). This definition refers to goods that are already public and global—a stringent requirement that might not be satisfied by any good. Hence, as suggested in the 1999 precursor to this volume, a less strict but more useful definition could be that a good qualifies as being globally public when it benefits more than one group of countries and does not discriminate against any population group or generation.

Global public goods are nothing new. Many, notably the global natural commons, predate human activity. They include the atmosphere, the geostationary orbit, the electromagnetic spectrum, and the high seas. And as long as humans have been around, there have been externalities—many traveling the world, often in a diffuse and not clearly traceable way, as with emissions of carbon dioxide and other greenhouse gases.

But externalities alone did not create the links and interdependencies among different parts of the world's growing population. International cooperation has also played an important role. The Earth's landmasses have been claimed by and assigned to various nations (turned into national and, from a global viewpoint, private property). Following futile attempts to do the same for the high seas, it was decided to declare them a common heritage of humankind accessible to all (Mendez 1992).

The 15th and 16th centuries ushered in a new epoch in international relations, marked by the appearance of sovereign states in Europe and the expansion of their colonial powers and trade links (Braudel 1986). But in recent centuries and especially recent decades the volume of externalities and intentionally created goods of global reach has surged, often growing exponentially:

- *New technologies* increasingly enhance human mobility as well as the movement of goods, services, and information around the world.
- *Economic and political openness* have provided further impetus to cross-border and transnational activity.[23]
- *Systemic risks* have increased. The accumulating environmental degradation caused by human activities poses many risks, including global climate change. Integrated financial markets pose the risk of boom and bust cycles. Growing socioeconomic inequities call into question the legitimacy of the global system.
- *International regimes* are becoming more influential, often formulated by small groups of powerful nations yet often claiming universal applicability.

Nations and groups have seen their public domains become interlocked and their living conditions become interdependent (Cerny 1995; Stiglitz 1995; Woods 2000). For example, an economic downturn in a major economy usually affects many others through trade and investment links. Financial crises can spread from one continent to another in a matter of hours, often not sparing economies with good fundamentals. Lax food safety standards in one area can create health problems in many distant places through international travel or trade. And new global public platforms, such as the Internet, blunt many conventional public policy tools, including those for controlling such public bads as tax evasion, money laundering, drug trafficking, commercial fraud, and child abuse. The public and policymakers all over the world increasingly find that public goods they would prefer to have locally—or for bads, not have—cannot be produced solely through domestic action. A growing number of national public goods have gone global.

Like figure 3, figure 5 classifies global public goods primarily according to their humanmade (social) properties. Bearing in mind the first section of this chapter and figures 2 and 3, one can discern the differences between the original and current properties of the goods in figure 5. As before, various goods have moved within or across quadrants or are slated to do so. These changes in status show that global public goods are public in two senses: public rather than private, and global rather than national.

Given the conditions often summarized by the term *globalization,* many decisions on whether and to what extent to make certain goods public or private—decisions on which it is often difficult enough to reach consensus at the national level—must now be made by nations together. Agreeing on policies can be difficult, as indicated by recent discussions of the World Trade Organization's agreement on Trade-Related Aspects of Intellectual Property Rights (TRIPS).

The goods in quadrants 2 and 4 of figure 5 require harmonization of national policies. Policy harmonization is often intended to encourage countries to internalize cross-border externalities: to help generate positive ones and to take back negative ones. Several goods in quadrant 2B involve such efforts. Efforts to increase the inclusiveness of such goods as international communication and transport systems are aimed at improving the worldwide availability of network externalities. The same intention usually drives initiatives to increase adherence to norms and standards, including for human rights, and foster respect for national sovereignty. Most of the goods in quadrant 2B are oriented toward unleashing what various national and transnational actors perceive as global benefits.

By contrast, many of the goods in quadrant 4 involve the internalization of negative cross-border externalities. These spillovers can be diffuse, emanating from almost all countries—as with carbon dioxide emissions, which combined create the risk of global warming. Or they can originate in certain countries but potentially affect all, as with the outbreak of a new contagious disease. The policy response to diffuse externalities could be to establish an international regime that all countries would be expected to comply with. The promotion of basic human rights, shown in quadrant 2B, is an example. But depending on the public good under consideration, alternative policy options might be preferable, as shown in quadrants 4A and 4B.

Quadrant 4A lists goods with policy responses that involve defining and assigning new (national) property rights, such as national pollution allowances or the exclusive economic zones created by the 1982 UN Convention on the Law of the Sea.[24] Quadrant 4B includes goods involving measures similar to those in the national context and are aimed at making certain crucial goods—such as basic education and health care—universally available. Moral and ethical concerns often motivate the international community to undertake such measures. But sometimes externalities also matter. For example, there might be concern that the potential global repercussions of failing states, including conflicts and wars, could impose much higher costs in the future than addressing today the root causes of political tension, such as extreme poverty and inequity.[25]

A further message of figure 5 relates to the pure public goods listed in quadrant 3. Many of the goods in this quadrant are the same as those in figures 2 and 3. As national borders become porous and cross-border economic activity increases, these goods become indivisible across borders, or transnational. All nations face the same international economic conditions. All face the same conditions in international financial markets. All face the same risk of global climate change. Because of this indivisibility, environmental sustainability is included in figure 5 as an umbrella concern whereby countries are encouraged to internalize the environmental externalities they generate. Environmental sustainability requires more than occasional, unfocused corrections. Fundamental changes are needed in global production and consumption patterns to avoid irreversible environmental damage and the possible foreclosure of future generations' development options.

FIGURE 5

The de facto mix of national goods and global public goods

	RIVAL	NONRIVAL

QUADRANT 1

PRIVATE GOODS
- National biodiversity and wildlife
- Languages and cultural traditions
- National public education programs
- National water resources
- National poverty eradication programs

QUADRANT 2

2A NONRIVAL GOODS MADE EXCLUSIVE
- Commercial knowledge

2B NONRIVAL GOODS KEPT OR MADE NONEXCLUSIVE
- International communication and transport networks
- Norms and standards
- Respect for human rights
- Respect for national sovereignty
- Multilateral trade agreements (such as the agreement on TRIPS)
- Harmonization of language
- Globalization of advertisements of lifestyles and other social norms and institutions

QUADRANT 4

4A RIVAL GOODS MADE (PARTIALLY) EXCLUSIVE
- Geographic territory: exlusive economic zones such as those established by the UN Convention on the Law of the Sea
- Ozone layer: targets for reducing emissions of ozone-depleting substances
- Atmosphere: targets or quotas for reducing emissions of carbon dioxide

4B RIVAL GOODS KEPT OR MADE NONEXCLUSIVE[a]
- Atmosphere
- Global gene pool to promote food security[b]
- High seas
- Basic education and health care for all[c]
- Freedom from extreme poverty[c]

QUADRANT 3

PURE PUBLIC GOODS
- Moonlight
- Peace and security/conflict
- Financial stability/excessive financial volatility
- Economic stabilization/global economic slowdown
- Efficient/inefficient (integrated) markets
- Environmental sustainability
- Communicable diseases controlled or eradicated/spreading

EXCLUSIVE — NONEXCLUSIVE — NATIONAL DOMAIN — GLOBAL PUBLIC DOMAIN

a. The goods in this quadrant are kept or made nonexclusive to current generations (as with education) and future generations (as with the atmosphere).
b. Refers to the International Treaty on Plant Genetic Resources for Food and Agriculture (see http://www.fao.org/ag/cgrfa/).
c. These goods are included in the Millennium Development Goals (to be achieved by 2015) adopted by the UN General Assembly (see http://www.un.org/millenniumgoals/).

The considerations in figure 5 make it possible to develop a typology of global public goods (table 1). This typology differentiates between goods based on the nature of their benefits—not the scope of their benefits (they are all global), but the type of their publicness. Differentiating between the types of publicness associated with particular classes of global public goods sheds new light on some of the political tensions accompanying globalization. It shows that understanding these tensions requires assessing globalization not just for cross-border private economic activity but also for what is happening to goods in the public domain: Why have some been taken out, partly or fully? Why are the benefits—or costs—of other goods increasingly becoming public? To what extent are global public goods a shared fate of all, making international cooperation compulsory?

International cooperation seems essential for global policy outcomes or conditions (see table 1). For global humanmade commons the international community has more latitude in pursuing international cooperation. In addition, international cooperation can often take the form of more concerted national policy action. Yet for global policy outcomes or conditions and the shaping of their indivisible benefits there is often a need for truly common action—raising all boats to the same level.

Provision of global public goods: politics and production

If so many global public goods are humanmade, and if even the elements of the natural global commons so often carry a social mantle (or should but do not as yet), key questions need to be studied to determine how well the three dimensions of publicness—consumption, decisionmaking, and distribution of benefits—are met for global public goods. That global public goods are largely national public goods that have gone global has important implications for the social aggregation strategies used to produce them.

Politics. Nations have been described as communities with shared tastes. To some extent this is correct. But consider the many political and other differences within nations, such as those between rich and poor people. Tastes and preferences vary even more between nations.

The world is globalizing. But are the various dimensions of today's realities—such as decisionmaking—globalizing in tandem and at the same pace? This question is especially important for global public goods because they affect all people. More precisely, the question is whether the global scope of these goods' benefits and costs has been accompanied by a corresponding publicness in national and international policymaking. This question is urgent because publicness in consumption is often a requirement, not an option.[26]

As noted, some people—notably the world's richer people—sometimes have the option of exiting from the public domain and protecting themselves through various private means. Where commercial airline travel is too unsafe, private jets

TABLE 1

A typology of global public goods by the nature of their publicness

Class of good	Nature of publicness
Global natural commons (such as the atmosphere or the high seas)	*Free (managed) access.* In their original state these goods are typically rival and nonexcludable. Some global natural commons (such as the ozone layer) have taken on the social form of a managed access resource. But they are usually still available for all to consume—though sometimes only in limited measure.
Global humanmade commons (such as global networks, international regimes, norms, and knowledge)	*Free access.* Noncommercial knowledge, for example, is often accessible to all. It is nonrival and difficult to exclude. It typically has limited (if any) commercial value but can be important to people's daily lives or to economic and political governance.
	Limited access. Patented knowledge, for example, may be in the public domain but its use is restricted, at least for a period. The rationale is that providing incentives to private producers of knowledge will enhance the economy's growth and its dynamic efficiency.
	Inclusiveness being promoted. Many efforts are under way to enhance the inclusiveness of goods with network characteristics and whose expansion promises "additional user" benefits or positive network externalities. Examples include international regimes (multilateral trade regime, Universal Declaration of Human Rights), global communication and transport systems, and informal norms. Efforts to increase the inclusiveness of these goods will widen the range of users, globalizing the benefits and costs. Globalization of public goods includes both top-down (from international to national) and bottom-up efforts.
Global policy outcomes or conditions (such as global peace, financial stability, and environmental sustainability)	*Universalization of essentially private goods.* Examples include global (national and international) efforts aimed at "for all" goals—basic education, health care, and food security.
	Indivisibility of benefits and costs. Goods in this category have indivisible benefits that form the core of the interdependencies among countries and people. These goods tend to be technically nonexcludable and so de facto inclusive and public.

can be used. Or where global warming occurs, it may be possible to escape some of its effects by retreating to air conditioned rooms. Poor people rarely have such private exit options.

As Hirschman (1970) emphasizes, when people have no exit options—when they cannot refuse consumption—they cannot help but belong to the community of stakeholders. Often the only strategy available to them is to seek a stronger voice and more direct participation in matters that affect their lives. Such "no exit" situations are often the case for global public goods. It is not surprising that civil society has become more active and determined, and in some cases more forceful, in making its voice heard. Developing countries are also becoming more concerned about gaining seats at the tables of international negotiations.

A stronger voice is often sought for its own sake, in the interest of democracy and pluralism. But it is often sought to enhance decisionmaking and increase the economic, technical, and political feasibility of policy actions. When international cooperation is required to curtail costly, inefficient global public bads, an effective voice for all is also critical. This is particularly evident in cases where international institutions are assigned to implement international standards to promote certain public goods (such as international security and international financial stability), often resulting in incursions on domestic policymaking and lawmaking. The legitimacy of such incursions hinges on more participatory decisionmaking (Woods 2000). Hence it is important to assess the main global public goods, notably those involving high interdependence, against the ideal triangle of publicness.

Figure 6 shows how select global public goods are likely to differ from the ideal triangle. In each case it would be important to define clear indicators and reliable measurement methodologies, but doing so is beyond the scope of this chapter. The triangles in figure 6 are intended to encourage research and debate.[27] The chapters in part 2 of this volume shed further light on the politics of global public goods provision, including its participatory nature and the fairness of negotiations. The case studies in part 4 provide additional information on decisionmaking and the distribution of benefits for specific global public goods.

Production. Few global public goods are "readymade." Even the few that are, such as the natural global commons, often require international management regimes for their sustainable use. Most global public goods follow a complex, multidimensional, multilayered, multiactor production path. Accordingly, many are also likely to comprise a variety of building blocks. These building blocks can include national public goods, which may require harmonization or upgrading for all to enjoy a higher level of provision.

But especially where externalities of activities undertaken by households and firms are involved, private goods and changed patterns of private behavior may also be among the key building blocks. These often call for complementary

FIGURE 6

Examining global public goods through the triangle of publicness

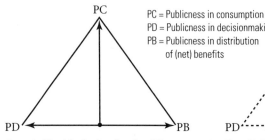

PC = Publicness in consumption
PD = Publicness in decisionmaking
PB = Publicness in distribution
of (net) benefits

Case A: The ideal triangle of publicness

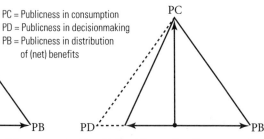

Case B: Decisionmaking is not completely public, but consumption and the distribution of benefits are.

Example: G-7 stabilization of major currencies.

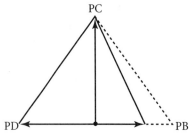

Case C: The distribution of benefits is not completely public, but consumption and formal decisionmaking are.

Example: The multilateral trade regime. The World Trade Organization (WTO) follows a one-country, one-vote procedure and so appears to satisfy publicness in decisionmaking. Yet many developing countries have limited influence in the trade negotiations process.

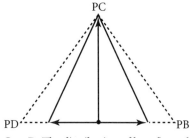

Case D: The distribution of benefits and decisionmaking are not completely public but consumption is.

Example: International financial architecture.

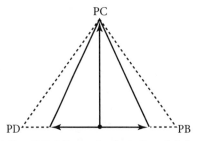

Case E: Public goods—including global public goods—often have limited benefits for women. Furthermore, there are very few women in leadership positions, leading to limited publicness in decisionmaking.

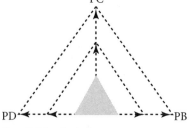

Case F: The shaded area represents a regional public good with growing externalities—making this good more public in consumption, globally. It would be interesting to examine if it also becomes more public in benefits and decisionmaking. Example: Water management.

national public policy actions, such as the provision of incentives. In addition, the production paths of global public goods are often likely to include international arrangements such as the World Trade Organization or the Global Fund to Fight AIDS, Tuberculosis, and Malaria (see http://www.globalfundatm.org/). The chapter on institutions by Kaul and Le Goulven (in this volume) discusses in more detail the production paths and building blocks of global public goods. Examples of elements that might enter the production cycles of global public goods are provided in table 2.

In many ways the process of assembling the various building blocks of global public goods is similar to that of producing national public goods. National public goods, however, can no longer be provided without due attention to their emerging international dimension. For example, international financial stability requires that every country be concerned with its own fundamentals as well as any threat of contagion from other countries. The same is true for goods such as communicable disease control and climate stability: without international cooperation, no amount of domestic spending could fully ensure the national public good. Hence, viewed from the production side, many global public goods can be seen as the sum of national public goods plus international cooperation.

Notwithstanding the importance of international cooperation, the issue of subsidiarity also needs to be raised: why would centralization—and thus international cooperation—be desirable? It is prudent to insist that the burden of proof be on those who advocate increased national policy harmonization or joint production at the international level. The reason lies in the tremendous diversity of conditions around the world. Increased provision of a global public good often requires all countries, even all people, to accept a change in global trends. But moving in the same direction is often best achieved through policy pluralism rather than standard approaches (as some of the case studies in this volume highlight). Allowing for policy pluralism increases the transaction costs involved in producing global public goods because it may entail more management support, monitoring, and reporting. Yet these costs could be modest relative to the deadweight losses of excess centralization and standardization. Policy pluralism would also be ideal when there is much debate on the best approach to providing certain goods, such as financial stability, for example.

Given the complexity of producing global public goods, there is no easy or standard formula for ensuring their adequate provision. International studies often note another handicap: the fact that there is no institution with coercive powers. Perhaps this is just as well. More important are efficient, effective measures to ensure proper feedback loops: from international agreements to implementation, from implementation to policymaking and if necessary renegotiation of agreements, and so on. The actors most likely to ensure that this process moves beyond narrow national self-interests might not always be governments, since

TABLE 2

Stages and examples of the production cycle of global public goods and their components

Global public good or component	Example
Final global public good	Peace or eradication of polio.
Intermediate global public goods	International regimes (agreements and organizations). These goods have significant properties of publicness and are also being consumed. But their consumption is often of an instrumental character. Thus the medical and pharmaceutical knowledge on which the polio vaccine is based is an intermediate global public good because it is fully in the public domain. Eradication of polio is the final global public good to which it is an input.
National public goods	National civil aviation regimes and facilities, which serve national purposes but, if in line with international agreements, also constitute important building blocks of a global public good: the international civil aviation network.
Private goods and activities and their externalities	Bed nets purchased by households as a contribution to the global public good of malaria control or use of solar energy panels by businesses as a contribution to climate stability.

they are territorially bound. They might be transnational businesses, civil society organizations, and members of the public. As Sen (1999) points out, these actors often pursue interests and concerns independently of their nationalities.

CONCLUSION

This chapter has suggested a rethinking of three notions underpinning the theory of public goods. First, it has shown that properties of (non)rivalry in consumption and (non)excludability of benefits do not automatically determine whether a good is public or private. "Public" and "private" are in many—perhaps most—cases a matter of policy choice: a social construct. Some goods lend themselves more easily to being either public or private. Nevertheless, it is important to distinguish between a good's having the potential of being public (that is, its having nonrival and nonexcludable properties) and its being de facto public (nonexclusive and available for all to consume).

Second, public goods do not necessarily have to be provided by the state. All actors can, and increasingly do, contribute to their provision. And third, a growing number of public goods are no longer just national in scope, having assumed cross-border dimensions. Many have become global and require international cooperation to be adequately provided.

Rethinking the concept of public goods along these lines has a number of implications for the theory of public goods and opens up an important new research agenda. This includes the question of how in various cases publicness in consumption is matched with publicness in decisionmaking and with equity in the distribution of a good's benefits—the issues raised by the triangle of publicness. Furthermore, recognizing the provision of public goods as a multiactor activity calls for reconsideration of the current concept of optimal provision as well as for renewed analysis of the production process of public goods.

These issues are even more urgent at the international level, particularly when one considers international cooperation in support of global public goods. The reasons are that at the international level there is no real equivalent to the institution of the state and that the global public has far more diverse interests and preferences than any national public. Furthermore, many people—indeed, entire countries—often find themselves in "no exit" situations. Under these conditions a decisionmaking and production process for global public goods that is more participatory and "bottom up" is perhaps most ideal.

In summary, Desai (in this volume) is correct when stating that the debate on global public goods cannot simply build on the existing theory of public goods. The theory must be updated to reflect current realities. This chapter has tried to do just that, and opens the door to debate and discussion on a host of new issues. The chapters that follow address many of these issues, offering the opening salvo in this debate.

NOTES

1. Arguably, civil society is emerging as a third coordinating mechanism—a role with long-standing historical precedents. For example, Desai (in this volume) discusses the coordinating role that churches and charities have played in providing health care, particularly in the 13th and 14th centuries.

2. For reasons of brevity, in this chapter *goods* refer to both goods and services.

3. Throughout this chapter, references to benefits also apply to costs. To be more precise, the objective is to derive positive net benefits from public goods—or to minimize the costs of public bads.

4. Unless otherwise specified, national public goods include local public goods.

5. For an overview of the literature, see Acocella (1998), Cornes and Sandler (1996), Cullis and Jones (1998), Musgrave and Musgrave (1989), Oakland (1991), Rosen (1999), Samuelson and Nordhaus (2001), Salanie (2000), and Stiglitz (2000).

For discussions on the evolution of the concept of public goods, see Desai (in this volume) and Buchanan and Musgrave (1999).

6. Pilot projects and schemes for greenhouse gas emissions trading are already under way; see Cozijnsen (2001), Sandor (2002), and Castro and Cordero (in this volume).

7. Quotas and other quantitative limits are often only one part of a comprehensive system of sustainable ecosystem management. See, for instance, the discussion in the Reykjavik Conference on Responsible Fisheries in the Marine Ecosystem at http://www.refisheries2001.org.

8. The Bolar provision under the World Trade Organization agreement on Trade-Related Aspects of Intellectual Property Rights (TRIPS) allows manufacturers of generic drugs to develop production and regulatory procedures before patents expire to shorten the long period of preparing generics for the market. Research on patented drugs is part of this provision (WTO 2001).

9. Respect for human rights and the norm of equity are viewed by some as pure public goods. The reason is that they are relational goods—no one can have them alone. For example, for a person to be treated equally, he or she needs to receive this treatment from others. Such goods exist only if a person can relate to others—so in that sense the goods are nonrival and nonexcludable. Furthermore, the more widespread is the acceptance of certain norms, the more established and firm they are for all individuals. Each additional user provides additional benefits to existing users (Rao 1999). So, all who accept a norm such as equity also benefit from it being shared as widely as possible—from being nonexclusive. But while it is nonrival and nonexcludable in the abstract, its application to the functioning of society often has distributional consequences and so encounters political opposition. As a result respect for human rights is sometimes an exclusive good—withheld from all or some population groups.

10. In figure 3 technically nonexcludable goods often fall into quadrant 3. Goods that are public by policy design—that are kept or made nonexclusive—fall into quadrants 2B and 4B. Goods (or bads) that are inadvertently public are those that have yet to be discovered. An example is HIV/AIDS in its nascent stages several decades ago.

11. For further information, see the British Antarctic Survey homepage at http://www.antarctica.ac.uk/.

12. Stiglitz (2000, p. 149) refers to "efficient government" as a public good.

13. For perspectives on the state and civil society in different cultures, see Rosenblum and Post (2002). For diverse ethical perspectives on the concept of boundaries, including political and jurisdictional ones, see Miller and Hashmi (2001).

14. Sandler (in this volume) explains how the risk of free riding and other types of collective action problems vary with the nature of the good. Barrett (in this volume) takes this discussion forward by showing how cooperation strategies can be designed to minimize noncompliance with international agreements.

15. For an illuminating dialogue between some of the main representatives of these two different schools of thought and approach, see Buchanan and Musgrave (1999).

16. Externalities are benefits conferred or costs imposed on others without compensation. Put differently, an externality is a phenomenon that arises when an individual or firm takes an action but does not bear all the costs (negative externalities) or receive all the benefits (positive externalities). In this chapter externalities are primarily seen as linked to and emanating from the activities of individual actors, making it feasible to take policy action to encourage positive externalities or discourage negative ones. Externalities can affect private well-being directly. (For example, water pollution can cause health problems.) But externalities can also affect public goods. (For example, air pollution can lead to global warming.) By diminishing—or enhancing, as the case may be—the availability of particular public goods, such externalities also change people's living conditions. Thus the difference between externalities and public goods is that externalities are seen here as a side effect of private activity, and public goods as a more deliberately designed and produced good, such as a legal framework or judicial system. For an extensive discussion of externalities, see Papandreou (1998).

17. As Arce M. and Sandler (2002) point out, three concerns can override the fiscal equivalence or subsidiarity principle: economies of scale, economies of scope, and the nonexistence of requisite organizational capacity.

18. For a feminist discussion on the concept of the public sphere, see Meehan (1995).

19. Thus publicness in consumption is distinct from publicness in the distribution of benefits. Publicness in consumption has to do with whether a good is nonexclusive in consumption. Publicness in the distribution of benefits has to do with how consumers derive benefits from the good.

20. For a more detailed discussion on these and other types of aggregation technologies, see Sandler (in this volume, 1998) and Arce M. and Sandler (2001, 2002).

21. Conceição (in this volume) offers a first attempt at such a broader assessment of the provision status of public goods.

22. It is important to differentiate the scope of a public good's benefits (or public bad's costs) and the level at which it may be situated or from which its effects may emanate. For example, pollution can arise locally but spread globally, affecting people in all parts of the world. The notion of reach or scope implies that the wider concept includes all others. Put differently, global includes regional, national, and local. By contrast, a good can be situated at the international level, such as a development assistance facility, but be designed to deliver a particular regional good, such as support for the management of a lake or forest system shared by several countries. Or a locally situated good, such as an outbreak of the Ebola virus, can have global consequences. In other words, levels are distinct and separate—but the wider is a good's reach, the more comprehensive it is of other areas.

23. As Risse-Kappen (1995) notes, international relations are often analyzed merely in terms of international, intergovernmental relations, ignoring direct links between societies and societal actors across national borders. But networks of transnational actors have become increasingly important.

24. The exclusive economic zones extend for 200 nautical miles from coastal baselines. In these zones, coastal states have "exclusive rights (1) for the purpose of exploring and exploiting, conserving, and managing the natural resources, whether living or nonliving, of the water superadjacent to the seabed and its subsoil, and (2) with regard to other activities for the economic exploitation and exploration of the zone such as the production of energy from the water, currents and winds" (Mendez 1992, p. 235).

25. There is, however, a fine line between parts of industrial countries' populations being concerned about severe human deprivation and other parts being concerned about spillovers, such as the risk of rising numbers of international economic migrants.

26. It would also be interesting to investigate, at the international level, the applicability (or inapplicability) of frameworks for analyzing public choice at the local and national levels—including, for instance, the median voter theorem.

27. In considering the triangle as an analytical tool, several interesting issues could be further explored. For instance, how exactly would each dimension be measured? What would be the conceptual optimum (maximum or minimum) for each axis for certain public goods? If there are ideal dimensions for the triangle of publicness, what are they and how are they determined?

REFERENCES

Acocella, Nicola. 1998. *The Foundations of Economic Policy: Values and Techniques.* Cambridge: Cambridge University Press.

Anheier, Helmut, Marlies Glasius, and Mary Kaldor, eds. 2001. *Global Civil Society 2001.* Oxford: Oxford University Press.

Arce M., Daniel G., and Todd Sandler. 2001. "Transnational Public Goods: Strategies and Institutions." *European Journal of Political Economy* 17 (3): 493–516.

———. 2002. *Regional Public Goods: Typologies, Provision, Financing, and Development Assistance.* Stockholm: Sweden Ministry for Foreign Affairs, Expert Group on Development Issues.

Barzel, Yoram. 1997. *Economic Analysis of Property Rights.* 2nd ed. Cambridge: Cambridge University Press.

Braudel, Fernand. 1986. *The Perspective of the World: Civilization and Capitalism, 15th–18th Century.* Vol. 3. New York: Harper & Row.

Breton, Albert. 1965. "A Theory of Government Grants." *Canadian Journal of Economics and Political Science* 31 (2): 175–87.

Bromley, Daniel W., ed. 1990. *Essays on the Commons.* Madison: University of Wisconsin Press.

Buchanan, James M., and Richard A. Musgrave. 1999. *Public Finance and Public Choice: Two Contrasting Visions of the State.* Cambridge, Mass.: MIT Press.

Cerny, Philip G. 1995. "Globalization and the Changing Logic of Collective Action." *International Organization* 49 (4): 595–625.

Cornes, Richard, and Todd Sandler. 1994. "Are Public Goods Myths?" *Journal of Theoretical Politics* 6 (3): 369–85.

———. 1996. *The Theory of Externalities, Public Goods and Club Goods.* New York: Cambridge University Press.

Cozijnsen, Jos. 2001. "The Development of Post Kyoto Emissions Trading Schemes in Europe: An Analysis in the Context of the Kyoto Process." In Malik Amin Aslam, Jos Cozijnsen, Svetlana Morozova, Marc Stuart, Richard B. Stewart, and Philippe Sands, eds., *Greenhouse Gas Market Perspectives: Trade and Investment Implications of the Climate Change Regime.* Geneva: United Nations Conference on Trade and Development. [http://www.unctad.org/ghg/Publications/GHG_MktPersp.PDF].

Cropper, Maureen L., and Wallace E. Oates. 1992. "Environmental Economics: A Survey." *Journal of Economic Literature* 30: 675–740.

Cullis, John, and Philip Jones. 1998. *Public Finance and Public Choice.* New York: Oxford University Press.

Cutler, A. Claire, Virginia Haufler, and Tony Porter, eds. 1999. *Private Authority and International Affairs.* Albany: State University of New York Press.

Demsetz, Harold. 1967. "Toward a Theory of Property Rights." *American Economic Review* 57 (2): 347–59.

Dixit, Avinash K. 1996. *The Making of Economic Policy: A Transaction-Cost Politics Perspective.* Cambridge, Mass.: MIT Press.

Giddens, Anthony, and Will Hutton. 2000. "In Conversation." In Will Hutton and Anthony Giddens, eds., *Global Capitalism.* New York: New Press.

Held, David, Anthony McGrew, David Goldblatt, and Jonathan Perraton. 1999. *Global Transformations.* Cambridge: Polity Press.

Hirschman, Albert O. 1970. *Exit, Voice, and Loyalty: Responses to Decline in Firms, Organizations, and States.* Cambridge, Mass.: Harvard University Press.

Hirshleifer, Jack. 1983. "From Weakest-link to Best-shot: The Voluntary Provision of Public Goods." *Public Choice* 41: 371–86.

Kaul, Inge. 2001. "Public Goods in the 21st Century." In *Global Public Goods: Taking the Concept Forward.* Discussion Paper 17. New York: United Nations Development Programme, Office of Development Studies.

Kaul, Inge, Isabelle Grunberg, and Marc A. Stern. 1999. "Defining Global Public Goods." In Inge Kaul, Isabelle Grunberg, and Marc A. Stern, eds., *Global Public Goods: International Cooperation in the 21st Century.* New York: Oxford University Press.

Keane, John. 2001. "Global Civil Society?" In Helmut Anheier, Marlies Glasius, and Mary Kaldor, eds., *Global Civil Society 2001*. New York: Oxford University Press.

Luttwak, Edward. 1999. *Turbo-Capitalism: Winners and Losers in the Global Economy*. New York: HarperCollins.

Malkin, Jesse, and Aaron Wildavsky. 1991. "Why the Traditional Distinction between Public and Private Goods Should Be Abandoned." *Journal of Theoretical Politics* 3 (4): 355–78.

Marmolo, Elisabetta. 1999. "A Constitutional Theory of Public Goods." *Journal of Economic Behavior and Organization* 38 (1): 27–42.

Meehan, Johanna, ed. 1995. *Feminists Read Habermas: Gendering the Subject of Discourse*. New York and London: Routledge.

Mendez, Ruben. 1992. *International Public Finance: A New Perspective on Global Relations*. New York: Oxford University Press.

Micklethwait, John, and Adrian Wooldridge. 2000. *A Future Perfect: The Challenge and Hidden Promise of Globalization*. New York: Times Books.

Miller, David, and Sohail H. Hashmi, eds. 2001. *Boundaries and Justice: Diverse Ethical Perspectives*. Princeton, N.J.: Princeton University Press.

Musgrave, Richard A., and Peggy B. Musgrave. 1989. *Public Finance in Theory and Practice*. 5th ed. New York: McGraw-Hill.

Nicholson, Walter. 1998. *Microeconomic Theory: Basic Principles and Extensions*. 7th ed. New York: Harcourt.

Oakland, William H. 1991. "Theory of Public Goods." In Alan Auerbach and Martin Feldstein, eds., *Handbook of Public Economics*. Vol. 2. Amsterdam: North-Holland.

Olson, Mancur. 1971 [1965]. *The Logic of Collective Action: Public Goods and the Theory of Groups*. Cambridge, Mass.: Harvard University Press.

Ostrom, Elinor. 1990. *Governing the Commons: The Evolution of Institutions for Collective Action*. Cambridge: Cambridge University Press.

Papandreou, Andreas A. 1998. *Externality and Institutions*. Oxford: Clarendon Press.

Rao, J. Mohan. 1999. "Equity in a Global Public Goods Framework." In Inge Kaul, Isabelle Grunberg, and Marc A. Stern, eds., *Global Public Goods: International Cooperation in the 21st Century*. New York: Oxford University Press.

Risse-Kappen, Thomas, ed. 1995. *Bringing Transnational Relations Back In: Non-state Actors, Domestic Structures and International Institutions*. Cambridge: Cambridge University Press.

Rosen, Harvey. 1999. *Public Finance*. 5th ed. New York: McGraw-Hill.

Rosenblum, Nancy L., and Robert C. Post. 2002. *Civil Society and Government*. Princeton, N.J.: Princeton University Press.

Salanie, Bernard. 2000. *The Microeconomics of Market Failures*. Cambridge, Mass.: MIT Press.

Samuelson, Paul A. 1954. "The Pure Theory of Public Expenditure." *Review of Economics and Statistics* 36: 387–89.

Samuelson, Paul A., and William P. Nordhaus. 2001. *Microeconomics*. 17th ed. New York: McGraw-Hill.

Sandler, Todd. 1998. "Global and Regional Public Goods: A Prognosis for Collective Action." *Fiscal Studies* 19 (3): 221–47.

Sandor, Richard. 2002. "Emissions Trading: Financing Environmental Public Goods at Least Cost." In Inge Kaul, Katell Le Goulven, and Mirjam Schnupf, eds., *Global Public Goods Financing: New Tools for New Challenges*. New York: United Nations Development Programme.

Sen, Amartya. 1982. *Choice, Welfare and Measurement*. Cambridge, Mass.: Harvard University Press.

———. 1999. "Global Justice: Beyond International Equity." In Inge Kaul, Isabelle Grunberg, and Marc A. Stern, eds., *Global Public Goods: International Cooperation in the 21st Century*. New York: Oxford University Press.

Stiglitz, Joseph E. 1995. *The Theory of International Public Goods and the Architecture of International Organizations*. Helsinki: United Nations University and World Institute for Development Economics Research.

———. 2000. *Economics of the Public Sector*. 3rd ed. New York: W. W. Norton.

Tobin, James. 1970. "On Limiting the Domain of Inequality." *Journal of Law and Economics* 13 (2): 263–77.

UNRISD (United Nations Research Institute for Social Development). 2000. *Visible Hands: Taking Responsibility for Social Development*. Geneva.

Wildavsky, Aaron. 1994. "Reply to Cornes and Sandler (1994)." *Journal of Theoretical Politics* 6 (3): 387–88.

Woods, Ngaire. 2000. "Globalization and the Challenge to International Institutions." In Ngaire Woods, ed., *The Political Economy of Globalization*. Basingstoke, U.K.: Macmillan. [http://users.ox.ac.uk/~ntwoods/Globalization%20and%20the%20 Challenge.pdf].

WTO (World Trade Organization). 2001. "Fact Sheet: TRIPS and Pharmaceutical Patents." Geneva. [http://www.wto.org/english/tratop_e/trips_e/factsheet_ pharm02_e.htm].

INTERNATIONAL ASPECTS OF PUBLIC GOODS PROVISION

AGNAR SANDMO

Paul A. Samuelson's (1954, 1955) original formulation of the theory of public goods contains few references to the jurisdictional framework in which decisions about public goods provision are assumed to occur.[1] A natural interpretation is that he primarily had in mind the nation-state. But it is also reasonable to assume that he saw the theory as being applicable to several jurisdictional frameworks. In later years such applications were mainly in the area of local public goods and local public finance.

Only recently has economists' attention turned to global public goods—goods that are public not only for the population of a particular country but also for the entire world (see Kaul, Grunberg, and Stern 1999). The qualitative properties of the global environment offer perhaps the most obvious examples of global public goods, but there are many others. Knowledge is an important example; public health is another. At the institutional level important examples of global public goods are the institutions required to promote world peace and international security and to sustain the global market economy.

Samuelson's formulation is cast in the framework of welfare economics. It postulates an individualistic welfare function that depends positively on the utility levels of the individual consumers in an economy, and the analysis aims to characterize an optimal allocation of resources when social welfare is maximized subject to a production possibility constraint. The most novel result from the analysis was the famous "Samuelson rule." This rule says that for the supply of a public good to be optimal, the sum of the marginal rates of substitution between that public good and some numéraire private good—for all consumers in society—must be equal to the marginal rate of transformation in production. An alternative interpretation is that the aggregate marginal willingness to pay for the public good must equal its marginal cost of production.

This chapter extends and interprets this theory in the context of global public goods. One focus of the analysis is whether the Samuelson rule is valid in a global context. Should the rule guide how we think about the provision of global public goods? If not, what changes are needed for the theory to be applied to global public goods? The most problematic part of extending the theory involves the desirability of global production efficiency and the separation of equity and efficiency conditions, which play an important role in Samuelson's formulation.

The discussion here emphasizes normative theory in the welfare economics sense, though it also considers implementation and incentives, particularly in the sections on implementation issues. The problem also could have been approached from a positive angle: that is, what kind of global public goods equilibrium emerges from voluntary cooperation between countries? Formal analysis of this problem is best left for separate treatment. But since an important focus of a positive theory would be the efficiency properties of the equilibrium, the normative theory provides an important benchmark for such a study.[2]

SOURCE OF AND INFLUENCES ON PUBLIC GOODS PROVISION

Among Samuelson's (1955) examples of pure public goods are an outdoor circus and national defense—somewhat tongue-in-cheek examples suggesting that these goods are provided through the explicit choice of some well-defined decision-maker. But for many public goods this is a simplified scenario. Whether in a natural or cultural environment, the availability of many public goods is determined partly by exogenous forces—by the laws of nature or by past human activities.

The current and future availability of public goods is also determined by the actions of many consumers and producers. Some of these actions are negative, as when private agents contribute to traffic congestion, greenhouse gas emissions, or the degradation of historical monuments by air pollution. Others are positive, as when private spending on architectural design contributes to the aesthetic value of the cultural landscape.

The availability of public goods is determined by public actions as well. Thus the provision of such goods takes both direct and indirect forms, reflecting their varying providers. In some cases individual consumers produce a public good as a by-product of other activities. In other cases public or private agencies increase the provision of a public good through explicit budget funding or through policies that modify the actions of private individuals.

The effects that individual production and consumption decisions have on the quantity and quality of public goods are called externalities. Much has been written about how governments can improve the functioning of markets when private goods have externalities like those of public goods (see Sandmo 2000 for a detailed discussion). The following discussion does not try to distinguish between pure public goods and private goods with externalities; the focus is on public goods. This approach is not as restrictive as it may seem, because many of the problems in this area—such as the method used to reveal willingness to pay—are of the same nature in both cases.

BASIC ASSUMPTIONS FOR A MODEL OF RESOURCE ALLOCATION

The notion of a social welfare function, central to Samuelson's theory of public goods, is viewed by many with considerable skepticism. The skepticism stems partly from Kenneth Arrow's (1963 [1951]) impossibility theorem and partly from criticism by James Buchanan and others from the public choice school that an aggregate social welfare function is inconsistent with the values of a democratic society (see Buchanan 1987 for a selection of his writings on this topic). Although such skepticism would seem to apply a fortiori to a global social welfare function, such a function is used below. The use of this concept does not in any way deny the power of Arrow's theorem. It is not meant to imply the existence of a political system for global preference aggregation or of a benevolent global planner managing the world's resources based on his or her ethical values. The social welfare function is simply intended to help show the limited significance of social efficiency or Pareto optimality as the sole guide to rational decisions. Thus it also helps explain the distinction between efficiency criteria on the one hand and ethical judgments on the other.

For simplicity, assume that the world has two countries: one rich and one poor. The rich country consists of n consumers with utility functions u^{iR}, where $i = 1,\ldots,n$. Similarly, the m consumers of the poor country have utility functions u^{jP}. For simplicity, assume that there is just one private good and one global public good, so that the utility functions can be written as:

$$(1) \qquad u^{iR} = u^{iR}(x^{iR}, g); \; i = 1,\ldots,n, \text{ and } u^{jP} = u^{jP}(x^{jP}, g); \; j = 1,\ldots,m.$$

Here x^{iR} is the private good consumption of the ith individual in the rich country, and x^{jP} is the private good consumption of the ith individual in the poor country. The global public good g enters into all utility functions, but valuations of it likely differ between individuals—both within and between the rich country and the poor country.

The public good, as modeled here, is a pure public good in the Samuelson sense. It is public both within and between the two countries—enjoyment of the good by citizen i in country R does not diminish its availability for citizen j in country P. This type of polar case makes it possible to focus on the problem of global public goods in its purest form.[3] This focus is motivated by the desire to extend Samuelson's model to a global context and to study the problem of incentives in a setting directly comparable to the original formulation of the theory.

The social welfare function is then:

$$(2) \qquad W = W(u^{1R},\ldots u^{nR}; u^{1P},\ldots u^{mP}).$$

Note that the maximum of the social welfare function (subject to the production possibilities constraint) is necessarily also a Pareto optimum, because if an allocation can make one consumer—such as the poorest individual in the poor country—better off without making anyone else worse off, the value of the social welfare function must increase. Thus such an allocation cannot be a welfare maximum.

The description of the production side of the economy proceeds in two steps. First, it is assumed that both countries devote some resources to providing the global public good and that the global provision is an increasing function of the countries' contributions. This can be written as:

(3) $g = \varphi(g^R, g^P).$

For simplicity, the analysis that follows uses the more specific assumption that:

(3′) $g = g^R + g^P.$

In this context the special assumption—that the amount of the global public good is equal to the sum of the two countries' contributions—is justified mainly by analytical simplicity. More generally, it is reasonable to assume that the two countries' contributions may have a different degree of efficiency in contributing to the global public good.[4] But at the present level of abstraction the special assumption does not detract from the general validity of the conclusions that can be drawn.

Second, each of the countries is constrained in its output of private and public goods by technology and factor supplies. These constraints are summarized as:

(4) $F^R(x^R, g^R) = 0$, and $F^P(x^P, g^P) = 0.$

Here x^R and x^P are the aggregate private goods produced and consumed in the rich country and the poor country, so that $\sum_i x^{iR} = x^R$ and $\sum_j x^{jP} = x^P$.

Equation 4 calculates, for each country, the maximum contribution to the global public good that can be achieved for any given amount of private good consumption. Behind the efficiency frontier, which is assumed to have the usual concavity properties, lie a number of assumptions about the efficient allocation of factors of production among subsectors of the economy. For reasons of space these are not discussed explicitly here. To facilitate an intuitive interpretation of the results, the analysis uses the quasi-linear forms:

(4′) $x^R + C^R(g^R) - R^R = 0$, and $x^P + C^P(g^P) - R^P = 0.$

Here R^R and R^P are constants representing the resource limitations of the two economies. The functions C^R and C^P are assumed to be continuous with positive first and second derivatives. This approach ensures that the production possibility curves have the usual properties. Moreover, the marginal rates of transformation, which generally should be written as F_g^R/F_x^R and F_g^P/F_x^P, now become simply C_g^R and C_g^P. (Here and elsewhere subscripts are used to denote partial derivatives in notations that should otherwise be self-explanatory.) C_g^R and C_g^P have an obvious interpretation as the marginal cost of producing the public good in terms of the quantity of private goods forgone.

Formally, the main difference between the present formulation and the standard one lies in the disaggregated treatment of the production side. It is reasonable to assume that factor supplies and technologies differ between rich and poor countries, and there is even more reason than in a single-country analysis to be explicit about conditions for production efficiency.

PRODUCTION EFFICIENCY

As a step toward solving the global welfare maximization problem, it is useful to examine the more limited issue of global production efficiency. In this context a global allocation of resources can be said to be productively efficient if, for some given total of world consumption of private goods, the provision of the global public good is at its maximum. This is obviously desirable given the wider objective of global welfare maximization because in the absence of production efficiency it would be possible to reallocate the world's resources to have more of the public good without suffering a loss of private goods output. Such a reallocation would have the potential to improve living standards for all.

Formally, the problem of characterizing production efficiency can be set up as:

(5)   Maximize g subject to $x^R + x^P = x^0$

where x^0 is some given amount of world consumption of the private good. Using equation 4, production efficiency can be characterized by these and the condition:

(6) $C_g^R = C_g^P.$

This condition simply says that for global production efficiency to hold, the marginal cost of producing the global public good must be the same in rich and poor countries. In other words, comparative advantages should be fully exploited. The country where factor endowments and technology make it cheaper to produce the public good should devote more resources to it.

It is worth noting briefly that if the more general contribution technology of equation 3 had been used instead of that in equation 3', condition 6 would become:

(6') $C_g^R / C_g^P = \varphi_R/\varphi_G$

where φ_R and φ_G are the partial derivatives of the function φ. The ratio of marginal costs of production should be equal to the ratio of contribution efficiencies. This involves a more complex notion of comparative advantage, which should be kept in mind in the interpretation of the results based on the simpler case in equation 3'. Comparative advantage is determined not only by relative production costs but also by the relative efficiency with which countries contribute to the global public good.

The production efficiency result is strongly reminiscent of a classic insight from the Heckscher-Ohlin theory of international trade,[5] where the exploitation of comparative advantage ensures global production efficiency.[6] In that theory the next step is to show that free international trade will establish relative producer prices that are uniform across countries. Since, in a competitive equilibrium, these will be equated to the marginal rate of substitution in each country, it follows that free trade will result in an efficient allocation of production between countries. But international trade theory is almost exclusively about trade in private goods. It is interesting to ask under what institutional conditions a similar result can be expected to emerge in the context of public goods—a question considered further below.

Is global production efficiency necessarily desirable? Welfare economics says that production efficiency is necessary for social welfare maximization: that if some outputs can be increased with no decrease in others, it must be possible to make things better for some consumers without making them worse for others. But in an international context it is not clear that this argument can be applied. The setup of the efficiency problem (equation 5) implicitly assumes that world output of the private good is available to satisfy consumer needs in both countries. If instead national consumption possibilities are constrained by national output, the present formulation of the problem loses much of its appeal. These issues can be clarified only by embedding the production efficiency problem in the wider framework of welfare maximization.

GLOBAL WELFARE MAXIMIZATION

Now consider the more general problem of global welfare maximization. Here this will be conceived as maximization of the social welfare function (equation 2) subject to technological constraints (equations 3' and 4'). In addition, the connection between world consumption and world production needs to be specified. To start, assume simply that world consumption must equal world production, so that:

$$(7) \qquad \sum_i x^{iR} + \sum_j x^{jP} = x^R + x^P.$$

Solving this problem of constrained optimization generates three sets of optimal conditions:

(8) $C_g^R = C_g^P \equiv C_g$.

(9) $\Sigma_i(u_g^{iR}/u_x^{iR}) + \Sigma_j(u_g^{jP}/u_x^{jP}) = C_g$.

(10) $W_{iR} \, u_x^{iR} = W_{jP} \, u_x^{jP}$ $(i = 1,....,n; j = 1,....,m)$.

Equation 8 is the condition for global production efficiency (condition 6), restated here for convenience. This condition ensures that the marginal cost of the public good—the opportunity cost of public goods provision in terms of private goods output—is the same in both countries. For convenience, this common value will be written as C_g. Equation 9 is a direct generalization of the Samuelson efficiency condition for public goods: The sum of the marginal rates of substitution between the public and private good—the sum of the corresponding sums for each of the countries—should be equal to the global marginal rate of transformation. Another way to write this condition is as the requirement that the marginal benefit-cost ratio—the ratio of marginal benefits to marginal costs—should be equal to unity, that is:

(9′) $[\Sigma_i(u_g^{iR}/u_x^{iR}) + \Sigma_j(u_g^{jP}/u_x^{jP})]/C_g = 1$.

Finally, the set of equations 10 is a requirement that the marginal utility of private goods consumption be the same for all consumers both within and across countries. Combined, conditions 8, 9, and 10 constitute a complete characterization of conditions for an optimal world allocation of resources. Conditions 8 and 9 are characterizations of efficiency or Pareto optimality, while equation 10 characterizes the just or equitable distribution of resources between individuals.

At this point the generalization of the Samuelson analysis to an international setting may seem straightforward. In particular, the condition for optimal provision of public goods has the same form as in the original model except for the splitting of the sum on the left-hand side into a sum for each country. This outcome may not be surprising if world welfare is being considered from a utopian perspective. But as indicated, the results are based on the assumption that private goods consumption in the two countries is constrained only by world output, not by output in each country. This assumption may be too utopian to be helpful.

It is true that international trade allows countries to choose consumption patterns outside their sets of production possibilities, but the assumption here is stronger than that. Because the single private commodity x represents all private consumption goods, national consumption can differ from national production only when there are transfers of consumption or income between countries. This feature of the analysis leads to the equity conditions in equation 10. In other words, the constraint in equation 7 is equivalent to an assumption of lump sum transfers not only within each country but also between countries, and that assumption allows the neat separation of efficiency and equity considerations in the optimal solution—exactly as in the Samuelson analysis. The formulation also implicitly requires that the net revenue from the transfers be positive and equal to the resource cost of public goods provision.

Such transfers should not be ruled out as irrelevant and uninteresting. Foreign aid is significant and could be increased. Moreover, some transfers could be seen as payments for providing public goods (see below). Still, most countries generally have to rely on their own resources—making it of obvious interest to examine the case where a country's consumption is constrained by its output. This assumption can be represented by the two constraints:

$$(11) \quad \sum_i x^{iR} = x^R, \sum_j x^{jP} = x^P$$

which should be compared with the single condition 7 for the previous case. It must be emphasized that assumption 11 does not imply that there is no international trade. The single private good in this model should be interpreted as an aggregate of all private goods; thus the assumption means that the value of production must equal the value of consumption. In other words, trade must be balanced. By contrast, assumption 7 allows a country's value of consumption to be higher or lower than its value of production—which can happen only through international transfers. Thus assumptions 7 and 11 are both consistent with an assumption of free trade. The difference is that assumption 11 rules out international transfers.[7]

How does this change affect production efficiency? The welfare case for national production efficiency remains valid. If one assumes the possibility of a national lump sum redistribution of income, output of the private good should be maximized for any given contribution of the public good. In other words, national welfare can always be improved by moving from inside the production possibility frontier to some point on it.[8]

Nevertheless, global production efficiency is generally undesirable—and it is easy to see why. Assume that at first the marginal cost of the public good differs between the poor country and the rich country. Then suppose that the concern for global production efficiency calls for the poor country to contribute more to the public good and for the rich country to contribute less. The poor country must then move along its production possibility frontier toward less production of the private good, while the rich country will produce more. On average, then, consumers in the poor country will see their consumption of private goods fall, while consumers in the rich country will see theirs increase. This change will likely involve a welfare loss for the poor country consumers and a corresponding gain for the rich country consumers.[9] If the rich country consumers could transfer some of their gain to the poor country consumers, everyone could gain—but the inability to make such transfers is precisely what assumption 11 implies.

Formally, the condition for the optimal supply of public goods in this case can be written as:

$$(12) \quad \Sigma_i(u_g^{iR}/u_x^{iR})/C_g^R + \Sigma_j(u_g^{jP}/u_x^{jP})/C_g^P = 1.$$

This equation, which is formally derived in the appendix at the end of the chapter, should be compared with equation 9′ for the case where international transfers are possible. Equation 9′ says that the optimal provision of the global public good implies that the global marginal benefit-cost ratio must equal 1. By contrast, condition 12 says that without transfers, the sum of national marginal benefit-cost ratios should equal 1.

Equation 9′ represents an obvious extension of the theory of public goods to a global context. But the interpretation of condition 12 is less obvious. The lower is a country's marginal cost of producing the global public good, the more its preferences for the good should count in the evaluation of global benefits. In this way the aggregation of preferences across countries takes some account of production efficiency, which is intuitively reasonable.

But a puzzling feature of condition 12 is the apparent absence of welfare weights. Since there is no equalization of the social marginal utility of consumption between the rich and poor countries, one would expect the benefits to be weighted by terms that reflect the distributional preferences embedded in the social welfare function. Recall that perfect lump sum transfers are assumed within but not between countries.[10] Consequently, the social marginal utility of consumption will be the same for all consumers in the poor country and for all consumers in the rich country. Formally, this can be written as:

$$(13) \quad W_{iR}\, u_x^{iR} = \gamma^R, \; W_{jP}\, u_x^{jP} = \gamma^P \qquad (i = 1,....,n; j = 1,....,m)$$

where γ^R and γ^P are the common social marginal utility of income for the two countries. From condition 12 the relative weight on the poor country's preferences is C_g^R/C_g^P. But from the solution to the optimization problem it follows that this is in fact equal to γ^P/γ^R, so that condition 12 has an alternative interpretation in terms of welfare weights. If the global welfare function has an egalitarian form, $\gamma^P/\gamma^R > 1$, more weight is attached to the preferences of the poor country's population in deciding on the optimal provision of the global public good.

The connection between cost weights and welfare weights has an intuitive economic explanation. If the social welfare function has an egalitarian bias, so that more weight is attached to the private goods consumption of the poor country, one would like the poor country to contribute less to the global public good. But since the marginal cost of providing the public good is increasing, this implies that the marginal cost in the poor country must, in an egalitarian optimum, be low relative to that in the rich country. The poor country should devote fewer resources to global public goods than indicated by considerations of comparative advantage.

An interesting question is whether the optimum without international transfers would entail a higher or lower solution value for the public good than the optimal solution when such transfers are possible. But at the purely "technological" level, abstracting from all incentive problems, no firm answer to this question can be given. Intuitively, whether a greater weight on the benefits derived by the poor country will increase or decrease the sum of marginal benefit-cost ratios depends on whether the poor country's benefits are high or low relative to those of the rich country.

A natural extension of the present analysis would be to the case where countries must finance their spending on global public goods through distortionary taxes. In that case countries' comparative advantage in the production of global public goods would be based not only on differences in their marginal production costs but also on differences in the efficiency of their tax systems. Such an extension of the literature on the marginal cost of public funds to an international context lies beyond the scope of this chapter and must be left for future research.

IMPLEMENTATION PROBLEMS: COST EFFICIENCY

The theory of public goods was formulated at a fairly high level of abstraction. Nevertheless, it has provided the theoretical foundations for applied cost-benefit analysis in a number of areas. In cost-benefit analysis one considers a public project socially profitable if the aggregate benefits exceed the aggregate costs; for a "marginal" project the benefits should equal the costs.[11] This criterion can be considered the practical interpretation of the optimality conditions 9 and 9′ in a national context.

But as noted, unless there is extensive international redistribution of income, global production efficiency for public goods is generally not optimal from a global welfare point of view. A realistic framework for viewing the policy issues is presumably one in which there is a limited degree of international redistribution, so that the consumption constraints 7 and 11 must be seen as polar cases of redistributional feasibility. This discussion begins with case 7, in which global production efficiency is a desirable feature of the global optimum.

The procedures used to ensure that one produces at the cost-minimizing level vary with the nature of the public good and the extent to which private incentives can be harnessed for this purpose. Many governments have formal guidelines for the selection of the most efficient producers, and units in charge of public procurement are subject to surveillance and possible sanctions if gross deviations from the guidelines are discovered. Competition between private firms for government contracts is a powerful system for promoting production efficiency.

In environmental policy many governments are showing an increased interest in incentive systems that have long been analyzed by economists—including Pigouvian taxes and transferable quotas. Suppose that the national government wishes to reduce the emissions of some pollutant into the air, water, or soil. One way to do so efficiently would be to levy a uniform tax on emissions for all polluters. Polluters then have an incentive to reduce emissions as long as the cost of doing so is less than the tax, so that cost minimization leads to equality between the tax rate and the marginal cost of pollution reduction. This ensures that pollution will be reduced most where the reductions are cheapest and that in equilibrium the marginal cost of reducing emissions is the same for all polluters.

An alternative is to introduce a system of transferable quotas. The aggregate volume of quotas should correspond to the target level of emissions. Suppose that the government first distributes the quotas among polluters according to some more or less arbitrary criterion, such as past levels of pollution. Then it allows trade in quotas. Firms with high costs of reducing pollution would then wish to increase their quotas, while those with low costs would be interested in selling some. A competitive market would establish a uniform price for quotas, and again the marginal cost of reducing pollution—or creating a less polluted environment—would be the same for all polluters.[12]

Now consider the implementation of similar policies in an international setting. In environmental policy much attention has been given to this problem in connection with the emission of greenhouse gases, such as carbon dioxide. An internationally uniform tax on carbon dioxide would ensure global production efficiency, while a system of international trade in emission quotas would result in the largest reductions of emissions being made in the countries where it is cheapest to do so. Under either policy, then, there will be one marginal rate of transformation—one marginal cost of producing the public good—for the world as a whole. The global public good of a cleaner environment will have been achieved at the minimum cost.

This solution is optimal only when there is perfect international redistribution of income. If that is not the case, the marginal cost of contributing to the global public good should be less in the poor country than in the rich country. But in the case of international green taxation this can be achieved only if the poor country has a lower tax rate than the rich country. Similarly, with tradable quotas, a quota must be cheaper in the poor country. The desire for global production efficiency must be tempered by considerations of equity. Such a modified system must be based on national tax policies or national markets for tradable quotas. This solution should be supplemented by international treaties to ensure a reasonable international tradeoff between efficiency and equity. How large should the difference in tax levels between rich and poor countries be? How should national quotas be set?

A possible objection to such a system is that polluting industries would have an incentive to relocate from rich to poor countries to avoid high taxes or expensive quotas. But as the model has been formulated, such a relocation would not lead to more pollution in the poor country because—by assumption—pollution is global and its source does not matter. Moreover, such a relocation might increase the poor country's capacity for producing private goods and raise private living standards. On equity grounds, therefore, the objection is not very convincing. Moreover, to the extent that a relocation contributes to the economic development of the poor country, the case for more favorable treatment on equity grounds would gradually become weaker, tax rates or quota prices would become more similar, and incentives to relocate would diminish.[13]

Tradable quotas for greenhouse gas emissions offer perhaps the most direct example of how economic institutions can be designed with a view toward global production efficiency. In other cases, such as the prevention of global epidemic diseases or the design of peacekeeping organizations, it is much less obvious that similar market institutions could be made to work. But at least the principles of production efficiency are there to guide thinking in such areas. The production of public goods should be allocated among countries so as to minimize the global opportunity cost, though taking into account distributional considerations. Whether the principle should be pursued all the way to ensure full global production efficiency depends on opportunities for international redistribution of income through transfers from rich to poor countries.

IMPLEMENTATION PROBLEMS: EVALUATION AND REVELATION OF BENEFITS

In the formulation of the global welfare maximization problem, perhaps the most utopian feature of the analysis is in equation 7—or, rather, in the absence of any further constraints on the division of the world's output between rich and poor countries. That the distribution of the world's consumption among rich and poor countries is constrained only by the world's total output is equivalent to the assumption in a national setting that the government can levy individualized lump sum taxes. Here it implies that lump sum transfers can also be used for international redistribution, and this assumption allows the perfect division between equity and efficiency concerns in the optimality conditions 8, 9, and 10.

The assumption is clearly unrealistic even in a national setting. The problem is that government does not have—indeed, cannot possibly have—the information needed to implement such a tax system. Instead, it must use distortionary taxes that create a need to trade off efficiency losses against equity gains. In the evaluation of public goods benefits it can no longer be assumed that total welfare benefits can be measured simply by willingness to pay or the marginal rate of substitution. Welfare weights need to be introduced to balance the inequities of the distribution of resources between individuals. These inequities will generally be present both within and between countries. But in the following, as in the analytical model above, this problem is ignored at the national level, and the focus is on the constraints on international redistribution.

Suppose that governments have found a way to estimate national benefits from global public goods. This means that they have overcome the difficulties that stem from individuals' private incentives to misrepresent their benefits to avoid paying for public goods.[14] The next step is to arrive at a measure of global benefits from public goods. Consider the governments of the world negotiating an environmental treaty. Each finds itself in a situation whose strategic considerations are similar to those of a single individual with respect to the national government. Within the international community each country is small relative to the world as a whole. By underreporting its aggregate willingness to pay, a country may conceivably reduce the amount that it will have to contribute to global public goods without appreciably influencing the global provision of such goods. But if all countries reason along similar lines, the result will be underprovision of global public goods.

How serious is this international free-rider problem? Again, a crucial consideration is the availability of policies for international redistribution. Consider first condition 9′ for optimal provision with unrestricted international transfers. If this condition is not satisfied, it is in principle possible to improve the situation for all countries through a combination of public goods adjustment and international transfers. One could envisage a system of international bargaining that would make it possible to convert a situation characterized by potential Pareto improvement to one of actual improvement, provided that the transfer mechanism were sufficiently fine-tuned and flexible. This would not eliminate the incentive problems; countries might still find it in their interest to report high costs and low benefits to increase their net gains from international transfers. Still, the combination of contributions to global public goods provision and income transfers would increase the possibility of achieving a global optimum relative to the case with no transfers.

The case with no transfers can be understood by considering condition 12, which generalizes easily to an arbitrary number of countries. In the absence of international transfers the marginal benefit-cost ratios should sum to unity. But this means that at the optimum each country's ratio must be less than 1. In other words, since some of the benefits generated by a country accrue to other countries, each country will be asked to contribute beyond the point where its marginal benefit-cost ratio equals 1. Suppose that each country considers only its own welfare. If marginal benefit-cost ratios decline with the amount of public goods available—a reasonable assumption[15]—no country would voluntarily use resources for global public goods beyond the point where its national benefit-cost ratio equals unity. But this would imply that the sum of these ratios would be on the order of the number of countries in the world, indicating a severe underprovision of global public goods.

One must conclude, therefore, that whatever the difficulties are of achieving efficient and equitable provision of global public goods in combination with international transfers of income, the difficulties become magnified in the absence of such transfers.[16]

Some modifications may be in order. It is not entirely realistic to assume that economic agents always take a narrow view of their self-interest when considering the allocation of resources to public goods. Even single individuals in large economies voluntarily donate time and money for the purpose of providing public goods. The increased concern for the environment in public policy has been caused largely by voluntary organizations acting as pressure groups. Many individuals obviously do not see themselves as being unable to influence aggregate outcomes such as the allocation of resources to public goods or the design of policies to modify the effects of unregulated private actions. What is true for a single individual in a national economy is also likely to be true for a single country in the community of nations—particularly since some countries are quite large relative to the world. One might therefore expect that, at least to some extent, these countries might be able to internalize the effects of their actions on the global environment.[17]

CONCLUSION

This chapter has shown how the theory of pure public goods can be generalized to an international setting where countries contribute to the provision of global public goods. At one level of discourse the generalization is straightforward. Under the assumption of global welfare maximization, the Samuelson optimality rule remains valid for global public goods: The sum of individuals' marginal benefits or marginal willingness to pay should equal the marginal cost of production, which should be the same in all countries. Equivalently, the marginal benefit-cost ratio should equal unity. The measure of global marginal benefits should be the sum of total individual benefits for every country.

But some of the assumptions required for the result to hold are distinctly less attractive in an international setting than in the context of the nation-state. The most crucial is the availability of individualized lump sum transfers. Politically, such transfers are hardly feasible even in the context of the nation-state—and even more doubtful in an international context. Nevertheless, the result is interesting because it shows the conditions under which the standard optimality conditions are valid in an international context.

To demonstrate the crucial role of international transfers, the analysis here has assumed that, as an alternative, lump sum transfers are feasible within nation-states but nonexistent between states. In that case the optimality conditions are altered. First, global production efficiency is no longer desirable; in the interests of equity, poor countries might not be required to contribute as much to global public goods as their comparative advantage would otherwise call for. Second, the optimality condition for public goods provision changes to the requirement that the sum of national marginal benefit-cost ratios be equal to 1. This condition brings to light an important incentive problem for the global economy, because each nation-state finds itself in a strategic situation similar to that of each individual in the nation-state. To ensure the maximal gain to the world as a whole, each country must contribute to a point that, at least at the margin, involves a loss to itself.

The two model alternatives—unrestricted lump sum transfers and no transfers at all—are theoretical polar cases of international income redistribution. The general conclusion that can be drawn from the analysis is that the incentive problem is easier to overcome when decisions on global public goods are combined with a policy of international transfers. Indeed, in a world with rich and poor countries a policy in which efficiency calls for poor countries to extensively provide global public goods—such as preservation of rainforests or of tropical biodiversity—would be easier to implement if it were combined with a policy of redistribution. The transfers could in principle be designed so that the overall gains from the provision of global public goods could be distributed among countries to ensure a gain for all.

An interesting perspective on such transfers is to see them as payments for services rendered to rich countries. Rich countries derive benefits from poor countries' provision of global public goods—and if poor countries have a comparative advantage in the production of such goods, rich countries can "buy" those goods more cheaply abroad than at home. Thus there are possible gains from trade. But to realize the gains, one must overcome the incentive problems inherent and inescapable in all problems of public goods allocation. Rich countries can obtain more worldwide biodiversity—a global public good—by paying poor countries to spend more on protecting endangered species. Nevertheless, a single rich country has free-rider incentives to let other rich countries foot the bill.

For income transfers to play the role envisaged here, they must differ in design from current foreign aid. Some economists argue that unconditional aid is the best way to overcome international inequality, and that approach would be consistent with the implications of the first version of the theoretical model presented in this chapter. But in the context of a more restricted and practical role for these particular income transfers, they should instead be conditional on contributions to global public goods.[18]

The main difference between public goods provision in the nation-state and that in the global economy lies in the link with tax payments. Two differences of principle are of crucial importance. The first is that in the nation-state a tax-financed increase in public goods could pass the benefit-cost test without providing gains to every citizen. The reason is that the nation-state has enforcement mechanisms that enable it to extract payments from citizens who are not net beneficiaries from such a policy. The world community of sovereign nations does not possess such policy instruments. Thus in the global community participation in such a policy must be voluntary, making it important to develop tools that distribute the gains to all participating nations. The second difference lies in the possibilities of developing credible enforcement systems. Even when all countries gain from a policy, individual countries have incentives to engage in activities—such as evasion, avoidance of taxes or quotas, or misrepresentation of benefits or costs—that further increase their net share of the global gains. A viable system of global public goods provision must to some extent be based on countries' acceptance of a notion of global welfare that goes beyond national self-interest.

APPENDIX. DERIVATION OF EQUATION 12

Consider the problem of maximizing the welfare function (equation 2) subject to constraints 3′, 4′, and 11. The Lagrange function can be written as:

$$\text{(A1)} \quad \Lambda = W(u^{1R},\ldots u^{nR}; u^{1P},\ldots u^{mP}) - \lambda(g - g^R - g^P) - \mu^R[x^R + C^R(g^R) - R^R]$$
$$- \mu^P[x^P + C^P(g^P) - R^P] - \gamma^R(\Sigma_i x^{iR} - x^R) - \gamma^P(\Sigma_j x^{jP} - x^P).$$

The first-order conditions for a maximum are as follows:

(A2) $\quad \partial\Lambda/\partial x^{iR} = W_{iR}u_x^{iR} - \gamma^R = 0.$ $\qquad (i = 1,\ldots,n)$

(A3) $\quad \partial\Lambda/\partial x^{jP} = W_{jP}u_x^{jP} - \gamma^P = 0.$ $\qquad (j = 1,\ldots,m)$

(A4) $\quad \partial\Lambda/g = \Sigma_i W_{iR}u_g^{iR} + \Sigma_j W_{jP}u_g^{jP} - \lambda = 0.$

(A5) $\quad \partial\Lambda/g^R = \lambda - \mu^R C_g^R = 0.$

(A6) $\quad \partial\Lambda/g^P = \lambda - \mu^P C_g^P = 0.$

(A7) $\quad \partial\Lambda/x^R = -\mu^R + \gamma^R = 0.$

(A8) $\quad \partial\Lambda/x^P = -\mu^P + \gamma^P = 0.$

Substituting from equations A2 and A3 into equation A4 yields:

(A9) $\quad \Sigma_i(u_g^{iR}/u_x^{iR})\gamma^R + \Sigma_j(u_g^{jP}/u_x^{jP})\gamma^P = \lambda.$

Equations A5–A8 can now be used to find that $\gamma^R = \lambda/C_g^R$ and $\gamma^P = \lambda/C_g^P$. Dividing by these expressions in equation A9 yields equation 12 in the main text. Note also that this implies that the ratio of marginal costs equals the inverse ratio of social marginal utilities of income—that is, $\gamma^P/\gamma^R = C_g^R/C_g^P$—establishing the link between cost weights and welfare weights.

Now assume that instead of the two constraints in equation 11 there is just the single constraint in equation 7. The last two terms of the Lagrange function (equation A1) then collapse into one, with the single multiplier γ. Equation A9 becomes:

$$(A10) \quad \sum_i (u_g^{iR}/u_x^{iR}) + \sum_j (u_g^{jP}/u_x^{jP}) = \lambda/\gamma.$$

From equations A5–A8 it then follows that $\lambda/\gamma = C_g^R = C_g^P$. With C_g being the common value of this, the result is equation 9 or 9′ in the main text.

NOTES

1. For an exposition of the Samuelson model and a short survey of some of the subsequent literature, see Sandmo (1987).

2. The treatment of this problem would have to draw on the literature on the private provision of public goods. For good introductions to this literature, see Oakland (1987, section 4) and Cornes and Sandler (1996).

3. A number of alternatives for theoretical modeling have a higher claim to descriptive realism. Air pollution may travel to other countries but still affect its country of origin more severely—so in this case the absence of air pollution is both a national and a global public good. And because air pollution is generated mainly by the consumption and production of private goods, it can also be treated as a case of private goods use with both national and international externalities (see Sandler in this volume for a more detailed discussion of such cases).

4. In theories of externalities and public goods several alternative assumptions have been explored on the relationship between individual contributions and the aggregate outcome, of which the case represented by equation 3′ is clearly a special but important one. Cornes and Sandler (1996), in a survey of a number of alternative models, refer to the present case as a "summation technology."

5. For their original work, see Heckscher (1949 [1919]) and Ohlin (1933).

6. This must be understood as relative to the assumption that factors of production are internationally immobile.

7. This formulation is similar to that in models of international trade with one traded and one nontraded good; for an exposition, see Bruce and Purvis (1985, pp. 814–17).

8. Indeed, Diamond and Mirrlees (1971) show that under certain conditions the case for production efficiency remains valid even when the only instruments for redistribution are distortionary taxes.

9. This will be true unless the poor country consumers have a much higher willingness to pay for the public good than do the rich country consumers.

10. This assumption is obviously unrealistic. Its use here should be seen as an attempt to capture the idea that national redistribution policy is more highly developed than redistribution between countries.

11. The formal model considers the scale of a project to be continuously variable—an analytical simplification that does not fit all practical cases. Sometimes the choice is between carrying out a project on a given scale or not at all. At other times the choice is between a few technologically feasible alternatives. In such cases the formal optimality criteria have to be restated in the form of inequalities, but here such complexities are left aside to focus on the basic economic insights that can be derived from the analysis.

12. For an examination of the validity of these results in the case of imperfect compliance on the part of polluters, see Sandmo (forthcoming).

13. In a more realistic setting where pollution is not entirely global, the location of industry would likely have additional consequences for the national environment and the argument would have to be modified.

14. For surveys of methods of benefits assessment, see Cropper and Oates (1992) and Sandmo (2000, ch. 4).

15. This follows if marginal benefits decline and marginal costs increase with the level of provision.

16. The combination of antipollution measures and international transfers has been discussed in a number of contributions to the literature on transfrontier pollution. For a theoretical analysis, see Chander and Tulkens (1992). Mäler (1991) discusses the problem of practical implementation with numerical illustrations for the case of sulfur emissions in Europe.

17. For a more detailed discussion of the incentive structures for global public goods provision, see Barrett (in this volume and 2001).

18. It is in this sense that these transfers can be viewed as payments, serving a distinctly different purpose than traditional foreign aid.

REFERENCES

Arrow, Kenneth J. 1963 [1951]. *Social Choice and Individual Values.* 2nd ed. New York: Wiley.

Barrett, Scott. 2001. "International Cooperation for Sale." *European Economic Review* 45: 1835–50.

Bruce, Neil, and Douglas D. Purvis. 1985. "The Specification and Influence of Goods and Factor Markets in Open-Economy Macroeconomic Models." In Ronald Jones and Peter Kenen, eds., *Handbook of International Economics*. Vol. 2. Amsterdam: Elsevier Science.

Buchanan, James M. 1987. *Economics: Between Predictive Science and Moral Philosophy*. College Station: Texas A&M University Press.

Chander, Parkash, and Henry Tulkens. 1992. "Theoretical Foundations of Negotiations and Cost Sharing in Transfrontier Pollution Problems." *European Economic Review* 36: 388–98.

Cornes, Richard, and Todd Sandler. 1996. *The Theory of Externalities, Public Goods, and Club Goods*. 2nd ed. Cambridge: Cambridge University Press.

Cropper, Maureen, and Wallace Oates. 1992. "Environmental Economics: A Survey." *Journal of Economic Literature* 30: 675–740.

Diamond, Peter A., and James A. Mirrlees. 1971. "Optimal Taxation and Public Production I–II." *American Economic Review* 61: 8–27 and 261–78.

Heckscher, Eli. 1949 [1919]. "The Effect of Foreign Trade on the Distribution of Income" (in Swedish). Ekonomisk Tidskrift 21: 497–512. Translated and reprinted in H. S. Ellis and L. Metzler, eds., *Readings in the Theory of International Trade*. Philadelphia: Blakiston.

Kaul, Inge, Isabelle Grunberg, and Marc A. Stern, eds. 1999. *Global Public Goods: International Cooperation in the 21st Century*. New York: Oxford University Press.

Mäler, Karl-Göran. 1991. "Environmental Issues in the New Europe." In Anthony B. Atkinson and Renato Brunetta, eds., *Economics for the New Europe*. London: Macmillan in association with the International Economic Association.

Oakland, William H. 1987. "Theory of Public Goods." In Alan Auerbach and Martin Feldstein, eds., *Handbook of Public Economics*. Vol. 2. Amsterdam: Elsevier Science.

Ohlin, Bertil. 1933. *Interregional and International Trade*. Cambridge, Mass.: Harvard University Press.

Samuelson, Paul A. 1954. "The Pure Theory of Public Expenditure." *Review of Economics and Statistics* 36 (4): 387-89.

———. 1955. "Diagrammatic Exposition of a Theory of Public Expenditure." *Review of Economics and Statistics* 37 (4): 350–56.

Sandmo, Agnar. 1987. "Public Goods." *The New Palgrave*. Vol. 3. London: Macmillan.

———. 2000. *The Public Economics of the Environment*. Oxford: Oxford University Press.

———. Forthcoming. "Efficient Environmental Policy with Imperfect Compliance." *Environmental and Resource Economics*.

ASSESSING THE OPTIMAL PROVISION OF PUBLIC GOODS: IN SEARCH OF THE HOLY GRAIL

TODD SANDLER

Over the past decade there has been a growing awareness of the negative spillovers from inadequate supply of transnational public goods, notably those stemming from communicable diseases, environmental degradation, spreading conflicts, and financial instability.[1] This realization is best illustrated by the United Nations High-Level Panel on Financing for Development (UN 2001), which recommends a significant increase in the financing of public goods. The panel suggests a four-fold increase from an estimated current level of $5 billion a year (UN 2001, p. 9). In *Global Development Finance 2001,* the World Bank (2001, p. 13) estimates that $5 billion a year is spent directly on global public goods, while another $11 billion is spent on "complementary activities."

Transnational public goods are those with benefits and costs that reach beyond one country and in some cases beyond one generation. If this reach is worldwide, the goods are global public goods. To understand the challenges posed by transnational public goods and how to address them, clear understanding is needed of the nature of these goods—especially of their benefits or costs and the type of cooperation required to provide them. Subtle differences in three dimensions of publicness—nonrivalry of benefits, nonexclusion of nonpayers, and the aggregation technology—can result in significant differences in how public goods are provided and by whom (Sandler 2001). These dimensions also affect the prognoses of provision efficiency by determining the incentives embodied in the implied strategic interactions as agents choose whether to contribute and contributors determine how much they are willing to pay (Sandler 1992, 1997, 1998; Sandler and Hartley 2001; Sandler and Sargent 1995). A related concern is the endogeneity of the dimensions of publicness, which may depend on institutional choices and so may not be an immutable property of a public good (Cornes and Sandler 1994).

This chapter develops two typologies of public goods that incorporate these dimensions of publicness and then uses the typologies to flag possibilities of undersupply, oversupply, or efficient supply. The chapter begins by examining the main classes of public goods from the viewpoint of how the nature of their benefits could affect the prognosis for their provision. It shows that judging provision efficiency becomes more complex when technologies of supply aggregation are taken into account. It then discusses two additional, special classes of public goods—club goods and joint products. Based on this analysis, the chapter suggests a few measures that could be employed in judging optimal provision, a discussion that leads to the two typologies of public goods, useful for supply prognoses. Finally, the chapter goes in search of the holy grail: an empirical measure of optimality.

Many of the issues raised apply to public goods in general, regardless of the geographic or temporal reach of their benefits and costs. Thus the chapter usually refers only to *public goods*. But given this volume's focus on global public goods, many examples are drawn from this category of goods and from the category of transnational public goods.

PURE AND IMPURE PUBLIC GOODS AND
SOME OF THEIR SUPPLY PROBLEMS

A pure public good, in its classical representation, possesses two properties: nonrivalry of benefits and nonexclusion of nonpayers. These properties distinguish pure public goods from those that can be traded in markets.

Pure public goods

A public good possesses nonrival benefits if one agent's consumption of it does not detract from the consumption opportunities available to others from the same unit of the good. Some economists equate nonrivalry of benefits with a zero marginal cost of extending consumption to additional users, meaning that no congestion cost or other associated cost—such as capacity building—is associated with additional consumers (Bruce 2001, ch. 3). If some consumers must be given the ability to enjoy a good, nonrivalry is not satisfied in this zero marginal cost sense because there is a cost in helping them partake in the benefits. The cleansing of a river can be enjoyed by all the nations along its banks; one nation's gain from the cleaner river does not diminish the same benefits available to others. Thus the cleansing is nonrival, and all potential consumers possess the ability to enjoy the improvement. Analogously, activities that degrade an environment or commons are public bads whose harm is nonrival among recipients and experienced by anyone who depends on the environmental asset.

The cleansing of a river also has nonexcludable benefits. Nonexclusion means that once a good is provided, payers and nonpayers alike can receive its benefits. Thus the provider cannot keep a nonpayer from consuming the good's benefits. This inability limits incentives for users to finance the provision of a good. If, for example, a nation were to clean a polluted lake shared with other nations and then ask those nations to reimburse the cleanup costs, voluntary contributions would be meager. Nonexclusion poses free-rider problems for a pure public good, resulting in a preference revelation problem. That is, when polled, people will have a strong incentive to understate or hide their true benefits if they believe that charges will be based on their responses. This means that efforts to judge the suboptimality of a pure public good by asking respondents to reveal what benefits they derive are doomed to failure: because their marginal willingness to pay (MWTP) is difficult to ascertain through solicitation, the optimal provision where ΣMWTP = MC is anyone's guess (where MC is the marginal cost of providing the good).[2]

Impure public goods
When transnational public goods possess benefits that are partly rival, partly excludable (that is, excludable at a cost), or both, they are impure public goods, as most kinds of public goods are. Partly rival benefits result in congestion or crowding costs if an additional user decreases the quantity or quality of the good available to others. Along the electromagnetic spectrum, for example, congestion takes the form of interference or noise—resulting in indecipherable signals—as the use of a given radiation band increases. Congestion means that extending the benefits of a public good to another user does not result in zero marginal cost.

If an impure public good is partially or fully rival but completely nonexcludable (as with a fishing commons or groundwater pool), the crowding externality that one user imposes on another may not be taken into account. This may result in overuse. Again, nonexclusion plays a crucial role in predicting underprovision or overprovision.

Next consider an impure public good that is completely nonrival but excludable at a negligible cost. Pay-per-view television is a good example. For transnational public goods a relevant example is the provision of satellite-based weather forecasts or surveys (such as LANDSAT) for different countries. Only those agents whose marginal willingness to pay is at least as great as the price charged will utilize the forecasting or surveying services. If the "hookup" costs are zero,[3] some inefficiency remains, because the marginal cost of additional users is negligible yet agents' marginal willingness to pay is greater than zero but less than the price charged. Social welfare can be augmented by including such agents.

This inefficiency is displayed in figure 1, which shows the demand of 180 countries for satellite-based weather forecasts. Line AB denotes the aggregate demand or marginal willingness to pay to subscribe to these forecasts. Suppose that the marginal cost of providing the forecasts to a subscriber is zero once the satellite is deployed. Each nation's choice is to subscribe or not to subscribe. If the provider charges $1 million per subscriber, 90 countries will subscribe (those whose marginal willingness to pay equals or exceeds $1 million), thereby generating $90 million in revenues for the provider. Those countries whose marginal willingness to pay is less than $1 million will not subscribe. This results in a wel-

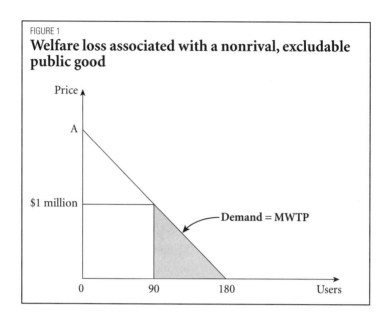

FIGURE 1
Welfare loss associated with a nonrival, excludable public good

fare loss of $45 million [= $1 million x (180 – 90)/2], represented by the shaded triangle, because providing the service to additional countries would be costless to achieve. A dilemma arises, since the revenue is required to finance the good's provision, but exclusion results in welfare losses. The solution to this dilemma is supranational provision financed by taxes.

Thus some public goods face a greater risk of suboptimal provision than others, and they do so for different reasons intimately linked to the nature of their benefits or costs.

AGGREGATION TECHNOLOGIES

This section turns from the benefits and costs of a good to a further dimension, which concerns the relationship between individual contributions and the good's overall supply level. This dimension is known as the *aggregation technology* (Cornes and Sandler 1996; Hirshleifer 1983; Kanbur and Sandler with Morrison 1999).

Summation and weighted-sum technologies

The most common aggregation technology is summation, where each unit contributed to a public good—or bad—adds identically and additively to the overall level available to all. For example, the accumulation of greenhouse gases abides by summation technology. If 200 nations each emit 1,000 metric tons of greenhouse gases into the atmosphere, 200,000 metric tons result, heating the atmosphere. Because each unit contributed has the same effect on the total for a summation technology, every unit is a perfect substitute for other units. This perfect substitutability drives the motivation to free ride and the standard prediction of underprovision.

A generalization of summation technology is that of weighted sum, for which the weights are no longer one. These weights reflect the marginal effect that a unit provided by one agent has on the total level of a public good. In efforts to reduce sulfur deposits falling on a country, the influence of cutbacks abroad depends on wind patterns, the sites of emission sources, and the pollution's airborne time. Emission cutbacks in one location do not necessarily have the same impact on deposits as do cutbacks in other locations, so a weighted-sum aggregation applies (Murdoch, Sandler, and Sargent 1997).

With weighted-sum technology, provision efforts are no longer perfect substitutes. Because some nations may receive a disproportionate share of the benefits of a transnational public good from their provision, such nations have stronger incentives to supply the good. For acid rain geographically larger countries experience a greater portion of the reduction in deposits that results from curtailing their emissions and so are more motivated to act. Thus underprovision may be eased.

Weakest-link and weaker-link technologies

Another important aggregation technology is that of weakest link, for which the smallest contribution determines the quantity of a public good for a group. Efforts to contain the spread of a disease adhere to weakest-link technology in that the country exercising the fewest precautions determines the extent to which the disease spreads. Similarly, the integrity of a network hinges on its least reliable component.

Incentives promote the efficient provision of a weakest-link public good. Matching behavior is likely, with providers giving only as much as the smallest contribution because giving more would exhaust resources without augmenting the public good. But if potential providers have similar tastes and endowments, they will desire a similar level of provision. That is, such agents will want the same security or minimal level of the public good, and the copying of other agents' contributions results in an efficient provision level. Free riding is not a problem because contributing nothing lowers to zero the quantity of the public good for everyone.

Low-income countries, however, may be able to afford only a small contribution to the public good. In such cases richer countries can either augment to an acceptable level the poorer countries' supply of the good or provide the good on their soil (Vicary and Sandler 2002). Multilateral institutions and nongovernmental organizations (NGOs) can also finance shortfalls. Weakest-link technology vastly attenuates the underprovision of a public good.

A less extreme form of a weakest-link public good is a weaker-link public good, for which the smallest contribution has the greatest impact on overall provision, followed by the second smallest contribution, and so on. The stability of financial markets can be seen as a weaker-link public good because the most unstable market has the most destabilizing effect, followed by the second most unstable market, and so on. For weaker-link public goods a country that exceeds the minimum (smallest) contribution can achieve additional gains, though these diminish at the margin as the contribution rises (Arce and Sandler 2001; Cornes 1993; Sandler 1998). The trend toward matching behavior is somewhat attenuated because some providers can obtain greater gains by supplying more than others. Thus there are fewer incentives to achieve acceptable standards globally or regionally. The good will likely be either efficiently supplied or somewhat undersupplied as a result of a coordination problem involving who does more.

Best-shot and better-shot technologies

The overall quantity of a best-shot transnational public good is determined solely by the largest contribution from among participating countries; contributions below that level add nothing. Some best-shot public goods either are obtained or are not; that is, they are discrete public goods. An example is finding a cure for a disease—once the breakthrough is made, it is accomplished for everyone. For other best-shot public goods the provision level is variable and corresponds to the largest capacity provided. Discrete best-shot public goods may be optimally supplied, while variable capacity best-shot public goods may be undersupplied because the provider may not account for the spillover benefits conferred on others. This failure can be corrected if exclusion can be practiced and a charge levied on users, as with a patent on medicine.

Better-shot public goods are a less extreme form of best-shot public goods. For better-shot public goods the largest contribution has the greatest impact on overall supply, followed by the second-largest contribution, and so on. Better-shot public goods are likely to have multiple suppliers because even a second-best effort may add to the overall quantity. The development of a treatment regime for a disease may abide by better-shot technology if a less desirable regime benefits patients who cannot tolerate the preferred regime. There is less need to concentrate resources than for best-shot public goods. As with best-shot public goods, better-shot public goods may be efficiently supplied or undersupplied depending on exclusion or the discreteness of the good.

The foregoing discussion reveals that the aggregation technology subdivides each of the major classes of public goods. The implication is that reliable provision prognoses must be undertaken on a good-specific basis.

TWO ADDITIONAL CLASSES OF PUBLIC GOODS

For the analysis in this chapter it is important to considers two other types of public goods: club goods and joint products.

Club goods

If exclusion costs are sufficiently small to allow utilization rates to be monitored and a toll or user fee to be levied, the users can form a collective called a club and provide themselves with a partially rival shared good (Buchanan 1965; Sandler and Tschirhart 1980, 1997). Transnational club goods—such as satellite communication networks, the electromagnetic spectrum's bandwidths, nature reserves, international airports, airplane corridors, orbital slots, and terrorist commando units—can be provided by members and financed through tolls that charge for the crowding costs at the margin. The toll mechanism forces payments that "internalize" or account for the marginal crowding costs suffered by the membership for an additional unit of use. Even taste differences among members are taken into account: members with a stronger preference for the club good will use it more often and thus pay more in total tolls. Toll revenues can then be earmarked to finance the club good.

Through their toll charges, clubs maintain the connection between benefits and financing, because only those members whose marginal willingness to pay justifies paying the toll will use the facilities and then only to the point at which their marginal willingness to pay just equals the toll. Anyone whose marginal willingness to pay is less than the toll does not receive sufficient benefits from a visit to compensate for the marginal crowding cost that the visit imposes on others. Unlike with nonrival public goods, there is an efficiency rationale for excluding such agents, because their use is not costless. The ability of clubs to fund an optimal provision level depends on the nature of the crowding function, the production function of the club good, and other considerations (Sandler and Tschirhart 1980, 1997).

Clubs can be privately owned and operated, as in the case of INTELSAT. Thus global clubs offer a private allocative mechanism that can supply an important class of transnational public goods without high transaction costs or the inefficiency that has come to characterize many forms of public provision. If some countries cannot afford membership, clubs may be associated with equity concerns, which must be addressed.

Joint products

A final class of public goods consists of joint products for which an activity simultaneously yields two or more outputs that may vary in their degree of publicness. For joint products an activity may result in a pure public output, agent-specific private outputs, and even a club good. By lessening threats to neighboring countries, peacekeeping activities yield regionwide public benefits from reduced instability along with country-specific benefits to the crisis-laden nation. International recognition and approval given to major peacekeeping nations (for example, Australia in East Timor) also constitute a nation-specific private benefit. Nation-specific benefits cannot be gained through free riding, so that a nation must contribute to the overall public activity if it is to obtain these private benefits. If, moreover, these nation-specific private benefits are complementary, in that nations desire to consume them along with the purely public benefits, spillovers of benefits may motivate more rather than less provision on behalf of the spillover recipient. Thus joint products figure in an essential way in any assessment of undersupply.[4]

THEORETICAL ISSUES IN JUDGING OPTIMAL PROVISION

The above classes of public goods can be used to develop a typology from which optimal provision can be inferred. Any nation providing a pure transnational public good G will equate only its own marginal willingness to pay ($MWTP_G$) with the associated marginal cost. That means that nation A, when deciding the provision of G, will ignore benefit spillovers to $n-1$ other nations; those spillovers equal $\sum_{i=2}^{n} MWTP_G^i$. The greater is the number of countries receiving the spillovers, the greater is the extent of suboptimal provision, because more countries' spillover benefits are ignored.

The presence of goods with benefits that are both nonrival and nonexcludable implies suboptimal provision in many but not all circumstances. As noted, pure public goods should be grouped according to their aggregation technology, because technologies such as weakest link may be consistent with optimality. Thus pure publicness is not a sufficient condition for suboptimality. Pure public bads, which have a negative sum of marginal willingness to pay, are best subsumed in the class of pure public goods,[5] where oversupply is implied by individual behavior because of the negative spillovers ignored by the provider. The greater is the number of these ignored negative spillovers, the greater is the oversupply of pure public bads.

Turning to impure public goods, consider open access resources, which are nonexcludable but often rival. Exploiters of a fishery, for example, are unlikely to account for the crowding externality that their exploitation creates for others. This crowding occurs because increased use of the fishery reduces the catch associated with a given level of effort. Because each user's catch hinges on doing as much as possible, a contest ensues and an oversupply of effort results. The extent of the oversupply of effort depends on how output from the commons is shared (Cornes and Sandler 1994, 1996). In the standard case users' shares of the output depend on their proportion of the total effort expended. That is, a firm with one-quarter of the fishing boats is apt to catch one-quarter of the fish.

But the distribution of the catch and thus the supply prognosis can depend on other sharing arrangements if a central authority or convention exists. In stark contrast to proportional sharing is equal sharing, where the catch is pooled and divided evenly among the group of exploiters. Such a setup leads to free riding, resulting in an undersupply of effort (Cauley, Cornes, and Sandler 1999). But if access to the commons is restricted, the crowding externality is taken into account resulting in an efficient supply of effort. Thus the supply prognosis for a commons hinges on the underlying institutional rules. When exclusion is not possible or is limited, some free riding and undersupply should be anticipated for impure public goods.

If an impure transnational public good is nonrival and exclusion is practiced, the good will be undersupplied because potential user nations will be denied entry if their marginal willingness to pay is less than the price. An example is the exclusion of knowledge through patent rights. In such cases the extent of suboptimal provision is equal to the area under the transnational demand curve and to the right of the quantity supplied (that is, the number of uses or visits). Because users must reveal their preference through entry fees—such as royalties paid to patent holders—the demand curve can be estimated and the extent of suboptimality determined.[6] The demand relationships can be determined by varying the user fee and ascertaining the quantity demanded. With the example of knowledge, however, the challenge of balancing dynamic and static efficiency concerns also has to be kept in mind (Stiglitz 1999).

As noted, club goods result when exclusion is complete. Member nations reveal their marginal willingness to pay through their use of the good. If there are more nations than can be accommodated in a single global club, multiple regional clubs can be created. The Suez Canal represents a single global club with nations as members. Clubs providing communication links among members can be organized at the national level, then tied together for global coverage (as with telephone and mail services). Advances in technology have transformed a growing number of public goods into club goods.

With joint products, optimality hinges on the ratio of excludable benefits to total benefits from the public activity. As this ratio approaches one, the share of excludable benefits increases, enabling markets and clubs to optimally allocate resources to the good's provision. As the ratio approaches zero, the share of purely public benefits increases, making it likely that the activity will be undersupplied (or oversupplied if public spillovers are negative). Joint products encompass a wide variety of scenarios and may include underprovision (when the share of purely public benefits is large), overprovision (when the share of purely public costs is large), or nearly efficient provision (when the share of nation-specific or club outputs, or both, is large). By proxying these shares, the extent of over- or undersupply can be estimated (Sandler and Murdoch 2000). This proxying has been done in practice for defense activities that are shared by NATO allies (Sandler and Hartley 1999).

TYPOLOGIES FOR PUBLIC GOOD SUPPLY PROGNOSES

There are many alternative typologies of public goods in the literature, with no single typology being best. In essence, typologies differ according to the purpose that they are intended to serve. This section reviews two typologies that could be useful for assessing the provision of public goods, notably that of transnational public goods. Both typologies build on, and in a way summarize, the foregoing discussion.

Transnational public goods according to the aggregation technology
This first typology captures three of the four classes of public goods that have been described, along with the six aggregation technologies discussed. Joint products are left out of this first typology because each of their outputs possesses potentially different private and publicness properties that can be further subdivided by the aggregation technologies. Thus a joint product activity such as peacekeeping may have a deterrence output that is the sum of the troops and arsenal provided, while peacekeeping also yields a conflict containment output that hinges on the smallest effort. If these complications are permitted, joint products could also be considered in the present context.

Table 1 indicates the supply prognosis for each of the resultant 18 classes of goods and gives an example of each. The examples listed for pure public goods were discussed when the aggregation technologies were presented. Among impure public goods, the overall effort to reduce transnational terrorism is the sum of the countries' individual actions. Since an oil spill at sea that threatens multiple countries may pose different risks depending on currents and wind, a weighted-sum technology applies, underscoring the lack of perfect substitutability among individual efforts to contain the spill. Weakest link applies to the surveillance of a disease outbreak, because the least adequate intelligence determines the overall level of preparedness. Impurity results because enhanced surveillance in one location may detract from efforts elsewhere. Eradicating a pest abides by a weaker-link technology if greater effort at home provides greater security than just matching the smallest effort elsewhere. Creating knowledge and compiling a database are categorized as best-shot and better-shot impure public goods, respectively. For a database efforts below the largest may still provide a marginal benefit by serving as a backup or by capturing additional information.

Just as pure and impure public goods can be distinguished by the aggregation technologies, so too can club goods. Since the overall availability of transnational parks depends on the total land allocated, these parks are classified as adhering to a summation technology. INTELSAT's capacity to transmit communications involves the placement of satellites, with those over the Atlantic Ocean more in demand because of the flow of communication between the continents. Thus the capacity and the number of transmissions carried by INTELSAT correspond to a weighted sum of the number of satellites, where higher weights are given to some positions. The use of a hub-spoke network for air transportation is a weakest-link club good, which is painfully apparent when the weather closes down a major airport, leading to repercussions throughout the network. Members that share

TABLE 1

Supply prognoses for and examples of selected transnational public goods, by aggregation technology

Aggregation technology	Pure public goods (nonrival and nonexcludable benefits)	Impure public goods (partially rival and partially excludable benefits)	Club goods (partially rival and partially excludable benefits)
Summation	Undersupplied *Curbing global warming*	Oversupplied or undersupplied *Reducing transnational terrorism*	Efficiently supplied *Transnational parks*
Weighted sum	Undersupplied to some extent *Reducing sulfur deposits*	Undersupplied *Cleaning up an oil spill*	Efficiently supplied *Communication satellites (such as INTELSAT)*
Weakest link	Supply may be efficient *Containing the spread of a disease*	Undersupplied or efficiently supplied *Surveillance of a disease outbreak*	Undersupplied or efficiently supplied *Air transport hub-spoke networks*
Weaker link	Undersupplied to some extent *Financial market stability*	Undersupplied to some extent *Eradicating a pest*	Efficiently supplied *Extension services*
Best shot	Undersupplied or efficiently supplied *Finding a cure for a disease*	Undersupplied or efficiently supplied *Creating new knowledge*	Efficiently supplied *Crisis management teams*
Better shot	Undersupplied or efficiently supplied *Developing treatment regimes*	Undersupplied or efficiently supplied *Compiling a database*	Efficiently supplied *BL-4 laboratory (study of highly contagious diseases)*

Note: Items in italics are examples.

extension services may also experience cuts in services caused by network problems. The disruption may, however, be less severe if network capacity differs among users. A crisis management force to address terrorist events or other exigencies may be a best-shot club good, whose premier force can be shared when needed for a deployment fee. A BL-4 laboratory for studying highly contagious diseases represents a better-shot club good, because a second-best backup facility for even the most secure laboratory may be needed if it becomes accidentally contaminated.

Three points are worth stressing:

- Even a pure public good may *not* be undersupplied for some aggregation technologies.
- A range of supply prognoses are associated with impure public goods, owing to their alternative publicness properties.
- Club goods can be efficiently allocated regardless of the underlying aggregation technology if the toll internalizes the crowding. This is true unless the club good has some externalities not properly taken into account.

*Transnational public goods according to geographic
and intertemporal spillovers*
Table 2 distinguishes six general classes of public goods in the left-hand column: pure public goods or bads, nonrival and excludable impure public goods, partially rival and partially excludable impure public goods, commons, club goods, and joint products. Commons are further distinguished by open access and limited access. Another means for subdividing each class of these goods is by its geographic range of spillovers; that is, by how far the benefits of the good extend.

In the case of pure public goods, impure public goods, and open-access commons, inefficiency worsens as the range of spillover of the benefits or costs increases—from national to regional and global. This follows because the relevant externalities that are ignored involve more people's marginal willingness to pay. Yet geographic range need not have any influence on either limited-access commons or club goods if means are in place for charging costs imposed on others. For joint products greater geographic breadth worsens inefficiency on the relevant pure and impure public outputs. For five out of six of the classes of public goods some aggregation technologies may alleviate the inefficiency caused by spillovers. Because there is almost no inefficiency in clubs, there is generally nothing for these technologies to alleviate.

The third column of table 2 distinguishes public goods by their temporal spillovers. Some public goods are assets that can have a short life span, say 10 years, such as communication satellites. Other public goods can have longer-lasting streams of spillovers that benefit many generations into the future (Sandler 1999). Failure to include these generations' gains from spillovers will mean that too lit-

TABLE 2

Transnational public goods by geographic and intertemporal spillovers and by aggregation technology

Type of good	Geographic range of spillovers	Intertemporal range of spillovers	Aggregation technology	Remarks
Pure public goods or bads	Worsens inefficiency	Worsens inefficiency	Some technologies alleviate inefficiency	Public goods (bads) tend to be undersupplied (over-supplied). Increases in the range of geographic or temporal spillovers can exacerbate the problem.
Impure public goods, nonrival and excludable	Worsens inefficiency	Worsens inefficiency	Some technologies alleviate inefficiency	Undersupply results when people with a positive marginal willingness to pay are excluded and there is no cost associated with their inclusion.
Impure public goods, partially rival, partially excludable, or both	Worsens inefficiency	Worsens inefficiency	Some technologies alleviate inefficiency	Exclusion promotes voluntary provision but some undersupply remains.
Commons				
1. Open access	Worsens inefficiency May be neutral	Worsens inefficiency May be neutral	Some technologies alleviate inefficiency	With open access, oversupply of effort is expected. As access becomes limited, more efficient supply of effort results. Sharing rule is important.
2. Limited access				
Club goods	No necessary influence	No necessary influence	Generally no influence	Toll mechanism can result in an efficient outcome, but there is an equity concern.
Joint products	Worsens inefficiency on purely and impurely public outputs	Worsens inefficiency on purely and impurely public outputs	Some technologies alleviate inefficiency	As the ratio of excludable to total benefits approaches one, markets and clubs can achieve an efficient allocation. Equity remains a concern.

tle of the good will be provided by the current generation. Of course, distant generations are not around to voice their preference or to consummate a trade with the current providers (Doeleman and Sandler 1998). These intertemporal spillovers act like geographic spillovers but are even more difficult to include. Finally, the last two columns of table 2 remark on the impact that aggregation technologies could have on the efficient provision of the various classes of goods.

Thus, in general, both transnational and intertemporal spillovers worsen inefficiency in the absence of club goods. But aggregation technologies can sometimes limit this inefficiency.

EMPIRICAL MEASURES OF OPTIMAL PROVISION

Empirical measures of the supply of public goods face many methodological challenges. Before discussing a possible index of optimal provision of public goods, this section reviews some of these challenges. This review helps better appreciate the usefulness of the suggested index, which also faces implementation difficulties.

How can the provision of a public good be measured empirically?

The most direct way to measure a public good (or bad) is by its physical properties and quantity—for example, acres of wilderness areas, miles of roads, or number of international conflicts or financial crises (see Conceição in this volume). But some public goods, such as defense or peacekeeping, do not have a well-defined unit of measurement. Moreover, if the goal is to calculate the overall level of diverse public goods, a common unit of measurement is required because it is not meaningful to add, say, the number of bridges to the number of immunization shots. Money provides a well-defined, common unit of measurement. Thus expenditures for each public good can be summed over all the public goods in a transnational region, providing an aggregate level of provision.

Measuring public goods in terms of expenditures still poses difficulties, however, because the goods may be produced by a government, an intergovernmental organization, or the private sector. (For example, peacekeeping tanks for United Nations missions are manufactured by private corporations and then purchased by the UN.) Public goods produced in the private sector have prices that reflect their opportunity costs better than do public goods produced in the public sector.[7] Consider national defense, where conscription allows governments to purchase soldiers at well below their market value, so that defense spending may underestimate soldiers' true opportunity costs. The UN pays about $1,000 a month for its peacekeepers, which is less than one-fifth of what a U.S. soldier costs but well above the pay for a soldier in Bangladesh or Pakistan (Sandler and Hartley 1999, ch. 4). Thus the true opportunity cost of UN peacekeeping hinges on which country is supplying the troops. In cases of public production, expenditures may have to be adjusted to better reflect opportunity costs.

Quality poses another concern, because the quality of a public good can vary across countries and over time. Consider how weather forecasting technologies have changed over the past 50 years. The higher quality of today's far more sophisticated equipment is reflected in its higher price. But forecasts are also more detailed and more reliable.

A final dimension of the measurement problem involves the level at which to calculate public goods—national, regional, or global. As calculations move beyond the national level, cross-country comparisons become an issue in terms of unit price and conversion to a common currency for comparison. It is easy to apply well-developed methods for converting to a common currency while adjusting for inflation rates. The challenge lies in getting spending figures from government budgets when different countries use different definitions and accounting procedures.

An index of optimality
The hardest thing to calculate for public goods is their degree of suboptimality, which is ideally measured as a shortfall in quantity because actual welfare losses are not comparable among different agents. Suppose that it is possible to measure the actual quantity supplied or the spending on a public good. This amount reflects voluntary behavior and, for a pure public good (bad), is typically expected to be less (more) than the optimal quantity. To determine the optimal quantity, each agent's marginal willingness to pay must be ascertained. But nations have no incentive to reveal their true marginal willingness to pay, leaving half a formula—the actual but not the optimal quantity of the pure public good. Even preference revelation mechanisms, such as taxes or other burden-sharing formulas, have myriad problems and would not be practical at the transnational level (Cornes and Sandler 1996, pp. 221–37). These schemes encourage truthful reporting of preferences by making honesty a dominant strategy, best no matter what others do. Judicious choice of taxes makes a respondent responsible for any shortfalls or oversupply—that is, exaggerating one's tastes results in paying too much, while understating one's tastes leads to too little of the public good. Similarly, direct valuation methods (such as contingent valuation) and indirect approaches (such as the travel-cost method or the hedonic approach; see Bjornstad and Kahn 1996) have serious limitations.

The proposed method for calculating an index of optimality, without a need to compute different agents' marginal willingness to pay or any proxy indicators, relies on the supply prognoses described above for the various classes of public goods. That is, pure public goods and nonrival impure public goods are undersupplied, club goods are supplied efficiently, and the optimality of joint products depends on the ratio of excludable benefits to total benefits from an activity.

For an illustration, assume that a regional economy has only three types of public goods: pure public, nonrival impure public, and club goods. The proposed index of optimality is:

$$(1)\quad I_{opt} = \frac{\$CLUB}{\$PP + \$NIM + \$CLUB}$$

which ranges from zero to one. In equation 1, $ indicates expenditures, $CLUB denotes total regional spending on club goods, $PP represents total regional spending on pure public goods, and $NIM indicates total regional spending on nonrival impure public goods. If this ratio is one, all public goods are club goods and there is effectively no suboptimality. If this ratio is zero, all public goods belong to the two classes where undersupply is anticipated and spending is far from optimal. This optimality index can serve as a proxy for the efficiency of public good supply at any jurisdictional level, so different levels can be compared. The denominator of equation 1 also serves as a measure of regional spending on public goods. The proposed index can be converted to an index of suboptimality by merely subtracting I_{opt} from one.

In a more complicated example, suppose that there is also a joint product activity with an expenditure of $JP. Further suppose that half the benefits of this activity are a club good and the other half are a pure public good. That is, $CLUB$_{JP}$ = $JP/2 and PP_{JP}$ = $JP/2, where the subscript JP ties these outputs to the joint product. The index of optimality with the joint product included is:

$$(2)\quad I_{opt} = \frac{\$CLUB + \$CLUB_{JP}}{\$PP + \$NIM + \$CLUB + \$JP}.$$

Any private good outputs stemming from a joint product activity must be properly apportioned and then placed in the numerator along with club spending, because markets can allocate these private outputs. For joint products, markets and clubs can efficiently allocate private and club good outputs, respectively, thus leaving any inefficiency to be associated with any other public good outputs. But this is not the entire story, because spending on weakest-link pure public goods and some discrete best-shot public goods may be sufficiently optimal to warrant inclusion in both the numerator and the denominator of I_{opt}.

The index can be used to judge the relative efficiency of two regions in providing public goods. If region 1 has a higher percentage of spending on club goods, joint products with mostly excludable outputs, and weakest-link public goods than region 2, the index can roughly calibrate how much more efficient region 1 is in supplying these public goods.

An index value of one indicates that the supranational community does not have to worry about allocative efficiency, but this does not imply that policy has no role to play (see below). The index simply helps flag optimal provision or possible underprovision. It is not making a normative statement. A jurisdiction—whether a country or the international community—may be interested in pursuing other goals and so might want to combine, for example, efficiency and equity considerations. But before returning to that issue, it is useful to consider some of the implementation problems of the proposed index.

Implementation problems
The optimality index has some implementation problems. First, public goods must be distinguished and assigned to their classes. This is easy for some public goods, such as club goods. But for others the required judgment is more difficult.

Second, joint product activities are a concern because their components must be identified and valued, which is challenging. Consider the valuation of a tropical forest that provides worldwide purely public benefits from biodiversity and the sequestration of carbon, as well as host-country benefits from a watershed, erosion control, tourism, and fruits and nuts. Apportioning a tropical forest into these jointly produced outputs requires that an overall value first be assigned to the forest. This value must then be divided among the various joint products—a formidable task.

Third, data requirements for computing any country's optimality index are daunting because of the presence of a wide range of public goods, all of which must be valued and assigned to their classes. This difficulty confronts any attempt to calculate a country's public good spending—the denominator of the optimality index. The index's numerator presents additional concerns. Finally, there is the problem of distinguishing within classes of public goods according to the aggregation technology. After making this determination, analysts must decide whether there are sufficient grounds for including the good's value in the numerator of the index, where efficiency is implied.

Despite its practical problems, the index serves some useful purposes. Foremost, it conceptualizes how the various classes of public goods can be used to derive a sense of the inefficiency of public good supply in a jurisdiction. The index can be applied at any jurisdictional level. It can also be used to ascertain the optimality of specific activities, especially when a ratio of excludable to total benefits can be computed. If it is known how technological and institutional changes affect the mix of public goods in a jurisdiction, the index signals how provision efficiency will be influenced. In many ways the optimality index poses fewer insurmountable problems than other techniques for evaluating the efficient provision of public goods.

Further observations on clubs and on the use and purpose
of the optimality index
As noted, potential recipients with insufficient income or capacity will not receive club goods and excludable goods. But as Sandmo (in this volume) argues, it is often harder to separate efficiency and equity concerns at the international than at the national level. Thus at the international level there could often be a role for

policy to ensure socially acceptable levels of access to such goods. For example, developing countries could be given foreign aid to join international clubs such as INTELSAT (Kanbur and Sandler with Morrison 1999).

An allocative mechanism such as a club should not be dismissed because the outcome may be inequitable. Allocative mechanisms should be chosen to increase efficiency and lower transaction costs. Once an allocative mechanism is in place, however, equity concerns can be addressed. Clubs are fine for efficiency—but, like markets, they may increase disparities.

However, it is important not to confuse technical clubs with political clubs. The first are organized for producing, delivering, and sharing excludable public goods once a (preferably participatory, nondiscriminatory) decision is made to do so. The term *political club* as sometimes used in political science and international relations theory (see, for example, Keohane and Nye 2001) describes exclusive and often discriminatory associations, such as the G-8, the United Nations Security Council, or, in the context of the World Trade Organization, the group of countries meeting in the "Green Room."

The index suggested here is a tool intended to assist in judging provision optimality. Its purpose is to facilitate empirical measurement of the supply of public goods, including that of transnational public goods. It is a possible measure of provision efficiency. Policymakers may have many other concerns, and thus measurement needs, with respect to public goods.

CONCLUSION

This chapter has clarified the notion of public goods and their prognosis for efficient supply. To place these goods in proper perspective, the chapter has developed two typologies. The first indicates how the aggregation technology subdivides each of the major classes of public goods. This subdivision may have a profound influence on suboptimality for the different classes of public goods. When, moreover, there is suboptimal supply, the aggregation technology influences policy options. The second typology furthers the analysis of supply adequacy by allowing for alternative geographic and intertemporal spillovers of benefits. Throughout the discussion, it is argued that an allocative mechanism such as clubs should not be dismissed because the outcome may be inequitable. Allocative mechanisms for public goods should be chosen on grounds of efficiency and a desire to save on transaction costs. Given the allocative mechanism, equity concerns can then be addressed.

An index of optimality has been devised to assess how well a jurisdiction has supplied its public goods and, in doing so, to alert us to underprovision. This index circumvents the difficult problem of ascertaining the difference between the efficient and the actual level of provision. Moreover, the index does not have to determine a consumer's marginal willingness to pay for the public good. Although the index confronts a number of implementation problems, it uses the nature of the classes of public goods as a rough means for comparing the adequacy of supply of public goods among jurisdictions.

NOTES

1. One of the first books that heightened this awareness was Sandler's (1997) *Global Challenges,* which made the link between transnational public goods and foreign assistance. Other relevant books include Kaul, Grunberg, and Stern (1999) and Kanbur and Sandler with Morrison (1999).

2. The marginal willingness to pay or marginal rate of substitution indicates the amount of a numéraire (or comparison) private good that an agent is willing to sacrifice for an additional unit of the public good while maintaining the same level of satisfaction. The efficiency condition for a pure public good is that the sum of the benefit recipients' marginal rates of substitution or their marginal willingness to pay equals the marginal cost (MC) of providing the good (see also Samuelson 1954, 1955).

3. A hookup cost results when there is an expense in making the good's benefits available to an additional user.

4. Olson (1965, 2000) called these jointly produced private benefits selective incentives and emphasized their importance in solving the collective action problem associated with public goods (see also Sandler 1992).

5. A public good can include some values of marginal willingness to pay that are negative or zero, provided that the overall sum of marginal willingness to pay is positive. Similarly, a public bad may still have some values of marginal willingness to pay that are positive or zero. It is the overall sum that differentiates public goods from public bads (Cornes and Sandler 1994).

6. This estimation is easier for a linear demand curve because observed points on a segment allow the entire curve to be drawn. When the demand is nonlinear, the extrapolation to unseen points may be subject to significant error.

7. The prices of public goods produced in the private sector may not be a perfect measure of opportunity costs because of asymmetric information, where the producer knows more about the goods' true costs than does the government purchaser. Incentive contracts are one way of circumventing this problem (Sandler and Hartley 1999).

REFERENCES

Arce M., Daniel G., and Todd Sandler. 2001. "Transnational Public Goods: Strategies and Institutions." *European Journal of Political Economy* 17 (3): 493–516.

Bjornstad, David J., and James R. Kahn, eds. 1996. *The Contingent Valuation of Environmental Resources: Methodological Issues and Research Needs.* Cheltenham, U.K.: Edward Elgar.

Bruce, Neil. 2001. *Public Finance and the American Economy*. 2nd ed. Reading, Mass.: Addison-Wesley.

Buchanan, James M. 1965. "An Economic Theory of Clubs." *Economica* 32 (1): 1–14.

Cauley, Jon, Richard Cornes, and Todd Sandler. 1999. "Stakeholder Incentives and Reforms in China's State-Owned Enterprises: A Common-Property Theory." *China Economic Review* 10 (2): 191–206.

Cornes, Richard. 1993. "Dyke Maintenance and Other Stories: Some Neglected Types of Public Goods." *Quarterly Journal of Economics* 108 (1): 259–71.

Cornes, Richard, and Todd Sandler. 1994. "Are Public Goods Myths?" *Journal of Theoretical Politics* 6 (3): 369–85.

———. 1996. *The Theory of Externalities, Public Goods, and Club Goods*. 2nd ed. Cambridge: Cambridge University Press.

Doeleman, Jacobus A., and Todd Sandler. 1998. "The Intergenerational Case of Missing Markets and Missing Voters." *Land Economics* 74 (1): 1–15.

Hirshleifer, Jack. 1983. "From Weakest-Link to Best Shot: The Voluntary Provision of Public Goods." *Public Choice* 41 (3): 371–86.

Kanbur, Ravi, and Todd Sandler with Kevin Morrison. 1999. "The Future of Development Assistance: Common Pools and International Public Goods." Policy Essay 25. Overseas Development Council, Washington, D.C.

Kaul, Inge, Isabelle Grunberg, and Marc A. Stern, eds. 1999. *Global Public Goods: International Cooperation in the 21st Century*. New York: Oxford University Press.

Keohane, Robert O., and Joseph S. Nye Jr. 2001. "The Club Model of Multilateral Cooperation and Problems of Democratic Legitimacy." In Robert B. Porter, Pierre Sauve, Arvind Subramanian, and Americo Beviglia Zampeti, eds., *Efficiency, Equity, Legitimacy: The Multilateral Trading System at the Millennium*. Washington, D.C.: Brookings Institution Press for the Center for Business and Government.

Murdoch, James C., Todd Sandler, and Keith Sargent. 1997. "A Tale of Two Collectives: Sulphur versus Nitrogen Oxides Emission Reduction in Europe." *Economica* 64 (2): 281–301.

Olson, Mancur 1965. *The Logic of Collective Action*. Cambridge, Mass.: Harvard University Press.

———. 2000. *Power and Prosperity: Outgrowing Communist and Capitalist Dictatorships*. New York: Basic Books.

Samuelson, Paul A. 1954. "The Pure Theory of Public Expenditure." *Review of Economics and Statistics* 36 (4): 387–89.

———. 1955. "A Diagrammatic Exposition of a Theory of Public Expenditure." *Review of Economics and Statistics* 37 (4): 350–56.

Sandler, Todd. 1992. *Collective Action: Theory and Applications*. Ann Arbor: University of Michigan Press.

————. 1997. *Global Challenges: An Approach to Environmental, Political, and Economic Problems.* Cambridge: Cambridge University Press.

————. 1998. "Global and Regional Public Goods: A Prognosis for Collective Action." *Fiscal Studies* 19 (3): 221–47.

————. 1999. "Intergenerational Public Goods: Strategies, Efficiency, and Institutions." In Inge Kaul, Isabelle Grunberg, and Marc A. Stern, eds., *Global Public Goods: International Cooperation in the 21st Century.* New York: Oxford University Press.

————. 2001. "On Financing Global and International Public Goods." Policy Research Working Paper 2638. World Bank, Economic Policy and Prospects Group, Washington, D.C.

Sandler, Todd, and Keith Hartley. 1999. *The Political Economy of NATO: Past, Present, and into the 21st Century.* Cambridge: Cambridge University Press.

————. 2001. "Economics of Alliances: The Lessons for Collective Action." *Journal of Economic Literature* 39 (3): 869–96.

Sandler, Todd, and James C. Murdoch. 2000. "On Sharing NATO Defence Burdens in the 1990s and Beyond." *Fiscal Studies* 21 (3): 297–327.

Sandler, Todd, and Keith Sargent. 1995. "Management of Transnational Commons: Coordination, Publicness, and Treaty Formation." *Land Economics* 71 (2): 145–62.

Sandler, Todd, and John T. Tschirhart. 1980. "Economic Theory of Clubs: An Evaluative Survey." *Journal of Economic Literature* 18 (4): 1481–1521.

————. 1997. "Club Theory: Thirty Years Later." *Public Choice* 93 (3–4): 335–55.

Stiglitz, Joseph E. 1999. "Knowledge as a Global Public Good." In Inge Kaul, Isabelle Grunberg, and Marc A. Stern, eds., *Global Public Goods: International Cooperation in the 21st Century.* New York: Oxford University Press.

UN (United Nations). 2001. "Recommendations of the High-Level Panel on Financing for Development." New York.

Vicary, Simon, and Todd Sandler. 2002. "Weakest-Link Public Goods: Giving In-Kind or Transferring Money." *European Economic Review* 46 (8): 1501–20.

World Bank. 2001. *Global Development Finance 2001: Building Coalitions for Effective Development Finance.* Washington, D.C.

ASSESSING
THE PROVISION STATUS OF
GLOBAL PUBLIC GOODS

Pedro Conceição

Samuelson (1954) argues that the level of resources committed to a public good is optimal when the sum of each individual's marginal willingness to pay equals the marginal cost of providing the good. Because a decentralized market lacks the incentives required to provide public goods, this condition was advanced by Samuelson as defining an optimal level of public spending, since the public good would have to be provided by the state.

This "Samuelson condition" has inspired a large volume of theoretical and empirical follow-up work. The empirical work has focused on how to use the Samuelson condition to determine whether a public good is optimally provided. Many studies have discussed how to encourage people to reveal their preferences and how to measure their willingness to pay.[1]

The issue of how to determine the costs of providing a public good—the flip side of the preference revelation problem—has been considered less problematic. The reason is that the debate has focused on local and national public goods, for which the state has been assumed to be the main provider or, if not the main provider, the main financier. But recent trends toward privatization and economic liberalization have changed the economic and political context—and with it the role of the state—in such a basic way that it is increasingly difficult to determine the full cost of a public good. Establishing the total cost associated with public and private agents' involvement in the provision of public goods is not always straightforward. Consider the multiple public and private funding mechanisms and providers in areas such as health and education, which have marked features of public goods.

When the discussion is taken to the level of global public goods, both issues (determining people's marginal willingness to pay and the costs of provision) become even more complex. Vast international differences in preferences and disparities in economic conditions make it harder to aggregate (and even to interpret) preferences than at the national level. Internationally there is no equivalent to the institution of the state, so there are fewer options (such as certain types of taxes) for preference revelation. The range of actors involved (both in expressing preferences and providing goods) is often larger and more diverse than at the national level. Sandler (in this volume) concludes that trying to determine whether global public goods are optimally provided is like searching for the Holy Grail. That is true if the focus is on determining the optimal spending level by all actors including states. But that is not the primary interest of this chapter.

Rather, this chapter focuses on assessing the provision status of global public goods, proposing an assessment methodology. In the appendix to this chapter that methodology is applied to seven global public goods, presenting a provision profile for each. The methodology and the profiles are first steps toward establishing a consolidated, quantitative picture of how global public goods are provided. The information here is preliminary, intended to illustrate how provision profiles can be constructed and the type of insights they can generate.

Around the world, deficient provision of global public goods costs billions of dollars a year, as suggested by the preliminary cost estimates presented in the provision profiles (which are partial both in the number of public goods assessed and in the costs accounted for). For the cases assessed here, corrective actions might cost just 1–10 percent of the cost of continuing inaction. All the provision profiles convey the same message: it is highly inefficient to continue allowing deficiently provided global public goods to cause global crises. In many cases there are technically feasible corrective actions. These can be considered investment opportunities that, if realized, would generate high social returns.

This chapter aims, above all, to encourage active follow-up research and policy debate so that the data presented here can be complemented to provide a more complete, reliable assessment of the provision status of global public goods. Follow-up work could establish a more persuasive foundation on which to build the case that enhancing the provision of global public goods is not just beneficial in its own right—it is also a highly rewarding investment.

METHODOLOGY TO ASSESS THE PROVISION STATUS
OF GLOBAL PUBLIC GOODS

Before describing the methodology used to assess the provision status of global public goods, it is informative to see how the international community has taken a growing interest in developing such methodologies and in knowing where things stand on global issues. For example, relative to previous decades the 1990s saw four times as many reports on global concerns by UN system agencies and international nongovernmental organizations (figure 1).

These reports cover a wide range of issues, with many referring to global public goods—and bads—such as financial stability, health and environmental issues, drug trafficking and others crimes, violence, human rights, corruption, immigration, and the Internet. The motivations behind such reports are often similar to

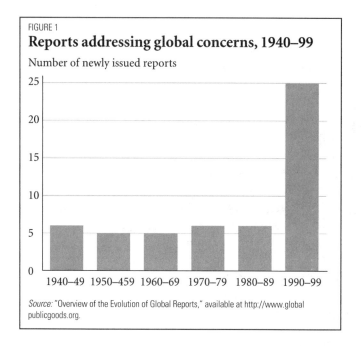

FIGURE 1

Reports addressing global concerns, 1940–99

Number of newly issued reports

Source: "Overview of the Evolution of Global Reports," available at http://www.global publicgoods.org.

those underpinning this chapter: determining the shortfall in the provision of the global public good concerned, assessing the costs of deficient provision—especially its effects on economic growth and development—and recommending corrective actions.

But few of the reports compare the costs of deficient provision with the costs of corrective actions. Though this task is complex, it is crucial because it provides policymakers with important information on the net benefits of increasing resources for a particular global public good.

Taxonomy of provision problems

Public goods are usually underprovided.[2] The reason lies in their publicness, which generates collective action problems. Hence it is important to define the types of provision problems for global public goods—not why they occur but their nature. Drawing on Kaul, Grunberg, and Stern (1999), the taxonomy proposed below differentiates between two main provision problems—underuse and underprovision:

- *Underuse.* An underused global public good exists, but some actors, countries, or people are unable to consume it, either in full or in part.
- *Underprovision.* An underprovided good does not exist or is not fully or adequately provided.

This distinction separates provision problems that arise on the consumption side from those on the production side (figure 2). For underuse it is important to determine what is hindering consumption of a global public good that has been provided. For underprovision the analysis must focus on supply problems.

Underuse can occur because of access problems or because the nature of a good's production makes consumption difficult or impossible. Access problems may result from a lack of (often private) means needed to consume a good (such as a computer to access the Internet) or from formal restrictions (such as patents that limit access to pharmaceutical technology).

Underprovision can result from:

- *Undersupply*, which results when a good is not provided or is provided only partially. The shortfall from complete or enhanced provision can be characterized quantitatively. For example, if some countries but not others ensure airport security, it may not exist as a global public good. If a disease surveillance system covers only 100 countries, it exists in a partial and incomplete way.

- *Malprovision*, meaning that a good is provided in a distorted way, generating benefits (or costs) that are systematically biased against groups of countries or people. The characterization of malprovision is predominantly qualitative. For example, the multilateral trade regime systematically benefits industrial countries far more than developing countries. In this case the provision problem is not a matter of access (as with underused global public goods). It is also not, or not only, a matter of undersupply. Rather, it is that some countries derive a lot of utility from consuming the good and others derive very little, or even incur net costs.

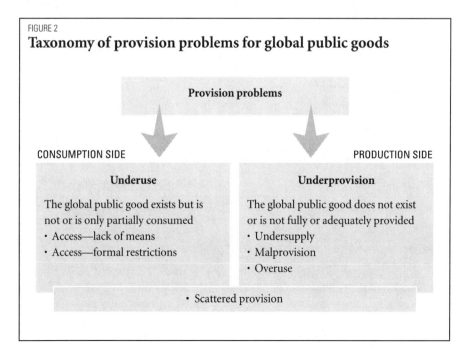

FIGURE 2

Taxonomy of provision problems for global public goods

Provision problems

CONSUMPTION SIDE

PRODUCTION SIDE

Underuse

The global public good exists but is not or is only partially consumed
- Access—lack of means
- Access—formal restrictions

Underprovision

The global public good does not exist or is not fully or adequately provided
- Undersupply
- Malprovision
- Overuse

- Scattered provision

Thus the provision problem has to be solved on the supply side: it calls for redesigning and reshaping the good.

- *Overuse* or destruction, which can be caused by excessive use of goods such as the global natural commons. For example, climate stability is an underprovided global public good because the global atmosphere is overused as an outlet for pollution.

When the provision of a global public good is scattered, it may suffer from both underuse and underprovision. As noted, underuse can result from the way a good is produced. For example, the global stock of knowledge, including practical and other unprotected knowledge, is in many cases so scattered that consuming it is difficult or impossible. Thus the good exists, but in inadequately packaged form. The supply of the good is incomplete, and extra steps may be needed to make it accessible. Noncommercial knowledge—for example, about how to undertake effective policy reforms—may have to be systematically collected, analyzed, categorized, and referenced so that interested users can locate and benefit from it. To make scattered knowledge useful, new knowledge may have to be produced.

This taxonomy makes it possible to identify the main provision problems facing specific global public goods. Table 1 lists the global public goods assessed in the second half of this chapter and the predominant provision problem affecting each.

Steps in profiling the provision status of global public goods
The provision profiles presented in the appendix follow four steps, serving several purposes. First, they show that from a technical perspective, global public goods are underprovided and underused—as indicated by measurements such as the number of financial crises or number of people without access to global communications infrastructure. This information provides an assessment of their provision status from a technical perspective.

The profiles then move toward an economic assessment of the goods' provision status. The second step involves establishing the costs associated with underprovi-

TABLE 1

Global public goods and their main provision problems

Global public good	Main provision problem
International financial stability	Underprovision (undersupply)
Multilateral trade regime	Underprovision (malprovision)
Global communications network and the Internet	Underuse (access problems)
Communicable disease control	Underprovision (undersupply)
Reducing the excessive disease burden	Underprovision (undersupply)
Climate stability	Underprovision (overuse)
Peace and security	Underprovision (undersupply)

sion or underuse, and the third involves assessing the costs of corrective actions aimed at improving provision.[3] Fourth, by comparing the costs of underprovision (or inaction) with those of corrective policy initiatives, the profiles serve as guideposts toward global public goods involving potentially high-return investments.

Characterizing current provision. To illustrate, consider the example of controlling a communicable disease. In this case the technical criterion that defines adequate (complete) provision is the elimination of the infectious agent from nature, reflected in part in the absence of cases of the disease.

Eradication can be looked at in a dichotomous way: either it has been achieved or has not. But the profile considers progress over time: if the world is 90 percent free from a certain infection (expressed as the reduction in the number of cases since the eradication program started), the shortfall is 10 percent (a measure of underprovision, since complete provision would entail a world entirely free of the disease). Not all global public goods lend themselves to such simple quantification of their provision status. Still, the example of communicable disease control is instructive. It indicates well the basic intention and purpose of the first part of the provision profiles.

Establishing the costs of underprovision or underuse. It is not always possible to assess the full costs of underprovision, but in most cases it is possible to estimate at least some. This is often due to the extensive databases that have been created as a result of, among other things, growth in global reporting initiatives. To stay with the example of communicable disease control, the number of cases corresponding to the 10 percent shortfall from eradication of a certain disease can be translated into a burden measured by the years of healthy life or productive time lost to disability and early death. This burden can then be converted, if desired, into economic costs.

Assessing the costs of corrective actions. The actions needed to improve the provision of a global public good—to the extent that they are or can be known—are associated with the good's production path.[4] The data required to estimate the costs of these actions, and so their resource implications, are available for very few global public goods. Still, estimates are possible for some. Using again the example of disease eradication, work by the Commission on Macroeconomics and Health (CMH 2001) shows that it is possible to estimate the costs of extending control measures to achieve eradication. Work being undertaken on financing for the Millennium Development Goals will provide further insight into this issue (Devarajan, Miller, and Swanson 2002).

Indicating the likely net benefits of enhanced provision. Enhancing the provision of a global public good eliminates, or substantially reduces, the costs associated with its underprovision. Comparing the costs of corrective actions with the elimination of the costs of underprovision provides a rough estimate of direct net benefits. But enhancing the provision of a global public good often generates indirect benefits. For example, reducing the burden of a disease produces spillovers that range from enhancing people's ability to learn to improving participation and performance in the workforce—changes that, in turn, generate substantial indirect social and economic benefits. In some cases there are estimates of these broader, indirect benefits. But it is often difficult to find such studies and datasets.

Because the provision profiles provide measures of corrective action costs and estimates of benefits, a natural next step would be to compare the two, with adequate discounting over time of future benefits, and perform a cost-benefit analysis. Goods promising high social returns would be prime candidates for investment. Cost-benefit analysis has long been used to assess the provision of public goods (see the classic article by Musgrave 1969). But taking this step requires considerable effort and in-depth analysis of concepts, measurements, and data. It also requires identifying the goods to be produced with great precision and, especially, decomposing them into manageable components. The approach used and profiles presented in the appendix are intended to illustrate the type of assessment that could facilitate policymaking on global public goods. They go in the direction of cost-benefit analysis, but they are not there yet.

Still, it is interesting to juxtapose the estimated costs of underprovision and corrective actions (table 2). For the trade regime and reduction in the excessive disease burden the costs of inaction (that is, the continuing costs of underprovision) are about 10 times the costs of corrective actions.

The table is intended to compare the annual costs of inaction with the annual costs of interventions that would significantly reduce (or even eliminate) the costs of inaction. The enormous scale of the differences makes it far more appealing to invest in corrective actions than to continue absorbing the costs of inaction.

CONCLUSION AND SUGGESTIONS FOR FURTHER STUDY

Economic theory usually identifies a public good as being optimally provided when the sum of individuals' marginal willingness to pay equals the cost of the good's production. Economic studies on provision optimality focus on whether the resources allocated to a good are in line with what the public is willing to pay. The good itself hardly figures in these analyses. The approach suggested in this chapter places the good at the center of the analysis.

This approach leaves several possible avenues for further development, especially in terms of more complete economic assessments. One aspect requiring further study is the co-evolution of the costs of corrective actions and the corresponding reduction in the costs of inaction. The costs of corrective actions often do not have to be incurred forever. For example, the costs of achieving lower car-

TABLE 2

Annual costs of inaction and corrective actions for provision problems of selected global public goods
(billions of U.S. dollars)

Type of costs	International financial stability	Multilateral trade regime	Reducing the excessive disease burden	Climate stability	Peace and security[a]
Inaction	50[b]	260[c]	1,138[d]	780[e]	358
Corrective actions	0.3[f]	20[g]	93[h]	125[i]	71

a. The costs for peace and security refer to just nine conflicts in the 1990s. These estimates are not annual costs—they are the costs incurred over the duration of the conflicts.

b. Includes only banking crises in developing and transition countries; excludes currency and twin crises.

c. Net benefits from removing distortions in goods markets of industrial and developing countries.

d. Refers only to Africa's excessive burden of communicable disease (relative to the burdens in Europe and North and South America) in 2000 in PPP exchange rates.

e. Indicates the midrange potential reduction in global GDP if the atmospheric concentration of carbon dioxide reaches twice the level of the pre-industrial era in PPP exchange rates.

f. This is a partial estimate; it includes only technical assistance spending by the International Monetary Fund (IMF).

g. The estimated costs of corrective actions for the multilateral trade regime are not annual and involve mostly one-time costs associated with capacity building.

h. Estimated funding required by 2007 for the interventions proposed in CMH (2001), including commitments by both industrial and developing countries, to scale up existing interventions. Annual commitments would have to increase to $119 billion by 2015. The interventions would significantly reduce the excessive disease burden in developing countries. There are no estimates of how long this level of commitment would have to be maintained.

i. Annual costs to industrial countries, over 10 years, of meeting Kyoto Protocol targets for carbon dioxide emissions. (Estimate assumes full emissions trading and a 0.1 percent annual loss in GDP from meeting the targets.)

Source: Provision profiles in this chapter's appendix.

bon dioxide emissions (contributing to climate stability) fall once predefined targets have been met and technology is available to maintain the target levels. Similarly, when a disease is eradicated there is no longer a need to continue vaccinations or other corrective interventions. In other cases the costs of corrective actions will have to continue well into the future, such as when a disease is not eradicable and control measures have to persist.

On the other hand, the costs of inaction are not entirely eliminated once corrective actions start. Quantifying and better specifying these time consistency issues are important steps in further developing the economic assessment of underprovision. Doing so would allow, for example, full cost-benefit analysis—taking into account the lower costs of corrective actions over time as well as the benefits of reducing (or eliminating) the costs of inaction.

Discounting, or appropriately weighting the stream of net benefits into the future, also requires further analysis. As Heal (1997) notes, the standard discounting methods used in cost-benefit analysis may not be adequate to deal with long-term benefits—such as those from sustainable development. Issues with benefits stretching well into the future may require placing more weight on future benefits. Economic assessments of the provision of global public goods, which typically yield permanent and manifold benefits, may require similar adjustments.

NOTES

1. For an overview of the literature, see Cornes and Sandler (1996, especially chapters 7 and 18) and Cullis and Jones (1998, especially chapters 3 and 4).

2. This chapter does not address what constitutes a public good or why certain goods are—or are not—provided as global public goods. These issues are discussed in Kaul and Mendoza (in this volume).

3. There are different ways to develop a full economic assessment, including considerations of static efficiency (the optimal use of available resources—greatest benefit at lowest cost) and dynamic efficiency (the introduction of new products and production processes over time). But given the varied nature of the studies and data sources used to construct the sample profiles, a more differentiated analysis is beyond the scope of this chapter.

4. See the chapter on institutions by Kaul and Le Goulven (in this volume) for a discussion of the production path of global public goods.

REFERENCES

CMH (Commission on Macroeconomics and Health). 2001. *Macroeconomics and Health: Investing in Health for Economic Development.* Report of the Commission on Macroeconomics and Health. Geneva: World Health Organization.

Cornes, Richard, and Todd Sandler. 1996. *The Theory of Externalities, Public Goods and Club Goods.* 2nd ed. Cambridge and New York: Cambridge University Press.

Cullis, John, and Philip Jones. 1998. *Public Finance and Public Choice: Alternative Perspectives.* New York: Oxford University Press.

Devarajan, Shantayanan, Margaret J. Miller, and Eric V. Swanson. 2002. "Goals for Development: History, Prospects, and Costs." World Bank, Washington, D.C.

Heal, Geoffrey. 1997. "Valuing Our Future: Cost-Benefit Analysis and Sustainability." ODS Discussion Paper 13. United Nations Development Programme, Office of Development Studies, New York.

Kaul, Inge, Isabelle Grunberg, and Marc A. Stern. 1999. "Global Public Goods-Concepts, Policies and Strategies." In Inge Kaul, Isabelle Grunberg, and Marc A. Stern, eds., *Global Public Goods: International Cooperation in the 21st Century.* New York: Oxford University Press.

Musgrave, Richard A. 1969. "Cost-Benefit Analysis and the Theory of Public Finance." *Journal of Economic Literature* 7 (3): 797–806.

Samuelson, Paul A. 1954. "The Pure Theory of Public Expenditure." *Review of Economics and Statistics* 36: 387–89.

Appendix. Provision Profiles of Selected Global Public Goods

Details on data and calculations are available in the full study from which this chapter is drawn, "Profiling the Provision Status of GPGs," available at http://www.globalpublicgoods.org. The profiles were written by Ronald U. Mendoza (international financial stability, multilateral trade regime), Vikas Nath (global communications network and the Internet), Pedro Conceição (communicable disease control, reducing the excessive disease burden), Katell Le Goulven (climate stability), and Grace Ryu and Frederick Nikiema (peace and security). The main data sources for each profile are listed in the references.

International financial stability

Current provision
The absence of financial crises—financial stability—is an underprovided global public good, given the prevalence of financial crises since the 1970s. Between 1975 and 1998 there were 158 currency crises, 54 banking crises, and 32 twin (currency and banking) crises. These crises were far more common in emerging markets, which suffered 116 currency, 42 banking, and 26 twin crises. Recent crises include the Russian Federation's 1998 debt crisis, Brazil's 1999 currency crisis, Turkey's 2001 currency crisis, and Argentina's current debt crisis.

Cost of underprovision
Countries that have experienced financial crises have suffered cumulative output losses ranging from 5–19 percent of annual GDP depending on the crisis type (banking, exchange rate, or twin) and location (industrial country or emerging market). The costs of a selection of banking crises between the late 1970s and 2000 illustrate the partial costs of underprovision. During this period lost output totaled $8.2 trillion, with more than $1 trillion accruing to developing and transition countries. This translates to an average loss of $50 billion a year for developing and transition countries—roughly equal to all official development assistance in 1999 ($56 billion) and slightly more than the total debt service of low-income countries in 1999 ($47 billion). Costs of recent crisis include:

- *East Asian financial crisis (1997–98).* In 1998 real GDP per capita dropped 15.1 percent in Indonesia, 6.7 percent in the Republic of Korea, 9.2 percent in Malaysia, and 10.3 percent in Thailand. In 1996 net private capital flows to the crisis countries—the four just mentioned plus the Philippines—were $65.8 billion. Between 1997 and 1999 these flows were –$70.6 billion, a $136 billion turnaround over just four years. Furthermore, unemployment increased in the crisis countries between 1997 and 1998: from 4.7 to 5.5 percent in Indonesia, 2.6 to 7.4 percent in the Republic of Korea, 2.7 to 3.2 percent in Malaysia, and 1.6 to 4.1 percent in Thailand.
- *Russian Federation debt crisis (1998).* The Russian Federation saw its GDP plunge by more than 30 percent in 1998, while inflation soared to 100 percent in early 1999.
- *Brazilian currency crisis (1999).* The floating of the Brazilian real in January 1999 was followed by a mild slowdown in the country's economy, with real GDP growing just 1 percent that year.
- *Turkish currency crisis (2001).* Due partly to political turmoil in January 2001, the Turkish lira plummeted 80 percent over the next three months, while the economy contracted 6.1 percent that year.

For details on the global public goods characteristics of international financial stability see Griffith-Jones, in this volume.

- *Argentine debt crisis (2001–present).* Analysts predict that Argentina's economy will shrink 5–10 percent in 2002, while the country faces $141 billion in public debt and unemployment above 20 percent.

Cost of corrective actions

Building countries' capacity in financial management and regulation is crucial to preventing future crises, so the International Monetary Fund (IMF) budget for technical assistance is a good place to initiate corrective actions. In 2000 the IMF allocated $115 million for technical assistance, about 19 percent of its total administrative expenses of $606 million. While it is simplistic to assume that increasing this budget alone will prevent future crises, this figure can be used as a preliminary estimate of the financing gap for capacity building. The IMF's technical assistance budget is only about 0.2 percent of $50 billion, the estimated average annual GDP loss from banking crises (that is, excluding currency and twin crises) in developing and transition countries. Even if technical assistance were tripled to $345 million, it would still be less than 0.7 percent of the conservatively estimated cost of inaction.

Benefits

Based on the partial cost estimate for banking crises and a tripling of the IMF technical assistance budget, a conservative estimate of the net benefits would be about $50 billion a year in reclaimed output.

References

BIS (Bank for International Settlements). 1999. *BIS 69th Annual Report.* Basel, Switzerland.

———. 2000. *BIS 70th Annual Report.* Basel, Switzerland.

Caprio, Gerald, and Daniela Klingebiel. 2002. "Episodes of Systemic and Borderline Financial Crises." In Daniel Klingebiel and Luc Laeven, eds. *Managing the Real and Fiscal Effects of Banking Crises.* World Bank Discussion Paper 428. Washington, D.C: The World Bank.

Honohan, Patrick, and Daniela Klingebiel. Forthcoming. "The Fiscal Cost Implications of an Accommodating Approach to Banking Crises." *Journal of Banking and Finance.*

IMF (International Monetary Fund). 1998. *World Economic Outlook 1998.* Washington, D.C.

———. 2000. *World Economic Outlook 2000.* Washington, D.C.

OECD (Organisation for Economic Co-operation and Development). 2001. *The DAC Journal for Development Cooperation: 2000 Report.* Paris.

UNCTAD (United Nations Conference on Trade and Development). 2000. *Handbook of Statistics, 2000.* CD-ROM. Geneva.

World Bank. 2000. *Global Economic Prospects and the Developing Countries 2000.* Washington, D.C.

————. 2001a. *Global Development Finance 2001: Building Coalitions for Effective Development Finance.* Washington, D.C.

————. 2001b. *Global Economic Prospects and the Developing Countries 2001.* Washington, D.C.

Multilateral trade regime

Current provision

Several factors substantially and systematically diminish the net benefits that developing countries receive from international trade, indicating that the multilateral trade regime is a malprovided global public good. Mechanisms are lacking to deal with terms of trade shocks to commodity-exporting countries. Moreover, industrial country markets continue to be heavily protected—particularly in textiles and agriculture. In addition, developing countries have not received adequate capacity-building support to interface more effectively with the multilateral trade regime.

Cost of malprovision

Agricultural protection in industrial countries imposes significant welfare costs on consumers and taxpayers in those countries as well as on producers in developing countries who are denied access to those markets. Removing Organisation for Economic Co-operation and Development (OECD) countries' price and trade distortions in agriculture and food processing could generate annual welfare gains of $44 billion (1992 dollars) for developing countries and $29 billion for OECD countries. Removing distortions in textiles and clothing markets could generate an additional welfare gain of $21 billion a year for developing countries. This translates into $65 billion in lost welfare for developing countries in agriculture and textiles alone.

More broadly, a recent estimate placed potential global welfare gains from post–Uruguay Round trade reforms at $260 billion a year, implying that such welfare gains are lost in the present system. Other costs of malprovision are associated with the impact of terms of trade shocks on real income (as a percentage of real GDP). Export earnings fell by almost 30 percent in Angola and Nigeria, by about 25 percent in Gabon and the Libyan Arab Jamahiriya, and by 10–15 percent in Burundi, Cameroon, the Democratic Republic of Congo, Equatorial Guinea, Ethiopia, Guinea, Rwanda, Uganda, and Zambia.

Cost of corrective actions

Resources freed by eliminating subsidies in industrial countries—about $170 billion a year in taxpayer money in OECD countries—could be used to provide adjustment assistance to displaced producers and workers in these countries. Broad capacity-building measures in developing countries would require at least $20 billion, estimated based on the amount it would cost developing countries to comply with the requirements of the Uruguay Round (about $150 million per developing country).

For details on the global public goods characteristics of the multilateral trade regime see Mendoza, in this volume.

Benefits
Net of the $20 billion cost of capacity building in developing countries, global welfare gains could reach $240 billion a year.

References
Anderson, Kym, Bernard Hoekman, and Anna Strutt. 2001. "Agriculture and the WTO: Next Steps." *Review of International Economics* 9 (2): 192–214.

Finger, J. Michael, and Philip Schuler. 2001. "Implementation of Uruguay Round Commitments: The Development Challenge." In Bernard Hoekman and Will Martin, eds., *Developing Countries and the WTO: A Pro-active Agenda*. 2001. Oxford: Blackwell.

IMF (International Monetary Fund). 1999. *World Economic Outlook (May)*. Washington, D.C.

Mendoza, Ronald U., and Chandrika Bahadur. Forthcoming. "Towards Free and Fair Trade: A global public good perspective." *Challenge: The Magazine of Economic Affairs.* Armonk, New York: M.E. Sharpe. [http://www.cid.harvard.edu/cidtrade/Papers/MendozaBahadurJune02.pdf]

OECD (Organisation for Economic Co-operation and Development). 2001. *Agricultural Policies in OECD Countries: Monitoring and Evaluation, 2001 Edition*. Paris.

UNCTAD (United Nations Conference on Trade and Development). 1999. *Trade and Development Report 1999*. Geneva.

———. 2000a. *Handbook of Statistics 2000*. CD-ROM. Geneva.

———. 2000b. "The Post-Uruguay Round Tariff Environment for Developing Country Exports: Tariff Peaks and Tariff Escalation." Geneva.

———. 2001. *World Investment Report 2001*. Geneva.

World Bank. 2000. *World Development Indicators 2000*. Washington, D.C.

———. 2001. *Global Development Finance 2001: Building Coalitions for Effective Development Finance*. Washington, D.C.

———. 2001. *Global Economic Prospects and the Developing Countries 2002*. Washington, D.C.

Global communications network and the Internet

Current provision

Despite the increasing capacity of the global communications network, the network and the Internet are underused: more than half of the world's people have never made or received a telephone call, and only one-sixth will be connected to the Internet by 2005. Yet international Internet bandwidth quadrupled in both 1998 and 1999, and tripled in 2001. Moreover, technological advances in optical fibers have dramatically increased the potential capacity of new cables. Given the network externalities of these two global public goods, enhancing access could offer higher returns for all. Having more telephone users means that a greater number of interconnections becomes possible. And on the Internet, each new user may be a potential supplier or consumer of goods and services, and can widen the market for electronic commerce. Access is even more nonuniform for the Internet than for the global communications network. In 2001 almost 50 percent of the U.S. population had access to the Internet but only 2.6 percent of Chinese and 0.85 percent of Africans did. Further, access to the Internet is 10 times more expensive in Africa than in Western Europe. Underuse results from access problems due to a lack of private goods (a telephone or computer) or an inability to pay access tolls (such as the cost of a telephone call).

Cost of underuse

Developing countries can lose $726 million in terms of trade and wage reductions if industrial countries increase their productivity by 1 percent through e-commerce (based on 1997 data). Countries with the average number of telephones for their income receive less foreign investment—on the order of 0.3 cents per $100 of GDP—than countries with one more phone per 100 people expected for their income. Almost half the difference between Africa's and East Asia's manufactured exports as a share of GDP is caused by Africa's weak communications. If India does not meet massive bandwidth requirements, it could be left out of at least 30 percent of its target export market, at a cost of $22.5 billion and 650,000 jobs.

The global communications network and the Internet exhibit network externalities: each additional user confers positive network externalities to existing users—up to a point of congestion. However, modern technologies often allow the congestion to be reduced. Thus, it is typically undesirable to exclude anyone from enjoying the benefits of these networks—and it is more desirable to make them inclusive. In both cases there are access problems: to enjoy the good, people often need to purchase a means of private access (such as a telephone or a computer) and pay monthly access fees. Still, it is important to distinguish these access problems from the goods' publicness. Once accessed, the goods are largely nonrival in consumption and nonexlusive in their benefits.

Cost of corrective actions

An additional 3 billion telephone lines are needed for developing countries to reach the same teledensity as industrial nations. If innovative technologies are used and connectivity is provided at the community level instead of at the individual level, the annual costs of enhancing connectivity would be $5.8 billion over 10 years (2002 prices). In India providing individual access could cost more than $706 billion a year. Switching to community access models and innovative technologies could lower those costs by $300 million a year over three years.

Benefits

The benefits of improving access to the global communications network and the Internet depend on the regions and countries being considered. In Asia a 1 percent increase in productivity through e-commerce, while productivity in all other regions remain unchanged, would result in welfare gain of $12 billion in the region. Similarly, a 1 percent increase in productivity in Latin America, Eastern Europe, and Africa would result in welfare gains of $7.6 billion, $1.8 billion, and $2.7 billion. The use of information technology, needed to access the Internet, accounted for about two-thirds of a 1 percent increase in productivity in the United States between the first and second halves of 2000.

Information and communications technology are constantly creating new job opportunities. In Senegal 10,000 jobs have been created through community telecenters, while in India cyber kiosks have created 600,000 jobs. In Israel about 21,000 jobs were related to information and communications technology in 1998, generating more than $7.4 billion in revenue. In South Africa such employment is projected to increase to 85,000 by 2003. By 2005 global business-to-business e-commerce will be worth more than $4 trillion. Corporations in the Asia-Pacific region, excluding Japan, will purchase more than $516 billion in materials over the Internet by 2005, a 3,900 percent increase over the $12.8 billion spent in 2000. Internet users in the region will increase by 275 percent, from 64 million users in 2000. E-commerce can have an especially strong influence on developing countries, because the scope for reducing inefficiency and increasing productivity is much larger than in industrial countries.

References

Afemann, Uwe. 2001. "Entwicklung und Zusammenarbeit (Development and Cooperation)." *Deutsche Stiftung für Internationale Entwicklung* 42 (4).

Forge, Simon. 1995. "The Consequences of Current Telecommunications Trends for the Competitiveness of Developing Countries." World Bank, Washington, D.C.

IDC (International Data Corporation). 2001. "IDC Predicts a Boom, Not Gloom for Asia's B2B eCommerce Markets." Press Release, 23 April.

ILO (International Labour Organization). 2001. *World Employment Report 2001.* Geneva: International Labour Office.

ITU (International Telecommunication Union). 1998. *World Telecommunication Development Report 1998.* Geneva.

———. 2001. "ITU Telecommunication Indicator Update." *ITU News 5.*

———. 2002. *World Telecommunication Development Report 2002.* Geneva.

NASSCOM (National Association of Software and Service Companies). 2001. "Nasscom's Handbook on IT Enabled Services." New Delhi.

NUA (National Users Association). 2001. "How Many Online Survey." [http://www.nua.com].

Oliner, Stephen, and Daniel Sichel. 2000. "The Resurgence of Growth in the Late 1990s: Is information Technology the Story?" *Journal of Economic Perspectives* 14 (4): 3–22.

Reynolds, Taylor, Charles Kenny, and Christine Qiang. 2001. "Networking and FDI." World Bank, Global Information and Communication Technologies Department, Washington, D.C.

TeleGeography. 2000. *International Bandwidth 2000.* Washington, D.C.

———. 2002. *Submarine Bandwidth 2002.* Washington, D.C.

UNCTAD (United Nations Conference on Trade and Development). 2001. *E-Commerce and Development Report 2001.* Geneva.

World Bank. 2000. "The Networking Revolution: Opportunities and Challenges for Developing Countries." InfoDev, Washington, D.C.

Communicable disease control

Current provision
Smallpox eradication is 100 percent provided, polio eradication is 99.9 percent provided, and dracunculiasis eradication is 98 percent provided (measured in terms of the number of current cases as a percentage of the number when eradication efforts began). HIV/AIDS control is severely underprovided, however. HIV/AIDS is the world's fourth leading cause of death: in 2001, 40 million people were living with the disease and 3 million were killed by it—about three-quarters of them in Sub-Saharan Africa. In Botswana HIV/AIDS has lowered life expectancy by 34 years; in Lesotho, Namibia, South Africa, and Zimbabwe by about 20 years. Malaria control is also underprovided: the disease killed 1.1 million people in 2000 and accounts for more than 10 percent of the global burden of communicable disease. Tuberculosis control is underprovided as well: the disease killed 1.7 million people in 2000 and also accounts for more than 10 percent of the global burden of communicable disease.

Cost of underprovision
Incomplete polio eradication requires vaccinations and other preventive measures costing $1.5 billion a year (to industrial and developing countries), an important part of the cost of underproviding the global public good of polio eradication. While dracunculiasis is a public health problem only in some parts of Africa—especially Sudan (which accounted for 73 percent of the cases reported in 2000), Nigeria, and Ghana—the costs are high in affected communities. In an affected area in Nigeria the costs of the disease reach $20 million a year. The burden of HIV/AIDS, due to illness and early death, lowers annual GDP by 35 percent in Sub-Saharan Africa. Underproviding malaria control in Sub-Saharan Africa cuts output by about 17 percent a year. Tuberculosis-related illness costs about 20 percent of annual household income for those who are cured and a full year of income when the disease is not detected. Potential losses at the country level range from 4–7 percent of annual GDP.

Cost of corrective actions
Smallpox eradication cost $300 million. Polio eradication would cost $2.5 billion; dracunculiasis eradication, $200 million; HIV/AIDS control, $14 billion a year by 2007; malaria control, $2.5 billion a year by 2007; and tuberculosis control, $500 million a year by 2007. (Control costs are incremental, above current interventions, to meet treatment and prevention targets.)

For details on the global public goods characteristics of communicable disease control see Arhin-Tenkorang and Conceição, in this volume.

Benefits

Smallpox eradication generated $168 billion (1997 dollars) in benefits between 1978 and 1997, for a rate of return of 46 percent a year. Polio eradication would generate savings of $1.5 billion a year (to industrial and developing countries). The rate of return for dracunculiasis eradication would be 29 percent a year.

References

Acharya, Arnab, Sarah England, Mary Agocs, Jennifer Linkins, and Bruce Aylward. 2001. "Producing a Global Public Good: Polio Eradication." Paper presented at the International Development Research Center Workshop on Global Public Goods for Health, 4–6 June, Ottawa, Canada.

Aylward, Bruce R., Karen A. Hennessy, Nevio Zagaria, Jean-Marc Olivé, and Stephen L. Cochi. 2000. "When Is a Disease Eradicable? 100 Years of Lessons Learned." *American Journal of Public Health* 90 (10): 1515–20.

CMH (Commission on Macroeconomics and Health). 2001. *Macroeconomics and Health: Investing in Health for Economic Development. Report of the Commission on Macroeconomics and Health.* Geneva: World Health Organization.

Gallup, John Luke, and Jeffrey D. Sachs. 2000. *The Economic Burden of Malaria.* Center for International Development Working Paper 52. Harvard University, Cambridge, Mass.

Kim, Aehyung, Ajay Tandon, and Ernesto Ruiz-Tiben. 1997. "Cost-benefit Analysis of the Global Dracunculiasis Eradication Campaign." Policy Research Working Paper 1935. World Bank, Washington, D.C.

UN (United Nations). 2001. *World Population Prospects: The 2000 Revision: Highlights.* UN publication ESA/P/WP.165. Department of Economic and Social Affairs, Population Division, New York.

UNAIDS (Joint United Nations Programme on HIV/AIDS). 2000. *Global Summary of the HIV/AIDS Epidemic 2000.* Geneva.

————. 2001. *Global Summary of the HIV/AIDS Epidemic 2001.* Geneva.

USGAO (United States General Accounting Office). 1998. *Infectious Diseases—Soundness of the World Health Organization Estimates for Eradication or Elimination.* GAO/NSIAD-98-114. Washington, D.C.

WHO (World Health Organization). 2001a. *Global Tuberculosis Control: WHO Report 2001.* WHO/CDS/TB/2001.287. Geneva.

————. 2001b. *World Health Report.* Geneva.

World Bank and UNAIDS (Joint United Nations Programme on HIV/AIDS). 2001. "HIV/AIDS at a Glance." [www.worldbank.org/hnp].

Reducing the excessive disease burden

Current provision
The burden of disease is most excessive in Africa, where in 2000 the average person lost more than half a year to illness-induced disability and early death—three times as much as in the Americas and Europe, and twice as much as in South-East Asia and the eastern Mediterranean regions (considering the geographic regions of the World Health Organizations). This excessive disease burden has adverse effects on countries other than those suffering the direct consequences of ill health, given that it generates negative global externalities ranging from the spread of multidrug resistant infections to risks of political instability and conflict.

Cost of underprovision
Not including the costs to peace and national security, in 2000 Africa's excessive burden of communicable disease—measured as the difference between its burden and those in Europe and the Americas—reduced the region's potential GDP by 95 percent ($1,138 billion in PPP exchange rates). The excessive disease burden also impairs the economic performance of affected countries. Comparing the growth rates of countries with different burdens of disease, controlling for other factors, a 1 percent increase in the adult survival rate (the probability, at age 15, of reaching age 60) is associated with a 0.05 percentage point increase in the growth rate of developing countries, and a one-year improvement in life expectancy increases output by 4 percent. Meanwhile, losing 10 years in life expectancy lowers economic growth (after controlling for other factors) by 0.3–0.4 percentage point a year, further contributing to global inequity.

Cost of corrective actions
Interventions proposed to control the main causes of the excessive disease burden would cost $93 billion a year by 2007. This level of spending would require an additional $27 billion a year from industrial countries. Of this, $22 billion would go to country programs to strengthen local capacity and provide local services, with about $8 billion going to a global fund to fight AIDS, tuberculosis, and malaria. Another $3 billion would fund research and development, split evenly between the development of new technologies for the diseases of poor people and the establishment of a global fund for health research. The proposed interventions would substantially increase prevention and treatment for the diseases most responsible for the excessive disease burden and should continue through 2015, when their annual cost would need to approach $119 billion.

For details on the global public goods characteristics of reducing the excessive disease burden see Arhin-Tenkorang and Conceição, in this volume.

Benefits

By 2015 the proposed interventions would save 8 million lives and $558 billion a year. And in the long run, as the control measures reduce infection loads, there would be less need to disburse such large sums on disease control—while the benefits would remain and even increase. In addition, reduced social and political strains in affected countries would limit threats to global peace and security—not to mention, the reduction in infection loads would decrease the likelihood of diseases spreading (including multidrug-resistant forms) around the world.

References

Becker, Gary, Tomas Philipson, and Rodrigo R. Soares. 2001. "Growth and Mortality in Less Developed Nations." University of Chicago, Chicago, Ill.

Bhargava, Alok, Dean T. Jamison, Lawerence J. Lau, and Christopher J. L. Murray. 2001. "Modeling the Effects of Health on Economic Growth." *Journal of Health Economics* 20: 423–40.

Bloom, David E., David Canning, and Jaypee Sevilla. 2001. "The Effect of Health on Economic Growth: Theory and Evidence." NBER Working Paper 8587. National Bureau for Economic Research, Cambridge, Mass.

IMF (International Monetary Fund). 2002. *World Economic Outlook.* Washington, D.C.

Mathers, Colin D., Christopher J. L. Murray, Alan D. Lopez, Joshua A. Salomon, Ritu Sadana, Bedirhan L. Ustün, and Somnath Chatterj. 2001. "Estimates of Healthy Life Expectancy for 191 Countries in the Year 2000: Methods and Results." Global Programme on Evidence for Health Policy Discussion Paper 36. World Health Organization, Geneva.

UNFPA (United Nations Population Fund). 2002. *The State of the World Population 2000.* New York.

Climate stability

Current provision
During the 20th century the global average surface temperature increased by 0.6 degrees Celsius, snow cover and ice extent decreased by 10 percent, and the sea level rose by 0.1–0.2 meters. Rainfalls are increasing by 0.3 percent a decade in the subtropical parts of the Northern hemisphere, the frequency of extreme low temperatures has decreased, El Niño oscillations are more frequent, intense, and persistent, and droughts have become more intense and more frequent in Africa and Asia. Climate changes are due to a mix of natural variability and human-induced pollution, but global warming over the past 50 years is attributable to human-induced greenhouse gas emissions—a result of the overuse of the atmosphere, a global common pool resource, as an outlet for pollution.

The most important greenhouse gas is carbon dioxide. Accordingly, emissions of carbon dioxide and its concentration in the atmosphere are used as proxies for the overuse of the commons resource that leads to underprovision of the global public good of climate stability. Before the industrial era, the atmospheric concentration of carbon dioxide was 280 parts per million by volume (ppm); since then it has risen continuously, reaching 367 ppm in 1999. This increase is due to rising anthropogenic carbon dioxide emissions: from 14 gigatons a year in 1980 to 16 gigatons in 1990 and 24 gigatons in 1997. Without question, climate stability is underprovided—and its underprovision is worsening.

Cost of overuse
The costs of climate change include economic losses, loss of life, changes in quality of life (need to migrate, conflict over resources, loss of cultural diversity), and biodiversity losses. If the concentration of carbon dioxide in the atmosphere reaches twice the pre-industrial level, global annual damages would reach 1.5–2.0 percent of world GDP ($670–890 billion based on world GDP in 2000 in PPP), with industrial countries losing 1.0–1.5 percent of their GDP and developing countries losing 2–9 percent. Poor people will be affected the most because developing countries tend to be more vulnerable, since their economies are more dependent on agriculture and several are located in climatic-stressed regions.

Cost of corrective actions
A first step toward corrective actions is for industrial countries to meet the targets agreed under the Kyoto Protocol—to reduce carbon dioxide emissions by an aver-

Climate stability (change) is a global condition with indivisible, nonexclusive, and nonrival properties. For example, if global warming occurs, the world as a whole faces a higher average world temperature. However, the consequences for different countries and population groups will vary. Thus, climate stability (change) is public in consumption, yet entails different benefits or costs across different population groups.

age of 5 percent below 1990 levels by 2008–12. With full emissions trading, the annual costs of meeting these targets are estimated at 0.5 percent of GDP, or $125 billion—equivalent to a 0.1 percent annual loss in economic growth over 10 years.

Benefits
Avoiding the damage from carbon dioxide emissions would save $670–890 billion a year. In addition, studies in Europe and the United States indicate that secondary benefits (mainly in the form of local air quality improvements) could offset 30–100 percent of abatement costs.

References

IPCC (Intergovernmental Panel on Climate Change). 1996. *Economic and Social Dimensions of Climate Change.* James P. Bruce, Hoesung Lee, and Erik F. Haites, eds. Cambridge: Cambridge University Press.

————. 2001a. *Climate Change 2001: Impacts, Adaptation and Vulnerability.* James J. McCarthy, Osvaldo F. Canziani, Neil A. Leary, David J. Dokken, and Kasey S. White, eds. Cambridge: Cambridge University Press.

————. 2001b. *Climate Change 2001: Mitigation.* Bert Metz, Ogunlade Davidson, Rob Swart, and Jiahua Pan, eds. Cambridge: Cambridge University Press.

Peace and security

Current provision
Peace and security is an underprovided global public good. In 2000 25 major violent conflicts (defined as those involving more than 1,000 deaths), all but 2 of which were internal. Yet peace and security are not only threatened by conflicts within or between states—they can also be fractured by terrorist attacks. Examples include the 1993 bombing of New York's World Trade Center, the 1995 poison gas attack in a Tokyo subway station, the 1995 bombing of a government building in Oklahoma City (United States), and the September 11, 2001, destruction of the World Trade Center.

Cost of underprovision
During the 20th century violent conflicts—the absence of peace—caused 110 million deaths, 59 percent of them civilians. In the 1990s the costs to the international community (including refugee costs, direct economic and opportunity costs, military costs, instability costs, and costs of international peace operations) of a selection of conflicts totaled $358 billion. (The conflicts considered were the Gulf War and those in Bosnia, Cambodia, El Salvador, Haiti, Rwanda, and Somalia; in addition, costs were estimated for conflicts that were prevented or halted in the former Yugoslav Republic of Macedonia and Slovakia.)

Not all countries are exposed to or bear the costs of conflict. Developing countries are far more likely to experience conflict and suffer its heaviest burden because they have so few means for economic and political self-protection. In 1999, 14 of the 30 countries with the lowest rankings on the UNDP's human development index had recently emerged from or were still embroiled in extended internal conflicts. And in the past decade nearly 1 million of the world's 4 million war-related deaths occurred in Sub-Saharan Africa.

In 2001, 348 international terrorist attacks caused more than 4,500 deaths—most of them due to the September 2001 attacks on the United States. The U.S. attacks led the United Nations to lower its projected growth rate for gross world product to 1.4 percent from 2.2 percent for 2001 and to 2.0 percent from 3.0 percent for 2002. The attacks cost $191 billion to U.S. metropolitan areas alone. Largely because of the attacks, the world's airline industry experienced an operating loss of 3.6 percent in 2001, down from a profit of 3.3 percent in 2000. In

---

Peace and security, if underprovided somewhere, may not only interrupt activities such as international trade and investment but may also lead to military engagement of third parties or inflict the costs of rehabilitating war-torn societies on the international community. Thus, war and conflict, as well as other types of political violence and unrest, can generate negative externalities far beyond the zone of turmoil and unrest. Once they exist, peace and security are nonrival and strongly nonexcludable and, therefore, also nonexclusive.

addition, the September 11 attacks increased insurance risk premiums by as much as 30 percent, accompanied by a reduction in coverage for terrorism risk.

Heightened security concerns are also affecting people's everyday lives. For example, the costs of international sporting events have risen because organizers face a 20–50 percent increase in insurance costs and added inconvenience to the public. In addition, new border restrictions could increase the costs of foreign trade by 1–3 percent, potentially reducing trade by 3–9 percent.

Cost of corrective actions

Prevention efforts for the conflicts considered above cost $71 billion. These costs included fact-finding missions, mediation missions, confidence-building measures, and traditional peacekeeping operations. In terms of reducing the threat of terrorism, consider the costs for full rehabilitation of Afghanistan, estimated at $25 billion over the next 10 years. And with renewed security concerns, U.S. antiterrorism efforts now exceed $60 billion a year—five times the spending before the September 11 attacks.

Benefits

Continuing to restrict the assessment to the conflicts for which costs of under-provision and corrective actions were estimated, the net benefits of conflict prevention total $287 billion.

References

Brown, Michael, and Richard Rosecrance, eds. 1999. *Prevention and Cure in the Global Arena.* Lanham, Mass.: Rowman & Littlefield.

Fram, Alan. 2002. "Anti-Terrorism Costs Exceed $60 Billion." *Associated Press,* 6 January.

ICAO (International Civil Aviation Organization). 2002. "Events of 11 September Had Strong Negative Impact on Airline Financial Results for 2001." News release, 28 May.

ICISS (International Commission on Intervention and State Sovereignty). 2001. *The Responsibility to Protect.* Ottawa: International Development Research Centre.

NCPA (National Center for Policy Analysis). 2002. "OECD Sees Lingering Economic Effects of Sept. 11." *Daily Policy Digest,* 7 June.

OECD (Organisation for Economic Co-operation and Development). 2002. "OECD Study Warns of Longer-term Economic Impact of 11 September Attacks." News release, 5 June.

SIPRI (Stockholm International Peace Research Institute). 2001. *SIPRI Yearbook 2001.* New York: Oxford University Press.

Sivard, Ruth. 1996. *World Military and Social Expenditures, 1996.* Washington, D.C.: World Priorities.

Thornhill, John. 2001. "Rehabilitation of Country May Cost $25 billion." *Financial Times.* 21 November.

UN (United Nations). 2001. "Global Economic Slowdown Aggravated by Attacks on the US." Department of Economic and Social Affairs, New York.

UNDP (United Nations Development Programme). Various years. *Human Development Report.* New York: Oxford University Press.

UNHCR (United Nations High Commissioner for Refugees). 2000. *Global Report 2000.* Geneva.

U.S. Department of State. 2002. *Patterns of Global Terrorism 2001.* Washington, D.C.

U.S. General Accounting Office. 2002. *Review of Studies of the Economic Impact of the September 11, 2001, Terrorist Attacks on the World Trade Center.* Report GAO-02-700R. Washington, D.C.

Yeager, Holly. 2001. "City Faces $83 billion Losses, Says Study." *Financial Times.* 16 November.

2

POLITICS: BRINGING THE PUBLIC BACK INTO PUBLIC POLICYMAKING

POLITICAL GLOBALIZATION: TRENDS AND CHOICES
David Held and Anthony McGrew

GOVERNING THE PROVISION OF GLOBAL PUBLIC GOODS:
THE ROLE AND LEGITIMACY OF NONSTATE ACTORS
Michael Edwards and Simon Zadek

THE GOVERNANCE OF THE INTERNATIONAL MONETARY FUND
Ariel Buira

STEPS TOWARD ENHANCED PARITY:
NEGOTIATING CAPACITY AND STRATEGIES OF DEVELOPING COUNTRIES
Pamela Chasek and Lavanya Rajamani

GETTING TO FAIRNESS: NEGOTIATIONS OVER GLOBAL PUBLIC GOODS
Cecilia Albin

COMBINING EFFICIENCY WITH EQUITY: A PRAGMATIC APPROACH
Odile Blanchard, Patrick Criqui, Alban Kitous, and Laurent Viguier

The provision of global public goods involves two closely related processes: political decisionmaking and production. The chapters in this part of the volume explore political decisionmaking.

Global public goods are goods with benefits—or, in the case of global public bads, costs—that potentially affect all people. For some analysts this is reason enough to argue that all parts of the global public should have the opportunity to express their preferences and help shape the content and structure of the global public domain. But there is another crucial reason for participatory decisionmaking on global public goods. When looked at not from the consumption side (that is, from the viewpoint of the goods' indivisible benefits) but from the production side (from the viewpoint of their constituent components), it is clear that many of these goods are also highly public in production. In many cases all parts of the global public have to contribute for a good to emerge. Moreover, there is no international equivalent of the national state to coerce actors to contribute. International cooperation in the provision of global public goods is largely voluntary. Thus international decisionmaking and agreements must be perceived as being fair—as improving people's lives.

David Held and Anthony McGrew's chapter discusses the emergence of global politics. They argue that globalization poses a fundamental challenge to the world order designed in accordance with the Westphalian principle of exclusive sovereign rule over bounded territories. With globalization, power is shared by diverse state and nonstate actors, nationally and internationally, interacting in multiple transborder networks and alliances. Held and McGrew emphasize that globalization is not, as some observers have suggested, narrowing or foreclosing political debate. Rather, it is demanding political reform and reinvigoration of the political terrain.

A critical element of political reform involves facilitating interaction between nonstate and state actors, particularly intergovernmental bodies, in global public policymaking. Businesses, the general public, and civil society organizations directly influence public policies and global public goods, individually or through interactions between them. But the state is still responsible for translating policy consensus into binding policy decisions and perhaps law. How prepared are intergovernmental bodies and nonstate actors for multiactor consultations? And are the public's views being heard in multilateral negotiations? Michael Edwards and Simon Zadek show that today's multi-stakeholder discussions are plagued with problems. The main reason is that state and nonstate actors lack clear rules for their interaction. Accordingly, Edwards and Zadek focus on the challenges of legitimacy for nonstate actors in the international system.

The chapters by Ariel Buira and by Pamela Chasek and Lavanya Rajamani examine the publicness of decisionmaking in the intergovernmental arena, with an emphasis on the participation of developing countries in multilateral institutions and in international negotiations, respectively. Buira's starting point is that transparency and accountability are important global public goods. They facilitate trust and confidence, bolstering international coopera-tion. His question is, how transparent and accountable are multilateral institutions? He examines this issue by analyzing decisionmaking in the International Monetary Fund—and concludes that developing countries deserve more seats at the decisionmaking table.

Yet Chasek and Rajamani show that even when developing countries have seats at negotiating tables, they may still be underrepresented. Data for a wide range of multilateral negotiations reveal a vast gap between the negotiating capacity and strength of industrial and developing countries. As a result devel-oping country delegations find it hard to cover all meetings and even harder, if not impossible, to play active roles in setting agendas and steering negotiations.

Thus the analyses in this part of the volume point to critical shortcomings in international decisionmaking. Many parts of the global public consider the outcomes of these processes unfair and the goods in the global public domain malprovided, sometimes constituting more of an obstacle to than a useful means for local and national development. But how can fairness be enhanced? Cecilia Albin offers a pragmatic approach. Based on extensive interviews with country representatives who have participated in multilateral negotiations, she concludes that an effective, politically feasible approach would be to focus on the fairness of the structure and process of negotiations that shape policy outcomes.

Using climate stability as an example, Odile Blanchard, Patrick Criqui, Alban Kitous, and Laurent Viguier show that modeling exercises could help negotiators see the possible policy outcomes of various decisions and the notions of fairness and justice to which they correspond. Thus epistemic communities could play an important role in international decisionmaking on global public goods. Bringing research and analysis into negotiations could also enhance their fairness, which Albin suggests. Blanchard, Criqui, Kitous, and Viguier show that it would then be possible to think beyond process fairness and to discuss in an informed way the likely outcomes of agreements—making those outcomes fairer as well.

POLITICAL GLOBALIZATION: TRENDS AND CHOICES

DAVID HELD AND ANTHONY MCGREW

The fortunes of political communities can no longer be understood just in national or territorial terms. Multiple cross-border challenges, interaction networks, and power systems increasingly shape the lives of such communities. Indeed, in the context of intense regional and global interconnectedness, the very idea of a political community as an exclusive, territorially delimited unit has become uncompelling. Accordingly, questions arise about the fate of the idea of political community and about the appropriate principles and institutions for effective governance of human affairs.

The emergence of a growing array of global issues—global public goods and bads—has been one of the transformative processes leading to today's reconfiguration of political power and policymaking. These processes have eroded clear-cut distinctions between domestic and foreign affairs. At the same time, an adequate provision of global public goods requires national political communities to be involved in all areas of regional and global policymaking. Growing interconnectedness and the emergence of global politics demand a reconsideration of current forms of democracy and accountability. If many contemporary forms of power are to become participatory, transparent, and accountable, and if many of the complex issues that affect all people—locally, nationally, regionally, and globally—are to be democratically regulated, people will have to have access to, and participation in, diverse political communities.

This chapter discusses three issues that highlight the changing constellation of politics. First it examines how globalization is altering state politics and policymaking. Then it explores the implications of these political transformations for the notion of political community. Finally, it discusses the policy choices available and required to govern, democratize, and civilize globalization more effectively than at present.

Contemporary processes of globalization present a fundamental challenge to the world order designed in accordance with the Westphalian principle of exclusive sovereign rule over a bounded territory. Of course, the nature and significance of this challenge are hotly debated. For some, referred to here as hyperglobalizers, these developments prefigure the demise of sovereign statehood and undermine a world order based on Westphalian norms (see Ohmae 1995; Perlmutter 1991;

and Guéhenno 1995). Among those with more skeptical minds, globalization is an enormous myth—because, they say, all the empirical evidence points to a world still dominated by geopolitics and increasingly divided by regional economic blocs (Brown 1995; Hirst and Thompson 1999; Krasner 1995).

Still others argue that contemporary globalization is reconstituting or transforming the power, functions, and authority of the state (Giddens 1990; Elkins 1995; Held 1995; Keohane and Milner 1996; Mann 1997; Rosenau 1997). For these transformationalists, globalization is associated with the emergence of a post-Westphalian world order in which the institutions of sovereign statehood and political community are being re-formed and reconstituted.[1] In this post-Westphalian order there is a marked shift toward heterarchy—a divided authority system—with states seeking to share the tasks of governance with a complex array of institutions, public and private, transnational, regional, and global, representing the emergence of overlapping "communities of fate."

This is not the place to review in detail the claims, counterclaims, and historical evidence on these competing accounts (for such a review, see Held and others 1999). Rather, the main task here is to examine the effects of contemporary globalization on political life. The focus is on politics, law, and security, to highlight the changing form and context of state power and the new patterns of governance associated with the pressing agenda of global public goods.

THE EMERGENCE OF GLOBAL POLITICS

Globalization is a process that transforms the spatial organization of social relations and transactions, generating transcontinental and interregional networks for interaction and the exercise of power (see Held and others 1999). Different historical forms of globalization can be identified, including the epoch of world discovery in the early modern period, the era of European empires, and the present era shaped by neoliberal global economics. These different forms of globalization have distinctive spatial, temporal, and organizational attributes—that is, particular patterns of extensity, intensity, velocity, and impact of global relations, flows, and networks, alongside different types of institutionalization and modes of stratification and reproduction. Thus to talk of globalization is to acknowledge that its different forms have been associated with quite different world orders.

While sharing many elements with past phases, contemporary globalization has several distinctive features. It is creating a world where the extensive reach of cross-country relations and networks is matched by their high intensity, velocity, and impact propensity across many facets of life, from economic and social to environmental. These changes have not occurred in an empty political space; there has also been a shift in the nature and form of political organization. The distinctive form that this has taken is the emergence of "global politics."

At the heart of this expansion of politics lies the rapid increase in transborder activities such as international trade, transport, travel, communications, and finance—as well as pollution, communicable diseases, drugs, and terrorism. Global politics is anchored not just in traditional geopolitical concerns but also in these diverse economic, social, and ecological issues, which are assuming an increasingly political character. It is focused on controlling and reducing global public bads, which cut across territorial jurisdictions and existing political alignments, and which require international cooperation to resolve. But there is also a long and lengthening agenda of international cooperation sought deliberately, not just in response to global public bads. This second strand of global politics is aimed at building connected and harmonized physical and institutional infrastructure, ranging from international communications and transport systems to international trade and financial architecture.

Thus political communities confront a growing number of policy issues that concern them all. Another change has been that sites of political action and decisionmaking have increasingly become linked, through rapid communications, into complex networks of political interaction. Political decisions and actions in one part of the world can quickly have worldwide ramifications. Associated with this "stretching" of politics is a frequent intensification or deepening of global processes such that "action at a distance" permeates the social conditions and cognitive worlds of specific places or policy communities (Giddens 1990, ch. 2). As a result international developments—economic, social, or environmental—can have almost instant local consequences, and vice versa.

New communication systems also form the basis for reorganizing political action and exercising political power over vast distances (see Deibert 1997). The revolution in computers, microelectronics, and information technology has established instant worldwide links, dramatically altering the nature of political communication by combining the technologies of the telephone, television, cable, satellite, and jet. From premodern to modern times, most political associations were distinguished by close links between physical setting, social situation, and politics. But those links have been ruptured; the new communication systems create new experiences, new modes of understanding, and new frames of political reference independent of direct contact with particular peoples, issues, or events. One poignant example is the speed at which the events of 11 September 2001 reached around the world and made mass terrorism a global issue. The expansion of international and transnational organizations, the extension of international rules and legal mechanisms, and the emergence of nonstate actors have all received an impetus from the new communication systems, and all depend on these systems to further their aims. The present era of global politics marks a shift toward multilayered regional and global governance.

The sovereign state now lies at the intersection of a vast array of international regimes and organizations established to manage areas of transnational activity (trade, financial flows, crime) and address collective policy problems. The rapid growth of these challenges, many of a global public goods nature, has involved a spread of layers of governance. It has been marked by the transformation of aspects of political decisionmaking based on territoriality—notably the development of regional and international organizations and institutions, the emergence of regional and international law, and increased involvement in policymaking by nonstate actors. Even for defense and security the notion of a singular, discrete, delimited political community now appears problematic.

Most obvious is the rapid emergence of an increasingly dense web of intergovernmental organizations, international nongovernmental organizations (NGOs), and a wide variety of other transnational pressure groups and networks. For example, at the beginning of the 20th century there were just 37 intergovernmental organizations and 176 international NGOs. In 1999 there were 6,415 intergovernmental organizations and 43,958 international NGOs (Union of International Associations 2001). In the mid-19th century there were two or three interstate conferences or congresses each year; today there are more than 4,000 a year.

There has also been a substantial increase in the number of international treaties and international regimes, altering the situational context of states (Held and others 1999, chs. 1–2). According to Ku (2001, p. 23), between 1648 and 1750 there were 86 multilateral treaties—whereas between 1976 and 1995 there were a whopping 1,619 treaties, 100 of which created international organizations.

Regional relations have also accelerated significantly. In remarkably little time the European Union has taken Europe from the disarray of World War II to a world where sovereignty is pooled across a growing number of areas of common concern. Judged in the context of state history, it is, for all its flaws, a remarkable political formation. Important trends toward regionalism have also occurred in the Americas, Asia and the Pacific, and to a lesser degree Africa. Regionalism in these parts of the world differs from the EU model. But it has also had significant consequences for political power.

The Asia-Pacific region has seen the formation of the Association of Southeast Asian Nations (ASEAN), Asia-Pacific Economic Cooperation (APEC), ASEAN Regional Forum (ARF), Pacific Basin Economic Council (PBEC), and many other groups. In the Americas regionalism has led to the Southern Common Market (Mercosur), North American Free Trade Agreement (NAFTA), Summits of the Americas, and proposals for a Free Trade Area of the Americas (FTAA) in 2006. In Africa renewed efforts at achieving development have been launched as a joint regional endeavor in the context of the New Partnership for Africa's Development (NEPAD). As regionalism has deepened, interregional diplomacy has intensified as well. Old and new regional groups are seeking to consolidate their relations with one another. In this respect regionalism has not been a barrier to political globalization but, on the contrary, has been a building block for it (see Hettne 1998).

The increasing internationalization and regionalization of politics have been accompanied by an important change in the scope and content of international law. Twentieth-century forms of international law—from the law governing war to laws on human rights, environmental issues, and crimes against humanity—have created components of what can be thought of as an emerging framework of "cosmopolitan" law circumscribing and delimiting the political power of individual states (Held 2002). In principle, states are no longer able to treat their citizens as they see fit. Although many states still violate these standards, nearly all accept general duties for protection and provision in their practices and procedures (Beetham 1999).

Another notable trend is the growing enmeshment of public and private agencies in the making of rules, setting of codes, and establishment of standards. Many new sites of rulemaking and lawmaking have emerged, creating a multitude of "decentred law-making processes" in various areas of the global order (Teubner 1997, p. xiii). Many of these have come into existence through self-validating processes related to technical standardization, professional rule production, and intraorganizational regulation in multinational corporations, and through business contracting, arbitration, and other elements of the global framework of commercial law (see Teubner 1997). Global public policy networks involving public and private actors are reshaping the basis on which national and international rules and regulations are made, and the results do not easily fit the traditional distinction between national and international law (Jayasuriya 1999; Reinicke 1999; Slaughter 2000). There is no longer a strict separation between public and private, domestic and international legal procedures and mechanisms; models of lawmaking and enforcement no longer simply fit the unified hierarchy of the state system.

Thus national governments are increasingly locked into an array of multilayered, multiactor governance systems—and can barely monitor them all, let alone stay in command. Foreign and domestic, public and private policy have become chronically intertwined, making national coordination and control of government policy increasingly problematic. Interlaced with these political and legal transformations are changes in the world military order. A key consideration for the argument supporting global politics and altering state politics made here is the fact that few states—except perhaps China and the United States—can contemplate unilateralism as a credible defense strategy.

With the proliferation of weapons of mass destruction, the demarcation between allies and enemies has become blurred. This distinction made sense during the period of massed battles, when battlegrounds were relatively contained. But with modern warfare technology, the impact of a war can be as devastating for a "friend" as for an "enemy." Furthermore, the paradox and novelty of the globalization of organized violence are that national security is becoming a collective or multilateral affair—making global and regional security institutions more salient (Clark 2001). As a result the thing that did the most to give modern nation-states a focus and a purpose and that has always been at the heart of modern statehood (as understood since Hobbes)—national defense and security—can now be realized only if nation-states pool resources, technology, intelligence, power, and authority.

Yet it is not just the problems and institutions of defense that have become multinational. The way military hardware is manufactured has also changed. The age of "national champions" has been superseded by a sharp increase in coproduction agreements, joint ventures, corporate alliances, and subcontracting (Held and others 1999, ch. 2). This means that few countries—not even the United States—can claim to have wholly autonomous military production capacity. This point is highlighted by key civil technologies, such as electronics, that are vital to advanced weapons systems and are the products of highly globalized industries.

Thus contemporary globalization and regionalization have given rise to global politics—cross-border policy challenges, overlapping networks and constellations of power, and an increasingly dense web of international regimes and organizations. Today's world differs markedly from the Westphalian principle of sovereign state rule over a bounded territory.

THE NEW CONTEXT OF POLITICAL COMMUNITY

National governments can no longer be assumed to be the locus of effective political power. Effective power is shared and bartered by diverse forces and agencies at the national, regional, and international levels. Consequently, the idea of a political community of fate—of a self-determining collectivity—also can no longer be meaningfully located in the boundaries of a single nation-state. Some of the most fundamental forces and processes that determine the nature of life chances within and across political communities are now beyond the reach of individual nation-states.

Thus political communities must be thought of as being embedded in complex structures of overlapping forces, relations, and networks. These structures are marked, within and among themselves, by manifold aspects of inequality and hierarchy. But even the most powerful of today's diverse political communities—including the most powerful states—are affected by the changing conditions and processes of regional and global entrenchment and interconnectedness. For all, there are stronger compulsions to engage in cross-border cooperation.

The political world at the start of the 21st century faces significant new political externalities, or "boundary problems." In the past, nation-states resolved most differences over boundary matters by pursuing state interests backed by diplomatic initiatives and, ultimately, coercive means. But this power logic is inadequate and inappropriate for resolving today's complex issues, from economic regulation to resource depletion and environmental degradation, which engender—at seemingly ever greater speeds—an intermeshing of "national fortunes." Political space for the development and pursuit of effective government and the accountability of power is no longer coterminous with a delimited political territory. Contemporary forms of political globalization involve a complex deterritorialization and reterritorialization of political authority (see Rosenau 1997).

Metaphors of the loss, diminution, or erosion of state power can misrepresent this change. Indeed, such language indicates a failure to properly conceptualize the nature of power and its complex manifestations, because it represents a crude zero-sum view of power. Such a conception is particularly unhelpful in attempting to understand the apparently contradictory position of states under contemporary globalization. For while globalization is engendering, for instance, a reconfiguration of state-market relations in the economic domain, states and international public authorities are deeply implicated in this process (for example, through the weakening or removal of national capital controls). Economic globalization by no means necessarily translates into a diminution of state power. Rather, it is transforming the conditions under which state power can be exercised (see Perraton and others 1997). The apparent simultaneous weakening and expansion of state power under contemporary globalization is symptomatic of an underlying structural transformation. This is nowhere so evident as with state sovereignty and autonomy, which form the ideological foundations of the modern state.

The position taken in this chapter is critical of both the hyperglobalizers and the skeptics. Although regional and global interaction networks are strengthening, they have variable and multiple impacts across diverse locales. Moreover, national sovereignty has not been wholly subverted, even in regions with intensive overlapping and divided authority structures. Rather, sovereignty has been transformed in such regions. It has been displaced as an illimitable, indivisible, and exclusive form of public power, embodied in an individual state, and embedded in a system of multiple, often pooled power centers and overlapping spheres of authority (see Held 2002). There has been, in other words, a reconfiguration of political power.

Many hyperglobalizers associate contemporary globalization with new limits to politics and the erosion of state power, but the argument developed here is critical of such political fatalism. Contemporary globalization not only has triggered or reinforced the significant politicization of a growing array of issue areas, it also has been accompanied by extraordinary growth in institutionalized arenas and networks of political mobilization, surveillance, decisionmaking, and regulatory activity that transcend national political jurisdictions. This has expanded enormously the capacity for and scope of political activity and the exercise of political authority. In this respect globalization is not, nor has it ever been, beyond regulation and control. Globalization does not prefigure the "end of politics" so much as its continuation by new means. Yet this is not to overlook the profound intellectual, institutional, and normative challenges that globalization presents to existing political communities.

Global developments have changed the concept of the political community—particularly the democratic political community—which often gets split into the "inner" and "outer" spheres of political life. But today national communities by no means determine policies exclusively for themselves when deciding on global issues, especially issues with important public, nonexcludable properties that can potentially affect everyone's lives. Consider the issues of health, the environment, international finance, and terrorism. Not only do national political communities no longer have the means to resolve these issues on their own, but their policy decisions are often not exclusively for them. In many cases the effects of these decisions spill across jurisdictional boundaries, with important implications for democracy.

Today it is readily understood that the quality of democracy depends on the accountability of political decisionmaking to citizens in a delimited political community. Moreover, it is well understood that the quality of democracy depends on more than citizens' formal access to the public sphere and the polity—to public deliberation and decisionmaking. But it is still too rarely acknowledged that the nature, form, and prospects of political communities are clouded by the multiplying interconnections among them. As more countries seek to establish national democracies, powerful forces affecting social, economic, cultural, and environmental welfare transcend the boundaries of nation-states. In this context fundamental questions are raised about the meaning of democracy and citizenship.

In existing liberal democracies consent to government and legitimacy for government action depend on electoral politics and the ballot box. Yet as soon as the nature of a "relevant" community is contested, problems arise for the notion that consent legitimates government and that the ballot box is the appropriate mechanism for citizens to periodically confer authority on government to enact the law and regulate economic and social life. What is the proper constituency and proper realm of jurisdiction for developing and implementing policy on narcotics, military security, the use of nuclear energy, the management of nuclear waste, health issues such as HIV/AIDS, the harvesting of rainforests, the use of nonrenewable resources, the instability of global financial markets, and the management and control of genetic engineering? Traditionally, national boundaries have demarcated the basis on which individuals are included and excluded from participation in decisions affecting their lives. If many socioeconomic processes, and the outcomes of decisions about them, now stretch beyond national frontiers, the implications of this are serious not only for consent and legitimacy but for all the key ideas of democracy. As fundamental processes of governance escape the categories of the nation-state, traditional national resolutions of the key questions of democratic theory and practice look increasingly threadbare.

Accordingly, the extent, intensity, and impact of a broad range of processes and issues—economic, political, and environmental—raise questions about where those issues are most appropriately addressed. If the most powerful geopolitical forces are not to settle pressing matters simply in terms of their own objectives and by virtue of their power, existing structures and mechanisms of accountability need to be reconsidered.

GOVERNING, DEMOCRATIZING, AND CIVILIZING GLOBALIZATION

Contemporary globalization is transforming the foundations of world order by reconstituting traditional forms of sovereign statehood, political community, and international governance. But these processes are neither inevitable nor fully secure. The contemporary world order is a highly complex, interconnected but still evolving and contested order in which the interstate system is increasingly embedded in an evolving system of multilayered regional and global political governance. Globalization is not, as some suggest, narrowing or foreclosing political debate. On the contrary, it is reilluminating and reinvigorating the political terrain. But what are the policy options for shaping globalization, and what are the directions in which policy reform could possibly move?

Given the growing number of global crises and the growing strength of social movements around the world pressing for more broadly based and equitable development, simply perpetuating existing socioeconomic arrangements is not a policy option to be seriously considered. Some hyperglobalizers (such as Ohmae 1995) have supported this option for some time. Yet it offers no real solutions to the market failure induced by globalization or to the growing backlash against it. At the same time, a radical approach of "globalization from below" (see Burnheim 1995; Walker 1992; and Falk 1995) is probably overly optimistic about the potential for localism to resolve or engage with the governance agenda generated by the forces of globalism.

Rather, policy reform should start from the finding that global politics and multilayered governance are fundamentally challenging the efficacy of national democratic traditions and institutions. The nature of a particular community and the nature of relations among communities are now interconnected, and new legal and organizational mechanisms must be created if democracy and political communities are to prosper. It would be fallacious to conclude from this that the politics of local communities or national democratic communities will be (or should be) wholly eclipsed by the new forces of political globalization. To assume this would be to misunderstand the complex, variable, and uneven impact of regional and global processes on political life. Of course, certain problems and policies should remain the responsibility of local and national governments. But others will be recognized as appropriate for specific regions, and still others—such as elements of environmental protection, security concerns, health questions, and economic regulation—will need to be addressed by new, cooperative institutional arrangements.

The reform of governance needs to be rethought as a "double-sided" process. A double-sided process—or process of double democratization—means deepening democracy within national communities, as well as extending democratic forms and processes across territorial borders. Democracy must allow all stakeholders to access and render accountable the social, economic, and political processes that cut across and transform their traditional community boundaries. This double-sided approach involves reconceiving legitimate political activity in a way that disconnects it from its traditional anchor in fixed borders and delimited territories. Basic democratic arrangements and basic democratic law can, in principle, be entrenched and drawn on in diverse, self-regulating associations— from cities and subnational regions to nation-states, regions, and global networks. The process of disconnection has already begun, with political authority and legitimate forms of governance diffused below, above, and alongside nation-states.

Some analysts argue that central to this notion of governance is that of a "cosmopolitan citizen" (see Archibugi, Held, and Köhler 1998; Held 1995; and Linklater 1998). Citizenship in a democratic polity of the future, it is argued, will likely require mediating between national traditions, communities of fate, and alternative forms of public life. Such a role encompasses dialogue with the traditions and discourses of others with the aim of expanding one's own framework of meaning and prejudice and increasing mutual understanding. Political agents who can reason from other people's points of view will be better equipped to resolve—and resolve fairly—the new and challenging transboundary issues that create overlapping communities of fate.

But if many contemporary forms of power are to become accountable and if many of the complex issues that affect us all—locally, nationally, regionally, and globally—are to be democratically regulated, people will also have to have access to and membership in diverse political communities. Put differently, a democratic political community of the future is one where citizens will enjoy multiple identities and citizenships. Faced with overlapping communities of fate, they will need to be not only citizens of their own communities but also members of the wider regions where they live and of the wider global order.

New political arrangements are not only a necessity but also a distinct possibility in light of the changing organization of regional and global processes, evolving political decisionmaking centers such as the European Union, and growing demands for new forms of political deliberation, conflict resolution, and transparency in international decisionmaking. In this new and emerging world, cities, national parliaments, regional assemblies, and international organizations could have distinctive but interlinked roles within a framework of accountability and public decisionmaking. There is a choice on how to proceed—and the choice is ours to make.

It would be easy to be pessimistic about the future of political communities, about the future of democracy, and about prospects for attaining effective accountability in the context of changing regional and global orders. There are plenty of reasons for pessimism, including the fact that the world's essential political units are still based on nation-states while some of the world's most powerful sociopolitical forces escape the boundaries of these units. Partly in response to this, new forms of fundamentalism have arisen along with new forms of tribalism—all asserting the superiority of a particular religious, cultural, or political identity over all others, and all asserting their own aims and interests.

Another reason for pessimism is the reform of global governance—such as the reform of the United Nations Security Council—currently envisaged by the most powerful countries. Proposals for the reform of the Security Council are too often focused on including other powerful countries, above all Germany and Japan. Such moves would consolidate the power of certain geopolitical interests at the expense of many other countries, including some with enormous populations and high economic growth rates. This approach is unsustainable in the long run. The challenge is to bring all countries—industrial and developing—and all stakeholders—business, civil society, and the general public—into decisionmaking on global issues, especially as it concerns the global public goods that affect us all.

Yet there are also forces that inspire a more optimistic reading of the prospects for political community and democratic politics. The first is the emergence, however halting, of international and regional institutions and mechanisms of governance. The United Nations is weak in many respects, but it is a relatively recent creation and provides an innovative structure on which to build. In addition, the development of the European Union as a powerful regional body is remarkable. Six decades ago Europe was at the point of self-destruction. Since then it has created new mechanisms of collaboration, new instruments of human rights enforcement, and new political institutions that hold member states accountable on a broad range of issues and pool aspects of their sovereignty.

Furthermore, new regional and global actors are contesting the terms of globalization—not just corporations but also new social movements, such as the environmental movement, the women's movement, and the World Social Forum. These are the new voices of an emerging "transnational civil society" heard, for instance, at the major conferences of the 1990s—the Rio Conference on Environment and Development, the Cairo Conference on Population Control, and the Beijing Women's Conference—and again, and probably even more clearly, at more recent international gatherings, such as the International Conference on Finance for Development, held in Monterrey, and the Johannesburg World Summit on Sustainable Development. In short, efforts are being made to establish new forms of public life and new ways of debating regional and global issues.

These are all in early stages of development, and there are no guarantees that the balance of political contest will allow them to develop. But they point in the direction of a more inclusive and just form of global governance, a direction that must be followed if some of democracy's most cherished notions—political accountability, social justice, the rule of law, and a self-determining people, to name just a few—are to retain their relevance and efficacy in the decades ahead.

Conclusion

Effective and accountable institutions of governance are central to the effective provision of global public goods. These institutions cannot just emulate the bounded, state-centered political communities of the past. At the beginning of the 21st century there are strong reasons to believe that the old order, in the words of E. H. Carr (1981, p. 237), "cannot be restored, and a drastic change of outlook is unavoidable." Avoiding global crises and managing the social, economic, and political dislocation arising from contemporary globalization "will require the articulation of a collaborative ethos based upon the principles of consultation, transparency and accountability. . . . There is no alternative to working together and using collective power to create a better world" (Commission on Global Governance 1995, pp. 2, 5).

Today's globalization is tying together in increasingly complex ways the fates of people, households, and communities in and across all regions of the globe. Even the most powerful actors—in traditional terms of income, technology, and military might—will not, in the long run, be able to pursue their goals unilaterally. But if cooperation is to succeed across community lines, democracy needs to be strengthened within and across borders, both territorial and others. Thus globalization does not signal the "end of politics" so much as its continuation through new means, at new locuses, and with new actors. Democracy must become a feature of the multiple interaction networks and decisionmaking forums—public and private, local, national, regional, and global—on which enhanced governance of globalization depends (McGrew 2002). It is through such an extended public dialogue about the provision of global public goods that new, more accountable and just forms of governance can be built and the forces of globalization shaped more in the interests of all.

Note

1. The concept of sovereignty lodges a distinctive claim to the rightful exercise of political power over a circumscribed realm. It seeks to specify the political authority empowered to determine the rules, regulations, and policies in a given territory and to govern accordingly. But in thinking about the impact of globalization on the modern nation-state, one needs to distinguish sovereignty—the entitlement to rule over

a bounded territory—from state autonomy—the actual power of the nation-state to independently articulate and achieve policy goals. In effect, state autonomy refers to the capacity of state representatives, managers, and agencies to articulate and pursue their policy preferences even if those preferences sometimes clash with the dictates of domestic and foreign social forces and conditions. Moreover, to the extent that modern nation-states are democratic, sovereignty and autonomy are assumed to be embedded in and congruent with the territorially organized framework of liberal democratic government: the "rulers" (elected representatives) are accountable to the "ruled" (citizens) within a delimited territory. There is, in effect, a "national community of fate" whereby membership in the political community is defined in terms of the people within the territorial borders of the nation-state. See the introduction to Held and others (1999) for a fuller analysis of these terms.

References

Archibugi, Daniele, David Held, and Martin Köhler, eds. 1998. *Reimagining Political Community*. Cambridge: Polity Press.

Beetham, David. 1999. *Democracy and Human Rights*. Cambridge: Polity Press.

Brown, Chris. 1995. "International Political Theory and the Idea of World Community." In Ken Booth and Steve Smith, eds., *International Relations Theory Today*. Cambridge: Polity Press.

Burnheim, John. 1995. "Power-Trading and the Environment." *Environmental Politics* 4 (4): 49–65.

Carr, Edward H. 1981. *The Twenty Years Crisis, 1919–1939*. London: Papermac.

Clark, Ian. 2001. *The Post–Cold War Order: The Spoils of Peace*. Oxford: Oxford University Press.

Commission on Global Governance. 1995. *Our Global Neighbourhood*. Oxford: Oxford University Press.

Deibert, Ronald. 1997. *Parchment, Printing and Hypermedia: Communication in World Order Transformation*. New York: Columbia University Press.

Elkins, David J. 1995. *Beyond Sovereignty: Territory and Political Economy in the Twenty-First Century*. Toronto: University of Toronto Press.

Falk, Richard. 1995. "Liberalism at the Global Level: The Last of the Independent Commissions?" *Millennium: Journal of International Studies* 24 (3): 563–76.

Giddens, Anthony. 1990. *The Consequences of Modernity*. Cambridge: Polity Press.

Guéhenno, Jean-Marie. 1995. *The End of the Nation-State*. Minneapolis: Minnesota University Press.

Held, David. 1995. *Democracy and Global Order*. Cambridge: Polity Press.

———. 2002. "Law of States, Law of Peoples: Three Models of Sovereignty." *Legal Theory* 8: 1–44.

Held, David, Anthony McGrew, David Goldblatt, and Jonathan Perraton. 1999. *Global Transformations: Politics, Economics and Culture.* Cambridge: Polity Press.

Hettne, Björn. 1998. "The Double Movement: Global Market versus Regionalism." In R. W. Cox, ed., *The New Realism: Perspectives on Multilateralism and World Order.* Tokyo: United Nations University Press.

Hirst, Paul, and Grahame Thompson. 1999. *Globalization in Question.* 2nd ed. Cambridge: Polity Press.

Jayasuriya, Kanishka. 1999. "Globalization, Law and the Transformation of Sovereignty: The Emergence of Global Regulatory Governance." *Indiana Journal of Global Legal Studies* 6: 425–56.

Keohane, Robert O., and Helen V. Milner, eds. 1996. *Internationalization and Domestic Politics.* Cambridge: Cambridge University Press.

Krasner, Stephen. 1995. "Compromising Westphalia." *International Security* 20 (3): 115–51.

Ku, Charlotte. 2001. "Global Governance and the Changing Face of International Law." The 2001 John W. Holmes Memorial Lecture, prepared for delivery at the annual meeting of the Academic Council on the United Nations System (ACUNS), 16–18 June, Puebla, Mexico. ACUNS Reports and Papers Series, no. 2. Academic Council on the United Nations System, New Haven, CT.

Linklater, Andrew. 1998. *The Transformation of Political Community: Ethical Foundations of the Post-Westphalian Era.* Cambridge: Polity Press.

Mann, Michael. 1997. "Has Globalization Ended the Rise and Rise of the Nation-State?" *Review of International Political Economy* 4 (3): 472–96.

McGrew, Anthony. 2002. "Transnational Democracy." In April Carter and Geoffrey Stokes, eds., *Democratic Theory Today.* Cambridge: Polity Press.

Ohmae, Kenichi. 1995. *The End of the Nation State: The Rise of Regional Economies.* New York: Free Press.

Perlmutter, Howard V. 1991. "On the Rocky Road to the First Global Civilization." *Human Relations* 44 (9): 897–920.

Perraton, Jonathan, David Goldblatt, David Held, and Anthony McGrew. 1997. "The Globalization of Economic Activity." *New Political Economy* 2 (2): 257–77.

Reinicke, Wolfgang. 1999. "The Other World Wide Web: Global Public Policy Networks." *Foreign Policy* (winter): 44–57.

Rosenau, James. 1997. *Along the Domestic-Foreign Frontier: Exploring Governance in a Turbulent World.* Cambridge: Cambridge University Press.

Slaughter, Anne-Marie. 2000. "Governing the Global Economy through Government Networks." In Michael Byers, ed., *The Role of Law in International Politics.* Oxford: Oxford University Press.

Teubner, Gunther, ed. 1997. *Global Law without a State.* Aldershot, U.K.: Dartmouth.

Union of International Associations. 2001. *Yearbook of International Organizations 2001–2*. Vol. 1B (Int–Z). Munich: K. G. Saur.

Walker, Rob B. J. 1992. *Inside/Outside: International Relations as Political Theory.* Cambridge: Cambridge University Press.

Governing the Provision of Global Public Goods: The Role and Legitimacy of Nonstate Actors

Michael Edwards and Simon Zadek

The successful provision of global public goods in the 21st century rests on two complementary tasks. First, increasing the involvement of nonstate actors in global governance, because governments will find it increasingly difficult to act alone in designing and implementing effective regimes. Second, ensuring that nonstate involvement is structured to avoid the dangers of special interest politics, because otherwise decisions may favor one group over another or lead to gridlock in the system. These two tasks must be approached together and will require a radical overhaul of the rules of global governance to ensure that state and nonstate capacities are combined effectively. Without such an overhaul, global governance is likely to degenerate into the worst of all possible outcomes—as at the 2001 G-8 summit in Genoa, Italy, which produced a crippling combination of overzealous policing, anarchist violence, stalemate in official discussions, and responsible nonstate voices drowned out in the general cacophony. The problems in providing global public goods cannot be solved in such an environment. New solutions must be developed.

This chapter shows how these two tasks can be addressed in tandem, a challenge that raises fundamental questions of political theory and democratic practice that take the debate on global public goods into largely uncharted territory. Fundamental to this challenge is the complicated issue of legitimacy: the sense that institutions and the decisions they make must be seen as fair and acceptable to all relevant stakeholders if they are to be effective in changing public and private behavior. Two dimensions of legitimacy are especially important. The first concerns the legitimacy of the international system for negotiating and delivering global public goods. As a result of the current system's perceived failure to achieve results and the appearance of its domination by governments and corporations from industrial countries, its legitimacy is being questioned by those who feel excluded, whether governments or citizen groups. For reasons explored in this chapter, nonstate actors are crucial to rebuilding the legitimacy of the international system for global governance. However, and this is the second dimension of the problem, nonstate actors are likely to be accepted and effective in this role only if they strengthen their own legitimacy in the eyes of governments, intergovernmental organizations, and the general public. Although these two dimensions of legitimacy are closely linked and cannot be resolved in isolation from each other, this chapter focuses on the challenges of legitimacy for nonstate actors in the international system.

THE RISE OF NONSTATE ACTORS

In this chapter the term *nonstate actor* covers both business and civil society. *Civil society* includes all organizations, networks, and associations between the level of the family and the level of the state, except firms. Nongovernmental organizations (NGOs), labor unions, and business associations form subsets of civil society, but firms are excluded because they are assumed to exist to make and distribute a private profit, while civil society groups are organized to defend or advance the interests they hold in common. This definition is helpful in clarifying the institutional and legally mandated aims of corporations like Shell or IBM. But it is less helpful in categorizing sections of the business community that exist, at least in part, to generate a social good or advance a collective interest, such as cooperatives, social and community enterprises, and partnerships that combine traditional businesses with public and nonprofit actors. Nevertheless, different types of nonstate actors have different mandates, interests, and characteristics, and these differences make it dangerous to generalize about the role of nonstate actors in securing global public goods. Thus, where necessary, this chapter deals separately with businesses and civil society organizations, and focuses on corporations and NGOs within these general categories.

Civil society organizations are enjoying an unprecedented upsurge in their profile and—to a lesser extent—their influence over global debates and decision-making (Florini 2000; Edwards and Gaventa 2001; Anheier, Glasius, and Kaldor 2001). Although it lacks coherence, the current wave of global citizen action is comparable with, and probably larger than, previous waves in the 1960s and earlier periods. John Cavanagh of the Institute for Policy Studies estimates that more than 49 million people have joined the Hemispheric Social Alliance against the Free Trade Agreement of the Americas (Cox's News Service, 12 April 2001), while the U.S. antisweatshop movement has chapters in 140 colleges and universities. More than 40,000 international NGOs are active on the world stage, along with about 20,000 transnational civil society networks—90 percent of which were formed in the past 30 years, an astonishing growth rate (Edwards 1999, 2000b).

These "epistemic communities" include associations of local authorities and mayors, federations of community groups like Shack Dwellers International (Patel, Bolnick, and Mitlin 2001), international networks of universities, and independent media groups, labor unions, and business federations. Successive international United Nations conferences have provided invaluable opportunities for these groups to mobilize and make connections in an international context that increasingly favors civil society and the national democratic openings that have been such a feature of the post–Cold War world. In particular, developing country groups like the Third World Network and Development Alternatives with Women for a New Era (DAWN) are now an established presence on the world stage (Bunch and others 2001). Of course, not all civil society organizations share the same normative agendas. The international terrorist networks that organized the attacks on the U.S. Pentagon and the World Trade Center on 11 September 2001 are the latest and most visible example of "uncivil society" at work, but this is an extreme example.

Parallel to the rise of civil society groups has been the emergence of business as a key player on the global stage. Most visible and significant in the context of any discussion of global public goods are the increased scope and influence of one part of the business community, corporations. Like civil society organizations, the corporate community has grown remarkably in recent decades. Some 60,000–70,000 multinational corporations operate in today's global economy, and these corporations have an additional 200,000–300,000 nationally and regionally based subsidiaries. The largest multinational corporations are large indeed. Of the world's 100 largest "economies," 51 are corporations (Anderson and Cavanagh 1996), and the top 200 corporations have sales equal to one-quarter of the world's economic activity (Wheeler and Sillanpää 1997). General Motors has annual sales equivalent to the GDP of Denmark, and the annual sales of Sears Roebuck are comparable to the annual income of more than 100 million Bangladeshis (Utting 2000). World trade, dominated by a small number of transnational corporations, has increased by more than 12 times since 1945—and now accounts for about one-fifth of the world's measured economic income. In addition, the 1990s witnessed a huge increase in private capital flows to developing countries. In 1990 public sources accounted for more than half the international resources flowing to these countries, but by 1995 more than three-quarters came from private sources (World Bank 1997). Private foreign direct investment into developing countries alone nearly quadrupled during this period, rising to $96 billion by 1995 (UNCTAD 1998; Zarsky 1999). Although fluctuating yearly, private capital flows into developing countries continue on an increasing trend (World Bank 2002, p. 354).

Of great significance to debates on global governance has been the increasing political mobilization of business on the world stage over the past 10 years. For example, U.S. and European corporations meet regularly through the Transatlantic Business Dialogue to plan and coordinate their lobbying strategies, and throughout 1999 the European Commission met with an Investment Network representing more than 60 leading corporations to establish priorities for a new investment agreement under the World Trade Organization (Edwards 2000b). According to some estimates, NGOs focusing on international development were outnumbered by NGOs representing business interests at the November 2001 World Trade Organization ministerial meetings in Doha, Qatar—including 26 industry committees advising the U.S. government (Denny 2001). The implications of this trend are considered below.

NONSTATE ACTORS AND GLOBAL PUBLIC GOODS

Securing global public goods increasingly requires cooperation between governments and business, international agencies, and civil society organizations (Kaul, Grunberg, and Stern 1999). The United Nations cannot prevent global warming unless citizens decide that their environment has to be protected from their actions and industry offers them energy-efficient products and services. Similarly, progressive labor regimes will not be viable unless there is buy-in from companies like Nike and Wal-Mart and from consumers who are willing to pay higher prices for the goods these companies produce, procure, and sell.

Civil society organizations already claim to have established a role for themselves in identifying and lobbying for the increased provision of global public goods, a role that governments and business have been unable or unwilling to fulfill. The landmines campaign (Scott 2001), debt relief (Collins, Gariyo, and Burdon 2001), international certification of the diamond trade (Smillie and Gberie 2001), and access to essential medicines are good examples. The last was illustrated most recently by the success of South Africa's Treatment Action Campaign in lowering the potential price of HIV/AIDS drugs and by the agreement between the drug company Aventis and the World Health Organization to provide five years' worth of drugs to African countries to treat sleeping sickness free of charge (*Guardian Weekly,* 10–16 May 2001). Citizen groups were also a significant source of pressure to establish the International Criminal Court in 2000 and to ratify the Kyoto Protocol on climate change in Bonn, Germany, in 2001—the culmination of 20 years of NGO campaigns on the environment.

Many of the most vocal self-identified members of "global civil society" assert their support for a common goal: to democratize rulemaking and ensure that poor people around the world have more opportunities to benefit from the application of those rules. In reality, however, the interests of citizens—including poor people—are often at odds once one moves beyond the most general call for equity. Trade is the clearest example: for instance, the interests of family farmers in the U.S. Midwest are unlikely to be the same as those of small farmers in Latin America who are trying to gain access to U.S. markets, yet both groups are associated with NGOs and labor unions that lobby for their cause. In this case the global public good at stake is a trading regime that tries to satisfy both sets of interests—a difficult but not impossible task if trade rules are graduated according to circumstance and compensation is provided to the losers. For civil society groups, however, such differences pose some difficult questions that are taken up below.

The relationship between business and global public goods is complex and multifaceted. At one end of the spectrum, business affects the provision of global public goods through its primary activity of creating and delivering private goods through the market (Zadek 2001c). Most obvious are the positive externalities that may be associated with a general increase in economic wealth. For example, economic prosperity is generally associated with an increase in spending on health, education, and environmental and social protection—all of which are global public goods or can have indirect impacts on such goods. As the United Nations Development Programme's *Human Development Report 1999* (UNDP 1999, pp. 129–30) concludes,

> *People in many countries live a much longer and healthier life than just two decades ago. In 31 of the 174 countries included in the HDI [human development index], life expectancy has increased by more than a fifth since 1975. . . . Between 1975 and 1997 most countries made substantial progress in human development, reducing their shortfall from the maximum possible value of the HDI.*

The potential link between these improvements and the key role of the corporate community in globalization underpins the argument of those who advocate market liberalization as the most effective means of enhancing the delivery of global public goods.

But the impact of globalization and corporations on economic prosperity and human development is contested. The Washington, D.C.–based Center for Economic and Policy Research recently published a study suggesting that the economic growth rates of most developing countries, as well as many of these countries' human development indicators, worsened during 1980–2000, a period of accelerated globalization (Weisbrot and others 2001). Much anecdotal evidence suggests that corporate activities can damage the health of local economies and communities (Korten 1999), exacerbate civil unrest, and contribute to sustaining war—as with the mining companies whose activities have effectively bankrolled the conflicts in Angola, the Democratic Republic of Congo, and elsewhere.[1] Corporations may also try to undermine public policies that enhance the delivery of global public goods. For example, the U.S. government's recent decision not to sign the Kyoto Protocol was undoubtedly rooted in lobbying by the powerful, energy-intensive U.S. business community. Conversely, businesses and business associations are active in lobbying for other forms of global public goods, such as technical standards that need to be harmonized to promote cross-border commerce. Hence the debate about corporate actors and global public goods extends to measuring potential negative impacts as well as positive contributions.

These ambiguities have underpinned the emergence of the philosophy and practice of "corporate citizenship" (Zadek 2001a), through which corporations have sought to gain broader public trust and legitimacy by enhancing their non-financial performance and wider contributions to society. The focus and scope of corporate citizenship have widened from localized philanthropy to embrace a far broader swath of social, environmental, and economic dimensions of corporate performance. In this way businesses are, in effect, adopting policies and practices that explicitly commit them to delivering public goods. For multinational corporations in particular this includes global public goods, such as corporate initiatives to bridge the "digital divide" (Zadek and Raynard 2001) and code-based voluntary initiatives like the Forest Stewardship Council, which seeks to preserve and replenish tropical and other forests.

The growing role of nonstate actors in the provision of global public goods presents major challenges. There are deeply rooted fears that initiatives like the UN Global Compact legitimize the increasing influence of corporations on public policy and practice. But there are also concerns about the legitimacy of NGOs that have mobilized against the business community. In this climate it is important to be clear about whether, and under what conditions, increased nonstate involvement is desirable.

NONSTATE ACTORS AND THE CHANGING SHAPE OF GLOBAL GOVERNANCE

International market integration, the Internet, and the increasing interconnectedness of citizens are gradually eroding the monopoly on power exercised by nation-states in the Westphalian system of international relations. Many scholars have commented on the implications of this shift for global governance and on the move away from "club" models of decisionmaking to frameworks built around multilayered, cross-society dialogue (Ruggie 1983; Edwards 1999; Nye and Donahue 2001). These frameworks are built on the premise that the involvement of nonstate actors is a precondition for ensuring institutional plurality and creating viable strategies and programs. In theory, nonstate actors can make two contributions to effective global governance:

- Improving the quality of debate and decisionmaking by injecting more information, transparency, and accountability into the system from a wider range of sources, and making space for unorthodox ideas and "reality checks" on the effects of policy on the ground. Governments have no monopoly on ideas or expertise.
- Strengthening the legitimacy and effectiveness of decisions and decisionmaking processes by involving a broader spectrum of those whose support is required to make them work—meaning the public, the media, and the business community. Governments can confer authority on

decisions but rarely a complete sense of legitimacy, especially in a "wired" world where information flows much more freely through the media and across the Internet. In this scenario the weight of public or business pressure will be felt much more keenly by decisionmakers, wherever they are, and buy-in from nonstate actors will be crucial in ensuring that decisions are actually implemented.

Over the past 10 years nonstate actors have put these contributions into practice in three ways:

- *Setting new agendas and changing the language of debates*—for example, on debt relief and how to spend the proceeds, where G-7 governments have increasingly adopted Jubilee 2000's proposals since a human chain surrounded their summit meeting in Birmingham, England, in 1998 (Collins, Gariyo, and Burdon 2001). Similarly, corporate social responsibility, social auditing, and ethical trade have become part of the new language in and through which the role of business and its renegotiated rights and responsibilities are played out (Zadek, Pruzan, and Evans 1998).

- *Negotiating the details of regimes*—for example, the Ottawa Treaty on Landmines, which was driven through by a global NGO alliance (the International Campaign to Ban Landmines) and a group of middle-power governments led by Canada (Scott 2001). Business is increasingly active in seeking to influence the terms on which global public goods are provided— for example, how best to create a bribery- and corruption-free trading environment through the Organisation for Economic Co-operation and Development (OECD) or to negotiate international labor conventions through the International Labour Organization (ILO).

- *Monitoring and enforcing international agreements*—for example, certification systems such as the Forest Stewardship Council, or the implementation of measures to combat child labor in Bangladesh and Pakistan, which were negotiated by NGOs, governments, and factory owners and backed up by onsite visits and NGO programs designed to provide alternative sources of income for the families of child workers (Harper 2001).

Each of these roles requires a different form of legitimacy from nonstate actors, linked to a particular form of politics. Voicing an opinion is very different from negotiating a treaty, but both are vital to the successful provision of global public goods. At the local and national levels representative and direct democracy go hand in hand in many societies. But at the beginning of a new century the balance between them is changing in favor of nonstate actors, driven by rising disaffection with conventional politics, the attractions of direct action (including street protest), and the opportunities for broader participation generated by the macro-level political changes highlighted above. At times of regime transition such as this, the space for nonstate actors tends to increase.

Traditionally, the role of representative democracy has been to aggregate private preferences among large numbers of individuals, enabling tradeoffs to be made in the interests of society as a whole. This is something that business and civil society cannot do, at least not with the same degree of transparent legitimacy and accountability. The role of direct or participatory democracy has been to generate and shape opinions, ensure that the interests of excluded groups are not ignored, and hold governments accountable for delivering on the commitments they make on election day. This is something governments rarely do without sustained public pressure. Effective democracies combine elements of both systems, but when one is sacrificed for the other, problems inevitably arise—the "dictatorship" of a government elected with a minority of the popular vote in a weak civil society, for example, or the gridlock effect of strong special interests pushing against a weak state.

At the international level this debate is further complicated by the fact that so few elements of a global polity or of global political structures exist—for example, the checks and balances provided by the separation of the executive, legislative, and judicial branches of government, or the direct links between elected representatives and their constituents that enable the exercise of accountability. As argued below, the absence of these structures exposes nonstate involvement to a set of dilemmas. In particular, there is a danger that national, representative processes will be eroded by the relative convenience and easy access of direct global engagement. As one civil society activist remarked following the street battles that took place around the 1999 World Trade Organization meeting in Seattle, Washington,

> The question that came to my mind while seeing delegates from mainly developing countries excluded from the talks by protestors—and being sporadically assaulted and intimidated by them—while the US and EU negotiated inside—is when does one group's right to free speech outweigh another's right to free assembly? And when does obstruction of legitimate activity stop being "non-violent"? (excerpted from comments made during a closed online debate, 7 December 1999)

These problems may undermine attempts to secure the provision of global public goods, because success depends on mutually reinforcing actions from the local level to the global. A successful campaign at the global level may achieve few concrete results if it is only weakly rooted in local and national politics—especially through government policy and regulation and a sense of ownership among the citizens. Examples include the Ottawa Treaty on Landmines, which has not led to a decrease in mine-laying (Scott 2001); the ineffectiveness of international regulations on labor rights (Harper 2001); and the failure of the international campaign against breast-milk substitutes to eradicate their use in Africa and elsewhere

(Chapman 2001). Conversely, successful experiments at the local or national level may be undermined if they take place outside an international framework, preventing the exploitation of one country's sacrifices by free riders elsewhere. Climate change is the obvious example. Not every nonstate policy position needs to be negotiated along the chain from the local to the global level; doing so would suck much of the energy out of global citizen action and lead to lowest common denominator consensus. But campaigns divorced from local and national politics will always be vulnerable to co-optation by external interests. Despite the gradual erosion of nation-states, states still negotiate the rules of global governance and provide the authority required to implement them. Therefore, reconstructing state authority through democratic means remains a key challenge for the 21st century.

THE DILEMMAS OF NONSTATE INVOLVEMENT

None of the contributions listed above will necessarily be realized in every context. The actual outcome of nonstate involvement depends on whose voices are represented in debates, how competing interests are reconciled, and whether civic groups and business are effective in playing the roles assigned to them in the evolving international system. History suggests that political pluralism produces effective outcomes when many voices are fairly represented and mechanisms are put into place to arbitrate between them when disagreements arise. But unless the involvement of nonstate actors is managed effectively, the result may be gridlock or chaotic policymaking processes open to manipulation by the loudest and strongest groups—a problem already seen in international negotiations and in the special interest politics of industrial democracies like the United States. The reasons are clear:

- The quantity and diversity of businesses and civil society groups make it impossible for each one to participate equally. "Global civil society resembles a bazaar, a kaleidoscope of differently sized rooms, twisting alleys and steps leading to obscure places" (Keane 2001, p. 23), not a body with a common identity or agenda. This produces obvious problems for civic engagement in global governance, but this same diversity protects the public sphere by offering more opportunities for the dispersal and diffusion of power.

- Nonstate actors (even if restricted to civil society) may lack a common agenda at the international level because the opinions and interests of different groups do not coincide. Some U.S. NGOs, for example, speak for family farmers (such as the Institute for Agriculture and Trade Policy, headed by Mark Ritchie), and others for agribusiness (such as Truth about Trade, headed by a former president of the American Farm Bureau Federation; Aaronson 2001).[2] These divisions are being replicated at the international level through the emergence of organizations such as

International Consumers for Civil Society, which aims to counter the influence of the antiglobalization movement in debates over the World Trade Organization (Charnovitz 2001). Similarly, businesses have different models of success that create diverse interests. It makes little sense to equate the interests of Shell and Talisman, for example, merely because both are energy companies that have to make a profit (Shell International 1999). The interests and approach of Rio Tinto today are not the same as those of Rio Tinto Zinc (its former name) 5 or 10 years ago, even though it continues to be a global, profit-making mining conglomerate. Wal-Mart's price minimization strategy has very different implications for international labor standards than do up-market brands such as the U.K.-based food retailer Sainsburys or the Canada-based clothing manufacturer Hudson Bay (Zadek 2000).

- Global nonstate networks are asymmetrical and often dominated by organizations based in industrial countries, despite the emergence of developing country networks such as the Third World Network. For example, only 251 of the 1,550 NGOs associated with the UN Department of Public Information are based in developing countries, and the ratio for NGOs in consultative status with the UN Economic and Social Council is even lower (Edwards 2000b). Businesses and multinational affiliates based in developing countries have a similarly weak voice in international business networks.

- Accountability is problematic. NGOs have no clear bottom line for results and no single authority to whom they must report on their activities. "Downward" accountability (to those on whose behalf the NGO is speaking or claiming to speak) is often weaker than "upward" accountability to the donors who fund the NGO's activities. For business, the financial bottom line and shareholder accountability are relatively clear, but other stakeholders have to struggle to find voice and adequate sources of accountability (Elkington 1998).

- NGO positions are often criticized as crude and simplistic, poorly researched, and driven by fashion and sensation rather than loyalty to the facts. In reality, many NGO positions are researched with considerable sophistication, but there is always a temptation to trade off rigor for speed and profile in campaigns—as with Jubilee 2000's lack of attention to issues of economic management outside of debt relief, or attacks by some labor unions against forms of child labor in South Asia that turned out to be nonexploitive and essential to household welfare (Harper 2001). Corporate "intelligence" is similarly weak, despite the vast budgets of multinational corporations and the access they have to the best brains and data. Corporations often do little more than regurgitate outdated thinking about the costs of environmental management, or seem totally unaware of the potential productivity gains that come from treating their employees better. These weaknesses translate into the public policy sphere, where few senior business executives are aware of leading-edge insights into the potential for translating the pursuit of global public goods into viable business propositions (Hawken, Lovins, and Lovins 1999).

- Weak mechanisms are used to arbitrate between nonstate interests at the international level and to negotiate levels of consensus above the lowest common denominator. NGOs and business lack an equivalent to the United Nations through which their differences might be resolved or even debated to a conclusion. The result, demonstrated by the NGO declaration to the 2001 World Conference against Racism in Durban, South Africa, is a mixed bag of particularistic views in place of a sense of the negotiated common interest—precisely the outcome that is supposed to emerge from civil society in its role as an arena for public deliberation between competing ideas.

- As noted, NGO advocacy on the international stage is often weakly rooted in local and national politics, especially in classic "pyramidal" campaigns with centralized control over messages and strategies (Chapman 2001). There is always a temptation to leapfrog over the national arena and go directly to Washington or Brussels, where it is often easier to gain access to senior officials and achieve a response. As Keck and Sikkink (1998) show, international pressure can unlock political gridlock at the national level when it is mobilized effectively, but when this route displaces national political engagement it may erode the domestic coalition building that is essential to sustained policy reform. This is the "two bites of the cherry" problem, implying that NGOs and business have plenty of opportunities to influence official policy at the national level, but when they lose out they move their arguments to the global arena and undermine positions that have been established by their governments through democratic processes (Charnovitz 2001). On what basis, for example, did business and nonprofit organizations create the U.K.-based Ethical Trading Initiative and the U.S.-based Fair Labor Association as collusive mechanisms to drive new labor standards down global supply chains—when governments had already decided not to create mandatory international standards (Zadek 2000)? On what basis was it legitimate for Phil Knight, chief executive officer of Nike, to advocate as follows at the launch of the UN Global Compact?

> We believe in a global system that measures every multinational against a core set of universal standards using an independent process of social performance monitoring akin to financial auditing. This would bring greater clarity to the impact of globalization and the performance of any one company. (Zadek 2001a, p. 90)

One can certainly argue that democracy requires individuals and associations to use as many channels as possible to secure their interests, especially if those interests are ignored by people in power or formal citizenship rights are weak. But the problems outlined above raise serious questions about the involvement of nonstate actors in global governance. Unless they are explicitly addressed, these problems and questions may erode the benefits that are predicted to flow from nonstate participation. At their root are the thorny issues of legitimacy, accountability, and connectivity.

LEGITIMACY, ACCOUNTABILITY, AND CONNECTIVITY AMONG NONSTATE ACTORS

What right do nonstate actors have to participate in global governance? Do different types of actors have different rights? And what responsibilities go with those rights? At their root these are questions of legitimacy, a controversial issue that arouses strong reactions. Critics of NGOs usually cite one or more of the following problems to justify their position: NGOs do not formally represent those on whose behalf they claim to speak, they are not accountable for their actions or for the results of the positions they take, their policy positions are often inaccurate and misleading, and they are active only at the international level and have no roots in national politics.

Similar criticisms are made about business, which is accused of exerting undue influence in pursuit of the narrow interests of managers and shareholders. From this perspective the right of business to participate in global governance is challenged on the basis of its institutionalized and often legally dictated disinterest in—and lack of accountability to—the stakeholders who would benefit from the enhanced delivery of global public goods. (After all, most global public goods have distributional effects even if they are in principle nonexclusive.) But what is legitimacy, and how is it claimed?

Legitimacy is generally understood as the right to be and do something in society, a sense that an organization is lawful, admissible, and justified in its chosen course of action or in the global arena, an "acknowledged right to exert influence in global politics" (Scholte 2001, p. 97). But there are many ways to validate these claims. The legitimacy of ideas, for example, is very different from the legitimacy of decisionmaking processes (Brown 2001). Claims to legitimacy can be based on one or more of the following criteria:

- *Representation.* In membership-based bodies legitimacy is claimed through the normal democratic processes of elections and formal sanctions that ensure that an agency is representative of and accountable to its constituents. Labor unions and some NGOs and business associations fall into this category, though whether these processes operate effectively is another matter. If nonstate actors claim to represent poor people, they must be specific about which poor people they are representing and how. In reality, most industrial country NGOs are more sophisticated than this and accept that their policy positions are their own, even if substantial consultation has taken place with "partners" in developing countries.

- *Legal bases.* Businesses, particularly those that are publicly listed, are generally legally obliged to represent the interests of their shareholders. In so doing, however, businesses also claim that they reflect the needs of consumers, whose interests must be served if shareholders are to be satisfied. Corporate citizenship has extended this argument further, with businesses claiming to act with broader social and environmental interests in mind. Civil society groups that are not membership-based organizations—and most are not—define their legitimacy primarily according to their compliance with nonprofit legislation and regulation in a particular country, and effective oversight by their trustees.

- *Competence.* It is common for nonstate actors to claim legitimacy through recognition by other legitimate bodies that they have valuable knowledge and skills to bring to the table. The United Nations, for example, can accord a certain degree of legitimacy to NGOs or businesses when it recognizes and accredits them to its Economic and Social Council or Global Compact. In such cases competence is key. No one expects Oxfam, for example, to be perfectly representative of developing country opinion in order to qualify for accreditation in this sense; only that its proposals on debt and other issues be useful to the debate, rooted in research and experience, and sensitive to the views and aspirations of its developing country partners. These views can be challenged on the grounds of accuracy or rigor, or simply by those who have a different opinion, but that does not make them illegitimate. The same is true for business: though its competencies may be weak where public policy issues are at stake, it may nevertheless qualify for a seat at the negotiating table by virtue of its expertise or material interest in the issues under discussion (ISEA 2000).

- *Moral legitimacy.* Civil society organizations seem to have struck a chord in the public imagination in voicing concerns about globalization and the rising influence of corporations. This is evidenced not just in the rise of street protest, but in opinion polls as well. A recent poll of 20,000 citizens in G-20 nations by Environics International found that only 10 percent viewed globalization as "positive"—and only 1 percent thought that current global governance structures were satisfactory (see http://www.environics.net/eil/). Even if civic groups are not formally representative or particularly sophisticated in their critiques, their empathy with large segments of the public awards them a degree of moral legitimacy. The moral legitimacy of business—particularly the corporate community—is a fragile affair. Public opinion surveys around the world repeatedly confirm that business is distrusted when it comes to the public good (ranking together with governments except in the Nordic region, where governments score far higher; Zadek 2001a). Unlike nonprofits, businesses often build brand identification and associated trust around relationships with individuals and with other organizations, such as Nike's link to Michael Jordan (LaFeber 1999) or the growing number of long-term partnerships between businesses, nonprofit organizations, and state bodies (Nelson and Zadek

2000; Zadek 2001b). Such trust remains little more than a distant cousin of a more deeply rooted moral legitimacy, however, despite attempts by leaders in corporate citizenship to attain the moral high ground through substantive investment, change, and collaboration with NGOs like Oxfam, Amnesty International, and the World Wildlife Fund (Zadek 2001a).

- *Public benefit.* Many nonstate actors, especially NGOs, claim a right to participate in debates by virtue of the fact that they are "public benefit" or "public interest" organizations. By definition, many assume civil society to be the defender of the public interest, in opposition to business and corrupt or partisan politicians. When considered analytically, however, the situation is not so clear. Civil society is the arena where the public interest is debated and negotiated, but the organizations that occupy it have different and sometimes conflicting views of what the public interest is and, especially, how to secure it through different combinations of public, private, and civic action (Edwards 2000a). There may be a conceptual difference between NGOs that lobby, for example, for gender equity in general and those that lobby for particular groups of women, but in practice it is difficult to categorize NGOs as either special interest groups or public interest groups. Similarly, a growing number of corporations claim to have a demonstrable public interest agenda and argue that unlike other nonstate actors they are well placed to deliver it. This does not mean that NGOs are the same as business, but it does mean that in principle business has a right to argue its case before legislative bodies that arbitrate between competing interests when making decisions.

Business and civil society organizations can answer their critics by facing up to the responsibilities that accompany their right to a voice. This means substantiating the criteria through which they claim legitimacy and being transparent and accountable for their actions. "NGOs do not have to be member controlled to be legitimate, but they do have to be accountable for their actions if their claims to legitimacy are to be maintained" (Edwards and Hulme 1996, p. 14). If legitimacy is claimed through representation, nonstate actors must be able to show who they represent and how they are held accountable to their constituents. If legitimacy is claimed through expertise, nonstate actors must be able to show how their positions have been derived and what depth of rigor has been used. If legitimacy is claimed through the ability to create change on the ground—the business argument—business must be able to show that it has the competencies and will and provide evidence on the ground that it has effectively applied both.

In addition, nonstate actors can build legitimacy by rooting their global activities in national and local action—for example, by pressuring national governments to represent the full range of public interests in international negotiations, by building dialogues with government that link local, national, and global activities, and by developing more democratic ways of deciding on strategies and messages. Jubilee 2000 provides some good examples of these innovations. In Uganda, for example, local NGOs developed a dialogue with the government on options for debt relief, supported by technical assistance from industrial country NGOs like Oxfam (Collins, Gariyo, and Burdon 2001). The results of this dialogue were then incorporated into the international debt campaign. Rede Bancos played a similar role in Brazil, joining forces with the Brazilian Congress to force the World Bank to publish its Country Assistance Strategy and agree to a public debate on the reform of social sector spending (Tussie and Tuozzo 2001). In the United Kingdom the World Development Movement (an NGO) persuaded the Scottish Parliament to hold its first-ever debate on the World Trade Organization's General Agreement on Trade in Services. These are ways of making global debates more responsive to ordinary citizens and of encouraging citizens to support the action needed to preserve global public goods. A similar example from business is the emergence of Instituto Ethos in Brazil as a significant player in driving through business-led local and national initiatives in response to daunting social and environmental challenges. In South Africa the business community created the New Business Initiative to channel a large, collective, one-time financial donation to support the government's social programs.

Above all, both enthusiasts and skeptics must be clear about how legitimacy is claimed and avoid conflating the requirements of different criteria, because doing so confuses the debate, makes solutions harder to find, and increases the likelihood that criticisms of legitimacy will be used to exclude rather than structure the involvement of dissenting voices. Any nonstate actor is entitled to voice an opinion. This is a basic human right that need only be subject to the minimum amount of regulation required to guard against slander, violence, or discrimination. No other legitimacy is required. But negotiating a treaty is a very different matter, and may require detailed rules to preserve genuine democracy in decisionmaking. In this case legitimacy through representation is essential. Transnational civil society is far from democratic, and few nonstate networks have democratic systems of governance and accountability. Nevertheless, the growing voice of nonstate actors adds essential checks and balances to the international system and helps ensure that excluded views are heard. Problems of legitimacy are not, therefore, a justification for turning back the tide of global citizen action. But they pose a challenge in structuring such action in ways that combat rather than accentuate existing social, economic, and political inequalities.

WAYS FORWARD: SOLUTIONS AND RECOMMENDATIONS

Solutions to the dilemmas of nonstate involvement in global governance must reconcile two potentially contradictory imperatives. The first is the need to give structure to the process in order to guard against the potentially distorting effects of those who shout loudest. The huge number and diversity of nonstate actors, and the inequalities of voice and resources among them, make rules, standards, and protocols essential. The second imperative is the need to ensure that these structures are as light and nonbureaucratic as possible, to avoid eroding the passion, spontaneity, and diversity that are the hallmarks of a healthy civil society (including nonviolent street protest) and a dynamic business community. Boxes 1 and 2 provide general principles to help in striking a balance between these two imperatives.

How might these principles be put into practice? Given the state of flux in the debate on global public goods, now is not the time for rigid or universal recommendations. Flexibility, innovation, experimentation, and learning from experience should be the top priorities, enthusiastically supported by governments and intergovernmental organizations. Some commentators have suggested that democratically elected nonstate bodies should be created to stand alongside intergovernmental structures, such as a Global People's Council to complement the UN General Assembly (Falk and Strauss 1997). The obvious obstacle is the question of representation and of how members would be elected across such a diverse set of constituencies. A number of options exist, including representation from national parliaments, direct elections from subnational constituencies (as in the European Parliament), and elections from nonstate bodies that already represent a constituency (such as labor unions, business federations, and national NGO umbrella bodies). However, there is little political support for these ideas from governments, which remain unconvinced of the rationale for parallel structures.

A less contentious alternative would be a series of nonrepresentative bodies designed to provide a space for debate on particular international institutions or regimes, with participants selected according to expertise or material interest. For example, a World Financial Forum could complement the International Monetary Fund, enabling nonstate actors to debate the Fund's policy and performance every two years, once the dust has settled on particular macroeconomic crises (Edwards 2000b). It is not difficult to envisage something similar on trade for the World Trade Organization, though in both cases such bodies would need to be given a real job—not just "talking shop"—and used to bring stakeholders together rather than separate them into the World Economic Forum, World Social Forum, and so on. (These other gatherings could obviously continue, but they serve a different purpose than joint decisionmaking.) These ideas enjoy more political support, but the resources and will to put them into practice are lacking. (The World Trade Organization's total budget is less than half the World Bank's budget for staff travel.)

Both of these proposals have strengths and weaknesses, but underlying them is a common conclusion: different models should be used for different contexts and purposes. The characteristics of a multistakeholder forum designed to resolve a dispute over a particular World Bank loan in Tanzania differ from those of a body designed to develop global policy guidelines on access to affordable medicines for HIV/AIDS. The criteria for nonstate involvement would need to vary

BOX 1

RULES OF THE ROAD FOR NONSTATE ACTORS

Nonstate actors can enhance their legitimacy by:
- Stating clearly in whose name they speak. (There is nothing wrong with nonstate actors speaking on their own behalf.)
- Ensuring transparency by providing information on their legal status, sources of funding, boards of trustees and advisers, and decisionmaking and reporting processes.
- Providing evidence of the added value they can bring to international debates and negotiations—for example, scientific or technical expertise, first-hand knowledge, or local experience.
- Offering information on past achievements and on how they will monitor the accuracy and effectiveness of their advice in order to promote accountability.
- Indicating links, forward and backward, to national and local policymaking processes.

In addition, networks of nonstate actors can strengthen their role in global governance by:
- Forming umbrella groups and federations to facilitate deliberations within civil society and the business community and, if desirable, formulate consolidated policy positions.
- Supporting the right of all people to be fairly represented—and to that end, self-monitoring the composition of civil society communities to encourage balanced participation (by race, gender, geography, and other relevant criteria) and providing financial support to nonstate actors with fewer resources.
- Offering advice to conference and agency secretariats on desirable consultation procedures and access by nonstate actors to international organizations.
- Adopting common codes of conduct—for example, a commitment to nonviolent advocacy and action.

Underlying these steps would be a clear recognition that the role of nonstate actors is not to replace governmental or intergovernmental decisionmaking but to complement it. Nonstate actors can present and deliberate on policy positions, but it is up to elected governments to balance different interests and arrive at policy decisions. Nonstate actors have a right to a voice but not necessarily to a vote in global governance.

BOX 2

Rules of the Road for International Organizations

To engage nonstate actors in global governance more systematically, international organizations may want to consider:

- Setting clear and transparent rules, equally applicable to all, for the accreditation of nonstate actors in different types of meetings.
- Applying all rules impartially, without political, religious, or other bias.
- Developing clear rules on nonstate actors' "right to know" (information disclosure policies).
- Reviewing and strengthening their accountability mechanisms to enable more effective engagement with nonstate actors.
- Wherever possible, convening multistakeholder dialogues between governments and nonstate actors around the same table.
- Facilitating nonstate actors' access to information about agendas and procedures before and during meetings and conferences and facilitating effective communication.
- Providing adequate financial support for nonstate actors' participation—especially to promote more equal participation by nonstate actors from developing countries.
- Experimenting with different ways of facilitating nonstate actors' involvement, such as scheduling joint meetings of governments and nonstate actors the day before intergovernmental sessions, using the "Arias formula" to give nonstate actors access to otherwise inaccessible intergovernmental bodies (such as the UN Security Council), and soliciting "alternative reports" from nonstate actors.

In addition, international organizations should consider establishing more joint bodies to facilitate open debate—such as a World Financial Forum to complement the work of the International Monetary Fund or a World Trade Forum linked to the World Trade Organization.

---

accordingly. Much more innovation is needed to develop and test such models so that the lessons of experience can be fed back into the international system. There are already many interesting experiments to build on, such as:

- Fully integrated decisionmaking bodies in place of structures reserved for governments, as long as clear and transparent processes exist to identify nonstate actors and their constituencies. The International Labour Organization shows that this is a possibility, at least in principle.
- Multistakeholder bodies that encourage honest debate among governments, business, and civil society organizations around the same table, without fear of co-optation. Many such bodies have already been organized around the implementation of Agenda 21 (Dodds 2001). A solid body of experience

exists to guide such efforts and help avoid the problems that can arise—such as the International Labour Organization's tripartite arrangements for considering labor standards (Hemmati 2001; Enayati and Hemmati 2000; Nelson and Zadek 2000).

- Meetings with nonstate actors on particular topics the day before official intergovernmental meetings, as in the committee process used by the Organisation for Economic Co-operation and Development or the "Arias formula" used to invite NGOs to address the UN Security Council outside its official sessions (Stanley Foundation 2001). Proposals already exist to extend NGO accreditation from the UN Economic and Social Council to the General Assembly for this purpose (United Nations 1999; WFUNA 2000).

- Solicitation of "alternative reports" from nonstate actors to be considered alongside country reports from governments. Some UN treaty bodies already do this (such as the Committee on the Rights of the Child of the UN Commission on Human Rights). The World Trade Organization could use the same principle to allow nonstate actors to submit *amicus curiae* (friend of the court) briefs to the appellate body (Charnovitz 2001).

- Internal codes of conduct that spell out minimum standards of behavior, accountability, and representation in global nonstate networks and coalitions. The U.K.-based New Economics Foundation has developed a "Code of Protest" that specifies nonviolence as a basic principle, alongside "remaining curious about perspectives other than our own" and "focusing on creative action" (that is, what NGOs are for, not just against).[3] Friends of the Earth–Europe has launched a similar set of "principles for peaceful protest." NGOs led by the U.S.-based Institute for Agriculture and Trade Policy worked to exchange their accredited places at the 2001 World Trade Organization ministerial meeting in Qatar with counterparts from developing countries, to ensure greater balance in NGO delegations. CIVICUS and the Hauser Center at Harvard University have produced a "legitimacy guide" that takes NGOs through the process of establishing their legitimacy (Brown 2001).

- Information and communication technology—such as "open space" technology and Webcasting—that facilitates discussion by and information inputs from large numbers of nonstate actors simultaneously or over short periods before an official gathering.

- Publicly accessible policies governing consultations with nonstate actors for all international agencies, meetings, and conferences.

Overall, there is a pressing need for regular forums at the international level that allow governments, intergovernmental institutions, civil society groups, and business to discuss these innovations and brainstorm new ideas. There is clearly a role for the United Nations here, especially since it has not been a target of the demonstrations that have affected the G-8 and the international financial institutions. The United Nations needs to be much more active in using its greater perceived public legitimacy to create opportunities for dialogue around these new "rules of the road." The next annual meeting between the United Nations and NGOs provides a good opportunity to host a discussion of this kind. Governments and intergovernmental organizations have the authority—and therefore the responsibility—to create structures that can promote nonstate involvement without falling prey to special interest politics.

CONCLUSION

Global public goods are arguably the most difficult public goods to provide in adequate, reasonably distributed quantities. Their scale is often daunting, and the large number of actors that need to reach agreement makes global governance a greater challenge than anything attempted before. But given the price of failure, this challenge cannot be evaded. Environmental security and social stability, to name just two examples, cannot be underprovided indefinitely without threatening the fabric of local and national communities and undermining the viability of businesses, the functioning of public agencies and democratic processes, and, ultimately, the lives of millions of people around the world.

In recent years nonstate actors have played a growing role in the provision of global public goods, and their influence will continue to increase. The issue is not whether but how best to realize the potential of nonstate actors and offset any associated costs. Nonstate actors offer enormous resources—in innovation and thought leadership, advocacy, popular mobilization, financial investment, and service delivery. But these resources do not come for free. All nonstate actors have institutional interests, ranging from narrow financial interests to broad, ideologically framed agendas for change. These interests may be invidious or even illegal, as with the production and sale of landmines targeted at civilians or the pursuit of sectarian interests using violent or otherwise unacceptable means. For the most part, however, the institutional interests of nonstate actors are perfectly legal, legitimate on their own terms, and openly declared and pursued.

In realizing the potential of nonstate actors, the core challenge is managing diverse interests so that the pursuit of some global public goods—such as health, education, security, and environmental protection—are not achieved at the cost of others—such as the fundamental rights of citizens to speak their minds, associate together, and participate in decisionmaking that affects them. This challenge is particularly pertinent for global public goods because the inability of current governance structures to secure and enforce agreements is most apparent at the international level. Indeed, that inability goes a long way toward explaining why nonstate actors have become so significant in the debate about and practice of delivering public goods across as well as within communities.

This is not a time for closure. The challenge of global governance needs to be faced head on, but solutions will take time to emerge. In the future the very notion of nonstate actors may seem outdated and unhelpful as today's emerging coalitions of businesses, nonprofit organizations, and public agencies become tomorrow's permanent institutions—blending the different forms of accountability that have historically separated state, civil society, and business. The proposals set out above are part of an emerging discussion about global governance that tries to frame the difficult problems associated with the provision of global public goods. The proposals emphasize the need to strike a balance between developing clear and enforceable rules and encouraging diversity, innovation, and the organic evolution of new patterns of governance. As they stand, the proposals reflect (rather than resolve) the tensions between the need to establish globally applicable rules and the need to create frameworks and processes that ensure that those rules can be constantly tested and challenged at the local and national levels.

The early years of the 21st century are witnessing a major transformation of world politics. The boundaries between direct and representative democracy and between local, national, and global governance are being tested and rearranged. These changes create new opportunities for the provision of global public goods, but we know little about how to manage them without succumbing to the pitfalls of statist inertia or special interest politics. The question for governments, business, and civil society is clear: do they have the courage and imagination to work out new answers in partnership—or only a mindset that sees a new space to be fought over for power or profit? The stakes are very high.

NOTES

1. One example is the link between war in the Democratic Republic of Congo and the continued mining in key parts of the country of coltan, a critical ingredient in the production of mobile phones (*The Guardian*, 20 August 2001, G2–3). Similarly, in 2001 corporate lobbyists tried to soften proposals for international certification of the diamond trade (Smillie and Gberie 2001).

2. Global Knowledge Partnership listserv, 19 December 2000.

3. Ed Mayo, openDemocracy Web site (http://www.openDemocracy.org.uk), 31 July 2001.

REFERENCES

Aaronson, Susan. 2001. *Taking Trade to the Streets: The Lost History of Public Efforts to Shape Globalization*. Ann Arbor: University of Michigan Press.

Anderson, Sarah, and John Cavanagh. 1996. *The Top 200: The Rise of Corporate Global Power*. Washington, D.C.: Institute of Policy Studies.

Anheier, Helmut, Marlies Glasius, and Mary Kaldor, eds. 2001. *Global Civil Society 2001*. Oxford: Oxford University Press.

Brown, L. David. 2001. "Civil Society Legitimacy: A Discussion Guide." In L. David Brown, ed., *Practice-Research Engagement and Civil Society in a Globalizing World.* Washington, D.C.: CIVICUS and Cambridge: Hauser Center on Non-Profit Organizations.

Bunch, Charlotte, with Peggy Antrobus, Samantha Frost, and Niamh Reilly. 2001. "International Networking for Women's Human Rights." In Michael Edwards and John Gaventa, eds., *Global Citizen Action.* Boulder, Colo.: Lynne Rienner Publishers.

Chapman, Jennifer. 2001. "What Makes International Campaigns Effective? Lessons from India and Ghana." In Michael Edwards and John Gaventa, eds., *Global Citizen Action.* Boulder, Colo.: Lynne Rienner Publishers.

Charnovitz, Steve. 2001. "Opening the WTO to Non-Governmental Interests." *Fordham International Law Journal* 24 (1–2): 173–216.

Collins, Carole, Zie Gariyo, and Tony Burdon. 2001. "Jubilee 2000: Citizen Action across the North-South Divide." In Michael Edwards and John Gaventa, eds., *Global Citizen Action.* Boulder, Colo.: Lynne Rienner Publishers.

Denny, Charlotte. 2001. "Row as WTO Lobbyists Keep Out the Poor." *The Guardian,* 3 September.

Dodds, Felix. 2001. "From the Corridors of Power to the Global Negotiating Table: The NGO Steering Committee of the Commission on Sustainable Development." In Michael Edwards and John Gaventa, eds., *Global Citizen Action.* Boulder, Colo.: Lynne Rienner Publishers.

Edwards, Michael. 1999. *Future Positive: International Cooperation in the 21st Century.* London: Earthscan.

———. 2000a. "Enthusiasts, Tacticians and Skeptics: The World Bank, Civil Society and Social Capital." *The Kettering Review* 18 (1): 39–51.

———. 2000b. NGO Rights and Responsibilities: A New Deal for Global Governance. London: Foreign Policy Centre.

Edwards, Michael, and John Gaventa, eds. 2001. *Global Citizen Action.* Boulder, Colo.: Lynne Rienner Publishers.

Edwards, Michael, and David Hulme. 1996. *Beyond the Magic Bullet: NGO Performance and Accountability in the Post–Cold War World.* London: Earthscan and West Hartford, Conn.: Kumarian Press.

Elkington, John. 1998. *Cannibals with Forks: The Triple Bottom Line of the 21st Century.* Oxford: Capstone.

Enayati, Jasmin, and Minu Hemmati. 2000. *Multi-Stakeholder Processes: Examples, Principles and Strategies: Workshop Report.* London: UNED Forum.

Falk, Richard, and Andrew Strauss. 1997. "For a Global People's Assembly." *International Herald Tribune,* 14 November.

Florini, Ann M., ed. 2000. *The Third Force—The Rise of Transnational Civil Society.*

Washington, D.C.: Carnegie Endowment for International Peace and Tokyo: Japan Center for International Exchange.

Harper, Caroline. 2001. "Do the Facts Matter? NGOs, Research and International Advocacy." In Michael Edwards and John Gaventa, eds., *Global Citizen Action.* Boulder, Colo.: Lynne Rienner Publishers.

Hawken, Paul, Amory Lovins, and Hunter L. Lovins. 1999. *Natural Capitalism: Creating the Next Industrial Revolution.* Boston, Mass.: Little Brown.

Hemmati, Minu, with contributions from Felix Dodds, Jasmin Enayati, and Jan McHarry. 2001. *Multi-Stakeholder Participation: A Methodological Framework.* London: UNED Forum.

ISEA (Institute of Social and Ethical AccountAbility). 2000. *Innovation through Partnership.* London. [http://www.accountability.org.uk].

Kaul, Inge, Isabelle Grunberg, and Marc A. Stern, eds. 1999. *Global Public Goods: International Cooperation in the 21st Century.* New York: Oxford University Press.

Keane, John. 2001. "Global Civil Society." In *The Global Civil Society Yearbook.* London: London School of Economics, Center for the Study of Civil Society.

Keck, Margaret, and Kathryn Sikkink. 1998. *Activists beyond Borders: Advocacy Networks in International Politics.* Ithaca, N.Y.: Cornell University Press.

Korten, David. 1999. *The Post-Corporate World: Life after Capitalism.* West Hartford, Conn.: Kumarian Press and Berret-Koehler.

LaFeber, Walter. 1999. *Michael Jordan and the New Global Capitalism.* New York: W. W. Norton.

Nelson, Jane, and Simon Zadek. 2000. *Partnership Alchemy: New Social Partnerships in Europe.* Copenhagen: Copenhagen Centre. [http://www.copenhagencentre. org].

Nye, Joseph, and John Donahue, eds. 2001. Governance in a Globalizing World. Washington, D.C.: Brookings Institution Press.

Patel, Sheela, Joel Bolnick, and Diana Mitlin. 2001. "Squatting on the Global Highway: Community Exchanges for Urban Transformation." In Michael Edwards and John Gaventa, eds., *Global Citizen Action.* Boulder, Colo.: Lynne Rienner Publishers.

Ruggie, John. 1983. "International Regimes, Transactions and Change: Embedded Liberalism in the Postwar Economic Order." In Stephen Krasner, ed., *International Regimes.* Ithaca, N.Y.: Cornell University Press.

Scholte, Jan Aart. 2001. "The IMF and Civil Society: An Interim Progress Report." In Michael Edwards and John Gaventa, eds., *Global Citizen Action.* Boulder, Colo.: Lynne Rienner Publishers.

Scott, Matthew. 2001. "Danger—Landmines! NGO-Government Collaboration in the Ottawa Process." In Michael Edwards and John Gaventa, eds., *Global Citizen Action.* Boulder, Colo.: Lynne Rienner Publishers.

Shell International. 1999. *The Shell Report 1999: People, Planet and Profits—An Act of Commitment.* London.

Smillie, Ian, and Lansana Gberie. 2001. "Dirty Diamonds and Civil Society." Background paper for CIVICUS World Assembly, Vancouver, Canada, 19–23 August.

Stanley Foundation. 2001. *Report of the Symposium on UN Civil Society Outreach.* New York.

Tussie, Diana, and Maria Fernanda Tuozzo. 2001. "Opportunities and Limits for Civil Society Participation in Multilateral Lending Operations: Lessons from Latin America." In Michael Edwards and John Gaventa, eds., *Global Citizen Action.* Boulder, Colo.: Lynne Rienner Publishers.

UNCTAD (United Nations Conference on Trade and Development). 1998. *World Investment Report 1998: Trends and Determinants.* New York.

UNDP (United Nations Development Programme). 1999. *Human Development Report 1999.* New York: Oxford University Press.

United Nations. 1999. *Views of Member States, Members of the Specialized Agencies, Observers, Intergovernmental and Non-Governmental Organizations from all Regions on the Report of the Secretary-General on Arrangements and Practices for the Interaction of Non-Governmental Organizations in All Activities of the United Nations System: Report of the Secretary-General.* Document A/54/329. New York.

Utting, Peter. 2000. *Business Responsibility for Sustainable Development.* Geneva: United Nations Research Institute on Social Development.

Weisbrot, Mark, Dean Baker, Egor Kraev, and Judy Chen. 2001. *The Scorecard on Globalisation 1980–2000: Twenty Years of Diminished Progress.* Washington, D.C.: Centre for Economic and Policy Research.

WFUNA (World Federation of United Nations Associations). 2000. *Resolution on NGO Accreditation to the General Assembly.* New York.

Wheeler, David, and Maria Sillanpää. 1997. *The Stakeholder Corporation: A Blueprint for Maximising Stakeholder Value.* London: Pitman.

World Bank. 1997. *World Development Indicators 1997.* Washington, D.C.

———. 2002. *World Development Indicators 2002.* Washington, D.C.

Zadek, Simon. 2000. *Ethical Trade Futures.* London: New Economics Foundation.

———. 2001a. *The Civil Corporation: The New Economy of Corporate Citizenship.* London: Earthscan.

———. 2001b. *Endearing Myths, Enduring Truths: Enabling Partnerships between Business, Civil Society and the Public Sector.* Washington, D.C.: Business Partners for Development. [http://www.bpdweb.org].

———. 2001c. *Third Generation Corporate Citizenship: Public Policy and Business in Society.* London: Foreign Policy Centre and AccountAbility.

Zadek, Simon, and Peter Raynard. 2001. *The Digital Divide.* London: BT plc. [http://www.groupbt.com/betterworld/TheDigitalDivide.htm].

Zadek, Simon, Peter Pruzan, and Richard Evans, eds. 1998. *Building Corporate AccountAbility: Emerging Practices in Social and Ethical Accounting, Auditing, and Reporting.* London: Earthscan.

Zarsky, Lyuba. 1999. "Havens, Halos and Spaghetti: Untangling the Evidence about the Relationship between Foreign Direct Investment and the Environment." Nautilus Institute for Security and Sustainable Development, Berkeley, Calif.

THE GOVERNANCE

OF THE INTERNATIONAL

MONETARY FUND

ARIEL BUIRA

At the end of World War II the Bretton Woods conference gave birth to the International Monetary Fund (IMF) and the International Bank for Reconstruction and Development—better known as the World Bank. These two international financial institutions have come to exert a major—some would say dominant—influence on economic policy in developing countries over the last half century. During the nineties these two institutions have placed significant importance on governance issues among their member countries. The IMF, in particular, has given increased attention to such issues, following the approval of the Guidance Note on governance by the Executive Board[1] five years ago (IMF 1997). The promotion of transparency and accountability are now at the core of the IMF's efforts to ensure the good use of public resources as well as the domestic ownership of IMF programs (IMF 2001b). In this respect, transparency and accountability are important global public goods in an increasingly interdependent and democratic world. These two factors facilitate trust and confidence, bolstering cooperation within the context of the international financial system.

In recent years the IMF has developed and applied its instruments for promoting these objectives to an extent well beyond what was envisaged at the time the Guidance Note was approved. Indeed, the IMF helps countries identify any weaknesses that may exist in their institutional and regulatory frameworks that could give rise to poor governance; it then provides support in the design and implementation of remedial reforms. Given the strength of vested interests that benefit from the lack of transparency and accountability in these situations, overcoming these weaknesses often requires that the countries undertake significant structural reforms. By the very nature of its work then, the IMF exerts considerable influence over the majority of its 183 member countries, on such economic

Preparation of this chapter was financed in part by a grant from the OPEC Fund for International Development. It is a condensed version of a paper presented at the September 2000 meeting of the Intergovernmental Group of 24 on International Monetary Affairs and is based on and develops several themes in a paper prepared for the United Nations Development Programme (UNDP).

and politically sensitive matters as wage policies, taxation and public expenditure levels, public sector prices and tariffs, subsidies and pensions, privatisation policies, the exchange regime and the exchange rate, interest rates and monetary policy, trade policy, financial sector regulations and others. With resources of over $280 billion and an expanded mandate, the IMF is probably today the most powerful of all international institutions.

In view of its influence, it is of interest to consider to what extent the IMF's own governance meets the standards of transparency and accountability required to ensure the ownership of programs by member countries and the prudent and effective use of international public resources. This chapter takes up that question, and begins with an analysis of the IMF's power structure and of the issues raised by its current patterns of decisionmaking. Given the similarities between the IMF's and the World Bank's composition of shareholding and the resulting decisionmaking structures, this analysis of the IMF can also be applied to the World Bank.

CURRENT PATTERNS OF DECISIONMAKING

The decisionmaking patterns of the IMF member countries involve three key areas: the distribution of voting powers, the rules for decisionmaking, and the management structure within the IMF. Each of these dimensions is examined below in terms of its potential and actual effects on IMF policies and operations.

Voting powers

Two aspects are remarkable in the distribution of voting power in the IMF. One is the skewed distribution of voting rights between industrial and developing countries, due in part to the diminished role of basic votes relative to quota-based votes. The other is that some of the variables used to determine quotas—a crucial element of voting powers—have not changed in more than 50 years. Both facts suggest that voting powers have not kept pace with changes in the global economy, undermining the IMF's capacity to pursue its cooperative mandate.

Basic votes and quota-based votes. IMF members do not have equal voting power. Instead, they have weighted voting, a departure from the traditional practice of international organizations. To clarify, the vote of an IMF member has two components. Each member has 250 basic votes simply by virtue of its membership, as a symbolic recognition of the principle of the legal equality of states. Each member also has one additional vote for every 100,000 Special Drawing Rights (SDRs) of its quota. Because the number of basic votes has not changed with successive quota increases, the ratio of basic votes to total votes has declined from 12.4 percent of the voting power of the countries participating in the Bretton Woods conference (IMF 1993, schedule A) to 2.1 percent today, despite the entry of 135 new member countries. In fact, as a proportion of the total, the basic votes of the original members have declined from more than 12 percent to less than 0.4 percent as a result of a 37-fold increase in total quotas. This has changed the power structure of the IMF since the importance of the basic vote of a country is inversely related to the size of its economy, as basic votes represent a substantially higher proportion of the voting power of small countries.

To illustrate: A country with a quota of 10 million SDRs would be entitled to 350 votes—100 votes due to its quota size and 250 basic votes for being a member. If the size of quotas is multiplied by ten, the country will have 1000 votes on account of its quota and 250 basic votes, for a total of 1250 votes. Thus the share of basic votes declines from over 70 percent to 20 percent of the total. Recall that in 1945 there were 14 countries—almost a third of the membership—whose quota was $10 million or less, and 28 countries—more than half the total—whose quotas were $50 million or less. With the passage of time, inflation and economic growth have combined to increase the size of the quotas. But since the number of basic votes has remained constant, their relative proportion to the total has declined, emasculating the role of basic votes and the relative influence of developing countries.

Determination of quotas. Because members' quotas are the main factor determining voting rights, the process for setting such quotas should also be examined. It has been said that the quotas of the United States, the United Kingdom, the Soviet Union, and China were politically determined at the Bretton Woods conference. Raymond Mikesell, who was asked by the U.S. Treasury to estimate the first quotas, writes:

> In mid-April 1943, White [i.e. Harry Dexter White, chief international economist at the U.S. Treasury in 1942–44] called me to his office and asked that I prepare a formula for the . . . quotas that would be based on the members' gold and dollar holdings, national incomes, and foreign trade. He gave no instructions on the weights to be used, but I was to give the United States a quota of approximately $2.9 billion; the United Kingdom (including its colonies), about half the U.S. quota; the Soviet Union, an amount just under that of the United Kingdom; and China, somewhat less. He also wanted the total of the quotas to be about $10 billion. White's major concern was that our military allies (President Roosevelt's Big Four) should have the largest quotas, with a ranking on which the president and the secretary of state had agreed. . . . I confess to having exercised a certain amount of freedom in making these estimates in order to achieve the predetermined quotas. (1994, pp. 22–23)

Subsequently, at the meeting of the Committee on Quotas, Mikesell was asked to explain the basis for his quota estimates, and he further writes:

> *I had anticipated this request and gave a rambling twenty-minute seminar on the factors taken into account in calculating the quotas, but I did not reveal the formula. I tried to make the process appear as scientific as possible, but the delegates were intelligent enough to know that the process was more political than scientific. (1994, pp. 35–36)*

Given these historical facts, it is remarkable that—with only some adjustments in the weighting and definition of the main variables—the IMF continues to use the original formula for determining members' quotas. It is certainly understandable that the lack of equity and rationality in the quota criteria continues to cause controversy and mistrust among members today, just as it did 50 years ago. The original formula is now combined with four other formulas, which give different weights to the same variables, and an element of discretion is used in selecting the formula to be applied in each case. (At times, the average of the various calculations is used to set a country's quota.) It is therefore not surprising that current quotas are far from representative of the actual sizes of economies—of their ability to contribute to the IMF or of their importance in the world economy.

This can be easily illustrated by the fact that such large countries as Brazil, Mexico, and the Republic of Korea, with real GNPs and populations much larger than those of Belgium, the Netherlands, and Switzerland, had quotas in 1999 that were only a fraction of those countries' and fewer votes (table 1). Thus their share in decisionmaking is not commensurate with the systemic importance of their economies.

It would be difficult to argue that the quota of China, the world's second largest economy in purchasing power parity (PPP) terms, should be smaller than that of the Netherlands and similar to that of Belgium. Or that Belgium's quota should be 52 percent larger than that of Brazil and 78 percent larger than that of Mexico. Moreover, it appears that many of the major differences arise between the quotas of industrial and developing countries and are not simply the result of history. For Switzerland, which recently joined the IMF, the quota was determined in line with those of industrial countries with similar economic structures and levels of development. As a result the distribution of quotas is skewed, as more recent quota numbers show (table 2).

Quotas are important not just because they confer decisionmaking power but also because they determine access to financing. But for some exceptional cases, a member can borrow only up to a total of 300 per cent of its quota under regular facilities. Thus the small quotas of developing countries limit both their share of voting power and their access to IMF resources. The consequences of the imbal-

TABLE 1

IMF quotas and GNPs for selected countries

Country	Quota, effective January 1999[a] (billions of Special Drawing Rights)	Purchasing power parity GNP, 1998 (billions of U.S. dollars)	GNP, 1998 (billions of U.S. dollars)
Russian Federation	5.945	580.3	337.9
Netherlands	5.162	339.3	388.7
China	4.687	3,983.6	928.9
Belgium	4.607	239.7	259
Switzerland	3.458	189.1	284.8
Brazil	3.036	1,021.4	758
Mexico	2.586	785.8	380.9
Denmark	1.643	126.4	176.4
Korea, Republic of	1.634	569.3	369.9

a. Following the IMF's Eleventh General Review of Quotas.
Source: IMF, various issues, *International Financial Statistics;* World Bank, various issues, *World Development Report.*

TABLE 2

Distribution of IMF quotas by country group, 2001

Country group	Special Drawing Rights (millions)	Share of total (percent)
24 industrial countries	130,567	61.4
Oil-exporting countries	20,307	9.6
Non-oil-exporting developing countries	61,527	29.0
Total	212,401	100.0

Source: IMF, various issues, *International Financial Statistics.*

ance of power have been further aggravated by the fact that since the late 1970s no industrial country has resorted to IMF support. This has changed the nature of the IMF: it has gone from being a credit cooperative from which all members draw resources from time to time, and therefore have an interest in credit being available on reasonable terms and conditions, to being an institution formed by two distinct groups of countries—industrial country creditors and developing country debtors. Hence, the fact that for over twenty years the IMF has only lent to developing countries has come to mean that the creditor countries try to lend as little as possible and therefore favor a hardening of conditionality, while the borrower countries, generally wanting to have ample access to financing on easy terms, tend to defend their short-term interests. The objectivity and impartiality of the Board,[2] assumed by the Articles of Agreement has been eroded to a significant extent.[3]

More troubling, some past changes in the quotas of the main industrial countries were not based simply on the formulas—questionable as they may be—but on political criteria. In the Ninth General Review of Quotas, for example, Germany and Japan were assigned the same quota (giving both countries the second largest quotas after the United States) even though at the time Japan's economy was twice the size of Germany's. Similarly, France and the United Kingdom were given the third largest quotas even though Italy's economy was larger than the United Kingdom's. More recently, the IMF approved China's request to increase its quota (following the resumption of Chinese sovereignty over Hong Kong), which has now been made equal—to the last decimal point—to Canada's: 6,369.2 million SDRs. Yet one would be hard pressed to find similarities between their two economies; China's economy is larger than Canada's whether measured in purchasing power parity terms or in terms of market exchange rates (see table A.2 in the appendix). The IMF's imbalanced allocations of quotas and voting powers necessarily raise questions about the legitimacy of access to its resources and of the decisions it makes.

Decisionmaking rules

The IMF's Articles of Agreement stipulate that some decisions require a qualified majority of the votes cast; that is, a particular proportion of the votes. At the Bretton Woods conference it was proposed that qualified majorities should be required in only two cases (one being quota adjustments), yet the subsequently accepted Articles of Agreement required qualified majorities for decisions in nine areas. With the first amendment to the Articles of Agreement, the number of these decisions rose to 18; with the second amendment, to 53. Forty of these are Executive Board decisions; 13 are Board of Governors[4] decisions.

The obvious explanation for this increase is the desire to protect some particular interest that might be affected by such decisions; decisions subject to a qualified majority can be taken only with the consent of the members having a high proportion of the total votes. Currently, the United States has 17.16 percent of total votes, Japan 6.16 percent, Germany 6.02 percent, and France and the United Kingdom 4.97 percent each, for a combined total of about 39 percent.[5] If the votes cast by the Belgian, Canadian, Dutch, Finnish, Italian, and Swiss executive directors are added, the total exceeds 60 percent (IMF 2001a). The result is that decisions on 18 subjects requiring 85 percent of the total vote can be vetoed by one member country alone. Decisions on 21 other questions that require a 70 percent majority can be collectively vetoed by the five countries with the most voting power.

Special majorities have been used to block decisions supported by an absolute majority of votes on increases in the size of the IMF (that is, quota increases) and in SDR allocations, sales of the IMF's vast gold holdings, and policies on access to IMF resources. This special-majority requirement often has the effect of inhibiting even the discussion of important issues that would be difficult to resolve. The developing countries have argued that because voting itself is weighted—a situation that favors the industrial countries in decisionmaking—there should be no need for special majorities. However, the countries that for various reasons have favored such majorities have not been prepared to do away with them.

Management structure

In principle, the staff and management of the IMF are subject to the political control of—and accountable to—the Board of Governors and its representatives, the executive directors. Thus the line of control and supervision runs from the Board of Governors, formed by the ministers of finance and central bank governors of member countries, to the executive directors who represent them, to the IMF management whom the executive directors appoint, and finally to the staff whom the management supervises. This management structure has three main weaknesses, involving the selection of the managing director, the role and functions of the executive directors, and the composition and background of the IMF staff.

The managing director. Formally, the Executive Board, on which all member countries are represented, appoints the managing director. However, there is an unwritten understanding among major industrial countries by which the United States appoints the president of the World Bank, while Europe appoints the managing director of the IMF. As a result a handful of European officials—primarily British, French, and German—feel that it is their prerogative to appoint the managing director, with the consent of the United States but little consultation with the rest of the membership. The widely publicized discussions and disagreements between the U.S. and German governments leading up to the appointment of the managing director in 2000—with a touch of black comedy, as the United States rejected the first German candidate—should have ended all illusions about the participation of most countries in the process. But as the *New York Times* editorialized, "The managing director is too important to be chosen in secret by a few self-selected European countries" (22 November 1999).

The selection process has to be opened up, considering the pivotal role the managing director plays in leading the IMF. Candidates for the position should state what their policies would be and how they would guide the IMF to attain its purposes. Since IMF operations are entirely with developing countries and transition economies, it is neocolonial to assume that only a European is capable of becoming managing director. It is also entirely implausible to suppose that there is no highly qualified developing country national who could take the position.

The issue is doubly important because the managing director and senior staff can in practice be held accountable only by the governments of a handful of countries.

The executive directors. Executive directors play two roles: they are national representatives, and they are IMF officials whose salaries are paid by the IMF. On the one hand they collectively determine the policies under which the organization is run and appoint the managing director, who in turn appoints and supervises the staff. On the other hand they represent member countries.

However, directors representing developing countries—most of which turn to the IMF for financial support from time to time—have a limited ability to hold the staff and, much less, the management accountable, for two reasons. The first reason for this is their limited voting power, which means that they have little say on staff promotion or removal. No less important, the second reason is that being the representatives of petitioner governments limits these directors' ability to question the staff. They are particularly limited in their ability to question staff in their area departments, since they have to rely on these same staff to prepare the papers presenting their (developing country directors') countries' case for financial support to the Board.

Not wishing to diminish their own effectiveness in securing financial support for the countries they represent often means directors will not challenge or antagonize senior staff, much less management, on whose judgment and goodwill their countries have to rely. A sensitive issue from the standpoint of transparency and accountability arises with the requirement of prior action or "pre-conditions" imposed by the staff and management on a country requesting a program, without the knowledge of the Board. In practice, the ability of developing country directors to exercise effective control over staff and management is seriously impaired. Indeed, directors who try to exercise their supervisory role run the risk that the staff or management complain about them to their authorities at the time financial support is negotiated, giving rise to a particularly delicate situation for directors from third countries, since the confidence of the authorities in them may be undermined.[6]

Furthermore, given their limited voting power, developing countries are forced to join other countries to muster a sufficient number of votes to elect an executive director to represent them on the Board. Consequently, developing country constituencies or "chairs" representing several countries usually rotate the positions of executive director and alternate executive director every two years among the several member countries they represent. While this practice permits a wide access of countries to the Board, it has two serious disadvantages. The first is that the rotation often means that newly appointed directors are not immediately familiar with the complexities and the policies of the IMF; they often need a year to become familiar with the modus operandi of the institution. It follows that in policy discussions they are at a disadvantage relative to the staff and to industrial country directors, with their greater tenure and experience. The second disadvantage of this rotating arrangement is that the staff, whose appointments are permanent, know that these directors will normally depart at the end of the two-year cycle. So if the directors request changes in the presentation of annual consultation reports (or on policy matters) the staff do not favor, the staff can simply wait them out until the Director in question departs from the scene.

Finally, in line with the imbalanced distribution of quotas noted earlier, country representation on the Board is necessarily skewed. Thus, while 24 industrial countries, none of which has an IMF-supported program, are at any one time represented by 10 or 11 executive directors—who generally receive considerable technical support from specialized offices in their capitals and are able to devote much of their time to policy issues—42 African countries (excluding Arab countries) are represented by only 2 executive directors. Consequently, those Directors each representing 20 countries or more are barely able to attend to the copious amount of bilateral business with the IMF of the countries they represent, several of which may be engaged in programs or the negotiation of programs at the same time. This provides little time to devote to the consideration of systemic policy issues.[7]

The staff. The IMF staff includes nationals from most (127 of the 183) member countries, but there has been a long-standing predominance of industrial country nationals among management and senior officers. These accounted for 26 of 31 such officials in 1996, improving slightly to 22 of 29 in March 2001 (IMF, various years). Moreover, since numerous developing country nationals in senior positions went directly from a US university to a position at the IMF, they cannot be said to have brought the experience and sensibility that come from work in their own countries. In addition, training in economics at the better graduate schools in Canada, the United Kingdom, and the United States—common among a large proportion of the staff—provides remarkable homogeneity in economic thought. This common approach facilitates IMF operations, but at times it may lead to a certain lack of pragmatism and innovation that creates difficulties in different environments.[8]

POLICY IMPLICATIONS

Clearly, the current power structure places a small number of countries in a dominant position, impairing the objectivity of IMF decisions and recommendations. In light of the power structure of the IMF and keeping in mind that economic policy is not an exact science, it is inconceivable that the staff are not influenced by the interests of the major quota-holding countries.

For example, the dramatic volatility of capital flows and the high costs of the Mexican crisis of 1994–95 should have been sufficient to lead the IMF to take a careful second look at the risks implied by full capital account liberalization and the integration of developing countries (particularly those without strong banking systems) into international capital markets. The IMF continued to vigorously pursue the amendment to the Articles of Agreement to demand the opening of the capital account of developing countries. Only well after the Asian crisis of 1997–98 did the IMF concede that such crises do raise questions about the desirability of completely free capital movements and full capital account convertibility (IMF 2000a). This policy shift came only after wide recognition of and broad public discontent with serious mistakes in the IMF's performance during the Asian crisis (Sachs and Radelet 1998; Bhagwati 2000).

However, belated correction of ineffective policies is not the only symptom of this problem. Technically questionable programs have sometimes been approved in order to support governments allied with the interests of the dominant country or countries, thereby placing the resources of the international community at risk. Furthermore, these cases have a demoralizing effect on the IMF staff, who are made to recognize that there are "special cases" based on non-economic considerations (Bordo and James 2000; Krueger 1997). The effectiveness of the staff could therefore be compromised, as they may impose a degree of self-censorship.[9] Thus, it is difficult, if not impossible, to examine and analyze objectively initiatives or proposals that go against the interests of the major industrial countries.

These facts cause even more concern given the international financial environment. In recent years, with the increase in capital mobility, developing countries have become much more vulnerable than in the past. They have frequently faced massive capital outflows leading to financial crises. The financial support required in such cases is much larger than that necessitated by traditional balance of payments crises and greatly in excess, both in absolute terms and as a proportion of quotas, of that contemplated by IMF policies. Although in a number of well known cases such exceptional support has been forthcoming—Mexico received $48 billion of which SDR 12.3 billion ($17 billion) came from the IMF; the Republic of Korea $57 billion, of which SDR 15.5 billion ($22 billion) came from the IMF; Indonesia $43 billion; and Thailand $17 billion—this support has been decided on an ad hoc, discretionary basis by major industrial countries outside the framework of IMF policies. Of course, such arrangements are unlikely to comply with the principle of equality of treatment for all members.

Moreover, it would seem that countries with the largest quotas—the creditor countries of the IMF—have opted to reduce their relative contributions and their exposure to IMF borrowing, thereby reducing the size of the IMF relative to world trade (table 3). As a result IMF quotas were equivalent to barely 6 percent of world imports in 1998, compared with almost 60 percent in 1944. Consequently, the

TABLE 3

IMF quotas as a proportion of world imports and GDP, selected years, 1944–98
(percent)

	1944	1950	1965	1970	1978	1990	1998
Quotas as a proportion of imports	58	17	15	14	9	6	6
Quotas as a proportion of GDP	4	2	2	2	1	1	1

Source: IMF 2000b, table 7.

IMF has inadequate resources to provide sufficient credit to member countries suffering payment imbalances.

As IMF resources have not kept pace with financing needs, countries do not know how much, if any, financial support may be forthcoming In fact, at times of crisis it is very difficult for any country to obtain significant financing from the markets and normally countries cannot. In such circumstances, in the absence of sufficient financial support from the IMF, bilateral assistance may come with conditions and strings attached that have no bearing on the resolution of the crisis. For example, support for the Republic of Korea was made conditional on that country implementing more than ninety structural reform measures, including allowing foreign investors to purchase Korean businesses, opening the domestic financial sector to foreign banks and insurance companies, and liberalizing imports of Japanese cars. Regarding this issue, Feldstein (1998, p. 4 of electronic copy) writes, "A nation's desperate need for short-term financial help does not give the IMF the moral right to substitute its technical judgments for the outcomes of the nation's political process."

As has become clear, the governance of the IMF falls short of its standards and recommendations for transparency and accountability in the programs of its member countries. Transparency requires that decisions be the result of open discussions with broad participation. Accountability requires that those making decisions face up to their consequences. Legitimacy requires that the views and interests of all IMF members be given appropriate consideration. Only with transparency, accountability, and legitimacy can international institutions like the IMF hope to reconcile each country's political and economic objectives with the international community's wider interests, including the provision of global public goods like financial stability and market efficiency. These objectives will not be attained if decisions are made by a small group of industrial countries meeting outside the purview of the IMF or if the power structure in the IMF is decidedly imbalanced. This situation must be rectified.

OPTIONS FOR GOVERNANCE REFORM

The decisionmaking patterns in the IMF illustrate a problem facing other multilateral institutions: the IMF was founded during an era in which most developing countries were still under colonial rule and economies were less interdependent than today. Initially evolving under a marked east-west divide, the international political and economic environment has now achieved unprecedented integration that has led more countries to seek membership in multilateral institutions such as the IMF. But the expansion of the IMF's membership has not led to a broadening of its decisionmaking base.

Recognizing these potential disparities, in 1999 the IMF's managing director asked an independent group of external experts—led by Richard Cooper, professor of economics at Harvard University—to provide the Executive Board with a report on the adequacy of the quota formulas, including proposals for changes where appropriate. But the "Cooper report" (IMF 2000b) left unresolved many issues pertaining to IMF governance. Thus the following reforms—restructuring the Executive Board, revising quota formulas, and restoring the role of basic votes—are offered in hopes of contributing to a more effective IMF.

Restructuring the Executive Board

The representation at the Executive Board could be undertaken in a way that an increase in the number of directors representing developing countries be matched by an equal reduction in the number of directors from industrial countries. The region with the greatest number of representatives on the Board is Europe, which currently holds eight chairs. Thus it is the obvious candidate for a reduction in the number of the chairs it holds. An additional reason for suggesting a reduction in the number of European directors is the process of unification that has resulted in a monetary union among 12 European countries, all now with a common interest rate and exchange rate policy. While one might think that all members of the European Monetary Union could be represented by one director, it would suffice to reduce the number of their directors to, say, two or three.[10]

Furthermore, in order to be able to give adequate attention to the needs of countries represented, no executive director should represent more than, say, 12–15 countries. In addition, the staff in the offices of executive directors representing more than one country should be strengthened significantly, in proportion to the number of countries represented. These measures should permit directors representing large constituencies to play a more active and effective role in policy discussions.

While important, increased voice at the Board for developing countries is not by itself sufficient. This author recalls occasions when directors representing a major industrial country would not engage in the discussion of an issue that they could lose on grounds of logic. The directors would simply state that, after listening to the arguments, they had not changed their position on the issue. Thus restructuring of the Executive Board should be accompanied by other reforms.

Revising quota formulas

A more technical aspect of reform relates to quota formulas. The work of the Quota Formula Review Group (QFRG), which produced the Cooper report, has prompted consideration of the issues involved in the revision of the quota formulas and of the variables that should be included. Despite the shortcomings of the formula proposed, the initiative for the simplification and increasing the transparency of formula posited by the QFRG has considerable merit. However, the proposals from the QFRG can be improved upon. Some suggestions are presented below:

- *Relate total quotas to world trade and capital movements or to world GDP.* A first approach would be to ensure that the size of the IMF should not fall below an agreed proportion of world trade or of world GDP. Note that simply establishing a ratio of say 15 percent of imports would more than double IMF resources, enabling it to reduce the costs of adjustment to members, making the institution far more relevant to their problems. Total quotas could be adjusted more or less automatically at three-year intervals to keep them from lagging significantly behind the expansion of the international economy. Additionally, the pattern of capital flows to prospective borrowing countries—all the IMF members except some 22 industrial countries—could also be considered in determining countries' potential need for IMF support.[11]

- *Include additional elements in the variable that measures the external vulnerability of countries.* The inclusion in the quota formula of a measure of openness of the economy and of the dependence of countries on international financial markets would appear to be necessary, considering the volatility of short-term capital flows, which as is widely recognized, has been the determining factor in the financial crises suffered by emerging market economies over the last few years.

- *Use PPP-based GDP estimates in the quota formulas.* For computation of the quotas, the figures used should be the PPP-based GDP estimates, since these are more stable and are unbiased compared to market exchange rate-based GDP. (See the appendix for a more thorough discussion of this issue.) More importantly, this should help correct the current underestimation of the economic size of developing countries and emerging market economies in the current quotas, as well as improve their representation at the Executive Board. There is no doubt that given the small size of quotas to GDP and that only a portion is contributed in hard currency (U.S. dollars), virtually all countries will be able to contribute to the IMF—which in any case is part of their reserves.[12] Broadening the stake of developing countries in the IMF should also increase their contribution and lessen the concern of current creditor countries over the risk of IMF credits.

Restoring basic votes to their original function

This reform measure could be initiated by increasing basic votes to an agreed proportion of total voting rights, say, 20 percent. Provision should then be made that in the future, basic votes will increase in the same proportion as total quotas, in order to preserve its role in the decisionmaking structure. It is important to note that the preservation of the share of basic votes in the total would not be an exceptional practice among international institutions. For instance, Article 33-1 in the Articles of Agreement of the Asian Development Bank provides that the relative importance of basic votes will remain constant over time as a proportion of the total vote. Similarly, the Articles of Agreement of the Inter-American Development Bank provide that no increase in the subscription of any member will become effective if it would reduce the voting power of certain countries or groups of countries below a given percentage of the total (IMF 2000b).

CONCLUSION

The world has changed considerably since the Bretton Woods conference of 1944. Developing countries now account for a much larger share of the world economy, with China, India, Brazil, Mexico, and Indonesia among the world's 15 largest economies measured in real terms. The Soviet Union has disappeared. Trade has grown beyond expectations and vastly expanded international capital markets have taken a major unforeseen role. During the past 20 years or so IMF operations have been conducted exclusively with developing countries and, recently, also with transition economies. Moreover, in recent years the IMF has extended its conditionality to issues of governance.

The divide among IMF members has widened during this period. On the one hand is a small group of creditor industrial countries with a majority vote; on the other is the large number of mostly prospective debtor developing countries with a minority vote and limited influence on policies. It is hardly coincidental that while the need for support of a significant group of developing countries has risen the size of the IMF has shrunk relative to world trade, and even more in relation to international capital movements. Over the last 20 years countries' access to IMF resources has become less predictable, conditionality has become gradually more restrictive—even for the compensatory financing facility—and SDR allocations have been suspended since 1981. Consequently, decisions on major IMF-supported programs are taken outside the IMF by a very small group of countries, on a discretionary basis, without rules. This power distribution raises questions on the legitimacy, transparency and accountability of IMF governance.

Clearly, the industrial countries no longer regard the IMF as being the center of the international monetary system but treat it instead as a specialized agency that assists the developing countries. Therefore, availability of sufficient support cannot be relied on. With this approach Keynes would disagree: "This [the IMF] is not a Red Cross philanthropic relief scheme, by which rich countries come to the rescue of the poor," he declared, "it is a piece of highly necessary business mechanism which is at least as useful to the creditor as to the debtor" (as quoted in Chandavarkar 1984, Introduction).

More broadly, the pressures of short-term self-interest and political expediency appear to have blurred the Bretton Woods vision of international cooperation as a means to improve the workings of the world economy. The notion that national goals are often best attained through international cooperation tends to be forgotten. This situation is unsatisfactory. To improve the governance of the IMF and the World Bank in terms of participation, transparency, and accountability—and to enable them to meet the new challenges of the world economy—reform of the shareholding and decisionmaking structures must be undertaken.

In thinking of this reform process one must note that a wider and more balanced participation of member countries is not contrary to the strict application of sound economic policies in the context of the IMF's crisis prevention and resolution work nor in the World Bank's project-related development work. In fact, member countries' ownership of IMF and World Bank programs, projects, and policies—as well as stake holding in the global financial system—require it.

APPENDIX. THE ADVANTAGES OF PPP-BASED GDP

There are two key reasons to favor the use of PPP-based GDP as the basis for quota estimation, rather than market exchange rate-based GDP. PPP-based GDP is more stable, and it is unbiased when compared to market exchange rate-based GDP:

More stable
PPP-based GDP is a far more stable basis for the quota formulas when compared to market exchange rate-based GDP. Consider the range of the exchange rate fluctuations and misalignments among major currencies. Simply recall that the

TABLE A.1

Ratio of Japan's GDP to U.S. GDP converted using various methods, selected years, 1985–96

(percent)

Conversion method	1985	1990	1993	1996
Annual average exchange rate	33	54	67	62
Five-year average exchange rate	39	59	65	61
PPP-based estimate	35	41	41	40

Source: OECD data [http://www.oecd.org].

exchange rate between the dollar and the euro has gone (since the latter's introduction in January 1999) from $1.16 per euro to $0.89 per euro (as of January 2002), a variation of over 20 percent in a period of three years.[13] This alone would introduce substantial distortions in market exchange rate conversions of GDPs measured in these currencies and in others linked to these currencies. The problem is only somewhat reduced but does not disappear with the use of three-year averages as proposed in the Cooper report (IMF 2000b). In the example of Japan and the United States below, even the use of five-year averages was not sufficient to eliminate significant fluctuations in market rate-based GDP estimates. Contrast these changes with the stability displayed by PPP-based GDP estimates (table A.1).

Unbiased
The use of market exchange rates substantially undervalues the GDPs of developing countries, as the prices and wages prevailing in the tradable goods sector

TABLE A.2

PPP-based and exchange rate-based GDPs of selected countries, 2000

Country	Share of world GDP (percent)		World ranking	
	PPP-based GDP	Exchange rate-based GDP	PPP-based GDP	Exchange rate-based GDP
United States	21.5	31.5	1	1
China	11.2	3.4	2	6
Japan	7.4	14.9	3	2
India	5.4	1.5	4	12
Germany	4.6	6.0	5	3
France	3.2	4.1	6	5
United Kingdom	3.1	4.5	7	4
Italy	3.0	3.4	8	7
Brazil	2.9	1.9	9	9
Russian Federation	2.7	0.8	10	17
Mexico	2.0	1.8	11	10
Canada	1.9	2.2	12	8
Korea, Republic of	1.8	1.5	13	13
Spain	1.7	1.8	14	11
Indonesia	1.4	0.5	15	26
Netherlands	0.9	1.2	19	15

Source: World Bank, World Development Indicators Database, 2001.

are higher than those prevailing in the non-tradable goods sector—a phenomenon that is not significant in industrial countries. This represents a major distortion inherent in the market exchange rate-based GDP, which would argue against its use in GDP comparisons between industrial and developing countries. Since PPP-based GDP estimates on the other hand, do not introduce a measurement bias against any group of countries, they would appear to be preferable for this purpose. To visualize the importance of the differences simply consider table A.2 which clearly shows how exchange rate-based GDP is a striking underestimation of the size of developing countries like China and India.

NOTES

1. The Executive Board is responsible for conducting the day-to-day business of the IMF. It is composed of 24 executive directors, who are appointed or elected by member countries or groups of countries. Some directors represent more than one country. The managing director serves as its chairman. Meeting several times a week, the Executive Board deals with a wide variety of policy, operational, and administrative matters, including surveillance of members' macroeconomic policies, provision of IMF financial assistance to member countries, and discussion of systemic issues in the global economy. (See http://www.imf.org/external/pubs/ft/survey/sup 2001/index.htm#2)

2. From hereon, unless otherwise stated, the *Board* refers to the Executive Board.

3. According to the Articles of Agreement, quotas are to be reviewed by the Board of Governors at intervals of no more than five years and if appropriate adjusted (IMF 1993, Art. III Sec. 2a). However, some 70 percent of all increases have been across the board, producing a substantial inertia in quota shares and failing to adequately reflect changes that have taken place in the world economy since 1944.

4. The Board of Governors of the IMF consists of one governor and one alternate for each member country. The governor, appointed by the member country, is usually the minister of finance or the central bank governor. The Board of Governors has delegated to the Executive Board all except certain reserved powers. It normally meets once a year. (See http://www.imf.org/external/pubs/ft/survey/sup2001/index.htm#2)

5. In the World Bank the same five countries control 38 percent of the total votes. If the votes cast by the Belgian, Canadian, Danish, Dutch, Italian, and Swiss directors are added, the total is around 60 percent. (See http://www.worldbank.org/about/organization/voting/librd.htm.)

6. The situation is no different in the World Bank. As Fidler (*Financial Times*, 28 August 2001, editorial page) writes,

> *Although no other member states come close to matching US power over the bank, all its influential owners—Britain, France, Germany and others—have borrowing governments whose interests they purport to sponsor, as well as key issues (such as the environment) that are viewed as important by their electorates. Otherwise, accountability and scrutiny from donor governments are*

uneven at best and non-existent at worst. Meanwhile, the few powerful bor-rowing nations that could exert some influence are afraid to voice their concerns lest they lose access to bank finance.

7. In the World Bank the problem may be worse given the large number and variety of projects and the fact that Sub-Saharan African countries are also represented by only two directors.

8. Again, this characteristic in the IMF can also be observed in the World Bank. As the World Bank's official history states,

> *The Americans had a secure enough lead in the Bank throughout the half century to help it avoid the clutter of country quotas in its hiring, to recruit personnel on merit from the developed and developing countries alike, and to build a work force that some saw as comparatively denationalized and homogeneous....One unmistakable factor that contributed to this homogenizing and that grew stronger over time was economics. As this work demonstrates, economics would become the Bank's hallmark scholarly discipline, and the economists who heavily shaped Bank operations as well as its research were recruited from an array of countries. To a large degree, however, they were the product of the graduate economics departments of English-speaking, but specially American, universities. This fact, as it played into the Bank's consulting, research, technical assistance and agenda setting, would enhance the US role in the institution beyond the apparatus of formal governance (Kapur, Lewis, and Webb 1997, p. 4).*

9. For example, David Finch, former director of the IMF's Exchange and Trade Relations Department, resigned under political pressure to relax IMF conditionality for Egypt and Zaire ("IMF Silent on Resignations," *Financial Times,* 21 March 1987).

10. The cumulative GDP of the 15 countries of the European Union is roughly equal to that of the United States; however, the European Union has seven directors (as of the end of April 2001), and its cumulative quota is about 70 percent larger than that of the United States.

11. This would not preclude any industrial country from turning to the IMF for support.

12. One argument for the use of GDP based on market exchange rates is that it is a better measure of a country's ability to contribute to the IMF. However, the relationship between actual contributions as determined by quotas and the ability to contribute as a proportion of GDP is far from being a binding restriction for three reasons. First, quotas are a very small proportion of GDP: only 1 percent at the time of the Eleventh Quota Review in 1998 and an even smaller proportion today. Second, since conversion of GDP at market rates produces significantly smaller GDP estimates than PPP-based conversion, the potential contributions by developing countries are such a small proportion of their GDP that the argument loses significance. Third, note that only 25 per cent of the member's contributions or quota is paid in foreign currencies. Taken together, these facts weaken the "ability to contribute" argument—the main argument against the use of PPP-based GDP—to the point at which it becomes irrelevant.

13. Data are from the Pacific Exchange Rate Service, as provided by Professor Werner Antweiler of the University of British Columbia (http://pacific.commerce. ubc.ca/xr/).

REFERENCES

ADB (Asian Development Bank). 1966. "Agreement Establishing the Asian Development Bank." Manila. [http://www.adb.org/Documents/Reports/Charter/charter.pdf].

Bhagwati, Jagdish N. 2000. "Lessons from the East Asian Experience: Opening Address." In Eric S. Rosengren and John S. Jordan, eds., *Building an Infrastructure for Financial Stability.* Conference Series, no. 44. Boston: Federal Reserve Bank of Boston.

Bordo, Michael, and Harold James. 2000. *The International Monetary Fund: Its Present Role in Historical Perspective.* NBER Working Paper 7724. Cambridge, Mass.: National Bureau of Economic Research.

Chandavarkar, Anand G. 1984. "The International Monetary Fund, Its Financial Organization and Activities." International Monetary Fund, Washington, D.C.

Feldstein, Martin. 1998. "Refocusing the IMF." *Foreign Affairs* 77 (2): 20–33.

IMF (International Monetary Fund). 1979. *Guidelines on Conditionality.* Decision 6056 (79/38). 2 March. Washington, D.C.

————. 1993. "Articles of Agreement." Washington, D.C. [http://www.imf.org/external/pubs/ft/aa/].

————. 1997. "IMF Adopts Guidelines Regarding Governance Issues." Washington, D.C. [http://www.imf.org/external/np/sec/nb/1997/nb9715.htm#I2].

————. 2000a. "Country Experiences with the Use and Liberalization of Capital Controls." Occasional Paper. Washington, D.C.

————. 2000b. "Report to the IMF Executive Board of the Quota Formula Review Group." Washington, D.C.

————. 2001a. "Annual Report of the Executive Board for the Financial Year Ended April 30, 2001." Washington, D.C. [http://www.imf.org/external/pubs/ft/ar/2001/eng/index.htm].

————. 2001b. "Review of the Fund's Experience in Governance Issues." Washington, D.C. [http://www.imf.org/external/np/gov/2001/eng/report.htm].

————. Various issues. *International Financial Statistics.* Washington, D.C.

Kapur, Devesh, John P. Lewis, and Richard Webb. 1997. *The World Bank: Its First Half Century.* Washington, D.C.: Brookings Institution Press.

Krueger, Anne O. 1997. *Whither the World Bank and the IMF?* NBER Working Paper 6327. Cambridge, Mass.: National Bureau of Economic Research.

Mikesell, Raymond F. 1994. "The Bretton Woods Debates: A Memoir." Essays in International Finance 192. Princeton University, International Finance Section, Princeton, N.J.

Sachs, Jeffrey, and Steven Radelet. 1998. "The East Asian Financial Crisis: Diagnosis, Remedies, Prospects." *Brookings Papers on Economic Activity.* Washington, D.C.: Brookings Institution.

World Bank. 2001. *World Development Indicators.* Washington, D.C.

———. Various years. *World Development Report.* New York: Oxford University Press.

STEPS TOWARD ENHANCED PARITY: NEGOTIATING CAPACITY AND STRATEGIES OF DEVELOPING COUNTRIES

PAMELA CHASEK AND LAVANYA RAJAMANI

Around the world, differences in living conditions and development levels translate into differences in policy priorities and strategies, including for global public goods. To reach consensus on the management of global public goods, perhaps through the creation of an international regime, governments work out agreements or treaties with other governments through multilateral negotiations. This chapter explores the participation of developing countries—as represented by government delegations—in such negotiations.

More often than not developing countries today enter multilateral negotiations at a disadvantage. They are either underrepresented or unrepresented in a number of international fora. This can result in agreements and regimes that do not fully reflect the policy priorities of developing countries. As a consequence there have been numerous calls for broader and deeper participation of developing countries in multilateral negotiations. It is argued not only that such participation would further the development of poor countries but that it is a necessity, not a charitable act, if there is to be firm consensus on global issues and strong commitment of all parties to the agreements reached. Yet the negotiating capacity of developing countries is already stretched to the limit.

The question is thus how to realize broader and deeper participation. To explore this challenge, the chapter first examines the characteristics of the multilateral negotiating process and procedures and the present composition and strength of developing country negotiating teams. Next it looks at some of the negotiating strategies and tactics currently employed by developing country delegations to cope with the process demands. While these coping strategies may help developing countries to participate, they have been less effective in enabling them to play an active role in setting agendas and in shaping issues under negotiation to their best advantage. But there are ways for developing countries to strengthen their negotiating capacity, and their development partners—civil society organizations, epistemic communities, multilateral agencies, donor countries—can support these efforts.

Current constraints on negotiating capacity often reflect a lack of national policy analysis, design, and management capacity. Thus one of this chapter's main recommendations is to increase national policymaking capacity. Without a nationally grounded approach, many delegates will continue to negotiate on weak grounds and sometimes even with "hollow mandates." Another important measure would be to improve networking among developing country negotiating teams—not only at negotiating sessions but also before, between, and after the sessions. Given the diversity among developing countries and thus the diversity of their national concerns and policy priorities, the chapter also suggests more differentiated coalition building. Emerging practical political experience indicates that to maximize their gains from multilateral negotiations and international cooperation, developing countries should more systematically explore opportunities for complementing broad-based negotiating coalitions, such as the Group of 77 (G-77), with coalitions focusing on special issues.

MULTILATERAL NEGOTIATIONS: PROCESS CHARACTERISTICS AND DEVELOPING COUNTRY CAPACITY

Multilateral negotiations are a complex process—and one that is becoming more complex as a result of recent changes such as globalization and increasing political pluralism and democracy. Such negotiations involve a multitude of actors, cover a multitude of issues, and often occur under conditions of great uncertainty. This section focuses on two questions. First, what are the features of the multilateral negotiating process, and what challenges does this process pose to delegations? Second, what are the characteristics of developing country delegations, and how well do they meet the demands of the negotiating process?

Process features and challenges

Multilateral negotiations may involve four processes or stages: issue definition, fact finding, bargaining, and implementation, review, and strengthening of agreements (table 1; see also Chasek 1997 and Porter and Brown 1996). The sequencing of these stages and the time that each takes vary greatly from negotiation to negotiation, and the stages are not always distinct. For example, the definition stage may overlap with the fact-finding stage, which could overlap with the bargaining stage. But each stage is crucial; thus it is also crucial for delegations to be fully involved in all stages.

Issue definition. Issue definition involves bringing an issue to the attention of the international community, identifying its scope and magnitude, illustrating the type of international action required, and, most important, explaining persua-

TABLE 1

Stages of multilateral negotiations

Stage	Purpose	Role of negotiators	Who has the power?
Issue definition	• To bring the issue to the attention of the international community • To reach general agreement on the desirability of multilateral negotiations • To set the international policy agenda	• To present evidence that there is a problem and a feasible solution to it • To convince other states of the need to negotiate an agreement	• Countries that have policy analysis and design capacity • "First movers" that bring the issue to the table
Fact finding	• To build consensus on the precise nature of the problem and on the most appropriate international cooperation actions to address it	• To establish the scope and seriousness of the problem • To examine possible policy options and the net benefits to be derived from an agreement • To explore negotiating coalitions	• Countries whose delegations include technical and political experts
Bargaining	• To assess alternative draft agreements in light of key criteria • To achieve, if desirable, consensus on a final agreement	• To evaluate options for the text of the agreement against the original bargaining position and in other comparative terms • To ensure that as far as possible and desirable, national or other relevant interests are reflected in the text	• Countries whose delegations include appropriate substantive depth • Countries skilled in both the art of negotiation and the issues
Strengthening of agreements	• To elaborate and make more precise particular dimensions • To adjust stipulations in the light of new evidence	• To identify, assess, and negotiate needed or proposed amendments, annexes, or protocols to the agreement	• Countries with policy analysis and design capacity • Countries with strong delegations

Source: Chasek 1997, 2001; Porter and Brown 1996.

sively why addressing the issue will deliver high social returns and net benefits for all. An issue may be placed on the international policy agenda by one or more state actors, an international organization (usually at the suggestion of one or more members), or a civil society organization. The actors who introduce and define the issue may publicize new scientific evidence or theories—as they did with ozone depletion. But issue definition may also involve identifying a radically different approach to international cooperation on a problem. One example is the incremental cost concept used by the Global Environment Facility. Another is the proposal for a global vaccine purchasing fund.

The issue definition stage is where the agenda is set. The countries that define the agenda are usually the ones that have the most power during subsequent phases of negotiation. If delegations are absent from this first stage, they risk losing the leverage to significantly influence later proceedings.

Fact finding. Fact finding involves efforts to build consensus on the nature and extent of the problem and on the most appropriate actions to address it. In practice, fact finding may vary from well developed to nonexistent. In the most successful cases, mediating international organizations have brought together key policymakers and experts in an attempt to establish baseline facts and figures. This stage often involves the participation of independent scientists and government-appointed technical experts rather than high-level diplomats or other government officials. In cases with no mediated process of fact finding and consensus building, facts may be challenged by states opposed to international action. Thus the fact-finding stage often becomes indistinguishable from the bargaining stage (see below).

The difficulty encountered by developing countries in this stage is that they have to assess complex scientific studies, examine the underlying assumptions, and test the robustness of the findings and conclusions. The studies often originate from industrial country or international think tanks and other non–developing country sources. Thus developing country representatives may find it hard to obtain comprehensive comments or alternative views on the analyses or even the facts and figures placed on the international negotiating table.

Bargaining. During bargaining, participants explore and debate alternative drafts of an agreement or a draft prepared by a neutral party such as the chair, facilitator, or secretariat. Before more difficult issues can be addressed by a plenary session, informal consultations are held where governments make proposals and counterproposals in an attempt to insert their positions into the debate—while, if desirable, also trying to reach consensus. Sometimes the chair, a member of the secretariat, or a neutral delegate steps in to mediate between groups. In other cases governments trade concessions on the agreement. The adoption of the agreement is often influenced by time pressure. As the final day of the conference or session approaches, governments must choose between finalizing the agreement and risking being blamed for the failure of the negotiations.

The bargaining stage draws the most participant countries. In fact, participation in international negotiations usually increases with each negotiating session. Again, countries that participate from the beginning usually have the most bargaining power during the crucial final days of negotiations. When countries send delegates only to the final session, their negotiators often lack institutional memory of the negotiations and risk making major errors, such as attempting to reopen issues on which agreement has been reached through a fragile compromise. It is also at this stage that consummate negotiators take control, often away from technical experts, meeting simultaneously in many small groups. Large delegations have a clear advantage at this stage.

Strengthening of agreements. The negotiating process does not always end with the signing of an agreement. Once established, an agreement can be strengthened, with its central provisions made clearer or more stringent through further bargaining. An agreement may be strengthened because new scientific evidence becomes available, because there are political shifts in one or more major states, or because the existing agreement is ineffective in bringing about meaningful actions. An agreement may also be strengthened because the parties have agreed in advance that such strengthening will form part of the agreement's evolution—as has become common with the growing practice of states' agreeing on framework conventions initially and protocols later.

Composition and strength of developing country delegations

Multilateral negotiations consist of many building blocks and often overlapping stages. To succeed in these processes, national delegations require technical expertise, diplomatic skills, good institutional memory, and strong policy analysis, design, and evaluation capacity. Because decisions are often made by consensus, negotiators also need effective communication, persuasion, and other interpersonal skills. In addition, expertise in outreach and consultation has become more important because of the stronger interest and increased participation of nonstate actors in international meetings. Finally, as expectations of transparency and accountability in governmental and intergovernmental decisionmaking have increased, multilateral negotiators have needed to strengthen their links with domestic authorities and constituencies. (For more on the complexities of multilateral negotiations, see Chasek 2001.)

The ability of developing countries to respond effectively to all these demands is often hampered by limitations in the size and composition of their delegations, especially when compared with those of industrial countries. Developing coun-

TABLE 2

Composition of delegations to selected multilateral negotiations

Number of delegations	Average and largest delegations	Number of one-person delegations	Share of delegation members from capitals
CSW-39 (March 1995, New York)[a]			
38 reporting names of delegates (279 delegates)	Average: 7 France, Spain, and Mexico: 17 China and the Philippines: 16	Total: 3 (all from developing countries)	—
IFF-2 (August 1998, Geneva)[b]			
37 reporting names of delegates (162 delegates)	Average: 4.4 Canada: 16 Brazil: 9	Total: 10 Developing countries: 9 Transition economies: 1	—
UNCTAD X (February 2000, Bangkok)[c]			
143 (1,265 delegates)	Average: 9 Japan: 53 Indonesia: 29 Thailand (host): 135	Total: 17 Developing countries: 11 Transition economies: 5 Industrial countries: 1	70 percent
IFF-4 (February 2000, New York)[d]			
44 reporting names of delegates (269 delegates)	Average: 6 United Kingdom: 18 Brazil: 12	Total: 5 (all from developing countries)	—
Montreal Protocol MOP-12 (December 2000, Burkina Faso)[e]			
111 (232 delegates, excluding observers)	Average: 2 Burkina Faso (host): 9	Total: 52 Developing countries: 40 Transition economies: 10 Industrial countries: 2	96 percent
CCD COP-4 (December 2000, Germany)[f]			
143 (597 delegates, excluding observers)	Average: 4 Germany: 40 Nigeria (G-77 chair): 14	Total: 39 Developing countries: 30 Transition economies: 5 Industrial countries: 4	87 percent
POPS INC-5 (December 2000, South Africa)[g]			
122 (330 delegates)	Average: 2.7 United States: 32 South Africa (host): 16	Total: 80 Developing countries: 67 Transition economies: 10 Industrial countries: 3	91 percent

TABLE 2 CONTINUED

Composition of delegations to selected multilateral negotiations

Number of delegations	Average and largest delegations	Number of one-person delegations	Share of dele- gation members from capitals
FfD PrepCom III (May 2001, New York)[h]			
109 reporting names of delegates (390 delegates)	Average: 3.6 Mexico (future host): 12 China: 9	Total: 8 Developing countries: 6 Transition economies: 1 Industrial countries: 1	—

— Not available.

a. Thirty-Ninth Session of the Committee on the Status of Women.

b. Second Session of the Intergovernmental Forum on Forests.

c. Tenth Session of the United Nations Conference on Trade and Development.

d. Fourth Session of the Intergovernmental Forum on Forests.

e. Twelfth Meeting of Parties to the Montreal Protocol on Substances That Deplete the Ozone Layer.

f. Fourth Meeting of the Conference of the Parties to the Convention to Combat Desertification.

g. Fifth Session of the Intergovernmental Negotiating Committee for an International Legally Binding Instrument for Implementing International Action on Certain Persistent Organic Pollutants.

h. Third Substantive Session of the Preparatory Committee for the International Conference on Finance for Development, Part I.

Source: Authors' compilation based on relevant documentation.

tries often send one-person delegations to multilateral negotiations (table 2). A one-person delegation is at a disadvantage for two main reasons: lack of expertise and inability to cover simultaneous negotiating sessions.

One person rarely possesses both the negotiating skills and the technical knowledge required for multilateral negotiations. Thus, for example, technical experts lacking multilateral negotiating experience may be ignored if their contributions are not couched in the proper language—even if what they say makes perfect sense.

Small delegations from developing countries are further taxed by the challenge of attending simultaneous meetings during the same negotiations, by the growing number of meetings (see Schechter 2001), and by the changing of venues when negotiations entail several sessions and stretch over long periods, as many do today. For example, the United Nations Framework Convention on Climate Change holds most of its meetings in Bonn, Germany, where its secretariat is located. But its conferences have also met in Berlin (Germany), Geneva (Switzerland), Kyoto (Japan), Buenos Aires (Argentina), The Hague (the Netherlands), and Marrakech (Morocco). A change of venue has advantages: it may enhance fairness and help level the playing field (see Albin in this volume), and it links host countries and regions more closely to the negotiating process and the issues under consideration. But changes in venue make it difficult for developing countries to send the same delegates and thus to build an institutional memory and consistent negotiating strategies and positions.[1] They also make it hard for developing country delegates to develop relationships with their colleagues from industrial countries—relationships that are vital to effective bargaining (Djoghlaf 1994).

Even if the same delegates attend, they sometimes participate for a limited period to minimize costs. For example, delegates may join only the final stages of a negotiating process. But as noted, entering a negotiating process late—say, during the bargaining phase—hinders delegates' capacity to intervene effectively. To facilitate developing country participation, some international organizations have occasionally paid the costs for technical experts to attend negotiations. Yet if the experts' participation is a one-time affair, it does little to remedy the situation.

The Intergovernmental Forum on Forests illustrates the consistency issue. The forum's second and third meetings were in Geneva, and the fourth was in New York. Of the 109 developing country delegates to the second and fourth meetings, only 9 (8 percent) attended both—while of the 223 industrial country delegates to the two meetings, 44 (20 percent) attended both (table 3). Of the 12 delegations from industrial countries, only 1—from Mexico[2]—did not include at least one of the same delegates for both meetings. Such change in membership places developing countries at a disadvantage. It slows the delegations' learning, weakens their institutional memory, and potentially limits their effectiveness.

NEGOTIATING STRATEGIES

The composition of a country's delegation is just one of several factors that determine how successfully it can pursue its interests in international negotiations. Another important factor is how ingenious negotiators are in overcoming resource constraints. Developing countries have used various strategies in this regard, including forming coalitions, setting priorities, pooling expertise, participating in prenegotiation sessions, and forming alliances with nonstate actors, particularly civil society organizations.

Forming coalitions

Coalition building can have several advantages. Among other things, it can add resources to each delegation, broadening expertise and allowing better coverage of—and leverage in—negotiations (Gupta 2000). Coalitions are more likely to be effective if they are homogeneous and cohesive, with members sharing a common history and identity (Boyer 2000).

The G-77, established in 1964, is a major coalition of developing countries (see http://www.g77.org/; Sauvant 1981; and CBI 2000). It emerged because developing countries believed that their individual development problems were actually a common problem that required a new international economic order—and that such an order could be created only by placing concerted political pressure

TABLE 3

Delegates sent to both the Second and Fourth Sessions of the Intergovernmental Forum on Forests

Country	Delegates at Second Session	Delegates at Fourth Session	Delegates at both sessions
Developing countries			
Algeria	1	2	1
Angola	0	3	0
Bolivia	1	0	0
Brazil	9	12	3
China	4	7	2
Colombia	3	6	0
Côte d'Ivoire	1	3	0
Cuba	0	7	0
Egypt	1	4	0
Guyana	1	3	0
India	1	3	1
Indonesia	7	8	0
Iran	3	7	1
Peru	3	5	1
Philippines	1	3	0
Total	36	73	9
Industrial countries			
Canada	16	17	10
Finland	4	14	4
France	5	6	2
Germany	13	14	5
Japan	8	9	3
Mexico	3	14	0
Netherlands	5	7	1
New Zealand	3	7	2
Portugal	6	12	3
Spain	4	4	1
United Kingdom	11	18	9
United States	8	15	4
Total	86	137	44
Transition economies			
Bulgaria	2	1	0
Czech Republic	2	3	0
Russian Federation	6	8	2
Total	10	12	2

Source: Authors' compilation based on relevant documentation.

on industrial countries (Williams 1991). Since then the number of developing countries has risen from 77 to 134. In addition, differences between developing countries have become more pronounced (see UNCTAD, various years; UNDP, various years; and World Bank, various years). As a result defining these countries' common interests and concerns has become increasingly difficult, calling for subcoalitions (such as the G-24) as well as alliances with industrial countries (such as the Cairns Group; see http://www.cairnsgroup.org/).

The G-77, often joined by China, has acquired considerable leverage in negotiations on newer issues, such as those involving environmental, social, and gender concerns. But negotiations on these concerns often touch on what divides countries, industrial and developing, compounding the difficulties facing the G-77 and China in maintaining a united front in multilateral negotiations.

In the climate change negotiations, for example, the coalition has been fractured by radically different national interests and priorities. At one end of the ideological spectrum lie the small island states and countries with low-lying coastal areas. These countries, members of the Alliance of Small Island States (AOSIS), are particularly vulnerable to climate change because a rise in sea level could destroy or render uninhabitable all or part of their territory (Bruce and others 1996). They have therefore endeavored to act as the "global conscience" in the negotiations on climate change. At the other end of the spectrum lie the members of the Organization of Petroleum Exporting Countries (OPEC; http://www.opec.org), which stand to lose substantial revenue from measures to avert climate change. A common G-77 position has to take all these interests into account (Grubb and Brack 1999; Rajamani 2000).

The initial negotiations on the Clean Development Mechanism (CDM), the only mechanism of the three under the Kyoto Protocol that opens up a channel of interaction between industrial and developing countries, provide a telling example of diverging positions among the G-77 members and China.[3] China and India wanted the CDM to include nuclear energy projects; AOSIS and OPEC were strongly opposed to their inclusion. While China and India believe that nuclear power will help meet the energy needs of their large populations, AOSIS members have negative historical associations with nuclear testing and OPEC does not wish to support non–fossil fuel energy sources. Meanwhile, Africa argued that the CDM should be designed to reward projects that avoid emissions and promote sustainable socioeconomic development using clean technologies, since Africa consumes less than 2–3 percent of global energy resources and therefore has few potential opportunities for CDM projects that reduce emissions from existing sources. As a result of these diverging interests, the G-77–China position papers on the CDM were phrased to leave these fundamental questions open (Rajamani 1999, 2000).

Similar examples could be found in many other issue areas. These examples show that the G-77 and China often find it difficult to formulate clear and consistent positions on issues in which some of the group's members have strong interests—because their interests are likely to diverge. But even though strong consensus positions are rare, they do happen—particularly on issues that are well-established policy priorities for the group or for its more powerful members (Jakobsen 1996). For example, the G-77 and China are united in arguing that environmental rules should not hinder their ability to develop. Thus since the early 1990s, beginning with the Montreal Protocol on Substances That Deplete the Ozone Layer, developing countries have called for financial assistance, technology transfers, and capacity building to help them implement multilateral treaties on environmental issues (Jakobsen 1996). Moreover, during the climate change negotiations the G-77 and China have maintained that the historical responsibility for climate change lies with industrial countries and that these countries should bear the main responsibility for correcting the problem (Bodansky 1993).

Interestingly, in recent years several smaller coalitions have emerged, focusing on specific interests of selected countries. While supporting positions of G-77 and China, these coalitions have assumed growing visibility in multilateral negotiations. One such coalition is AOSIS. Another is the Group of Independent Latin American Countries (GRILA), an informal group of 16 Latin American countries that coalesced primarily to ensure that forests are included in the mechanisms foreseen under the Kyoto Protocol. Yet another is the group of least developed countries (LDCs). These and similar examples show that while forming broad coalitions and broadly shared positions can be a powerful strategy for advancing developing country interests, creating smaller, issue-based coalitions can often be an important complement. Multiple memberships in both broad coalitions and small ones appear to confer greater leverage: while the small, issue-focused groups help define, voice, and protect the shared interests of its members, the broad coalitions may offer more general support. This observation is significant, as most leverage theorists believe that in environmental negotiations, for example, the real leverage among developing countries rests with India, China, and, in some cases, Brazil (Beukel 1993; Young 1990; Rajan 1992; Porter and Brown 1996; Ravenhill 1990).

Setting priorities
A complementary strategy is the effort by developing countries to keep multilateral negotiations manageable by focusing on policy priorities. For example, prominent among the agreed concerns of developing countries is the need for new and additional financial and technological resources, a need that permeates virtually all issue areas (see Hurrell and Kingsbury 1991 and Jakobsen 1996). Priority setting has in some instances clearly benefited developing countries. For example, the recognition today of the principle of "common but differentiated responsibilities" of industrial and developing countries in the climate change negotiations—

in the text of both the United Nations Framework Convention on Climate Change and the Kyoto Protocol—is a result of the G-77 and China bringing their combined and not inconsiderable weight to bear on this issue. They put the principle forward in the early years of the negotiations and got it reaffirmed in subsequent decisions (Rajamani 2000).

Priority setting can work, but it can also have drawbacks. Focusing on a few issues to the exclusion of others could lead to the loss of opportunities that a more detailed coverage of the issues on the negotiating table could open up. For example, focusing on new and additional resources may divert attention from aspects of an international regime entailing high costs that could never be adequately compensated for through additional official development assistance or aid. And as noted, developing countries may not have the capacity to identify priorities or participate in relevant sessions during complex multilateral negotiations—resulting in outcomes or agreements that run counter to their interests. Although priority setting is desirable when resources are limited, it requires a narrowing of the focus of delegations. As this must often be done under severe time constraints, it frequently means reverting to established policy positions and thus risking the loss of opportunities to strike better deals.

Pooling expertise
Pooling expertise allows countries with small delegations and limited expertise to focus on areas of particular interest to them, with the confidence that others are representing the interests of the group. Sometimes this works well, as in the Kyoto Protocol negotiations under the United Nations Framework Convention on Climate Change. Although Tanzania was the chair of the G-77 and China, it did not place the burden of representing the group's views exclusively on the shoulders of its three-member delegation. Instead, coordinators for the different agenda items were identified from among other developing country delegations. These coordinators had a mandate to articulate the position of the group (arrived at in the plenary session of the G-77 and China), report back to the group and advise it on the best strategy to follow, and, under the guidance of the chair, prepare position papers for the group (Mwandosya 2000). Developing countries have used this strategy for other negotiations on climate change as well as for negotiations on financing and desertification.

Participating in prenegotiation sessions
Developing countries need to fully understand the issue under consideration simply to determine how best to organize their participation in negotiations. They also need to know the policy positions of their potential coalition partners and the strengths of their delegations. Effective strategizing requires prenegotiation meetings, sometimes held before major meetings and conferences.

Although prenegotiation briefings are important, they often occur too late to be truly useful. For example, prenegotiation sessions held the weekend before negotiations start can help delegations select coordinators and consolidate their positions in a minimal way. But such sessions do not help delegations strategize effectively, because by then the delegations have often had to clear their positions with their governments and other stakeholders. As a result agreements with coalition partners often stay within the realm of the well known.

Forming alliances with nonstate actors

As Edwards and Zadek (in this volume) discuss, a growing number of nonstate actors are becoming involved in multilateral negotiations. Nonstate actors can bring important resources and expertise to the negotiating process. Building strategic alliances with nonstate actors is yet another strategy developing country delegations employ to strengthen their negotiating capacity, create a level playing field, and thereby ensure more equitable and progressive outcomes in international environmental negotiations.

Alliances need to be chosen carefully, however. Sometimes nonstate actors are part of the official delegation and may enter into negotiations themselves. In such cases they may substitute for capacity in developing country delegations. In addition, developing country representatives may leave a particular item to nonstate actors to pursue, especially when they feel that the nonstate actors might be better equipped to articulate their concerns. They often do so if they have only general instructions from their capitals, for example, so that the risk in delegating the negotiating function is limited. Again, however, the nonstate actors merely substitute for the negotiating capacity of developing countries. So while relying on nonstate actors may ensure that the interests of developing countries are well represented in a particular negotiation, it is not a long-term solution to the problem of inadequate negotiating capacity.

Thus the benefits and risks of such alliances must be carefully and constantly balanced. Forming alliances with nonstate actors raises issues of trust and confidence as well as legitimacy and accountability (see Edwards and Zadek in this volume). Nonstate actors—civil society organizations as well as businesses—may not be disinterested global players. In technically complex negotiations, for example, relying on other entities' briefing papers, statistics, and scientific assessments could prove problematic because such documents may incorporate value judgments (easily obfuscated in technical language) that could significantly affect policy outcomes (Friends of the Earth International 1997; Newell 2000; Yamin 2001).

Summary

The coping strategies employed by developing country delegations thus have both merits and limitations. They offer developing countries the opportunity to participate more effectively than they otherwise could. In some instances they have even helped delegations to pursue certain issues more decisively. Yet many of the tactics are ad hoc and reactive. They seldom aid proactive agenda setting. And while they help developing country delegations to cope, they are a poor substitute for strong policy analysis and design capacity—domestically, in the national ministries concerned, and internationally, in their multilateral negotiating teams. Moreover, some of the coping strategies were designed at a time that a clearer divide existed between the North and the South. They are less suited for today's more issue-based and global public goods–focused international agenda.

These findings lead to the question of what corrective steps could be taken to strengthen the capacity of developing countries to participate in multilateral negotiations.

Policy options

Fair negotiations require both a level playing field (see Albin and Buira in this volume) and players that have a more equal starting position, at least in terms of negotiating capacity. Yet international cooperation and negotiation efforts are a part of national policymaking, just as global public goods are often just national public goods—or bads—with cross-border dimensions. For any significant change to occur in the capacity of developing country delegations, issues related to international cooperation must figure more prominently in domestic politics. As Gupta (1997, p. 133) notes, many developing country delegations have a "hollow mandate," attending negotiations without clear instructions. Although developing countries are not unique in this respect, this situation is often beyond their control—dictated by circumstances rather than by policy neglect or low concern.

In light of the many challenges that still face developing countries, new and additional support measures are necessary. The following recommendations represent first steps that could enhance the participation of developing countries in multilateral negotiations within the existing system.

- *Strengthen long-term capacity building.* Several initiatives are under way to bring delegates to meetings and ensure that they are briefed shortly before or sometimes even at the meetings. Capacity building efforts would be more effective if they were focused instead at the country level. They could help domestic researchers and policy think tanks undertake studies in time for national policy debates preceding international negotiations, allowing developing countries to prepare policy positions and consult strategic partners inside and outside the country. Capacity could also be built by providing support for better networking among concerned groups of (or all) developing country delegations before, between, and after negotiating sessions. Enhancing capacity in both respects would enable developing country negotiators to receive fuller briefs and enter negotiations with a stronger mandate—and thus a better bargaining position.

This goal could be achieved by creating an independently administered or self-administered participation fund for developing countries, as suggested by Kaul, Grunberg, and Stern (1999). Rather than solely support participation in larger conferences, as similar initiatives do today, the fund could sponsor more regional and preparatory meetings among developing countries. The policy coordination that would develop through these meetings would help developing countries change the negotiating dynamics and influence agenda setting. The fund could also be used to improve access to the latest communication technology (computers, the Internet, and the like), to strengthen coordination among countries before meetings. Finally, the fund could be used for providing issue-specific training; for acquiring environmental, trade-related, or other expertise; or for building national, regional, or joint capacity.

- *Improve coordination between national policymaking and multilateral negotiations.* Greater coordination between ministries relevant to negotiating sessions would make for more effective delegations. For example, if a developing country intends to participate in a meeting of the World Trade Organization's Committee on Trade and Environment, it would be useful for the country's ministries of trade, environment, foreign affairs, and perhaps even finance to coordinate their positions along with those of the country's Geneva-based diplomats and others who might be attending the session. One subject at such consultations could be negotiating strategies—with other countries and with nonstate actors. It might also be useful for each relevant ministry to have an international cooperation unit responsible for ensuring proper links between the domestic and international components of national policymaking.

- *Increase support from international conference secretariats.* Developing countries should have easier access to policy-oriented background documentation offering a menu of clear policy alternatives. The availability of studies and reports on the Internet has helped, but many developing country governments lack reliable, high-speed Internet connections—and in some cases even computers. Postal delivery of documentation is often slow, and in some cases developing country delegates have arrived at meetings without having had an opportunity to review reports internally or with their coalition partners. One potential solution would be to have United Nations Development Programme (UNDP) country offices with high-speed Internet connections download conference documentation and make it available to country delegations.

- *Adjust alliance-building strategies to new realities.* Each country will, of course, have to make its own assessment of which alliances are worth pursuing, bearing in mind the issue and the forum, weighing short- and long-term interests, and balancing economic, political, and other international cooperation concerns with national self-interests and interests in a balanced, peaceful world. Given the diversity among countries, it seems desirable for developing countries to explore how to complement current coalition and alliance-building strategies with more issue-focused strategies.

Conclusion

The complexity of multilateral negotiations is unlikely to ease as long as the topics remain complex and the number of actors and interests continues to increase. The prevalent trend favors the negotiation of more global regimes and the convening of global rather than regional conferences. This in itself contributes substantially to the complexity of the negotiations. Therefore, rather than seeking to simplify the process or the issues under negotiation—an effort that cannot but be artificial and that may not serve anyone's interest—it would be better to focus change on the developing countries themselves.

Hampered by enduring structural inequities and limited resources, developing countries have fashioned innovative techniques and drawn help from unexpected quarters to maximize their leverage in multilateral negotiations. These strategies have helped them cope with the immediate challenges of multilateral negotiations. But they have proved less successful in helping developing countries contribute to shaping the agenda or participate proactively, creatively, and constructively in the negotiation of issues in which they have significant interests. The measures suggested in this chapter are mere first steps. They are not meant to generate the fundamental structural changes that some argue are necessary to create a level playing field. But if implemented, they would significantly broaden and deepen developing country participation in multilateral negotiations and thereby enhance the provision of global public goods.

Notes

1. Also interesting in this context is that delegations tend to be larger across the board when meetings take place at United Nations centers such as New York or Geneva (see table 3). The reason is that countries maintain permanent representative offices in these centers.

2. Here Mexico is considered an industrial country based on its membership in the Organisation for Economic Co-operation and Development.

3. The Clean Development Mechanism allows industrial countries to invest in project activities in developing nations and to use the certified emission reductions that accrue from the project toward compliance with their commitments under the Kyoto Protocol (Article 12, Kyoto Protocol to the United Nations Framework Convention on Climate Change, 1997). For a detailed description of the politics of

the Clean Development Mechanism and the current state of play in the negotiations, see Rajamani (2001, pp. 218–21).

REFERENCES

Beukel, Erik. 1993. "Global miljøbeskyttelse som kollektivt gode i internal politik." *Politologiske Skrifter* 2. Odense Universitet, Institut for Erhvervsret og Politologi, Odense, Denmark.

Bodansky, Daniel. 1993. "The United Nations Framework Convention on Climate Change: A Commentary." *Yale Journal of International Law* 18 (2): 451–558.

Boyer, Brook. 2000. "Groups and Coalitions: Negotiating within the G-77 and Outside." Paper presented to the Negotiating Skills Workshop, Center for Sustainable Development in the Americas, Miami, Florida, July. [http://www.csdanet.org/English/miami/sessionfour.pdf].

Bruce, James P., Hoe-Song Yi, Erik F. Haites, and Hoesung Lee, eds. 1996. *Climate Change 1995: Economic and Social Dimensions of Climate Change.* Cambridge: Cambridge University Press.

CBI (Consensus Building Institute). 2000. "The Group of 77: Building Global Negotiating Capacity: A Provisional Report." Cambridge, Mass.

Chasek, Pamela S. 1997. "A Comparative Analysis of Multilateral Environmental Negotiations." *Group Decision and Negotiations* 6 (5): 437–61.

———. 2001. *Earth Negotiations: Analyzing Thirty Years of Environmental Diplomacy.* Tokyo: United Nations University Press.

Djoghlaf, Ahmed. 1994. "The Beginnings of an International Climate Law." In Irving M. Mintzer and J. A. Leonard, eds., *Negotiating Climate Change.* Cambridge: Cambridge University Press.

Friends of the Earth International. 1997. "Lobbying for Lethargy—The Fossil Fuel Lobby and the Climate Change Negotiations." Press briefing. [http://www.foe.co.uk/pubsinfo/briefings/html/19971215150450.html].

Grubb, Michael, and Duncan Brack, eds. 1999. *The Kyoto Protocol: A Guide and Assessment.* London: Royal Institute of International Affairs and Earthscan.

Gupta, Joyeeta. 1997. *The Climate Convention and Developing Countries: From Conflict to Consensus.* London: Kluwer.

———. 2000. *On Behalf of My Delegation, . . . A Survival Guide for Developing Country Climate Negotiators.* Washington, D.C.: Center for Sustainable Development in the Americas.

Hurrell, Andrew, and Benedict Kingsbury. 1991. *The International Politics of the Environment: Actors, Interests and Institutions.* Oxford: Clarendon Press.

Jakobsen, Susanne. 1996. "North-South Relations and Global Environmental Issues." Working Paper 96.3. Centre for Development Research, Copenhagen.

Kaul, Inge, Isabelle Grunberg, and Marc A. Stern. 1999. "Defining Global Public Goods." In Inge Kaul, Isabelle Grunberg, and Marc A. Stern, eds., *Global Public Goods: International Cooperation in the 21st Century.* New York: Oxford University Press.

Mwandosya, Mark J. 2000. *Survival Emissions: A Perspective from the South on Global Climate Change Negotiations.* Dar-es-Salaam, Tanzania: DUP Ltd. and Centre for Energy, Environment, Science and Technology.

Newell, Peter. 2000. *Climate for Change: Non-State Actors and the Global Politics of the Greenhouse.* Cambridge: Cambridge University Press

Porter, Gareth, and Janet Welsh Brown. 1996. *Global Environmental Politics.* 2nd ed. Boulder, Colo.: Westview Press.

Rajamani, Lavanya. 1999. "Kyoto to Buenos Aires, Bonn, and Beyond." *Tiempo: Global Warming and the Third World* 33: 20.

———. 2000. "The Principle of Common but Differentiated Responsibility and the Balance of Commitments under the Climate Regime." *Review of European Community and International Environmental Law* 9 (2): 120–31.

———. 2001. "Re-negotiating Kyoto: A Review of the Sixth Conference of Parties to the Framework Convention on Climate Change." *2000 Yearbook of the Colorado Journal of International Environmental Law & Policy* (summer): 201–38.

Rajan, Mukund Govind. 1992. "Bargaining with the Environment: A New Weapon for the South?" *South Asia Research* 12 (2): 135–47.

Ravenhill, John. 1990. "The North-South Balance of Power." *International Affairs* 66 (4): 731–48.

Sauvant, Karl P. 1981. *Group of 77: Evolution, Structure and Organization.* Dobbs Ferry, N.Y.: Oceana Publications.

Schechter, Michael. 2001. *United Nations–Sponsored World Conferences: Focus on Impact and Follow-Up.* Tokyo: United Nations University Press.

UNCTAD (United Nations Conference on Trade and Development). Various years. *Trade and Development Report.* Geneva: United Nations Publications.

UNDP (United Nations Development Programme). Various years. *Human Development Report.* New York: Oxford University Press.

Williams, Marc. 1991. *Third World Cooperation: The Group of 77 in UNCTAD.* London: St. Martin's.

World Bank. Various years. *World Development Report.* New York: Oxford University Press.

Yamin, Farhana. 2001. "NGOs and International Environmental Law: A Critical Evaluation of the Roles and Responsibilities." *Review of European Community and International Environmental Law* 10 (2): 149–67.

Young, Oran R. 1990. "Global Environmental Change and International Governance." *Millennium: Journal of International Studies* 19 (3): 337–46.

GETTING TO FAIRNESS: NEGOTIATIONS OVER GLOBAL PUBLIC GOODS

Cecilia Albin

At their July 2001 summit meeting in Genoa, Italy, the Group of Eight (G-8) defended free trade as the key to global prosperity and to poverty alleviation in developing countries. These representatives of the world's wealthiest countries also confirmed their commitment to development aid. Meanwhile, the world's attention was drawn to confrontations involving tens of thousands of demonstrators against the summit. The Genoa demonstrations followed similar protests against meetings of international financial institutions in Washington, D.C., in April 2000 and of the World Trade Organization (WTO) in Seattle, Washington (United States), in December 1999. These and other disputes suggest that some people—and sometimes many people—perceive certain international organizations, along with the negotiations that they initiate or host and the resulting outcomes, as one-sided and unfair.

Such perceptions are in many ways ironic. After all, international meetings and agreements are often focused on global public goods. Theoretically, such goods could be provided to all of the world's people. So what explains the demonstrations and the concerns about justice and fairness? This chapter addresses that question. More important, it proposes a framework for defining and implementing fair negotiation practice. The main message is this: to manage and provide global public goods effectively, we need to ensure that considerations of justice and fairness are better reflected in negotiations and agreements concerned with them. Thus a more explicit focus is needed on such considerations. A good and politically feasible approach would be to start not with outcome justice but with the fairness of the structure and process of negotiations, where, in important ways, the outcome is often shaped considerably.

NEGOTIATING GLOBAL PUBLIC GOODS

Parties enter and conduct negotiations when they expect this to serve their own interests better than unilateral options (Zartman and Berman 1982; Grieco 1988). Negotiation and cooperation are seen as tools to further self-interest. All parties come to the table with their own concerns and objectives, so successful negotiations must achieve a mutually advantageous outcome. This requirement is widely recognized. Yet sharp disagreements often riddle the process as negotiators seek to maximize their benefits. The type and extent of disagreement depend partly on the issues. Some issues are more "zero sum" than others, in that one party's gain may entail the other's loss. An example is the delineation of territorial borders.

Other issues entail more positive-sum situations and provide much scope for mutually advantageous agreements. Negotiations over global public goods often fall into this category, as these goods tend to be largely nonexcludable and nonrivalrous in consumption. Once such a good exists, everyone (countries, firms, individuals) should, in principle, be able to enjoy it fully. Yet, as noted, fierce protests have arisen in recent years over the provision of global public goods. Frequently, the contentious issue was not whether to produce these goods, but how to shape and provide them so that they have positive utility for all.[1]

So why these controversies? From a negotiation perspective, three factors shed light on this question.

The need for active involvement in setting agendas

Parties to international negotiations have different interests and priorities with regard to global public goods. Therefore, each party needs to ensure that it is actively involved in setting global agendas; otherwise a party may end up discussing merely the concerns of others at the expense of its own interests.

Efforts to launch another round of multilateral trade talks at the 1999 WTO meeting in Seattle collapsed partly over this matter. Major industrial countries suggested negotiations on issues of little immediate priority for developing countries, such as electronic commerce, investment policy, and labor and environmental standards. Developing countries, for their part, insisted on the need for further progress in removing barriers to their exports of textiles and agricultural products before debating new concerns. Only two years later, at a meeting in Doha, Qatar, did delegations manage to formulate a reasonably broad and balanced agenda (WTO 2001; see also de Jonquieres 2001). So while the provision of global public goods offers significant potential for mutual gains, it also raises important questions of fairness and distributive justice.

The distribution of costs

The benefits of global public goods are largely public. But the costs of providing them have to be shared, that is, distributed among countries and groups within countries. In negotiations over such goods, parties often seek to minimize the burden (for example, financial costs and policy adjustments) that they will have to bear themselves. They reason that the smaller is the price of their contribution to the provision of the goods, the more they will benefit from the overall agreement.

Various criteria can be used to calculate benefits (Kanbur 2001). Governmental and nongovernmental representatives, with their different political constraints and agendas, often do not rely on the same measuring rods. As a result they can expect or demand divergent measures and policies on an issue even if they are from the same country. For example, U.S. environmental experts and civil society representatives have criticized the Bush administration's withdrawal from the Kyoto Protocol on cutting greenhouse gas emissions. During the negotiation in 2002 of a final document to be adopted by the International Conference on Financing for Development, nongovernmental organizations headquartered in Europe strongly advocated the adoption of a common carbon tax or a currency transaction tax. Among the official delegations of the European Union, however, such tax measures remained highly controversial.

Some parties may try to delay or avoid contributing to the provision of global public goods. The European Union was seen as doing this when it sought to preserve the Common Agricultural Policy for so long in multilateral trade negotiations (see Albin 2001). When this happens, other parties may claim a right to compensation and, if it is not fulfilled, consider withdrawing altogether from joint ventures involving negotiation and cooperation. In the negotiation of the 1987 Montreal Protocol on Substances That Deplete the Ozone Layer, compensation and incentives had to be extended to developing countries to encourage them to participate (Barrett 1999).

The global impact

Global public goods affect not only the parties or individuals seated around an international bargaining table, but also the lives of people worldwide. Indeed, deliberations over such goods ultimately concern not distant foreign affairs but people's daily lives. This raises difficult issues of justice and fairness that need to be considered and resolved in the negotiation process. Much can (and does) go wrong in that process, given the distributive obstacles and challenges. But it also offers win-win opportunities. A primary incentive for parties to work to exploit these opportunities is that few global public goods can be produced or provided on a unilateral basis. Cooperation on a large scale is required, and this is rarely possible to get under way or to sustain without some measure of justice and fairness. These values play an important role in bringing the parties to the negotiating table, keeping them there, and motivating them to honor agreements. What then do these values mean? How are they defined?

CONCEPTS OF JUSTICE

Justice can be viewed as a "macro" concept that refers to general criteria of what is right and wrong. Its exact meaning in practical contexts is often unclear. Fairness, by contrast, can be seen as a "micro" concept that suggests what is right and wrong in particular circumstances, for individual parties and specific issues (Albin 1993). Principles of fairness are often applications and interpretations of more general notions of justice. An outcome can therefore be fair to a group of parties within a local or issue-specific context, but unjust from a broader (global, for example) perspective. Conversely, an arrangement may be just in the sense of being based on a general distributive principle, but unfair in how the principle has been applied in a particular case.

The importance of mutual advantage has been put forward as a principle of justice (Gauthier 1986). The idea that justice has something to do with mutual gains is far less controversial among parties to international negotiations than in the relevant literature (see Barry 1989, 1995; and Albin 2001). From a broader, pragmatic viewpoint, it is also widely recognized that successful negotiations and agreements depend to a large extent on their ability to deliver net benefits to all those whose participation and cooperation are needed.

Another principle is reciprocity, that is, the responsiveness of parties to one another's concessions. Again, the extent to which this behavior has anything to do with justice or fairness is contested in the scholarly literature. Some authors endorse this principle as intrinsically just (Gauthier 1986; Gouldner 1960) and as instrumental in achieving cooperation in an anarchic world (Axelrod 1984). Elsewhere it is rejected for leaving people who are unable to reciprocate and offer benefits to others, such as people who are very poor or disabled, outside the bounds of justice and outside cooperative ventures (Barry 1995). Delegates to international negotiations tend to agree that reciprocity is essential to fairness but also that variations in resources and circumstances need to be taken into account. They often appear to aim for an overall balance of reciprocal benefits, which requires parties to contribute and concede as far as they are able rather than exactly to the same extent or in equal measure (Albin 2001).

Reciprocity and mutual advantage are notions defined in particular contexts, within a negotiation. After all, adequate reciprocity and mutual advantage are whatever the parties themselves define them to be. The next few principles discussed here have a basic meaning that is more external to and independent of specific situations (box 1).

The principle of equality calls for parties to receive identical or comparable treatment, rewards, and burdens. It poses the question of what exactly is to be equalized and how equality is to be achieved when, as is so often the case, the parties are unequal to begin with. For example, should we focus on equalizing opportunities and treatment, allocations and contributions, or should we aim to equalize the outcome in terms of the welfare and resources of parties? The notion of equality as equal shares advocates the uniform distribution of resources regardless of differences in needs, preferences, or other considerations (Pruitt 1981). It does not take into account the fact that parties often gain unequal utility from acquiring equal amounts of the same good. Some argue for "equality in the

---

BOX 1

Principles of Justice

Internal (contextual) principles
- *Reciprocity:* Parties should respond to one another's concessions.
- *Mutual advantage:* Agreements should have positive net benefits for all.

External principles
- *Equality:* Parties should receive identical or comparable treatment, rewards, and burdens.
- *Proportionality:* Resources, opportunities, benefits, and costs should be allocated in proportion to relevant inputs, such as contributions (actions and efforts adding value to a collective or disputed good) or assets (skills, wealth, income, status).
- *Entitlement:* Benefits should be distributed in line with entitlements acquired—for example, through a purchase, gift, bequest, discovery, achievement, or cooperative effort.
- *Compensatory justice:* Resources should be distributed to indemnify undue costs inflicted on a party in the past or present.
- *Needs:* Resources should be allocated relative to need, so that those in most need receive the greatest share.

Impartial principles
- *Justice as fairness:* Principles of justice are those that parties would adopt if they were ignorant of their own identity and position or, put differently, if they were to decide from a detached viewpoint.
- *Voluntary acceptance:* Decisions must be reached without the use of heavy-handed coercion or manipulation if they are to be considered just.

---

weights attached to the welfare of all individuals" (Ng 2000, p. 141), while others advocate equalizing the opportunities that people have to create decent, meaningful lives for themselves (Arneson 1989; Cohen 1993; Dworkin 1981).

The principle of proportionality, by contrast, holds that resources, opportunities, benefits, and costs should be allocated in proportion to relevant inputs. These inputs may be contributions in the form of actions and efforts adding value to a collective or disputed good, or they may be assets such as skills, wealth, income, and status. The principle originates in Aristotle's proposition that equal treatment is just only if parties already are equal in ways relevant to the resource distribution; otherwise they should be treated unequally. Among many interpretations of the proportionality principle is that of "shared but differentiated responsibility," which entails parties making concessions and accepting burdens in proportion to their ability to do so (Kelley, Beckman, and Fischer 1967). Countries' contributions to the regular budget of the United Nations are based on their ability to pay, as measured by and proportional to their gross national product.

An argument about proportionality also underpins entitlement approaches to justice. Some suggest a notion of acquired rights and entitlements (Godard 1997) or merit (Van Parijs 1991, 1998; Dupuy 1992). Along these lines, those who have made more effort to reduce pollution, for example, should be rewarded accordingly. This type of approach, and perceived violations of it, can be very contentious. When a global resource is a pure public good (such as the global climate), it provides many tempting opportunities for free-riding by some on the efforts undertaken by others (such as reductions in carbon dioxide emissions).

The principle of compensatory justice stipulates that resources should be distributed to indemnify undue costs inflicted on a party in the past or present (Shue 1992). It is distinct from the principle of needs, which aims to meet basic wants regardless of their origin and is based on some supposed universal standard to which all people or countries are entitled. A compensatory approach focuses on victims. A needs-driven approach would instead target the world's poorest people or countries, regardless of other considerations. A notion of compensatory justice is especially important when considering the growing number of transboundary threats to human security and health, including cross-border air and water pollution.

In addition to the internal and external principles discussed so far, there are also so-called impartial principles. These concern notions of justice that parties would supposedly endorse if they were to assess a situation from a detached viewpoint. The theory of "justice as fairness" (Rawls 1958, 1999) is based on such a notion. It holds that justice is what parties would select and agree on "behind a veil of ignorance"—that is, if they were ignorant of their own identity and position and thus of how their decisions would affect their own situation. This procedure is meant to purge the process of all inequalities in resources and other advantages, including skills and power. Drawing on Rawls and on Scanlon (1982), another theory holds that justice is "what can freely be agreed on" by parties who are equally well placed, notably in the sense of being able to reject and veto an agreement (Barry 1995, p. 51). Just decisions are reached without the need to use heavy-handed threats or rewards or other forms of coercion or manipulation. They can be justified on impartial grounds. A detached outside observer could not reasonably reject them as unjust.

The scholarly debate on justice has generated a voluminous literature. Even the very limited and selective review provided here demonstrates that there are numerous principles and concepts, many of which are competing and controversial. If the question of what justice is and requires is traced back to Plato, the debate has already lasted well over 2,000 years. This makes it all the more interesting to examine how parties to international negotiations have defined justice and fairness and how they have managed and settled differences in perceptions.

JUSTICE AND FAIRNESS IN PRACTICE

Interviews with senior participants in negotiations have revealed that notions of justice and fairness were not the primary driving force or objective behind their deliberations or decisions. Depending on the area, the main goals have instead been such matters as climate stability, clean air, disarmament, market access, financial stability, and economic development. Yet in structuring negotiations and formulating broadly acceptable agreements on cooperation to reach these objectives, it has almost always been necessary to take justice and fairness into account. A long list of widely endorsed principles has thus emerged from negotiations, including nondiscrimination, "no harm," polluter pays, shared but differentiated responsibility, the duty of compliance, and no free-riding (Albin 2001). Many of these are variations on the principles of equality, proportionality, and impartiality discussed above.

But the most striking finding from these interviews, and from observations of recent negotiations over different global public goods, is that justice is effectively defined as a combination of and balance among several principles. Negotiators clearly believe that justice and fairness entail representing, protecting, and promoting the needs and concerns of all parties. They also recognize that as problems become more intricate and parties more unequal, a wider range of considerations needs to be accommodated and this can rarely be done while relying on a single standard (Earle 1998; Tran 1998).

Thus international agreements are often "package deals" based on many criteria. This is seen as right and reasonable, not only as required on pragmatic grounds. The 1987 Montreal Protocol on Substances That Deplete the Ozone Layer, one of the most successful environmental agreements ever negotiated, combined several norms to take into account the varied conditions and concerns of signatory states. The proportionality principle drove the protocol's call for reductions, beginning in 1993, in chlorofluorocarbon emissions in relation to each country's emissions level in 1986. It thereby imposed a greater (unequal) cost of regulation on industrial countries. Compensatory justice underlay the provision for financial and technical assistance to developing countries, and the principle of need their exemption from the stipulated emission reductions for the first 10 years for purposes of economic development. Finally, the equality norm was expressed in the long-term goal of industrial countries and developing countries sharing regulation costs on a basis of parity.

In practice, then, justice and fairness mean a balanced settlement of conflicting claims (Albin 2001). This approach takes into account the interests of parties but constrains the raw pursuit of self-interest. It allows for some power inequalities between parties but does not simply mirror the prevailing balance of forces. Thus it highlights the importance of the structural and process dimensions of negotiations. Although never a guarantee of a fair outcome, fairness in the negotiation structure and process does facilitate a more balanced result. Without it, parties are unlikely to accept the outcome as legitimate.

GETTING TO FAIRNESS: HOW TO ARRANGE AND CONDUCT NEGOTIATIONS

Negotiations involve a structure and a bargaining process, including procedures that the parties use in working toward an agreement. All these elements can be designed to reflect notions of justice.

To achieve a balanced settlement of conflicting claims, two issues among many others matter: ensuring as far as possible that all parties have an effective voice in representing their interests and concerns and that all claims are considered fully in the negotiation process. How then can negotiations be organized and conducted to make this possible?

Creating a just and fair negotiating structure

The structural components of negotiation concern the issue-related as well as the social and physical constraints under which the talks unfold and participants operate (Rubin and Brown 1975). The structural elements are typically givens that have been determined earlier, in preparatory consultations or by extraneous factors. Most remain constant throughout the bargaining—unlike the process issues, which may fluctuate. Among the important structural elements are agenda setting; parties, relations between them, and their participation; and the negotiation rules and venue.

Formulating a broad, inclusive agenda. What issues and priorities are placed on the agenda, and how they are ordered and linked, can significantly affect subsequent deliberations and their eventual outcome. Negotiators naturally seek to ensure maximum coverage of issues that are of most interest to themselves and favor linkages that may bolster their own bargaining position. The concept of justice as a balanced settlement of conflicting claims calls for a reasonably broad and balanced agenda that includes, orders, and links issues in a way that considers the essential interests and concerns of all parties.

The preparatory meetings for the International Conference on Financing for Development provide a successful example of inclusive agenda setting. They led to an agenda that incorporated concerns of industrial countries (such as enhanced resource mobilization and implementation of financial codes and standards in developing countries), priorities of the poorest countries (such as increased development assistance), and interests of advanced emerging market economies (such as improved participation in international financial forums). The agenda also reflected concerns that international organizations brought to the table and issues of interest to nonstate actors.

Ensuring that all parties are represented. Offering all stakeholders a seat at the bargaining table (as far as possible) is another important element of justice, which helps to ensure that all interests are considered (Susskind and Cruikshank 1987). It also enhances the perceived legitimacy of the outcome and facilitates implementation. Parties with a genuine opportunity to be represented and have an input into the negotiations are more likely to identify with the outcome and to be motivated or feel obliged to ensure effective follow-up.

The international community (especially intergovernmental organizations) faces at least two challenges on the question of representation in negotiations.[2] One is the issue of whether developing countries are adequately represented and what can be done to tackle disadvantages effectively. The other is the issue of defining and agreeing on criteria and procedures for involving parties, state and non-state, in deliberations (Albin 1995, 1999; Helleiner 2000). Traditional criteria, such as statehood and sovereignty, are inadequate because negotiations over global public goods often concern more parties and interests than governments can fully or credibly represent alone. Yet for practical reasons *all* affected parties can rarely participate, one reason being that they are far too numerous.

Justice as a balanced settlement of conflicting claims therefore calls for a principled and consistent, yet cautious and incremental, expansion of the opportunities for concerned parties to participate in negotiations over global public goods. Participation should be based on criteria that relate directly to what the parties (whether state or nonstate) can contribute in enhancing the representativeness, legitimacy, and effectiveness of the process and outcome. During the turbulent WTO meeting in Seattle in 1999, U.S. President Clinton pointed out that "the public must see and hear and, in a very real sense, actually join in the deliberations. . . . That's the only way they can know the process is fair and know their concerns were at least considered."[3]

Crafting clear, transparent rules. Negotiations are governed by rules for a range of matters, including modes of communication and decisionmaking (such as rule of consensus and voting rules), any involvement of outside observers or interested parties, and the use of deadlines. Concerns about fairness will arise if, for example, some parties do not have a chance to take part in selecting the rules or are disadvantaged by them.

Rules are important in negotiations over global public goods, which so often are multilateral and large scale. The rules help to organize the deliberations, coordinate expectations, and facilitate agreement. They can also enhance fairness in various respects. For example, the rule of decisionmaking by consensus in the WTO and the Conference on Disarmament gives every country a power of veto, which encourages taking a broad range of interests into account and convincing all needed parties. The chief U.S. negotiator on services in the Uruguay Round noted in an interview that the WTO consensus rule "gives all countries, big and small

... a fair degree of equality when it comes to things like decisionmaking. . . . All parties feel that they . . . require reciprocity from other parties" (Self 1998). Informal decisionmaking procedures and understandings almost always emerge simultaneously in complex multilateral negotiations, partly as a means to overcome the complexity of the process and make an agreement possible. These may or may not compromise the formal agreed rules and fairness. The U.S. chair of the WTO meeting in Seattle decided to hold so-called Green Room meetings with a small number of delegations to resolve important issues. This forum became widely regarded as unrepresentative, however, and the WTO consensus rule enabled developing countries in particular to reject its recommended agenda for a new round of trade talks.

Choosing a neutral and accessible venue. The venue concerns the location and sponsoring organization of the negotiations. It has a bearing on fairness because it influences participation, performance, and transparency (Rubin and Brown 1975; Susskind and Cruikshank 1987). For example, the venue affects the provision of services and facilities and access for directly involved parties as well as interested observers, including nongovernmental organizations and the media. Therefore, the selection of a neutral site outside the home territory of parties or their close allies may be appropriate. Alternatively, when negotiations continue over a period of time, they may be alternated between partisan sites. This can prove costly and undesirable, however, especially for small delegations from developing countries (see Chasek and Rajamani in this volume).

Ensuring a fair negotiation process

Process fairness here refers to how parties relate to and treat one another during negotiations. The process is governed in part by procedures that reflect how the negotiators hope to arrive at an agreement (Young 1994). Often, some rules have been established in earlier preparatory talks or agreements or by the host organization. But the parties can also agree to adopt additional complementary or entirely new procedures for a specific negotiation. Assessing process fairness requires observing the nature of the rules, the manner in which they were adopted (and changed, if applicable), and the extent to which parties honor them during deliberation and bargaining.

Giving all parties a say in selecting procedures. Procedures concern a range of matters, including the creation and use of negotiating or consultation groups (for example, formal subcommittees and informal gatherings of certain parties selected by the chair), the assignment of issues and tasks to these, and the manner in which draft proposals will be discussed, concessions exchanged, and decisions adopted. They may be explicit and well-established regulations or more subtle guidelines or expectations for the parties to interpret and apply as they go along. Whatever the case, giving all parties an adequate chance to participate in selecting and defining them is essential from a fairness perspective. The way in which large-scale multilateral negotiations over global public goods are organized and handled through procedures is perhaps particularly important for smaller and poorly resourced delegations, which often struggle to keep up with the process. For example, they may be adversely affected if numerous meetings on technical issues requiring mastery of extensive background documentation are conducted in parallel or over too short a time.

Giving all parties an effective voice. Every party should have a real chance to put forward its case and have an input into all stages of the negotiation process (Susskind 1994; Susskind and Cruikshank 1987). To have an effective voice, parties must be well informed and able to enjoy full access to relevant information about the issues under negotiation. Again, this requires trained staff and material resources. For this reason many developing countries, especially the very poorest with small delegations, have limited capacity to participate fully in the process even if formally given the chance to do so. One method used to help reduce the impact of such differences on the eventual outcome is a common negotiating text, prepared by the conference secretariat or a facilitator appointed from among the negotiating parties. That method was used in the International Conference on Financing for Development.[4]

Fair input and fair hearing are not just of intrinsic value; they are crucial to successful negotiations. Parties are unlikely to sign or implement agreements voluntarily if they were denied the chance to be heard and play a meaningful role. A full hearing of all concerns also brings out divergent interests and perspectives, including on justice and fairness. This can enhance the effectiveness of the outcome in a technical as well as a political way. Moreover, it can facilitate progress toward a final agreement by providing parties with opportunities to trade concessions on issues that they value differently. When the issues under consideration are very complex, outside expertise may have to be enlisted, such as epistemic communities and data generated by computer models (see Blanchard, Criqui, Kitous, and Viguier in this volume). This goes back to the point made earlier, that effective and fair negotiations require parties to be fully informed and knowledgeable.

Ensuring fair play. Fair negotiations are also about fair play, which requires compliance with agreed rules and procedures, whether formally established or informally understood. Heavy-handed coercion and pressure should be avoided so that all parties, including weak ones, can freely accept or reject proposals for an agreement. All participants have, however, an underlying obligation to negotiate in good faith and work toward and contribute to an agreement. In other words, a party cannot in the name of fairness pursue its narrow self-interests in an uncompromising way. Parties ranging from India (in the negotiation of the 1996 Comprehensive Test Ban Treaty) to the United States (in recent climate change talks) have been accused of holding or attempting to hold all others and an entire process hostage by threatening to block an agreement unless their high demands were met.[5]

Some elements in the framework for fair negotiation practice outlined here (and summarized in figure 1) may appear secondary to larger considerations of justice in the provision of global public goods. But many cases have demonstrated that the real difficulties and challenges are found in the details. Fairness matters in all phases of negotiations, from setting the agenda to implementing and ensuring compliance with any agreement reached. If this is not recognized, the prospects may be limited for achieving outcomes that all needed parties will accept. In the case of global public goods, cooperation and provision are likely to suffer, to the ultimate detriment of everyone.

Concluding note

What then can be done to encourage fair negotiation practice, along the lines discussed here? A number of possibilities emerge from this discussion, though only two are mentioned here.[6]

Agreeing in advance on standards for fair negotiation practice
Parties could discuss and agree on certain criteria for fair negotiation, to be observed when the actual talks are arranged and conducted. The framework set forth in this chapter provides criteria that could serve as a starting point. Subsequent adherence to agreed standards could then be reviewed at critical junctures. A detached party, such as a committee of subject experts and representatives of the host organization, could help to undertake these reviews impartially.

The observance of agreed criteria for fair negotiations could also be examined across issue areas at regular intervals. Organizations sponsoring negotiations over global public goods would be well placed to institute such a procedure. In the United Nations it could be done by the General Assembly. Such broader reviews might reveal patterns and trends that would not, within a single issue area, be apparent or seem serious enough to evoke concern and action. For example, from a fairness perspective, it would be important to examine whether or to what extent the interests and priorities of weaker parties (such as poor developing countries) are neglected.

Linking issues to enhance fairness
In the absence of shared and agreed priorities among countries, many global resources are valued differently and thereby provide a basis for trading. This allows a party to exchange concessions on its lower-priority issues, if these are

FIGURE 1
A framework for fair negotiation practice

Fair structure

- All parties represented (as far as possible)
- Inclusive and balanced agenda setting
- Clear, transparent rules agreed on by all
- Neutral venue

Fair process

Fair hearing	Fair play
• Negotiating procedures selected or agreed on by all • All parties having a say and an input into the process • Needed information and expertise available to all • All interests and concerns fully considered	• Adherence by all to agreed rules and procedures • Avoidance of force and coercion • All parties prepared to reciprocate, compromise, and contribute to an agreement

Enhance

Fair outcome

- Voluntary agreement (obligations entered into freely)
- Balanced settlement of conflicting claims (with a balance of net benefits for all)
- Implementation and compliance by all parties
- Outcome accepted as legitimate and balanced by parties and outside observers

more important to another party, for concessions on matters that it values more. Linkage can also be used to promote fairness (as defined in this chapter) when negotiations are planned and conducted. Indeed, weak parties to negotiations over global public goods have used this method effectively on a number of occasions to secure a more balanced agenda and terms of agreement than they otherwise would have been able to achieve. An example is the United Nations special session on HIV/AIDS in 2001. Developing countries, in exchange for a greater commitment to fight their high infection rates, secured financial transfers and concessions on intellectual property rights that industrial countries had long resisted (United Nations 2001). Since AIDS cannot be fought successfully without the collaboration of developing countries, their call for a better balance between intellectual property rights and the rights of people to good health and proper medical care was influential.

*   *   *

These are only two of several strategies available to enhance fairness in the negotiation and provision of global public goods. The degree of interdependence and need for cooperation among parties in these processes are almost always considerable. This means that it should be possible to use such strategies far more extensively than they have been used to date, to everyone's ultimate benefit.

Is the framework proposed here likely to appeal to those who feel dissatisfied with today's international negotiation practice and agreements? It might, because fair negotiations are more inclusive and offer better prospects for balanced outcomes. But it can at best facilitate, not substitute for, various policy choices that have to be made. This chapter has pointed to a major one: whether international negotiators and their host organizations should begin to address justice and fairness considerations more systematically rather than continuing to do so only on an ad hoc and case-by-case basis. If this choice is made, justice and fairness in the provision of global public goods is an excellent place to start, given the importance of these goods and the great potential they offer for mutual gains.

NOTES

1. See also the chapters by Griffith-Jones and by Mendoza in this volume.

2. See further discussions in the chapters by Buira, Chasek and Rajamani, Edwards and Zadek, Griffith-Jones, Held and McGrew, and Mendoza in this volume.

3. Quoted in "Clinton Calls for a More Transparent WTO," India Abroad News Service, 2 December 1999 (http://www.indiainfo.com/news/1999/12/2/us.html).

4. See, for example, the draft agreement prepared by a facilitator at this conference at http://www.un.org/esa/ffd/aac257_25.htm.

5. See, for example, "A Stern Warning on Warming" (editorial, *The New York Times*, 8 June 2001) for reactions in different parts of the world to the Bush administration's withdrawal from the Kyoto Protocol.

6. For a more in-depth discussion of these and other proposals, see Albin (forthcoming) and, in this volume, the chapters by Chasek and Rajamani as well as Edwards and Zadek.

REFERENCES

Albin, Cecilia. 1993. "The Role of Fairness in Negotiation." *Negotiation Journal* 9 (3): 223–44.

———. 1995. "The Global Security Challenge to Negotiation: Toward the New Agenda." In Cecilia Albin, ed., *Negotiation and Global Security: New Approaches to Contemporary Issues*. Special issue of American Behavioral Scientist 38 (6): 921–48.

———. 1999. "Can NGOs Enhance the Effectiveness of International Negotiation?" In Cecilia Albin, ed., *Negotiating Effectively: The Role of Non-Governmental Organizations*. Special issue of International Negotiation 4 (3): 371–87.

———. 2001. *Justice and Fairness in International Negotiation*. Cambridge: Cambridge University Press.

———. Forthcoming. "Negotiating International Cooperation: Global Public Goods and Fairness." University of Reading, Reading, UK.

Arneson, Richard. 1989. "Equality and Equal Opportunity for Welfare." *Philosophical Studies* 56: 77–93.

Axelrod, Robert. 1984. *The Evolution of Cooperation*. New York: Basic Books.

Barrett, Scott. 1999. "Montreal versus Kyoto: International Cooperation and the Global Environment." In Inge Kaul, Isabelle Grunberg, and Marc A. Stern, eds., *Global Public Goods: International Cooperation in the 21st Century*. New York: Oxford University Press.

Barry, Brian. 1989. *Theories of Justice*. Berkeley: University of California Press.

———. 1995. *Justice as Impartiality*. Oxford: Clarendon Press.

Cohen, Gerald. 1993. "Equality of What? On Welfare, Goods, and Capabilities." In Martha Nussbaum and Amartya Sen, eds., *The Quality of Life*. Oxford: Clarendon Press.

de Jonquieres, Guy. 2001. "All Night Haggling in Doha Ends in Agreement." *Financial Times*, 15 November, p. 6.

Dupuy, Jean-Pierre. 1992. *Libéralisme et justice sociale*. Paris: Hachette Littérature.

Dworkin, Ronald. 1981. "What Is Equality?" *Philosophy and Public Affairs* 10: 185–246, 283–345.

Earle, Ralph. 1998. Personal interview. Acting head of the U.S. delegation to the 1995 Nuclear Nonproliferation Treaty Review and Extension Conference. 30 June.

Gauthier, David. 1986. *Morals by Agreement.* Oxford: Clarendon Press.

Godard, Olivier. 1997. " De Rio à Kyoto: pourquoi la convention sur le climat devrait intéresser ceux qui ne s'intéressent pas au climat. " *Futuribles* 224: 31–68

Gouldner, Alvin W. 1960. "The Norm of Reciprocity: A Preliminary Statement." *American Sociological Review* 25 (2): 161-178.

Grieco, Joseph M. 1988. "Anarchy and the Limits of Cooperation." *International Organization* 42: 485–508.

Helleiner, Gerald Karl. 2000. "Markets, Politics and Globalization: Can the Global Economy Be Civilized?" Tenth Raul Prebisch Lecture, delivered at the Palais des Nations, Geneva, 11 December. United Nations Conference on Trade and Development, Geneva.

Kanbur, Ravi. 2001. "Economic Policy, Distribution and Poverty: The Nature of Disagreements." *World Development* 9 (6): 1083–94.

Kelley, Harold H., Linda L. Beckman, and Claude S. Fischer. 1967. "Negotiating the Division of a Reward under Incomplete Information." *Journal of Experimental Social Psychology* 3: 361–98.

Ng, Yew Kwang. 2000. *Efficiency, Equality and Public Policy: With a Case for Higher Public Spending.* New York: St. Martin's.

Pruitt, Dean. 1981. *Negotiation Behavior.* New York: Academic Press.

Rawls, John. 1958. "Justice as Fairness." *Philosophical Review* 67: 164–94.

———. 1999 [1971]. *A Theory of Justice.* Cambridge, Mass.: The Belknap Press of Harvard University Press.

Roemer, John E. 1996. *Theories of Distributive Justice.* Cambridge, Mass.: Harvard University Press.

Rubin, Jeffrey Z., and Bert Brown. 1975. *The Social Psychology of Bargaining and Negotiation.* New York and London: Academic Press.

Scanlon, Thomas. 1982. "Contractualism and Utilitarianism." In Amartya Sen and Bernard Williams, eds., *Utilitarianism and Beyond.* Cambridge: Cambridge University Press.

Self, Richard. 1998. Personal interview. Chief U.S. negotiator on services in the Uruguay Round, overseeing the drafting of the text of the General Agreement on Trade in Services (GATS) and the market access commitments of more than 90 countries. 29 April.

Shue, Henry. 1992. "The Unavoidability of Justice." In Andrew Hurrell and Benedict Kingsbury, eds., *The International Politics of the Environment.* Oxford: Clarendon Press.

Susskind, Lawrence. 1994. *Environmental Diplomacy: Negotiating More Effective Global Agreements.* Oxford: Oxford University Press.

Susskind, Lawrence, and Jeffrey Cruikshank. 1987. *Breaking the Impasse: Consensual Approaches to Resolving Public Disputes.* New York: Basic Books.

Tran, Van-Thinh. 1998. Personal interview. Head of and chief negotiator for the European Commission permanent delegation to the Uruguay Round of the General Agreement on Tariffs and Trade in all areas (from 1979 to 1994). 25 March.

United Nations. 2001. "Declaration of Commitment on HIV/AIDS." Adopted by the General Assembly special session on HIV/AIDS. New York, 2 August. [http://www.unaids.org/whatsnew/others/un_special/Declaration020801_en.htm].

Van Parijs, Philippe. 1991. *Qu'est-ce qu'une société juste?* Paris: Seuil.

———. 1998. "Inégalité, justice et protection socials." *Problèmes économiques* 2565–66: 88–89.

WTO (World Trade Organization). 2001. "Doha WTO Ministerial 2001: Ministerial Declaration." WT/MIN(01)/DEC/1. Geneva, 20 November. [http://www-chil.wto-ministerial.org/english/thewto_e/minist_e/min01_e/mindecl_e.htm].

Young, Peyton. 1994. *Equity: In Theory and Practice.* Princeton, N.J.: Princeton University Press.

Zartman, Ian William, and Maureen Berman. 1982. *The Practical Negotiator.* New Haven, Conn., and London: Yale University Press.

COMBINING EFFICIENCY
WITH EQUITY:
A PRAGMATIC APPROACH

ODILE BLANCHARD, PATRICK CRIQUI, ALBAN KITOUS,

AND LAURENT VIGUIER

As Sandmo (in this volume) shows, under some circumstances efficiency and equity concerns must go hand in hand to avoid further inequity. The challenge is to strike the appropriate balance between efficiency and equity—with equity largely determined by society's notions of justice and fairness.

At the same time, Albin (in this volume) points out the wide range of often conflicting views that people and scholars hold when it comes to justice and fairness. Views on justice and fairness for environmental issues—the focus of this chapter—are no exception. The international community has acknowledged that industrial and developing countries have "common but differentiated responsibilities" and different capabilities for contributing to the provision of climate stability, a global public good (UNFCCC 1992, art. 3). A first step toward applying this principle was the decision to define binding commitments for industrial countries to reduce greenhouse gas emissions by 2008–12.

But greenhouse gas emissions from developing countries are expected to grow rapidly over the coming decades. Thus future international negotiations on climate stability—and the reductions in greenhouse gas emissions needed to achieve it—will have to address developing country contributions to this global public good. What notions of justice and fairness should guide policy proposals and targets for emission limits in developing countries? This question has no easy answer, and negotiations on these issues face several challenges.

The basic principle of common but differentiated responsibilities and different capabilities has been translated into a series of specific differentiation rules.

The authors are grateful to Nikolas Kouvaritakis (Institute of Communication and Computer Systems, National Technical University of Athens) for contributions to the POLES model and the first draft of the carbon constrained scenario, to Silvana Mima and Anh Tuan Nguyen (Institut d'Economie et de Politique de l'Energie) for contributions to the POLES modeling exercises, and to anonymous referees for insightful comments. Funding for the research underlying this chapter was provided by the Institut Français de l'Energie and the National Center of Competence in Research–Climate.

But analysis of these rules leads to a conclusion similar to that of Albin (in this volume)—that no single rule is likely to achieve broad political acceptance in the foreseeable future. This is the first challenge facing negotiators.

A second challenge is that the goal is not to achieve merely equity but also efficiency. The current international regime for stabilizing the climate, the Kyoto Protocol (UNFCCC 1997), proposes "flexibility mechanisms" so that countries can achieve emission targets in efficient, affordable ways. These mechanisms— international emissions trading, joint implementation, and the Clean Development Mechanism—involve interntional trading of permits to emit greenhouse gases (for more details, see Castro and Cordero in this volume). So, even if negotiators succeeded in agreeing on a principle of equity, what would happen to distributive justice once trading occurs? In other words, how fair will the ultimate policy outcome be?

These challenges cannot be resolved without scenario building and modeling efforts. In the past, negotiators often had to make decisions despite uncertainties about the realities of climate change. Today, however, extensive data are available to generate well-informed analyses.

Indeed, this chapter's purpose is to demonstrate the possibilities for better, more informed decisionmaking. Such decisionmaking opens new avenues for political pragmatism, making it possible to explore the effects of incremental policy changes resulting from possible decisions—concessions—made by one negotiating party or another. Most important, this chapter shows that it is possible to do what many have considered difficult: to combine efficiency and equity considerations and even to satisfy various rules on differentiation and various notions of justice.

The approach proposed here is pragmatic and politically feasible because it does not require agreement on specific criteria at the outset. The model can be based on different assumptions, and the assumptions can be changed through an iterative process until the negotiating parties are satisfied with the projected outcome. Moreover, there is a greater likelihood that the parties will agree on the projected outcome because it will likely satisfy several of the expectations that they bring to the bargaining table. With current analytical tools, there is no longer a need to wait three or four decades to see the consequences of today's policy choices. It is now possible to determine likely outcomes before embarking on certain policy paths.

COMMON BUT DIFFERENTIATED RESPONSIBILITY: AN ACCEPTED PRINCIPLE LEADING TO CONTESTED RULES

This section first examines the differentiation of countries' commitment to contribute to global climate stability as indicated by the United Nations Framework Convention on Climate Change (UNFCCC) and its Kyoto Protocol. The section then reviews various proposals on how this principle could be translated into rules to guide policymaking. Finally, it discusses the dilemma that this multiplicity of rules creates for policymakers—and why this dilemma is less of a problem than it would appear at first sight.

Differentiation: a key component of the climate change regime
The UNFCCC uses the term *differentiation* in the broad sense of taking into account national characteristics in order to achieve the convention's ultimate goal. Here, however, the term is used in the more restrictive sense of differentiating countries' quantified objectives for limiting and reducing emissions, because the analysis focuses on how these objectives can be shared among the parties to the convention.

As noted, climate stability is the global public good in question, and its properties are nonrival and nonexcludable. But climate stability is based on another, impure global public good (a "common pool" resource): an atmosphere protected against excessive emissions of anthropogenic greenhouse gases. Carbon dioxide emissions are a major component of anthropogenic greenhouse gases. So, one of the tasks facing the international community in achieving climate stability is reducing these emissions.

Accordingly, countries have an incentive to maximize the emissions allowance granted to them and to minimize the costs of achieving required emission reductions. Thus while the final good of climate stability is public and available for all to enjoy, the effort of producing it needs to be apportioned. The production effort involves two tasks: quantifying emission allowances (that is, creating rules for sharing the scarce good—the "entitlement" to emit greenhouse gases) and sharing the costs of achieving emissions reduction targets. These tasks are closely intertwined, because the costs of a country's efforts depend, among other things, on its emissions allowance.

The UNFCCC differentiates emissions reduction targets by country groups. Annex 1 countries—industrial countries and transition economies—have agreed to stabilize greenhouse gas emissions by 2000 at 1990 levels. Non–Annex 1 countries—developing countries—have no such obligation. This setup reflects the parties' differing historical responsibilities for creating the greenhouse effect. The distinction between Annex 1 and non–Annex 1 countries can be called the primary differentiation.

The Kyoto Protocol, adopted in 1997, introduces a secondary differentiation. The protocol stipulates that between 2008 and 2012, Annex 1 countries must, as a group, cut greenhouse gas emissions by at least 5 percent below 1990 levels. Emissions reduction requirements are similar for the European Union (–8 percent), the United States (–7 percent), and Japan (–6 percent). Elsewhere, however, reduction rates are more differentiated, and some are actually growth rates. Examples include Iceland (+10 percent), Australia (+8 percent), Norway (+1 percent), and New Zealand, the Russian Federation, and Ukraine (no change). No clear rule led to this differentiation; it was more the result of political haggling (Babiker and Eckaus 2000; Viguier 1999). Still, the differentiation roughly reflects the parties' different economic, technological, and energy situations.

Proposed differentiation rules for achieving climate stability
Thus recent negotiations and existing agreements provide limited guidance on exactly how to implement the principle of common but differentiated responsibilities and different capabilities for contributing to climate stability. Little concrete policy advice is available on options for the possible inclusion of developing countries in future agreements on emission targets. So, in assessing options, one should start by examining various proposals put forward by policymakers and scientists since the late 1980s, in preparation for and in response to the 1992 United Nations Conference on Environment and Development (the Earth Summit).

These proposals address the two main tasks, identified above, in the production effort for climate stability—quantifying emission allowances and sharing the costs of achieving emissions reduction targets. Most of the differentiation rules proposed by country representatives in negotiations refer to emission allowances, because emission levels are easier to monitor than mitigation costs. Some of the most frequently proposed rules include (see also table 1):

- *Equalizing per capita emission limits.* This rule would inevitably lead to lower emission allowances for industrial countries and higher emission allowances for developing countries, compared with current levels.[1] Thus developing countries would be allowed to increase per capita emissions for a certain period.[2]

- *Allocating emission allowances based on current or cumulative emissions.* This rule is also known as that of "inherited quotas" or "grandfathering." It would undoubtedly benefit industrial countries because current emissions would be considered an "acquired right" (Godard 1997). Developing countries would be severely disadvantaged because there would be no way for them to increase emissions over the next few decades.

- *Differentiating emission allowances or mitigation costs based on contributions to climate change.* If responsibilities for climate change were determined solely on the basis of past emissions, under this rule developing countries would be expected to contribute less to corrective action than would industrial countries.[3]

- *Differentiating commitments based on the intensity of emissions relative to GDP.* This rule would require the greatest efforts from countries with energy systems emitting relatively high levels of greenhouse gases. Thus it is often seen as unfavorable not only to industrial but also developing countries—China, India, the United States—with greenhouse gas–intensive energy systems.

TABLE 1

Proposed differentiation rules, criteria, and most favored beneficiaries

Rule	Differentiation criteria	Most favored party
Equalizing per capita emission limits	Per capita emissions	Developing countries
Allocating emission allowances based on current or cumulative emissions (grandfathering)	Current or cumulative emissions	Industrial countries
Differentiating emission allowances or mitigation costs based on contributions to climate change	Current or cumulative emissions Share of responsibility for global warming	Developing countries
Differentiating commitments based on the intensity of emissions	Emissions/GDP	Countries whose energy relative to GDP systems emit low levels of greenhouse gases
Differentiating commitments based on per capita GDP	Per capita GDP	Developing countries
Equalizing marginal abatement costs	Marginal abatement costs	Depends on the reduction level
Differentiating abatement costs based on expected benefits from lower greenhouse gas emissions and climate stabilization	Benefits from mitigation of climate change	Industrial countries

- *Differentiating commitments based on per capita GDP.* This rule would allow policymakers to take into account both the ability of industrial countries to pay and the priority that developing countries place on such goals as economic growth and poverty reduction. But because the rule is not directly related to emission levels or mitigation costs, it might not provide the right incentives to reduce greenhouse gas emissions.
- *Equalizing marginal abatement costs.* This rule is sometimes claimed to establish relatively severe emissions reduction targets for countries with inefficient energy systems. The reason is that such countries have greater potential for low-cost emission cuts than do countries with efficient energy systems. But this approach should be qualified by taking into account the

structure and dynamics of each country's energy system, because countries with already efficient energy systems may encounter high marginal costs while reducing emissions.

- *Differentiating abatement costs based on expected benefits from lower greenhouse gas emissions and climate stabilization.* Because developing countries will likely suffer most of the negative effects of climate instability, the benefits of prevention might be more important for these countries. The implication is that developing countries should be willing to pay the highest abatement costs. In a way it would require that the "victims" pay. But this approach must take into account the fact that developing countries have limited financial resources for their development needs and would probably not view investments in global climate stabilization as deserving priority over other investments. Moreover, because this rule ignores past emissions, it may not be very feasible politically.

All of these rules will likely generate a divergence of interests (see Shue 1992). Even among developing countries, under certain rules some countries would be better off than others, depending on their characteristics. Thus any international negotiations using these rules would face multiple dividing lines cutting across various subgroups. Moreover, the rules are partly based on different principles of justice. Some reflect principles of equality (such as the rule calling for equal per capita emission limits). Others are based on the principle of proportionality but use varying reference criteria (such as emissions intensity or per capita GDP). These different principles of justice add another source of potential disagreement, further limiting the possibility of an easy settlement between competing expectations and claims.

The impossibility of identifying just one fair solution

Given the array of differentiation rules, coupled with the lack of consensus on any one of them, it is easy to understand why the literature depicts the application of principles of justice in international relations as a hotly debated, disputed, and often unattempted solution.[4] So, is there a way forward? To begin answering that question, it is useful to explain some of the hurdles on the way.

No single criterion will be feasible. Theory tells us that some principles of justice are "configurational" in that fair allocation is determined by characteristics of the negotiating parties (Dupuy 1992). Albin (in this volume) uses the term "internal" in this sense. In theory, nonconfigurational principles are more likely to lead to an agreement. In practice, parties involved in climate change negotiations want an agreement that takes into account their positions. The more the characteristics of the parties differ, the less an agreement based on a nonconfigurational principle can be expected, and the less such an agreement might derive from a single configurational principle. Thus any future burden-sharing agreement involving developing countries will probably be based on a complex differentiation scheme combining different basic rules.

In fact, in past negotiations countries often advocated not just one rule but a combination (see, for example, UNFCCC 1996). Proposals for an approach using multiple rules have also begun to emerge in the literature (see Blanchard and others 1998; Helm and Simonis 2001; and Müller 1998, 2001). But they generally fail to simultaneously define equitable and efficient policy options for providing climate stability.

Initial decisions will not necessarily deliver intended outcomes. Assume, for the sake of argument, that negotiators agree to blend several differentiation rules. As noted, the question immediately arises of how emissions trading will affect the agreed arrangement. The flexibility mechanisms incorporated in the Kyoto Protocol are designed to achieve emission reductions at the lowest possible costs. If these international mechanisms are used, the final distribution of actual emissions will necessarily differ from the initial allocation of allowances. Thus it should be determined how market outcomes are deviating from the agreed initial allocation pattern. One could argue that, at least in theory, the market process will be set up from behind a "veil of ignorance" (Rawls 1971). That is, at the outset parties would agree on trading rules and emission allocations without being able to forecast trading actions and thus final outcomes. But according to Dupuy (1992), the outcomes of trade are efficient and fair because the market is free from human will, conscience, and control.

In practice, however, parties know more or less what they can expect from greenhouse gas emissions trading under different initial allocation schemes.[5] The "veil of ignorance" is partly removed because parties have some information about their current and future abatement costs (through modeling exercises, for example) as well as such costs in other countries. But the market may become a new source of disputes—this time about the fairness of the distribution of gains from trade, making policy consensus even harder to obtain.

In other words, final outcomes can look quite different from initial agreements. Thus it may be a waste of time to debate distribution formulas and related policy choices without analyzing how they might be affected by other conditions along the way.

Ex post validation of pragmatic policy scenarios. Given the impossibility of agreeing on a single criterion and the inadvisability of reaching an initial agreement without regard to final outcomes, how can the current negotiation dilemma be resolved?

Clearly, a large group of countries cannot be expected to share the same concepts of distributive justice. As Fishkin (1986) points out, the ethics of international relations are confronted with the need to find an equilibrium between immeasurable considerations and thus with the impossibility of satisfying absolutist expectations—a point that Albin (in this volume) corroborates. This realization guides this chapter's approach to the challenge of reducing greenhouse gas emissions. The main premise is that several differentiation rules must be combined to achieve climate stability as efficiently as possible.

If, in addition, there is a desire to know the likely final outcomes of various policy choices, this complex analytical challenge can be tackled only through scenario building and modeling. In fact, this chapter argues that one way to advance climate change negotiations is to support them more systematically with insights from policy research and analysis. More concretely, it provides a scenario building and modeling exercise with two main features. First, the exercise is based on realistic assumptions—ethical, political, economic, and technical—about global climate stabilization. Second, the exercise provides an ex post (model run) validation of the outcome against a number of criteria that might already enjoy broad support among different negotiating parties.[6]

A PRAGMATIC SCENARIO FOR STABILIZING GREENHOUSE GAS EMISSIONS BY 2030

This section explores a pragmatic "post Kyoto" (beyond 2010) scenario in which developing countries (along with industrial countries) may be included in a commitment to emission limits. The goal is not to propose a normative solution to the climate change equity dilemma or to test the likelihood of success for any agreement. Rather, it is to demonstrate the usefulness of scenario building and modeling as tools for decisionmaking on complex, contested issues.

The pragmatic scenario is built around a few basic assumptions. The first is that the Kyoto Protocol emission reductions will be achieved by 2010. The scenario then takes into account the total emission restrictions aimed at limiting climate change and the economic, energy, and demographic constraints of developing countries. It is called a "soft landing" scenario because it will allow all countries to contribute to the global goal and global public good of climate stability in a way that is politically, technically, and economically feasible. The assumptions underlying the scenario are described in more detail below.

A first set of constraints: meeting a common target to stabilize emissions
The latest report from the Intergovernmental Panel on Climate Change (IPCC) reviews a wide variety of possible trajectories for changes in emissions of the most important greenhouse gas—carbon dioxide from the burning of fossil fuels—from 1990 onward, leading to the stabilization of atmospheric concentrations by 2100 or later. The scientifically defined trajectories generally aim to stabilize carbon dioxide concentrations at 550 parts per million by volume (ppmv). Although "it does not imply an agreed-upon desirability of stabilization" (IPCC 2001, p.

124), this target is often used in political discussions. Thus the scenario for allocating emission allowances is based on this stabilization hypothesis.

Most of the trajectories for stabilizing concentrations at 550 ppmv by 2100 follow an inverted U-shaped curve for fossil fuel carbon dioxide emissions. After an initial growth period, emissions peak between 2020 and 2060, briefly stabilize at that point, then decline to different levels at different rates. The maximum of this curve most frequently ranges between 9 and 12 gigatons of carbon (IPCC 2001, pp.130, 150).

Scenario assumption 1: fossil fuel carbon dioxide emissions will peak and briefly stabilize at 10 gigatons of carbon by 2030.
Based on this assumption, the scenario develops along the lines of the Kyoto Protocol's primary differentiation between industrial and developing countries for the first commitment period (2008–12). This approach is used to take into account extremely different energy and economic dynamics.

For Annex 1 countries the scenario proposes the same emissions reduction rates as those in the Kyoto Protocol for Canada, the United States, and the European Union. For other countries the targets are adjusted slightly. The reduction rate for Eastern European countries matches that of the European Union (–8 percent) because these countries are expected to join the union. The target rate for all the former Soviet republics (–5 percent) is more stringent than that under the Kyoto Protocol (no change) because the region may benefit from better economic conditions after 2010. In addition, the region may transfer its large surplus of emission allowances from the first commitment period to the second. Australia and New Zealand are supposed to stabilize emissions during 2010–30.

Scenario assumption 2: in Annex 1 countries the emissions reduction rate will average –6.5 percent between 2010 and 2030.
For non–Annex 1 countries, based on the condition in assumption 1 that world emissions will peak and stabilize by 2030, the scenario projects that emissions will stabilize between 2015 and 2045.

A second set of constraints: stabilizing emissions from developing countries
For non–Annex 1 countries the proposed assumptions involve no a priori allocation principles. Rather, they require defining:

- A *departure year* for determining the initial situation and dynamics of these countries. This year is defined as 2010. By then these countries' emissions under a "business as usual" scenario will be about twice the level in 1990.
- *Initial emissions growth rates,* differentiated to account for regional population growth between 2000 and 2010. Gradual reductions in these rates—along with the expected absolute reductions in Annex 1 countries (assumption 2)—lead to overall stabilization.

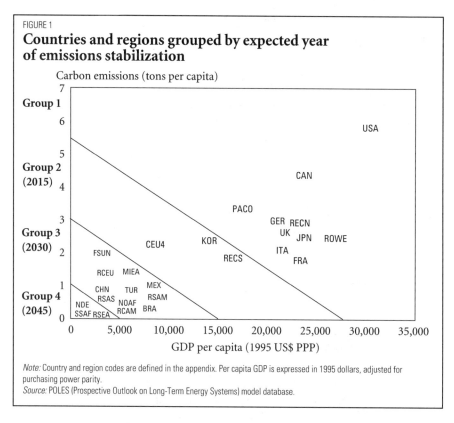

FIGURE 1

Countries and regions grouped by expected year of emissions stabilization

Carbon emissions (tons per capita)

Note: Country and region codes are defined in the appendix. Per capita GDP is expressed in 1995 dollars, adjusted for purchasing power parity.

Source: POLES (Prospective Outlook on Long-Term Energy Systems) model database.

- *Future years by which emissions must stabilize.* To define these years, developing and industrial countries were grouped according to two criteria: per capita GDP and per capita carbon dioxide emissions in 2000. These criteria are used not to allocate emission allowances but to define stabilization horizons for each of the four resulting groups (figure 1).

Group 1 in figure 1 consists of Annex 1 countries. Although the rest of the southern European Union (RECS); the Czech Republic, Hungary, Poland, and the Slovak Republic (CEU4); the former Soviet Union (FSUN); and the rest of Central European countries (RCEU) fall into groups 2 and 3 in the figure, they are Annex 1 countries and regions. Thus they are included in group 1 in the analysis below for consistency with assumption 2. The resulting picture shows why the primary differentiation of the Kyoto Protocol (between Annex 1 and non–Annex 1 countries) may—in hindsight and with today's data—be considered legitimate.

Meanwhile, non–Annex 1 countries fall into groups 2 (relatively high income and emissions), 3 (intermediate income and emissions), and 4 (low income and emissions). Why such groupings? To define a horizon of stabilization, the higher are a country's income and emissions, the sooner should its emissions be stabilized. Conversely, a poor country with low per capita emissions should not be required to stabilize emissions until much later.

Scenario assumption 3: countries in group 2 will stabilize emissions by 2015, those in group 3 by 2030, and those in group 4 by 2045.
With the three preliminary assumptions in place, how can emissions allowance profiles be designed for non–Annex 1 countries, leading from the nonbinding situation in 2010 to the country-specific stabilization horizon? The initial emissions growth rate in 2010 is taken as the sum of an across-the-board annual growth rate of 3 percent in per capita emissions for all developing countries[7] and of the average annual population growth rate in each country between 2000 and 2010 (see Blanchard and others 2000 for mathematical details on this growth rate). Then this initial growth rate decreases until it reaches zero in the stabilization year (2015, 2030, or 2045) defined for each group of developing countries. For each group the reduction in the growth rate follows the same linear function, resulting in a "soft landing" of the growth rate to zero.

So, to summarize the structure of the soft-landing scenario:

- It aims to achieve a stable 10 gigatons of carbon emissions by 2030.
- It assumes that the Kyoto targets will be achieved by Annex 1 countries and reapplied (with minor adjustments) for the second period (2010–30).
- It proposes reducing linearly the emissions growth rates for developing countries at different horizons, taking into account their per capita GDP, per capita carbon dioxide emissions, and population growth rates.

In addition, the model will be run without and with the assumption that international emissions trading occurs.

In defining the stabilization rate for developing countries, no particular differentiation rule has been chosen. So, the intriguing question is, what allocation patterns (of emission allowances or costs of emission reductions) result from the assumptions and constraints for realistic, pragmatic considerations? And are they fair? This is the subject of the next section.

ASSESSING THE RESULTS OF THE SOFT-LANDING SCENARIO

Figure 2 shows emissions under the scenario for 2000–50, differentiated by country group. The scenario achieves the overall target: combined emissions are stabilized at 9.5 gigatons of carbon in 2030. In addition, the global stabilization target is reached: emissions from Annex 1 countries decrease over the entire period, while emissions from group 2 countries stabilize in 2015, those from group 3 countries in 2030, and those from group 4 countries in 2045. Of the 9.5 gigatons of carbon in 2030, 3.7 gigatons are endowed to Annex 1 countries and 5.8 gigatons to developing countries.

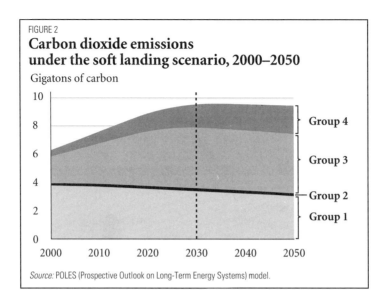

FIGURE 2
Carbon dioxide emissions under the soft landing scenario, 2000–2050

Gigatons of carbon

Group 4

Group 3

Group 2

Group 1

Source: POLES (Prospective Outlook on Long-Term Energy Systems) model.

One requirement for the soft-landing scenario is that it be politically accept-able to most of the negotiating parties. This goal could be achieved only if the sce-nario were compatible with several of the differentiation rules described above. Accordingly, this section evaluates the results of the scenario by answering several questions. How equitable are the final outcomes? How does the scenario address efficiency concerns? And does the scenario achieve the overall objective of com-bining efficiency with equity?

Equity considerations
Gauging the equity of a distribution depends on the principle of justice used to define equity (Blanchard and others 2000). One way is to consider the changes in the distribution of per capita emissions over the period.

Figure 3 shows Lorenz curves and Gini coefficients for world carbon dioxide emissions in 1990, 2010, and 2030.[8] The 1990 curve represents real carbon dioxide emissions, or de facto allowances for that year. The 2010 curve shows the de jure distribution of emission allowances as called for in the Kyoto Protocol. The 2030 curve is based on the allocation of allowances under the soft-landing scenario.

When a Lorenz curve is a straight line, the distribution is considered per-fectly egalitarian. In the allocation of allowances such a distribution would reflect universally equal per capita emissions. Thus figure 3 shows that the situ-ation in 1990 was the most unequal, the situation in 2010 will be less unequal, and the hypothetical situation in 2030 even less unequal. These observations are confirmed by the Gini coefficients, which drop from 0.52 in 1990 to 0.40 in 2010 and 0.33 in 2030.[9] Thus the soft-landing scenario would reduce inequalities

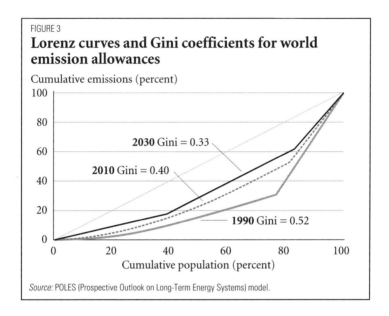

FIGURE 3

Lorenz curves and Gini coefficients for world emission allowances

Cumulative emissions (percent)

2030 Gini = 0.33

2010 Gini = 0.40

1990 Gini = 0.52

Cumulative population (percent)

Source: POLES (Prospective Outlook on Long-Term Energy Systems) model.

among countries by moving toward more equal per capita emission allowances. The scenario does not, however, achieve equality. If further equality is desired, some initial assumptions would have to be modified or further constraints introduced.

Efficiency considerations

Governments and other stakeholders are seriously concerned about reducing abatement costs as much as possible. What do the results of the soft-landing scenario indicate about this concern?

Abatement costs have been calculated using the POLES (Prospective Outlook on Long-Term Energy Systems) model, a partial equilibrium model of the world energy system.[10] This model is situated between the "top down" approach of general computable equilibrium models and the "bottom up" approach of analytical engineering studies. In the POLES model abatement costs are estimated by introducing a shadow carbon tax—a "carbon value"—in all the energy consumption transformation modules. This shadow tax induces adjustments in final energy demand through technological progress or behavioral change, as well as substitutions in energy conversion systems for which the technologies are explicitly identified. By first projecting a reference case in which the shadow tax is zero, it is possible to perform iterative simulations to calculate the emissions associated with a shadow tax that gradually increases from, say, $0 to $600 per ton of carbon. The marginal abatement costs for a particular level of emissions are then deduced (Criqui and Kouvaritakis 1997).[11]

No trading allowed. Abatement costs under the soft-landing scenario are listed in table 2. These costs assume that countries pursue fully autarkic policies—that is, that they cannot trade emission allowances. Annex 1 countries are highlighted to ease reading, and countries are ordered according to abatement costs as a percentage of GDP.

Under the scenario, by 2030 world emissions would be reduced by about 2,500 million tons of carbon relative to the reference situation. Annex 1 countries would account for almost 1,400 million tons of emission reductions, or about 55 percent, and incur 66 percent of total abatement costs. The annual sectoral cost of complying with the commitments for 2030 would range between 0.01 and 1.1 percent of GDP for Annex 1 countries and between 0 and 1 percent for non–Annex 1 countries.[12] The marginal cost of the projected reductions would vary considerably by region, and in extreme cases would exceed $600 per ton of carbon, with the highest values found in Europe and Central America.

The analysis of total abatement costs recalls that costs are built up from the combination of a price effect and a quantity effect. Thus some regions can face a similar cost stemming from either:

- A limited amount of reductions combined with high marginal costs (the Netherlands, rest of Western Europe).
- A greater volume of reductions achieved at low marginal costs (India).

Trading allowed. Now consider a situation where emissions trading is possible. Numerous studies have demonstrated the economic rationale of developing a market for emission permits (see Criqui, Mima, and Viguier 1999; *Energy Journal* 1999; and UNCTAD 2001). This section uses the soft-landing scenario to support this approach.

With trading, the emissions reduction target is still about 2,500 million tons of carbon below the reference level by 2030 (table 3). The world marginal cost of compliance—or the permit price—comes out to $95 per ton of carbon. More than 750 million tons of carbon would be traded, representing 30 percent of the emissions reduction required by the scenario, at a total value of about $71 billion. A dozen countries and regions would export permits, the main ones being China and the former Soviet Union. The main permit buyer would be the United States, with 288 million tons of carbon ($27 billion). Other Annex 1 countries would buy about 250 million tons, and permit-importing non–Annex 1 countries would buy just over 200 million tons.

Taking the situation with no trading as a benchmark, it is possible to analyze the potential gains from introducing international emissions trading. Table 3 confirms the efficiency gains from trade at the global level (a cost of 0.11 percent of GDP instead of 0.2 percent in the no-trade case) and at the national level for all countries. The net gains compared with the no-trading situation are significant

TABLE 2

Abatement costs under the soft-landing scenario, with no trading

| Country or region | Emissions in 2030 (millions of tons of carbon) | | | Abatement costs | | |
	Business-as-usual scenario	Soft-landing scenario	Emission reductions	Marginal costs (1995 U.S. dollars per ton of carbon)	Total costs (millions of 1995 U.S. dollars)	Share of GDP (percent)
Rest of Western Europe	40	20	20	>600	6,634	1.14
Rest of Central America	88	61	27	>600	7,131	1.01
Netherlands	63	38	25	>600	6,528	0.99
Korea, Republic of	249	153	96	529.3	15,643	0.84
Ireland	16	9	7	591.7	1,361	0.65
Sweden	25	14	11	471.9	2,015	0.60
Canada	170	101	69	311.0	7,759	0.54
Greece	39	22	17	230.3	1,436	0.52
Austria	18	13	6	>600	1,666	0.49
Finland	23	13	9	266.7	966	0.43
Australia and New Zealand	158	85	74	220.5	5,217	0.42
United States	1,951	1,155	796	221.6	63,634	0.41
Denmark	17	11	7	362.0	920	0.39
Rest of Southeast Asia	921	626	295	208.8	23,207	0.31
Belgium and Luxembourg	39	28	12	286.3	1,350	0.30
France	136	94	42	409.1	7,362	0.29
Spain	91	62	28	307.3	3,326	0.26

Japan	331	259	73	322.1	10,315	0.22
United Kingdom	189	129	60	204.0	4,930	0.22
Brazil	226	181	45	212.0	4,329	0.16
Italy	116	91	25	253.4	2,440	0.13
Rest of South Asia	179	144	35	125.0	1,944	0.11
Middle East (Mediterranean)	88	74	14	115.2	694	0.09
Germany	238	194	44	118.1	2,406	0.08
Sub-Saharan Africa	587	519	68	72.1	2,105	0.08
India	1,180	989	191	65.8	5,967	0.07
Turkey	130	106	24	72.3	772	0.05
Rest of South America	210	190	20	103.5	998	0.03
Portugal	16	13	3	70.4	87	0.03
Central Europe 4[a]	184	168	15	32.3	237	0.02
Rest of Central Europe	98	91	6	34.3	104	0.02
Gulf states	473	445	28	25.1	338	0.02
China	2,395	2,122	274	32.2	4,230	0.02
Egypt	51	48	3	42.3	53	0.01
Morocco and Tunisia	26	24	2	32.4	26	0.01
Former Soviet Union	944	913	32	12.9	204	0.01
Mexico	183	188	–4	0.0	0	0.00
Algeria and Libyan Arab Jamahariya	52	55	–3	0.0	0	0.00
World	11,941	9,444	2,498	94.8	198,333	0.20

Note: Annex 1 countries are shaded.

a. Czech Republic, Hungary, Poland, and Slovak Republic.

Source: POLES (Prospective Outlook on Long-Term Energy Systems) model using ASPEN (Analyse des Systèmes de Permis d'Emissions Négociables) software.

TABLE 3

World market for emission allowances: an equilibrium price of $95 per ton of carbon

(millions of 1995 U.S. dollars unless otherwise specified)

Country or region	Emissions in 2030 (millions of tons of carbon)			Domestic reductions (percent)	Volume of trade (millions of tons of carbon)	Value of trade	Domestic cost	Total cost	Total cost without trading	Gains from trading	Cost after trading (% of GDP)
	Business-as-usual scenario	Soft-landing scenario	With trading								
Korea, Republic of	249	153	207	44	-54	5,115	1,701	6,815	15,643	8,828	0.37
Greece	39	22	28	62	-6	614	416	1,031	1,436	405	0.37
Australia and New Zealand	158	85	106	71	-21	2,015	2,059	4,074	5,217	1,143	0.33
Rest of Central America	88	61	83	20	-22	2,062	265	2,328	7,131	4,803	0.33
Canada	170	101	136	49	-35	3,326	1,316	4,642	7,759	3,117	0.32
Netherlands	63	38	57	27	-19	1,764	293	2,056	6,528	4,472	0.31
United States	1,951	1,155	1,442	64	-288	27,265	20,149	47,414	63,634	16,220	0.30
Rest of Western Europe	40	20	36	21	-16	1,480	180	1,660	6,634	4,973	0.28
Finland	23	13	18	52	-5	427	210	637	966	329	0.28
Ireland	16	9	13	38	-4	423	112	535	1,361	826	0.26
Sweden	25	14	22	29	-8	738	146	884	2,015	1,131	0.26
Rest of Southeast Asia	921	626	727	66	-101	9,590	8,319	17,908	23,207	5,299	0.24
Denmark	17	11	14	45	-4	362	125	487	920	433	0.21
Belgium and Luxembourg	39	28	34	48	-6	589	246	835	1,350	514	0.18
United Kingdom	189	129	152	61	-24	2,235	1,537	3,772	4,930	1,159	0.17
Spain	91	62	77	49	-15	1,387	563	1,950	3,326	1,377	0.15
Austria	18	13	17	26	-4	412	64	476	1,666	1,190	0.14
France	136	94	123	31	-29	2,750	560	3,310	7,362	4,052	0.13

Japan	331	259	303	39	−44	4,173	1,229	5,402	10,315	4,913	0.12
Brazil	226	181	203	52	−22	2,061	1,052	3,113	4,329	1,215	0.12
Rest of South Asia	179	144	150	81	−7	624	1,222	1,846	1,944	98	0.11
Italy	116	91	102	56	−11	1,061	590	1,651	2,440	789	0.09
Middle East (Mediterranean)	88	74	76	87	−2	174	501	675	694	19	0.09
Germany	238	194	201	85	−7	643	1,687	2,330	2,406	76	0.07
Sub-Saharan Africa	587	519	505	121	14	−1,339	3,283	1,944	2,105	161	0.07
India	1,180	989	923	135	66	−6,277	11,263	4,986	5,967	981	0.06
Turkey	130	106	101	119	5	−433	1,152	719	772	53	0.05
Portugal	16	13	13	112	0	−35	118	82	87	5	0.03
Rest of South America	210	190	191	93	−1	137	855	992	998	6	0.03
Egypt	51	48	46	167	2	−218	209	−9	53	62	0.00
Morocco and Tunisia	26	24	22	222	2	−198	153	−45	26	71	−0.01
Rest of Central Europe	98	91	83	226	8	−764	611	−154	104	257	−0.03
Central Europe 4[a]	184	168	146	244	22	−2,098	1,614	−485	237	721	−0.04
China	2,395	2,122	1,748	237	374	−35,436	27,164	−8,272	4,230	12,502	−0.04
Gulf states	473	445	392	289	53	−5,022	3,369	−1,653	338	1,991	−0.08
Mexico	183	188	151	—	37	−3,471	1,416	−2,055	0	2,055	−0.10
Algeria and Libyan Arab Jamahariya	52	55	47	—	8	−780	217	−564	0	564	−0.18
Former Soviet Union	944	913	751	613	162	−15,353	8,058	−7,296	204	7,500	−0.26
World	11,941	9,444	9,444	n.a.	−754	−71,427	104,023	104,023	198,333	94,310	0.11

— Not available.

n.a. Not applicable.

Note: Annex 1 countries are shaded.

a. Czech Republic, Hungary, Poland, and Slovak Republic.

Source: POLES (Prospective Outlook on Long-Term Energy Systems) model using ASPEN (Analyse des Systèmes de Permis d'Emissions Négociables) software.

for certain regions: $67 billion for buying countries (including $16 billion for the United States) and $27 billion for selling countries (including $12 billion for China), for a total of $94 billion.[13]

The gains in cost efficiency stem from the savings that result from the equalization of marginal abatement costs across countries and regions. Thus a world market for emissions trading produces a more efficient outcome than the no-trading approach.

Of course, the values in tables 2 and 3 are indicative. The relative levels are more significant than the absolute figures. Furthermore, the results are largely theoretical. Like most assessments of this kind, they rely on the assumption that all the potential reductions can be achieved and that the flexibility mechanisms will operate perfectly. In other words, they are based on a pure, perfect, competitive market without transaction costs. In this context the value of the tradable permit should be interpreted as a minimum or floor value, while the volume traded is a maximum volume.

That said, how does the distribution of the abatement costs interfere with the trend toward enhanced equity seen earlier?

Combining efficiency and equity

As noted, the soft-landing scenario leads toward a convergence of per capita emissions over time. When trade is allowed, it is also consistent with utilitarian justice, as it lowers the costs of providing climate stability and so increases global welfare.

Furthermore, as a group the least advantaged countries bear a smaller burden in terms of total costs per unit of GDP. This outcome resembles Rawls's notion of justice, and especially the "difference principle" (or "maximin"), which gives priority to maximizing the expectations of the least favored members of society. Again, the soft-landing scenario does not strictly apply any one notion of justice, but from the perspective of the most commonly held notions of justice, it is moving in the right direction.

CONCLUSION

This chapter has addressed the efficient and equitable provision of global public goods using climate stabilization as an example. But the scenario suggested here is just one possibility—other scenarios and models could be developed.[14] The accuracy of the assumptions made and constraints adopted is not the key point. Of greater relevance is that the proposed approach would allow policymakers to explore the effects of various policy choices in an incremental way and, most important, to more clearly see the final outcomes. Those outcomes could then be assessed in terms of various equity and efficiency considerations and objectives. If the first set of likely outcomes is not satisfactory, initial assumptions could be modified to move toward more desirable but still realistic objectives and policy paths. This iterative, incremental approach to policy change could ultimately generate a satisfactory outcome for negotiating parties with very different notions of justice, fairness, and equity.

APPENDIX. COUNTRY AND REGION GROUPS FOR EXPECTED EMISSIONS STABILIZATION

Group 1: In compliance with objectives defined in the Kyoto Protocol
USA: United States
CAN: Canada
PACO: rest of Pacific OECD countries
GER: Germany
RECN: rest of northern European Union
RECS: rest of southern European Union
JPN: Japan
UK: United Kingdom
ITA: Italy
FRA: France
ROWE: rest of Western Europe
CEU4: four Central European countries (Czech Republic, Hungary, Poland, Slovak Republic)
FSUN: former Soviet Union
RCEU: rest of Central European countries

Group 2: Emissions stabilize in 2015 (non–Annex 1 countries)
KOR: Korea, Republic of

Group 3: Emissions stabilize in 2030 (non–Annex 1 countries)
MIEA: Middle East
MEX: Mexico
TUR: Turkey
CHN: China
RCAM: rest of Central America
BRA: Brazil
RSAM: rest of South America
NOAF: North Africa
RSEA: rest of Southeast Asia

Group 4: Emissions stabilize in 2045 (non–Annex 1 countries)
SSAF: Sub-Saharan Africa
RSAS: rest of South Asia
NDE: India

NOTES

1. The text does not refer to Annex 1 and non–Annex 1 countries in this section because some countries—such as the Republic of Korea and Singapore—that are not in the Annex 1 group could easily be part of the industrial country group based on GDP per capita and per capita emissions of greenhouse gases.

2. The Global Commons Institute refers to this proposal as "contraction and convergence" (GCI 1996). Agarwal and Narain (1991), along with the institute, were the first to propose it. Their approach is developed in Agarwal (1998) and Agarwal and Narain (1998).

3. Claussen and McNeilly (1998) consider the possibility of taking into account future emissions (rather than past emissions) when determining each country's responsibility. But even if problems in deciding how to measure future emissions are discounted, the result in terms of differentiation would be opposite to that based on past emissions and unacceptable to developing countries.

4. On this issue, see Hassner (1996, pp. 1278–85) and Hoffmann's comments on Rawls (in Rawls 1996). On the specific use of justice principles and greenhouse gas emissions, see Godard (1992), Grubb (1995), Harris (2001), Rose (1992), and Paterson (1996).

5. For example, Russia knows that it would be the main exporter of emission permits if trading were limited to Annex 1 parties, based on Kyoto targets. In the same way, Russia knows that China would be its main competitor in a world trading market.

6. As some analysts (such as Müller 2001) point out, making explicit ex ante reference to certain equity principles may help prevent disagreements in future negotiation steps. This is an important practical and political insight. The model in this chapter responds to this requirement by including consensus-based principles and rules in the scenario. In addition, negotiating parties can decide on the precise criteria that they want to see used in the ex post validation of the results.

7. Note that a per capita emissions growth rate of 3 percent corresponds to 3 percent growth in per capita GDP at a constant intensity of emissions per unit of GDP. In fact, since $E/POP = (E/GDP)*(GDP/POP)$, a first approximation indicates additivity of the growth rates of E/GDP and GDP/POP, with negligible differences.

8. The Lorenz curve and the Gini coefficient were created to measure inequality in a population's income distribution. But they can also be used to measure equity in the distribution of other assets, such as emission allowances.

9. A Gini coefficient of 0 indicates a perfectly equal distribution; a coefficient of 1 indicates a fully unequal distribution.

10. For more information on the POLES model, see European Commission (1996).

11. The costs calculated in the POLES model are sectoral costs, or "gross" costs that relate only to the adjustments needed in the energy sector. They differ from

macroeconomic costs, which register the costs supported by a country's entire economic system. They also do not include the costs countries incur to monitor and report their emissions, although these actions would be preliminary obligations for countries accepting binding commitments.

12. According to this scenario, two non–Annex 1 regions would have emission targets slightly less stringent than their reference emissions. Although the amount of such "hot air" is fairly small, it implies that the scenario should be better adjusted for these regions.

13. Some countries and regions even achieve a net gain relative to the no carbon constraint or reference case.

14. UNCTAD (2001), for example, reviews various flexible ways for developing countries to participate in an international emissions trading system.

REFERENCES

Agarwal, Anil. 1998. "Attribution des quotas: équité ou loi du plus fort?" *Courrier de la Planète/Global Chance* (March–April): 31–32.

Agarwal, Anil, and Sunita Narain. 1991. *Global Warming in an Unequal World.* New Delhi: Centre for Science and Environment.

―――. 1998. *The Atmospheric Rights of All People on Earth.* New Delhi: Centre for Science and Environment.

Babiker, Mustafa, and Richard Eckaus. 2000. "Rethinking the Kyoto Emissions Targets." Report 65. Massachusetts Institute of Technology, Joint Program on the Science and Policy of Global Change, Cambridge, Mass.

Blanchard, Odile, Patrick Criqui, Michel Trommetter, and Laurent Viguier. 1998. "Différenciation, équité internationale et efficacité dans la lutte contre le changement climatique global." IEPE (Institut d'Economie et de Politique de l'Energie) Cahier de Recherche de l'IEPE 14. Grenoble.

―――. 2000. "Au-delà de Kyoto: Enjeux d'équité et d'efficacité dans la négociation sur le changement climatique." *Economie et Prévision* 143–44 (2–3): 15–35.

Claussen, Eileen, and Lisa McNeilly. 1998. *The Complex Elements of Global Fairness.* Washington, D.C.: Pew Center on Global Climate Change.

Criqui, Patrick, and Nikolas Kouvaritakis. 1997. "Les coûts pour le secteur énergétique de la réduction des émissions de CO2: une évaluation internationale avec le modèle POLES." IEPE (Institut d'Economie et de Politique de l'Energie) Cahier de Recherche de l'IEPE 13. Grenoble.

Criqui, Patrick, Silvana Mima, and Laurent Viguier. 1999. "Marginal Abatement Costs of CO2 Emission Reductions, Geographical Flexibility and Concrete Ceilings: An Assessment Using the POLES Model." *Energy Policy* 27 (10): 585–602.

Dupuy, Jean-Pierre. 1992. *Libéralisme et justice sociale.* Paris: Hachette Littérature.

Energy Journal. 1999. *The Costs of the Kyoto Protocol: A Multi-Model Evaluation.* Special issue.

European Commission. 1996. *Poles 2.2.* Joule II Programme, Directorate General XII Science, Research and Development EUR 17358 EN. Brussels.

Fishkin, James. 1986. "Theories of Justice and International Relations: The Limits of Liberal Theory." In Anthony Ellis, ed., *Ethics and International Relations.* Manchester: Manchester University Press.

GCI (Global Commons Institute). 1996. *Draft Proposals for a Climate Change Protocol Based on Contraction and Convergence: A Contribution to the Framework Convention on Climate Change.* Ad Hoc Group on the Berlin Mandate AGBM/1996/14. London.

Godard, Olivier. 1992. "Des marchés internationaux de droits à polluer pour le problème de l'effet de serre: de la recherche de l'efficacité aux enjeux de légitimité." *Revue Politique et Management Public* 10 (2): 101–31.

———. 1997. "Les enjeux des négociations sur le climat. De Rio à Kyoto: pourquoi la convention sur le climat devrait intéresser ceux qui ne s'intéressent pas au climat." *Futuribles* 224: 33–66.

Grubb, Michael. 1995. "Seeking Fair Weather: Ethics and the International Debate on Climate Change." *International Affairs* 71 (3): 463–96.

Harris, Paul. 2001. *International Equity and Global Environmental Politics: Power and Principles in US Foreign Policy.* Aldershot, U.K.: Ashgate.

Hassner, Pierre. 1996. "Relations internationales." In Monique Canto-Sperber, ed., *Dictionnaire d'éthique et de philosophie morale.* Paris: Presses Universitaires de France.

Helm, Carsten, and Udo E. Simonis. 2001. "Distributive Justice in International Environmental Policy: Axiomatic Foundation and Exemplary Formulation." *Environmental Values* 10: 5–18.

IPCC (Intergovernmental Panel on Climate Change). 2001. *Climate Change 2001: Mitigation. Contribution of Working Group III to the Third Assessment Report of the Intergovernmental Panel on Climate Change.* Cambridge: Cambridge University Press.

Müller, Benito. 1998. "Justice in Global Warming Negotiations: How to Obtain a Procedurally Fair Compromise." Oxford Institute for Energy Studies, Oxford.

———. 2001. "Varieties of Distributive Justice in Climate Change." *Climatic Change* 48 (2–3): 273–88.

Paterson, Matthew. 1996. "International Justice and Global Warming." In Barry Holden, ed., *The Ethical Dimensions of Global Change.* London: Mcmillan.

Rawls, John. 1971. *A Theory of Justice.* Cambridge, Mass.: Harvard University Press.

———. 1996. *The Law of Peoples.* Cambridge, Mass.: Harvard University Press.

Rose, Adam. 1992. "Equity Considerations of Tradeable Carbon Entitlements." In Scott Barrett, Michael Grubb, Kjell Roland, Adam Rose, Richard Sandor, and Tom Tietenberg, eds., *Combating Global Warming: A Global System of Tradeable Carbon Emission Entitlements.* Geneva: United Nations Conference on Trade and Development.

Shue, Henry. 1992. "The Unavoidability of Justice." In Andrew Hurrell and Benedict Kingsbury, eds., *The International Politics of the Environment.* New York: Oxford University Press.

UNCTAD (United Nations Conference on Trade and Development). 2001. *Greenhouse Gas Market Perspectives: Trade and Investment Implications of the Climate Change Regime.* UNCTAD/DIT/TED/Misc.9. New York and Geneva.

UNFCCC (United Nations Framework Convention on Climate Change). 1992. New York.

————. 1996. *Strengthening the Commitments in Article 4.2 (A) and (B): Quantified Emissions Limitation and Reduction Objectives within Specified Time-Frames: Review of Possible Indicators to Define Criteria for Differentiation among Annex I Parties.* Ad Hoc Group on the Berlin Mandate, Note by the Secretariat FCCC/AGBM/1996/7. New York.

————. 1997. *Kyoto Protocol to the United Nations Framework Convention on Climate Change.* New York.

Viguier, Laurent. 1999. "L'environnement en économie communiste et post-communiste: de la crise systémique à l'agenda global." Ph.D. diss. Université Pierre Mendès France, Grenoble.

3

PRODUCTION: GETTING TO THE GOOD

The provision of global public goods partly depends on political decision-making, as explored in part 2. But it also depends on how these goods are produced—financed, assembled, and delivered. Even if there is political agreement on which goods to produce, they will not necessarily be adequately provided. The issue of how to produce them, addressed in this part of the volume, also matters.

Viewed from the production side, the provision of global public goods is hindered by two fundamental gaps: in institutions and in tools. Public management has not fully adjusted to current realities. And many policy tools, designed for a compartmentalized world of nation-states, economic sectors, and rivalry between markets and the state, are being stretched to respond to new global challenges in an increasingly multiactor world. The chapters in this part offer practical proposals for bridging both the institutions and the tools gaps. Despite considerable incompatibility between the nature of the policy challenges and the workings of public management, institutional and organizational molds are breaking open and innovation is occurring. Thus many of the policy recommendations in this part are aimed at nurturing new approaches to management.

The production of global public goods would be much less complex if, wherever possible, implementation of international agreements were left to nation-states to pursue in a decentralized fashion, through domestic policy action. But few international agreements are designed to be self-enforcing. As a result nation-states often pursue avoidance strategies instead of compliance. Monitoring compliance has thus become an important task for international organizations. Scott Barrett, however, recommends that international agreements do a better job of manipulating incentives and making compliance a matter of parties' self-interest. Doing so is a highly technical craft. Moreover, the approach should be flexible, because no two goods are the same.

In the first of their two chapters Inge Kaul and Katell Le Goulven address the financing of global public goods, a crucial component of their production. The authors present an inventory of current policy tools and sources tapped for financing. Most of the tools used to finance public goods in the national context are also used internationally. But there is a big difference between national and international financing. Nationally, public finance has an allocation branch concerned with the financing of public goods and a distribution branch concerned with equity and social protection. At the international level these two branches are confounded. Kaul and Le Goulven offer proposals for resolving this problem and moving toward a more systematic theory and practice of financing for global public goods.

In their second chapter Kaul and Le Goulven examine the institutions involved in producing global public goods. The analysis focuses on two issues. The first is the need to bridge the traditional divide between domestic and foreign policymaking. In particular, the authors discuss coordination between national technical ministries and ministries of foreign affairs. The second issue pertains to the overall structure of global public goods management. The authors note the emergence of a growing number of global public policy partnerships and argue that the role of these partnerships is akin to that of firms in markets. Both constitute a coordination mechanism for mobilizing diverse inputs and combining them to produce a final good. The chapter suggests moving toward a second generation of partnerships run by issue-focused chief executive officers (CEOs).

Production of global public goods often also requires knowledge—seen here as a resource akin to financing and management capacity. Many elements of knowledge have features of global public goods. But here the focus is on knowledge as a means and an input in the production of other global public goods. Carlos Correa shows how international regimes for knowledge management can affect the provision of goods such as global health. He addresses the challenge of balancing static efficiency (ensuring that available knowledge is widely available and used by current generations) and dynamic efficiency (ensuring the development of new ideas and new technologies for future generations).

CREATING INCENTIVES
FOR COOPERATION:
STRATEGIC CHOICES

Scott Barrett

There is a world of difference between the provision of national public goods and transnational public goods. National public goods are mainly provided by the state. Indeed, part of the reason states exist is to supply public goods. The state is unique among institutions in having the authority to coerce—an authority usually needed if public goods are to be supplied efficiently. For example, a state's first priority is to protect its citizens, and national defense is a national public good. It is a public good because protection of one citizen does not diminish the protection afforded to others and because no citizen can be excluded from being protected. It is a national public good because it is supplied only to citizens of the state. International collective defense, such as that provided by the North Atlantic Treaty Organization, is a transnational public good. National defense is costly and is financed by taxes, not voluntary donations. Citizens are required to pay taxes; if they do not, they are sent to prison. Conscription may also be deemed necessary to national defense and is another example of the state's coercive power.

Why does the state coerce? It does so because if goods like national defense were financed entirely by voluntary contributions, not enough money would be made available and the goods would be underprovided. (If people can benefit without having to pay, why should they pay?) The provision of public goods thus requires getting the incentives right. The state typically solves this problem by means of its visible—and sometimes very heavy—hand.[1]

The provision of transnational (regional and global) public goods also poses a challenge for incentives. The difference between national and transnational public goods lies in the institutional response. There is no world government with the authority to coerce states into supplying transnational public goods. Sovereignty safeguards the independence of individual states in this sphere as in others. A state can be pressured but not forced to contribute to the supply of a transnational public good. Provision of transnational public goods must be voluntary.

How can the incentive problem be resolved for transnational public goods, especially global public goods? Unilateralism can provide an alternative to world government—but only when a country's self-interest in a good is so strong that it will provide it regardless of whether others contribute. Another alternative is voluntary international cooperation achieved by restructuring incentives, typically through strategy. This chapter explains the considerations that matter when devising incentive-based cooperation strategies (see Barrett forthcoming for a more comprehensive treatment of this topic).

The chapter is divided into two main sections. The first examines different incentive structures that can underlie the provision of global public goods. The second shows how these structures could be manipulated to foster international cooperation and increase the provision of these goods. The concluding section summarizes the chapter's main messages.

INCENTIVE STRUCTURES FOR THE PROVISION OF GLOBAL PUBLIC GOODS

Not all public goods are alike (Sandler 1992, 1998, 2001, in this volume). Some global public goods have close substitutes in national public goods. In such cases national provision, or self-provision, can discourage international cooperation. Other global public goods yield countries such huge benefits relative to the costs of provision that they will supply them unilaterally.[2] Coordination of national policies can help provide some global public goods. For others, international cooperation—and enforcement—is needed. This section analyzes these different incentives for and approaches to provision—and shows that where incentives differ, the remedies for underprovision also differ.

Self-provision and cooperative provision

The provision of national and transnational public goods is often interrelated. When a transnational public good is undersupplied, increased provision of a national public good may help compensate. But provision of a national public good can also undermine incentives to supply a transnational public good. That is, national and transnational public goods may be substitutes.

Consider efforts to control measles, a highly infectious disease that kills up to 1 million children a year in developing countries but that rarely infects (and almost never kills) children of privilege. Thanks to extensive childhood vaccination campaigns, measles is no longer endemic in industrial countries. A few cases occur in the United States every year, but these are imported. National elimination of the disease is a national public good. But it has implications for other countries. Once industrial countries have immunized their children against measles, they have fewer incentives to help control the disease abroad.

There may still be a collective benefit from global eradication, which would obviate the need for national vaccinations. But the risk that a disease will be reintroduced, accidentally or maliciously, means that countries should probably maintain surveillance programs and vaccine stockpiles—dulling incentives to invest in global eradication. The global eradication of smallpox remains perhaps the greatest achievement of international cooperation. But its success has been blighted by current worries about bioterrorist attack. Sadly, this is what makes smallpox eradication a bittersweet victory (Committee on the Assessment of Future Scientific Needs for Live Variola Virus 1999).

For countries that can afford national immunizations, helping to control a disease abroad may best be described as an act of charity.[3] Indeed, major donors to the Global Polio Eradication Initiative include Rotary International, the United Nations Foundation, and the Bill and Melinda Gates Foundation (see http:// www.polioeradication.org/). These organizations are presumably investing in this initiative not just because they think the effort worthy, but also because they do not believe that governments will foot the entire bill. Given that the global public good of polio eradication is underprovided, the efforts of these institutions are to be welcomed. But at the same time, the involvement of these institutions is an indicator of underprovision by nation-states—an outcome not entirely to be cheered.

As it turns out, the measles problem is different in developing countries. In industrial countries children are exposed to measles when they are school-aged. In developing countries children are exposed much earlier. Newborns inherit from their mothers a natural immunity to measles. But this immunity wears off when babies are about 9 months old—making the timing of vaccination tricky. If the vaccine is given too early, it will not take effect, and the baby will be vulnerable when the inherited immunity wears off. If the vaccine is given too late, the baby may already have been exposed. Getting the timing right is hard enough for a single baby—and even harder for an entire population. In developing countries vaccines are normally given to all children of a given age cohort (but not precisely the same age) on national immunization days—usually once or twice a year. This kind of program works well for some diseases but leaves too many children vulnerable to measles.

Obviously it would be desirable to have a vaccine that could be given early and that would "switch on" when the inherited immunity has worn off. But such a vaccine would mainly benefit children in developing countries, and has not yet been developed. Knowledge of how to make such a vaccine would be another transnational public good, and could dramatically increase the supply of the global public good of measles eradication.

Global climate change provides another example of how national protection diminishes the incentive to supply a transnational public good. Climate change mitigation is a global public good. But countries can reduce the damage from climate change by investing in adaptation—building sea walls (a local public good), changing the varieties of seeds planted (private goods), and so on. Having this option reduces national returns to mitigation efforts. As a result countries do not sufficiently reduce their greenhouse gas emissions (a global public bad); instead they spend too much on adaptation. This approach is inefficient and especially harmful to countries least able to adapt.

To sum up, when provision of a global public good is inadequate, countries have incentives to take defensive measures at home. This is to be welcomed given that global (cooperative) provision is inadequate. But the ability to take defensive measures at home also dulls the incentive to provide the global public good, and this outcome can be inefficient. In a sense some global public goods (including measles eradication) are underprovided because they are not public enough. This leaves the countries that are least able to act at home the most vulnerable.

Unilateral (best shot) provision

Some global public goods, called best shot public goods, only need to be supplied by one country (see Sandler 1998 and in this volume). These goods will be supplied without the need for international cooperation as long as the national benefit of their provision exceeds the cost for the providing country. An example is the knowledge supplied by some government-funded research—leading, for example, to the development of safe, effective vaccines for diseases such as polio (Stiglitz 1999). Countries fund such research primarily to benefit their own citizens, but the knowledge acquired can be used around the world.

However, public goods do not always have to be supplied by the state. (Coercion is not essential to the supply of all public goods, even transnational public goods.) Edward Jenner, a British physician, discovered that vaccination with cowpox provided lasting immunity to smallpox. This discovery, one of the most important in the history of science, was made by an inquisitive doctor, apparently without state funding.

Basic research and development is an essential part of innovation and is typically provided by the state either directly (as with the research conducted by the U.S. National Institutes of Health) or indirectly (as with university research). But some research and development, as well as most product development, is usually left to the private sector. Thus the push of state-funded research is complemented by the pull of the market and the patent system.

The patent system has recently attracted much attention. As discussed by Correa (in this volume), AIDS-suppressing antiretroviral drugs are available worldwide. But the drugs are too expensive for millions of HIV-infected people in developing countries, and the companies that make the drugs have been pressured to lower their prices. The pressure is coming from different directions. It is coming from public protests in developing countries. It is coming from copycat producers, who can offer essentially the same drugs at much lower prices. And it is coming from countries threatening to force manufacturers to license their drug recipes on favorable terms to domestic producers or to allow parallel imports.

The marginal cost of making a drug is usually very low—perhaps pennies a pill. The high cost is in carrying out the research and testing needed to develop a drug and bring it to market. Static efficiency demands that drugs be sold at marginal cost, an outcome more or less guaranteed by competition. But if there is competition in drug manufacturing, research and development will be unprofitable. Dynamic efficiency demands that companies have the incentive to invest their capital, at considerable risk, in the development of new drugs. The patent system provides this incentive by essentially granting a monopoly on new drugs for the short to medium term. Thus it sacrifices static efficiency for dynamic efficiency.

Two problems can result. The first is that the drug is priced so that some people cannot afford it—a problem for intragenerational equity as well as static efficiency. The second is that if the patent system were not respected, pharmaceutical companies would have little incentive to develop new drugs—a problem for intergenerational equity as well as dynamic efficiency. Discussions in the media have focused almost exclusively on the first problem.

But the problem is actually more complicated. Monopolies maximize profits by selling goods to different people at different prices. Thus drug companies in industrial countries would probably like nothing better than to sell their drugs at low prices in developing countries. As long as a drug's price exceeds its marginal cost, its manufacturer would make money. The problem is that international arbitrage undercuts manufacturers' ability to do this. A secondary market may develop, with drugs sold cheaply in Africa being shipped back to a higher-price market. A related problem is that drug companies may have trouble defending their prices to bodies such as the U.S. Congress. It is not difficult to imagine a congressperson asking the chief executive officer of a pharmaceutical company why U.S. consumers are being charged so much more for a drug than foreign consumers.

Price discrimination is good for the consumers who pay the lowest price and bad for the consumers who pay the highest price. But such discrimination is often good for overall efficiency. Hence an insistence by industrial countries that drugs sell for the same price worldwide may impair efficiency. For the moment, stopgap measures are being taken to address these pricing problems, but in the future a fair, efficient international regime for drug pricing needs to be established.[4] (Even the United States arm-twisted the manufacturer of the antibiotic Cipro into lowering its price in the wake of the October 2001 anthrax attacks.)

Dependence on the weakest link
All disease eradication campaigns begin with the disease being eliminated from a certain area, such as the Western Hemisphere. As a campaign advances, the disease is eliminated from other regions and, finally, from particular countries. The disease will usually have a few last strongholds, such as countries being torn apart by civil war or very poor countries with inadequate public health and transportation infrastructure. The challenge is not how to eliminate the disease in the

first few countries. The real challenge always lies in eliminating the disease in the last country. Almost by definition, this is where elimination is hardest to achieve. And this is where the eradication effort will succeed or fail. If the disease cannot be eliminated in the last country, it cannot be eradicated (globally) at all.

Now imagine a world where all countries are more or less alike. For each country the cost of eliminating the disease locally far exceeds the benefit—not least because, even if the disease is eliminated locally, vaccination efforts will have to continue indefinitely. But for all countries collectively the benefit of global eradication far exceeds the cost of local elimination. In that case, if every country believes that all others will eliminate the disease, each has an incentive to eliminate it at home. These are weakest link games, where the weakest link in the chain determines whether the chain will hold when put to the test (see Sandler 1992, 1998, and in this volume).

The problem just described may also be a coordination game (see Sandler 1992). In a coordination game each country wants to do what all other countries are doing. If all others are not eliminating the disease at home, then each will not eliminate the disease at home—because, by assumption, the cost of doing so will exceed the local benefit. But if all others are eliminating the disease at home, then each will eliminate the disease at home—because doing so will ensure that the disease is eliminated globally and (again, by assumption) the benefit of global elimination exceeds the cost of local elimination for each country.

Because they do not require enforcement, coordination problems are easier for the international system to deal with than cooperation problems (discussed in the next section). The assurance by others that a disease will be eliminated at home is sufficient to impel every country to eliminate the disease. To be sure, there is no guarantee that eradication will be sustained by the international system. But if countries recognize a problem together, there is a good chance they will succeed. What each country needs is an assurance that others will coordinate. Unfortunately, coordination will not always suffice. Eradication will sometimes require international enforcement, the focus of the discussion below (see also Barrett 2002).

Summation public goods

The final kind of public good is the hardest for the international system to supply. These are goods where the total supply is the sum of the amounts supplied by individual countries. An example is climate change mitigation. Climate change depends on the total greenhouse gases in the atmosphere, not the releases of individual countries. Each country has a unilateral incentive to supply only limited quantities of these kinds of public goods. But all countries would be better off if every country supplied more. These are prisoner's dilemma games (see Sandler 1998).

Countries have mixed motives in prisoner's dilemma games. Each would prefer that others supply the good. But each also recognizes that if everyone depended on others to supply the good, the result would be bad for everyone. Thus there is a collective advantage in collective provision. The challenge is enforcing an agreement for collective provision. Sovereignty means that countries do not have to become parties to such agreements. Supplying summation public goods requires restructuring incentives, the subject of the next section.

STRATEGIES FOR RESTRUCTURING INCENTIVES

The preceding analysis shows that a strategic approach is required to foster international cooperation in the provision of public goods. Different players may have different priorities for a certain global public good, and the properties of global public goods vary. For both reasons a remedy that works for one good may not work for another.

Threshold effects

In many cases it may benefit a country to take action X only if enough other countries (or certain other countries) do the same; otherwise it may benefit every country to take action Y. That is, there may be threshold effects. If such effects are strong enough, they may tip the balance from noncooperative to cooperative behavior (see Schelling 1978 and Gladwell 2000).

Such a situation may be especially likely where countries are interconnected. An example is the decision of which side of the road to drive on. In most countries people drive on the right. Countries that drive on the left usually do so because they are not interconnected with countries that drive on the right. In Britain and Australia (a former British colony) people drive on the left; in Canada (another former British colony) they drive on the right. Britain and Australia are islands; their roads are not interconnected with other countries. Canada, by contrast, shares a long border with a large neighbor (the United States) that drives on the right.

Whether to drive on the right or the left is a standard, and standards are public goods. (One person's use of a standard does not preclude others from using it, and no one can be excluded from using it.) Other examples include the location of a car's steering wheel (chosen according to whether the car is driven on the left or the right) and its bumper height (which should be similar for all cars because otherwise a collision would cause greater damage to both vehicles).

In networks every country has an incentive to adopt the same standards as others. That is, there is a tendency toward harmonization. An important example is the use of unleaded gasoline and catalytic converters in automobiles (Heal 1999). Catalytic converters can only reduce harmful emissions from vehicles fueled by unleaded gasoline. A country can require the use of unleaded gasoline at home, but if the residents of that country drive to neighboring countries that do not use unleaded gasoline, the catalytic converters will soon become damaged.

Thus highly interconnected countries will want to adopt the same standards. This is a major reason for EU directives on the environment.

Importantly, however, catalytic converters are quickly becoming an international standard. This is happening for several reasons. One is interconnectedness—a consequence of globalization. Another is economies of scale. It is much cheaper for a manufacturer to produce cars fitted with catalytic converters for the home market if it is already producing such cars for export. A final reason is that catalytic converters will help reduce pollution emissions at home. Thus the local government may require that all new cars be fitted with catalytic converters.

So far, so good. But standards can also pose problems for efficiency. One is that the wrong standard may get chosen. And because of interconnectedness, a country will want to use the wrong standard if its neighbors do so. Another problem is that, once a standard has been adopted, it may be hard for a new standard to gain a foothold. A new international agreement on vehicle standards has been negotiated to deal with this last problem.[5]

Reciprocity
A strategy of reciprocity is often of limited effectiveness in enforcing an agreement to cooperate. The main reason is that when a country is punished for not cooperating, the countries that impose the punishment hurt themselves in the bargain.

Consider the control of pollution at sea by oil tankers. Most people think that oil spills are accidents. But historically that has not been the case: most oil used to be released deliberately. After a tanker unloaded its cargo, it needed to take on ballast to make the return journey, and so filled its tanks with water. Yet before returning home to reload a cargo of oil, it emptied its ballast into the sea. Because the ballast water was held in the same tanks as the oil, oil-water mixtures were released.[6]

In the 1920s maritime nations began trying to negotiate a treaty that would limit oil pollution at sea. They failed, largely because they could not devise a means for enforcing an agreement (Mitchell 1994)—just the kind of result one would expect from a prisoner's dilemma situation. Realizing that they could all do better by cooperating, maritime nations met to negotiate an agreement. But being unable to enforce the agreement, it never entered into force.

However, the real problem here requires a more subtle analysis. As is well known, if a game is repeated, it may be possible for countries to prop up a degree of cooperation through a strategy of reciprocity. The countries could agree that, should any country fail to behave in the manner prescribed by the treaty, the others will reciprocate and release their oil at sea. But to implement this strategy it must be possible to observe the actions of all the players, and tanker skippers could unload their ballast when no one was looking. Another difficulty is that the threat to reciprocate may not be credible. After all, when other countries release their oil at sea, they harm not just the party they intend to punish, but also themselves.

This is the problem with using such strategies to promote the supply of transnational public goods. When relations are bilateral, reciprocity works fine. The multilateral trading rules of the World Trade Organization (WTO), for example, allow a country to retaliate in the event of a trade rule being broken by another WTO member. The act of trade (as distinguished from the multilateral trading rules) is a bilateral exchange. The country harmed by a rule violation experiences a national (private) cost and can similarly punish the violator without affecting third parties or the overall trade agreement.

For this reason it is natural to contemplate the trade weapon as a means of enforcing cooperative agreements. The International Commission for the Conservation of Atlantic Tunas (ICCAT; http://www.iccat.org) provides an example. Tunas are highly migratory. They also spend much of their lives beyond countries' exclusive economic zones. Open access fishing has depleted tuna populations and so reduced the value of the fishery.[7] ICCAT has tried to correct the overfishing but has run into two familiar problems. Some fishing nations have declined to join the agreement (a problem of nonparticipation), and some parties to the agreement have refused to comply with ICCAT rulings (a problem of noncompliance).

To address the second problem, ICCAT decided that tuna and swordfish imports from noncomplying countries should be banned by other ICCAT members. The advantage of this strategy is that it is credible; it really is in the interests of these nations to ban the imports (the ban is certainly popular with the members' fishermen). The disadvantage is that the import ban may not cause serious harm to the offending nations. Most countries are not ICCAT members, so a country that chooses to violate ICCAT rules can still serve a huge market. To change behavior, sanctions must be both credible and severe.

Participation and compliance
ICCAT's problems notwithstanding, international agreements enjoy almost universal compliance. But does this mean, as Chayes and Chayes (1995) argue, that compliance is not a problem? Or does it mean, as Downs, Rocke, and Barsoom (1996) contend, that countries only negotiate and participate in treaties that they would comply with anyway?

The answer is not immediately obvious. But it is important to frame the problem correctly. Compliance cannot be divorced from participation; they are linked problems. But compliance and participation cannot be conflated; they are different problems. If the two problems are distinguished yet analyzed together, it turns out that compliance must be enforced but that participation is the binding constraint on cooperation (Barrett 1999c).

The reasoning is as follows. The problem with enforcement is that when cooperating countries punish noncooperating countries by cutting back on their provision of a public good, they harm themselves. The bigger the deviation that must be deterred, the larger must be the punishment—but larger punishments are the first to bump up against the credibility constraint. The biggest deviation that can credibly be contemplated is withdrawal from a treaty. Obviously this must be deterred. But once nonparticipation has been deterred, smaller acts of non-compliance will be easy to deter through the credible threat of smaller punishments. Hence once nonparticipation can be deterred, noncompliance can be deterred free of charge.

There is another way of looking at this issue. International law does not compel countries to belong to ICCAT. So, countries that belong to ICCAT but that are failing to comply can withdraw from the agreement. When they do so, they are free (more or less) to act as they please. But under current ICCAT rules they will be treated the same whether they withdraw or fail to comply (either way, they will be subject to the same trade restrictions). This probably explains why noncomplying countries have not withdrawn from this agreement. At the same time, ICCAT actions have done little to change behavior. They are likely to have an effect only on countries that trade extensively with other ICCAT members.

The Kyoto Protocol provides another illustration of the difficulty in enforcing international cooperation. The agreement negotiated in December 1997 left many details unsettled. At the conference of the parties held in The Hague in November 2000, a proposal was made for enforcing compliance with the treaty's main provisions. The proposal said that in the event that a country did not meet the emission targets that had been set for it in the first control period (2008–12), it would be required to reduce its emissions by an additional amount in the next control period. Not only would this country have to make up for its previous shortfall, but it would also have to reduce its emissions by an additional amount. (At the meetings held in Bonn in 2001, it was agreed that this amount should be 30 percent of the initial shortfall.) And if the country did not comply with this requirement, then in the third control period it would have to make up for the previous shortfalls and pay yet another penalty.

There are a number of problems with this approach, each on its own enough to weaken the agreement—and all taken as a group enough to undermine it entirely. First, the punishment for noncompliance is always deferred, and a punishment that is always deferred is never carried out. Second, countries that fail to meet their emission limits are expected to punish themselves. There is no mechanism in the current agreement that would punish a country for failing to punish itself for failing to comply. Third, the emission limits for future control periods have not been decided. They are thus endogenous to this process. A country that is having problems complying, whether for lack of trying or for more legitimate reasons, can therefore negotiate higher future emission ceilings, effectively relaxing the constraint of the compliance penalty. Fourth, the Kyoto Protocol already says that any binding compliance mechanism cannot apply except by means of an amendment. An amendment is basically a new treaty. Hence not only would the compliance mechanisms proposed thus far not work, but they could not even be applied to the first control period. At best they could only be incorporated in a follow-on protocol, and thus apply only beginning with the second control period. Finally, and perhaps most important, the Kyoto Protocol does little to promote participation (Barrett 1999b). Thus a country worried about future compliance and enforcement can take the safe option of not ratifying the agreement.

Strategic substitutes and complements

In a (one shot) prisoner's dilemma game, every country wants to not supply the good regardless of what other countries do. This is in contrast to a coordination game, where each country's best strategy depends on what other countries do.

Other situations require different strategies. In some cases where one country provides a public good, others become more inclined to do so. In these cases provision is a strategic complement. Such positive feedback facilitates the supply of transnational public goods. If there is no threshold, formal cooperation may not even be needed (see Heal 1994).

But in other cases feedback may be negative. As one country supplies a public good, others may respond by supplying less. In these situations provision is a strategic substitute. A treaty may help, but it may not be able to sustain full cooperation (see Barrett 1994).

These kinds of interdependencies are common. Take the example of disease control. As the prevalence of a disease falls globally, the risk of infection to any one country falls. After one country controls a disease, others may relax their controls. Eradication, by contrast, has the opposite effect. As explained previously, the benefit to one country of eradicating a disease may increase (nonlinearly) with the number of others that eradicate it.

One way of facilitating cooperation is to change the rules of the game. In the cooperation games described above, cooperation entails direct provision of the public good, and punishment strategies are limited to reducing provision levels. But the International Convention for the Prevention of Pollution from Ships (the MARPOL agreement) suggests a different approach. As noted, direct attempts failed to reduce oil dumping at sea. So, in the early 1970s a different approach was tried. The MARPOL agreement requires oil tankers to have separate tanks for ballast water and oil. As a result monitoring at sea is no longer a problem; port inspections of hulls are sufficient (Mitchell 1994). Moreover, coastal countries—seeking to prevent harmful oil releases—have strong incentives to ban from their ports ships not fitted with separate ballast tanks. Finally, ship owners have an incentive to adopt this standard because otherwise they would be shut out of major ports. By focusing on the technical standard of separate ballast tanks, the oil dumping problem was transformed: the underlying prisoner's dilemma game was turned into a coordination game.

The shift to separate ballast tanks required an international agreement. If only one country had adopted the new tanker standard, it is unlikely that others would have followed—and deliberate oil releases at sea would hardly have been reduced. Only if enough countries adopted the new standard would there be a strong enough incentive for all countries to do so, and only in that case would oceans be protected. The strategic challenge for the MARPOL agreement was not just to negotiate standards rather than emission limits. It was also to ensure that the threshold for coordination would be crossed—or that the demand for separate ballast tanks would be tipped.

Trade linkages and leakages
As noted, there are strong reasons for linking the provision of a public good to international trade. In fact, nearly every successful incentive restructuring has exploited trade linkages. Participation in the MARPOL agreement, for example, is encouraged by a trade restriction. To enforce the agreement, ports merely need to ban entry by oil tankers that violate it. Enforcement is facilitated by the fact that the agreement is linked to bilateral relationships between the port state and the flag state.

The Montreal Protocol on Substances that Deplete the Ozone Layer, perhaps the most successful international treaty ever adopted, functions in a similar way. The treaty restricts trade in ozone-depleting substances and in products containing them. Once again, it works by transforming the game (Barrett 1999b).

Ozone protection is a summation public good and so vulnerable to the usual free rider incentives. Imagine now a situation in which some countries reduce their emissions of ozone-depleting substances. Comparative advantage in using or producing such substances may then shift to other countries—a phenomenon known as trade leakage. As a result of some countries reducing their emissions, other countries may increase theirs. In this case the linkage to trade actually weakens the incentive to supply the public good unilaterally.

But once the parties to the Montreal Protocol agreed to ban trade in ozone-depleting substances and products containing them, countries that failed to participate in the treaty would suffer a loss in trade. If only a few countries had participated, this loss might not have been enough to make participation attractive to others. But once enough countries signed the agreement, the loss became big enough to foster participation. Again, there was a tipping point or threshold to be crossed. Even if the sanction did not make free riders want to participate, it at least stopped the trade leakage.

Ironically, although the trade leakage undermined unilateral attempts to provide the public good, it helped multilateral efforts (Barrett 1999a). The underlying prisoner's dilemma was transformed into a coordination game. If enough countries supply the good, all countries want to supply it. But how did supporters of the treaty ensure that enough countries would supply the good? The answer is simple: the treaty merely had to state that it became binding on parties only if it was ratified by a certain number of countries (and in some cases by certain countries). Thus the minimum participation level served as a coordinating device (Barrett 1997).

Carrots and sticks

Punishments are negative incentives. Can positive incentives work too? Positive incentives are needed when countries are asymmetric; they ensure that every country gains from an agreement. For example, when the parties to the North Pacific Fur Seal Treaty of 1911 struck a deal banning the hunting of seals at sea, the oceanic sealing nations—Canada and Japan—had to be compensated for agreeing to close their industries. The compensation came partly in cash and partly in shares of pelts from seals killed on land by Japan, Russia, and the United States (Mirovitskaya, Clark, and Purvey 1993).

Side payments are also made by the Montreal Protocol Fund. This agreement treats developing countries differently from industrial countries in two ways. First, in allowing more time before achieving the same ultimate goal of eliminating the production and consumption of ozone-destroying chemicals. Second, in compensating developing countries for the agreed incremental costs of compliance. Together these features give expression to the notion that industrial and developing countries have shared but distinct responsibilities.

It might seem that this formula should work more generally. But there is reason to think that the Montreal Protocol may be a special case (Barrett 1999b). Countries are strongly asymmetric in their responsibilities for the depletion of the ozone layer. When the protocol was written, developing countries were not important to ozone layer protection in the short run; they used little of the offending chemicals and produced even less. In the long run, however, these countries would be very important, partly because their consumption of chlorofluorocarbons (CFCs) was predicted to increase dramatically. Moreover, production might have shifted to these countries if the Montreal Protocol only restricted production in industrial countries (leakage). Thus industrial countries knew that they had to negotiate an agreement attracting close to full participation.

But while industrial countries very much wanted developing countries to participate, developing countries had few compelling reasons to do so. Many were not especially concerned about ozone depletion—because they had different priorities, because ozone depletion would be worse near the poles than near the equator, and because ozone depletion would affect fair-skinned people more than dark-skinned people.

This asymmetry meant that developing countries could credibly claim to prefer not to participate. The cooperation problem facing industrial countries was not so much how to agree to cut their emissions. Rather, the problem was to agree to supply the funds needed to pay developing countries to prevent their emissions from rising. This asymmetry ratcheted up the cooperation problem (Barrett 2001). Where asymmetries are less stark, this opportunity to expand cooperation will not exist. When one country pays another to participate, the gains from an agreement are redistributed. The country that is paid gains, but the country that pays loses.

Is the offer to pay incremental costs fair? It might not seem to be. Though determining incremental costs is as much art as science, the basic concept means that developing countries should be compensated for complying but given no surplus (in the form of cash payments or technology transfers) on top of that. This might seem to give the entire surplus to industrial countries. But there is a difference between the marginal and the total surplus. Because the offer to pay incremental costs is made to every developing country, each will gain a surplus in benefits from ozone protection. As noted, developing countries benefit less from ozone protection than do industrial countries—but they do benefit. Ozone depletion suppresses the immune system, causes cataracts, and reduces the productivity of agriculture and fisheries. The offer to pay incremental costs would have a nonmarginal effect on each developing country if it was accepted by all of them.

Informal institutions

The state is the primary actor in international affairs. But it is not the only actor. Nor is it a monolith, as the discussion to this point has implicitly assumed.

The introduction to this chapter noted how the state uses its power to supply national public goods. Other sections have emphasized the importance of treaties in supplying transnational public goods. But states and treaties are formal means of supplying public goods, and their effectiveness significantly depends on informal mechanisms.

Perhaps the best illustration is the study by Putnam, Leonardi, and Nanetti (1993) of northern and southern Italy after World War II. Both regions were given the same formal institutions, but the north achieved a must faster economic transformation. The reason seems to be that citizens of the north made better use of formal institutions. They read newspapers, voted, and complained when public services fell short of expectations. Formal institutions work best when they are used, but their use poses a collective action problem and needs to be supported informally—by a culture of civic engagement.

Effective treaty-making also requires civic involvement. Concerned citizens must learn about what is going on in the world, form judgments on what should and should not be done about important issues, and convey those preferences to their representatives. The Mine Ban Treaty is probably the best example of a treaty taking strength from global civic engagement. The International Campaign to Ban Landmines, a nongovernmental organization affiliated with more than a thousand civil society organizations, spearheaded the effort. The campaign influenced the negotiation and ratification of the treaty and in 1997 won the Nobel Peace Prize.

Nationally, there is a link between political institutions and the supply of public goods. Democracies are more likely than dictatorships to supply the kinds of goods that most benefit citizens. For example, Barrett and Graddy (2000) find that local air and water quality is higher in countries with greater civil and political freedoms, even after controlling for differences in income and geography. Presumably there is also a link between these institutions and the provision of transnational public goods. The evidence for this is mixed, however (see Congleton 1992; Murdoch and Sandler 1997; Murdoch, Sandler and Sargent 1997; Fredriksson and Gaston 1999). One reason may be that the decision to participate in a treaty is strategic: participation depends on what other countries do and on what a treaty requires of its parties.

Treaty remedies are also more effective if monitoring of compliance is supported by civil organizations. A recent example is the ICCAT treaty, discussed previously. To monitor compliance, fishermen are expected to monitor the behavior of others at sea and report suspected breaches of the treaty back to their national authorities.

Some businesses have voluntarily pledged to reduce their greenhouse gas emissions. A few have even established internal systems for emissions trading.[8] By doing so, these companies are demonstrating their concern for the environment. They are acknowledging their responsibility to contribute to the global mitigation effort. They are learning how emissions trading can be made to work. And they may be anticipating first mover advantages. Such actions and intentions are to be welcomed. But it would be wrong to believe that this behavior will do much to help the environment.

If the aim of the Framework Convention on Climate Change is to be realized—that is, if atmospheric concentrations of greenhouse gases are to be stabilized at an acceptable level, whatever that may be—the global economy will need to be restructured. Market forces have sparked technological revolutions in the past. But in the case of climate change, new technologies have to be developed and adopted even while cheap fossil fuel energy remains abundant.

Even in the case of stratospheric ozone depletion, where CFC substitutes cost only a little more than the ozone-destroying chemicals they were meant to replace, government intervention—and especially international cooperation—was needed to effect a transformation. For climate change the need for government regulation and international cooperation is much greater because the costs of substituting away from carbon-based fuels are much larger. Indeed, international cooperation was relatively easy to effect in the case of ozone depletion precisely because the costs of ozone protection were low (Barrett 1999b). Global climate change poses a much greater challenge to the international system.

Application to global climate change

If international cooperation is needed to mitigate global climate change but the Kyoto Protocol's enforcement mechanisms are inadequate, what should be done? The first thing to understand about international cooperation is that it may not be possible to sustain a first best outcome every time. The Kyoto Protocol was designed to be a kind of first best remedy. Its overall emissions reduction target is justified by cost-benefit analysis, and the treaty incorporates "flexible mechanisms" aimed at minimizing the costs of achieving this target (Barrett 1999b). However, the treaty negotiated in December 1997 ignored enforcement.[9] This was something that the negotiators thought they could add later. But this problem should be viewed from the other direction. Negotiators should first ask what can be enforced, then build a treaty around that. Enforcement is the main challenge, and it needs to be addressed directly.

Two aspects of global climate change make enforcement of a Kyoto-like treaty difficult. The first is that abatement is costly. The second is that climate change is a global problem. Costly abatement makes nonparticipation (noncompliance) attractive to every country. The global nature of the problem means that the stiff punishments needed to deter nonparticipation and noncompliance will not be credible. The Montreal Protocol worked because abatement was not very costly and because trade restrictions could be used to promote participation. With climate change the situation is not so accommodating.

The MARPOL agreement (on the design of oil tankers) may be a better model for addressing global climate change. Recall that international negotiations first tried to control oil pollution at sea by setting limits on oil dumping. That approach failed because the limits could not be monitored or enforced. The MARPOL agreement took the radical step of focusing instead on a technology standard. A treaty on climate change should do something similar.

A superior climate change treaty should:

- Promote cooperative research and development on technologies needed to substitute away from carbon-based fuels or to safely capture and store carbon. Climate change is a long-term problem that requires a long-term solution.
- Based on the fruits of this collaborative research and development, create follow-on protocols that establish technology standards for electricity generation, carbon capture and storage, and vehicles. Technology standards are easy to monitor and, unlike emission limits, create positive feedback. If there are network externalities, the more countries that embrace a standard, the greater will be the incentive for others to adopt the same standard. Technology standards also establish automatic, easily administered trade restrictions that conform to the rules of the World Trade Organization.
- Promote transfers of these technologies to developing countries. Climate change is a global problem and requires global action. But it is unreasonable

to expect—and unfair to ask—developing countries to foot the bill for their abatement efforts. As with the Montreal Protocol, abatement should be facilitated by a system of transfers.

- Establish a protocol for the short run. Because of the enforcement problem, legally binding emission limits should be abandoned. Instead countries should pledge to take certain actions—such as instituting carbon taxes, raising energy efficiency standards, and subsidizing renewable energy. The Kyoto Protocol has not only failed to support international cooperation, it has also taken pressure off countries to do much unilaterally.

- Recognize that climate change will likely occur no matter what is done to mitigate it. As a result some countries will suffer related damages. Developing countries are more vulnerable, yet they contributed little to the problem. Thus industrial countries have a responsibility to reduce the damages suffered by developing countries and to ease their adjustment. Designing such transfers will not be easy, not least because it will be impossible to determine whether any particular change in the climate was caused by humans. Still, this problem needs to be acknowledged and addressed.

Although this proposal would improve matters, it falls short of an ideal treaty on climate change. But it is not meant to be ideal. The ideal outcome for climate change is unlikely to be enforceable, and an outcome that cannot be enforced cannot be attained. The above proposal is enforceable (as well as fair and oriented to the long term). Thus it is attainable. Though not ideal, it may be the best climate outcome that the international system is capable of sustaining.

CONCLUSION

Some transnational public goods are supplied unilaterally. But many are not, and so require multilateral efforts to restructure incentives for their provision. Because of the constraint of sovereignty, this is a colossal institutional challenge.

There is no universal solution. Different public goods pose different problems and require different remedies. Some problems pose a challenge only for coordination. Because coordination does not require enforcement, these problems are relatively easy for the international system to fix.

Enforcement is a bigger challenge because sovereignty requires that multilateral approaches be self-enforcing. Strategy must be used to restructure the game, perhaps changing it from one requiring cooperation (and hence enforcement) to one requiring only coordination. This can sometimes be achieved by carefully choosing the instrument of policy. The MARPOL agreement, for example, shows how relying on a technical standard (on the design of oil tankers) rather than an emissions standard (on the dumping of oil) completely changed the game of reducing oil pollution at sea.

In other cases the switch from a cooperation to a coordination game can be achieved by linking the provision of public goods to international trade. The Montreal Protocol, for example, was transformed into a coordination game by imposing the credible threat of restricting trade with nonparties. Finally, cash payments and technology transfers can help when there are substantial asymmetries. This was another approach used by the Montreal Protocol. It was this combination of strategies that helped ensure protection of the stratospheric ozone layer.

Unfortunately, these successes are special cases. Too often, multilateralism fails or succeeds only partially. Remedies that work for one problem do not work for another. The international regime for regulating catches of Atlantic tuna, for example, has incorporated trade restrictions as a means of enforcing both compliance and participation. However, it is not clear that this approach will work because it is relatively easy for some countries to reduce the impact of the restrictions. The Kyoto Protocol was styled after the Montreal Protocol in that it established targets and timetables for reducing emissions of a global public bad. The difference is that the Montreal Protocol was able to enforce both participation and compliance by means of a trade restriction. The Kyoto Protocol has tried an alternative approach to enforcement—one that is almost certain to fail. The alternative treaty design proposed above has a greater chance of success.

This might seem a depressing note on which to end. But the international system is resilient—and occasionally ingenious—and with each failure new approaches are tried. Regulation of oil pollution at sea, for example, started out on the wrong foot but was adjusted after this failure became apparent. And although trade restrictions on tuna imports may not work as intended, they are being buttressed by other approaches. For example, the 1993 Agreement to Promote Compliance with International Conservation and Management Measures by Fishing Vessels on the High Seas acknowledges that all states have a duty not to undermine the conservation objectives of fisheries agreements. This agreement has not entered into force. But were it to do so and to attract substantial participation, countries would be further constrained from acting as they please on the high seas.

The international system is not static: it evolves. The challenge is to use strategy to ensure that it evolves toward greater provision of transnational public goods. An important first step is to know well the good in question, particularly its underlying incentive structures.

NOTES

1. The need for coercion is not always apparent. Ostrom (1990), for example, shows that community groups can often manage common property resources efficiently without direct interference by the state. Yet even in these cases, state coercion plays a role. First, effective management by the community depends on noncommu-

nity members being excluded from using the resources. For common property resources, exclusion is often enforced by the state. For public goods, of course, exclusion is not possible. Second, the state must recognize the community's authority to govern its affairs. Third, community groups are almost always homogeneous assemblages. Nations exist because of the differences that divide people. Baland and Platteau (1996) argue that even such community-based mechanisms work best in conjunction with the visible hand of government.

2. Olson (1965) calls such countries "privileged."

3. To the extent that the citizens of all countries care about the well-being of the citizens of other countries, assistance to reduce child mortality in developing countries may be a transnational public good.

4. International spillovers complicate the pricing problem, however. To the extent that antiretrovirals suppress the transmission of HIV, their use in one country will benefit others. But misuse of such drugs may also hasten resistance, imposing a cost on other countries. What is needed is not just a policy for pricing and trade but an effective global infrastructure for public health.

5. This is the 1998 Agreement Concerning the Establishing of Global Technical Regulations for Wheeled Vehicles, Equipment and Parts Which Can Be Fitted and/or Used on Wheeled Vehicles.

6. By a similar means, biological specimens are transported around the world, sometimes leading to ecologically destabilizing invasions; see Elton's (2000) classic study.

7. International fisheries are common property resources and thus a type of impure public good—nonexcludable but rival in consumption. Conservation by each country benefits the others that share the resource. But the two problems are otherwise different. Consumption of a fish by one party depletes the resource, leaving one less fish for others. In both cases, however, there is an incentive to free ride, and this is the feature of the fisheries problem focused on here.

8. The companies most prominent in this area are the 36 members of the Business Environmental Leadership Council, a group affiliated with the Pew Center on Global Climate Change.

9. The treaty has other flaws. Its "flexible mechanisms" are likely to be saddled with large transactions costs, preventing cost-effective implementation. The treaty also requires that substantial emission cuts be made in the short term—even though costs would be much lower (without much sacrifice in benefits) if abatement were postponed until capital could be turned over more cheaply.

REFERENCES

Baland, Jean-Marie, and Jean-Philippe Platteau. 1996. *Halting Degradation of Natural Resources: Is There a Role for Rural Communities?* New York: Food and Agriculture Organization of the United Nations.

Barrett, Scott. 1994. "Self-Enforcing International Environmental Agreements." *Oxford Economic Papers* 46: 878–94.

———. 1997. "The Strategy of Trade Sanctions in International Environmental Agreements." *Resource and Energy Economics* 19 (4): 345–61.

———. 1999a. "The Credibility of Trade Sanctions in International Environmental Agreements." In Per G. Fredriksson, ed., *Trade, Global Policy, and the Environment.* World Bank Discussion Paper 402. Washington, D.C.

———. 1999b. "Montreal versus Kyoto: International Cooperation and the Global Environment." In Inge Kaul, Isabelle Grunberg, and Marc A. Stern, eds., *Global Public Goods: International Cooperation in the 21st Century.* New York: Oxford University Press.

———. 1999c. "A Theory of Full International Cooperation." *Journal of Theoretical Politics* 11 (4): 519–41.

———. 2001. "International Cooperation for Sale." *European Economic Review* 45 (10): 1835–50.

———. 2002. "Global Disease Eradication." Johns Hopkins University, School of Advanced International Studies, Washington, D.C.

———. Forthcoming. *Environment and Statecraft: The Strategy of Environmental Treaty-Making.* Oxford: Oxford University Press.

Barrett, Scott, and Kathryn Graddy. 2000. "Freedom, Growth, and the Environment." *Environment and Development Economics* 5: 433–56.

Committee on the Assessment of Future Scientific Needs for Live Variola Virus. 1999. *Assessment of Future Scientific Needs for Live Variola Virus.* Washington, D.C.: National Academy Press.

Chayes, Abram, and Antonia Handler Chayes. 1995. *The New Sovereignty.* Cambridge, Mass.: Harvard University Press.

Congleton, Roger D. 1992. "Political Institutions and Pollution Control." *Review of Economics and Statistics* 74 (3): 412–21.

Downs, George W., David M. Rocke, and Peter N. Barsoom. 1996. "Is the Good News about Compliance Good News about Cooperation?" *International Organization* 50 (3): 379–406.

Elton, Charles S. 2000. *The Ecology of Invasions by Animals and Plants.* Chicago: University of Chicago Press.

Fredriksson, Per G., and Noel Gaston 1999. "The Importance of Trade for Ratification of the 1992 Climate Change Convention." In Per G. Fredriksson, ed., *Trade, Global Policy, and the Environment.* World Bank Discussion Paper 402. Washington, D.C.

Gladwell, Malcolm. 2000. *The Tipping Point: How Little Things Can Make a Big Difference.* Boston: Little, Brown & Company.

Heal, Geoffrey. 1994. "Formation of International Environmental Agreements." In Carlo Carraro, ed., *Trade, Innovation, Environment*. Dordrecht, the Netherlands: Kluwer Academic Publishers.

———. 1999. "New Strategies for the Provision of Global Public Goods: Learning from International Environmental Challenges." In Inge Kaul, Isabelle Grunberg, and Marc A. Stern, eds., *Global Public Goods: International Cooperation in the 21st Century*. New York: Oxford University Press.

Mirovitskaya, Natalia S., Margaret Clark, and Ronald G. Purvey. 1993. "North Pacific Fur Seals: Regime Formation as a Means of Resolving Conflict." In O. R. Young and G. Osherenko, eds., *Polar Politics: Creating International Environmental Regimes*. Ithaca, N.Y.: Cornell University Press.

Mitchell, Ronald B. 1994. *Intentional Oil Pollution at Sea: Environmental Policy and Treaty Compliance*. Cambridge, Mass.: MIT Press.

Murdoch, James C., and Todd Sandler. 1997. "The Voluntary Provision of a Pure Public Good: The Case of Reduced CFC Emissions and the Montreal Protocol." *Journal of Public Economics* 63 (3): 331–49.

Murdoch, James C., Todd Sandler, and Keith Sargent. 1997. "A Tale of Two Collectives: Sulphur versus Nitrogen Oxides Emission Reduction in Europe." *Economica* 64 (254): 281–301.

Olson, Mancur. 1965. *The Logic of Collective Action: Public Goods and the Theory of Groups*. Cambridge, Mass.: Harvard University Press.

Ostrom, Elinor. 1990. *Governing the Commons: The Evolution of Institutions for Collective Action*. Cambridge: Cambridge University Press.

Putnam, Robert D., with Robert Leonardi, and Rafaella Y. Nanetti. 1993. *Making Democracy Work: Civic Traditions in Modern Italy*. Princeton, N.J.: Princeton University Press.

Sandler, Todd. 1992. *Collective Action: Theory and Applications*. Ann Arbor: University of Michigan Press.

———. 1998. "Global and Regional Public Goods: A Prognosis for Collective Action." *Fiscal Studies* 19 (3): 221–47.

———. 2001. "Financing Global and International Public Goods." In Christopher D. Gerrard, Marco Ferroni, and Ashoka Mody, eds., *Global Public Policies and Programs: Implications for Financing and Evaluation*. Washington, D.C.: World Bank.

Schelling, Thomas C. 1978. *Micromotives and Macrobehavior*. New York: W.W. Norton.

Stiglitz, Joseph E. 1999. "Knowledge as a Public Good." In Inge Kaul, Isabelle Grunberg, and Marc A. Stern, eds., *Global Public Goods: International Cooperation in the 21st Century*. New York: Oxford University Press.

FINANCING
GLOBAL PUBLIC GOODS:
A NEW FRONTIER
OF PUBLIC FINANCE

INGE KAUL AND KATELL LE GOULVEN

"Public finances, in both theory and practice, do not stand still . . ."
—Musgrave and Musgrave 1989, p. xv

Reflecting on the changing realities of the 1970s and 1980s, Musgrave and Musgrave made this observation in the preface to the fifth edition of their *Public Finance in Theory and Practice.* This remark still holds true: public finance is starting to adjust to the growing importance of global public goods. Four main trends, developed in this chapter, are evident:

- *Most financing of global public goods continues to happen nationally.* Only $1 of every $200 spent on global public goods involves public spending at the international level.

- *International financing of global public goods is mainly an option for industrial countries.* Industrial countries tend to enjoy a higher provision of national public goods, which can often be maintained or improved only through cross-border cooperation, and these countries possess more assets to encourage other countries to cooperate.

- *International financing of global public goods often follows a "beneficiary pays" principle.* For many key global concerns, the payers ("donor" countries) are also the main beneficiaries of their spending on international cooperation.

- *International financing of global public goods often comes disguised as aid.* At the international level, global public goods are financed through official development assistance. In fact, nearly 30 percent of aid is spent on purposes related to global public goods. But aid is supposed to fight

The authors are grateful to Daniel G. Arce M., Keith Bezanson, Henk-Jan Brinkman, Anthony Clunies-Ross, Isabelle Grunberg, Raghbendra Jha, John Quiggin, Eugene Smolensky, and Paul Bernd Spahn for helpful comments.

poverty—not enhance the provision of global public goods, especially when such goods mainly benefit rich people.

The intermingling of aid and financing for global public goods constrains the effectiveness of both—hurting, in particular, poor people. Thus this chapter's main policy recommendation is to disentangle aid and financing for global public goods and to establish a distinct international component for each: the distribution branch and the allocation branch of public finance. The growing importance of global public goods should be seen as an added argument for aid, not a reason to forget about it. To the extent that aid enables developing countries to enhance the provision of national public goods, it diminishes the risk of negative cross-border spillovers and thus the need for international cooperation to control global public bads. Increasing aid frees resources that can be used to produce goods with positive utility, benefiting all people. From this main recommendation four others follow:

- *Reestablish a clear rationale for aid*—with aid defined as support to developing countries to help them foster development.
- *Increase international cooperation on financing for global public goods*— covering both inward-oriented cooperation (harmonizing national policies on public finance for global public goods) and outward-oriented cooperation (providing joint fiscal incentives at the international level).
- *Ensure resource additionality*—by making technical ministries responsible for meeting the resource implications of both the national and international components of global public goods.
- *Shift resources from controlling bads to providing goods*—to significantly enhance social returns on investments in global public goods.

Following Musgrave (1959), public economics theory distinguishes three main branches of public finance, corresponding to three main roles of government:

- *Allocation*—to encourage an adequate overall allocation of resources, private and public, to public goods.
- *Distribution*—to transfer resources that help society realize notions of fairness and justness.
- *Stabilization*—to promote full employment and price stability.

Stabilization was the first branch to emerge at the international level with the creation of the Bretton Woods system—the World Bank and International Monetary Fund—in 1946. But in practice the main industrial countries have retained power over this function, and exercise it unilaterally or through the G-7 and G-10 "clubs" (see Bordo and Eichengreen 1993 and Mendez 1992).

The international component of the distribution branch also originated in the 1940s. The precursor to the current system of official development assistance, the Marshall Plan, was created by the United States in 1948 to help European countries rebuild and expand their wartorn economies (De Long and Eichengreen 1993). Yet as with the stabilization branch, industrial countries have retained the key role in distribution. The Development Assistance Committee (DAC) of the Organisation for Economic Co-operation and Development (OECD) serves as the focal point for official development assistance. About three-quarters of aid flows through bilateral channels, directly between donor and recipient countries. One-quarter flows through multilateral channels such as the World Bank, regional development banks, and UN funds and programs (OECD 2001).

Today the growing importance of global public goods—and the serious and increasingly costly underprovision of some—calls for the creation of an international component of the allocation branch of public finance. Nationally, governments allocate funds to global public goods through a panoply of instruments. Some, such as taxes and subsidies, encourage private actors to align their economic activities more closely with societal goals. Regulation, new property rights, and other measures to promote new and more complete markets are also among the policy tools used for allocation purposes. So is spending on goods and services provided directly by government entities or through outsourcing to private providers.

Because the costs and benefits of global public goods cut across borders, international cooperation is required on these and similar instruments. Production of such goods also often requires inputs from multiple jurisdictions. So even if a country is willing and able to provide a global public good unilaterally, for technical reasons it may not be able to do so. Many—if not most—global public goods require cross-border cooperation, including cooperative financing arrangements.

This chapter explores how policymakers have responded to the growing importance of global public goods, particularly to the need for international cooperation on resource allocations. The analysis shows that international cooperation on financing for global public goods is a reality. Thus an international component of the allocation branch of public finance exists de facto, but it has grown in an ad hoc fashion. Because financing for global public goods is intertwined with aid in manifold ways, it is a policy option mainly exercised by industrial countries. Indeed, financing for global public goods is increasingly crowding out development assistance.

This situation presents a double jeopardy. First, at a time when global inequity is extreme and poverty still pervasive, the world risks losing its international distribution branch—a true development assistance function. Aside from domestic policies in recipient countries, this may contribute to ineffective aid—an issue of growing concern to both donor and recipient countries. Second, at a time when a growing number of global public goods suffer from serious underprovision, the international allocation branch continues to be constrained by having to function within the mold of aid. As a result concerned actors often lack incentives to tackle global crises, and crises are allowed to linger and worsen.

THE CHALLENGE: SPOTTING WHERE INTERNATIONAL COOPERATION IS THE BEST POLICY OPTION

Most global public goods follow a summation process, meaning that all countries must contribute for the good to emerge. Put differently, national building blocks are an important—if not the main—component of the production function of many global public goods.[1] But national building blocks are usually not, or not merely, created to feed into global public goods. Instead, they are produced because they generate important national benefits. National public goods become transnational—regional or global—when they cannot be maintained or improved solely through domestic policy action. Thus global public goods can be seen as comprising national public goods plus international cooperation. This is an important point because it suggests that the country level is the most appropriate starting point for analyzing the financing of global public goods.

This section first examines various motivations for cross-border cooperation. It then assesses the financing strategies and tools used to support international cooperation on global public goods—and how these differ from aid. The second point arises because aid, intended to help developing countries help themselves, is often used to pay for global public goods.

Why cooperate?

Various forms of international cooperation are summarized in table 1. National public goods can "go global" for many reasons, all of which indicate that cooperating is preferable to "going it alone." Whether international cooperation is desirable depends on many variables that must be assessed on a good-by-good basis. The main types of cooperation are[2]:

- *Outward-oriented cooperation.* Policymakers may seek cross-border cooperation when national public goods are widely provided, when national provision cannot be maintained or improved solely through domestic policies, or both. Country A may encourage other countries to enhance their provision of a good to avoid negative cross-border spillovers that could jeopardize provision in country A. In such cases further spending in country A would not yield additional benefits. Alternatively, the aim could be to encourage all countries to increase provision in a concerted manner. In both cases the rationale for cross-border cooperation is to encourage others—or all, including the requesting party—to internalize externalities. Promoting financial stability is a case in point.

- *Inward-oriented cooperation.* The outward-oriented cooperation initiatives of some countries translate into demands for inward-oriented cooperation by others. At the same time, if outward-oriented cooperation leads to international agreement, it may have a boomerang effect: it may return to the originating country as an international norm to be met. This second category of international cooperation thus demands policy coordination

TABLE 1

Forms of international cooperation—seen from the national level

Type of cooperation	Motivation	Illustration	Examples
Outward-oriented cooperation	Cooperation with others perceived as necessary to enjoy a good domestically	Country A / Rest of the world	Improving codes and standards in financial markets to enhance financial stability
Inward-oriented cooperation	Global exigencies or regimes requiring national policy adjustments	Country A / Rest of the world	Sustainable management of natural commons
Joint intergovern-mental production	Production of a good assigned to an international organization	GPG / IO / Country A Country B Country I	Harmonization and publication of standardized statistics
Networked cooperation	National policy adjustments to meet the access require-ments of joining a network, to capture its benefits	Country A / Rest of the world	International system of civil aviation/ International trade regime
Aid[a]	Transfer of resources from a richer country to a poorer country	Country A (rich) / Country B (poor)	A project assisted by a donor country to build schools in a developing country
International trade and investment[a]	Goods and services exchanged for payments of equivalent value	Country A / Country B	Trade in commodities/ Foreign investment

a. Aid and international trade and investment are listed here for purposes of comparison. Although they are forms of international cooperation, they are distinct from international cooperation in support of global public goods.

behind national borders, possibly including harmonization of fiscal policies. Requests emanating from international agreements—for instance, on food safety standards or reduction of chlorofluorocarbons (CFCs)—fall into this category.

- *Joint intergovernmental production.* Countries may find it more efficient to assign the production of public goods to an international organization rather than produce them individually at the national level. Countries may also find it more rational to assign the task to an existing agency rather than create a new one—to make the fullest use of existing international capacity for cooperation. Examples are global disease surveillance and generation of global meteorological data.
- *Networked cooperation.* Networked cooperation is a combination of the first two types. International networks, such as those for communication and transport, generally require an "entrance fee" from members. This fee often consists of requirements to standardize national policies and technical and regulatory norms, and to put in place adequate physical infrastructure. In such cases countries usually choose to cooperate—to pay the access costs to capture the benefits of network membership. An example is when countries decide to link themselves to the international system of civil aviation.

National interest in cross-border cooperation is likely to be stronger in the first, third, and fourth categories, which call for some form of outward-oriented cooperation. It is up to each country to decide whether to seek such cooperation and to what extent to do so—as well as what strategies to use in international policymaking to get more goods as cheaply as possible. For the second category, inward-oriented cooperation, the impetus to cooperate depends on whether and to what extent not addressing global exigencies or reneging on international commitments would generate net costs for important domestic stakeholders.

Of course, many countries are guided by a notion of responsible sovereignty. They voluntarily accept international standards and see cooperation and common rules as something that goes with being part of a community, nationally or internationally. For them outward-oriented and inward-oriented cooperation fall together. Still, the distinction between these two types of cooperation is important, because in many other countries they may be separate and so associated with different incentives.

A further distinction is critical to understanding why, when, and how countries cooperate in the provision of global public goods. Some national-level contributions, such as reductions in carbon dioxide emissions, have anonymous properties: any country's contribution is a perfect substitute for any other's. So it does not matter which country makes the input: actor A can agree to contribute on behalf of actor B. What matters is the total amount of the contributions, regardless of their source. Because of anonymous contributions, global public goods tend to face serious problems of free riding. But such goods also offer opportunities for trading: Country A can buy components from country B to make its contribution to the global good. And if country B can provide the good at lower cost than country A, such trade will be attractive—certainly for country A and, if an adequate price is paid, for country B as well.

Other national contributions have defined properties and are location-specific, often giving rise to a weakest link situation. Polio eradication is an example. It requires efforts in every country. Country A cannot contribute on behalf of country B (say, by vaccinating its own citizens twice). If a national contribution is underprovided, in situ corrections are required. (See also the discussion on biodiversity conservation in Perrings and Gadgil in this volume.) The link of the public good to a particular location makes it possible for other actors to encourage internalization of its cross-border externalities through targeted measures such as incentives or compensatory payments. Thus different goods require different policy responses and financing arrangements.

Allocating resources to promising global public goods

From the foregoing it is clear that financing global public goods requires more than just money, and certainly more than just increased public revenue mobilization and spending at the international level. It also requires ensuring through financial and nonfinancial ways that all concerned actors, public and private, allocate adequate resources to global public goods that promise a high social return—high relative to spending on and investment in other private and public goods.

The state has an important role in aligning private activities with social objectives. It is no longer expected to foot the entire bill of providing desired goods, as it was in previous decades, notably the 1950s and 1960s. Direct financing of public goods out of public revenue remains important where pure public goods are involved and goods require the authority of the state. But in many other cases the state's role lies more in providing incentives to enable individual actors to contribute to the production of public goods—for example, to be able to afford solar energy to help reduce greenhouse gases or to be able to afford vaccination to help control a communicable disease.

A powerful tool for effecting behavioral change is regulation, including assigning new property rights and creating or strengthening markets. Or the state can advance payments for services (such as by investing in road construction), then recoup some of the costs through user fees and other levies (such as by collecting a road toll). Yet in many cases financial incentives, such as subsidies, are needed. Financial incentives are especially important for leveraging private finance and making it focus on issues that affect poor people, not just for poor people's sake but also for the general public's. Private philanthropic money often provides such incentives, and even leverages public revenue for such purposes. Consider the role played in medical and pharmaceutical research and development by the Rockefeller Foundation (http://www.rockfound.org/) and the Bill and Melinda Gates Foundation (http://www.gatesfoundation.org/).

So, focusing on public finance and on the role of governments in financing global public goods does not mean that governments will always take the lead role in providing such incentives. Indeed, governments often need nudging from other actors. Besides foundations, the impetus for governments to get their spending priorities "right" can come from the general public, civil society, and business. As shown throughout this volume, this is especially the case for global public goods with benefits and costs that extend beyond the jurisdictional boundaries of the national state, creating problems of fiscal equivalence. Transnational nonstate actors often have to pressure governments to think beyond the national decisionmaking domain. They do so (rather than find their own private solutions) because the state is the only actor that can enforce cooperative solutions and is most answerable and accountable to the public. That is also why this chapter focuses on public financing of global public goods—as an incentive for and complement to private spending.

But public finance does not play only a positive role. It can also hinder the financing of public goods. As the debate on perverse subsidies has shown (Myers and Kent 2001; Van Beers and De Moor 2001), fiscal policy sometimes encourages the production of global public bads—for example, by subsidizing polluting sources of energy.

An interesting question explored in the following sections is whether international cooperation, either outward- or inward-oriented, pertains to all or only some of the tools used nationally to promote a desirable allocation of resources, public and private, to public goods. Have these tools been globalized in step with the globalization of the goods at which they are directed? Outward-oriented cooperation could be expected to be associated with the use of public finance tools, such as subsidies, at the international level. And inward-oriented cooperation could be accompanied by behind the border or national-level harmonization of public finance policies.

In international debates the financing issue is often narrowed down to just one modality: direct money flows between governments. As the analysis below shows, this narrow focus is largely due to the frequent obfuscation of aid and financing for global public goods. Aid is a distribution matter and constitutes a resource transfer—and mostly a flow of money from richer to poorer countries (table 2).

By contrast, global public goods are an allocation issue for which the state may use a range of public finance tools—nonfinancial instruments such as regulation or assignment of property rights; and financial instruments such as taxes, fines, subsidies, user fees and charges, and direct spending by state entities on services they provide through government agencies or private contractors. Adequate financing of public goods, global or national, may require using not just one measure but a battery of instruments, as the case studies in this volume demonstrate. The reason lies in the complex production function of many goods and their multiactor, multisector, multilevel features (see the institutions chapter by Kaul and Le Goulven in this volume). Other major differences between aid and global public goods financing lie in the fact that aid is country focused and aims at enhancing the development of developing countries, while global public goods financing is issue focused and aims at enhancing global development.

Although fair policymaking often requires that resource mobilization and public revenue allocation be seen together, this chapter does not deal with resource mobilization, which is seen as a national function. The assumption is that when matching their marginal willingness to pay with the marginal cost of a good, nation-states bear in mind that the cost may include national and international components. Certainly, economic theory and international relations theory, confirmed by empirical studies, tell us that nation-states are likely to consider spending on international cooperation only if it is in their national self-interest. Thus there is a risk that resource allocations will fall short of required funds. But the policy response cannot be automaticity of international resource mobilization, as some authors suggest (such as Mendez 1992). Such automaticity would curtail the role of national policymaking by predetermining, in a way, the repartition between domestic and international spending. Preferable would be to enhance the public's and politicians' awareness of interdependence and of the need to cooperate.

Action has to be taken to enhance people's willingness to pay—not to decide on their behalf. It is the function of fully participatory and democratic international cooperation to minimize through political consultation and bargaining the risks of free riding by individual nations on others. Automaticity of international resource mobilization entails risks of overly centralized provision just as overly decentralized, purely national provision can lead to welfare losses (box 1). Considering the wide differences and diversity in the world, it seems best to follow the subsidiarity principle and place the onus of proof on those who suggest centralization.

TABLE 2

Differences between aid and financing for global public goods

Issue	Aid	Financing for global public goods
Rationale	Equity	Efficiency
Branch of public finance	Distribution	Allocation
Policy tool	Transfer of resources	Panoply of instruments
Policy focus	Country	Issue (public good)
Main net beneficiary	Developing countries	Potentially all countries and all generations

---

BOX 1

WELFARE GAINS FROM MULTIPLE FISCAL UNITS:
THE DECENTRALIZATION THEOREM

The welfare gains from decentralization are often considered by reference to those deadweight losses that result from centralization (Oates 1972). Assume that the population of a particular nation-state is divided into two distinct localities. A local public good is to be provided in each locality, and it is assumed that there are no inter-jurisdictional spillovers. The cost is to be shared equally by residents. The figure below illustrates the demand for the local public good of two "representative" individuals, one from each locality. D_A represents the demand of individuals in locality A, and D_B represents the demand of individuals in B. The marginal costs of providing this particular local public good G are assumed to be constant. The price each individual is asked to pay is shown as $P = MC$ in the diagram. (This would be each individual's share of the overall marginal costs.)

The welfare loss of centralization

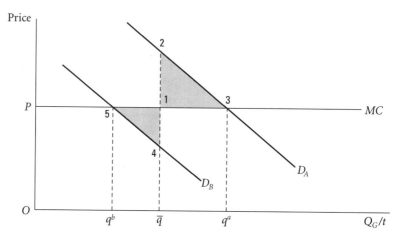

In this diagram, if a centralized regime provided a single uniform level of the good, the level of output provided could be shown as a compromise between the demands of the individuals in each locality, i.e. a level of $O\bar{q}$. Such a quantity is lower than the amount that would be demanded by the representative individual A but more than would be demanded by the representative individual B. Inevitably, welfare losses are experienced by each of these two individuals. The losses are shown as triangles 123 and 145. Triangle 123 indicates the loss that arises because individual A does not consume as much as she would choose if there were no need to compromise. She would gladly pay $\bar{q}\,23q^a$ for the addi-

BOX 1 CONTINUED

tional units $\overline{q}q^a$, but these would cost only $\overline{q}\,13q^a$ to be made available. Triangle 145 indicates the welfare losses that are experienced by individual B because he is consuming more than he would otherwise choose. He pays $q^b51\overline{q}$ for the additional units $q^b\overline{q}$ but he values them at only $q^b54\overline{q}$.

If each area could provide itself with just the quantity of the good that it requires, these deadweight losses could be avoided. Decentralization permits each locality to provide itself with the quantity of the good it prefers.

Source: Excerpted from Cullis and Jones 1998, pp. 293–94.

So where do matters stand on extending the allocation branch to the international level? What are the motivations and rationales for cooperation in the provision of global public goods? What policy approaches and instruments are used, and what policy experiences are gained?

CURRENT FINANCING FOR GLOBAL PUBLIC GOODS

Again, global public goods are often complex, with many components. Most goods follow a summation process, and among their key ingredients are national components, which can be national public goods or activities related to private goods.[3] This section begins by assessing the provision of national components of global public goods. It then reviews a step that sometimes comes between noncooperative and cooperative provision—unilateral provision of global public goods components. Finally, the section examines the cooperative financing instruments that exist internationally.

More or less, the instruments from the national context of public goods financing can also be found at the international level: financial incentives, compensatory payments, property rights assignments, trade in public goods and services, regulation, user fees and charges for global services, and direct spending on intergovernmental service facilities. The allocation branch of public finance is reaching into the international realm. But this becomes obvious only if one assesses some of the activities that present themselves as aid, and if one adopts a cross-cutting, multi-issue, multisector perspective.

National financing of global public goods

Considering the private and local benefits of many national components of global public goods, it is not surprising to find that in almost every country, significant spending—public and private—contributes to creating global public goods. Examples include controlling communicable diseases, improving human rights (reducing, among other things, the stream of international refugees), enhancing national bank regulation and supervision (reducing the risk of financial crisis), and building up national weather stations (improving the global system of meteorological information). The list goes on, extending into areas such as ensuring better food safety standards, building national ports, and strengthening statistical services.

The 1:200 ratio. It is difficult to find accurate, comparable data on national public spending on public goods, but a rough estimate suggests a worldwide figure of about $6 trillion. Of this, $5 trillion occurs in industrial countries and $1 trillion in developing countries.[4] By comparison, international spending on operational activities related to global public goods is estimated to range from $7.5–24.0 billion (table 3; see also Te Velde, Morrissey, and Hewitt 2002; Raffer 1999; and World Bank 2001).[5] Financing for the regular budgets of international organizations absorbs another $8 billion (UN 2000).

Thus the ratio of international to national public spending ranges between 1:400 and 1:200. Comparisons of national and international punitive measures, such as taxes and regulations to influence the behavior of economic actors, reconfirm the importance of national policy incentives. And if private spending is taken into account, international public spending becomes an even more minuscule part of the total. For example, the money that people spend on medicines, keeping their living spaces clean, and other protective measures may contribute to communicable disease control and so should be counted as well. Thus international cooperation is often a critical complement of national action—but it is not a substitute. Except for best-shot goods, such as the creation of new knowledge, national building blocks form the foundation of global public goods.

Provision of national building blocks. The provision of national building blocks for global public goods varies significantly among countries. Consider the differences

TABLE 3

International financing in support of global public goods

Financing	U.S. dollars (billions)
Resources for operational activities	
Official development assistance for international-level initiatives	3
Official development assistance for country-level initiatives	13
Official financing from national sector ministries or ministries of finance	8
Funding for core functions of international organizations	8
Total	32

Source: World Bank 2001, p. 112; Te Velde, Morrissey, and Hewitt 2002; UN 2000.

in the capacity of national banking systems (and hence their contributions to global financial stability) or national levels of basic education (and hence their contributions to slowing world population growth).[6] Yet the approaches and tools used to encourage resource allocations to the national building blocks of global public goods are increasingly similar across countries. They mostly involve a mix of private and public funding, of market and state-based activities. Within the government's role, preference is increasingly accorded to market-based instruments rather than regulation or direct spending. Where direct government spending occurs, "marketization" strategies—such as outsourcing to the private sector or levying user fees and charges—are widespread.[7]

Given these broad similarities in the public-private mix of national building blocks, what explains the different supply levels across countries? Are they caused by free riding, the concern usually highlighted in studies on public goods? Perhaps to some extent. But four other factors are also critical, together or in combination: poverty, private and public; weaknesses in national policy management; differences in country preferences; and exposure to and weak capacity to cope with negative cross-border spill-ins.

First, where income poverty is widespread, people cannot contribute to addressing national and thus global challenges. For example, if people are too poor to afford bed nets, they cannot protect themselves from—or help others avoid—malaria. If people are too poor to send their children to school, they cannot reap the benefits of educating girls—or foster reproductive health and slower population growth. Similarly, if governments lack adequate revenue, public services that could mitigate people's income poverty might be underprovided—such as law and order or public access to the Internet and other global communication and transportation systems.

Second, poverty-related underprovision can be magnified if countries lack sufficient capacity for policy analysis and design. It is sometimes difficult to strike the right balance between the private and public benefits of a good, or to find the right incentives for private agents to internalize the externalities of their activities, especially during periods of major policy reform and economic transition (World Bank 2001). This problem is not limited to developing countries. The chapters by Desai and by Kaul and Mendoza (in this volume) point to the need for the public and for policymakers to regain—or establish—a clear notion of publicness and of their desired balance between private and public goods. But in industrial countries people can generally substitute for public goods, such as law and order, with private goods, such as more locks on their doors. There are also more resources for the state to reclaim privatized goods and place them back in the public domain.[8] Such options are limited in developing countries.

Third, just as for private goods, people and nations have different preferences for public goods, including global public goods. These preferences depend on such factors as norms and values, political and economic environments, and, notably, development levels. Many developing countries find themselves confronted with global public goods demands from industrial countries that may not reflect their immediate policy priorities. An example is global climate change. All countries share this concern, but for developing countries it raises two issues. First, they have not contributed as much as industrial countries to the problem. Second, except for some small island states, addressing the problem is not necessarily a top policy priority. So from the perspective of industrial countries—and from a technical viewpoint, such as that of the Intergovernmental Panel on Climate Change—there appears to be an underprovision of global climate stability, while from the perspective of developing countries there appears to be an overproduction of a global public bad by a particular group of countries. As international negotiations on climate stability have shown, this difference in perspective translates into different notions of what the problem is, whose responsibility it is, and what constitutes an efficient and fair solution (see also Albin; Blanchard and others; and Chasek and Rajamani in this volume).

Similar differences of perception—and consequently, of willingness to act and pay—exist on many other issues, from financial codes and standards (see Griffith-Jones in this volume) to protection of intellectual property rights (see Correa and Mendoza in this volume). Thus the low supply of certain national public goods in developing countries often reflects not merely collective action problems, but also preference and capacity gaps. These gaps could be bridged through cooperative efforts that make economic sense, not just international transfers and not just norm and standard setting.

Fourth, national contributions to global public goods can be undermined by negative cross-border spill-ins. This risk has increased with the growing economic openness of countries and is especially high for developing countries due to their limited capacity to protect and insure themselves against external shocks. If hit by financial contagion, unexpected interest rate movements in the major currency areas (as happened in the 1970s and 1980s), trade shocks (as Mendoza in this volume discusses), or natural disasters, developing countries may see many of their development gains reversed overnight. Even the best national social safety nets would not have been strong enough to cushion the devastating effects that, for example, the financial crises of the 1990s had on several developing countries. The same is true of the devastating effects that changes in interest rate policies in industrial countries in the 1970s and 1980s had on developing countries and their external debt situation. Under such conditions developing countries may retrench rather than cooperate. A global optimum thus requires that such spillover effects be taken into account in the national decisionmaking of industrial countries (Frenkel, Goldstein, and Masson 1996) or that global safeguards be designed (as suggested by Griffith-Jones and Mendoza in this volume).

But concerns about spill-ins from abroad also run high in industrial countries. Consider the enormous effects that the September 11, 2001, terrorist attacks have had on many of them—including increased fears of bioterrorism and a back-lash against globalization. In addition, with a large volume of their investments and trade linked to foreign markets, people in industrial countries are closely fol-lowing economic trends abroad. But governments do not just seek each other's cooperation. They also compete with each other, and often do so with respect to public goods to attract private capital (Musgrave 1995; Strange 1988). Even tax competition has become a fact of life for many countries, with some exploiting at the expense of others the common "world tax base" (Tanzi 1999, p. 183)—that is, the ability of governments to mobilize the national revenue needed to perform the roles of the state in an adequate manner. Thus a range of factors contributes to people in developing and industrial countries today feeling more exposed and vulnerable. Yet many, though certainly not all, remain keen on staying engaged with the world beyond their national borders.

Developing and industrial countries share many concerns about globaliza-tion and interdependence. Yet the above analysis suggests that developing coun-tries are probably more preoccupied with providing national private and public goods for their own purposes. They may—and do—turn to the outside with cooperation requests. But in these cases they are generally asking for more assis-tance to develop, and not (or not just) for help to provide global public goods that interest industrial countries. Policymakers in industrial countries may face more demands from their constituencies to be outward-oriented, improving not only the local but also the global environment, or building not only local but also global markets. Developing country policymakers may also face demands from domestic constituencies for international cooperation to reduce the risk of exter-nal shocks to their economies. But unlike their counterparts in industrial coun-tries, as the following discussion shows, they often lack the resources to offer effective incentives or place attractive bargaining chips on the table in interna-tional negotiations.

Unilateral financing of global public goods components:
doing good while doing well
The more national public goods that countries provide for themselves, the more interested they may be in seeking cooperation with others. The reason for this apparent contradiction is that they stand to lose a lot if their domestic achieve-ments are undermined by other countries' underinvestment in global public goods and the resulting global public bads. This risk is particularly great where the production of a good follows a weakest link path. Consider the epidemics of bovine spongiform encephalopathy (mad cow's disease) and foot and mouth dis-ease in Europe in 2001. Or think of the potentially disastrous effects of the reemergence of smallpox. In such cases the overall provision of a good is equal to that achieved by the weakest link. To safeguard their accomplishments, it is rational for countries with high levels of national provision to support interna-

tional efforts to help other countries increase their national contributions to global public goods.

But recognizing dependence on others in achieving national goals does not necessarily increase countries' willingness to engage in more international cooperation. In between lie efforts aimed at unilaterally providing the lacking critical inputs for global public goods. Several such initiatives have emerged in recent years. The United Kingdom and the United States, for example, have introduced subsidies to encourage and enable their pharmaceutical companies to pay more attention to diseases that disproportionately affect the world's poor people, particularly communicable diseases such as HIV/AIDS, malaria, and tuberculosis (United Kingdom 2001; Summers 2000). Some industrial countries are also considering revising orphan drug legislation so that it covers not only neglected diseases at home but also certain diseases of poor people abroad (CMH forthcoming).

Similar national fiscal incentives have also been offered to deal with global environmental challenges—for example, to encourage wider use of clean energy technology. Such initiatives are often not just charitable measures but also make economic sense for the providing country, in that they protect its people from a global public bad while creating business opportunities for its pharmaceutical or energy companies. In addition, the providing country may enhance its international image and standing.

Unilateral provision can also occur unintentionally. Many technological innovations, for example, have benefited development worldwide, including in developing countries (Helpman 1999). This includes the spread of traditional knowledge from various cultures—which in many cases has been a contribution of developing countries to the global stock of knowledge.

Unilateral provision is a policy option primarily when three factors come together. First, the missing key ingredient (such as a vaccine) is based on a relatively certain best-shot technology. Second, corrective action has to be taken by a weak-link country that cannot afford the costs involved. Third, providing the ingredient is cheaper than continued inaction. When these three conditions are met, it makes economic sense for the best-shot provider to share the input more widely. This also means that unilateral provision is a strategy available primarily to industrial countries or major philanthropic actors with the means to finance and provide whatever is required—out of enlightened self-interest or concern for the global common good.

Cooperative financing of global public goods: the emerging international component of the allocation branch of public finance

When countries feel that neither domestic action nor unilateral provision can guarantee a desired policy outcome, international cooperation stands a good chance of being seen as a desirable approach. The international alliance against terrorism formed in response to the terrorist attacks of September 11, 2001, demonstrates this. So do many other recent international cooperation initiatives, such as those involving Internet-based crime, money laundering, drug trafficking, and international accounting standards. In addition, in many cases the private sector moves ahead with self-regulation (Cutler, Haufler, and Porter 1999) or civil society organizations push the envelope of international negotiations (Edwards and Zadek in this volume).

But whether in a proactive way or spurred by other actors, the state is often challenged. The task then is to choose the right instrument to encourage other actors—state and nonstate—to make complementary contributions to national components of a desired global public good. But as the following discussion shows, there is a caveat. Effectively pursuing national interests in international cooperation often requires more than making a persuasive argument in international negotiations, and more than voting power. It also requires resources—often financial resources—to motivate others to cooperate. As a result outward-oriented cooperation often flows from industrial to developing countries, and developing countries are often takers of inward-oriented cooperation.[9]

Several tools are used to facilitate the allocation of resources to global public goods (table 4). These tools indicate a variety of international cooperation instruments that closely resemble the tools that policymakers use for the provision of national public goods. Thus a new pattern exists in international public finance (see Sweden Ministry for Foreign Affairs 2001). But the stated rationale for using these tools is often based not on public economics and finance considerations but rather couched in aid terms. Put differently, international cooperation in support of global public goods financing is happening—but not always intentionally and so not in the most efficient way.

International (pooled) financial incentives. If things were to operate internationally exactly as they do nationally, international financial incentives would include such standard policy tools as taxes, fines, subsidies, and other types of side payments. Disincentives such as taxes would be intended to make individual actors—whether countries or private actors—internalize negative externalities. Positive incentives such as subsidies would be aimed at enabling individual actors to internalize negative externalities or encouraging them to produce positive ones.

Two possible international taxes are attracting attention from experts and civil society advocates at the international level: a currency transaction tax—the so-called Tobin tax—and a common carbon tax.[10] Today, however, there is no form of international taxation. When disincentives are used internationally, they may take the form of economic sanctions (Kaempfer and Lowenberg 1992) or withdrawal of aid, directed more against developing than industrial countries. For example, aid cancellation has become a common tool with the increased emphasis on aid conditionality that emerged in the 1980s and 1990s (Raffer and Singer

TABLE 4

Tools and purposes for financing global public goods

Purpose	Tools				
	International (pooled) financial incentives	Incremental cost payments or compensation	International regulation	Direct spending on intergovernmental service facilities	User fees and charges for global services
To back requests to internalize specific externalities (outward cooperation)	X	X			
To encourage internalization of diffuse externalities (requiring inward cooperation by all)	X		X		
To share the costs of intergovernmental joint production and purchase of global services				X	
To build and maintain national components of international networks					X

1996; Stokke 1996). Aid is sometimes withdrawn when recipient countries fail to meet certain norms (such as in terms of human rights). Conversely, aid is increased when recipient countries support certain endeavors, such as fighting illicit drug trafficking.

Subsidies are the preferred financial incentive at the international level. But most such payments, which seek to encourage an internalization of externalities, are neither designed nor presented as such. They typically appear in the guise of aid to developing countries, but they are aimed at doing what no country wants to do alone. They are "pooled" subsidies. The purpose of such subsidies is, for example, to facilitate anticorruption initiatives or to preserve biodiversity hotspots—that is, projects that yield pure global public goods from which a variety of actors may benefit and that no donor country necessarily wants to pay for on its own. Since the 1970s the share of such spending in official development assistance has doubled (World Bank 2001). Depending on the definitions used, it now ranges from $5–16 billion (Te Velde, Morrissey, and Hewitt 2002; Raffer 1999; World Bank 2001). Global environment issues attract about half, with health, knowledge management, governance, and conflict prevention sharing the other half.[11]

The aid flowing into global purposes would be considerably higher if one were to include aid provided with conditionality attached. For example, the conditionality linked to structural adjustment loans has often been aimed at—and contributed to the creation of—the institutional framework for international market integration. It has encouraged significant policy convergence behind national borders, including extensive harmonization—even globalization—of such national public goods as legal frameworks and judiciary systems. This harmonization significantly reduces risk and transaction costs for market participants.[12] For those who support the so-called Washington consensus, it illustrates an effort to encourage positive, useful externalities.[13] The growing international policy emphasis on poverty reduction can be seen in a similar light. If poverty were to reach even more excessive proportions, it could result in a rising number of failing states, civil strife, international conflict, and international terrorism and crime. So, even aid to reduce extreme poverty can be considered relevant to the goals of global public goods.[14]

International subsidies can be targeted at different groups. They can flow between donor governments and recipient governments if the externality emanates from public policy failure. The transmission channels can be bilateral or multilateral agencies as well as civil society organizations. For example, civil society organizations have often been the channel of support payments to countries where government violations of human rights or corruption were the troubling issue. But in growing measure, subsidies also flow to private corporations. Such subsidies often come bundled with philanthropic funds as well as contributions from the private sector itself, in the form of public-private partnerships. Several such partnerships have recently sprung up in the health sector, among them the Global Alliance for Vaccination and Immunization, the International AIDS Vaccine Initiative, and the Medicines for Malaria Venture. The purpose of these partnerships is, in part, to facilitate the availability of existing medicines for the poor and, in part, to encourage research and development that in particular help the poor.[15]

At the international level medical research and product development for neglected diseases are preferred investments of private foundations and philanthropic organizations. The Rockefeller Foundation and the Bill and Melinda Gates Foundation have been especially active in this respect. Evidently such partnerships find it easier to garner political support than more systematic approaches to the problem, as, for example, proposed by Kremer (2001a,b; 2002). His suggested vaccine purchasing commitment would cost several billion dollars and require a binding legal commitment over about 10 years.[16]

These and other public interventions in health aim to correct some of the adverse effects on the poor of the current international patent regime (see Arhin-Tenkorang and Conceição in this volume). Their objective is to make medicines more publicly affordable and medical research and development more focused on the diseases of the poor. This is needed to ease the crushing disease burden facing many developing countries, notably in Africa, and to avert the risk of a growing number of failing states. Put differently, these interventions seek to make some aspects of knowledge (which have, through the intellectual property rights regime, been privatized and taken out of the public domain) more public by design and to foster a better balance between dynamic and static efficiency (Stiglitz 1999). A similar effect could be achieved through some of the legal modifications to the patent regime suggested by various experts.[17] But again, these measures would be binding on pharmaceutical companies; public-private partnerships are a complement, and this is probably why they have not met with political acceptance.

The international community is concerned about a better balance between dynamic and static efficiency in the area of knowledge for health. But should one not explore other types of knowledge that might be overprivatized? For example, does an annual allocation of some $300 million suffice for the Consultative Group on International Agricultural Research (CGIAR) to ensure that enough research results of critical importance to the poor are in the public domain (http://www.cgiar.org/)? And why not encourage wider use of clean energy technologies and help develop the market for these goods?[18] Such a step would probably prove to be a "no regret" option in the battery of measures to help avert global warming (see also Barrett in this volume). This means it would be a measure that one might want to undertake in any case, whether or not global warming occurs, because of its many other potential benefits—including its positive effects on people's health. In many instances it seems "perverse," as some experts argue (Myers and Kent 2001; Van Beers and de Moor 2001), that governments grant fossil fuel subsidies of some $200 billion annually, adding to global warming, while clean energy markets have such a hard time taking off.

Besides being targeted at individual actors, state or nonstate, subsidies are also designed to support the expansion and hence the overall benefits from global networks. As mentioned, structural adjustment loans have fostered cross-border integration of markets. Similarly, the G-8's Digital Opportunity Taskforce (http://www.dotforce.org/) supports developing countries in making global communications networks accessible to wider population segments. And a number of aid projects aim at enhancing developing countries' access to markets for goods, services, and finance.

Markets, communication and transportation systems, and other international regimes are goods that entail important externalities between users (Heal 1999; Katz and Shapiro 1985; Spar 1999). Additional network members bring added value to the existing ones. Yet many networks pose access problems. Countries, for example, need institutions, physical infrastructure, and management capacity to link to a network and benefit from it; and individual households need to be able, for instance, to afford a computer to access the Internet. Aid to help developing countries overcome these problems is a good investment for all— current as well as new members. These initiatives make all better off. According to World Bank (2001, p. 112) estimates, about two-thirds of the aid flowing to global public goods consists of such complementary support intended to "prepare countries to consume the international public goods."[19]

Financial—or potentially "cashable"—incentives come in many "currencies." The gamut of measures can run from subsidies and payoffs to trade favors, military and diplomatic rewards, and regulation. But most of the time providing incentives requires having something to promise—or threaten—the other side. Thus incentives, especially financial ones, are more readily available to industrial countries or wealthy private actors than to developing countries, just as unilateral provision is easier for industrial countries or actors.

Incremental cost payments or compensation. There are many similarities between subsidies and compensatory payments. Both seek to provide positive incentives. But there is an important difference: compensatory payments have a stronger contractual character. With compensation, actor A reimburses actor B for the costs of providing a clearly defined service. The UN Framework Convention on Climate Change and the Convention on Biological Diversity have given prominence to the concept of compensatory payments, notably for incremental costs.

Here incremental costs are defined as the costs a country incurs in taking actions that generate global environmental benefits and that exceed what the country would do if guided solely by national self-interest (GEF 1998; King 1993). These two conventions and Agenda 21 (UN 1992) also stipulate that incremental costs should be paid out of new and additional resources. The Global Environment Facility (GEF) was created to make such payments (GEF 1998). But for the most part, donor countries' contributions to the facility have come out of official development assistance. This has occurred despite the fact that since the mid-1990s official development assistance has fallen and falls far short of the international target of 0.7 percent of industrial countries' GNP (OECD 2001).[20]

The Global Environment Facility has helped mobilize other public as well as private funding that exceeds its official contributions (http://www.gefweb.org). But that is not the point. The point is that the use of aid in projects supported by the facility negates the concept of incremental costs. The concept of incremental costs was introduced because global environmental activities are not aid. Rather, they are global services that countries provide to the world. These services can include maintaining forests for carbon sequestration or preserving biodiversity hotspots (see Castro and Cordero as well as Perrings and Gadgil in this volume). Because of the diffuse benefits of such services, donors tend not to buy them individually but seek burden-sharing arrangements with others through mechanisms such as the Global Environment Facility.

Paying for these increasingly scarce and valuable services through the lens of aid may lead donors to focus on the direct costs of the services rather than determine their true utility and value to society. This approach places sustainable development at risk of being underpriced and underprovided. But given the current international debate on global climate stability, the concept of incremental costs may prove to be merely a precursor to more efficient, equitable trade in global environment services. These trading arrangements form part of the discussion in the next section.

International regulation. Setting norms and standards is probably the approach used most extensively at the international level to motivate or, more precisely, urge states to internalize externalities and contribute to intergovernmental initiatives. Regulation usually encourages governments to consider harmonizing either the public finance instruments they are using nationally (say, by giving preference to market-based mechanisms over regulatory instruments) or to adjust public spending levels (such as on basic education).

In many cases international regulation is the only way to address problems that have sources and effects caused by diffuse externalities. To deal with diffuse externalities, all states must often agree to follow international norms to avoid a prisoner's dilemma. An example is the Montreal Protocol on Substances that Deplete the Ozone Layer (http://www.unep.ch/ozone/index.shtml). But states also resort to international regulation for specific, traceable externalities to broaden acceptance of certain norms and standards. The Universal Declaration of Human Rights, for example, allows the international community to pinpoint national shortfalls from agreed international norms.

Yet many international relations experts doubt the effectiveness of international regulation in influencing public and private behavior at the country level because of great difficulties in observing, determining, and enforcing compliance (see Barrett in this volume). Moreover, regulation is not the preferred approach of economists, because the suggested norms are often uniform. They require the same response from all actors and so can lead to inefficient resource allocations (see box 1). This concern is confirmed by the effects on poor people's health of the World Trade Organization agreement on Trade-Related Aspects of Intellectual Property Rights (TRIPs; see Correa in this volume). In addition, regulation is likely to be ineffective if some actors lack the capacity and means to comply, as is the case in today's world of huge development disparities between countries.

But promising new efforts are being made to overcome some of the traditional weaknesses of regulation guided by international agreements. Three important features of recent agreements include legalization, linking entitlement or allowance trading to international norm and standard setting, and attaching cost estimates to international action plans to know their "price" and facilitate resource mobilization.

First, international relations scholars suggest that there is a trend toward legally binding agreements on many issues, including trade and intellectual property rights, human rights, arms control, and the environment. Rules are becoming more obligatory and precise, and a growing number of agreements assign monitoring, interpretation, and dispute settlement to third parties (Goldstein and others 2001). Examples include the World Trade Organization's Dispute Settlement Mechanism (www.wto.org), the International Criminal Court (http://www.igc.org/icc/), and the trade sanctions used by the Montreal Protocol to deter noncompliance (Barrett 1999).

The hardening of international norms is linked to growing concern about risks and uncertainty in an open, globalizing, interdependent world. It is especially common where strong private interests or systemic risks are involved. The international trade regime is an example involving private interests, the Kyoto Protocol (on global warming) is an example of systemic risks, and the Cartagena Protocol on Biosafety (http://www.biodiv.org/biosafety/) is an example of both.[21]

Legally binding norms reduce transaction costs. Just imagine the number of legal battles that international traders and patent holders would have to fight if trade rules were less obligatory. But who gains from new international laws? Reflecting on the growing trend toward patenting nature and traditional knowledge, *The Economist* (2001) notes that few people in developing countries have the $20,000 required to obtain a patent in the United States—or the $1.5 million it costs to challenge one. For them legalization makes owning intellectual property difficult, if not impossible, to afford.

Second, to overcome the inefficient deadweight burden resulting from the top-down, centralized decisionmaking that often marks international norm and standard setting, efforts have been made to link regulation with market mechanisms and trading where anonymous (substitutable) externalities are involved. The Kyoto Protocol (http://unfccc.int/resource/docs/cop3/07a01.pdf), in addition to seeking lower emissions in industrial countries, foresees various emissions trading options—both among industrial countries and between industrial and developing countries—to increase flexibility in meeting regulatory targets. Other proposals have also recommended such trade (see Chichilnisky 1997).

But for such trade to occur, actors must first be assigned new property rights. And for that to happen, new products must be designed, such as "emission permits" or "certified carbon dioxide reduction." Various emissions trading schemes have already emerged.[22] Yet many unresolved questions remain about the efficiency and equity of such schemes and about how they compare with alternative policy tools such as a common carbon tax (see Cline 1992; Pearson 2000; Sandmo 2000; and UNCTAD 2001).

Yet whether the establishment of global and national emission targets leads to a common international policy mechanism or to policy pluralism—with countries choosing their own approach to reducing emissions—in both cases the purpose would be to place a price on use of the atmosphere. This could also encourage governments to carefully review their environmental subsidies. Canceling some perverse subsidies could free resources for new subsidies better attuned to the goal of global sustainable development. So, establishing emission targets could help rebalance national and global resource allocations in favor of global climate stability. It could do for the atmosphere what the Law of the Sea's establishment of a 200-mile exclusive economic zone did for fish stocks: facilitate a more rational use of an open-access resource (Mendez 1992; Pearson 2000).

Third, international agreements are giving thought to the cost implications of new regulation. Until recently most of these agreements came "empty handed," with no cost plans or funds for implementation. (The Montreal Protocol is a rare exception.) Unfunded agreements result in incentives without firm mandates. Donors tend to pick and choose from international agreements the stipulations that they want to support financially. Increasingly their focus is on the goals set in the Millennium Declaration adopted at the 2000 UN summit of heads of state (UN General Assembly resolution 55/2, 8 September 2000). But even this declaration initially came without financial backing. Only now are studies assessing its resource implications (Devarajan, Miller, and Swanson 2002).[23] This could mean an important shift in international negotiations: governments holding each other more accountable to match stated preferences with willingness to pay. Multiplying global crises—particularly extreme poverty and ill health—undoubtedly contributed to this shift in attitude and behavior.

Thus international regulation seems to be at a crossroads. In some ways it is gaining new importance, and institutionalization and legalization of international politics translate into policy convergence behind national borders. As a result the global public increasingly feels the influence of international agreements. Consequently, as several of the chapters in part 2 of this volume show, the public also seeks greater say in how international regimes are designed. In a sense they are also revealing their willingness to pay.

But there is a simultaneous trend, especially among powerful nations, not to get their hands tied if international agreements may affect their national interests or those of certain constituencies. Institutions must and do change as political, social, and economic realities and technological opportunities develop. There must be room and encouragement for such adjustments. Still, norms of international cooperation must be honored by all parties to an agreement. Otherwise cooperation will turn into competition, leading to situations like the prisoner's dilemma.

Direct spending on intergovernmental service facilities. International organizations such as UN agencies can be considered international service facilities. They provide an arena in which nation-states can meet, share experiences, and negotiate international agreements. Many also have a mandate to collect information and statistics from around the world, survey global trends, monitor states' compliance with agreements, and assist in operational follow-up action. It makes sense for countries to rely on one set of such institutions rather than replicate such tasks nationally. Joint, intergovernmental provision generates significant economies of scale. And because many international organizations perform multiple tasks, joint provision also generates economies of scope.

Nation-states perceive a basic set of international organizations performing certain core functions as important and indispensable. Reducing the possibility of their free riding on each other, member states have agreed that their contributions to the regular budgets of such organizations are obligatory and proportional to their national incomes, reflecting their ability to pay (Klein and Marwah 1997; Laurenti 2001; UN 2001c). These obligatory, assessed contributions are often funded by relevant national ministries. For example, the ministry of health finances a country's contribution to the regular budget of the World Health Organization, the ministry of agriculture finances the contribution to the Food and Agriculture Organization, and the ministry of labor finances the contribution to the International Labour Organization.[24] This setup distinguishes the financing of international organizations from the subsidies, compensatory, and other international payments reviewed above. Most of those other payments come from development assistance budgets or voluntary contributions by donor countries—although international organizations also receive voluntary funds for various purposes.

The International Monetary Fund (IMF) and World Bank are among the core international organizations, with finance ministries and central banks providing the main resources for their operations (see Buira in this volume). The first amendment to the IMF's Articles of Agreement, passed in 1969, introduced the Special Drawing Right (SDR) to increase the availability of official liquidity and avoid deflationary tendencies (Allen 2002). But while experts and policymakers have identified a growing need for such liquidity in the wake of financial openness and market integration (Buira 2002; Soros 2002; UN 2001b), no new SDRs have been issued since 1981. As a result developing countries are forced to undertake costly self-insurance—to accumulate high reserves at the expense of higher investment, growth, and consumption (Buira 2002).

Although an SDR issuance would have low costs, developing countries have found it hard to gain support for this proposal from industrial countries and those countries' financial markets. The reason is that some industrial country analysts question the continuing relevance of some IMF functions as well as the need for World Bank loans (IFIAC 2000). In the same vein, contributions to the regular budgets of other international organizations, notably the United Nations, are increasingly subject to requested reforms and proof of effectiveness.[25] Firm, long-term commitments by all governments thus seem to exist for only one global—and purely public—good: the role of international organizations as arenas for joint policy dialogue and negotiation.

User fees and charges for global services. In most countries natural monopolies (due to increasing returns to scale) have resulted in the public production of such essentially private goods as postal services, telecommunications, harbors, and civil aviation infrastructure. These services have progressively been standardized and integrated with global networks. Prospects of clear national benefits have driven countries' acceptance of the need for such cooperation—that is, standardization as a price for being able to jump on the bandwagon and capture network externalities.

But as noted in the discussion of subsidies, a network benefits from additional members. Thus it makes sense for industrial countries that are part of an international network to help developing countries join it, whether through aid or other means. In the past, international communication and transport systems received massive aid—showing the synergies between aid and global public goods provision.[26] Aid helped developing countries establish the building blocks needed to link to international networks, and being part of these networks has bolstered their development.

Certainly, more remains to be achieved, as indicated by the "digital divide." Determined aid could narrow this divide. Networks benefit from having a national organizational anchor, usually the concerned technical government authority, and from having an international organization focused on their development—as the International Civil Aviation Organization did for civil aviation.

Members of communication and transport networks recognize that networks are only as strong as their weakest members. Thus for a network to develop, the weaker links have to be brought along. For example, developing countries enjoy free access to some satellite systems, such as EUMETSAT (www.eumetsat.de). Similarly, member states of the Universal Postal Union have created a Quality of Service Fund intended to help developing countries upgrade their postal services. Contributions to the fund are mandatory and are mobilized by making industrial countries pay an extra 7.5 percent of the terminal dues they owe developing countries for delivering mail from industrial countries to its final destination (Mazou 2002). Such an arrangement is only possible because governments have long-standing international agreements on various user fees and charges, whether for postage costs, airport taxes and over-flying charges for aircraft (ICAO 2001), or lighthouse fees collected when a ship docks in a harbor. These agreements enable governments to recoup some of their considerable up-front investment and maintenance costs.

Such charges are based on the fact that many of the services provided by communication and transport networks are private goods for which people are willing to reveal their preferences. Many of these services were once publicly provided but have since been privatized, due in part to changing technology and in part to the general shift toward liberalization and transnationalization of production (Drake 2001; Lee 1996; Zacher and Sutton 1996). One attraction for the new owners is the revenue associated with the services.

But in many cases governments have stayed involved not just through regulation, but also through service provision. Thus governments retain the overarching responsibility for both the domestic and international components of these networks. This distinguishes these more established global public goods from those that have come to the fore since the 1970s—including the environment, international finance, new and reemerging communicable diseases, and growing global inequity. National ministries tend to handle the domestic components of these new goods as well as international negotiations on them. Yet when it comes to operational dimensions of international cooperation, aid agencies enter the picture in industrial countries—as with the Global Environment Facility—separating the domestic and international aspects of the goods' production functions.

Undoubtedly, more instances of global public goods financing could be identified and this inventory of examples extended. But what overall picture emerges from this array of details?

Summary and conclusion

International cooperation to enhance the financing of global public goods is a reality. The tools that governments use nationally to encourage the provision of public goods are increasingly evident internationally. But it seems that reality is ahead of theory and policy intent. Much of the financing of global public goods today is happenstance. Sometimes it works well, yet many other times it does not. The challenge thus is to enhance our understanding of when and why cooperation pays, and of the policy instruments, financial and nonfinancial, that could be used to channel more adequate resource to global public goods—where new investments promise high social returns at the global level. In more detail, the findings and policy recommendations of this chapter are as follows.

Main findings
Three findings summarize where things stand on international cooperation and financing for global public goods. First, an international component of the allocation branch of public finance exists, but not in a structured way. This is not sur-

prising, because the concept of global public goods is rather new. As a result financing for each global public good is more or less considered in isolation. It is rare to see cross-references between issues—such as a comparison of the policy experience gained with using the concept of incremental costs for transport issues and for environmental issues.

If there were a more structured notion of the international component of the allocation branch, there would be more debate on the links between national and international public financing for the same goods. At present it is extremely difficult to find data on such issues as what groups of countries and the world as a whole are undertaking in terms of public finance to encourage the use of clean energy. As noted, a rough estimate suggests that national public spending on public goods is 200–400 times international public spending on global public goods. If tax measures—which mainly if not exclusively exist nationally—are considered, national financing becomes even more important. The report by the World Health Organization's Commission on Macroeconomics and Health (CMH 2001) is a rare exception in that it provides a comprehensive picture of national and international financing arrangements for health, including some of the main challenges for global communicable disease control. Similar assessments for other global public goods would be extremely useful.

Second, international cooperation on financing for global public goods is often presented as, and financed by, aid. This is especially common for issues that have emerged or reemerged since the 1970s—such as those related to the environment, health, and the creation and strengthening of international markets. In fact, global public goods absorb nearly one-third of aid.

Closely related is the fact that extending the allocation branch of public finance to the international level is primarily a policy option for industrial countries (table 5). As a result industrial countries are more involved in outward-oriented international cooperation on global public goods (and self-engineered

TABLE 5

Financing of global public goods: an option primarily for industrial countries

Type of financing	Importance in overall financing	Availability to industrial countries	Availability to developing countries
National financing	High	High	Medium
Unilateral financing	Low	High	Unlikely to exist or be exercised
International cooperative financing	Medium	Medium	Low

inward-oriented cooperation), while developing countries mostly experience (externally driven) inward-oriented cooperation. Moreover, preferences for public goods, including global public goods, are likely to vary with a country's income and other circumstances. Given this fact and the analyses in part 2 of this volume—and their observations about the limited negotiating capacity of developing countries—it is reasonable to assume that industrial country policy preferences often translate into international public spending priorities. Even if developing countries sought international cooperation on certain issues involving global public goods, their limited resources and lack of voting power in international organizations would probably not allow them to translate such needs into policy demands.

Because much of the financing for global public goods is presented as aid, there is a widespread perception that countries' ability to pay determines the financing they receive to defray the costs of international cooperation projects—and even that such projects have donors and beneficiaries. Yet that may not be at all true when country preferences for a good are taken into account. In such cases the ability-to-pay principle can and often does translate into the beneficiary-pays principle (Mendoza 2002). To better understand the net benefits of responses to some key global concerns, it would be useful to analyze the distribution of utility among different groups. That way, the general public in "donor" countries could see that quite a bit of spending on international cooperation is in their self-interest—or at least in their and the recipients' mutual interest.

Third, although much of the international policy debate and the literature on global public goods concern goods supported by official development assistance, there are many "self-running" global public goods—that is, goods that find adequate financing from such sources as national sector and finance ministries and private financing. Examples include international communication and transport systems. Such goods offer important policy lessons. Because the properties of goods are often not innate and immutable, it would be interesting to study what contributes to the success of such goods and how other public goods that have gone global, or are expected to go more global, could benefit from these experiences.

Policy recommendations: disentangling aid and global public goods to benefit both
Given the preceding analysis, what is the best way to move forward with the financing of global public goods? There is clearly an enormous need for further research and policy debate. Some issues meriting additional study have already been mentioned. Scholars interested in fiscal federalism and subsidiarity will see many other issues that could be examined, as will international relations scholars. Clarifying the financing of global public goods requires bringing together many disciplines. Such a multidisciplinary view, which this chapter could only begin to

suggest, would reveal many contributions that could form the cornerstones of a beginning theory of global public goods financing.

Given the urgency of many global challenges, it is also desirable to identify practical policy steps to bolster the international component of the allocation branch of public finance. The most critical next step is to disentangle agendas for aid (the distribution branch) and global public goods financing (the allocation branch)—in the same way suggested to distinguish the two branches at the national level.[27] The reason is that the allocation agenda is increasingly suffocating the aid agenda. At the same time, the allocation branch is becoming overburdened with global public bads resulting from extreme poverty and severe underprovision of the national components of many global public goods, such as communicable disease control. Moreover, using aid for global public goods sends, notably in the environment area, the wrong price signals to both industrial and developing countries—a disconcerting fact given the global risks on this issue.

Disentangling agendas for aid and global public goods would involve four main policy choices. First, it would be important to reestablish (or perhaps, finally establish) a clear rationale for aid—and once accepted, to abide by it. Aid should be what it is often stated but rarely practiced as: support to help developing countries build a foundation for development. But aid should also enable these countries to pursue development in the spirit of today's interdependence, internalizing as much as possible any negative cross-border externalities that emanate from their jurisdictions. Accordingly, aid should be an unrequited transfer of resources (Kanbur 2001), country-driven and country-specific. Developing countries should be allowed to decide whether and to what extent they want to use aid for outward- or inward-oriented international cooperation. If industrial countries or other developing countries feel that certain countries need to do more to externalize certain externalities, they could consider doing what central governments do nationally—offering support through matching grants. But this would have to be non-aid money.

Second, establishing a clear rationale for aid would free the way to define a rationale for international cooperation in support of global public goods. This rationale would be similar to that for the role of the allocation branch nationally: to enhance resource allocations to and provision of public goods. Put differently, the focus of concern would be a global issue or public good, not a country as with aid. As the foregoing analysis has shown, governments can enhance resource allocations to a particular issue in three main ways: by harmonizing national allocation policies (say, by introducing an energy tax), by assigning new property rights and creating or strengthening markets, and by pooling public revenue internationally to finance intergovernmentally provided services or joint incentives (for other states or nonstate actors).

Third, separating agendas for aid and global public goods requires addressing resource additionality. If not from official development assistance, then from what sources could international cooperation linked to the provision of global public goods be financed? "Self-running" global public goods provide a possible answer: from national technical ministries that also handle the domestic component of the good, or from national finance ministries. If this route were taken, the international community could finally live up to a commitment made repeatedly over the past decade—to finance global public concerns, such as environmental concerns, out of new and additional resources.[28]

Fourth, funding aid adequately and finding new and additional resources for global public goods must not and should not involve inflating public budgets. In most national budgets there is scope for reallocating resources. In particular, it would be desirable to shift resources from controlling global public bads to producing global public goods. Certainly, the former is often a stepping stone toward the latter. But, for example, defense capacity alone will not necessarily generate peace. Similarly, financial market surveillance is a necessary but insufficient condition for financial stability. Budget restructuring often faces political obstacles. Thus the losers will have to be compensated. Shifting the emphasis from controlling bads to producing goods may, for some time, entail true additionality. The same would apply to reducing perverse subsidies. But considering the costs and benefits suggested by the provision profiles of Conceição this volume, the resource requirements seem affordable and worth incurring. Spending on corrective actions may require tens of billion of dollars—compared with the hundreds of billions that could result from continued underprovision.[29] In fact, well-chosen investments in global public goods could yield high social returns and add significantly to economic growth and development.

Many years of experience have led policymakers worldwide to follow nationally a public finance system that usually recognizes the three standard branches of public finance: allocation, distribution, and stabilization. Though there are many linkages between the three branches, capturing the synergies between them requires each branch to perform its role. Internationally there is no reason the same logic would not apply. So as an immediate next step it would be desirable to develop the international components of the distribution and allocation branches. The next chapter, on managing the production of global public goods, explores in more detail the institutional and organizational choices that will have to be made to build a more systematically organized international component of the allocation branch.

NOTES

1. The literature on public goods usually differentiates between three main provision or aggregation technologies: summation, best shot, and weakest link. Hirshleifer (1983) originally suggested this typology. For a more detailed discussion on how aggregation technologies relate to and vary with the nature of particular pub-

lic goods, see Sandler (1998 and in this volume) as well as Arce M. and Sandler (2002) for a discussion on this issue relating, in particular, to regional public goods. This chapter uses a slightly modified definition of aggregation technologies. It suggests that the production of most public goods follows a summation process, with the difference that depending on the good in question, some may contain weakest link or best shot providers.

2. Each component of a global public good may require a different type of cooperation. In other words, the production and financing of one good may call for a variety of cooperation strategies. In addition, the categories of cooperation distinguished here are not necessarily mutually exclusive—as highlighted by the discussion below on capturing network externalities. Nevertheless, the different categories are likely to affect countries' willingness to cooperate in different ways, so it is useful to distinguish them.

3. Interested readers may want to refer in this connection to the institutions chapter by Kaul and Le Goulven (in this volume) and the production trees for food safety and climate stability depicted therein. These production trees demonstrate the complexity of global public goods and the type of actions and inputs they may require at different levels and from different groups.

4. These figures are based on OECD (1997); Tanzi and Schuknecht (2000); and UNDP (various years). They mainly reflect government purchases of goods and services and subsidies.

5. Because spending on official development assistance is not classified according to global public goods and genuine aid purposes, analyses such as these have to rely on rough judgments based on descriptions of projects that also have not been formulated in terms of global public goods. Hence the variation in assessments of official development assistance allocated to global public goods in the various studies.

6. Interested readers may want to refer to Kaul and Mendoza (in this volume) for a more detailed discussion on the public properties of the various goods mentioned in this chapter.

7. For a more detailed discussion and assessments of the experiences gained with some of these measures, see Colclough (1997) and Kaul (1999).

8. Examples include free public health services and access to public libraries (including free Internet connections) for low-income groups.

9. This fact could explain why countries often prefer regional cooperation to interregional or universal cooperation. See Lawrence (1996) and Ocampo (2001).

10. For overviews of various taxation proposals that have surfaced in international debates, see Mendez (1992); Najman and d'Orville (1995); and UN (2001b). For discussions on a common carbon tax, see Cline (1992); Cooper (2000, 2002); and Tietenberg (1998). For a recent study on the currency transactions tax, see Spahn (2002).

11. As shown later in this chapter, not all of the official development assistance for global public goods takes the form of subsidies—especially money allocated to the

environment, which is often also used for compensatory payments or such activities as emissions trading.

12. For discussions on the main components of these programs, see Burki and Perry (1998) and Williamson (1990, 2000). Most assessments of structural adjustment loans focus on their contributions to national economic growth and development—which are often negative. But the programs' results in bringing about policy convergence have been quite significant.

13. The Washington consensus refers to neoliberal, free market policies promoted by the International Monetary Fund, World Bank, and U.S. government, among others.

14. As discussed in by Kaul and Mendoza (in this volume), extreme poverty—nationally and internationally—has the property of a public bad. But after a certain level of poverty reduction, when externalities subside, improving one's well-being is perceived as a private responsibility and a rival good. Thus during the process of fiscal decentralization in recent years, even functions of distribution were sometimes reassigned from central to lower levels of government. As Musgrave (1997) notes, countries making such policy choices have to decide "how much union" (p. 71) and social cohesion they seek. This is a difficult matter to determine ex ante. Ex post it is often easier to know that not enough resources—political attention, money, and opportunities— were allocated to a public good such as equity or social cohesion.

15. For brief descriptions of the activities of these and other partnerships, see Arhin-Tenkorang and Conceição (in this volume).

16. But a payment would only have to be made if a vaccine were actually developed. For a summary description of Kremer's proposal, see Arhin-Tenkorang and Conceição (in this volume).

17. These proposals suggest, for example, allowing under certain conditions a flexible interpretation of the World Trade Organization's agreement on Trade-Related Aspects of Intellectual Property Rights (TRIPS) (see Correa in this volume), creating a generalized system of differential pricing (WHO 2001), or granting patents on medicines for diseases (such as cardiovascular diseases) that affect people in all countries—either industrial or developing countries but not both (Lanjouw 2001). On the last proposal, Lanjouw explains that "because the profit potential offered by rich country markets is far greater, firms will naturally relinquish...[patent protection] in poor countries" (p. 7). Thus the policy may help making medicines more affordable in developing countries.

18. For a discussion and review of the literature on barriers to and opportunities and market potential for clean technologies, see IPCC (2001), especially chapter 5.

19. As the discussion in part 2 of this volume shows, the public—whether states, civil society organizations, business, or the general public—do not necessarily enjoy consuming public goods that they had no opportunity to help select and shape.

20. Denmark and the Netherlands as well as developing country donors to the Global Environment Facility—such as China and Egypt—deserve special mention in

this connection. Their contributions to the facility constitute, at least in part, new and additional resources, according to information obtained by the authors.

21. But just as strong private and national interests in some cases encourage firmer agreements, in other cases they oppose the adoption of binding international rules. The withdrawal of the United States from various treaty obligations, including the Kyoto Protocol, provides evidence of these contending forces.

22. The present situation on emissions trading confirms the analysis by Demsetz (1967) of the creation of new property rights. He pointed out that new property rights tend to be created when economic circumstances change, increasing the value of a common property resource. Barzel (1997) refines this insight by showing that individuals tend to delineate rights more carefully as the value of those rights increases and less so as their value declines. If this holds in the present case, then in a number of years, when new technology lowers pollution levels and the value of emission permits, the actors now so keenly interested in developing this new market may also be fast in walking away from it. On this point see also Chichilnisky (1997).

23. Intriguingly, the empty-handedness of international agreements is not being remarked on in studies and reports reviewing the progress—or lack thereof—in their implementation. See Schechter (2001) and UN (2001a).

24. In some cases core contributions as well as contributions to, for example, international peacekeeping or even the Global Environment Facility are paid for by the ministry of foreign affairs. It is difficult to determine which government entity budgets for which international cooperation expenditure. A survey is required to determine this. The information presented here is based on personal communications between the authors and select governments and multilateral organizations. If in the future there were, as recommended later in this chapter, efforts to record global public goods spending on international cooperation, many of the current data problems could be resolved and intergovernmental and governmental transparency and accountability enhanced.

25. Another function close to being within the set of recognized international core functions is UN peacekeeping. Peacekeeping is financed through special assessed contributions. Yet contributions are made on an ad hoc basis, and proposals to include the resources required for international peacekeeping in national defense budgets have met with decided resistance—not from the military but from ministries of foreign affairs (Gizewski and Pearson 1993). In addition, some functions of international organizations that used to be accepted as core activities—such as providing global survey and statistical information—are increasingly being "marketized" and included in cost recovery schemes. As a result these organizations now charge for many of their publications and data sets. One international organization that is fully self-financing is the World Intellectual Property Organization (www.wipo.int). A user fee approach is also being tried in the area of biodiversity for food and agriculture. The Multilateral System for Plant Genetic Resources for Food and Agriculture (MSPGRFA) will charge for the resources it provides (Gerbasi 2002). But there is an important difference between the services provided by WIPO and the MSPGRFA:

WIPO offers publicly produced private services by promoting the protection and use of intellectual property rights, MSPGRFA charges for private access to a common good—a global gene pool for food and agriculture.

26. See, for example, the history of the International Civil Aviation Organization (http://www.icao.int/) and UNDP (1985).

27. Musgrave and Musgrave (1989) state that even if theoretically an omniscient planner could resolve distribution and allocation simultaneously, it is not feasible in practice. "Least this [disentangling] is done, the efficient provision of public services tends to be distorted by distributional considerations, and vice versa. The two-step procedure thus remains a useful (if not perfect) model" (p. 71).

28. For these commitments, see chapter 33 of Agenda 21 (http://www.un.org/esa/sustdev/agenda21chapter33.htm), article 20 of the Convention on Biodiversity (http://www.biodiv.org/convention/articles.asp?lg=0&a=cbd-20), article 20 of the UN Convention to Combat Desertification (http://www.unccd.int/convention/text/convention.php), and section F of the Marrakesh Accords (http://unfccc.int/cop7/documents/accords_draft.pdf).

29. A rough estimate suggests that an annual expenditure level of about $ 28.5 billion would, for example, make it possible to undertake the following global public good-related initiatives:

- $10.5 billion to complement TRIPS with facilities aimed at improving static efficiency in the area of global knowledge management, e.g. R&D and technology dissemination in health ($3 billion as proposed by the Commission on Macroeconomics and Health, see CMH 2001), clean energy ($7 billion as initial investment proposed by Le Goulven 2002) and agricultural research ($0.5 billion);

- $8 billion to compensate developing countries for adjustments in their policy priorities, which industrial countries might want to request, e.g. to facilitate the implementation of the TRIPS regime, adoption of financial codes and standards, labor standards or norms of airport security;

- $2 billion for international peacekeeping (United Nations 2000);

- $8 billion for core services provided directly by intergovernmental agencies (New Zealand 2001 and United Nations 2000).

The first two sets of investments would be additional to existing expenditures, whereas the last two reflect current expenditures on these items. In reality industrial countries would probably meet most of this total $28.5 billion a year. However, it would also be desirable for developing countries to establish international cooperation budgets for the global public goods they wish to see better financed. If aid were provided in an unrequited form, and indeed, reach the now discussed figure of some $ 65–70 billion per year, developing countries could use part of the ODA to create for example, their own international incentive instruments, such as a vaccine purchasing fund—rather than have donors doing it for them.

REFERENCES

Allen, Mark. 2002. "Financing the Global Public Good of International Financial Stability." In Inge Kaul, Katell Le Goulven, and Mirjam Schnupf, eds., *Global Public Goods Financing: New Tools for New Challenges.* New York: United Nations Development Programme, Office of Development Studies. [http://www.undp.org/ods].

Arce M., Daniel G., and Todd Sandler. 2002. *Regional Public Goods: Typologies, Provision, Financing, and Development Assistance.* Stockholm: Almqvist & Wicksell International.

Barrett, Scott. 1999. "Montreal versus Kyoto: International Cooperation and the Global Environment." In Inge Kaul, Isabelle Grunberg, and Marc A. Stern, eds., *Global Public Goods: International Cooperation in the 21st Century.* New York: Oxford University Press.

Barzel, Yoram. 1997. *Economic Analysis of Property Rights.* 2nd ed. Cambridge: Cambridge University Press.

Bordo, Michael D., and Barry Eichengreen, eds. 1993. *A Retrospective on the Bretton Woods System: Lessons for International Monetary Reform.* Chicago and London: University of Chicago Press.

Buira, Ariel. 2002. "Allocating Special Drawing Rights to Increase International Financial Stability." In Inge Kaul, Katell Le Goulven, and Mirjam Schnupf, eds. *Global Public Goods Financing: New Tools for New Challenges.* New York: United Nations Development Programme, Office of Development Studies. [http://www.undp.org/ods].

Burki, Shahid Javed, and Guillermo E. Perry. 1998. *Beyond the Washington Consensus: Institutions Matter.* Washington, D.C.: World Bank.

Chichilnisky, Graciela. 1997. "Development and Global Finance: The Case for an International Bank for Environmental Settlements." Discussion Paper 10. United Nations Development Programme, Office of Development Studies, New York.

Cline, William R. 1992. *The Economics of Global Warming.* Washington, D.C: Institute of International Economics.

CMH (Commission on Macroeconomics and Health). 2001. *Macroeconomics and Health: Investing in Health for Economic Development.* Geneva: World Health Organization.

———. Forthcoming. *Final Report of Working Group 2.* Geneva: World Health Organization.

Colclough, Christopher, ed. 1997. *Marketizing Education and Health in Developing Countries: Miracle or Mirage?* Oxford: Clarendon Press.

Cooper, Richard N. 2000. "International Approaches to Global Climate Change." *World Bank Research Observer* 15 (August): 145–72.

————. 2002. "The Double Dividend of Emissions Taxes: Greenhouse Gas Reductions and Revenue." In Inge Kaul, Katell Le Goulven, and Mirjam Schnupf, eds. *Global Public Goods: New Tools for New Challenges.* New York: United Nations Development Programme, Office of Development Studies. [http://www.undp.org/ods].

Cullis, John, and Philip Jones. 1998. *Public Finance and Public Choice.* 2nd ed. New York: Oxford University Press.

Cutler, A. Claire, Virginia Haufler, and Tony Porter, eds. 1999. *Private Authority and International Affairs.* New York: State University of New York Press.

De Long, J. Bradford, and Barry Eichengreen. 1993. "The Marshall Plan: History's Most Successful Structural Adjustment Program." In Rudiger Dornbusch, Wilhelm Nölling, and Richard Layard, eds., *Postwar Economic Reconstruction and Lessons for the East Today.* Cambridge, Mass.: MIT Press, pp. 32–72.

Devarajan, Shantayanan, Margaret J. Miller. and Eric V. Swanson. 2002. "Goals for Development: History, Prospects, and Costs." World Bank, Washington, D.C.

Demsetz, Harold. 1967. "Toward a Theory of Property Rights." *American Economic Review* 57 (2): 347–59.

Drake, William J. 2001. "Communications." In P. J. Simmons and Chantal de Jonge Oudraat, eds., *Managing Global Issues: Lessons Learned.* Washington, D.C.: Carnegie Endowment for International Peace.

The Economist. 2001. "The Right to Good Ideas." June 21.

Frenkel, Jacob A., Morris Goldstein, and Paul R. Masson. 1996. "International Coordination of Economic Policies." In Jacob A. Frenkel and Morris Goldstein, eds., *Functioning of the International Monetary System.* Vol. 1. Washington, D.C.: International Monetary Fund.

GEF (Global Environment Facility). 1998. *Incremental Costs.* Washington, D.C.

Gerbasi, Fernando. 2002. "Sharing Commercial Benefits to Support Global Public Goods: The Multilateral System of the International Treaty on Plant Genetic Resources for Food and Agriculture." In Inge Kaul, Katell Le Goulven, and Mirjam Schnupf, eds., *Global Public Goods Financing: New Tools for New Challenges.* New York: United Nations Development Programme, Office of Development Studies. [http://www.undp.org/ods].

Gizewski, Peter, and Geoffrey Pearson. 1993. *The Burgeoning Cost of UN Peacekeeping: Who Pays and Who Benefits?* Ottawa: Canadian Centre for Global Security.

Goldstein, Judith L., Miles Kahler, Robert O. Keohane, and Anne-Marie Slaughter, eds. 2001. *Legalization and World Politics.* Cambridge, Mass.: MIT Press.

Heal, Geoffrey. 1999. "Price and Market Share Dynamics in Network Industries." In Graciela Chichilnisky, ed., *Markets, Information and Uncertainty: Essays in Economic Theory in Honor of Kenneth J. Arrow.* Cambridge: Cambridge University Press.

Helpman, Elhanan. 1999. "R&D and Productivity: The International Connection." In Assaf Razin and Efraim Sadka, eds., *The Economics of Globalization: Policy Perspectives from Public Economics.* Cambridge: Cambridge University Press.

Hirshleifer, Jack. 1983. "From Weakest-Link to Best-Shot: The Voluntary Provision of Public Goods." *Public Choice* 3: 371–86.

ICAO (International Civil Aviation Organization). 2001. *ICAO's Policies on Charges for Airports and Air Navigation Services.* 6th ed. Montreal.

IFIAC (International Financial Institution Advisory Commission). 2000. "Meltzer Commission Report." Washington, D.C. [http://www.bicusa.org/usgovtoversight/meltzer.htm].

IPCC (Intergovernmental Panel on Climate Change). 2001. *Climate Change 2001: Mitigation.* Cambridge: Cambridge University Press.

Kaempfer, William H., and Anton D. Lowenberg. 1992. *International Economic Sanctions: A Public Choice Perspective.* Boulder, Colo.: Westview Press.

Kanbur, Ravi. 2001. "Cross-border Externalities, International Public Goods and Their Implications for Aid Agencies." [http://www.people.cornell.edu/pages/sk145/papers.htm].

Katz, Michael, and Carl Shapiro. 1985. "Network Externalities, Competition and Compatibility." *American Economic Review* 75: 424–40.

Kaul, Inge. 1999. "Towards a Paradigm of Embedded Financial Liberalization: Interlocking the Wheels of Private and Public Finance." Policy Paper 13. Development and Peace Foundation, Bonn, Germany.

King, Ken. 1993. "The Incremental Costs of Global Environmental Benefits." Working Paper 5. Global Environment Facility, Washington, D.C.

Klein, Lawrence R., and Kanta Marwah. 1997. "Burden Sharing in Support of the United Nations." Yale University Library and Social Science Statistical Laboratory, New Haven, Conn. [http://www.library.yale.edu/un/burdnshar/].

Kremer, Michael. 2001a. "Creating Markets for New Vaccines: Part I: Rationale." In Adam Jaffe, Josh Lerner, and Scott Stern, eds., *Innovation Policy and the Economy.* Vol. 1. Cambridge, Mass.: MIT Press.

———. 2001b. "Creating Markets for New Vaccines: Part II: Design Issues." In Adam Jaffe, Josh Lerner, and Scott Stern, eds., *Innovation Policy and the Economy.* Vol. 1. Cambridge, Mass.: MIT Press.

———. 2002. "A Purchase Commitment for Vaccines." In Inge Kaul, Katell Le Goulven, and Mirjam Schnupf, eds., *Global Public Goods Financing: New Tools for New Challenges.* New York: United Nations Development Programme, Office of Development Studies. [http://www.undp.org/ods].

Lanjouw, Jean O. 2001. "A Patent Policy Proposal for Global Diseases." Paper presented at Annual World Bank Conference on Development Economics, 2 May, Washington, D.C. [http://econ.worldbank.org/files/1733_lanjouw.pdf].

Laurenti, Jeffrey. 2001. *Financing the United Nations.* New Haven, Conn.: Academic Council of the United Nations.

Lawrence, Robert Z. 1996. *Regionalism, Multilateralism, and Deeper Integration.* Washington, D.C.: Brookings Institution.

Lee, Kelley. 1996. *Global Telecommunications Regulation: A Political Economy Perspective.* London: Pinter.

Le Goulven, Katell. 2002. "Proposal for a Clean Energy Access Fund." Working paper. United Nations Development Programme, Office of Development Studies, New York.

Mazou, Moussibahou. 2002. "A User-Pay Approach to Providing World Postal Services." In Inge Kaul, Katell Le Goulven, and Mirjam Schnupf, eds., *Global Public Goods Financing: New Tools for New Challenges.* New York: United Nations Development Programme, Office of Development Studies. [http://www.undp.org/ods].

Mendez, Ruben P. 1992. *International Public Finance: A New Perspective on Global Relations.* New York: Oxford University Press.

Mendoza, Ronald U. 2002. "International Cooperation and Cost-Sharing: Who Benefits and Who Pays?" Working paper. United Nations Development Programme, Office of Development Studies, New York.

Musgrave, Peggy B. 1995. "Pure Global Externalities: International Efficiency and Equity." In Lans Bovenberg and Sijbren Cnossen, eds., *Public Economics and the Environment in an Imperfect World.* Dordrecht: Kluwer Academic Publishers.

Musgrave, Richard A. 1959. *The Theory of Public Finance: A Study in Public Economy.* New York: McGraw-Hill.

———. 1997. "Devolution, Grants, and Fiscal Competition." *Journal of Economic Perspectives* 11 (4): 65–72.

Musgrave, Richard A., and Peggy B. Musgrave. 1989. *Public Finance in Theory and Practice.* 5th ed. New York: McGraw-Hill.

Myers, Norman, and Jennifer Kent. 2001. *Perverse Subsidies: How Tax Dollars Can Undercut the Environment and the Economy.* Washington, D.C.: Island Press.

Najman, Dragoljub, and Hans d'Orville. 1995. *Towards a New Multilateralism: Funding Global Priorities—Innovative Financing Mechanisms for Internationally Agreed Programmes.* New York: Independent Commission on Population and Quality of Life.

New Zealand Ministry of Foreign Affairs and Trade. 2001. *United Nations Handbook 2001.* Wellington, New Zealand.

Oates, Wallace E. 1972. *Fiscal Federalism.* New York: Harcourt, Brace, Jovanovich.

———. 1999. "An Essay on Fiscal Federalism." *Journal of Economic Literature* 37 (September): 1120–49.

Ocampo, José Antonio. 2001. "International Asymmetries and the Design of the International Financial System." *Serie Temas de Coyuntura* 15. United Nations Economic Commission for Latin America and Caribbean, Santiago, Chile.

OECD (Organisation for Economic Co-operation and Development). 1997. *Economic Outlook.* Paris.

————. 2001. *Development Co-operation Report for 2001; Chapter III: Perspectives on Financing the Millennium Development Goals.* Document DCD/DAC(2001) 21/CHAP3.

Pearson, Charles S. 2000. *Economics and the Global Environment.* Cambridge: Cambridge University Press.

Raffer, Kunibert. 1999. *Official Development Assistance and Global Public Goods: A Trend Analysis of Past and Present Spending Patterns.* New York: United Nations Development Programme, Office of Development Studies.

Raffer, Kunibert, and Hans Wolfgang Singer. 1996. *The Foreign Aid Business: Economic Assistance and Development Co-operation.* Cheltenham, U.K.: Edward Elgar.

Sandler, Todd. 1998. "Global and Regional Public Goods: A Prognosis for Collective Action." *Fiscal Studies* 19 (3): 221–47.

Sandmo, Agnar. 2000. *The Public Economics of the Environment.* Oxford: Oxford University Press.

Schechter, Michael G., ed. 2001. *United Nations–sponsored World Conferences: Focus on Impact and Follow-up.* Tokyo: United Nations University Press.

Soros, George. 2002. *George Soros on Globalization.* New York: Public Affairs.

Spahn, Paul Bernd. 2002. "On the Feasibility of a Tax on Foreign Exchange Transactions." Report commissioned by the German Federal Ministry for Economic Cooperation and Development. [http://www.wiwi.uni-frankfurt.de/professoren/spahn/tobintax/].

Spar, Debora L. 1999. "The Public Face of Cyberspace: The Internet as a Public Good." In Inge Kaul, Isabelle Grunberg, and Marc A. Stern, eds., *Global Public Goods: International Cooperation in the 21st Century.* New York: Oxford University Press.

Stiglitz, Joseph E. 1999. "Knowledge as a Global Public Good." In Inge Kaul, Isabelle Grunberg, and Marc A. Stern, eds., *Global Public Goods: International Cooperation in the 21st Century.* New York: Oxford University Press.

Stokke, Olav. 1996. *Foreign Aid toward the Year 2000: Experiences and Challenges.* London: Frank Cass.

Strange, Susan. 1988. *States and Markets: An Introduction to International Political Economy.* New York: Basil Blackwell.

Summers, Larry. 2000. "Treasury News." Statement to the Development Committee of the World Bank and International Monetary Fund. Washington, D.C.

Sweden Ministry for Foreign Affairs. 2001. *Financing and Providing Global Public Goods: Expectations and Prospects.* Report prepared by Francisco Sagasti and Keith Bezanson on behalf of the Institute of Development Studies. Stockholm. [http://www.utrikes.regeringen.se/inenglish/policy/devcoop/financing.htm].

Tanzi, Vito. 1999. "Tax Harmonization, Tax Coordination, and the 'Disappearing Taxpayer: Is There a Need for a World Tax Organization?" In Assaf Razin and Efraim Sadka, eds., *The Economics of Globalization: Policy Perspectives from Public Economics.* Cambridge: Cambridge University Press.

Tanzi, Vito, and Ludger Schuknecht. 2000. *Public Spending in the 20th Century: A Global Perspective.* Cambridge: Cambridge University Press.

Te Velde, Dirk Willem, Oliver Morrissey, and Adrian Hewitt. 2002. "Allocating Aid to International Public Goods." In Marco Ferroni and Ashoka Mody, eds., *International Public Goods: Incentives, Measurement, and Financing.* Dordecht: Kluwer.

Tietenberg, Tom. 1998. *Environmental Economics and Policy.* 2nd ed. Boston: Addison-Wesley Educational Publishers.

UN (United Nations). 1992. *Earth Summit Agenda 21: The United Nations Programme of Action from Rio.* New York.

———. 2000. *Basic Facts about the United Nations.* New York.

———. 2001a. *Implementing Agenda 21.* Report of the Secretary-General. Economic and Social Council Document E/CN.17/2002/PC.2/7. New York. [http://www.johannesburgsummit.org/html/documents/no170793sgreport.pdf].

———. 2001b. "Note by the Secretary General: Technical Notes on Existing Proposals for Financing for Development." General Assembly Document A/AC.257/xx. [http://www.un.org/esa/ffd/aac257_27a1.pdf].

———. 2001c. *Report of the High-level Panel on Financing for Development* ("Zedillo Report"). Document A/55/1000. New York. [http://www.un.org/esa/ffd/a55-1000.pdf].

UNCTAD (United Nations Conference on Trade and Development). 2001. *Greenhouse Gas Market Perspectives: Trade and Investment Implications of the Climate Change Regime.* Report UNCTAD/DITC/TED/Misc 9. New York and Geneva.

UNDP (United Nations Development Programme). 1985. *Generation: Portrait of the United Nations Development Programme.* New York.

———. Various years. *Human Development Report.* New York: Oxford University Press.

United Kingdom. 2001. "Tackling the Diseases of Poverty." Final Report. Cabinet Office, Performance Innovation Unit, London. [http://www.cabinet-office.gov.uk/innovation/healthreport].

Van Beers, Cees, and André de Moor. 2001. *Public Subsidies and Policy Failures: How Subsidies Distort the Natural Environment, Equity and Trade, and How to Reform Them.* Cheltenham, U.K.: Edward Elgar.

Williamson, John. 1990. "What Washington Means by Policy Reform." In John Williamson, ed., *Latin American Adjustment: How Much Has Happened?* Washington, D.C.: Institute for International Economics.

———. 2000. "What Should the World Bank Think about the Washington Consensus?" *World Bank Research Observer* 15(2): 251–64.

World Bank. 2001. *Global Development Finance: Building Coalitions for Effective Development Finance.* Washington, D.C.

Zacher, Mark W., with Brent A. Sutton. 1996. *Governing Global Networks; International Regimes for Transportation and Communications.* Cambridge: Cambridge University Press.

INSTITUTIONAL OPTIONS FOR PRODUCING GLOBAL PUBLIC GOODS

INGE KAUL AND KATELL LE GOULVEN

For even the simplest private good—such as a pencil—a product design is developed before the good is manufactured. For a complex good, such as a car or medicine, billions of dollars are typically invested in research and development before the good is brought to the market. Moreover, private firms are increasingly concerned about better understanding and exploiting their operating environments—efforts that include finding the best ways to obtain, bundle, and convert resources and market goods and services. During the 1980s strategic management of private businesses evolved from an art practiced by some specialists to an essential responsibility of product managers (Montgomery and Porter 1991).

Many public goods—notably global public goods—do not benefit from such thorough product development and management. Global public goods are usually seen simply as concerns: as issues that call for international debates, agreements, or both. Seldom are they recognized as goods that need to be produced. As a result there are few comprehensive analyses of the production function of global public goods, such as a review of the inputs required, actors involved, and responsibilities assigned for the process and the final outcome.

Certainly, there are differences between, say, fostering financial stability and manufacturing an airplane. But there are also important similarities. Both processes are complex, based on contributions from a diverse range of actors, and require taking into account a multitude of stakeholders. And both processes are aimed at achieving a clear outcome. Forgetting to attach the tail rudder to a plane would be a major failure and would probably lead to the ruin of the manufacturer. But what happens when the international community forgets, for example, that orderly debt workouts require (among other things) international bankruptcy procedures? The answer is: not much—because there is no notion of a production path for the global public good of financial stability. Thus there is also no concept of forgotten and missing components, or of incomplete and poorly provided

The authors are grateful to Marco Ferroni, Isabelle Grunberg, Ahmad Kamal, Jacques Martin, and Francisco Sagasti for helpful comments.

goods. Yet the missing components of global public goods can have consequences as costly and catastrophic as those of trying to fly a poorly constructed airplane.

This chapter explores the production process for global public goods. The main issue examined is what happens after international agreements have been made to enhance the provision of global public goods. How is the follow-up to agreements managed? Or, put differently, how does the production process of global public goods function?

International relations scholars have conducted extensive research on the follow-up to and implementation of such agreements. A number of studies offer strategies for promoting compliance, including how to make agreements more self-enforcing (see Barrett in this volume; Chayes and Chayes 1998 [1995]; and Martin 1999). Other studies address how international agreements influence national policymaking and the effects of domestic variables on this process, including the state's strengths and weaknesses, the role of political parties, the costs of different aspects of policymaking (such as planning, implementation, and monitoring), and public perceptions and attitudes.[1]

This chapter takes the discussion on agreement implementation a step further by focusing on the compatibility—or incompatibility—of the institutions and organizations involved in the production of global public goods. One issue is how, and how well, national government and public management structures allow international cooperation agreements to filter back into national policymaking. A second, related issue is the extent to which international public management structures are designed to perform follow-up tasks resulting from agreements to provide global public goods. For both issues the chapter discusses how follow-up and production processes currently work and how they could be improved.

Important public management reforms are happening both nationally and internationally. Institutions and organizations are adjusting to the requirements of producing global public goods, with a clearer focus on issues and results. National reforms are primarily aimed at bridging the traditional divide between domestic and foreign affairs. Internationally, there is growing reliance on partnerships and networks, reaching across conventional dividing lines based on country borders, economic sectors, and groups of actors. Both trends are making it easier to bring together the different components that make up global public goods—and for the goods to emerge.

But further measures are needed to consolidate current reforms. Nationally, the most pressing task is to systematically link the management of the domestic and international cooperation components of global public goods—making international cooperation an integral part of public policymaking wherever a public good has cross-border dimensions. This goal could be achieved by appointing national lead agencies for key global public goods. Internationally, the production of global public goods would be greatly aided by establishing implementation councils for all major agreements, clarifying rules for global public policy partnerships, and fostering policy entrepreneurship—with issue-focused chief executive officers (CEOs) appointed to manage the production of crucial goods.

Such reforms could help ease the discrepancies between the global nature of a growing number of policy issues and the fractured nature of public policymaking and management along country, sector, actor (private and public), and other conventional dividing lines. Many issues have gone global as a result of public policy decisions such as those to remove trade barriers and dismantle capital controls. Yet policy processes and tools have hardly changed in recent decades and so do not reflect the increased openness and interdependence among countries. The full picture of global public goods will emerge only if policymaking takes a more integrated, cross-border approach—aligning itself with the benefit range of the public goods it has decided to globalize.

THE CHALLENGE OF PRODUCING GLOBAL PUBLIC GOODS IN A COMPARTMENTALIZED WORLD

In this chapter the production of global public goods is seen as a process that follows multilateral agreements. Global public goods can also be provided in other ways, such as through unilateral action or through a club—that is, when a limited number of private or public actors make a good (say, a new technology or medical insight) available to all people free of charge or for a fee, as Intelsat does.[2] But because public goods are in the public domain and often affect all people, it is usually desirable for all concerned parties to be involved in decisionmaking on their provision.[3] For global public goods that means undertaking multilateral negotiations and basing provision decisions at least partly on international agreements. This approach helps strike the right balance between the private and public nature of a good's production and provision. It also helps ensure that public goods are public in consumption and, as much as possible, in benefits (utility). Once an agreement has been reached—that is, once the political process has been concluded—the production process starts.

Requirements of the production process

The political process and the production process are not one-time events. They are iterative, intertwined processes that can span several years or even decades, with agreements building on agreements and policy outcomes building on policy outcomes (figure 1). In addition, different production paths generate different costs and distributions of benefits, so policy choices must be made even during the production stage. Thus the political process influences the production process, and production issues influence the political process. Effective follow-up to a first agreement can lead to easier negotiations on a second. Nevertheless, as suggested by Musgrave (1999), for analytical purposes it is useful to distinguish the political and production processes when analyzing the provision of global public goods.

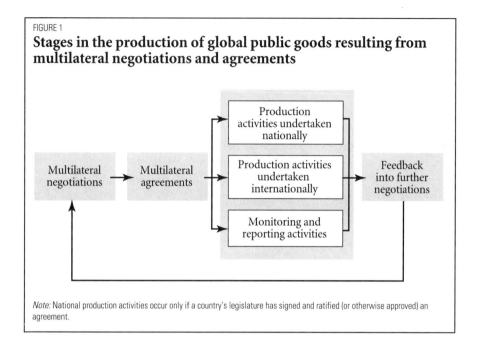

FIGURE 1
Stages in the production of global public goods resulting from multilateral negotiations and agreements

Note: National production activities occur only if a country's legislature has signed and ratified (or otherwise approved) an agreement.

The production process involves assembling and implementing the numerous inputs that a good typically requires. Some of the building blocks for climate stability are shown in figure 2, and for food safety in figure 3. The figures show the complexity of the production process. They also show that every good follows a unique production path—so production requires focusing on the specific goods involved.

Not all goods have to be built from scratch. Production of a global public good often only requires adding another building block. Still, even individual building blocks can be highly complex. Just consider all the elements involved in a land use management system, a component in figure 2.

The building blocks of global public goods can comprise local, national, regional, and international inputs, contributions from various economic sectors, and contributions from various groups of actors: the state, businesses, civil society organizations, and households. Figures 2 and 3 show some of the ways that different actors can contribute to the production of the goods depicted. Private goods come into play as much as public goods. Moreover, production can involve different types of public goods—pure or impure—and different aggregation technologies.[4] Multilayeredness is another production requirement, with efforts spanning regions, countries, sectors, and actor groups.

Public policy incentives are often a key ingredient, enabling individual actors to make needed contributions. Kaul and Le Goulven (in the financing chapter in this volume) show the wide variety of incentives and financing measures increas-

FIGURE 2

Building blocks of climate stability

FINAL GLOBAL PUBLIC GOOD	**Climate stability** (balanced gas composition in the atmosphere)		

⬆

INTERNATIONAL BUILDING BLOCKS	International regime—implemented and enforced by institutions and organizations—to avoid excessive greenhouse gases in the atmosphere

⬆

NATIONAL AND REGIONAL BUILDING BLOCKS	Systems to promote energy efficiency	Systems to promote clean energy	Systems to promote carbon fixation and capture greenhouse gases
	More efficient energy use (better fossil fuel yields) Individual saving habits and new behaviors	New forms of affordable clean energy	Well-managed land use and land changes Evaluation of potential for carbon sequestration New technologies to fix carbon
	Research and development and product development	Research and development and product development	Research and development and product development
	Public policy incentives for firms and households	Public policy incentives for firms and households	Public policy incentives for research institutes
	Information and public awareness programs	Supply networks	Land use management systems

Role of major actors

- *Households* can adopt energy-saving habits and can support and choose clean production and consumption technologies
- *Governments* at the local, national, and international levels can establish norms, provide incentives (taxes, subsidies, performance standards), and help manage regime implementation
- *Firms* can improve their energy efficiency, develop new technology based on clean energy, and adopt international standards
- *Civil society organizations* can set agendas, act as watchdogs, and promote initiatives aimed at adopting clean technology, saving energy, and conserving forests

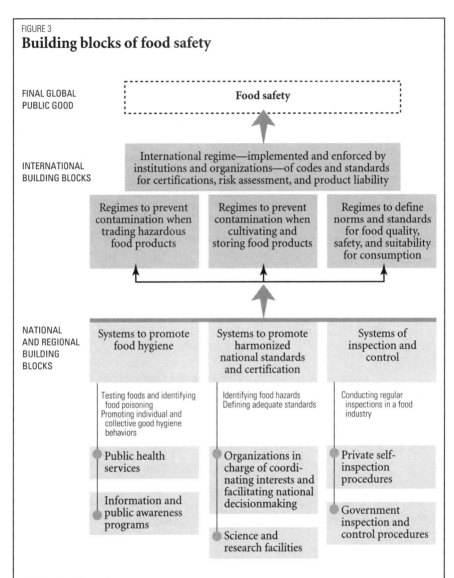

FIGURE 3

Building blocks of food safety

FINAL GLOBAL PUBLIC GOOD

Food safety

INTERNATIONAL BUILDING BLOCKS

International regime—implemented and enforced by institutions and organizations—of codes and standards for certifications, risk assessment, and product liability

Regimes to prevent contamination when trading hazardous food products

Regimes to prevent contamination when cultivating and storing food products

Regimes to define norms and standards for food quality, safety, and suitability for consumption

NATIONAL AND REGIONAL BUILDING BLOCKS

Systems to promote food hygiene

Systems to promote harmonized national standards and certification

Systems of inspection and control

Testing foods and identifying food poisoning
Promoting individual and collective good hygiene behaviors

Identifying food hazards
Defining adequate standards

Conducting regular inspections in a food industry

Public health services

Organizations in charge of coordinating interests and facilitating national decisionmaking

Private self-inspection procedures

Information and public awareness programs

Government inspection and control procedures

Science and research facilities

Role of major actors

- *Households* can encourage labeling, demand information and certification, and adopt good hygiene behaviors
- *Governments* can develop standards, certification and inspection procedures (national institutes of health, veterinary services), and regulation on product liability
- *Firms* can adopt certification standards and develop self-regulation (internal inspection and control systems)
- *Civil society organizations* can contribute to certifications and inspections (consumer associations)

ingly used nationally and internationally to encourage international cooperation on global public goods. Many choices may have to be made in selecting the right incentives and financing arrangements. Such choices usually need to be made not just for the good as a whole but also for each of its building blocks and even for the components of each building block. Incentives are the lubricant of cooperation, nationally as well as internationally. But concerted action also requires orchestration: strategic, results-oriented management so that all parts come together in the right way at the right time.

Thus the production of a global public good is highly complex. The process has three main features:

- It is issue-specific, with each good requiring a unique design and production path.
- It calls for a multilayered approach, reaching across national borders, economic sectors, and actor groups.
- It is results-oriented, aimed at making the desired good emerge.

These features raise several questions about the fit between global public goods and public management institutions and organizations: Do these entities rely on issue-specific production management? Are they open to the multilayered approach that production of these goods entails? And do they use results-oriented production strategies?

Many of the national building blocks that global public goods require would be produced in any event, for purely national reasons. Thus international cooperation usually complements national efforts, calling for stronger actions within countries, more harmonized approaches across countries, or joint measures among countries. The following analysis focuses on how well public management institutions and organizations foster follow-up to multilateral agreements—particularly in terms of national and international production activities (see figure 1).

Incompatibility between production efforts and today's institutions and organizations

Institutions provide structure to everyday life, including policymaking. Following North (1990), this chapter defines institutions as the norms, rules, conventions, and codes of behavior that provide a framework for human interaction. They can be informal or formal. Especially when formal, they often involve organizations as players. Organizations include political bodies and state entities (parties, legislatures, offices of the executive branch) as well as nonstate entities, including economic bodies (private businesses, trade unions, cooperatives) and civil society organizations.[5]

Institutions are intended to facilitate human activity by making it more predictable and reliable. But the features that make institutions an asset—being entrenched and firm—can become an impediment, at least temporarily, when reality changes. Institutions and organizations tend to evolve slowly (Davis and North 1970; North 1990; Alston, Eggertsson, and North 1996; Harris, Hunter, and Lewis 1995; Milner and Keohane 1996). This "institutional path dependence" (North 1990, p. 92) can lead to discrepancies between the structures of policymaking and the nature and scope of important issues.

Global public goods give rise to such incongruity because their existence and growing importance are only beginning to be fully recognized. Their benefits and costs cut across borders, yet policymaking remains focused on the national level. Although global public goods are increasingly public in both production and consumption, economic activity is usually organized along the lines of the main groups of actors. (Partnerships are on the rise but remain more the exception than the rule; see below.) And while global public goods generally require inputs from various actors and sectors, they rarely fall clearly under the mandates of government and intergovernmental entities, many of which were created to help develop specific economic sectors. Thus information and coordination problems can arise, hampering effective and efficient provision. Sector compartmentalization also characterizes the structures of many international organizations—notably those in the UN system, much of which was designed to mirror national government structures (Righter 1995; Urquhart and Childers 1990).

Moreover, international organizations traditionally fall into one of three categories. The first is made up of organizations that set international norms and standards. Examples include the United Nations and its specialized or technical agencies, such as the Food and Agriculture Organization and the World Health Organization. These agencies usually serve as the main arenas and secretariats for multilateral negotiations.

The second category of international organizations comprises operational aid agencies such as the United Nations Children's Fund, United Nations Development Programme, United Nations Population Fund, International Fund for Agricultural Development, World Food Programme, Office of the United Nations High Commissioner for Refugees, and World Bank. Whereas norm and standard setting focus on international issues—those between countries—operational activities have traditionally been expected to be country-driven. Thus there have been few links between these efforts.

The third category includes global service providers such as the International Monetary Fund (IMF) and World Intellectual Property Organization (WIPO). But the IMF is an exception among international organizations, having combined a normative role and a service delivery role.

The distinctions and limited interactions among these three types of organizations have resulted in deeply fractured public management systems, nationally and internationally. This setup creates a risk that global public goods will fall between mandates and not be acted on, be dealt with only partially, or lead to duplicated efforts.[6]

Yet while the concept of global public goods is relatively new and faces many institutional constraints, some global public goods have existed for quite some time. As Kaul and Le Goulven (in the financing chapter in this volume) show, several "self-running" global public goods are adequately financed and provided. These are primarily network-based goods such as international communication and transport systems. Obviously these goods managed to overcome the constraints or "lock-ins" (David 1985, 2000) of conventional public management structures. In addition, more recent global concerns—overuse of the global commons, communicable disease control—are being addressed, as evidenced by the Global Environment Facility, established in 1991, and the Global Fund to Fight AIDS, Tuberculosis, and Malaria, created in 2001.[7]

Thus some global concerns have generated new institutional responses. So how have conventional public management patterns changed? The following sections trace some of the reforms and suggest how these processes could be reinforced. Ensuring that the institutional and organizational framework evolves in line with policy challenges is critical. Such "adaptive efficiency," as North (1990, pp. 80–82) calls it, must complement allocative efficiency so that societies can respond effectively to changing conditions and new developments.

BRIDGING THE DOMESTIC-FOREIGN DIVIDE: NATIONAL PUBLIC MANAGEMENT REFORMS

Until foreign ministries began to be created in the 17th and 18th centuries, the same government department or ministry usually managed domestic and foreign policies related to specific concerns (Hocking 1999). As nation-states became more firmly established and national borders more clearly defined, the notion of foreignness emerged and government structures became compartmentalized to address internal and external concerns. Current reforms aim at reversing this trend at least partially, linking domestic and foreign affairs.

According to international relations scholars, "it is the *territoriality* of sovereignty as an instrument of public policy that is becoming contested, not the concept of sovereignty itself. The latter will only face a crisis if public policy cannot replace territoriality with a functional equivalent that is better equipped to meet the challenges of globalization"(Reinicke 1998, p. 228, emphasis in the original). It appears that a functional equivalent—or more appropriately, complement—is emerging. Current reforms seek to add a stronger focus on issues to conventional territorial (including sectoral) principles of organization—resulting in new areas of diplomacy and more networked, matrix-based public management.

Current trends: a growing focus on issues
A growing number of line ministries and subnational government entities in both industrial and developing countries are establishing international relations

departments.[8] These departments often participate directly (without going through ministries of foreign affairs) in intergovernmental and other international networks, promoting cross-border cooperation at the technical rather than the political level (Slaughter 2000, 2002). At the same time, many foreign affairs ministries are creating units focused on global policy issues to complement units focused on general country, regional, and international relations issues.[9] Economic and social issues, once perceived as "low" politics, are appearing next to and in some cases above peace and security concerns, which had been "high" politics (Baylis and Smith 1997) and the preserve of foreign affairs ministries. Diplomacy is entering new and specialized issue areas, and domestic policy is becoming more internationalized.

Emerging diplomacy issues and approaches. Among the new and specialized issue areas are environmental diplomacy (Broadhurst and Ledgerwood 1998; Susskind 1994), human rights diplomacy, and trade and financial diplomacy (Marshall 1997). Many countries are appointing special issue ambassadors[10] and nominating ambassadors to head their delegations to major international conferences, such as those on trade or disarmament.

The growing importance of issue diplomacy is also evident from the composition of embassy staff abroad. More than 60 percent of the staff in U.S. embassies abroad are employed by technical government agencies rather than by the State Department (Kennan 1997; Talbot 1997). Technical ministries are increasingly involved in not just the negotiations but also the operational aspects of international cooperation (Melissen 1999). Commenting on these trends, Hocking (1999) concludes that foreign affairs ministries will continue to play a crucial role in international cooperation—but their functions will no longer be exclusive. Talbot (1997) even suggests that the term *foreign* has become obsolete.

As Langhorne and Wallace (1999) point out, foreign affairs efforts are moving beyond gate keeping to coordinating cross-border relations. Thus Putnam's (1988) two-level game of international cooperation is no longer played out entirely by delegation—by sector ministries delegating foreign affairs staff to negotiate on their behalf. Instead, technical staff are playing more active roles in international cooperation, in both negotiations and follow-up, at home and abroad (Lancaster 2000). In addition, subnational governments such as states, provinces, and municipalities are increasingly engaged in direct foreign relations.

Thus diplomacy is being performed by a growing number of government entities and is no longer the sole province of foreign affairs ministries. Moreover, as diplomacy moves beyond its traditional focus on facilitating intergovernmental relations and becomes involved in promoting peace and security, it comes in contact with new actors such as businesses. These new actors then create additional new branches of diplomacy. A growing number of corporations have set up offices for business diplomacy—building long-term relations with countries as well as civil society organizations (see Stopford and Strange 1991).

Employing matrix management. The changing roles of government departments are also reflected in new management approaches. For example, based on a comprehensive review of its foreign policy, the Netherlands has chosen a matrix management approach to enhance coordination between sector ministries and the Ministry of Foreign Affairs:

> *Domestic policy is gaining an increasingly international dimension. Where any activities of this nature once belonged exclusively to the domain of the Ministries of Foreign Affairs/Development Cooperation and Defence, other ministries are now increasingly confronted with an international component in their work. . . . Exchanges of experience and knowledge are thus gaining increasing significance. [Accordingly, the] core of the new organisation will be a matrix model, with . . . "warps and wefts" in which knowledge of a country or region can be linked to . . . knowledge of subjects and themes. (Netherlands Ministry of Foreign Affairs 1995, pp. 46, 49)*

The resulting redistribution of responsibilities between sector ministries and the foreign affairs ministry might look like the setup in figure 4. Importantly, in the Netherlands these new organizational arrangements have been supported by corresponding adjustments in budget procedures. All spending on international

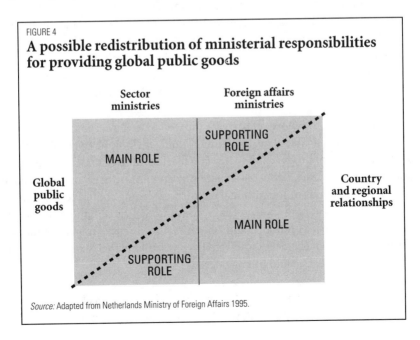

FIGURE 4

A possible redistribution of ministerial responsibilities for providing global public goods

Sector ministries

Foreign affairs ministries

SUPPORTING ROLE

MAIN ROLE

Global public goods

Country and regional relationships

MAIN ROLE

SUPPORTING ROLE

Source: Adapted from Netherlands Ministry of Foreign Affairs 1995.

cooperation is funded by a consolidated "homogeneous" budget coordinated by the Ministry of Foreign Affairs but tapped by all relevant government entities (Netherlands Ministry of Foreign Affairs 1995, pp. 57–59). The budget clearly identifies allocations to different international cooperation activities—such as spending on development assistance (aid), peacekeeping operations, international environmental policy, Ministry of Foreign Affairs administration, and contributions to international organizations (http://www.minbuza.nl).

Similarly, a report by Sweden's Parliamentary Commission on Swedish Policy for Global Development (2002, p. 10) concludes that:

> More and more specialised ministries are becoming active internationally and more and more issues are taking on transnational dimensions. The number of different government authorities participating in international forums and representing Sweden is growing. The increased demands for both vertical and horizontal coordination can be noted. . . . The Committee therefore proposes that a coordination unit for the policy of global development be established at the Government Offices.

Such changes signal a gradual closing of the "jurisdictional gap"—between the global nature of many policy issues and the often national focus of policymaking—that has long inhibited production of global public goods (Kaul, Grunberg, and Stern 1999, p. 466).

But in many countries, including most developing countries, foreign affairs entities retain traditional structures and act mainly as gate keepers. This is not surprising. Approaches such as matrix management require well-functioning, well-staffed government entities, which many developing countries are struggling to develop and afford (see Chasek and Rajamani in this volume).

Possible next steps: making international cooperation integral to national policymaking

Though on the rise, the above reforms are still isolated innovations in public management. A practical first step for national policymaking to catch up with the growing openness of borders and increasing market integration would be to consolidate and broaden such efforts—notably, by appointing issue ambassadors for all global public goods of top national concern, assigning staff of technical ministries to embassies abroad (and, perhaps, conventional career diplomats to technical ministries back home), and encouraging matrix management and consultation between all parties interested in particular global issues. In addition, the following measures could be considered.

Appointing national lead agencies. Many countries fail to assign clear institutional responsibilities for individual global public goods. For some goods, such as control of money laundering, this sometimes happens because addressing the issues involved requires the efforts of several agencies, but one would have to be designated to take the lead to avoid duplication and ensure complementarity of efforts.[11] In other cases, as with global environmental issues, the relevant national ministry may deal with just one part of international cooperation, such as norm and standard setting. Industrial countries often consider related operational activities undertaken abroad to be part of development assistance activities (and finance them with aid money, as Kaul and Le Goulven show in the financing chapter in this volume). In other countries operational follow-up to international agreements may be limited or nonexistent.

By contrast, "self-running" global public goods benefit from having national lead agencies: clear organizational homes within government. These agencies are responsible for both the domestic and international components of a good. They are also responsible for obtaining budget resources for both components and for maintaining links with concerned actors and stakeholders.

This approach could be used to enhance the provision of other global public goods. Selecting national lead agencies for all "unowned" global public goods would strengthen the links between the domestic and international cooperation components of global public goods. It would also facilitate more integrated management, including more integrated budgeting.

Making line ministries and other government entities responsible for the operational part of international cooperation does not mean requiring that they all engage in project work abroad. They could be responsible only for ensuring that international agreements are implemented and that resources are available to translate agreements into concrete policy action. In fact, implementation could be paid for by lead agencies but subcontracted to special operational agencies. In industrial countries, to exploit economies of scale and scope, implementation tasks could be assigned to aid agencies. Developing countries might want to consider creating new, specialized organizations for this purpose.[12]

Achieving institutional change often requires behavioral change. Would sector ministers want to accept responsibility for activities abroad that might be good for their countries, perhaps even for the world, but that may not bring them much credit nationally? Without new incentives, such as the matching grants proposed in the next section, appointing lead agencies might not result in more integrated, cohesive production of global public goods.[13]

Creating national funds for international cooperation. Many central governments provide matching grants to help subnational governments internalize externalities—say, to support public health or clean up the environment—beyond what they would do when considering only local preferences (Oates 1994). These grants are justified by spillovers from and to other jurisdictions that affect activities supported by public spending. The grants perform an important coordinating function between different jurisdictional entities (Mieszkowski 1994; Cullis and Jones 1998).

Drawing on this approach, countries could create national funds to encourage government entities (such as line ministries, other central government agencies, or subnational jurisdictions) to engage in international cooperation—both inward- and outward-oriented—that offers potential benefits to the entire country. Such a fund could be attached to the ministry of foreign affairs or to the office of the chancellor or prime minister. Its board might include representatives of all concerned government entities or be composed of high-level advisers.

Efforts are already being made in this direction. For instance, France has established the French Global Environment Facility as a complement to the Global Environment Facility. The French fund is jointly managed by the French Agency for Development and the ministries of foreign affairs, finance, environment, and research. The fund's resources are drawn from a line in the national budget called "common charges" that provides financing for initiatives involving more than one ministry (http://www.ffem.net/). The consolidated "homogeneous" budget coordinated by the Netherlands Ministry of Foreign Affairs, described above, is a similar example; its activities receive programming advice from a Council for European and International Affairs.

In the same vein, it would be useful to review national grant programs for subnational jurisdictions to see whether they adequately reflect global externalities emanating from or affecting local communities. For example, some countries face international criticism because some local communities neglect environmental standards or human rights. A national fund for international cooperation could foster more cooperation among sector agencies as well as among levels of government. In addition, a fund's board could advise the ministry of finance on fiscal incentives for international cooperation that the ministry might want to include in its budget proposals.

Strengthening legislators' involvement in international cooperation. To improve management of global issues, institutional and organizational reforms must affect both the executive and legislative branches of government. The reforms proposed above primarily involve the executive branch. But many such changes require the approval of legislatures and yield the desired results only if corresponding changes are made in the functioning of lawmaking bodies.

A recent study found that "institutionalized legislative participation in international cooperation enhances the credibility of states' commitments, thus leading to more stable and deeper patterns of international cooperation" (Martin 2000, p. 3; see also Putnam 1988). At the same time, systematic involvement of national legislators reduces the risk of governments endorsing international agreements and then finding it difficult—or impossible—to get them ratified and implemented by their national legislatures.

Yet when they are part of national conference teams, legislators often only accompany them and do not directly participate in negotiations. More active involvement would be desirable and important because "foreign affairs" has become less of a representational function and more of a policymaking one. Given the tight schedules of legislators, it would be difficult to have them exercise policymaking sovereignty more flexibly by participating in both national and international decisionmaking. But any support they need to cope with the expanding realm of global issues would be a worthwhile investment. It would allow legislatures to avoid the Scylla of mere rubber-stamping of international agreements and the Charybdis of having to reject negotiating results with which they cannot identify.

A further crucial reform might be to assess how well committee structures enable legislators to gain—or retain—a grip on public goods issues that have gone global. As on the executive side of government, organizational arrangements on the legislative side tend to be marked by a division between domestic and foreign affairs.

Parliamentarians recognize this challenge. Members of the Inter-Parliamentary Union, for example, have initiated a review of "how best to make use of current parliamentary procedures so that parliaments, with an active input by all parties and members, can make an appropriate contribution to governmental negotiations at the international level" (IPU 2001, p. 57).

Ensuring regular consultations between national negotiators and stakeholders. As Edwards and Zadek (in this volume) show, intergovernmental arenas increasingly serve as venues for consultations between various actors and stakeholders, notably between state and nonstate actors. Businesses and civil society organizations often find it easier to meet country delegations in these arenas than nationally.

Moreover, national delegations to international negotiations do not always debrief domestic constituencies and explain the implications of various agreements. Only potential beneficiaries may learn about certain decisions made abroad. Losers may not find out until later, when the consequences of policy change are felt. Not surprisingly, the general public sometimes feels that globalization is creating a "runaway world" (Giddens 2000). But it is usually negotiators—not globalization—who are running away.

Links with domestic actors and stakeholders could be strengthened if national negotiating teams engaged in full consultations before and after international negotiations. Such consultations could involve legislators, central government agencies, subnational authorities, and nonstate actors. Some government entities are required to engage in such consultations. For instance, the U.K. Department for International Development arranges discussions with civil society before and after major international meetings (http://www.dfid.gov.uk/). In Mexico nongovernmental organizations are closely involved in government preparations for major international conferences (Rozental 1999). For both the forging and implementation of international agreements on global public goods, it would be desirable if national negotiating teams thoroughly briefed and consulted with domestic constituencies before attending and after returning from international meetings. Doing so would make international agreements better reflect domestic policy concerns, promote policy ownership, and facilitate follow-up action by state and non-state actors.[14]

Creating trust funds to help developing countries manage interdependence. Most developing countries will require special support to adjust their public management structures to the challenges of global public goods and other exigencies of today's globalizing world. In fact, many developing countries face a dual challenge: fostering economic growth and development while contributing and adjusting to international regimes.

Looking at this challenge from the political decisionmaking angle, Chasek and Rajamani (in this volume) point to the critical need to strengthen developing countries' public management capacity, including negotiating capacity. Equally critical is strengthening these countries' capacity to assess international agreements in terms of their national implications. That way, fully informed decisions can be made when deciding how to translate such agreements into national laws or other follow-up initiatives. Ideally, all major agreements should include an implementation support fund for this purpose. But intergovernmental decisions are just one strand of international regime formation; international law and self-regulation by the private sector are two others of growing importance. Thus there is a need for broader support in this area. Important precedents in this regard include the Integrated Framework for Trade-related Technical Assistance.[15]

Should such support be funded by official development assistance or by new and additional resources? If a policy matter clearly reflects the interests of industrial countries, as with the new Basle proposals on financial codes and standards, it would be appropriate to tap new funding sources such as those countries' central banks or finance ministries. If an issue is in all countries' mutual interest, official development assistance could be used if developing countries agreed to fund at least part of the costs. But any such aid should be additional, because globalization has been promoted primarily by industrial country actors.

Box 1 summarizes the reforms discussed above to narrow the traditional divide between foreign and domestic affairs. To the extent that these reforms are institutionalized, consideration should also be given to renaming ministries of foreign affairs. A more appropriate name would be ministries of foreign affairs and international cooperation. This is not just wordplay: it could help convey to concerned national constituencies that the challenges of globalization are being actively addressed.

BOX 1

BRIDGING THE DIVIDE BETWEEN DOMESTIC AND FOREIGN AFFAIRS

More international agreements were signed in the past 50 years than in the past 500. In 1750 there were 86 multilateral treaties. In 1950 there were 1,200. Today there are more than 2,100 (Ku 2001; UIA 2001). Clearly, cross-border issues are being addressed.

But many agreements have not been implemented effectively and, too often, their goals remain elusive. Weak follow-up has many causes. International relations theory shows the importance of treaty design and monitoring in encouraging signatories not to renege on their commitments.

Also of crucial importance is how governments are organized to deal with global policy issues, particularly follow-up to international agreements. The traditional divide between foreign affairs and domestic policymaking often prevents international agreements from influencing national policymaking. But several policy reforms could close the foreign-domestic divide, including:

*   Creating special issue ambassadors to represent a country's global concerns, abroad and at home.
*   Assigning staff members of technical ministries to embassies abroad.
*   Using matrix management to enhance collaboration between the ministry of foreign affairs and other government entities involved in international cooperation.
*   Appointing national lead agencies to manage both the domestic and international components of global public goods, including securing budget resources.
*   Creating a national fund for international cooperation.
*   Involving national legislators and legislatures more closely in international cooperation issues and processes.
*   Reviewing the committee structure of legislatures.
*   Establishing regular consultations between country delegations to international negotiations and all concerned domestic actors and stakeholders.
*   Providing international financial support to enable developing countries to foster development while strengthening their capacity to manage globalization.

Such reforms would create the interface and incentives needed for enhanced national follow-up to international agreements.

GETTING TO THE GOOD: INSTITUTIONAL AND MANAGERIAL
INNOVATIONS AT THE INTERNATIONAL LEVEL

Even if matters were perfectly managed nationally, there would still be a risk of global public goods being underprovided, because each nation would be guided primarily by its own interests and not necessarily take into account possible spillovers of its actions on other countries or on transnational actors. Countries could also be tempted to try to free ride. Or, due to poverty and other shortfalls, they could be unable to contribute to a global public good. And without international coordination, initiatives risk being scattered, not fitting together, and not adding up to a fully assembled good. Hence, as noted, adequate provision of global public goods often depends on adequate provision of their national components as well as on effective international cooperation. International cooperation may be a small part of the total effort—but it is often crucial.

Following the structure of the previous section, this section first tracks current institutional innovations, then suggests possible next steps to consolidate and advance these reforms.

Current trends: focusing on results

Institutional and organizational reforms at the international level are, like reforms at the national level, aimed at fostering issue specificity—or, put differently, at encouraging specialization among multilateral agencies. Agencies with broad mandates are being called on to focus their activities, and new, single-issue agencies are emerging. In addition, increased emphasis is being placed on translating words—decisions—into action: making agreements operational. The overall objective is to strengthen the results orientation of international cooperation, lest global public bads continue to roam the global public domain.

Narrowing the focus. As discussed, the multilateral system was designed to mirror national government structures, essentially along sector lines, with the main differentiation being between norm and standard setting organizations and operational agencies. Norm and standard setting agencies have tended to have broad mandates, and many of the agreements they have helped negotiate have been nonbinding: left to governments to implement—or not.

These agencies are usually large, with thousands of employees administering the ever-increasing number of resolutions and decisions passed by the multilateral system's legislative bodies.[16] As secretariats of these bodies, the agencies are generally expected to function as backstopping bureaucracies rather than as policy initiators and policymakers. They primarily serve the intergovernmental process—and so, from the global public goods perspective, more the political than the production part of the provision process.

In recent years, however, multilateral agencies have increasingly been called on to prove their effectiveness. This has encouraged many to become more focused on achieving tangible results on specific issues. For example, in 1999 the International Labour Organization launched a campaign and Convention on the Worst Forms of Child Labour.[17] Similarly, the World Health Organization has initiated targeted health campaigns such as its recent Tobacco Free Initiative (http://www5.who.int/tobacco/). For most agencies the Millennium Declaration adopted by the UN General Assembly in 2000 (UN 2000)—particularly the declaration's Millennium Development Goals—provides the main framework for current activities (http://www.un.org/millenniumgoals/).

There has also been a trend toward creating new, single-issue agencies. Several recent international conventions—among them the Convention on Biological Diversity, UN Framework Convention on Climate Change, and Convention to Combat Desertification—have established secretariats to service their negotiation and follow-up processes. This approach was spearheaded by initiatives related to the environment, but similar efforts have been made for other issues, such as HIV/AIDS control.[18]

As a result of these and other efforts, many recent multilateral agreements have been more focused and often more binding, if not legally than at least by setting clear targets and making it possible to identify when those targets have been met. Limiting and more precisely defining intended objectives make it easier to implement multilateral agreements and facilitate more results-oriented production.

Translating agreements into policy actions and operational achievements. Despite the sharpened focus of multilateral agreements, actual implementation of international norms and standards is a subject of growing concern. Various steps have been taken to aid such efforts. For example, the Montreal Protocol on ozone-depleting substances has a fund attached to facilitate its implementation.[19] Similarly, the Global Environment Facility helps developing countries implement other environmental agreements. Other such bodies include the Council for Trade-Related Aspects of Intellectual Property Rights (TRIPS)[20] and the working groups on biosafety and traditional knowledge resulting from the Convention on Biodiversity.[21] In addition, the costs of achieving the Millennium Development Goals are being estimated to ensure that sufficient resources are channeled to them (UN 2002a, b).

The line dividing international norm and standard setting and operational activities is increasingly blurred. And it is in these areas that the international component of the allocation branch of public finance is emerging as a new operational strand of international cooperation, complementing official development assistance (see the financing chapter by Kaul and Le Goulven in this volume).

This change is also influencing the international cooperation efforts of traditional operational agencies—that is, conventional aid agencies. These agencies' programs are increasingly expected to link international and national concerns, matching the supply of and demand for international cooperation.[22] These agencies have also seen the emergence —and in some cases, encroachment—of highly issue-specific global public policy partnerships focused on getting things done in a flexible, time-bound manner.

Fostering global public policy partnerships. Global public policy partnerships have been created for many purposes (see Reinicke and Deng 2000; Keck and Sikkink 1998; Risse-Kappen 1995; Rosenau 1990; World Bank 2001b; and UN 2002a). Many play an advocacy role. But a growing number also work on the production side, contributing to concrete policy outcomes. Arhin-Tenkorang and Conceição (in this volume) cite some for global health, including the International AIDS Vaccine Initiative and the Medicines for Malaria Venture,[23] while Mehta (in this volume) refers to the Global Water Partnership (box 2). These partnerships typically involve multiple actors—not just governments—and seek to strengthen national operational activities, and in some cases to produce international complements. They operate in ways that would be difficult and often inappropriate for the main multilateral organizations discussed earlier. Such partnerships are product-driven and functionally oriented, crossing conventional lines of organization, mandate, and authority when necessary and desirable. In some cases multilateral organizations have spurred the creation of these partnerships and are among their members. Other actors, notably foundations, have also taken the lead in several cases.

The increasing focus on issues and growing number of partnerships have prompted and been encouraged by the more widespread use of trust funds— special accounts established to finance specific cooperation initiatives such as the promotion of human rights or clean energy technologies. Such trust funds receive some $2 billion a year in public funding (World Bank 2001b). This figure will increase significantly if the recently created Global Fund to Fight AIDS, Tuberculosis, and Malaria attracts, as envisioned, $7–10 billion a year. Trust funds tend to attract considerable funding from foundations and other private sources.

The growing number of trust funds indicates that the international community is seeking financing mechanisms that channel resources to specific concerns—in addition to allocations to organizations, sectors, and countries. The reason might be that, as various chapters in this volume show, international cooperation aimed at enhancing the provision of global public goods often entails targeted efforts aimed at eliminating specific negative externalities from the global public domain. Because a good's desired provision level will emerge only if this result is achieved, it is useful to make cooperation initiatives and resource allocations traceable. Doing so makes it easier to monitor results. Partnerships and trust funds both meet these performance criteria.

Not all partnerships are focused on single issues. They are also used by international organizations involved in setting international norms and standards, including the United Nations (see UN 2001a, 2002a), International Organization for Standardization (ISO), Intelsat, and Inmarsat (see notes 2 and 3).

BOX 2

HOW DO GLOBAL PUBLIC POLICY PARTNERSHIPS MANAGE?

The *Medicines for Malaria Venture (MMV)* was created to develop new drugs to treat malaria. This public-private partnership "brings together members of civil society (academia, NGOs [nongovernmental organizations], philanthropists and other not-for-profits), public sector (government agencies and inter-government agencies) and the for-profit sector (pharmaceutical companies, biotech companies and other commercial companies from related industries), to select, fund, coordinate and drive research projects that address the R&D [research and development] gap. Public-private partnerships in health are distinct from project management agencies that sit within an established inter-government agency because they base their management structures on the private company model. There is a board of directors with representatives who can address public, private and civil sectors, generally a very lean executive management, a scientific advisory committee and a stakeholder council."

"It is important that whatever their governance or accountability structure, public-private partnerships remain flexible enough so that these ventures can reach their missions as rapidly and efficiently as possible....Public-private partnerships share the common challenge of motivating different groups with widely disparate values, mandates and cultures to focus on a shared public health goal. Their ultimate success is in part dependent on their ability to override differences to achieve the common goal."

The International Crisis Group (ICG) is a "multinational organization committed to strengthening the capacity of the international community to anticipate, understand and act to prevent and contain conflict."

- *Operating in the field.* "ICG's board decides, on the recommendation of the President, what field projects will be commenced and continued....ICG professional field staff and consultants are recruited mainly from former diplomats, journalists, humanitarian NGO personnel and academics."
- *Proposing policy.* "The policy recommendations attached to nearly all ICG reports are settled by the President on the basis of advice from field staff and program directors, and consultation with Board members and a wide variety of governments, intergovernmental organizations, academic specialists and think-tanks and other NGOs."
- *Advocating action.* "The first task of effective advocacy is dissemination of [ICG reports and briefing papers]. The next task is to ensure that policy makers hear the message. So far as possible ICG tries to communicate it directly. Face to face briefings of ministers, officials, legislators, UN/EU/World Bank/NATO personnel and others are regularly conducted, locally and in major capitals."

continued overleaf

BOX 2 CONTINUED

The Global Water Partnership (GWP) is an "international network open to all organizations involved in water resources management: developed and developing country government institutions, agencies of the United Nations, bilateral and multilateral development banks, professional associations, research institutions, NGOs, and the private sector....The GWP network focuses on persuading decision makers to move away from the present fragmented, sectoral approach to water resources management....Through its network, the GWP fosters integrated water resource management (IWRM) to ensure the coordinated development and management of water, land and related resources....The GWP is forming water partnerships and enhancing dialogue between stakeholders at global, regional, area, national and local levels to promote IWRM."

The International Organization for Standardization (ISO) is "a network of national standards institutes from 140 countries working in partnership with international organizations, governments, industry, business and consumer representatives. [It is] a bridge between the public and private sectors....The mission of ISO is to promote the development of standardization and related activities in the world with a view to facilitating the international exchange of goods and services, and to developing cooperation in the spheres of intellectual, scientific, technological and economic activity....The technical work of ISO is highly decentralized, carried out in a hierarchy of some 2,850 technical committees, subcommittees and working groups. In these committees, qualified representatives of industry, research institutes, government authorities, consumer bodies, and international organizations from all over the world come together as equal partners in the resolution of global standardization problems. Some 30,000 experts participate in meetings each year."

Thus global public policy partnerships manage by envisioning, strategizing, focusing, adopting proactive initiatives, crossing borders and sectors, networking, and—last but not least—exercising leadership.

Source: Excerpted from MMV's Website (http://www.mmv.org); ICG's Website (http://212.212.165.32/default.cfm) and annual report (http://212.212.165.32/annual/2001/2001.pdf); GWP's Website (http://www.gwpforum.org/) and highlights of its 2001 activities (http://www.gwpforum.org/servlet/PSP?iNodeID=215&itemId=89); and ISO's Website (http://www.iso.ch/iso/en/ISOOnline.frontpage).

Possible next steps: promoting strategic management
Most of the above reforms have occurred spontaneously and incrementally, responding to political pressures and global exigencies. Some of these developments are desirable: partnerships, for example, provide an effective framework for enhancing the provision of certain public goods. Partnerships are especially useful for goods that require one-time corrective actions, such as producing a vaccine against a global disease. Still, the current approach to partnerships needs to be improved, as discussed below.

Others reforms may need to be rethought. For example, the mandates of multilateral agencies should be systematically reviewed to strike the proper balance between agencies and mandates focused on country and sector issues and those focused on global issues. All these are important if the multilateral system is to be responsive to the full agenda of international cooperation. Global public goods are a growing part of this agenda—and rightfully so. Still, global public goods should not crowd out other concerns—particularly development assistance concerns, which require a clear focus on developing countries.

Three steps appear to be especially important to increase production of global public goods: establishing implementation councils for all major agreements, consolidating and regularizing the modality of global public policy partnerships, and creating room for and appointing high-level policy entrepreneurs—issue-focused chief executive officers (CEOs)—to lead such partnerships.

Establishing implementation councils. There is no general, defined approach to implementing multilateral agreements. As noted, some—such as the Convention on Biodiversity and the agreement on Trade-Related Aspects of Intellectual Property Rights (TRIPS)—have special working groups or implementation arrangements. Many call on a range of national and international actors to take follow-up actions. Others benefit from global public policy partnerships. As a result implementation rates, including signature and ratification, vary considerably from agreement to agreement (UN 2001d).

In addition, when implementation is advanced through mechanisms such as global policy partnerships, the arrangements can encounter skepticism and raise concerns—particularly about their legitimacy (Amrith 2001; Evans and Chen 2001; Mkandawire and Soludo 1999). One reason is that there are no clear criteria for deciding which multilateral agreements should receive follow-up action and funding and which are lower priorities. Agreements and other policy statements have been issued for every global issue of concern to one actor or another, public or private. Thus willing funders can choose from a host of existing objectives. But about 90 percent of multilateral treaties are not clearly linked to any international organization (Ku 2001) and so do not offer the de facto guidance provided when an agency decides—or declines—to be the focal point for their implementation.

This problem could be addressed by requiring all major agreements to establish participatory implementation councils representing all major actors and stakeholders. Working with the concerned multilateral agency or convention sponsor, these councils could develop comprehensive strategies for producing the global public good. The councils could offer advice on which issues or aspects of issues may require partnerships. They could also identify countries that may require support to make informed decisions on signing and ratifying agreements and to fulfill implementation requirements.

Moving toward second generation partnerships. Many global public policy partnerships are first generation, exploratory models that have evolved in an ad hoc fashion. More systematic approaches are needed because such partnerships are probably indispensable for addressing some of today's main policy challenges. [24] Partnerships facilitate horizontal and networked management of multidimensional policy tasks (Reinicke and Deng 2000; Rischard 2002; Sproule-Jones 2000). They can make results more observable and so enhance transparency and accountability. And once they have achieved their goals (or proven incapable of doing so), they can be ended more easily than traditional bureaucratic structures (see Dixit 1996, especially chaps. 2.1–2.3). [25] Thus partnerships are an ideal organizational form for fostering the production of certain global public goods, responding to the three key features of this process—issue specificity, multilayeredness, and a results orientation.

But to realize their advantages, skepticism about partnerships must be allayed. The second generation of partnerships requires at least four modifications:

- *Grounding partnerships in multilateral agreements.* To respond to concerns about legitimacy, partnerships could be clearly linked to issues identified in multilateral agreements—and by the implementation councils suggested above—as ripe for and deserving priority in implementation. Figure 5 shows how a partnership arrangement can be firmly embedded in a multilateral agreement (represented by the shaded square).
- *Ensuring broad representation on supervisory boards.* The multilateral agency that serves as the secretariat for an international agreement on which a partnership is founded would remain ultimately responsible for follow-up. Thus the agency should be an ex officio member of the partnership's supervisory board. Other board members would represent various concerned actors and stakeholders (see figure 5).
- *Facilitating, not substituting.* All concerned actors should feel that the partnership is supporting their activities, not taking responsibilities away from them. Similarly, partnerships should not shift funds from the national to the international level. It would be useful for all actors and stakeholders to discuss partnership mandates and functions, to subject them to rigorous subsidiarity considerations. Second generation partnerships should often have a network structure and facilitate other entities' efforts to produce a

good (see figure 5). But if needed, they could also provide building blocks, especially if production entails economies of scale.

- *Making clear contractual arrangements.* Second generation partnerships would often be "satellites" outside the main multilateral agencies. Thus clear contractual arrangements—on which goods to produce, over what period, and in consultation with whom—are important for all parties to the contract. Transaction cost and principal-agent theories offer insights on contracting approaches (see Laffont 2001; Pratt and Zeckhauser 1985; and Williamson 1985).

Of course, any actor group can create a global public policy partnership whenever and however it sees fit. A more standardized, multilateral approach to the use of partnerships will have to be prepared for and face this healthy compe-

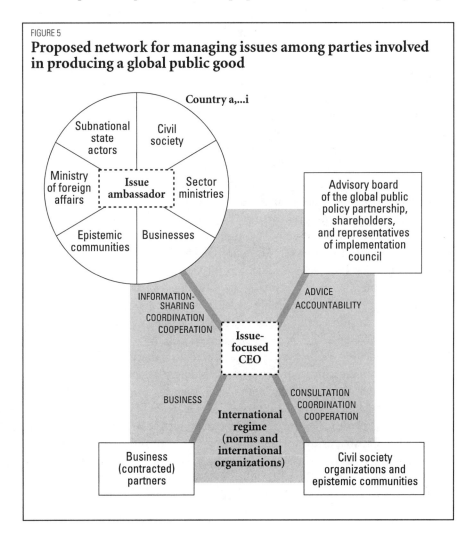

FIGURE 5

Proposed network for managing issues among parties involved in producing a global public good

tition. A better-defined, more business-like approach to partnerships will also be important if they are to become more widely used in making international agreements operational—and if they are to attract effective, high-level leadership. [26]

Creating room for policy entrepreneurship. Global public policy partnerships share an obvious structural similarity with networked, horizontally organized corporations (Wheelen and Hunger 2000). This similarity is not altogether surprising given that the activities of both involve many interactions between various groups of actors. The similarity may reflect the parallels between the tasks of a firm and those of an operational agency engaged in international cooperation: both are charged with producing concrete results, or goods.[27] Given this similarity, how can strategic management—an increasingly crucial component of corporate success in recent decades—be applied to global public policy partnerships and, more broadly, to the production of global public goods?

Ronald Coase, in his famous article "The Nature of the Firm" (1990 [1937]), refers to the "entrepreneur-coordinator" (p. 35) who sees the big picture and guides the process of turning myriad inputs into an output. Some analysts, among them Soros (2002), argue that the operational side of international cooperation could use such entrepreneur-coordinators.[28] In fact, policy entrepreneurship—"personal weight," in the words of Schumpeter (1962 [1934], p. 88)—likely led to the creation of many current partnerships.[29]

But whether and to what extent policy entrepreneurs step forward to help address global challenges largely depends on whether the multilateral system allows and encourages policy innovation, flexibility, and risk taking—in short, leadership and policy entrepreneurship. Given a conducive political environment, high-level CEOs with a public policy interest could spontaneously emerge[30] or respond to requests from the UN Secretary-General or heads of the UN system's technical agencies. Precedents exist: for example, the UN Secretary-General has appointed numerous special representatives and personal envoys to promote peace and security. Those responsible for leading peacekeeping missions have had to perform a role quite similar to the one suggested here for issue-focused CEOs (see Goodpaster 1996 and Vance and Hamburg 1997).

An issue-focused CEO would strategically facilitate the production of a global public good—anticipating, coordinating and linking, planning and restructuring, providing incentives, purchasing inputs, and accepting responsibility to shareholders and stakeholders in the venture. These CEOs could be aided by the issue ambassadors that countries appoint to bridge the divide between domestic and foreign affairs as well as by a wide range of other state and nonstate actors. By managing a special issue partnership outside the bureaucratic structures of national and international organizations, an issue-focused CEO would be better positioned to overcome problems related to mandates and procedures. The

---

BOX 3

MANAGING GLOBAL PUBLIC GOODS MORE EFFICIENTLY
AND EFFECTIVELY

A plethora of international resolutions and agreements call for action to enhance the provision of global public goods. Though these calls have been supported by follow-up initiatives, many of the initiatives have been adopted by numerous actors in multiple agencies. There is little information on if and how they have come together. Yet repeated expressions of concern about the ineffectiveness of international cooperation suggest room for improvement. Thus consideration should be given to:

- *Establishing implementation councils*—to oversee and support implementation of major multilateral agreements. These councils would represent major groups of actors and draw on extensive consultations with stakeholders.
- *Creating second generation, issue-focused public policy partnerships*—for global public goods concerns that achieve policy consensus and are well-defined and manageable, and thus "ready to move." These partnerships would have defined lifespans and complement, as needed, the efforts of existing multilateral agencies. Features that would make them second generation include, in particular, being firmly rooted in multilateral agreements and based on clear contractual arrangements.
- *Appointing issue-focused CEOs*—to facilitate strategic management of policy partnerships, including networking among all concerned stakeholders, shareholders, and business partners.

  Pressing issues that could benefit from these efforts include dissemination of clean energy technology and provision of science and technology for neglected diseases. Reinforcing existing, essential partnerships such as the Consultative Group on International Agricultural Research could also be among the priorities. So could efforts to ensure food safety, control money laundering, and promote financial codes and standards.

Global Alliance for Vaccines and Immunization, for example, helped the international community overcome the double jeopardy facing many global public goods—suffering from both market and government failures (http://www.vaccinealliance.org/).[31]

At this point efforts should focus not on deciding details but on defining basic principles. One important issue involves dealing with institutional and organizational compartmentalization. It should not be abandoned; rather, dividing lines should be bridged and policy coordination and cohesion enhanced. Partnerships, complemented by issue-focused CEOs, could respond to this challenge (box 3).

Conclusion

A number of reforms are under way to foster the production of global public goods by public management institutions and organizations, nationally and internationally. National reforms are focused on bridging the traditional divide between domestic and foreign affairs. At the international level changes are aimed at building partnerships across actor (state and nonstate), sector, and state lines. Together the national and international reforms allow for closer links between the multiple components that enter into the production of global public goods—allowing the goods to emerge.

Additional reforms could reinforce these efforts. They include creating national funds for international cooperation in all countries, establishing implementation councils for major multilateral agreements, designing a second generation approach to global public policy partnerships, and creating the conditions—notably room for maneuver—needed to attract high-level, issue-focused CEOs to manage these partnerships.

Global public policy partnerships are more appropriate for some global public goods than others. This approach is best suited to production efforts aimed at well-defined outputs and intended to achieve specific results within a certain period. Put differently, it would be appropriate when the goal is to control specific cross-border externalities such as pollution, communicable disease, financial crisis, or armed conflict. Partnerships could be especially useful when a good's production follows a summation process, including a weakest link strategy. Production of such goods typically involves many diverse actors, making networking and strategic management particularly important.

Other goods would be better handled by existing multilateral agencies or new, more permanent intergovernmental bodies. The reason might be that the good (for example, health surveillance) needs to be provided on a continuing basis—or because no country acting alone would have the legitimacy to provide the goods. An example is the recently established International Criminal Court (http://www.un.org/law/icc/). Because such a court requires neutrality, it is best set up as an open, fully transparent intergovernmental facility. Yet if the implementation councils suggested above were to become a standard feature of multilateral agreements, they would offer excellent opportunities for systematic analysis and debate on which institutional arrangement is best suited for a particular global public good.

Ad hoc arrangements, including partnerships, can be useful precursors of potential new organizations. Among their benefits is helping to establish whether there is a need for more permanent organizational arrangements. The International Criminal Court, for example, was preceded by a number of special war crime tribunals. Similarly, many partnerships for health are engaged in medical and pharmaceutical research and development. Some are focused on specific products or diseases (say, creating a vaccine for HIV/AIDS or medicines for malaria). Such partnerships need not become permanent because they may fulfill their missions.

At the same time, there may be an organizational deficit in terms of basic research on global health problems. Such research requires a long-term, sustained approach. Thus there may be a need for a global institute of health, coordinating an international network of national health institutes and drawing on their experience and knowledge (CMH 2001, p. 82). Similarly, international cooperation on financial issues could benefit from a world financial authority, as recommended by Eatwell and Taylor (2001). But in these and similar cases the critical question is, how the net benefits of more institutionalized, long-term centralization compare with those of more flexible, temporary networking arrangements.

As noted, institutions and organizations tend to evolve slowly. Thus this chapter emphasizes gradual reform—reinforcing current trends. Yet around the world, public management institutions and organizations have shown that they can undergo fundamental change in relatively short periods. In the past two decades there has been a major rebalancing between markets and states and a corresponding recasting of the state's role in both industrial and developing countries.[32] Swift public management reform is possible when governments receive the right signals from their constituencies. Although politics leads production, enhancing the efficacy of production can facilitate the politics of providing global public goods.

NOTES

1. Contributions to this topic come from a wide variety of disciplines. See Dixit (1996); Haas, Keohane, and Levy (1993); Keohane and Nye (2000); Neuman (1998); Rodrik (1997); Rosenau and Czempiel (1992); Sassen (1996); Schreurs and Economy (1997); Simmons and de Jonge Oudraat (2001); and Smith, Solinger, and Topik (1999).

2. Intelsat is a commercial company that provides international communication services under the supervision of an intergovernmental entity, the International Telecommunications Satellite Organization (ITSO). See http://www.intelsat.com and http://www.itso.int.

3. In this context it is interesting to note that Intelsat and the International Telecommunications Satellite Organization (ITSO) were created in tandem. ITSO's primary role is to ensure that despite being a commercial operation, Intelsat provides public services (see again http://www.itso.int). A similar arrangement exists for Inmarsat, which provides international communication services to ships, vehicles, aircraft, and portable terminals. An intergovernmental organization supervises the company's public service obligations for the maritime and aviation communities. See http://www.inmarsat.org.

4. For brief definitions of the different types of public goods and aggregation technologies, see the glossary in this volume. For more detailed discussions, see Kaul and Mendoza (in this volume) and Sandler (in this volume).

5. See also Young (1989) on the definitions of institutions and organizations and the importance of differentiating between the two concepts.

6. Similar problems beset the political process for providing these goods—that is, the channeling to the international level of national requests for cooperation. Such problems may be one reason that nonstate actors often collaborate in international networks and seek to collectively influence multilateral negotiations.

7. For further examples of institutional and organizational changes in response to various global issues and multilateral agreements, see the UN reports on implementing Agenda 21 and the Millennium Declaration (UN 2001b, d) as well as Ku (2001) and New Zealand Ministry of Foreign Affairs and Trade (2001).

8. The terms *technical ministry, sector ministry,* and *line ministry* are used interchangeably in this chapter.

9. Some ministries of foreign affairs have also created units in charge of global matters. See, for instance, the organizational charts of the German Federal Minister for Foreign Affairs (http://www.auswaertiges-amt.de/www/en/infoservice/download/pdf/organigramm.pdf) and the U.S. Department of State (http://www.state.gov/r/pa/ei/rls/dos/7926.htm). Other countries, such as Egypt, do not have full-fledged global affairs units, but diplomats of ambassador rank advise their governments on global issues.

10. For instance, the Netherlands has an ambassador for human rights issues. Australia, China, and Sweden, among others, have ambassadors for disarmament issues. Australia, Canada, and Sweden, among others, have ambassadors for global environmental issues.

11. For example, in 2001 the Philippines created a central Anti–Money Laundering Council to work with foreign jurisdictions and Philippine representatives in international organizations. See http://www.thetrustguru.com/act2001b.htm.

12. Development in developing countries depends, as in industrial countries, on numerous global and regional public goods. Thus it can also be more efficient for these countries to contribute to international cooperation efforts rather than to spend resources domestically. Regional cooperation efforts might be a priority for developing countries. But to enhance national well-being, these too need to be well-managed and systematically linked to domestic policy initiatives.

13. For a discussion on the incentives facing politicians and bureaucrats, see Nordhaus (1975) and Mueller (1989).

14. To provide fuller information to various cooperation partners, domestically and internationally, ministries of foreign affairs could also prepare periodic reports describing the government's priorities for and spending on international cooperation. Some countries have pursued such initiatives, though mostly as one-time efforts. See France Ministry of Foreign Affairs and Ministry of the Economy, Finance, and

Industry (2002); Germany Study Commission (2001); G-77 (2000); Sweden Parliamentary Commission on Swedish Policy for Global Development (2002); and U.K. Secretary of State for International Development (2000).

15. The Integrated Framework for Trade-related Technical Assistance seeks to increase the benefits that least developed countries derive from the trade-related assistance available to them from six multilateral agencies: the International Monetary Fund, International Trade Centre, United Nations Conference on Trade and Development, United Nations Development Programme, World Bank, and World Trade Organization. See http://www.wto.org/english/tratop_e/devel_e/framework.htm.

16. Such conditions give rise to "common agency" and "multiple principals" problems, such as competition among sponsors of various resolutions and mandates for agency resources and staff attention. Such rivalry may be difficult to observe; and lack of follow-up action may be noticeable only after some time. See Wilson (1989) for an analysis of the general point raised here. For a discussion focused on the functioning of international organizations, see Barnett and Finnemore (1999).

17. See http://www.ilo.org/public/english/region/asro/bangkok/newsroom/pr9906.htm.

18. For a comprehensive overview of new multilateral agencies and bodies, see New Zealand Ministry of Foreign Affairs and Trade (2001).

19. See http://www.unep.org/ozone/Montreal-Protocol/Montreal-Protocol2000.shtml.

20. The council monitors the operation of the World Trade Organization's TRIPS agreement and gives member states the opportunity to consult on matters relating to its implementation. See http://www.wto.org.

21. The parties to the Convention on Biodiversity created such working groups to shape recommendations on implementing elements of the convention. The working group on biosafety, established to offer recommendations on preventing biotechnology hazards, ultimately developed the Biosafety Protocol—a separate, binding international agreement governing transboundary movements of modified living organisms. See http//www.biodiv.org.

22. See the programming principles guiding the preparation of such documents as the UN Development Assistance Framework (http://hdrc.undp.org.in/undafmptoc.htm) and the World Bank's Comprehensive Development Framework (http://www.worldbank.org/cdf/cdf-text.htm) and Poverty Reduction Strategy Papers (http://www.worldbank.org/poverty/strategies/). Some agencies have always had a strong issue focus. Examples include the United Nations Children's Fund, with its focus on children's well-being, and the United Nations Population Fund, with its focus on reproductive health and related issues.

23. See also the *Bulletin of the World Health Organization* 79 (8) (2001), which focuses on public-private partnerships (www.who.int/bulletin).

24. Proposals have also been made to move in the opposite direction—toward larger, more integrated organizations with multiple mandates. Most such proposals

relate to organizations involved in global environmental issues (see Bierman 2000 and Newell and Whalley 1999). But it seems like the balance between global issues that a global environmental organization might help foster could be better achieved through periodic high-level policy reviews such as the Global Ministerial Environment Forum of the United Nations Environment Programme (http://www.unep.org). Especially when viewed from the perspective of agreement implementation, the need for a more centralized intergovernmental organization is not immediately obvious. Even within a single subject area such as the environment, issues differ widely in terms of political consensus, technical feasibility, and economic desirability of various policy options. Consider, for example, the tasks of preserving biodiversity and averting global warming. Each should be pursued in its own way—perhaps even by forming specialized partnerships for different aspects of each issue on which there is agreement to act.

25. A recent assessment by McKinsey & Company (at the request of the Bill and Melinda Gates Foundation), focusing on the health sector, highlights the main benefits of global alliances: avoiding duplicated investments and activities, gaining scale economies, sharing or reducing risks to allow new initiatives that individual partners or donors might not have been able or willing to pursue, sharing knowledge and resources to increase effectiveness, accelerating momentum, and attracting funding by building a common "brand" that gains legitimacy (Bill and Melinda Gates Foundation 2002).

26. In devising a second generation approach to global public policy partnerships, it will be important to heed Feachem's (2001, p. 693) advice : "It would be a mistake to try to over-manage the process. . . . Progress will come from diversity, from risk taking, and from numerous points of energy and initiative. [In addition,] we must accept failure. Some PPPs [public-private partnerships] will achieve little and should be terminated; and some brave private ventures will go bankrupt. We should regard a certain amount of failure as a sign that we are probably doing the right thing and are on the right track."

27. See also Wilson's (1989) typology of organizations, which distinguishes between product, procedural, craft, and coping organizations.

28. Similar ideas have been advanced by Coleman and Perl (1999), who present the concept of an issue mediator; Frohlich and Oppenheimer (1978), who define the political entrepreneur as "an individual who invests his own time and effort or other resources to coordinate and combine factors of production to supply collective goods" (p. 68); Kingdon (1984), who puts forward the concept of a policy entrepreneur; Sabatier (1993), who mentions the notion of a policy broker; and Young (1991), who differentiates between types of leadership—structural (based on possession of material resources), entrepreneurial, and intellectual.

29. Glaeser and Shleifer (2001) show that most nonprofit organizations are created by entrepreneurs.

30. Entrepreneurship is not motivated solely by pecuniary objectives. Additional motives identified by Schumpeter (1962 [1934]) include the desire to conquer and

the joy of creating and achieving things. Such motivations could encourage the emergence of CEOs for global public goods.

31. There is a precedent for the "CEO approach" to international cooperation. Paul G. Hoffman, the former president of Studebaker Corporation, was appointed by U.S. President Harry Truman as administrator of the Marshall Plan in 1948. He later became the first administrator of the United Nations Development Programme (UNDP).

32. For discussions of national policy experiences and the "new public management" literature that has emerged to analyze and advance policy reforms, see Barzelay (2001); Kamarck (2000); and Kettl (1999).

References

Alston, Lee J., Thrainn Eggertsson, and Douglass C. North. eds. 1996. *Empirical Studies in Institutional Change*. Cambridge: Cambridge University Press.

Amrith, Sunil. 2001. "'Post-Democratic Politics' and Africa: The Case of Health." Cambridge University, Cambridge.

Barnett, Michael N., and Martha Finnemore. 1999. "The Politics, Power and Pathologies of International Organizations." *International Organization* 53 (4): 699–732.

Barzelay. Michael. 2001. *The New Public Management: Improving Research and Policy Dialogue*. Berkeley: University of California Press and New York: Russell Sage Foundation.

Baylis, John, and Steve Smith, eds. 1997. *The Globalization of World Politics: An Introduction to International Relations*. Oxford and New York: Oxford University Press.

Bierman, Frank. 2000. "The Case for the World Environment Organization." *Environment* 42 (9): 22–31.

Bill and Melinda Gates Foundation. 2002. *Developing Successful Global Health Alliances*. Seattle, Wash.

Broadhurst, Arlene Idol, and Grant Ledgerwood. 1998. "Environmental Diplomacy of States, Corporations and Non-Governmental Organisations: The Worldwide Web of Influence." *International Relations* 14 (2): 1–19.

Chayes, Abram, and Antonia Handler Chayes. 1998 [1995]. *The New Sovereignty: Compliance with International Regulatory Agreements*. Cambridge, Mass.: Harvard University Press.

Coase, Ronald H. 1990 [1937]. "The Nature of the Firm." In Ronald H. Coase, *The Firm, The Market, and The Law*. Chicago: University of Chicago Press .

Coleman, William D., and Anthony Perl. 1999. "Internationalized Policy Environments and Policy Network Analysis." *Political Studies* 47 (4): 691–709.

CMH (Commission on Macroeconomics and Health). 2001. *Macroeconomics and Health: Investing in Health for Economic Development.* Geneva: World Health Organization.

Cullis, John, and Philip Jones. 1998. *Public Finance and Public Choice.* New York: Oxford University Press.

David, Paul A. 1985. "Clio and the Economics of QWERTY." *American Economic Review* 75 (2): 332–37.

———. 2000. "Path Dependence, Its Critics and the Quest for 'Historical Economics.'" Working paper. All Souls College, Oxford.

Davis, Lance, and Douglass North. 1970. " Institutional Change and American Economic Growth: A First Step Towards a Theory of Institutional Innovation." *Journal of Economic History* 30 (1): 131–49.

Dixit, Avinash K. 1996. *The Making of Economic Policy: A Transaction-Cost Politics Perspective.* Cambridge, Mass. and London: MIT Press.

Eatwell, John, and Lance Taylor. 2000. *Global Finance at Risk: The Case for International Regulation.* New York: New Press.

Evans, Tim G., and Lincoln C. Chen. 2001. " Partnerships for Global Health: Progress or Setbacks in Democratic Practice?" Rockefeller Foundation, New York.

Feachem, Richard G. A. 2001. "Infotech and Biotech: Learning the Lessons." *Bulletin of the World Health Organization: The International Journal of Public Health* 79 (8): 693.

France Ministry of Foreign Affairs and Ministry of the Economy, Finance and Industry. 2002. *Global Public Goods.* Paris.

Frohlich, Norman, and Joe A. Oppenheimer. 1978. *Modern Political Economy.* Englewood Cliffs, N.J.: Prentice Hall.

G-77 (Group of Seventy-Seven). 2000. "Havana Programme of Action." Declaration of the South Summit of the Group of 77, Havana. [http://www.g77.org/main/docs.htm].

Germany Study Commission. 2001. "Globalization of the World Economy— Challenges and Responses." Interim report by commission appointed by the German Bundestag. (Only introduction available in English; report in German.) [http://www.bundestag.de/gremien/welt/welt_zwischenbericht/index.html].

Giddens, Anthony. 2000. *Runaway World: How Globalization Is Reshaping our Lives.* New York: Routledge.

Glaeser, Edward L., and Andrei Shleifer. 2001. "Not-for-profit Entrepreneurs." *Journal of Public Economics* 81: 99–115.

Goodpaster, Andrew J. 1996. *When Diplomacy Is Not Enough: Managing Multinational Military Interventions.* Report to the Carnegie Commission on Preventing Deadly Conflict. New York: Carnegie Corporation of New York.

Haas, Peter M., Robert O. Keohane, and Marc A. Levy, eds. 1993. *Institutions for the Earth: Sources of Effective International Environmental Protection.* Cambridge, Mass.: MIT Press.

Harris, John, Jane Hunter, and Colin M. Lewis, eds. 1995. *The New Institutional Economics and Third World Development.* London: Routledge.

Hocking, Brian, ed. 1999. *Foreign Ministries: Change and Adaptation.* Houndmills, U.K.: Macmillan.

IPU (Inter-Parliamentary Union). 2001. *Activities of the IPU in 2000: Report of the Secretary General.* Geneva.

Kamarck, Elaine Ciulla. 2000. "Globalization and Public Administration Reform." In Joseph S. Nye and John D. Donahue, eds., *Governance in a Globalizing World.* Washington, D.C.: Brookings Institution Press.

Kaul, Inge, Isabelle Grunberg, and Marc A. Stern. 1999. "Conclusion: Global Public Goods—Concepts, Policies and Strategies." In Inge Kaul, Isabelle Grunberg, and Marc A. Stern, eds., *Global Public Goods: International Cooperation in the 21st Century.* New York: Oxford University Press.

Keck, Margaret, and Kathryn Sikkink. 1998. *Activists beyond Borders: Advocacy Networks in International Politics.* Ithaca, N.Y.: Cornell University Press.

Kennan, George F. 1997. "Diplomacy without Diplomats?" *Foreign Affairs* 76 (5): 198–212.

Keohane, Robert O., and Joseph S. Nye Jr. 2000. "Globalization: What's New? What's Not? (And So What?)." *Foreign Policy* 118 (spring): 104–19.

Kettl, Donald. 1999. *The Global Public Management Revolution: A Report on the Transformation of Governance.* Washington, D.C.: Brookings Institution Press.

Kingdon, John W. 1984. *Agendas, Alternatives and Public Policy.* Boston: Little Brown.

Ku, Charlotte. 2001. "Global Governance and the Changing Face of International Law." ACUNS Reports and Papers 2. Yale University, Academic Council of the United Nation System, New Haven, Conn.

Laffont, Jean-Jacques. 2001. *Incentives and Political Economy.* New York: Oxford University Press.

Lancaster, Carol. 2000. *Transforming Foreign Aid: United States Assistance in the 21st Century.* Washington, D.C.: Institute for International Economics.

Langhorne, Richard, and William Wallace. 1999. "Diplomacy towards the Twenty-first Century." In Brian Hocking, ed., *Foreign Ministries: Change and Adaptation.* Houndmills, U.K.: Macmillan.

Marshall. Peter. 1997. *Positive Diplomacy.* New York: Macmillan.

Martin, Lisa L. 1999. "The Political Economy of International Cooperation". In Inge Kaul, Isabelle Grunberg, and Marc A. Stern, eds., *Global Public Goods: International Cooperation in the 21st Century.* New York: Oxford University Press.

————. 2000. *Democratic Commitments: Legislatures and International Cooperation.* Princeton, N.J.: Princeton University Press.

Melissen, Jan, ed. 1999. *Innovation in Diplomatic Practice.* Basingtoke, U.K.: Macmillan.

Mieszkowski, Peter. 1994. "Comments on Chapter 5." In John M. Quigley and Eugene Smolensky, eds., *Modern Public Finance.* Cambridge, Mass.: Harvard University Press.

Milner, Helen V., and Robert O. Keohane. 1996. "Internationalization and Domestic Politics: An Introduction." In Robert O. Keohane and Helen V. Milner, eds., *Internationalization and Domestic Politics.* Cambridge: Cambridge University Press.

Mkandawire, Thandika, and Charles C. Soludo. 1999. *Our Continent, Our Future: African Perspectives on Structural Adjustment.* Trenton, N.J.: Africa World Press.

Montgomery, Cynthia A., and Michael E. Porter, eds. 1991. *Strategy: Seeking and Securing Competitive Advantage.* Cambridge, Mass.: Harvard Business School Press.

Mueller, Dennis C. 1989. *Public Choice II.* Cambridge: Cambridge University Press.

Musgrave. Richard A. 1999. "The Nature of the Fiscal State: The Roots of My Thinking." In James M. Buchanan and Richard A. Musgrave, eds., *Public Finance and Public Choice: Two Contrasting Visions of the State.* Cambridge, Mass. and London: MIT Press.

Netherlands Ministry of Foreign Affairs. 1995. *The Foreign Policy of the Netherlands: A Review.* The Hague.

Neuman, Stephanie G., ed. 1998. *International Relations Theory and the Third World.* New York: St. Martin's Press.

New Zealand Ministry of Foreign Affairs and Trade. 2001. *United Nations Handbook 2001.* Wellington.

Newell, Peter, and John Whalley. 1999. "Towards a World Environment Organization?" In Peter Newell, ed., *Globalization and the Governance of the Environment. IDS Bulletin* 30 (3): 16–24 (special issue).

Nordhaus, William D. 1975. "The Political Business Cycle." *Review of Economic Studies* 42 (2): 169–90.

North, Douglass C. 1990. *Institutions, Institutional Change and Economic Performance.* Cambridge: Cambridge University Press.

Oates, Wallace E. 1994. "Federalism and Government Finance." In John M. Quigley and Eugene Smolensky, eds., *Modern Public Finance.* Cambridge, Mass.: Harvard University Press.

Pratt, John W., and Richard J. Zeckhauser, eds. 1985. *Principals and Agents: The Structure of Business.* Cambridge, Mass.: Harvard Business School Press.

Putnam, Robert D. 1988. "Diplomacy and Domestic Politics: The Logic of Two-Level Games." *International Organizations* 42 (3): 427–60.

Reinicke, Wolfgang. 1998. *Global Public Policy: Governing without Government?* Washington, D.C.: Brookings Institution Press.

Reinicke, Wolfgang, and Francis Deng. 2000. *Critical Choices: The United Nations Networks and the Future of Global Governance.* Ottawa: International Development Research Centre.

Righter, Rosemary. 1995. *Utopia Lost: The United Nations and World Order.* New York: Twentieth Century Fund Press.

Rischard, Jean-François. 2002. *High Noon: Twenty Global Problems, Twenty Years to Solve Them.* New York: Basic Books.

Risse-Kappen, Thomas. 1995. *Cooperation Among Democracies: The European Influence on US Foreign Policy.* Princeton, N.J.: Princeton University Press.

Rodrik, Dani. 1997. *Has Globalization Gone Too Far?* Washington, D.C.: Institute for International Economics.

Rosenau, James N. 1990. *Turbulence in World Politics: A Theory of Change and Continuity.* Princeton, N.J.: Princeton University Press.

Rosenau, James N., and Ernst-Otto Czempiel, eds. 1992. *Governance without Government: Order and Change in World Politics.* Cambridge: Cambridge University Press.

Rozental, Andrés. 1999. "Mexico: Changes and Adaptation in the Ministry of Foreign Affairs." In Brian Hocking, ed., *Foreign Ministries: Change and Adaptation.* New York: St. Martin's Press.

Sabatier, Paul. 1993. "Policy Change over a Decade or More." In Paul Sabatier and Hank Jenkins-Smith, eds., *Policy Change and Learning: An Advocacy Coalition Approach.* Boulder, Colo.: Westview.

Sassen, Saskia. 1996. *Losing Control? Sovereignty in an Age of Globalization.* New York: Columbia University Press.

Schreurs, Miranda, and Elisabeth Economy. 1997. *The Internationalization of Environmental Protection.* Cambridge: Cambridge University Press.

Schumpeter, Joseph A. 1962 [1934]. *The Theory of Economic Development: An Inquiry into Profits, Capital, Credit, Interest and the Business Cycle.* Cambridge: Harvard University Press.

Simmons, P. J., and Chantal de Jonge Oudraat, eds. 2001. *Managing Global Issues: Lessons Learned.* Washington, D.C.: Carnegie Endowment for International Peace.

Slaughter, Anne-Marie. 2000. "Governing the Global Economy through Government Networks." In Michael Byers, ed., *The Role of Law in International Politics: Essays in International Relations and International Law.* Oxford: Oxford University Press.

———. 2002. "Global Government Networks, Global Information Agencies, and Disaggregated Democracy." Working Paper 18. Harvard Law School, Public Law, Cambridge, Mass.

Smith, David A., Dorothy J. Solinger, and Steven C. Topik, eds. 1999. *States and Sovereignty in the Global Economy.* London and New York: Routledge.

Soros, George. 2002. *George Soros on Globalization.* New York: Public Affairs.

Sproule-Jones, Mark. 2000. "Horizontal Management: Implementing Programs Across Interdependent Organizations." *Canadian Public Administration* 43 (1): 92–109.

Stopford, John, and Susan Strange, with John S. Henley. 1991. *Rival States, Rival Firms: Competition for World Market Shares.* Cambridge: Cambridge University Press.

Susskind, Lawrence E. 1994. *Environmental Diplomacy: Negotiating More Effective Global Agreements.* New York: Oxford University Press.

Sweden Ministry for Foreign Affairs. 2001. "Financing and Providing Global Public Goods: Expectations and Prospects." Study 2001:2. Prepared by Francisco Sagasti and Keith Bezanson on behalf of the Institute of Development Studies, Sussex, U.K. Stockholm. [http://www.utrikes.regeringen.se/inenglish/policy/devcoop/financing.htm].

Sweden Parliamentary Commission on Swedish Policy for Global Development. 2002. "Towards a More Equitable World Free from Poverty." Swedish Government Official Report SOU 2001: 96. Stockholm. [Executive summary available in English at http://www.globkom.net/betankande/summary.pdf].

Talbot, Strobe. 1997. "Globalization and Diplomacy: A Practitioner's Perspective." *Foreign Policy* 108 (fall): 69–83.

UIA (Union of International Associations). 2001. *Yearbook of International Organizations.* Vol. 1. Brussels: K.G. Saur Verlag.

U.K. Secretary of State for International Development. 2000. "Eliminating World Poverty: Making Globalization Work for the Poor." White paper presented to Parliament. London. [http://www.globalisation.gov.uk/].

UN (United Nations). 2000. *United Nations Millennium Declaration.* Resolution adopted by the General Assembly. Document A/55/L.2. New York.

———. 2001a. *Cooperation between the United Nations and All Relevant Partners, in Particular the Private Sector.* Report of the Secretary-General submitted to the 56th session of the General Assembly. Document A/56/323. New York.

———.2001b. *Implementing Agenda 21.* Report of the Secretary-General. Economic and Social Council Document E/CN.17/2002/PC.2/7. New York: [http://www.johannesburgsummit.org/html/documents/no170793sgreport.pdf].

———. 2001c. *Report of the High-level Panel on Financing for Development* ("Zedillo Report"). Document A/55/1000. New York. [http://www.un.org/esa/ffd/a55-1000.pdf].

———. 2001d. *Road Map towards the Implementation of the United Nations Millennium Declaration.* Report of the Secretary-General. Economic and Social Council Document A/56/326. New York.

————. 2002a. *Building Partnerships: Cooperation between the United Nations System and the Private Sector.* New York.

————. 2002b. *The Contribution of Human Resources Development, Including in the Areas of Health and Education to the Process of Development.* Report of the Secretary-General. Economic and Social Council. Document E/2002/46. New York. [http://www.un.org/documents/ecosoc/docs/2002/e2002-46.pdf].

Urquhart, Brian, and Erskine Childers. 1990. *A World in Need of Leadership: Tomorrow's United Nations.* Uppsala, Sweden: Dag Hammarskjold Foundation.

Vance, Cyrus R., and David A. Hamburg. 1997. *Pathfinders for Peace: A Report to the UN Secretary-General on the Role of Special Representatives and Special Envoys.* Carnegie Commission on Preventing Deadly Conflict. New York: Carnegie Corporation of New York.

Wheelen, Thomas L., and J. David Hunger. 2000. *Strategic Management and Business Policy.* Upper Saddler River, N.J.: Prentice Hall.

Williamson, Oliver E. 1985. *The Economic Institutions of Capitalism.* New York: Free Press.

Wilson, James Q. 1989. *Bureaucracy: What Government Agencies Do and Why They Do It.* New York: Basic Books.

World Bank. 2001a. "Financing for Development—Update Note." Prepared for the Development Committee Meeting, 5 November. Washington, D.C. [http://lnweb18.worldbank.org/dcs/devcom.nsf].

————. 2001b. *Global Development Finance: Building Coalitions for Effective Development Finance.* Washington, D.C.

Young, Oran R. 1989. *International Cooperation: Building Regimes for Natural Resources and the Environment.* Ithaca, N.Y. and London: Cornell University Press.

————. 1991. "Political Leadership and Regime Formation" *International Organization* 45 (3).

Managing the
Provision of Knowledge:
The Design of
Intellectual Property Laws

Carlos M. Correa

Intellectual property rights are intended to stimulate innovation and creation by offering the prospect of a monetary reward that allows a titleholder to recover investments in research and development and possibly make a profit. Intellectual property rights generally confer exclusive rights to exploit the protected subject matter. Exclusive rights empower a titleholder to prevent third parties from making commercial use of the protected knowledge without authorization. But exclusive rights also impede the diffusion and use of knowledge.

By its nature, knowledge is nonrival (Stiglitz 1999, p. 309). Nonrival goods can be made available for public use, usually at low cost and sometimes at no cost. But knowledge can be made excludable through actions by its possessor or through legal means. A company may prevent its competitors from knowing how a particular manufacturing process operates by, for instance, tightly controlling access to its physical premises and preventing the disclosure of relevant data by its employees. In biotechnology, genetic use restriction technologies (GURTs) render sterile the subsequent generation of seeds (FAO 2001). Such actions may be encouraged or supported by legal means.

In some cases purely legal means are used to exclude third parties from using information that otherwise would be accessible, as with patents and published copyright works. In these cases policy creates a deliberate mode of exclusion for the use of knowledge, based on the recognition of an intellectual property right.

Intellectual property rights evolved in the Middle Ages and obtained universal recognition during the 20th century. (For their history, see David 1993 and Granstrand 1999, pp. 27–30.) Over the past 20 years in particular, large industrial and knowledge-based companies and governments of industrial countries joined forces to broaden and strengthen the rights of knowledge owners (Ryan 1998). A notable result of this concerted effort was the adoption, as part of the Uruguay Round, of the Trade-Related Aspects of Intellectual Property Rights (TRIPS) agreement.

The TRIPS agreement was a major objective of industrial countries during the Uruguay Round. One of the agreement's main goals is to establish high international standards for intellectual property rights. During the Uruguay Round it was argued that broader, stronger intellectual property rights would foster creativity and innovation on a global scale. Industrial countries also claimed that stronger protection of these rights would increase flows of technology and investment to developing countries. Both facts would justify having the international community—particularly developing countries—assume the costs associated with granting such rights.

This chapter considers the efficiency effects of intellectual property rights, with a focus on patent rights.[1] Specifically, it examines the dilemma facing policymakers in fostering innovation: how to reconcile the restrictions that intellectual property rights impose on the use of innovations—to encourage their creation by knowledge providers—with society's interest in maximum use of innovative products.

The chapter first discusses the two types of efficiency—static and dynamic—and the different considerations for achieving them. It then examines how intellectual property rights can influence the balance between static and dynamic efficiency. Next it considers the options available under the TRIPS agreement to increase static efficiency, dynamic efficiency, or both. Finally, the chapter discusses the possibility of compulsory licensing as way of increasing static efficiency.

The main finding is that measures to enhance static and dynamic efficiency can go hand in hand. Because enhanced static efficiency often increases equity, the analysis also suggests that efficiency and equity can be combined—and should be so that in the long run inequity does not jeopardize efficiency.

STATIC AND DYNAMIC EFFICIENCY, INTELLECTUAL PROPERTY RIGHTS, AND INDUSTRIAL AND DEVELOPING COUNTRIES

Welfare economics examines the impact of intellectual property rights on economic efficiency. There are two main types of efficiency:

- Static efficiency is achieved when there is an optimal use of existing resources at the lowest possible cost.
- Dynamic efficiency is the optimal introduction of new or better products, more efficient production processes and organization, and (eventually) lower prices.

In general, static efficiency is best achieved through competitive markets. In terms of consumer welfare, competition may lead to allocative efficiency when the price of a product is equal to the marginal cost of producing a unit of it. In this scenario there is maximum diffusion of existing products. When the products are essential for life—as with food and pharmaceuticals—allocative efficiency becomes an important objective on both economic and equity grounds.

But a competitive environment may deter investment in the production of knowledge. Intellectual property rights provide the opportunity for profits over and above marginal costs both to finance ongoing research and development and as an incentive for further research and development. Thus a basic policy question is how to reconcile providing short-term benefits to consumers (static efficiency) with the need to ensure that long-term benefits are obtained as a result of innovation (dynamic efficiency).

The loss of static efficiency should be set against the growth and welfare benefits accruing from the future introduction of new products and processes. Exclusive rights can be imposed at the cost of sacrificing static efficiency, but they should be subject to strict limits because intellectual property rights lead to underutilization of information—including for the generation of subsequent innovation.

Intellectual property rights are just one appropriation method for the results of research and development. Depending on the technologies and sectors involved, other methods may be far more relevant to innovators. Many studies indicate that patent protection is usually not the driving force behind research and development.[2] Alternative protection from imitation may result, for instance, from lead time, from the innovator's ability to move ahead on the learning curve quicker than competitors, from the customer loyalty derived from superior sales and services, and from the structure of the market, as with oligopolistic market structures (see Scherer and Ross 1990, pp. 627–28, and Scherer 1999, p. 59).

Thus policymakers face difficult choices, and achieving both static and dynamic efficiency requires them to fine-tune the tools they use. A fair balance between private and social benefits requires policies that ensure the creation of new technologies as well as their dissemination so that competitors can improve on them. As taught by evolutionary theory on technical change, innovation and diffusion are two sides of the same coin: innovation leads to diffusion, which influences the level of innovative activity (OECD 1992, p. 51). Moreover, from an equity perspective it is essential for policies to ensure that innovations reach those who need them. Obvious examples include pharmaceuticals, diagnostic kits, and other products crucial for human health.[3]

Considerable emphasis has been placed on the limits of intellectual property rights in generating dynamic effects. Since knowledge is both an output and an input of its production process, a conflict arises between first- and second-generation producers—because the greater are the rights (and hence incentives) of the first generation, the greater are the costs (and hence the lower the incentives) of the second generation (Benkler 2001).

The extent to which static efficiency is sacrificed and dynamic efficiency is attained depends on factors such as market structure and the availability of substitutes for the material protected by intellectual property rights. It also depends on features of intellectual property laws, such as the scope of exclusive rights and the duration of protection. In other words, the reduction in static efficiency and the deleterious effects of intellectual property rights on future innovations can be attenuated by designing intellectual property laws in a way that reconciles the conflicting social interests underlying the recognition of such rights.

The validity of arguments about the need to sacrifice static efficiency in order to increase dynamic efficiency depends on the context in which they apply. Thus patent protection may be justified when the consumer surplus from new products, albeit limited by the presence of monopoly, outweighs the consumer surplus from current products in the absence of patent protection.

However, intellectual property rights may force some consumers to pay higher prices today without benefiting from the future innovations that their sacrifice is supposed to secure. With pharmaceuticals, for instance, full implementation of the TRIPS agreement will mean that consumers in developing countries are contributing to the research and development budgets of pharmaceutical companies in industrial countries. Such companies focus on producing profitable drugs and neglect those needed in developing countries (Lanjouw and Cockburn 2001; Médecins Sans Frontières 2001). Consumers in developing countries are unlikely to benefit from future innovations to the same extent as consumers in industrial countries—if at all.

Deardorff (1992) offers a model for extending patent protection from one country to another. He shows that when patent protection is extended to a "non-inventing" country, that country's welfare decreases while the welfare of the "inventing" country increases. Deardorff also shows that while patents involve a tradeoff between technological progress (inducing research and development) and consumer surplus, this tradeoff can be balanced by establishing patent protection only in part of the world. Thus, he concludes, worldwide patent protection may not be desirable—and at the least, the very poorest countries should be exempted from any new agreement to extend patent protection under the General Agreement on Tariffs and Trade (GATT).[4]

In addition, extending intellectual property rights to developing countries may not have the claimed positive effects on innovation, particularly if broad patent rights are recognized. Innovation in those countries is mainly based on incremental developments based on existing technologies rather than on original contributions to the state of the art. Innovation systems are weak in most developing countries, and would not be suddenly transformed by the introduction of stronger intellectual property rights. The development of technological capabilities is a cumulative process that takes time and—contrary to the prediction of "leapfrogging" theory—requires step-by-step upgrading in scientific infrastructure and education, as well as effective learning at the firm level.

As argued by Anderson (1998), in countries where follow-on innovation is most important, narrower (though not necessarily shorter) protection is better than broader. Hence, to accumulate technological capabilities, firms in those countries will benefit from a strict definition of patent requirements that allow them to develop from existing technology.

Similarly, Panagariya (1999) argues that the geographic extension of patents will increase monopoly power with adverse allocative and transfer effects, and will not increase research and development in developing countries. In his view, "the extension of North's patent law to South will lead to both efficiency loss and transfer of benefits from Southern consumers to innovators. Since innovators are mainly located in the North, the South will lose on both counts: monopoly distortion and the transfer from its consumers to innovators in the North. Global welfare will also decline" (quoted in Dumont and Holmes 1999, p. 23).

To summarize, intellectual property rights affect different countries in different ways. The static-dynamic efficiency rationale applicable to an industrial country does not necessarily hold where inequality is high. Strong protection for intellectual property rights may have significant negative allocative consequences in developing countries without contributing to—and even impeding—their technological development (Stiglitz 1999).

HOW FAR SHOULD INTELLECTUAL PROPERTY RIGHTS GO?
THE BALANCE BETWEEN STATIC AND DYNAMIC EFFICIENCY

Broad, long-lasting intellectual property rights provide strong incentives to innovate. But there are significant tradeoffs—the broader and longer-lasting are such rights, the higher is the cost of knowledge for society. Broad protection (in terms of the subject matter covered or rights of exclusion conferred) and long-lasting rights reduce competition and static efficiency as well as the diffusion of knowledge and dynamic efficiency (see Welfens and others 1999, p. 143). This section discusses how decisions on the coverage of protection, the extent of exclusive rights, and the duration of rights influence the static allocation and dynamic creation of knowledge.

Coverage of protection

Expanding protectable subject matter—as required by the TRIPS agreement in many areas—takes information out of the public domain. Hence one key issue affecting societal welfare is the coverage of the monopoly rights conferred to owners of intellectual property rights. Today's inventions provide not only the capability to produce new and better products and to produce them more effectively today, but also concepts and starting points for inventive efforts tomorrow. Thus the broader is the coverage of patents, the greater will be the reductions in static as well as dynamic efficiency.

The impact of the patent system on dynamic efficiency crucially depends on the range to which patent claims can be applied. The original intent of the patent system to reward inventiveness assumes that inventions marked by considerable originality are produced and protected, rather than technical developments that just build on and add little to existing knowledge—such as when the "invention" results from path-down experimentation that was obvious to many (Barton 2000). As a general rule, if a patent has a broad scope, competitors are deterred from innovating in the field covered by the patent. This outcome is particularly likely when, as is often the case, large companies aggressively use their patent portfolios to discourage competition from other companies. But if the scope of protection is narrowly defined, competitors may safely compete in the next round of inventing.

The breadth of patent protection depends on national legislation, particularly the criteria for judging the patentability of inventions, and on the terms that determine the "equivalence" of inventions. There are few guidelines in international treaties binding states to follow a more or less strict approach to patentability. Some jurisdictions grant patents using very lax patentability standards.[5] The United States, for instance, grants about 160,000 patents a year—twice the number 10 years ago. Many are for minor, sometimes trivial developments, or for substances (including genes) that already exist in nature and that have merely been discovered, not invented.

This proliferation of patents is the result of loose criteria for patentability,[6] of the excessive flexibility of patent offices in assessing the innovation, novelty, and usefulness of the applications submitted to them,[7] and of shortcomings in examination procedures.[8] In addition, new areas have come under the reach of the patent system, such as "methods of doing business," for which the number of patents has surged in the past 10 years (Gleick 2000, p. 44).

If patent policies lead, through loose criteria for protection, to monopolistic market structures, owners of intellectual property rights can maintain high price-cost margins, retard innovation, and deny access to innovative products. In contrast, some degree of competitive threat induces firms to innovate and keep prices low. Monopolistic elements should diminish, in particular, where diffusion creates important technological opportunities and where it is needed to satisfy essential societal needs.

An efficiency-enhancing patent system—one that fosters both static and dynamic efficiency—can rely on several policy options for the coverage of protection:

- Patentability requirements should be defined and applied such that exclusive rights are limited to truly "inventive" and novel contributions to the state of the art. Ineffective enforcement of patentability requirements enables inventors to protect inventions that cost considerably less than the value of the monopoly provided by patent law.
- Easily accessible, inexpensive mechanisms should be available to challenge the validity of wrongly granted patents. In some countries such challenges may be brought before patent offices at any time[9] or within a certain period

after a patent has been granted,[10] avoiding costly judicial procedures.

• Procedures can involve third parties to reduce the granting of improper monopolies. Such procedures may provide for the right of a third party to file an opposition to the grant of a patent or to submit observations on the patentability of an invention after publication of its application[11] and before granting.[12] In Japan allowing pre-grant opposition encouraged patent applicants to license their innovations, to discourage competing firms from opposing patent applications. The opposition phase also created incentives for early bargaining between innovators and potential rivals who would be disadvantaged if the patents were granted. Japan's patent system was designed to expedite the diffusion of knowledge contained in patents while maintaining incentives to invest in research and development (Ordover 1991, p. 48).

• Setting boundaries for protected inventions determines the scope of the rights conferred by a patent. National legislation should define when products or processes not literally described in a claim may be deemed equivalent and so infringing on patent rights. Both static and dynamic efficiency are enhanced if a narrow doctrine of equivalents is used, because it allows more room for competition and follow-on innovation.

Extent of exclusive rights

The power conferred to owners of intellectual property rights vary depending on the type of intellectual property involved. Patents confer the exclusive right to make, use, or sell an invention, generally for 20 years. Patents may be granted for processes and products. Patent protection of a product grants significant market power because the patent owner can prevent third parties from producing or selling the product even if it is obtained through different processes. In contrast, protection of a manufacturing process, unless it is the only possible or feasible approach, does not impede others from obtaining the same product through alternative processes. This distinction explains why large pharmaceutical companies, which only had process patents in many developing countries before the TRIPS agreement, actively sought and ultimately obtained an obligation for all members of the World Trade Organization to protect both pharmaceutical processes and products (see article 27.1 of the TRIPS agreement).

The breadth of patent claims is a key element in determining the degree of competition and the flow of future innovations. Broad patents can be used to stifle competition (reducing static efficiency) and can have adverse long-run effects on innovation (and dynamic efficiency).

Patent claims determine the control that patent holders can exercise over subsequent inventions. The broader is the original patent, the more likely that new inventions in closely related areas will be deemed infringing. Broad patent claims generate greater rewards to primary innovators, but they may discourage subsequent innovations.[13] For example, there is no pervasive evidence that even in the United States the greater breadth of patent claims has led to greater innovation (Dumont and Holmes 1999, p. 27).

Patent offices in some countries have recently tended to admit increasingly broad claims. The drafting of patent claims has become "more an art than a science under current law." Today's patent agents "make every effort to phrase claims such that they cover every conceivable improvement of an invention while, at the same time, steering the claims clear of the prior art" (Hart 1994, p. 230). In some cases protection is granted to inventions that embrace all ways of solving a problem. For instance, the first utility patent granted to a plant in the United States described the increase in the plant's tryptophan content rather than particular genes (Plowman 1993, p. 35). In other cases patents include claims that can extend to many plant varieties or even to entire plant species, such as an Agracetus patent related to any manipulation of cotton regardless of the germplasm used (Correa 1999, p. 5).

Merges and Nelson (1990) note that in many industries the efficiency gains that might be achieved through the granting of exclusive rights to the pioneer firm are likely to be outweighed by the loss of competition in developing improvements to the basic invention. Thus they advocate creating a competitive environment for improvements, rather than an environment dominated by the pioneer firm, taking into account the nature of technical advance in the specific industry. The patenting of research tools (such as reagents, DNA sequences, instruments, and other biomedical techniques) is another area where exclusive rights may diminish static and dynamic efficiency because of the time and energy required to avoid infringing on patents and to obtain licenses (see Heller and Eisenberg 1998 and Barton 2002).

In sum, the breadth of patent protection determines the extent to which patent owners can deter other firms from pursuing follow-on innovations and impose unwarranted costs on society.[14] Broad patent claims may defeat the intent of the patent system by stifling competition and delaying follow-on innovation.

Duration of rights
Given its implications for allocative efficiency, economists have extensively discussed the optimal length of a patent grant (Scherer 1972). The duration of exclusive rights is a key element in determining the balance between appropriability and use. A long patent life permits the titleholder to obtain extraordinary profits at the expense of optimal use, because of pricing above marginal cost. On the other hand, a short patent life may not provide incentives to invest in innovation.

The current patent term is largely a function of historical factors that no longer have any relevance.[15] The TRIPS agreement sets forth as a minimum standard a 20-year patent term counted from the date of application, obliging many countries to extend the protection previously granted under national laws. There is no economic justification for this standard. The pattern and rate of imitation vary substantially between industries, as do the initial expectations of investors.

Though it would be very complex to differentiate patent terms by sector, it may be possible to differentiate between fundamental advances in knowledge and logical, somehow predictable extensions of existing knowledge (Thurow 1997, p. 98). In addition, when a major invention achieves rapid acceptance in the marketplace and quickly permits its titleholder to recover research and development costs and make a profit, the period of patent protection could be shortened. The rationale is that the inventor would have received an adequate reward, and any extension of exclusive rights could exacerbate the potential allocative problems of the original patent (Gutterman 1997, p. 67).

Latitude in the application of patentability requirements has sometimes allowed, as in the pharmaceutical industry, artificial extensions of patent term protection well beyond the expiration of the original patent, based on the patenting of secondary developments (box 1).[16] The extension of a patent term reduces allocative efficiency and can also undermine dynamic efficiency, since new

---

BOX 1

EXTENSIONS OF PATENT TERMS FOR PHARMACEUTICALS

Pharmaceutical companies use many means to artificially delay the marketing of competing products, including the patenting of:

- *Pharmaceutical forms*—particular ways of administering an active ingredient that may be unpatented,[17] in combination with certain additives.
- *"Selection" inventions*—when an element or group of elements of a known large group are patented based on, for example, a feature that was not specifically described in an earlier patent for the larger group.
- *"Analogy" processes*—processes that are not in themselves innovative but that allow a product with innovative features to be obtained.
- *Combinations* of known products.
- *Optical isomers*—this takes advantage of the property of many chemical compounds to present two mirror forms. Often, after the mixture of both forms has been patented (racemic mixture), a patent application is made for the most active isomer.
- *Active metabolites*—patenting the active metabolite of a compound that produces the desired effect in the body.[18]
- *Parent substances*—compounds that, although themselves inactive, produce a therapeutically active "parent substance" when metabolized in the body.
- *New salts* of known substances.
- *Variants of known manufacturing processes.*
- *New uses* for known products.[19]

entrants are discouraged. There is considerable evidence that prices fall significantly after a patent elapses (Viscusi, Vernon, and Harrington 1997, p. 853).

Exceptions to exclusive rights

The exclusive rights conferred by patents may be subject to general, unpaid, automatic exceptions. Such exceptions may permit, among other things:

- Activities engaged in privately, on a noncommercial scale or for a noncommercial purpose.
- Use of the invention for scientific research or for teaching purposes.
- Commercial experimentation on the invention (for example, to test or improve it).
- Preparation of medicines under individual prescriptions.
- Experiments performed for the purpose of seeking regulatory approval to market a product after the expiration of a patent (known as the Bolar exception).
- Use of the invention by a third party that had bona fide use of it before the patent application.
- Import of a patented product that has been legitimately marketed in another country (known as parallel imports).

Depending on their formulation under national patent laws, these exceptions are permissible under article 30 of the TRIPS agreement (Correa 2000). Some are particularly important for increasing static (allocative) efficiency, while others are mainly relevant to dynamic efficiency.

Experimental use

The experimental use (research) exception permits any third party to experiment on a patented invention without the authorization of the titleholder. In some countries (such as the United States) this exception is allowed only for scientific research. It permits investigators to use previously patented inventions in their research without having to request permission and pay for them, lowering the costs of research and fostering scientific progress.

In many jurisdictions experimental use by third parties is also legitimate for commercial purposes—for instance, to request a license or to test whether the patent has been rightly granted (Correa 2000, p. 76). The adoption of this exception expedites follow-on innovation and technological progress. The exception may allow innovation based on "inventing around" or improving on the protected invention. It clearly enhances dynamic efficiency without reducing static efficiency.

Early working

The early working (Bolar) exception allows manufacturers of generic products to start, where necessary, seeking marketing approval before the expiration of another company's patent, and permits the introduction of competitive products as soon as the patent expires. Thus it increases static efficiency. In the absence of such an exception, the introduction of generic copies may be delayed for months or years, during which the patent owner might charge high prices despite the expiration of the patent.

This exception was introduced by the United States in 1984 and has since been established in Argentina, Australia, Canada, and Israel, among other countries.[20] The U.S. Drug Price Competition and Patent Term Restoration Act permits testing to establish the bioequivalency of generic products before the expiration of the relevant patent. This exception was intended to help generic drug producers place their products on the market as soon as a patent expired, allowing consumers to obtain medicines at much lower prices. In exchange for this exception, the patent term of the original drug could be extended up to five years. An analysis of the welfare implications of this act indicated that "from the perspective of economic welfare, the Act is the source of large potential positive gains of two types. First, it eliminated costly scientific testing which served no valid purpose. Second, the Act lowered prices to consumers with some elimination of deadweight losses and large transfers from producers to consumers" (Viscusi, Vernon, and Harrington 1997, p. 857).

After the act was adopted, the average generic product was introduced at a price equal to 61 percent of the brand name product's price—and after two years fell to 37 percent (table 1). Despite these lower prices, after two years generics had just 49 percent of market share (in terms of units sold), and former patent owners were able to maintain and even raise their prices (Viscusi, Vernon, and Harrington 1997, p. 853).

In sum, the early working exception has positive effects on allocative efficiency. And because the patent holder is able to keep its monopoly until the patent expires, the exception is unlikely to reduce dynamic efficiency.

Parallel imports

The admission under national law of parallel imports (as allowed under article 6 of the TRIPS agreement) implies a partial derogation of the exclusive right to import generally granted to owners of intellectual property rights. This derogation is justified under the doctrine of exhaustion of rights, according to which titleholders have no right to control the use or resale of goods that they have put on a foreign market directly or through a licensee.[21]

Parallel imports can be a powerful tool for increasing allocative efficiency. If consumers can get legitimate products from foreign countries at prices lower than those charged locally by the owners of the products' intellectual property rights, it increases static efficiency and does not necessarily reduce dynamic efficiency—because the owners of the rights have been remunerated (in the foreign market) for their intellectual contributions. The profits may be lower than those obtain-

TABLE 1

Average prices of brand name and generic drugs after the expiration of patent protection in the United States, 1984–88

Indicator	At date of entry	One year after entry	Two years after entry
Brand name price index	1.00	1.07	1.11
Generic price index	1.00	0.78	0.65
Ratio of generic price to brand name price	0.61	0.46	0.37
Generic market share in units (percent)	9	35	49

Note: Prices are based on unweighted averages for 18 categories of drugs.
Source: Grabowski and Vernon 1992.

able if the owners were able to fragment markets and charge higher prices in the importing countries, but that does not mean that the owners will not be able to recover their spending on research and development.

The pharmaceutical industry has claimed that parallel imports may endanger research and development. The industry has argued that exports of drugs sold at low cost in developing countries to higher-priced markets will affect its ability to fund future research and development.[22] That may be true if parallel trade becomes significant, but there is no indication that this is likely to happen. Trade in medicines is subject to stringent national regulations that erect effective barriers to market access. Moreover, parallel imports occur only where price differences are significant. To make parallel imports difficult or unattractive, pharmaceutical firms could reduce such differences or sell patented products under different trademarks or packaging in major markets (Watal 2000). Further, any country can adopt legislation to prevent parallel imports.

It has been suggested that, to maintain tiered pricing and prevent low-priced medicines in developing countries from flowing to industrial countries, developing countries should adopt measures to prevent their exportation.[23] But such export restraints may not be consistent with World Trade Organization rules, particularly in light of article XI of the General Agreement on Tariffs and Trade (GATT).

COMPULSORY LICENSES

A compulsory license is an authorization that a national authority gives a person to exploit—without the consent of the titleholder—information protected by a patent or other intellectual property rights.[24] During the 20th century compulsory licenses became a common feature of patent laws worldwide. In the early 1990s about a hundred countries recognized such licenses based on, for example, the lack or insufficient working of a patented invention, public interest, government use, and anticompetitive behavior. In addition, some countries (Canada, France, the United Kingdom) allowed compulsory licenses specifically for certain products such as food, medicines, and surgical or curative devices.

Compulsory licenses can enhance static efficiency, as when they are granted to remedy anticompetitive practices or to address public health emergencies by ensuring access to cheaper drugs. The granting of such licenses will force prices down, benefiting consumers.[25] And when the licensee undertakes production, such licenses can also increase dynamic efficiency.[26] The use of the patented process or the manufacturing of the patented product can lead to follow-on innovations or new innovative concepts. As evolutionary theory on innovation has shown, routine productive activities and cumulative learning at the plant level are important sources of innovation (Cooper 1994, p. 8). Hence, while improving allocative efficiency, compulsory licenses can also increase future flows of innovations and dynamic efficiency. As noted by Gutterman (1997, p. 69):

> Compulsory licensing might be considered as a means for reducing some of the adverse costs of the patent system. For example, requiring compulsory licensing at reasonable rates may reduce the underutilization costs of the patent system; however, uses of lesser value than the royalty rate would still not be covered. Compulsory licensing might also reduce to some extent the contribution of the patent system to monopoly power, the wasteful duplication of research efforts, the problem of blocking patent strategies, and the concerns about research in areas that may well already be covered by patents.

Some observers—such as the research-based pharmaceutical industry—argue that to the extent that compulsory licenses lower the prices of patented products and the expected profits of patent owners, such licenses undermine incentives to undertake future research and development (Rozek and Rainey 2001). But Scherer (1998, pp. 107–08) analyzed the extent to which compulsory licenses affected spending on research and development, and particularly whether such licenses diminished or destroyed incentives for patent holders to undertake research and development. His findings, based on 70 companies, showed no negative effect on research and development in companies subject to compulsory licenses. On the contrary, such companies showed a significant increase in research and development relative to companies of comparable size not subject to such licenses.[27]

Moreover, according to Tandon (1982, p. 485): "Firms spend large sums of money on efforts to 'invent around' the patents of their competitors. Under generalized compulsory licensing, these expenditures would be unnecessary, which might increase the welfare benefits." Hence compulsory licenses may increase both static and dynamic efficiency.

TABLE 2

Elements of patent law that enhance static and dynamic efficiency

Element	Static efficiency	Dynamic efficiency
Strict standards of patentability	X	X
Limited breadth of claims	X	X
Narrowly defined doctrine of equivalents	X	X
Experimental exception		X
Early working exception	X	X[a]
Parallel imports	X	
Compulsory licenses		
With manufacturing	X	X
Without manufacturing	X	

a. Mainly in relation to manufacturing processes and new applications.

CONCLUSION

This chapter has showed that patent law may be designed to increase static efficiency, dynamic efficiency, or both (table 2). The intensity of a law's effects depend on the context in which protection is applied and, particularly, on the market structure and the characteristics of the national innovation system.

Static and dynamic efficiency may be promoted by strict standards of patentability, a limited breadth of patent claims, a narrowly defined doctrine of equivalents, an early working exception, and in some cases by compulsory licenses. Parallel imports and compulsory licenses may increase static efficiency in developing countries without affecting global dynamic efficiency since the development of new products and processes is likely to be only marginally affected by such measures.

NOTES

1. The economic effects of patents have been considered more extensively than any other intellectual property right (Benkler 2001).

2. For example, a classic study by Levin, Klevorich, and Nelson (1987) found that firms in 130 lines of business reported that patents were the least important means of securing competitive advantage for new products. Still, a firm may obtain a patent even if an innovation would have occurred without it. In such cases a patent represents a windfall gain for the firm at the expense of social efficiency (Hart 1994, p. 232)

3. A resolution approved (with 52 votes and 1 abstention) on 23 April 2001 at the 57th session of the United Nations Commission on Human Rights calls on govern-

ments to ensure the accessibility of pharmaceuticals and medical treatments used to treat pandemics such as HIV/AIDS, as well as "their affordability for all," in accordance with international laws and agreements. The resolution also calls on governments "to safeguard access to such preventive, curative or palliative pharmaceuticals or medical technologies from any limitations by third parties."

4. See Deardoff (1992, p. 37). The TRIPS agreement does not accord such an exemption to the least developed countries. Such countries can delay the application of the agreement until 2006 and subsequently request extensions of that term (article 66.1). The Doha Ministerial Declaration on TRIPS and Public Health, adopted on 14 November 2001 by the members of the World Trade Organization (WTO), authorized least developed countries to further delay the patenting of pharmaceutical products until 2016 (see WT/MIN(01)/DEC/W/2, para. 7).

5. Ongoing negotiations (under the auspices of the World Intellectual Property Organization) on an international treaty to harmonize certain substantive aspects of patent law, if successful, may eventually limit states' freedom to decide on this matter.

6. The notion of "local" innovation disseminated by media other than publication outside the United States has led, for example, to the patenting of plants and knowledge widely used and developed in developing countries (Correa 1999).

7. Examples of patents granted in the United States include one for an "invention" consisting of elastic bands worn across the mouth, allowing wearers to breathe but preventing the intake of food (US 4,883,072); a patent for a hunting device consisting of a cape and a hat serving as a decoy for prey (US 5,197,216); and a patent for a hat for four-legged animals (US 4,967,317). From Feinberg (1994).

8. For example, less than half of the examinations conducted by the U.S. Patent Office refer to relevant background bibliographies; examinations are largely limited to analyzing previous patents (Aharonian 2000).

9. In the United States patent holders can ask the Patent Office to reexamine earlier patents before or during an infringement lawsuit, to determine whether prior art invalidates one or more new patent claims (33 USC 302).

10. The European Patent Office provides for an opposition procedure after a patent has been granted.

11. Most countries publish applications before granting patents. The United States recently adopted this rule (Public Law 106-113, of 29 November 1999), but only for inventors who filed abroad before applying in the United States.

12. This procedure is provided for in some laws, such as in Argentina and in Decision 486 of the Andean Group countries.

13. One reason broad patents discourage follow-on innovation is that the negotiation of patent rights for such innovation could be difficult. In addition, cross-licensing is likely to occur, discouraging follow-on innovation.

14. The optimal solution from society's perspective would be to determine the breadth of each patent based on the nature of the innovation and the relevant mar-

kets—an approach that is not easy to build into intellectual property law (see Scotchmer 1998 and Thurow 1997).

15. See Gutterman (1997, p. 67) and Hart (1994, p. 231), who argues that "to be efficient, a patent term should also reflect the costs of research and development involved. Current patent law awards the same patent term no matter what the inventive process costs; this cannot be efficient. The higher the cost of research and development, the longer the patent duration that is need to induce efficient investment, and therefore, the longer the patent term should be."

16. This practice is often called "evergreening" of patents.

17. This type of patent may have significant practical consequences. For example, in Thailand there was no patent for didanosine (ddl) as such. Nevertheless, Bristol Myers Squibb (which did not discover the product but obtained a license for it from a federal U.S. laboratory) patented a formulation of ddl, blocking the Thai government's attempts to purchase the drug at a much lower price.

18. For example, after terfenadine had been on sale for several years, a patent was obtained for its active metabolite. The courts decided that this was an unacceptable attempt to extend the original patent.

19. An example of a patent for the use of a known drug is AZT (Retrovir), which was synthesized in 1964 by the Karmanos Cancer Institute (formerly known as the Michigan Cancer Foundation) as a possible anticancer drug. Another more recent example is sildenafil (Viagra).

20. In European countries an early working exception has been gradually admitted by case law based on the right of a third party to conduct experiments without the authorization of the patent owner (Cook 1997; NERA 1998).

21. Under some formulations of this doctrine the consent of the titleholder in the exporting country is needed for "exhaustion" to occur ("consent theory"). Legally, however, exhaustion may be considered to have occurred when the titleholder was rewarded in the exporting country ("reward theory"), including through a compulsory license.

22. Another argument against parallel imports is that they increase opportunities for "counterfeit and substandard products to enter the market" (Bale 2000, p. 18), but this is essentially a law enforcement problem that can be addressed under normal procedures.

23. At the WTO TRIPS Council first special session on intellectual property and access to medicines, held on 20 June 2001, the U.S. delegation argued that "In our view, advocates of parallel importation overlook the fact that permitting such imports discourages patent owners from pricing their products differently in different markets based upon the level of economic development because of the likelihood that, for example, products sold for low prices in a poor country will be bought up by middle men and sent to wealthiest country markets and sold at higher prices, for the benefit primarily of the middle men. The lack of parallel import protection can also have significant health and safety implications. Our law enforcement and regulatory agencies,

especially the Food and Drug Administration, have commented on how very difficult it is for them to keep counterfeit and unapproved drugs out of our country even with the strong parallel import protection provided in the United States. Advocating parallel imports, therefore, could work to the disadvantage of the very people on behalf of whom the advocates purport to be speaking. As World Health Organization Director-General Dr. Brundtland in Oslo recently noted, 'For differential pricing to work on a large scale, I think we can all agree that there must be watertight ways of preventing lower priced drugs from finding their way back into rich country markets.'"

24. Compulsory licenses are often also called "nonvoluntary licenses." The TRIPS agreement (article 31) refers to "Other use without the authorization of the right holder."

25. According to the Paris Convention (article 5A) and the TRIPS agreement (article 31), compulsory licenses must be nonexclusive—meaning that licenses to use a patent may be given to more than one company.

26. A compulsory license can apply to manufacturing or importation of the protected product. Both options are admissible under the TRIPS agreement.

27. Scherer's studies also indicated a decline in patenting activities among firms subjected to compulsory licensing. However, that result does not necessarily mean that that the firms' spending on research declined—but rather that the firms could rely on alternative methods of protection, such as trade secrets.

REFERENCES

Aharonian, Greg. 2000. "Patent Examination System Is Intellectually Corrupt." Patnews, 1 May. [http://swpat.ffii.org/vreji/prina/patrupt.pdf]. March 2002.

Anderson, Robert D. 1998. "The Interface between Competition Policy and Intellectual Property in the Context of the International Trading System." *Journal of International Economic Law* 1 (4): 655–78.

Bale, Harvey. 2000. "TRIPS, Pharmaceuticals and Developing Countries: Implications for Drug Access and Drug Development." Paper presented at the World Health Organization workshop on the TRIPS Agreement and Its Impact on Pharmaceuticals, 2 May, Jakarta.

Barton, John. 2000. "Reforming the Patent System." *Science* 287 (17 March): 1933–34.

———. 2002. "Research-tool Patents: Issues for Health in the Developing World." *Bulletin of the World Health Organization* 80 (2): 121–25.

Benkler, Yochai. 2001. "A Political Economy of the Public Domain: Markets in Information Goods versus the Marketplace of Ideas." In Rochelle Dreyfuss, Diane Zimmerman, and Harry First, eds., *Expanding the Boundaries of Intellectual Property.* Oxford and New York: Oxford University Press.

Cook, Trevor. 1997. "Pharmaceutical Patents and the Generic Sector in Europe." *Patent World* (February).

Cooper, Charles, ed. 1994. *Technology and Innovation in the International Economy.* Hants, U.K. and Brookfield, Vt.: Edward Elgar and Tokyo: United Nations University Press.

Correa, Carlos. 1999. "Access to Plant Genetic Resources and Intellectual Property Rights." Background Study Paper 8. Food and Agriculture Organization, Commission on Genetic Resources for Food and Agriculture, Rome.

———. 2000. *Intellectual Property Rights, the WTO and Developing Countries.* Penang, Malaysia: Zed Books/Third World Network.

David, Paul A. 1993. "Intellectual Property Institutions and the Panda's Thumb: Patents, Copyrights, and Trade Secrets in Economic Theory and History." In M. Wallerstein, M. Mogee, and R. Schoen, eds., *Global Dimensions of Intellectual Property Rights in Science and Technology.* Washington, D.C.: National Academy Press.

Deardorff, Alan. 1992. "Welfare Effects of Global Patent Protection." *Economica* 59: 35–51. Reprinted in Kym Anderson and Bernard Hoekman, eds., 2000, *The Global Trading System,* New York: I. B. Tauris.

Dumont, Béatrice, and Peter Holmes. 1999. "The Breadth of Intellectual Property Rights and Their Interface with Competition Law and Policy: Divergent Paths to the Same Goal." Paper presented at the International Conference on Innovation, Appropriation Strategies and Economic Policy, 19 November, Paris.

FAO (Food and Agriculture Organization). 2001. "Potential Impacts of Genetic Restriction Technologies (GURTs) on Agricultural Biodiversity and Agricultural Production Systems." CGRFA/WG-PGR-1/01/7. Commission on Genetic Resources for Food and Agriculture, Rome.

Feinberg, Rick. 1994. *Peculiar Patents.* New York: Citadel Press.

Gleick, James. 2000. "Patently Absurd." *The New York Times Magazine,* March 12: 44–49.

Grabowski, Henry G., and John M. Vernon. 1992. "Brand Loyalty, Entry, and Price Competition in Pharmaceuticals after the 1984 Drug Act." *Journal of Law and Economics* 35 (2): 331–50.

Granstrand, Ove. 1999. *The Economics and Management of Intellectual Property.* Clentenham, U.K. and Northampton, Mass.: Edward Elgar.

Gutterman, Alan. 1997. *Innovation and Competition Policy: A Comparative Study of Regulation of Patent Licensing and Collaborative Research & Development in the United States and the European Community.* London: Kluwer Law International.

Hart, Michael. 1994. "Getting Back to Basics: Reinventing Patent Law for Economic Efficiency." *Intellectual Property Journal* 8 (2).

Heller, Michael A., and Rebecca S. Eisenberg. 1998. "Can Patents Deter Innovation? The Anticommons on Biomedical Research." *Science* 280: 698–701.

Kaul, Inge, Isabelle Grunberg, and Marc A. Stern. 1999. "Defining Global Public Goods." In Inge Kaul, Isabelle Grunberg, and Marc A. Stern, eds., *Global Public*

Goods: International Cooperation in the 21st Century. New York: Oxford University Press.

Lanjouw, Jean, and Ian Cockburn. 2001. "New Pills for Poor People? Empirical Evidence after GATT." *World Development* 29 (2): 265–89.

Levin, Richard, Alvin Klevorick, Richard Nelson, and Sidney Winter. 1987. "Appropriating the Returns from Industrial Research and Development." *Brookings Papers on Economic Activity 3.* Washington, D.C.: Brookings Institution.

Médecins Sans Frontières. 2001. *Fatal Imbalance: The Crisis in Research and Development for Drugs for Neglected Diseases.* Geneva.

Merges, Robert, and Richard Nelson. 1990. "On the Complex Economics of Patent Scope." *Columbia Law Review* 90 (4): 839–916.

NERA (National Economic Research Associates). 1998. *Policy Relating to Generic Medicines in the OECD: Final Report for the European Commission.* London.

OECD (Organisation for Economic Co-operation and Development). 1992. *Technology and the Economy.* Paris.

Ordover, Janusz A. 1991. "A Patent System for Both Diffusion and Exclusion." *Journal of Economic Perspectives* 5 (1): 43–60.

Panagariya, Arvind. 1999. "TRIPS and the WTO: An Uneasy Marriage." Seminar paper prepared for the World Trade Organization, Geneva. Quoted in Dumont and Holmes 1999.

Plowman, Ronald. 1993. "Intellectual Property Protection of Plants"—The Agricultural Research Service Perspective." In *Intellectual Property Rights: Protection of Plant Materials.* CSSA Special Publication 21. Madison, Wisc.: Crop Science Society of America.

Rozek, Richard, and Renee Rainey. 2001. "Broad-based Compulsory Licensing of Pharmaceutical Technologies—Unsound Public Policy." *Journal of World Intellectual Property* 4 (4).

Ryan, Michael. 1998. *Knowledge Diplomacy: Global Competition and the Politics of Intellectual Property.* Washington, D.C.: Brooking Institution Press.

Scherer, Frederic M. 1972. "Nordhaus's Theory of Optimal Patent Life: A Geometric Reinterpretation." *American Economic Review* 62.

———. 1998. "Comments." In Robert Anderson and Nancy Gallini, eds., *Competition Policy and Intellectual Property Rights in the Knowledge-based Economy.* Alberta: University of Calgary Press.

———. 1999. *New Perspectives on Economic Growth and Technological Innovation.* Washington, D.C.: Brookings Institution Press.

Scherer, Frederic M., and David Ross. 1990. *Industrial Market Structure and Economic Performance.* Dallas, Tex.: Houghton Mifflin.

Scotchmer, Suzanne. 1998. "Incentives to Innovate." In P. Newman, ed., *New Palgrave Dictionary of Economics and the Law.* London: Macmillan.

Stiglitz, Joseph E. 1999. "Knowledge as a Global Public Good." In Inge Kaul, Isabelle Grunberg, and Marc A. Stern, eds., *Global Public Goods: International Cooperation in the 21st Century.* New York: Oxford University Press.

Tandon, Pankaj. 1982. "Optimal Patents with Compulsory Licensing." *Journal of Political Economy* 90 (3).

Thurow, Lester. 1997. "Needed: A New System of Intellectual Property Rights." *Harvard Business Review* (September–October).

Viscusi, W. Kip, John Vernon, and Joseph Harrington. 1997. *Economics of Regulation and Antitrust.* Cambridge, Mass.: MIT Press.

Watal, Jayashree. 2000. "Pharmaceutical Patents, Prices and Welfare Losses: A Simulation Study of Policy Options for India under the WTO TRIPS Agreement." *World Economy* 23 (5).

Welfens, Paul, John Addison, David Audretsch, Thomas Gries, and Hariolf Grupp. 1999. *Globalization, Economic Growth and Innovation Dynamics.* Berlin: Springer.

4

CASE STUDIES: APPLYING THE CONCEPT OF GLOBAL PUBLIC GOODS

INTERNATIONAL FINANCIAL STABILITY AND MARKET EFFICIENCY
AS A GLOBAL PUBLIC GOOD
Stephany Griffith-Jones

THE MULTILATERAL TRADE REGIME:
A GLOBAL PUBLIC GOOD FOR ALL?
Ronald U. Mendoza

BEYOND COMMUNICABLE DISEASE CONTROL:
HEALTH IN THE AGE OF GLOBALIZATION
Dyna Arhin-Tenkorang and Pedro Conceição

GLOBAL TRADE FOR LOCAL BENEFIT:
FINANCING ENERGY FOR ALL IN COSTA RICA
René Castro and Sarah Cordero

CONSERVING BIODIVERSITY:
RECONCILING LOCAL AND GLOBAL PUBLIC BENEFITS
Charles Perrings and Madhav Gadgil

Problems of Publicness and Access Rights: Perspectives from the Water Domain
Lyla Mehta

Corruption and Global Public Goods
Peter Eigen and Christian Eigen-Zucchi

Earlier chapters in this volume examine the provision of global public goods from a cross-cutting perspective, exploring various dimensions of the process. The case studies in this part, by contrast, look at the provision process from an issue-specific perspective.

The studies show how global public goods are embedded in and matter to people's daily lives. Several authors analyze goods from the perspectives of local communities and developing countries. The analyses show that global public goods are not a luxury desired—and needed—only by rich people. Because of their globalness and publicness, most of these goods reach deep into all corners of the world. As Stephany Griffith-Jones stresses, poor people may lack income and barely participate in formal financial markets. Yet financial crises—through multiple transmission channels—can hurt them badly. Thus international financial stability is important for all people.

Moreover, poor people are often less able to cope with the crises and conflicts that accompany severe underprovision of global public goods. They also find it hard to live with malprovided goods—those shaped in a way that severely constrains the room for policy maneuver available to developing countries and local communities. Ronald U. Mendoza's chapter on the multilateral trade regime addresses this issue. Thus it is important to distinguish between publicness in form (consumption) and in substance. The relevant question is, does the global public good offer net benefits for all?

Lyla Mehta, in her chapter on water, also finds that this distinction is crucial. Water is a heavily embattled issue. Its properties are highly context-specific. As Mehta argues, water basically is not a public good. But given its increasing scarcity, it could be desirable to make water a global public good by policy design. Doing so could help ensure, at least to some extent, that it is available to all people. The notion of global public goods can thus be seen as an important policy tool for a rights-based approach to development.

Another theme emerging from the chapter analyses is the struggle between local and global interests in a particular good. Charles Perrings and Madhav Gadgil, for example, explain how the international community's desire for biodiversity conservation has been focused on the narrow goal of maintaining a global gene pool, whether through zoos and botanical gardens in industrial countries or through the preservation of biodiversity hotspots in developing countries. Yet what matters for local communities is maintaining ecosystems as a whole. Fortunately for poor people, the ex situ approach is of limited effectiveness and is being modified to emphasize integrated, comprehensive ecosystem management. This strategy will benefit local communities as well as the international one.

Different interests and approaches often arise because global interconnectedness is not well understood. Many policies are still conceived in terms of national self-interest and countries going it alone—in stark contrast to the indivisibility of fate in a globalizing world. For example, as Griffith-Jones shows, all countries have an interest in international financial stability. But many often fail to recognize this, or at least to act in ways that enhance such stability.

The same is true of the negative global spillovers that can result from the excessive disease burden in developing countries, as discussed by Dyna Arhin-Tenkorang and Pedro Conceição. Such spillovers transcend the health threats that have long been associated with high infection loads of communicable diseases. Global public goods are less likely to be adequately provided when their benefits and costs are not recognized and their importance is not sufficiently assessed.

Even when mutually beneficial arrangements are identified, their realization may be problematic. René Castro and Sarah Cordero show how Costa Rica's ability to provide carbon dioxide sequestration services could be matched with the desire of some industrial countries to buy such services. The revenues could help Costa Rica finance national policy objectives such as providing clean electricity to remote areas. But the evolving intricacies of this arrangement indicate that its implementation is complex and subject to uncertain interactions among countries.

Finally, Peter Eigen and Christian Eigen-Zucchi show how difficult it can be for individual actors, state or nonstate, to break out of a policy dilemma—however irrational and costly it may be. Corruption, the misuse of public office for private gain, undermines the provision of many public goods, nationally and internationally. Corruption control is a global public good that hinges on enhanced publicness and often enhanced globalness—namely, cross-border cooperation.

INTERNATIONAL FINANCIAL STABILITY AND MARKET EFFICIENCY AS A GLOBAL PUBLIC GOOD

STEPHANY GRIFFITH-JONES

Global public goods can be shaped and provided in different ways. Their utility for different parts of the world's population depends on both their quantitative levels (in terms of issues such as adequate spending) and their qualitative properties (involving areas such as ownership of policy reforms).

This chapter examines the global public good of financial stability and market efficiency by focusing on one if its main elements, the international financial architecture. The current international financial architecture is of limited utility—and sometimes even disutility—for developing countries. Most reforms of this architecture have focused on crisis prevention and management, emphasizing efforts by developing countries rather than industrial countries or private financial actors.

But there are ways to correct this situation. All stakeholders have an interest in financial stability and all are at least somewhat interested in economic growth in developing countries. Achieving such growth requires more than just financial stability: it also requires increased financial efficiency. But most industrial countries and private actors have only a moderate interest in increased financial efficiency in developing countries. Thus further reforms require developing country initiatives such as advocacy, building coalitions with the development community and civil society organizations, and pooling expertise and forming strategic alliances.

FINANCIAL STABILITY AND MARKET EFFICIENCY: AN IMPORTANT GLOBAL PUBLIC GOOD FOR DEVELOPING COUNTRIES

Normal financial volatility is priced through higher risk premiums or higher required returns and so requires no public intervention. But excess volatility that

The author is grateful to Arnab Acharya, Amar Bhattacharya, Ricardo Gottschalk, and John Langmore for stimulating discussions.

leads to crises cannot be appropriately priced. When foreign investors run to the exit in some or all emerging markets because of trouble in one, contagion transforms a national public bad into a regional and eventually global public bad.

If excess volatility is the global public bad, what is the corresponding global public good? Much of the literature on this topic focuses on financial stability, notably crisis prevention and management (see Rosengren and Jordan 2000 and Little and Olivei 1999). But while international financial efficiency cannot be achieved without market stability, stability without efficiency is pointless. The provision of both is a global public good. Once achieved, international financial stability and market efficiency are nonrivalrous and nonexcludable, and so possess the properties of a pure global public good. Yet as explained by Kaul and Mendoza in this volume, the publicness of a good simply means that it is public in consumption, affecting all. It does not necessarily mean that it has the same utility for all actors.

So how are the costs of financial instability and excess volatility and the benefits of financial stability and efficiency distributed across countries and groups? For instability, a growing literature—World Bank (2001, pp. 73–74), Reisen and Soto (2000), Obstfeld (1998), and Hausmann (1996)—suggests a strong negative link between financial and macroeconomic volatility and economic growth. Caprio and Klingebiel (2002), Conceição (in this volume), Honohan and Klingebiel (forthcoming) and IMF (1998) document the significant costs of crises in terms of lost output and show how developing countries are particularly vulnerable and suffer high economic costs from financial instability.

Financial efficiency, by contrast, can contribute to development through lower intermediation costs and more sustainable allocations of scarce capital. An efficient international financial architecture also implies that developing countries have better access to capital needed for development and growth. Theoretical and empirical analyses suggest that such capital may be the main benefit of participating in a stable, efficient international financial market (see Agénor 2001; Soto 2000; and Feldstein 1999).

Industrial countries also gain from financial stability and efficiency, including through higher returns on investments in developing countries. In addition, stable growth in developing countries provides new markets for industrial country exporters and increasingly profitable opportunities for industrial country investors, particularly multinational corporations.

More important, poor people in developing countries are also likely to gain from financial stability and market efficiency. As the financial crises of the 1990s showed, the poor often shoulder significant costs during financial instability, despite being innocent bystanders (Friedman and Levinsohn 2001; Berry, Friedman, and Levinsohn 1999; Walton and Manuelyan 1998; Chomthongdi 1998). Such crises hurt the poor in many ways, including through cuts in social spending, slower economic growth, and rising unemployment. Even during stable periods many developing countries lack adequate access to private and official flows, impeding growth and poverty reduction. Hence poor people in these countries are also hurt by inefficient capital markets—perhaps more silently but no less severely than by "loud" financial crises.

REQUIRED NEW ARCHITECTURE AND PROGRESS SO FAR

International financial stability and market efficiency result from many elements. Among the most important are the workings of the international financial architecture. This section first examines the elements that this architecture should include to foster growth in developing countries, then compares today's architecture with the desired one. Though a lot of progress has been made on international financial reform since the financial crises of the late 1990s, significant gaps remain.

Essential features

Given the dramatic changes—and crises—in international financial markets over the past decade, industrial and developing countries face a difficult challenge in creating an international financial architecture that supports growth and development. International private capital flows have become large and extremely volatile, and international financial institutions play a smaller role. Though there is no clear blueprint for the new architecture, its key functions have emerged from international discussions and from parallels in mature national credit and capital markets. The international financial architecture should:

- Promote transparency and regulation of international loan and capital markets.
- Provide sufficient official liquidity in times of distress or crisis.
- Develop mechanisms for debt standstills and orderly debt workouts at the international level.
- Provide mechanisms for development finance.

Transparency and regulation will help prevent crises. Official liquidity and debt standstills and workouts will help manage crises better, minimizing their damage. Development finance will channel more public flows to developing countries, particularly those with minimal access to private capital markets. Development finance can also help finance other global public goods and bolster social protection schemes, which are crucial to protect poor people in times of distress. For the international financial architecture to perform these functions, multilateral lending will have to increase.

For at least three reasons, these international mechanisms should be complemented at the regional level (Ocampo 2000). First, growth in intraregional trade and investment has significantly increased macroeconomic links, increasing the potential for regional contagion during crises. One advantage of a regional approach is that information asymmetries are smaller than at the international level. Hence some policies and functions, such as mutual surveillance, can be better performed at the regional level. Second, contagion during crises almost always starts within regions (Sachs and Radelet 1998). Thus regional mechanisms can complement international mechanisms, particularly for liquidity provision, as a first line of defense. Such a mechanism is being developed by the Association of South-East Asian Nations plus China, Japan, and the Republic of Korea (ASEAN+3) and has existed for several decades in the European Union. Third, regional mechanisms will give smaller developing countries access to a broader range of institutions for crisis management and help them negotiate a more inclusive international financial architecture.

Still, no matter how significant regional arrangements may become, they should be seen as complements to—not substitutes for—international financial institutions such as the International Monetary Fund (IMF), World Bank, and Bank for International Settlements. In addition, some national measures are indispensable, because the provision of financial stability and efficiency must start at the national level. Furthermore, national and international measures are mutually reinforcing. But national measures alone would not be adequate or desirable (Fernandez-Arias and Hausmann 2000; Schneider 2001).

Progress to date
Since the late 1990s several steps have been taken to strengthen the international financial architecture. The IMF's lending facilities for crisis prevention and management have been expanded and adapted, and its total resources have been increased (see www.imf.org/external/np/exr/facts/quotas.htm). Institutional innovations such as the Financial Stability Forum[1] have been introduced to identify vulnerabilities and systemic risks, fill gaps in regulations, and develop consistent regulations for all types of financial institutions. And in 1999 the G-20, with representatives from both industrial and developing countries, was created to advance international financial reform.[2]

In addition, developing countries have taken steps to reduce their vulnerability, including by pursuing more prudent macroeconomic policies and adopting internationally accepted financial codes and standards—though there are concerns that there are too many standards (64) and that they are too uniform. Some analysts have called for greater flexibility in using these standards (Pistor 2000; UN 2000). Others have argued for a more inclusive process for their development, because developing countries are asked to implement them without being involved in their design (Griffith-Jones and others 2001).

Thus while there has been progress in reforming the international financial architecture, serious problems remain. First, efforts have been insufficient given the changes required. For example, there is no framework for debt standstills or workouts. Second, no significant initiatives have been made to ensure stable, long-term capital flows to the developing world. Third, there are concerns about a possible reversal on international financial reform should the G-7 take positions like those in the March 2000 report to the U.S. Congress by the International Financial Institutions Advisory Commission (IFIAC 2000). Better known as the Meltzer Report, it argued for drastic cuts in the scale and functions of international financial institutions, particularly the IMF. Such a reversal would be deeply counterproductive, particularly for developing countries. Finally, reform of the international financial architecture has been marked by stark asymmetries in three key areas: strong reform pressures on developing countries but inadequate reforms at the international level, more attention to crisis prevention and management than financial efficiency, and better representation for industrial countries and private market actors than developing countries.

Strong reform pressures on developing countries but inadequate reforms at the international level. More progress has been made on changes at the national level—in developing countries—than at the international level. For example, developing countries are being urged to adopt financial codes and standards to enhance transparency for market actors. But there are few if any corresponding obligations for disclosure by private financial institutions, including highly leveraged ones such as hedge funds.

Furthermore, while developing countries are making impressive progress in improving regulation of their financial systems, large gaps remain in international regulation of institutions such as hedge funds. Moreover, progress has been slow on changing bank regulations that favor short-term flows to developing countries. Some proposed changes to international regulation also present problems. Increasing reliance on banks' risk assessment models—a proposed reform of Basel capital adequacy requirements—will likely amplify the procyclical nature of international bank lending. It will also likely increase loan costs and reduce bank lending to developing countries (Griffith-Jones and Spratt 2001).

In recent years many developing countries have adopted more prudent macroeconomic policies, which is positive. But some are also implementing costly self-insurance against crises (UNCTAD 2001b), including high foreign exchange reserves and deflationary biases in macroeconomic policies. For example, according to the Report of the High-Level Panel on Financing for Development (UN 2001), also known as the Zedillo report, developing countries hold about $300 billion more in foreign reserves today than they did before the East Asian crisis—an increase of about 60 percent. These self-insurance policies are needed largely because an appropriate international financial architecture is not in place. Thus they are second-best policies—and they hamper growth and poverty reduction. Furthermore, not all countries can pursue such a costly strategy. For example, East Asia's crisis countries have had varying capacity to accumulate reserves since the

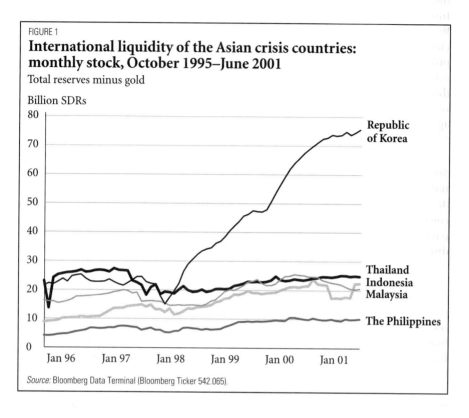

FIGURE 1

International liquidity of the Asian crisis countries: monthly stock, October 1995–June 2001

Total reserves minus gold

Source: Bloomberg Data Terminal (Bloomberg Ticker 542.065).

region's financial crisis began in July 1997. Of the five main crisis countries, only the Republic of Korea has been able to significantly increase reserves (figure 1).

Moving from crisis prevention to crisis management at the international level, it seems important to increase IMF resources to meet the financing needs of a systemic crisis involving several countries without compromising the liquidity needed to meet normal demands on IMF resources. Former IMF Managing Director Michel Camdessus and others—including the influential U.S. Council on Foreign Relations and representatives from developing countries—have suggested that this increase in emergency financing be partly funded by temporary, self-liquidating issues of IMF Special Drawing Rights (SDRs). This proposal merits further consideration because it would compensate for reductions or reversals in private flows and only temporarily boost world liquidity (Ocampo 2000).

Further modifying the IMF's Contingency Credit Line is a more modest but also important change to facilitate rapid liquidity support. This facility could automatically disburse credit when a crisis occurs in a country that has received favorable recent evaluations from the IMF (that is, during Article IV consultations[3]). This change would make a large number of countries eligible for the Contingency Credit Line—though few would necessarily ask for disbursements—eliminating the stigma on its use.

Finally, faster progress is needed on an international framework for debt standstills and workouts. UNCTAD (2001a) suggests combining voluntary mechanisms for debt restructuring with internationally sanctioned standstills. Krueger (2001, 2002) offers useful proposals in this regard.

More attention to crisis prevention and management than financial efficiency. Current reforms of the international financial architecture are focused on crisis prevention and management. Though important for middle-income countries with access to capital markets, the focus on these issues has neglected equally—if not more—important issues of liquidity and development finance for low-income countries. For liquidity, IMF facilities for low-income countries (such as the Compensatory Financing Facility and the Poverty Reduction and Growth Facility) should be made more flexible given the volatility in oil prices and the vulnerability of these countries to trade shocks.

For development finance, low-income countries need more multilateral lending and official flows, as well as speedy debt relief. Yet multilateral lending to low-income countries, especially in the form of official development assistance, has fallen sharply. Total official development assistance fell from $55 billion in 1998 to $45 billion in 1999, then to $39 billion in 2000 (World Bank 2001). The cyclicality and volatility of these important flows are also cause for concern. One study found that more than two-thirds of 38 African countries receive procyclical aid, and these flows are about twice as volatile as the recipients' GDP (Pallage and Robe 2000). Both features inhibit the consumption-smoothing effects of these flows and should be addressed.

Furthermore, donors, low-income countries, and international organizations—including international financial institutions—should collaborate so that more developing countries attract international flows of private capital. Sufficient, stable development finance from private and official sources is essential for growth and poverty reduction in the poorest countries. Foreign direct investment is important in this regard because it is more stable and long term than other capital flows (Lipsey 1999). Foreign direct investment is also strongly correlated with growth in developing countries (Soto 2000). Yet in 2000, 10 countries received 77 percent of all foreign direct investment in developing countries; 7 of the 10 were also among the top 10 recipients in 1985 (UN 2001, p. 52). Thus mechanisms are needed to broaden access to such flows and to encourage private flows to developing countries more generally.

Better representation for industrial countries and private market actors than developing countries. Developing countries are poorly represented in international financial decisionmaking, particularly in the IMF, World Bank, and Bank for International Settlements (see Buira in this volume). These international financial institutions need to consider more representative governance in parallel with a redefinition of their functions. And although developing countries are represented in some of the Financial Stability Forum's working groups, they are not included in its plenary meetings. It is particularly urgent that developing countries be fully represented in the forum because the issues discussed there have potentially profound effects on the their economies, and their insights could contribute to the forum's valuable work.

As noted, developing countries should also be represented on standard-setting bodies such as the Basel committees. The progress being made on new "soft" international law involves a small number of national authorities—usually from G-7 or G-10 countries—agreeing to certain standards.[4] These standards are then implemented in those countries and passed on as international standards that are broadly implemented in developing countries, often as a result of IMF or World Bank loan conditions or market pressures. This approach has been effective in spreading some regulatory measures but not others. Moreover, regulatory concerns in developing countries are unlikely to be reflected in the process for designing new standards, leading many developing countries to argue that there should be "no standardization without representation."[5]

Both the quantity and the quality of developing country representation need to be addressed. Developing country representatives at the IMF and World Bank, for example, are required to represent too many countries on too many issues. This is partly due to the small number of developing country representatives on the executive boards of these institutions. In addition, developing country representatives do not receive sufficient technical support from their countries or from the other developing countries they represent. Industrial country representatives, by contrast, often receive the full support of the research units in their central banks and finance ministries.

THE POLITICS OF INTERNATIONAL FINANCIAL REFORM

It is not for lack of ideas that international financial reform has not gone farther. Goldstein (2001) and Eichengreen (1999) review numerous reform proposals on such issues as an international lender of last resort, an international bankruptcy court, private sector bail-ins, transparency, the size and role of the IMF, and standards and regulations. So what is impeding further progress? To answer that question, this section first examines how different stakeholders view the goals of enhanced financial stability and market efficiency and of enabling developing countries to share more of the benefits of this global public good. It then explores which reforms the different stakeholders support.

Political support for enhanced reform
Many stakeholders participate, officially or unofficially, in international debates and negotiations on financial reform and the development of a new international

financial architecture. These participants usually include government officials from industrial and developing countries—mainly representing central banks and finance ministries—as well as representatives of banks and financial markets. Other participants may include representatives of national aid agencies, parliaments, trade unions, nonfinancial multilateral agencies, and international financial institutions. Only recently have civil society organizations started to focus on international financial architecture issues other than developing countries' debt (Scholte 2001). To keep the analysis manageable, the focus here is on the three main groups of actors: government representatives from industrial countries, government representatives from developing countries, and bank and financial market representatives. (Civil society organizations are considered in the next section, on policy options.)

All the key stakeholders share two objectives: international financial stability and economic growth in developing countries (table 1). Growth is the main objective for developing countries, but for industrial countries and financial market participants it is a secondary concern. Stability is also a secondary concern of market actors. But the crucial point is that there are shared concerns and common ground for beneficial policy reform—making the limited progress on such reform all the more puzzling.

TABLE 1

Objectives of key stakeholders in efforts to reform the international financial architecture

Stakeholder	Main objectives	Secondary objectives
Industrial country governments[a]	• Growth in their economies and other major economies • Profits for their financial sectors • International financial stability and market efficiency	• Growth in developing countries • No international financial crises and no requests for large bailouts
Developing country governments[a]	• Growth in their economies • International financial stability and market efficiency • Stable, sufficient capital flows	• Growth in industrial countries
Banks and financial markets	• Large profits	• International financial stability[b] • Growth in industrial and developing countries

a. Mainly representatives of central banks and finance ministries.
b. Though most financial stakeholders share this objective (in a relatively weak way), some (such as hedge funds) benefit from a certain amount of volatility.

Political support for specific measures
Underlying the general consensus on the broad goals of financial reform are very different views on the desirability of specific reforms. (Table 2 lists the most common of these reforms, some of which are considered below.) Consider capital account liberalization. Banks, which wield enormous influence in industrial countries, seek large profits as their main objective. Hence they strongly prefer open capital accounts, which allow them to move funds quickly across countries. Other participants in international financial markets (hedge funds, mutual funds, options traders) also benefit from this setup.

If such movements are determined by the economic fundamentals of the host country, they enhance efficiency and should be welcomed. But this open environment can also generate excess volatility in arbitrage and speculation, undermining the efficiency of resource allocation and provoking costly crises. Indeed, some financial actors—such as hedge funds—exploit increased exchange rate volatility during crises. Such actors will resist measures to restrict or regulate capital account openness.

Industrial country governments generally share this preference for open economies and free markets (though recent crises have somewhat tempered their views on capital account liberalization). Developing countries, on the other hand, stand to gain more from a gradual opening of their capital accounts. These countries will only benefit from this process if it favors long-term flows and if they are prudent about liberalizing short-term and easily reversible flows, to help avoid crises. Most developing countries that have opened their capital accounts have done so as part of World Bank and IMF programs, reflecting the pressures and preferences of industrial countries and their financial sectors.

On the proposals to provide sufficient liquidity during crises by adapting the IMF's Contingency Credit Line or by issuing temporary, self-liquidating Special Drawing Rights (SDRs), implementation is lacking because industrial country governments oppose both measures.[6] The U.S. government, which has veto power on the IMF board, is especially resistant. One reason is that industrial countries can borrow in international capital markets on terms similar to what they would receive with such an allocation. But this option is not available to developing countries, which must borrow at a premium (UNCTAD 2001b, p. 22).

As for increased development finance, developing countries clearly support it. Market participants vaguely support it because they benefit indirectly from development finance that helps strengthen banking systems or stock markets in developing countries. But several of the main industrial country governments oppose more development finance. Indeed, the Meltzer Report (IFIAC 2000) recommends significantly reducing development lending. As a result there has been no increase in development finance, and there is even a risk of a decrease (as noted earlier with trends in official development assistance).

TABLE 2

Attitudes of key stakeholders toward specific reforms of the international financial architecture

Reform	Industrial country governments	Developing country governments	Banks and financial markets	Outcome
Capital account liberalization	Support	Reluctant	Support	Implemented[a]
Codes and standards	Support	Some oppose or have reservations	Vaguely support	Implemented
Sufficient official international liquidity	Reluctant	Support	Support	Not implemented[b]
Increased development finance	Very reluctant	Support	Vaguely support	Not implemented
Sufficient, appropriate international regulation	Lukewarm	Lukewarm, linked to representation	Do not support	Not implemented
Debt standstills and orderly workouts	Support, some quite strongly	Support is weak but interest varies	Do not support	Not implemented
Increased developing country participation	Very reluctant	Support	Indifferent	Not implemented

a. By most developing countries. Some major ones—such as China and India—have taken a more gradual, prudent approach.
b. Though IMF resources have been increased and new facilities have been created since the East Asian crisis of the late 1990s, there is insufficient liquidity for quick disbursements should crises occur and spread.

Despite extensive discussions on a rule-based framework for debt standstills and workouts, including in the G-10 and the IMF, there has been little action thus far. Some industrial country governments, backed by the IMF and World Bank, are eager for progress in this area (Brown 2001; Krueger 2001). But most market participants are strongly opposed because of fears that such a framework will make it easier for developing countries to postpone or reduce debt servicing or other capital outflows. Some developing countries, especially Latin American ones and the Russian Federation, also oppose such a framework because they fear that it would discourage new private flows, increase their costs in normal times, and accelerate initial outflows during crises.

Progress has also been limited on increasing developing country participation in global governance. The creation of the G-20 is a welcome development, but it does not appear to be a decisionmaking body. Moreover, international groups such as the Financial Stability Forum have been created with almost no developing country representation—because most industrial country governments oppose it. Canada, the Netherlands, and Scandinavian countries tend to be far more open to such participation, as are most foreign affairs and development cooperation ministries or departments. And the September 2000 Commonwealth Finance Ministers Meeting, which included Australia, Canada, New Zealand, the United Kingdom, and many developing countries, explicitly endorsed developing country participation. Yet the treasuries and central banks of some of the main industrial countries, and especially their civil servants, resist such participation.

Thus when industrial country governments and market participants support reforms, they tend to be implemented. When developing countries support reforms, no action occurs. Industrial country governments seem to be the key stakeholder group, though banks and market actors are also influential. This pattern persists because the reforms of primary interest to developing countries would require industrial countries to provide resources or take other policy action.

SHAPING THE REFORM AGENDA: POSSIBLE INITIATIVES FOR DEVELOPING COUNTRIES

To accelerate and deepen international financial reform, developing countries will have to adopt measures that change the incentives of the two other main stakeholder groups—especially industrial country governments.

Demonstrate win-win opportunities

Developing country governments could argue that a new international financial architecture would provide a key pillar for their sustained economic growth and poverty reduction—in the context of a well-managed global economy—and that such growth would contribute to higher global growth, benefiting all actors. The global public good nature of financial stability and market efficiency also needs to be emphasized. Indeed, developing countries should be guided by a vision—of the possible and the desirable—that industrial and developing countries can jointly achieve.

Adopt and present common positions

Developing countries should try to develop strong common positions on reforms of the international financial architecture. This is a challenging task because there is considerable diversity across developing countries in development levels and patterns as well as in main needs and priorities for a new financial architecture. Different needs should be packaged and alliances formed so that different groups of developing countries support each other's interests. Developing countries and other concerned stakeholders should build more on what unites them than what divides them, particularly in terms of their joint global interests and the common goal of convergence (South Centre 2001). The leadership of larger, more influential developing countries—Brazil, China, India, Republic of Korea, Mexico, the Russian Federation, and South Africa—will prove crucial in this regard.

Strengthen and pool developing country expertise

To elaborate these common positions, developing countries need to focus their efforts and pool technical capacities. This can be done through existing institutions such as the G-24 or G-77, or by creating a new high-level panel of developing country politicians and experts to develop an integrated vision of international financial architecture reform (South Centre 2001).[7] Developing countries also need stronger capacity to respond to proposed changes and undertake reforms. As noted, developing country representatives—particularly in international financial institutions—would benefit greatly from increased research capacity.

Build coalitions with the international development community and civil society organizations

Some actors in industrial countries are more sympathetic than others to developing country concerns. Potential allies include development cooperation ministries, trade and industry ministries (if they are looking for new markets and opportunities), and nonfinancial international companies such as multinational corporations (if they support stable, rapid growth in developing countries). A dialogue between developing countries and political parties in key industrial countries—especially parliamentarians—is also important, because many seem likely to be sympathetic to developing country positions and to the common pursuit of financial stability and market efficiency. Groups such as Parliamentarians for Global Action could play an important role in this respect.

Civil society organizations and UN agencies would also be important dialogue counterparts. Civil society organizations in industrial countries are particularly important because they are often influential with their countries' governments, media, and international financial institutions. When focused on a specific issue, such as development or poverty reduction, civil society organizations can be highly effective—as with the strong influence of Jubilee 2000 on debt relief for heavily indebted poor countries.[8]

Promote regional institutions and complements to international financial institutions

Developing countries could also construct more regional institutions and mechanisms to complement international institutions. For instance, existing mechanisms created by regional institutions such as ASEAN+3 need to be developed further and replicated in other regions. As noted, such entities are particularly relevant in areas such as regional surveillance, coordination of macroeconomic policies, and mechanisms for liquidity provision. Regional mechanisms can also strengthen the bargaining position of developing countries for a better international financial architecture.

Link commitments to national reforms to international reforms

Finally, developing country markets—including their financial ones—are of great interest to industrial country investors, lenders, and exporters. The extent to which developing countries strengthen and regulate their financial systems, as well as liberalize their capital accounts, directly affects these interests. Thus developing countries could say that they would be far more willing to implement initiatives of interest to industrial countries (such as financial regulation or more open capital accounts) if industrial countries started reforming the international financial architecture in ways that facilitate more stable capital flows to developing countries.

Similarly, developing countries could argue that their implementation of codes and standards should be linked to new regulations of industrial countries' financial markets that help avoid excessive surges of potentially reversible capital flows. These regulations could complement mechanisms that encourage long-term capital flows and be accompanied by international liquidity mechanisms—with few or no conditions attached—that protect developing countries from crises and prevent contagion. Thus developing countries with prudent macroeconomic policies and regulatory systems could have almost automatic access to sufficient IMF lending if hit by contagion or terms of trade shocks. Low-income countries in that group should be given sufficient access not just to international liquidity but also to development finance. Collective action problems can be overcome if genuine concessions are made by both industrial and developing countries.

Conclusion

Developing countries could draw useful lessons from the bargaining tactics used and the vision presented by John Maynard Keynes in the Bretton Woods negotiations, which led to the creation of the postwar international financial order (Skidelsky 2001a, b). In bargaining, Keynes presented two alternatives: an "ideal" scheme with key international elements (such as a large, capable IMF) and a "second best" case in which the international financial system was not properly developed and the United Kingdom would reluctantly follow a far more closed approach to trade and the capital account. A similar argument, adapted to the features of today's world economy, could be made by developing countries. The two options for the international community are to:

- Construct an international financial architecture that supports development and makes crises far less likely and less costly—not just for developing countries but for the world economy as a whole. Developing countries can contribute to this new architecture by implementing standards, pursuing sound macroeconomic policies, and fully liberalizing their capital accounts.

- Tolerate an incomplete, lopsided international financial architecture that cannot guarantee support for developing countries' aims. Under such a system developing countries will not be able to fully open their capital accounts and integrate with the world economy. Instead they will have to defend their policymaking autonomy to protect their interests in a "second best" international financial system.

Developing countries—like Keynes in the 1940s—could show that the "first best" international financial architecture is superior because it would benefit all actors. It would support more stable growth in developing countries as well as benefit many actors in industrial countries. Perhaps more important, it would immediately increase international financial stability and efficiency. Just as Keynes appealed to U.S. internationalism and liberalism to help overcome opposition to his proposals, developing countries could appeal to U.S. ideals of supporting and deepening the market economy around the world. Also like Keynes, developing countries should prepare a clear vision and blueprint of the elements that would need to be included in a "first best" international financial system.

NOTES

1. The Financial Stability Forum was convened in April 1999 to promote international financial stability through information exchange and international cooperation in financial supervision and surveillance. It brings together on a regular basis national authorities responsible for financial stability in significant international financial centers, international financial institutions, sector-specific international groupings of regulators and supervisors, and committees of central bank experts. It seeks to coordinate the efforts of these bodies in order to promote international financial stability, improve the functioning of markets, and reduce systemic risk (http://www.fsforum.org/).

2. The G-20 is a forum for industrial countries and emerging markets to discuss and assess policy issues, with a view to promoting international financial and economic stability. This international forum of finance ministers and central bank governors includes 19 countries, the European Union, and the Bretton Woods Institutions (the International Monetary Fund and the World Bank). The G-20 member countries include Argentina, Australia, Brazil, Canada, China, France, Germany, India, Indonesia, Italy, Japan, Republic of Korea, Mexico, the Russian Federation, Saudi Arabia, South Africa, Turkey, the United Kingdom, and the United States (http://www.g20.org/indexe.html).

3. In accordance with Article IV of its Articles of Agreement, the IMF holds consultations, normally every year, with each of its members. These consultations are not limited to macroeconomic policies, but touch on all policies that significantly affect the macroeconomic performance of a country, which, depending upon circumstances, may include labor and environmental policies and the economic aspects of governance. (http://www.imf.org/external/np/exr/facts/surv.htm)

4. The G-10 is composed of the countries that participate in the General Arrangements to Borrow. These arrangements were established in 1962, when the governments of eight IMF members—Belgium, Canada, France, Italy, Japan, the Netherlands, the United Kingdom, and the United States—and the central banks of two others—Germany and Sweden—agreed to make resources available to the IMF for drawings by participants and, under certain circumstances, nonparticipants. The G-10 was strengthened in 1964 with the addition of Switzerland, then a nonmember of the IMF, but its name remained (http://www.imf.org/external/np/exr/facts/groups.htm#G10).

5. This phrase was coined by Gerry Helleiner.

6. SDRs have not been issued since 1981.

7. Established in 1971, the G-24 on International Monetary Affairs has one main objective: aligning the positions of developing countries on monetary and development finance issues. For a complete list of member countries, see http://www.g24.org/. Established in 1964, the G-77 is composed of developing countries that signed the Joint Declaration of the Seventy-Seven Countries, issued at the end of the first session of the United Nations Conference on Trade and Development (UNCTAD) in Geneva. For a complete list of member countries, see http://www.g77.org/.

8. For more information, see, for instance, http://www.jubilee2000uk.org and http://www.jubileeusa.org.

REFERENCES

Agénor, Pierre-Richard. 2001. "Benefits and Costs of International Financial Integration: Theory and Facts." Paper prepared for the conference on Financial Globalization: Issues and Challenges for Small States, 27–28 March, Saint Kitts. [http://www1.worldbank.org/wbiep/macro-program/agenor/pdfs/Benefits_and_Costs.pdf].

Berry, Steven, Jed Friedman, and James Levinsohn. 1999. "Impacts of the Indonesian Economic Crisis: Price Changes and the Poor." NBER Working Paper 7194. National Bureau of Economic Research, Cambridge, Mass. [http://papers.nber.org/papers/W7194].

Bloomberg Data Terminal. Bloomberg Professional Service. [http://about.bloomberg.com/professional/profservice.html]

Brown, Gordon. 2001. Speech given by Chancellor of the Exchequer to the Federal Reserve Bank of New York, 16 November, New York.

Caprio, Gerald, and Daniela Klingebiel. 2002. "Episodes of Systemic and Borderline Financial Crises." In Daniel Klingebiel and Luc Laeven, eds. *Managing the Real and Fiscal Effects of Banking Crises*. World Bank Discussion Paper 428. Washington, D.C.: The World Bank.

Chomthongdi, Jacques-Chai. 1998. "Overview of Social Impacts of the Economic Crisis." Paper prepared for the Thai Development Support Committee and Focus on the Global South, Bangkok, Thailand. [http://www.worldbank.org/eapsocial/library/socimpacts.pdf].

Eichengreen, Barry. 1999. *Toward a New International Financial Architecture: A Practical Post-Asia Agenda*. Washington, D.C.: Institute for International Economics.

Feldstein, Martin. ed. 1999. *International Capital Flows*. National Bureau of Economic Research conference report. Chicago: University of Chicago Press.

Fernandez-Arias, Eduardo, and Ricardo Hausmann. 2000. "The Redesign of the International Financial Architecture from a Latin American Perspective: Who Pays the Bill?" Working Paper 440. Inter-American Development Bank, Research Department, Washington, D.C.

Friedman, Jed, and James Levinsohn. 2001. "The Distributional Impacts of Indonesia's Financial Crisis on Household Welfare: A 'Rapid Response' Methodology." NBER Working Paper 8564. National Bureau of Economic Research, Cambridge, Mass. [http://papers.nber.org/papers/W8564].

Goldstein, Morris. 2001. "An Evaluation of Proposals to Reform the International Financial Architecture." Paper prepared for the National Bureau of Economic Research conference on Management of Currency Crises, 28–31 March, Monterey, Calif. [http://www.nber.org/books/mgmtcrises/goldstein5-2-01.pdf].

Griffith-Jones, Stephany. 1999. "A New Financial Architecture for Reducing Risks and Severity of Crises." University of Sussex, Institute of Development Studies, Brighton.

Griffith-Jones, Stephany, and Stephen Spratt. 2001. "Will the New Basel Capital Accord Have a Net Negative Effect on Developing Countries?" University of Sussex, Institute of Development Studies, Brighton. [http://www.ids.ac.uk/ids/global/finance/intfin2.html].

Griffith-Jones, Stephany, José Antonio Ocampo, and Jacques Cailloux. 1999. "The Poorest Countries and the Emerging International Financial Architecture."

Expert Group on Development Issues, Stockholm, Sweden. [http://www.ids. ac.uk/ids/global/Finance/pdfs/ocampo.pdf].

Griffith-Jones, Stephany, Ricardo Gottschalk, Brigitte Granville, and Stephen Spratt. 2001. "Reform of the International Financial Architecture: Views, Priorities and Concerns of Governments and the Private Sector in the Western Hemisphere and Eastern Europe." U.K. Department for International Development, London. [http://www.ids.ac.uk/ids/global/finance/intfin2.html].

Hausmann, Ricardo. 1996. "Macroeconomic Volatility and Economic Development: Institutional Dimensions." Inter-American Development Bank, Washington, D.C.

Honohan, Patrick, and Daniela Klingebiel. Forthcoming. "The Fiscal Cost Implications of an Accommodating Approach to Banking Crises." *Journal of Banking and Finance.*

IFIAC (International Financial Institutions Advisory Commission). 2000. *Report of the International Financial Institutions Advisory Commission* [also known as the Meltzer Report]. Washington, D.C.: U.S. Congress. [http://www.house.gov/jec/ imf/imfpage.htm].

IMF (International Monetary Fund). 1998. *World Economic Outlook 1998.* Washington, D.C.

Krueger, Anne. 2001. "International Financial Architecture for 2002: A New Approach to Sovereign Debt Restructuring." Address given at the National Economists Club Annual Members Dinner at the American Enterprise Institute, 26 November, Washington, D.C. [http://www.imf.org/external/np/speeches/ 2001/112601.htm].

———. 2002. *A New Approach to Sovereign Debt Restructuring.* Washington, DC: International Monetary Fund. [http://www.imf.org/external/pubs/ft/exrp/ sdrm/eng/sdrm.pdf].

Lipsey, Robert E. 1999. "The Role of Foreign Direct Investment in International Capital Flows." In Martin Feldstein, ed., *International Capital Flows.* National Bureau of Economic Research conference report. Chicago: University of Chicago Press.

Little, Jane Sneddon, and Giovanni P. Olivei, eds. 1999. *Rethinking the International Monetary System.* Conference Series 43. Boston, Mass.: Federal Reserve Bank of Boston.

Obstfeld, Maurice. 1998. "Financial Shocks and Business Cycles: Lessons from outside the United States." In Jeffrey C. Fuhrer and Scott Schuh, eds., *Beyond Shocks: What Causes Business Cycles?* Conference Series 42. Boston, Mass.: Federal Reserve Bank of Boston.

Ocampo, José Antonio. 2000. "Developing Countries' Anti-Cyclical Policies in a Globalised World." *Temas de Coyuntura* 13. Economic Commission for Latin America and the Caribbean, Santiago, Chile.

Pallage, Stéphane, and Michael Robe. 2000. "Foreign Aid and the Business Cycle." Working paper. University of Quebec at Montreal, Department of Economics, and American University, Kogod School of Business. [http://fmwww.bc.edu/ cef00/papers/paper107.pdf].

Pistor, Katharina. 2000. "The Standardization of Law and Its Effect on Developing Economies." G-24 Discussion Paper. Geneva. [http://www.unctad.org/en/docs/ pogdsmdpbg24d4.en.pdf].

Reisen, Helmut, and Marcelo Soto. 2000. "The Need for Foreign Savings in Post-Crisis Asia." Paper presented at the Asian Development Bank and OECD Development Centre Sixth International Forum on Asian Perspectives, 3 July, Paris.

Rosengren, Eric S., and John S. Jordan, eds. 2000. *Building an Infrastructure for Financial Stability.* Conference Series 44. Boston, Mass.: Federal Reserve Bank of Boston.

Sachs, Jeffrey, and Steven Radelet. 1998. "The East Asian Financial Crisis: Diagnosis, Remedies, Prospects." *Brookings Papers on Economic Activity.* Washington, D.C.: Brookings Institution.

Schneider, Benu. 2001. "International Financial Architecture: Have We Done Enough to Set It Right?" Paper presented at the Overseas Development Institute meeting on Financing for Development, 11 April, London. [http://www.odi.org.uk/ speeches/schneider7b.html].

Scholte, Jan Aart. 2001. "The Globalization of World Politics." In John Baylis and Steve Smith, eds., *The Globalization of World Politics: An Introduction to International Relations.* 2nd ed. Oxford: Oxford University Press.

Skidelsky, Robert. 2001a. *John Maynard Keynes: Fighting for Britain, 1937–1946.* London: Macmillan.

————. 2001b. "Keynes' Road to Bretton Woods: An Essay in Interpretation." Warwick Economics Research Paper Series. University of Warwick, Department of Economics, U.K.

Soto, Marcelo 2000. "Capital Flows and Growth in Developing Countries: Recent Empirical Evidence." Paper produced as part of the research program on Capital Movements and Development. Organisation for Economic Co-operation and Development, Development Centre, Paris. [http://www1.oecd.org/dev/PUBLI-CATION/tp/TP160.pdf].

South Centre. 2001. "Multilateral Funding for Middle Income Countries." In *Financing Development: Key Issues for the South.* Geneva.

UN (United Nations). 2000. "Towards a Stable International Financial System, Responsive to Challenges of Development, Especially in the Developing Countries." Report of the Secretary General. A/55/187. New York.

————. 2001. "Report of the High-Level Panel on Financing for Development [also known as the Zedillo Report]." New York. [http://www.un.org/reports/financ-ing/full_report.pdf].

UNCTAD (United Nations Conference on Trade and Development). 2001a. *Trade and Development Report 2001*. Geneva.

—————. 2001b. *World Investment Report 2001*. Geneva.

Van Wincoop, Eric. 1998. "How Big Are Potential Welfare Gains from International Risksharing?" *Journal of International Economics* 47: 109–35.

Walton, Michael, and Tamar Manuelyan. 1998. "Social Consequences of the East Asian Financial Crisis." World Bank. Washington, D.C. [http://www.world-bank.org/eapsocial/library/socconsq/index.htm].

World Bank. 2001. *Global Development Finance 2001: Building Coalitions for Effective Development Finance*. Washington, D.C.

THE MULTILATERAL TRADE REGIME: A GLOBAL PUBLIC GOOD FOR ALL?

RONALD U. MENDOZA

"[Like] putting a rabbit and a tiger in the same cage."
—A Sri Lankan activist, when asked about
free trade between developing and industrial countries

International trade continues to be a defining feature of national development policies. But the breakdown of the World Trade Organization (WTO) ministerial conference in Seattle, Washington (United States), in 1999 and the difficulties (if not near failure) of the conference in Doha, Qatar, in 2001 highlight the strained relations among WTO members—at times polarized by a divide between industrial and developing countries.[1] Both critics (see, for example, Rodrik 2001; Third World Network 2001; OXFAM International 2002) and supporters (see, for example, Srinivasan and Bhagwati 1999; Ben-David 2001; Greenaway, Morgan, and Wright 2002) of international trade do not see trade itself as the problem. All agree that trade has the potential to benefit developing countries. But disagreements arise on the structure of arrangements for multilateral trade.

This chapter responds to this problem by reviewing the multilateral trade regime through the lens of the global public goods concept. The analysis suggests that the trade regime is a global public good in form but not substance. The regime is largely public in consumption, but the distribution of its net benefits is skewed in favor of industrial countries. Correcting this imbalance would not only be good for developing countries, it would also enhance the functioning and stability of the trade regime—benefiting industrial countries.

The first section of the chapter examines the evolution of the multilateral trade regime since 1947. During that time the trade regime has taken on the form of a global public good. Yet the regime's increasing publicness has generated tensions between various groups of states as well as other stakeholders—notably in

_____

The author is indebted to Chandrika Bahadur, Mumtaz Keklik, and Kamal Malhotra of the United Nations Development Programme, Bureau for Development Policy, for enlightening discussions on the topic, as well as to anonymous referees for their comments and suggestions on earlier drafts.

terms of questions about its fairness. The main issue is whether and to what extent all countries derive a net benefit from trade rules and mechanisms. The evidence presented in the second section indicates problems of fairness. Relative to industrial countries, developing countries—and especially the least developed countries—derive smaller benefits and incur higher costs from the trade regime. The third section proposes reforms that could correct this situation, making the multilateral trade regime a global public good in form and substance. The overarching reform is to recast trade negotiations and rules in a way that recognizes the primacy of national development policies and provides flexible support for developing countries. More specific reforms are suggested to make this approach operational. The conclusion presents the chapter's main messages.

THE MULTILATERAL TRADE REGIME:
FROM CLUB GOOD TO GLOBAL PUBLIC GOOD

International regimes are often composed of rules and of organizational mechanisms to facilitate the negotiation and implementation of those rules. Today's multilateral trade regime is governed by the WTO, which was established in 1995 as the successor to the General Agreement on Tariffs and Trade (GATT). The GATT was created in 1947 but for nearly five decades functioned without a formal organizational arrangement.[2] Current multilateral trade rules are composed primarily of the GATT, the agreement on Trade-Related Aspects of Intellectual Property Rights (TRIPS), the General Agreement on Trade in Services (GATS), and the Dispute Settlement Understanding (DSU).[3] The WTO's main organizational elements include the Ministerial Conference, General Council, Dispute Settlement Body and Appellate Body, and Trade Policy Review Body (see Blackhurst 1998; Ruggie 1998; and Woolcock 1999).

An analysis of the regime fittingly begins with a description of its evolution over time. The analysis in this section covers both the "GATT period" and the "GATT/WTO" period. The discussion shows how membership in the regime has increased and become more diverse and how the issues covered by the regime have continuously widened.[4]

The trade regime from 1947 to today
The evolutions of the two international market systems—for trade and finance—are strikingly similar. In 1944, 45 countries created the International Monetary Fund (IMF) and World Bank, together known as the Bretton Woods institutions. Today these two institutions have 183 members and form the cornerstone of the international financial architecture. Similarly, the multilateral trade regime began in 1947 with 23 parties to the Protocol of Provisional Application of the GATT.[5] If the 1947 GATT is considered a club, then club membership and club rules have changed dramatically since its inception.

Club membership. In 1948 the 23 original parties to the GATT accounted for 60 percent of world merchandise trade. By 1994, coupled with new trade agreements from the Uruguay Round of negotiations, the number of contracting parties had quintupled. Today the WTO has 144 member countries that account for more than 90 percent of world merchandise exports and imports.[6]

Membership has become far more diverse. More than 70 percent of WTO members are developing countries, yet more than 80 percent of world merchandise exports come from just 30 countries—indicating wide disparities in trading capacity (World Bank 2001, p. 21). In 1992 the dispersion in per capita GDP (measured by the coefficient of variation) for a sample of GATT member countries was 0.92, up from 0.61 for a sample in 1950 (figure 1). With the accession of about 40 developing countries since 1992 and the pending accession of 27 more, this pattern of highly differentiated trading capacities will likely become more pronounced.[7]

Club rules. The scope and depth of the original GATT were quite minimal, dealing only with some provisional rules and giving member countries the flexibility to select sectors for liberalization. But the eight rounds of negotiations over the GATT's more than 50-year history have covered increasingly larger volumes and more aspects (such as dispute settlement, technical barriers, and so on) of international trade. The 1947 GATT was eventually replaced by the expanded 1994 GATT.[8] At the 1994 ministerial conference in Marrakech it was decided that the 1994 GATT, the TRIPS agreement, and the GATS would form the core legal

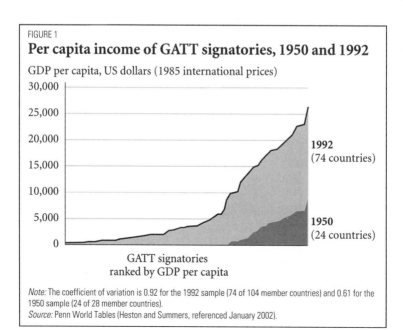

FIGURE 1

Per capita income of GATT signatories, 1950 and 1992

GDP per capita, US dollars (1985 international prices)

Note: The coefficient of variation is 0.92 for the 1992 sample (74 of 104 member countries) and 0.61 for the 1950 sample (24 of 28 member countries).
Source: Penn World Tables (Heston and Summers, referenced January 2002).

TABLE 1

Issues addressed by multilateral trade negotiations, 1947–present

Issue	First five rounds 1947–61[a]	Kennedy Round, 1963–67 (62 countries)	Tokyo Round, 1973–79 (102 countries)	Uruguay Round, 1986–94 (123 countries)	World Trade Organization, 2002–present (144 countries)[b]
Tariffs	•	•	•	•	•
Customs duties		•	•	•	•
Antidumping		•	•	•	•
Agriculture		•	•	•	•
Subsidies and countervailing duties		•	•	•	•
Technical barriers to trade			•	•	•
Import licensing			•	•	•
Public procurement			•	•	•
Safeguards			•	•	•
GATT articles			•	•	•
Dispute settlement			•	•	•
Code on civil aircraft (subsidies)			•	•	•
Rules of origin				•	•
Preshipment inspection				•	•
Textiles and clothing				•	•

GATT functions •••••

WTO (organizational issues) •••••

Investment •••••

TRIPS •••••

Services •••••

Industrial tariffs •••• ••••

Regional trade agreements ••••

Trade and the environment ••••

Capacity building ••••

Implementation issues[c] ••••

"Singapore issues"[d] ?

a. The first five rounds were the Geneva Round, 1947 (23 countries); Annecy Round, 1948 (13 countries); Torquay Round, 1950 (38 countries); Geneva Round, 1956 (26 countries); and Dillon Round, 1960–61 (26 countries).

b. As of January 2002.

c. Include, among other issues, further liberalization of textiles and agriculture (see http://www.wto.org/english/tratop_e/devel_e/d5prop_e.htm).

d. Include investment and public procurement (both of which were also covered by the Uruguay Round), competition policy, and trade facilitation. No formal decision has been made to start negotiations on these issues.

Source: Woolcock 1999, table 1.1; WTO 1999; http://www.wto.org.

ground rules for international commerce, facilitated by GATT's successor, the WTO. Under the single undertaking introduced in the Uruguay Round, member countries are to adhere to nearly these same rules. The next round of negotiations will cover even more aspects of international trade, further expanding this set of rules (table 1).

The Uruguay Round signaled a paradigm shift in the nature and structure of the trade regime. From being a minimalist set of agreements on reducing tariffs and nontariff barriers on traded goods, the regime grew to encompass both border and domestic issues for trade in both goods and services. The expanded GATT, together with the GATS, TRIPS agreement, and DSU, are now administered by the WTO, a full-fledged international organization with a mandate and vested authority to monitor and regulate specific trade matters. These changes have introduced a level of determinacy in the trade regime that was not present in the 1947 GATT.

Is the multilateral trade regime a global public good?

These changes in the scope and membership of the multilateral trade regime make it a global public good in form. The regime is available to a large group of member countries, and it has strong properties of nonrivalrous consumption and nonexcludable benefits.

In terms of nonrivalry, having more countries join the trade regime does not detract from the benefits to existing members. Common, established rules for trade can benefit all consumers and producers across countries and over time. In fact, having more members makes the regime's rules more valuable, increasing their legitimacy and credibility. This is especially important for the work of WTO units such as the Trade Policy Review Body and Dispute Settlement and Appellate bodies.

In terms of nonxcludability, there are two dimensions to consider: publicness of consumption and nonexclusivity (that is, potential openness to all countries). A number of WTO benefits are nonexcludable, with high publicness of consumption. For example, because the multilateral trade regime promotes a rule-based framework, it restrains inefficient protectionism and minimizes the probability of costly trade wars, both of which could disrupt international trade. The absence (or minimization) of these disruptions benefits all countries, members and nonmembers alike. Moreover, because the regime has a large (and growing) membership and covers a large (and growing) portion of international trade, its impact is likely to be significant and felt across all countries and regions. The regime's benefits (and costs) are available for the global public to consume—to some extent whether they choose to or not.

Furthermore, as more countries join, the portion of the market governed by the regime becomes larger and more diverse. Hence there are also benefits from network externalities and greater product variety (Funke and Ruhwedel 2001; Hummels and Klenow 2002; Rutherford and Tarr 2002). As a result better, cheaper products are enjoyed by more consumers. But perhaps most important, trade provides many countries with important development and growth benefits.[9] For all these reasons the rules of the club emphasize the expansion and nonexclusivity of membership, as long as new members accept existing rules.[10]

Tensions about trade between and within countries
Despite its properties as a global public good in form, the trade regime has started to see tensions arise on two main fronts. At the international level the dispersed development levels of member countries indicate varying capacities to combine participating in international trade with pursuing effective national development policies. There is growing concern in developing countries about the "bounced check" of the Uruguay Round, because industrial country markets continue to be highly protected—despite promises of greater access (Vajpayee 2001). Developing countries also often see themselves as "ruletakers," importing burdensome standards and regulations (such as the TRIPS agreement) that may not be compatible with their development policies (see Finger and Schuler 2001; Helleiner 2001; Ostry 2002; and Rodrik 2001).

Pressures have also increased within countries. There is growing awareness of the "social cost comparative advantage" of developing countries. As a result issues such as pollution-intensive manufacturing, unsustainable harvesting of natural resources, and child labor have resulted in a backlash (primarily in industrial countries) against "ecodumping" and "social dumping" (Birdsall and Lawrence 1999, pp. 132–42). Furthermore, the proliferation of nonstate actors in both industrial and developing countries has helped push for a broader agenda and more participatory trade negotiations. The increasing spread of democratic norms within countries has also created demand for their application at the international level, because many observers perceive the problems of globalization as stemming partly from this "democratic deficit." This issue has become even more important with the WTO's continued expansion into areas with a direct impact on domestic policymaking and lawmaking (see Helleiner 2001; Kennedy and Southwick 2002; Scholte, O'Brien, and Williams 1999; and Third World Network 2001).

Production of the multilateral trade regime—like production of all global public goods—requires national and international inputs, and the tensions above indicate that some of these inputs may be in jeopardy. Examples of national inputs for the trade regime include domestic trade policy reform, institutional capacity building, and provision of trade adjustment assistance and safety nets. International inputs include the 1994 GATT and other trade agreements as well as the WTO's ministerial conferences and Dispute Settlement and Appellate bodies. How the international inputs are shaped (and to begin with, their existence or absence) critically determines, by supporting or hindering, each country's capacity to provide national inputs. If a country's welfare gains from trade are small or shrinking—due in no small measure to the structure of international trade agree-

---

BOX 1

DEVELOPMENT REQUIRES MORE THAN FREE TRADE

The move toward freer international trade has its roots in David Ricardo's classical theory of comparative advantage, which is driven by inherent differences in countries' capacity—and hence cost—to produce different products and services. But much has changed since Ricardo's 1817 world of Portuguese wine and British clothing. Today's trade patterns reveal that comparative advantage, on which specialization in production and trade is based, can no longer be taken as a given. Beyond inherent differences in factor endowments, possible sources of comparative advantage now include increasing returns to scale, product differentiation, and technological differences. Enhancing comparative advantage in retainable industries—those with high startup costs, making small-scale entry difficult—can lead to more gains from trade and robust economic development. In retainable industries, market forces tend to bolster the status quo, suggesting the need for active government support of domestic industries. This also implies that some protection may be required to nurture and develop comparative advantage in these industries.

Source: Antweiler and Trefler 2002; Dollar 1993; Gomory and Baumol 2000; Hummels and Levinsohn 1993; Leamer 1993; Tybout 1993.

---

ments, as shown in the next section—it faces an added constraint on its social, economic, and institutional adjustments related to trade. This point has not been adequately considered as the trade regime has expanded and evolved into a global public good, causing it to come under severe stress.[11]

IS THE MULTILATERAL TRADE REGIME FAIR?

As with all goods, private and public, the multilateral trade regime is valuable only to the extent that it generates utility for its providers and users. Growing concern about its welfare effects on the different actors and stakeholders in trade is perhaps the unifying theme behind all the current tensions related to the regime. Developing countries in particular have reason to reevaluate the regime, taking into account the trade and development nexus that national and international policymakers have repeatedly emphasized.

Development and growth require more than just free trade—a costly lesson for many developing countries that have liberalized trade yet failed to reap its potential benefits (box 1). Making matters worse, these countries often face import-led consumption booms, appreciating real exchange rates (due to capital inflows), social dislocation, rising income inequality (between workers in export sectors and the rest of the population), and even deindustrialization (see

Wood 1995; Taylor 2001; and UNCTAD various years). Several fundamental questions have been raised about the multilateral trade regime: Do all countries benefit from trade? Is the trade regime balanced in terms of benefits and costs? Is the regime fair?

This section provides some preliminary answers to these questions. It first proposes some notions of fairness, then uses these to assess, in a tentative way, the fairness of the multilateral trade regime. Two aspects of the regime are examined. The first is whether and to what extent the projected outcomes of major Uruguay Round agreements benefit all regime members. The second is whether the regime addresses the main concerns of all country groups or whether it suffers gaps.

Measures of fairness

As Albin (in this volume) points out, the notion of fairness remains contested. Still, three aspects of fairness seem useful for evaluating the trade regime:

- *Neutrality.* Pareto efficiency is achieved if no individual can be made better off without making another individual worse off. If this notion of efficiency is recast as a notion of fairness, one could argue that the trade regime is fair in this limited sense—if it does not make any country worse off when it makes some countries better off. This minimalist or neutral notion of fairness requires, at the least, that the regime do no harm. Fairness, in this sense, would require that each country be at least as well off with the trade regime as it would be without it.

- *Net benefit for all.* One welfare-maximizing approach is to achieve the greatest good for all. Under this notion of fairness the multilateral trade regime (or its expansion) is fair if all member countries derive positive net benefits. In fact, if industrial countries were to benefit immensely from the regime through larger and faster-growing gains from trade (and leave behind developing countries in the process), the regime would still be fair in this sense if all countries were better off relative to the "no trade regime" scenario.

- *Maximin rule.* If the rules of the trade regime were chosen to maximize the gains to the least well-off member countries, the Rawlsian notion of fairness as process would obtain.[12] From the point of view of developing countries, particularly the least developed ones, fairness could reasonably mean nothing less than increasing net benefits from the trade regime—or alternatively, growth and development.

With these fairness measures, the chosen trade regime could be one that simply does not harm the progress of developing countries, implying a minimalist approach. Yet WTO policy statements suggest that the international community has chosen a more active approach to development. Under the WTO Articles of Agreement (WTO 1994, p. 9) all member countries recognize that "there is need for positive efforts designed to ensure that developing countries, and especially the least developed among them, secure a share in the growth in international trade commensurate with the needs of their economic development" (see Bhagwati 1998; Kapstein 1999; and Shafaeddin 2000 for other discussions of fair trade). The next step is to evaluate the net benefits from specific agreements in the Uruguay Round—the building blocks of the trade regime.[13]

Projected effects of Uruguay Round agreements

The Uruguay Round negotiations, in essence, was intended to give developing countries increased access to the protected agricultural, textiles, and manufacturing markets of industrial countries—in exchange for introducing agreements on investments, intellectual property rights, and trade in services, which primarily benefited industrial countries through increased rents and market access (see Ostry 2002). Measuring the cross-country distribution of the gains from this bargain would be a considerable task, requiring a cost-benefit examination of all the agreements. To keep the task manageable, the analysis here compares the welfare gains from all the agreements that were supposed to benefit developing countries (that is, the agreements requiring agricultural, textiles, and manufacturing reforms) with the costs of just one agreement that primarily interested some industrial countries (the agreement on TRIPS). The analysis shows that the projected net benefit is negative for developing countries (see McCalman 1999 for a similar analysis).

The likely cost for developing countries of the TRIPS agreement. Although the full implications of the TRIPS agreement—in terms of access to technology, transfers of rents, and changes in prices of patented products—will not be apparent for some time, some estimates of potential outcomes are available. If the TRIPS agreement were fully implemented, annual net rent transfers to the five main technology-creating countries (France, Germany, Japan, the United Kingdom, and the United States) alone would be about $38 billion in 2000 dollars (World Bank 2001, table 5.1).

What developing countries might gain in agriculture, textiles, and manufacturing. Harrison, Rutherford, and Tarr (1996) present one of the few disaggregated studies of the welfare impact of the Uruguay Round across regions. In their base (constant returns to scale) model they project that complete implementation of agricultural, textiles, and manufacturing reforms in both developing and industrial countries (based on the trade agreements negotiated) would provide developing countries with annual welfare gains of about $18 billion in 1992 dollars, or about $22 billion in 2000 dollars (table 2). Using a static increasing returns to scale model, developing countries' annual projected gains are about $24 billion, while under a steady-state increasing returns to scale model they are about $68 billion (in 2000 dollars).[14]

Net gains for developing countries. Assuming that full implementation of the TRIPS agreement would cost developing countries $38 billion (excluding the additional costs of price increases and implementation), a back-of-the-envelope calculation shows that under the base model the Uruguay Round causes a net annual loss of $16 billion for developing countries. Under the static increasing returns to scale model, developing countries stand to lose about $14 billion, while under the steady-state model they stand to gain $30 billion (see table 2).

TABLE 2

Projected annual effects of full implementation of trade-related agriculture, textiles, and manufacturing reforms agreed to under the Uruguay Round

(billions of U.S. dollars)

Region/country group	Base model	Static increasing returns to scale model	Steady-state increasing returns to scale model
	1992 dollars	1992 dollars	1992 dollars
Sub-Saharan Africa	−0.4	−0.3	−0.7
Middle East and North Africa	−0.4	−0.3	1.5
Eastern Europe and former Soviet Union	−0.4	−0.2	1.2
South Asia	3.3	3.7	6.7
	1992 dollars / 2000 dollars	1992 dollars / 2000 dollars	1992 dollars / 2000 dollars
World	92.9 / 114.0	96.0 / 117.9	170.6 / 209.5
Industrial countries	75.2 / 92.4	76.6 / 94.1	115.4 / 141.7
Developing countries	17.7 / 21.6	19.4 / 23.8	55.2 / 67.8
	2000 dollars	2000 dollars	2000 dollars
Effect of Uruguay Round on developing countries	21.6	23.8	67.8
Cost of TRIPS agreement	38.0	38.0	38.0
Net effect on developing countries	−16.4	−14.2	29.8

Note: Calculations for 2000 data assume an average U.S. inflation rate of 2.6 percent.
Source: World Bank 2001; Harrison, Rutherford, and Tarr 1996, tables 8.2, 8.6, and 8.7.

Harrison, Rutherford, and Tarr (1996) also forecast some scenarios for developing regions in which Sub-Saharan Africa, the Middle East and North Africa, and Eastern Europe and the former Soviet Union would lose out even without the TRIPS agreement. Sub-Saharan Africa suffers losses in all three models, ranging from $0.3–0.7 billion in 1992 dollars. The authors attribute some of these losses to worsened terms of trade for net food importers and to inefficient developing country producers (of textiles and clothing) losing market share. If these countries had to comply with the TRIPS agreement under these conditions, there would be little reason to expect any net benefits.[15]

In analyzing these results, several points are worth noting. First, industrial countries' annual gains—ranging from $92–142 billion in 2000 dollars—may be misleading under the common mercantilist notion of "concessions" because most of the gains are due to reductions in these countries' protectionist measures. Second, the gains of developing countries (without the TRIPS agreement) range from about a quarter (under the base and static models) to half (under the steady-state model) those of industrial countries—reasonably high given that developing countries accounted for only about a quarter of global trade at the time of the Uruguay Round. Third, these simple country groups mask the fact that a small group of developing countries receive most of the gains. Of the $17.7 billion a year that developing countries gain in the base model, $4.6 billion goes to the Republic of Korea, while China, Indonesia, Malaysia, the Philippines, Singapore, and Thailand together gain about $8.6 billion. Finally, net rent transfers from developing countries could be lower since some industrial countries could also be net importers of technology. Further research is required to ascertain the exact cost of the TRIPS agreement for the developing world.

Still, it is clear that some developing countries, such as those in Sub-Saharan Africa, are projected to receive negative net benefits from agricultural, textiles, and manufacturing reforms. In addition to their rent transfers, Sub-Saharan countries will also likely be more adversely affected by the TRIPS agreement, given the HIV/AIDS epidemic in that region.[16] And as the base and static models show, developing countries as a group could lose out in the short run, using the preliminary figure on net rent transfers.

These numbers are not conclusive by any means and are quite sensitive to modeling assumptions and revisions in implementation schedules. For instance, for most developing countries implementation of the TRIPS agreement has already been delayed until 2006 (and until 2016 for the least developed countries). In addition, liberalization of industrial countries' agriculture and textiles sectors has fallen short of expectations (World Bank 2001).[17] Still, these figures are useful indicators that the current multilateral trade regime, largely formed during the Uruguay Round, likely fails the neutrality (minimalist) measure of fairness. Its projected effects appear to be loaded against developing countries. (See Perroni 1998 and World Bank 2001 for an overview of other modeling results.)

TABLE 3

Variance in the growth rates of terms of trade, by region and country group, 1980–97

Variance	Region/country group
0.0308	West Asia
0.0299	Major petroleum exporters
0.0204	Oceania
0.0199	North Africa
0.0083	Africa
0.0038	Asia
0.0034	Other Africa
0.0030	All developing countries
0.0030	Non-major petroleum exporters, major exporters of manufactures
0.0028	Americas: non-major petroleum exporters, non-major exporters of manufactures
0.0026	Other Asia
0.0026	Other Asia: non-major petroleum exporters, non-major exporters of manufactures
0.0025	All heavily indebted countries
0.0022	Americas
0.0021	Non-major petroleum exporters, non-major exporters of manufactures
0.0021	All least developed countries
0.0018	West Asia: non-major petroleum exporters, non-major exporters of manufactures
0.0015	Non-major petroleum exporters
0.0014	Africa: non-major petroleum exporters, non-major exporters of manufactures
0.0008	All industrial countries

Note: Except for the last row, all regions and country groups refer to developing countries. Countries may belong to more than one country group.
Source: UNCTAD 2000.

Protection against trade shocks: a gap in the regime
The pattern of a country's terms of trade is a good indicator of its welfare gains from trade over time. Many developing countries' terms of trade—and hence their gains from trade—are volatile and shrinking, not necessarily because of faulty development policies but more likely because of international trade patterns beyond their control. For instance, developing countries in West Asia,[18] Oceania, and Africa, as well as major petroleum exporters, are exposed to more trade shocks—as implied by the relatively high variance in the growth rates of their terms of trade (table 3).[19] This fact, coupled with their growing trade as a share of GDP and in the context of low per capita incomes, leaves these countries extremely vulnerable. This vulnerability was evident in the aftermath of the 1997–98 finan-

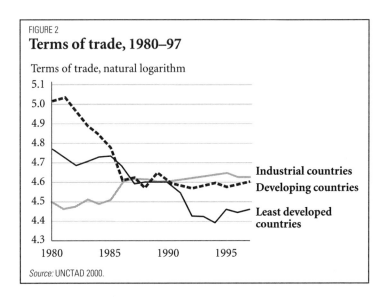

FIGURE 2
Terms of trade, 1980–97

Terms of trade, natural logarithm

Industrial countries

Developing countries

Least developed countries

Source: UNCTAD 2000.

cial crisis on the Asian countries and the effects of the commodity terms of trade shocks on the African countries in the late 1990s (UNCTAD, *Trade and Development Report 1999*).

The vulnerability of developing countries is even clearer from the direction of their terms of trade over time. Since the mid-1980s industrial countries' terms of trade have improved dramatically (figure 2). As a result developing countries— specifically the least developed countries—have seen their terms of trade decline, shrinking their gains from trade.

Are developing countries as likely to face such terms of trade shocks inside the trade regime as they would outside it? That is, does the trade regime pass the neutrality notion of fairness? (Recall that this notion of fairness requires that the country be at least as well off with the regime as without it.) While the counter-factual is difficult to ascertain, it is reasonable to expect terms of trade shocks to be just as prevalent without the trade regime as long as these countries remain exporters of primary products. In this sense the trade regime passes the minimal fairness condition of neutrality.

Over time, however, unabated terms of trade decline and volatility shrink developing countries' gains from trade and weaken their development prospects (UNCTAD, *Trade and Development Report 1999*)—violating the two other notions of fairness defined above. If the multilateral trade regime is intended to promote development and ensure conditions under which all member countries share in the benefits of international trade, one could reasonably argue that the regime should include mechanisms—such as international trade agreements or financing facilities—that help developing countries deal with terms of trade shocks more effectively. Such issues have not been dealt with effectively in trade negotiations and can be seen as gaps in the regime. (See Conceição in this volume for more empirical data on the adverse effects of terms of trade shocks, particularly on developing countries.)

Hence the evidence indicates that the multilateral trade regime is imbalanced in terms of its benefits and costs. Judging from the main agreements under the Uruguay Round, the trade regime appears to fail even the minimal neutrality notion of fairness. That these imbalances have not been corrected indicates underprovision of this global public good (box 2).

The vulnerability of developing countries to terms of trade shocks—coupled with the lack of adequate mechanisms to respond to such shocks—also indicates underprovision of the trade regime as a global public good. Under these conditions the trade regime passes the minimal neutrality notion of fairness but probably fails the two others. To the extent that developing countries' development concerns are not adequately reflected in the design of the trade regime (and its underlying decisionmaking process), this is also proof of malprovision.

MAKING THE TRADE REGIME A GLOBAL PUBLIC GOOD IN FORM AND SUBSTANCE

These imbalances show that the multilateral trade regime is fast advancing as a global public good in form (due to its increased membership and broader scope) but is lagging in substance (due to the imbalanced welfare gains from trade). This explains why developing countries advocate a fair trade regime. But why would all countries necessarily want to pursue a fair regime?

BOX 2

WHY DID DEVELOPING COUNTRIES JOIN THE WORLD TRADE ORGANIZATION?

Beyond the concessions (such as longer timetables to implement reforms) and the promised support (for example, for capacity building and technology transfers) that come with WTO membership, many developing countries have based their development strategies on outward-oriented trade policies—part of a broader approach heavily promoted by the World Bank and International Monetary Fund. And the multilateral trade regime, however flawed, is likely preferable to unilateral actions by industrial countries. Nevertheless, developing countries probably overestimated the improved market access and underestimated the compliance and implementation costs resulting from the Uruguay Round.

Source: Finger and Schuler 2001; Ostry 2002; Taylor 2001.

Beyond the policy statements by WTO member countries seeking to promote development through trade—on which developing countries can legitimately anchor their demands for a fair trade regime—the regime requires ex ante and ex post fairness in order to be stable. Ex ante fairness in processes and procedures (trade negotiations, dispute settlements, and so on) is needed because it underpins trade-related reforms, which are key national inputs for this global public good. For instance, if a proposed agreement on competition policy would affect policymaking (and lawmaking) in developing countries, those countries should have a say on how (and whether) it is drafted. Such participation would make for a better agreement (if one is drafted), since all possible policy options are more likely to be considered, and would bolster each country's commitment to the reforms needed for that agreement.

Ex post fairness in outcomes is also important because defection is always a possibility. Evidence of this comes from the past experiences of Brazil and South Africa—and the more recent experiences of Canada and the United States—with the TRIPS agreement, as well as the growing disappointment in trade outcomes from the Uruguay Round.[20] As noted, trade outcomes (that is, welfare gains) largely determine each country's capacity to provide inputs for this global public good. Imbalanced outcomes can therefore jeopardize these inputs. Thus the trade regime should be reevaluated over time, in light of emerging information on the gains from and development impact of trade.

Appropriate provision of this global public good requires a better balance between constructing a free trade regime and a fair trade regime, with a fair regime promoting a more equitable distribution of the gains from trade, including those that directly bolster development policies. To bring this about, two areas of reform have already received significant treatment in the literature: the need to rebalance the results of the Uruguay Round, primarily through liberalization of agriculture and textiles markets in industrial countries (Finger and Schuknecht 2001; Hertel and Martin 2001; Ostry 2002), and the need to bolster developing country participation in the WTO (Helleiner 2001; Shafaeddin 2000; Third World Network 2001). The first reform responds to the underprovision of this global public good, while the second responds to its malprovision at the decisionmaking stage. (See Chasek and Rajamani in this volume for a discussion of developing country strategies to enhance their bargaining power and the effectiveness of their participation.)

However, through the lens of global public goods these reforms alone will likely prove insufficient. Even with the liberalization of agriculture and textiles markets, many developing countries may still be left out—if not harmed outright, as shown earlier. Furthermore, the bargaining framework is a limited vehicle from which to construct a more development-oriented trade regime. Improved bargaining capacity for developing countries does little to change this fact (Mendoza and Bahadur forthcoming).[21] Appropriate recognition of the basic flaws in the bargaining framework is missing in much of the trade discourse; yet some economists—notably Helleiner (2001) and Rodrik (2001)—have begun to hint at this by calling for the primacy of development goals in viewing trade issues, instead of the other way around.

The following recommendations on safeguards, additional foreign aid, and Rawlsian policies are presented to elicit further discussion. To facilitate a clear outline of policy options, each reform is linked to one of the fairness notions established earlier. What surfaces is a hierarchy of reforms that progressively bring about a fairer multilateral trade regime.

Safeguards: minimizing the negative impact of trade on development

Perhaps the first building block toward a fair trade regime would be to establish safeguards to help protect particularly vulnerable countries from adverse impacts from international trade. This move would ensure the minimal notion of fairness discussed earlier: neutrality. In essence, this responds to the declining net benefits from trade by limiting the "cost" side.

To illustrate, think of the trade regime as a national public highway used by both car drivers and bicyclists. Providing space for a bike path would protect bikers from being run over by cars. Some of the special and differential treatment clauses in WTO agreements—such as lower obligations and more flexible implementation timetables for developing countries—can be seen as serving this purpose. The GATT also includes language on economic development and infant industry protection that enables developing countries to opt out of many provisions (see Article XVIII on Special and Differential Treatment and GATT Part IV on Trade and Development). But both types of protections have proven inadequate. (See Birdsall and Lawrence 1999 and Michalopoulos 2000 for discussions of special and differential treatment issues.) The proposal by Rodrik (2001) to recast the Agreement on Safeguards (pursuant to Article XIX of GATT 1994) into a broader Agreement on Development and Social Safeguards could be a more effective "bike path" for developing countries and should be studied further.

Income transfers: ensuring net benefits for all

The process of specialization in the Ricardian world is supposed to produce an optimal collective outcome as world production increases well beyond autarkic levels. But in the real world this process is far from automatic and painless, generating social costs that are much higher among developing countries. Their benefits from trade are also likely to be smaller, due to their various capacity constraints mentioned earlier. Indeed, some least developed countries were projected to lose out, on balance, from the Uruguay Round.

With national public goods, winners normally compensate losers so that welfare levels increase for all. Ensuring gains from trade for all member countries—the second notion of fairness identified above—is therefore a similar concern.

Within each country, adjustment assistance programs (such as trade adjustment assistance and the National Emergency Grants programs in the United States) serve this purpose of ensuring that adversely affected sectors also gain, by enhancing the competitiveness of those sectors or facilitating the adjustment of individuals in those sectors to transfer to other, more competitive sectors. But in the international context of trade, there is no such income transfer arrangement across countries, and the closest—and imperfect—equivalent is foreign aid.

As a means to build capacity for better interface with the multilateral trade regime, foreign aid could help increase developing countries' gains from trade in the long run, and so should not be readily discounted. In the short run an additional justification for income transfers could be to temporarily assist and partly compensate commodity exporters for the decline in their export earnings. Cheaper commodities, after all, amount to a net welfare transfer from commodity exporters to commodity importers. The failure of commodity export boards in the 1960s and 1970s, the ineffectiveness of IMF lending facilities (such as the Compensatory Financing Facility), and the limitations of other market-based approaches—such as the commodity price insurance proposed by the International Task Force on Commodity Risk Management in Developing Countries[22] and the fair trade movement[23]—underscore the need to explore this income transfer option. Such an arrangement departs from the traditional motivation for aid, and so should not crowd out existing aid. This income transfer can be thought of as a sort of compensation for agreeing to more international trade integration, which has declining and more volatile commodity prices as inevitable features.

While helpful, foreign aid and safeguards for developing countries still constitute a relatively neutral stance on growth and development. If increased participation in the multilateral trade regime is intended to promote the development of the least developed member countries, a more active stance is required. The objective is not just to protect the bicyclists in the short run, but also to ensure that they eventually become car drivers in the long run—responding to the net benefits issue by boosting the "benefit" side.

Rawlsian policies: ensuring development

The development of comparative advantage—that is, developing supply capacity (Shafaeddin 1994) and nurturing retainable industries (Gomory and Baumol 2000)—is one of the primary challenges for developing countries, particularly the least developed ones, that hope to eventually diversify out of commodity exports.[24] Such strategies would enable them to permanently respond to terms of trade shocks, increase their gains from trade, and, most important, generate more robust growth.

Such development strategies are difficult enough without giving up policy maneuverability in the context of the trade regime. Rawlsian measures that preserve—and even enhance—policy maneuverability could therefore be undertaken. One such measure would be continuing the Generalized System of Preferences (GSP), of which the EU Everything but Arms initiative is a good example. Expected to increase the revenues of least developed countries by 10 percent and trade from Sub-Saharan Africa by 14 percent (World Bank 2001, p. 162), this initiative will be an important first step in supporting developing countries' transition from "bike" to "car."[25]

More generally, the key to a development-oriented approach would lie primarily in ensuring sufficient policy maneuverability for developing countries to generate innovative development policies and foster the initial conditions for robust development that are not likely to occur under laissez-faire approaches and that ultimately are more crucial than trade liberalization alone (see Gomory and Baumol 2000; Hausmann and Rodrik 2002; and Rodrik 1999).[26] This approach is not unreasonable, as industrial countries enjoyed considerable maneuverability in their earlier stages of development (see Chang 2002 for a detailed historical discussion on this point). And even with their higher development levels today, these countries have occasionally reclaimed policy maneuverability. For example, after several cases of anthrax were reported in the United States in the fall of 2001, Canada and the United States considered compulsory licensing of the generic equivalent of Cipro, the antibiotic. If industrial countries sometimes require policy maneuverability, shouldn't developing countries be granted the same leverage—if not more?

To operationalize this Rawlsian approach, a trade and development review mechanism could be incorporated into the multilateral trade regime. Additional pro-development policies that enhance policy maneuverability could also be pursued.

A trade and development review council. Preserving policy maneuverability is admittedly a somewhat vague notion. Ex ante, it would be difficult to tell which agreements (and which of their aspects) would hamper development policies. Experience from the TRIPS agreement and the way it constrained policy responses to HIV/AIDS showed that the development impact of some agreements could become evident only over time. How would policy maneuverability be legitimately reclaimed as such?

One solution would be to create a trade and development review council in the WTO to allow developing countries, individually or collectively, to make the case for possible reforms in the trade regime. Such a review mechanism could help assess the impact of trade-related issues that now plague developing countries (such as terms of trade shocks) and facilitate policy responses. Thus it could prove invaluable in enabling member countries to fill in gaps in the regime that may not have been covered during negotiations. Such a facility could also enable member countries to fine-tune the trade rules, in order to more appropriately take account of specific country conditions.[27]

More important, this demand-driven review mechanism could facilitate an immediate response to trade-related development crises.[28] Certainly, any proposal brought to this member-constituted panel for peer review would need to be agreed to by all WTO members, under a transparent and participatory process. Hence it could also serve the important function of providing a safety valve for the multilateral trade regime. Whether the facility responds in the context of the trade regime (as it probably would with terms of trade shocks) or whether it calls on other international organizations for a more coordinated effort (as it might with labor or environmental issues), its key advantage would be that development and trade concerns would be adequately and appropriately deliberated based on their merits.[29]

Additional pro-development policies. The WTO discipline could prove useful from a political economy vantage point if it binds developing country governments to sound and consistent development strategies. But in the absence of such strategies, this same discipline would amount to nothing more than a self-inflicted constraint on policy maneuverability, amplified by internationally binding agreements. Immediately bringing all these countries within the expanding discipline of the WTO could therefore prove detrimental to their development, particularly if the tail (trade policy) starts wagging the dog (development policy).

It is in this light that further expansion of the trade regime into "beyond-border issues" (such as "Singapore issues" and labor standards) must be slowed and reviewed more carefully. Instead, development policies can be bolstered by certain measures in the WTO, including but not limited to the following proposals:

- Subsidies implemented by developing countries are part of their arsenal of development tools, and should not be removed nor limited.
- The transfer of technology provisions under the TRIPS agreement (articles 7, 8, and 66.2) need to be operationalized to improve developing country access to needed technologies (Third World Network 2001).

CONCLUSION

As Sandmo (in this volume) explains, an extension of the public goods concept in the international setting reveals that efficiency and equity cannot simply be disentangled. Perhaps for no global public good is this truer than the multilateral trade regime. Trade is inherently redistributive, as specialization triggers intra- as well as international adjustment by consumers and producers. Throughout this process, developing countries increasingly find themselves caught between shrinking gains from trade and decreasing policy maneuverability—a combination that is anathema to robust development.

The WTO meetings in Seattle and Doha and the growing backlash against globalization indicate that the future of the trade regime rests on a more equitable distribution of gains from trade between and within countries. For developing countries the development impact of trade is a primary concern. Hence the provision of this global public good is more properly seen as striking a better balance between a free trade regime and a fair trade regime. Bargaining and negotiations are inherently poor vehicles for accomplishing such a task. A combination of a more balanced trade negotiations process and more development-focused policies and mechanisms in the WTO may be more effective. Certainly, opt-out clauses are needed to protect developing country gains, and additional foreign aid can be used to help build capacity in developing countries (as well as partly compensate them for the costs related to this regime).

But these policies alone might not be enough. To reconcile WTO member countries' proclamations on trade and development with the realities of international trade, Rawlsian policies that actively advance development need to be investigated. Perhaps as a start, industrial and developing country policymakers should reexamine the totality and the components of the multilateral trade regime under the fairness notions introduced earlier, to determine which level of fairness is in effect—and more important, which level they are willing to pursue. If such reforms are not accomplished, expectations for the trade and development nexus—as well as optimistic forecasts on the integration of international goods and services markets—need to be ratcheted downward, if only to defuse some of the tensions on the trade regime.

"Trade theory is not a guarantee of Santa Claus gains for all. Its classical and neoclassical versions do preclude *losses for all*. Still, the winds of economic history can warm some and freeze others with no regard for *distributive justice*" (Samuelson 2001, p. 1209). The stability of the multilateral trade regime will hinge on a more balanced distribution of benefits from this global public good. Ultimately, only a regime that promotes both free and fair trade will endure.

NOTES

1. Though trade talks in Doha were scheduled to conclude on 13 November 2001, "green room" meetings were held well into that night to hammer out an agreement (Reddy 2001).

2. That is, the GATT is a set of rules, with no institutional foundation, applied on a provisional basis. The WTO is a permanent institution with a permanent framework and its own secretariat. (http://www.wto.org)

3. These rules form the core of the multilateral trade regime. Other parts of the regime include the agreement on trade policy reviews and agreements on plurilateral trade (such as those on civil aircraft and government procurement) not signed by all WTO members (http://www.wto.org).

4. The discussion in this chapter focuses on the multilateral trade regime as embodied by the WTO. Other analysts refer to this as the "multilateral trading sys-

tem" or the "WTO trade regime." Note that the multilateral trade regime does not cover every aspect of international trade, nor does it cover regional trade agreements. Although regional trade agreements are important, they are beyond the scope of this chapter. Throughout the chapter, the term *trade regime* refers to the multilateral trade regime.

5. The 1947 GATT followed directly from the unsuccessful attempt to establish an international trade organization at the UN Conference on Trade and Employment held in Havana, Cuba, in 1947.

6. Technically, some members are customs territories, but for brevity this chapter refers to all members as countries.

7. Comparable data from the Penn World Tables (Heston and Summers, referenced January 2002) end in 1992. The author's calculation of 1999 per capita GDP data (in purchasing power parity terms) from the World Bank (Data and Statistics, referenced January 2002) for 122 WTO members resulted in a coefficient of variation of 1.02.

8. GATT is an international agreement on trade in goods as well as an ad hoc international agency created later to support the agreement. It was never ratified in the parliaments of its contracting parties; and it contained no provision for the creation of an organization. GATT no longer exists as an agency—it was replaced by the WTO, a more formal international organization, after the Uruguay Round. The WTO has an expanded mandate that includes reviewing trade policies and a stronger role in settling trade disputes (see http://www.wto.org/english/res_e/doload_e/tif.pdf).

9. "The multilateral trading system…has contributed significantly to economic growth, development and employment throughout the past fifty years. We are determined…to maintain the process of reform and liberalization of trade policies, thus ensuring that the system plays its full part in promoting recovery, growth and development" (Doha Ministerial Declaration, 20 November 2001, p. 1; see http://www.wto.org/english/thewto_e/minist_e/min01_e/mindecl_e.htm).

10. At the micro level the regime is nonexcludable among member countries' producers and consumers, all of whom share in its benefits and costs to varying degrees. At the international level the regime is made conditionally nonexclusive for nonmember countries, because the terms of accession can be considered membership fees. But nonmembers are actively being encouraged to join, particularly by the Group of Eight (G-8) countries and by the World Bank and International Monetary Fund. For instance, the accessions of Mexico and Morocco were supported with World Bank lending (Hoekman and Kostecki 1995, p. 52).

11. Trade agreements reflect the commitment of member countries to WTO rules and their intention to subject themselves to WTO discipline. National policies implemented in light of these agreements (whether because the policies were required by the agreements or were affected nonetheless) are important inputs for the trade regime. In a way national and international inputs cannot be disentangled. International rules are useful only to the extent that they are complied with in light of national policies.

12. According to philosopher John Rawls (1999), the principles of justice as fairness are those that would be selected from a detached viewpoint. Rawls argues that individuals are risk averse and that, if they were not certain about their position in society, they would opt for a welfare criterion that departs from perfect equality only if the worst-off individual under an unequal utility distribution would be better off than under equality.

13. Adverse outcomes from trade may also result from bad policies or from purely exogenous factors (such as weather) unrelated to the trade regime. Hence it is important to distinguish the rules and institutions of the game (the trade regime) from the game itself (trade).

14. Harrison, Rutherford, and Tarr (1996) quantify the impact of the Uruguay Round based on four reforms: reduced tariffs on manufactured products, tariffication of nontariff barriers in agriculture as well as binding commitments to reduce agricultural protection, reduced export and production subsidies in agriculture, and elimination of voluntary export restraints and the Multifibre Agreement. Their base model is a comparative static model based on constant returns to scale. Their static increasing returns to scale model introduces scale economies at the plant or firm level across several sectors. Their steady-state increasing returns to scale model accounts for dynamic gains from trade due to scale economies, in the presence of imperfect competition. Unlike other studies, theirs bases counterfactual simulations on actual reform commitments, and their more disaggregated model offers better insight into regional effects.

15. In addition, Page and Davenport (1994) argue that exporters of primary goods would not only lose the preferential terms on their few nontraditional primary and manufacturing exports, they would also lose any possible future preferences to help them break into foreign markets. This trend has been reversed somewhat with the renewed discussion on special and differential treatment and the Cotonou waiver, successfully negotiated by the 78 African, Caribbean, and Pacific countries as a deal breaker at the WTO conference in Doha.

16. A year's supply of patented HIV/AIDS antiretroviral drugs costs $10,000 –12,000 in industrial countries, while their generic versions sell for $350 in developing countries. Once the TRIPS agreement is implemented, patents are expected to increase drug prices in some developing countries by 12–68 percent (see World Bank 2001; Fink 2000; Watal 2000; Lanjouw 1997; and Subramanian 1995). In addition, the administrative costs of developing a patent system that complies with the agreement—that is, the costs of setting up the system, training personnel, and creating the capacity to manage records—could cost between $250,000 and $1.2 million per country (UNCTAD 1996). Finger and Schuler (2001) provide much higher estimates of broader Uruguay Round compliance costs: $150 million a country.

17. The Uruguay Round Agreement on Agriculture left broad margins for continued subsidies, while much of the liberalization due to the Agreement on Textiles and Clothing (ATC) has been slowed and back-loaded.

18. West Asian countries include Bahrain, Cyprus, and Jordan, among others. For a complete list of countries in each region, see UNCTAD (2000, pp. 2–8).

19. This discussion refers to the "net barter" terms of trade, defined as the ratio of the export unit value index to the import unit value index.

20. Potentially violating the TRIPS agreement, Brazil and South Africa explored options to manufacture cheaper versions of HIV/AIDS drugs.

21. Mendoza and Bahadur (forthcoming) argue that the bargaining framework is inherently unequal (given unequal bargainers) and usually characterized by coercion, incentives to overload the negotiating agenda, and flawed agreements in the context of cross-bargaining.

22. The task force's proposal focuses on price risk, though not income protection; alleviates short-term price fluctuations but not declining price trends; and covers only some commodities (http://www.itf-commrisk.org/)

23. This refers to efforts by organizations such as the Max Havelaar Foundation, Cafedirect, and Kuapa Kokoo (a Ghanaian cocoa cooperative) to develop a niche in the commodity market that ensures minimum prices for producers. But these organizations' purchases are quite minimal (Cowe 2002).

24. On this point the debate has also begun to shift in focus from terms of trade between primary commodities and manufactures to relative movements in the prices of manufactures exported by developing relative to industrial countries. See UNCTAD's *Trade and Development Report 2002* for a discussion.

25. In its present form this initiative is still limited—with some critics referring to it as "everything but farms."

26. In addition, Jones (2000) argues that in the presence of factor mobility (such as capital flows), a comparison of government policies will have a first-order effect on where that factor locates itself. Government interventions, such as subsidies, may be welfare enhancing even in competitive settings (p. 140). Moreover, Wood and Ridao-Cano (1999) provide evidence that more openness might actually widen country differences in skill stocks, increasing divergence in per capita incomes.

27. This proposal differs from the existing WTO Committee on Trade and Development, which discusses and monitors trade agreements rather than filling gaps in WTO rules. Focusing broadly on improving the governance of the WTO, Ostry (2001) makes a similar proposal to establish a policy forum or executive committee that would study and foster comprehensive structural reform. In the same vein, Helleiner (2001) advocates an immediate independent review of the content, implementation, and development consequences of existing trade agreements.

28. Decisions made for individual countries could also be seen as setting precedents.

29. There are obviously many more issues to consider for this proposal to differ from the current process. One key issue for further discussion would be how to strike the appropriate balance between a technocratic approach (as in the dispute settlement process) and a more democratic (bargaining) approach. But discussing and facilitating policies on trade and development issues outside normal trade negotiations would be a welcome change in and of itself. In the longer term this review facility could

decouple the most pressing development issues from traditional trade negotiations, preventing legitimate development-related issues from being treated as bargaining chips.

REFERENCES

Antweiler, Werner, and Daniel Trefler. 2002. "Increasing Returns and All That: A View from Trade." *The American Economic Review* 92 (1): 93–119.

Bhagwati, Jagdish. 1998. "Free Trade: What Now?" Keynote address delivered at the International Management Symposium, 25 May, University of St. Gallen, Switzerland. [http://www.columbia.edu/~jb38/papers/freedom_speech.pdf].

Ben-David, Dan. 2001. "Trade Liberalization and Income Convergence: A Comment." *Journal of International Economics* 55: 229–34.

Birdsall Nancy, and Robert Z. Lawrence. 1999. "Deep Integration and Trade Agreements: Good for Developing Countries?" In Inge Kaul, Isabelle Grunberg, and Marc A. Stern, eds., *Global Public Goods: International Cooperation in the 21st Century*. New York: Oxford University Press.

Blackhurst, Richard. 1998. "The Capacity of the WTO to Fulfill Its Mandate". In Anne O. Krueger, ed., with the assistance of Chonira Aturupane, *The WTO as an International Organization*. Chicago and London: University of Chicago Press.

Chang, Ha-Joon. 2002. *Kicking Away the Ladder: Development Strategy in Historical Perspective*. London: Anthem Press.

Cowe, Roger. 2002. "Poor Farmers Taste Success." *Financial Times,* 5 March, p. 11.

Dollar, David. 1993. "Technological Differences as a Source of Comparative Advantage." *The American Economic Review* 83 (2): 431–35.

Finger, J. Michael, and Philip Schuler. 2001. "Implementation of Uruguay Round Commitments." In Bernard Hoekman and Will Martin, eds., *Developing Countries and the WTO: A Pro-active Agenda*. Oxford: Blackwell Publishers.

Finger, J. Michael, and Ludger Schuknecht. 2001. "Market Access Advances: The Uruguay Round." In Bernard Hoekman and Will Martin, eds., *Developing Countries and the WTO: A Pro-active Agenda*. Oxford: Blackwell Publishers.

Fink, Carsten. 2000. "How Stronger Patent Protection in India Might Affect the Behavior of Transnational Pharmaceutical Industries." Policy Research Working Paper 2352. World Bank, Washington, D.C. [http://econ.worldbank.org/docs/1106.pdf].

Funke, Michael, and Ralf Ruhwedel. 2001. "Export Variety and Export Performance: Empirical Evidence from East Asia." *Journal of Asian Economics* 12: 493–505.

Gomory, Ralph E., and William Baumol. 2000. *Global Trade and Conflicting National Interests*. Cambridge, Mass.: MIT Press.

Greenaway, David, Wyn Morgan, and Peter Wright. 2002. "Trade Liberalization and Growth in Developing Countries." *Journal of Development Economics* 67 (1): 229–44.

Harrison, Glen, Thomas Rutherford, and David Tarr. 1996. "Quantifying the Uruguay Round." In Will Martin and L. Alan Winters, eds., *The Uruguay Round and the Developing Countries*. Cambridge: Cambridge University Press.

Hausmann, Ricardo, and Dani Rodrik. 2002. "Economic Development as Self-Discovery." Working Paper. Harvard University, John F. Kennedy School of Government, Cambridge, Mass. [http://ksghome.harvard.edu/~.drodrik. academic.ksg/selfdisc.pdf].

Helleiner, Gerald. 2001. "Markets, Politics and Globalization: Can the Global Economy Be Civilized?" *Global Governance* 7 (3): 243–63.

Hertel, Thomas W., and Will Martin. 2001. "Liberalizing Agriculture and Manufactures in a Millennium Round: Implications for Developing Countries." In Bernard Hoekman and Will Martin, eds., *Developing Countries and the WTO: A Pro-active Agenda*. Oxford: Blackwell Publishers.

Heston, Allan, and Robert Summers. Referenced January 2002. "Penn World Tables." [http://datacentre.chass.utoronto.ca/pwt/pwt.html].

Hoekman, Bernard, and Michel Kostecki. 1995. *The Political Economy of the World Trading System*. Oxford: Oxford University Press.

Hummels, David, and Peter J. Klenow. 2002. "The Variety and Quality of a Nation's Trade." NBER Working Paper 8712. National Bureau of Economic Research, Cambridge, Mass. [http://papers.nber.org/papers/w8712.pdf].

Hummels, David, and James Levinsohn. 1993. "Product Differentiation as a Source of Comparative Advantage." *The American Economic Review* 83 (2): 445–49.

Jones, Ronald W. 2000. *Globalization and the Theory of Input Trade*. Cambridge, Mass.: MIT Press.

Kapstein, Ethan. 1999. "Distributive Justice and International Trade." *Ethics and International Affairs* 13: 175–204.

Kennedy, Daniel L. M., and James D. Southwick, eds. 2002. *The Political Economy of International Trade Law: Essays in Honor of Robert E. Hudec*. Cambridge: Cambridge University Press.

Lanjouw, Jean. 1997. "The Introduction of Pharmaceutical Product Patents in India: 'Heartless Exploitation of the Poor and Suffering'?" NBER Working Paper 6366. National Bureau of Economic Research, Cambridge, Mass. [http://papers. nber.org/papers/w6366.pdf].

Leamer, Edward. 1993. "Factor-Supply Differences as a Source of Comparative Advantage." *The American Economic Review* 83 (2): 436–39.

McCalman, Phillip. 1999. "Reaping What You Sow: An Empirical Analysis of International Patent Harmonization." Working Paper in Economics and Econometrics 374. Australian National University, Canberra.

Mendoza, Ronald U., and Chandrika Bahadur. Forthcoming. "Towards Free and Fair Trade: A Global Public Good Perspective." *Challenge: The Magazine of Economic Affairs.* Armonk, New York: M.E. Sharpe. [http://www.cid.harvard.edu/cidtrade/Papers/MendozaBahadurJune02.pdf]

Michalopoulos, Constantine. 2000. "The Role of Special and Differential Treatment for Developing Countries in GATT and WTO." Policy Research Working Paper 2388. World Bank, Washington, D.C. [http://econ.worldbank.org/docs/1143.pdf].

Nicholson, Walter. 1998. *Microeconomic Theory: Basic Principles and Extensions.* 7th ed. New York: Dryden Press.

Ostry, Sylvia. 2002. "The Uruguay Round North-South Grand Bargain: Implications for Future Negotiations." In Daniel L. M. Kennedy and James D. Southwick, eds., *The Political Economy of International Trade Law: Essays in honor of Robert E. Hudec.* Cambridge: Cambridge University Press.

———. 2001. "World Trade Organization: Institutional Design for Better Governance." In Roger B. Porter, Pierre Sauve, Arvind Subramanian, and Americo Beviglia Zampetti, eds., *Efficiency, Equity, Legitimacy: The Multilateral Trading System at the Millennium.* Washington, D.C.: Brookings Institution Press.

OXFAM International. 2002. *Rigged Rules and Double Standards: Trade, Globalization and the Fight against Poverty.* [http://www.maketradefair.com/]

Page, Sheila, and Michael Davenport. 1994. "World Trade Reform: Do Developing Countries Gain or Lose?" ODI Special Report. London: Overseas Development Institute.

Perroni, Carlo. 1998. "The Uruguay Round and Its Impact on Developing Countries: An Overview of Modeling Results." In Harmon Thomas and John Whalley, eds., *Uruguay Round Results and the Emerging Trade Agenda.* Geneva: United Nations Conference on Trade and Development.

Rawls, John. 1999. *A Theory of Justice.* revised ed. Cambridge: Belknap Press of Harvard University Press.

Reddy, Rammanohar. 2001. "Shenanigans at Presidential Suite 11 at Doha." *The Hindu,* 16 November. [http://www.hinduonnet.com/thehindu/2001/11/16/stories/03160009.htm].

Rodrik, Dani. 1999. "The New Global Economy and Developing Countries: Making Openness Work." Economic Development Policy Essay 24. Overseas Development Council, Washington, D.C.

———. 2001. "The Global Governance of Trade as if Development Really Mattered." Background paper to the United Nations Development Programme Project on Trade and Sustainable Human Development, New York.

Ruggie, John Gerard. 1998. *Constructing the World Polity: Essays on International Institutionalization.* London and New York: Routledge.

Rutherford, Thomas F., and David G. Tarr. 2002. "Trade Liberalization, Product Variety and Growth in a Small Open Economy: A Quantitative Assessment." *Journal of International Economics* 56: 246–72.

Samuelson, Paul A. 2001. "A Ricardo-Sraffa Paradigm Comparing Gains from Trade in Inputs and Finished Goods." *Journal of Economic Literature* 39 (4): 1204–14.

Scholte, Jan Aart, with Robert O'Brien and Marc Williams. 1999. "The World Trade Organization and Civil Society." In Brian Hocking and Steven McGuire, eds., *Trade Politics: International, Domestic, and Regional Perspectives.* New York: Routledge.

Shafaeddin, Mehdi. 1994. "The Impact of Trade Liberalization on Export and GDP Growth in Least Developing Countries." Discussion paper. United Nations Conference on Trade and Development, Geneva.

———. 2000. "Free Trade or Fair Trade?" UNCTAD Secretariat Working Paper. United Nations Conference on Trade and Development, Geneva. [http://www.unctad.org/en/docs/dp_153.en.pdf].

Srinivasan, TN, and Jagdish Bhagwati. 1999. "Outward-Orientation and Development: Are Revisionists Right?" Columbia University, Economics Department, New York. [http://www.columbia.edu/~jb38/Krueger.pdf].

Subramanian, Arvind 1995. "Putting Some Numbers on the TRIPS Pharmaceuticals Debate." *International Journal of Technology Management* 10 (2): 252–68.

Taylor, Lance, ed. 2001. *External Liberalization, Economic Performance, and Social Policy.* New York: Oxford University Press.

Third World Network. 2001. "The Multilateral Trade System: A Development Perspective." Background paper to the United Nations Development Programme Project on Trade and Sustainable Human Development, New York.

Tybout, James R. 1993. "Internal Returns to Scale as a Source of Comparative Advantage: The Evidence." *The American Economic Review* 83 (2): 440–44.

UNCTAD (United Nations Conference on Trade and Development). 1996. "International Trade in Goods and Services, and Commodities." Geneva.

———. 2000. UNCTAD *Handbook of Statistics 2000.* Geneva.

———. Various years. *Trade and Development Report.* Geneva.

Vajpayee, Atal Behari. 2001. "Address to the 56th session of the U.N. General Assembly." 10 November. New York. [http://meadev.nic.in/speeches/pm-unga.htm].

Watal, Jayshree. 2000. "Pharmaceutical Patents, Prices and Welfare Losses: Policy Options for India under the WTO TRIPS Agreement." *World Economy* 23 (5): 733–52.

Wood, Adrian. 1995. *North-South Trade, Employment and Inequality: Changing Fortunes in a Skill-driven World.* Oxford: Oxford University Press.

Wood, Adrian, and Cristobal Ridao-Cano. 1999. "Skill, Trade and International Inequality." Institute for Development Studies Working Paper 47. University of Sussex, Brighton. [http://www.ids.ac.uk/ids/bookshop/wp/WP47.pdf].

Woolcock, Stephen. 1999. "The Multilateral Trading System into the New Millennium." In Brian Hocking and Steven McGuire, eds., *Trade Politics: International, Regional and Domestic Perspectives.* New York: Routledge.

World Bank. 2001. *Global Economic Prospects 2002: Making Trade Work for the World's Poor.* Washington, D.C.

———. Referenced January 2002. "Data and Statistics." [http://www.worldbank.org/data/].

WTO (World Trade Organization). 1994. "Agreement Establishing the World Trade Organization." Geneva. [http://www.wto.org/english/docs_e/legal_e/04-wto.pdf].

———. 1999. "Trading into the Future." Geneva.

———. 2001. *International Trade Statistics 2001.* Geneva.

BEYOND COMMUNICABLE DISEASE CONTROL: HEALTH IN THE AGE OF GLOBALIZATION

DYNA ARHIN-TENKORANG AND PEDRO CONCEIÇÃO

Health concerns have triggered systematic international cooperation for more than 150 years. Disease control was also the core concern of the first formal international organizations. After World War II this tradition of international cooperation was strengthened with the creation of the World Health Organization and expanded with the establishment of official development assistance. During the 1950s medical science and technology progressed, and ambitious initiatives for the eradication of communicable diseases were launched, creating great optimism that such diseases would be eliminated. Today, however, communicable diseases remain a challenge. Old diseases have reemerged, and new infectious diseases—especially HIV/AIDS—are causing living and health standards to regress in many developing countries. Why has this happened, and what is being done about it? Moreover, how can current responses be improved? These questions propel this chapter's analysis.

The chapter starts by summarizing international efforts to fight communicable diseases in the 19th century and the first half of the 20th century. It then describes the results of international cooperation on public health since the 1950s. To help understand why some communicable diseases have been tamed while others remain a problem, the chapter analyzes three health challenges. The main finding is that problems tend to persist when the publicness of the response is limited. Here publicness refers to three inputs crucial for controlling disease: available and accessible medical knowledge, a national public health infrastructure, and private household spending on complementary goods and services. The chapter's analysis focuses on the first two inputs. It then explains why health concerns have returned to the top of the international agenda and characterizes current actions to address international health challenges as efforts to enhance the publicness of responses. The chapter concludes by suggesting steps to consolidate and improve these responses.

A BRIEF HISTORY OF COMMUNICABLE DISEASE CONTROL

For the purposes of the analysis in this chapter, international efforts to control communicable diseases can be divided into two periods: responses before the 1950s and those since.

Focusing on "at the border" controls: responses until the 1950s

Past epidemics have led to an increasingly coordinated, centralized approach to communicable disease control. Desai (in this volume) describes how care for sick people evolved beyond the realm of the family and the church into the hands of public authorities—first local governments, then central governments.

As human activity expanded geographically, so did the spread of communicable diseases. Technological developments in transportation throughout the 19th century (the steam engine, railroads) made the global spread of communicable diseases easier than ever before. For example, in the early 19th century a cholera epidemic took eight years to spread globally: it broke out in India in 1826, reached eastern Russia in 1827, moved to Germany, Hungary, and Austria through 1831, and hit Paris, London, and New York in 1832, the U.S. Pacific coast in 1833, and Mexico City in 1834, where it apparently stopped (Cooper 1989, pp. 107–08).

The public policy response to global epidemics started by imposing strict quarantines at ports (Cooper 1989, pp. 103–07). But with each country fending for itself, quarantine requirements were often redundant, imposing a great burden on commerce and travel. As a result in 1834 the French government issued the first call for international cooperation to prevent the spread of diseases. But it took another global epidemic of cholera, in 1848–49, for the first international sanitary conference to be held, in 1851 (Lyons 1963, p. 240). Three more conferences followed—in 1859, 1866, and 1874.

Across the Atlantic yellow fever (of little worry in Europe) was as much a concern as cholera. Endemic to West Africa, yellow fever reached the Americas in the 17th century, becoming "the disease that sparked the greatest fear, claimed enormous numbers of lives, and ignited public health policies for decades to come" (Garrett 2000, p. 281). After a continentwide epidemic in the 1870s, and because the European-led sanitary conferences had failed to address yellow fever, a fifth international conference, called by North and South American states, was held in 1881 in Washington, D.C. (PAHO 1992).

None of these conferences resulted in binding agreements between countries. The main obstacle was a lack of understanding of diseases and of how communicable diseases were transmitted. Only as science and practical knowledge progressed was it possible to reach consensus. In 1892 countries finally adopted an International Sanitary Convention, agreeing on steps to fight the cross-country transmission of cholera (Cooper 1989, p. 210). Although the measures adopted continued to focus on quarantine, there was an effort to rationalize quarantine requirements and to improve the reporting and communication of the health condition of travelers. Thus international coordination focused on "at the border" controls, but countries were also starting to build national public health systems.

In 1902 North and South American nations went further, establishing the International Sanitary Bureau—the precursor to the Pan-American Health Organization (PAHO), the first formal international organization for public health (PAHO 1992). In Europe a second international organization dealing with international health issues was created in 1907: the International Office of Public Hygiene, based in Paris. The Health Organization of the League of Nations, created after World War I, became the third entity devoted to international public health. All three organizations became engaged in monitoring diseases and in sharing epidemiological and other scientific information (Zacher 1999). Still, their focus remained on at-the-border controls (especially quarantine regulations)—so much so that because influenza could not be quarantined and smallpox was considered a universal disease, neither was among the diseases addressed by these international organizations (Cooper 1989, p. 228).

International cooperation in health was not limited to governments and formal intergovernmental organizations. Volunteers and nongovernmental organizations have always played important roles, contributing to the diffusion of ideas and to the development of actions to mitigate ill health in the context of social, religious, and humanitarian movements (Loughlin and Berridge 2002, p. 9). For example, the International Committee of the Red Cross (created in 1863) contributed to the establishment of the Geneva Convention on the treatment of combatants, setting ethical standards and safeguards that were a precursor to later international health regimes (Dodgson, Lee, and Drager 2002). In 1913 the Rockefeller Foundation became active in the international promotion of public health, including by financing the Health Organization of the League of Nations.

Under these initial international arrangements for communicable disease control, action tended to follow crises. The first responses came at the local or national level, but as the ineffectiveness and difficulties of these uncoordinated actions became clear, calls for international cooperation emerged. International cooperation focused on limiting the international spread of diseases, especially by harmonizing border controls. The second half of the 20th century saw a new era of international cooperation in health: meeting diseases at their sources.

Meeting diseases at their sources: the creation of the World Health Organization and the emergence of aid

After its creation in 1948, the World Health Organization (WHO) became the locus of international cooperation on health. The WHO absorbed the International Office of Public Hygiene and the Health Organization of the League of Nations. The International Sanitary Bureau was renamed PAHO and became the WHO's regional office for the Americas (PAHO 1992, p. 42). In a period of great vitality in the scientific understanding of infectious diseases and of progress in medical technology—in vaccines for prevention and drugs for treatment—the WHO added eliminating communicable diseases at their sources to its mandate of containing their spread through its more traditional functions of coordinating international health regulations and serving as an information clearinghouse.

Addressing diseases at their sources required a new type of interaction between governments and the WHO. National health authorities provide most of the control of diseases at their sources. But for developing countries without the capacity or resources to control communicable diseases, the WHO helped do so— a move made possible by the recent creation of official development assistance, funded by industrial countries. The WHO's expanded mandate, coupled with official development assistance, also made possible systematic attempts to eradicate diseases, which require international coordination beyond the capacity of any one country.

POLICY RESPONSES AND ACHIEVEMENTS: LIMITED PUBLICNESS

So what have been the results of this new international framework for addressing communicable diseases? Some impressive achievements have been made. For example, the Onchocerciasis Control Programme was created in 1968 to control river blindness in 11 West African countries—and is ending in 2002 having achieved its goal. The program has also established national capacity so that countries can continue to control the disease.

In addition, smallpox has been eradicated. In 1967, when the eradication effort was intensified, smallpox infected 15 million people and caused 2 million deaths. Had smallpox not been eradicated, between 1967 and 1998 there would have been 350 million infections and more than 40 million deaths (http://www. who.int/archives/who50/en/smallpox.htm). Smallpox eradication cost nearly $300 million, with industrial (donor) countries paying for about one-third. It is estimated that the United States recoups the costs it incurred once every 26 days— every 26 days the benefits accruing from not having to deal with smallpox are equal to the total U.S. eradication cost (http://www.unfoundation.org/campaigns /polio/challenge.asp).

Other eradication efforts were less successful. In the mid- to late 1950s initiatives were launched to eradicate malaria. Although malaria was eliminated in some parts of the world (Southern Europe, Jamaica), in others (India, Sri Lanka) it recurred after eradication efforts stopped. The strategy for eradicating malaria presumed that its vector—certain mosquitoes—could be eliminated using the chemical DDT. But mosquitoes' ability to develop resistance to DDT was underestimated, and subsequent concerns about DDT's environmental effects made this strategy impossible to pursue. Aylward, Hennessey, and others (2000) find that successful eradication depends on a number of conditions: biological (no non-human reservoir for the infectious agent), technical (availability of an effective vaccine or treatment), economic (with benefits exceeding costs), political (political commitment), and social (social support). Malaria eradication was impeded by imperfect understanding of its biological feasibility and dwindling support for its strategy.

Today we know that the optimism of the mid-20th century was premature: communicable disease control is an enduring challenge. Communicable diseases account for one-third of the global disease burden (WHO 2001b, table 3) and in 1998 were the leading cause of premature death, causing nearly half of all deaths before age 45 (WHO 2000, p. 1). Old "killer diseases" have resurged: in 2000 malaria caused more than 1 million deaths, childhood infectious diseases caused 1.4 million deaths, and tuberculosis killed more than 1.5 million people (WHO 2001b, table 2). In 1999 there were 8.5 million new tuberculosis infections (WHO 2001b, table 10). And new diseases, especially HIV/AIDS (see below), are killing several million people a year. All of this is happening in a context where resistance to treatments for communicable diseases is limiting the available options for disease control.

To understand the challenges of communicable disease control, the analysis below focuses on three health challenges, chosen for the intriguingly different policy responses to them: poliomyelitis (polio), acquired immunodeficiency syndrome (AIDS) caused by the human immunodeficiency virus (HIV), and infections with antimicrobial-resistant agents. (Later in the chapter a noncommunicable condition, sickle cell disease, is also considered.) These three cases are of worldwide reach, and resolving any of them constitutes a condition-specific global public good: eradicating polio, controlling HIV/AIDS, and containing antimicrobial-resistant infections (table 1). Protecting a single individual from

TABLE 1

Characteristics of and responses to the four cases

Case	Criterion for adequate provision	Global reach?	Global awareness?	Inputs developed?	Global access to inputs?
Polio	Eradication	Yes	Yes	Yes	Yes
HIV/AIDS	Control	Yes	Yes	Yes, partially	Limited
Infections with antimicrobial-resistant agents	Containment	Yes	Yes	Minimally	Limited
Sickle cell disease	Control	Yes	No	Minimally	Very limited

infection has positive externalities because it constrains the spread of communicable diseases ("herd immunity"). Thus eradicating (when possible) or controlling communicable diseases that can spread globally is a global public good (Sandler and Arce M. 2002).

The difference among the first three cases in table 1 lies in the extent to which inputs to control them have been developed and deployed. Thus the analysis of the cases focuses on the three types of inputs that communicable disease control (or containment of antimicrobial-resistant agents) typically requires:

- Type 1: available medical knowledge (implying the generation of scientific knowledge and production of medical technologies) and access to pharmaceutical and other medical technologies (including their affordability in developing countries).

- Type 2: a functioning public health care system to detect disease outbreaks, channel interventions, and monitor and report progress on communicable disease control.

- Type 3: private spending—even if the previous two inputs are available and affordable, individuals and households need to have the means to make complementary expenditures.

In this analysis a disease is considered to have been met with a fully public response if all three types of inputs are developed and made available. Most of the analysis focuses on the first two. The first, medical knowledge and drugs for treatment or vaccines for prevention, can be considered global public goods for health (Sandler and Arce M. 2002; Mills 2001). These global public goods are often necessary (though insufficient) for communicable disease control. Knowledge about how a disease is transmitted can be used to control it. For example, the strategy for dracunculiasis (guinea worm) eradication is based largely on the knowledge that infection occurs after drinking contaminated water. Infection can be prevented through measures as simple as using water filter cloths. Because dracunculiasis control was associated with safe water, guinea worm eradication was one of the objectives for the International Water Supply and Sanitation Decade (the 1990s). The number of infections dropped from 3.6 million in 1986 to 75,000 in 2000, mostly as a result of providing access to filtered drinking water (http://www.who.int/ctd/dracun/progress.htm).

In other cases, as discussed below, effective control intervention requires developing and deploying medical technologies, including drugs for treatment and vaccines for prevention. Underprovision of or limited access to these global public goods reflects a limited publicness in the policy response. In many cases access is limited because the needed medicines are unaffordable in developing countries, even if there are no formal restrictions on access. However, the publicness of the response—and thus its success—also depends on the other two types of inputs, especially the public health care system.

Policy response to polio: public, determined, and inclusive

Polio is caused by three strains of polioviruses that destroy nerve cells, causing paralysis. Historically, polioviruses infected almost all infants, paralyzing and permanently disabling about 0.5 percent of all children (Aylward, Hull, and others 2000). Of those, 4–10 percent died. Before its accelerated control through vaccination, polio had global reach, affecting both industrial and developing countries—and within countries, both rich and poor people (Woodward, Smith, and others 2001).

The response to polio was spearheaded in the United States in the 1930s, driven by public concern accentuated by the fact that the disease affected public figures and mobilizing a strong response from civil society.[1] In the early 1950s polio figured in public opinion polls as the second most important concern of Americans, right after the threat of a nuclear confrontation (Seavey, Smith, and Wagner 1998). The National Foundation for Infantile Paralysis (known as the March of Dimes) funded treatment and vaccine research, leading to the development of the first polio vaccine in the mid-1950s by Jonas Salk. The March of Dimes also funded initial clinical tests for and mass delivery of the vaccine in the United States. The research outcomes funded by the March of Dimes were not allowed to be patented: they were made public by design.[2] Thus access to the vaccine was not impeded by a patent—so medical knowledge and technology (type 1 inputs) were widely available.

Mass vaccination reduced the number of polio cases in industrial countries by 86 percent between 1955 and 1957, but developing countries were excluded from the response. Polio had not been immediately recognized as a threat in developing countries. As a result, even in 1988, 350,000 cases of polio were detected in 125 countries. Making the formulation of the vaccine public was a crucial step toward controlling polio in industrial countries but was not sufficient in developing countries. Most of the costs of polio vaccination stem from support staff, vehicles, storage facilities, and other equipment—not from the vaccine—so successful vaccination initiatives depend on local health facilities and the ability to buy private goods (type 2 and 3 inputs). Lack of access to these inputs excluded many developing countries from benefiting from the polio vaccine.

In 1988 a combination of national self-interest and commitments from international organizations (WHO, United Nations Children's Fund) and philanthropic foundations (Rotary International) led to the Polio Eradication Initiative.[3] The initiative, still under way, mobilizes resources to deliver the vaccine even where public health facilities are inadequate. Between 1988 and 2000 the incidence of polio around the world was reduced by 99.9 percent (from the 350,000 cases in 1988 to less than 500 in 2001; WHO 2002, p. 100; http://www.polioeradication. org/all/news/_files/pdf/PN15-05-02.pdf). Almost half a century had passed since a similar response had been provided in industrial countries.

Action on eradication was driven by the technical feasibility of the endeavor (made possible by past investments in technology and a track record of success associated with the response to the disease in industrial countries) and by its significant health and economic benefits (prospects of future, and permanent, health and financial gains). Looking at polio eradication as a disease-specific global public good helps in understanding the evolving structure of incentives that led to the eradication effort. After the initial vaccination effort in industrial countries, incentives for eradication became different for industrial and developing countries. Successfully controlling polio in industrial countries amounted to national elimination of the disease. National elimination is a national public good. Once a country is disease-free, its incentives to invest in global eradication are limited— and in fact diminished if only health benefits are considered (see Barrett in this volume and Philipson 1999).

Because polio-free countries had fewer health-related incentives, the effort to eradicate polio at the global level moved toward an "international effort." International organizations and foundations assumed a leadership role in eradicating polio, in conjunction with countries not yet free of it.[4] Does that mean that global eradication has no benefits for countries already free of polio? There are benefits, but less of a health nature, since polio does not represent a direct health threat to polio-free countries. Whether global eradication is achieved or not, polio-free countries will not have the disease. But without global eradication, they will still have to pay a price: they have to continue to vaccinate. Providing the national public good of national elimination is costly to a country as long as the disease exists elsewhere. At the global level, polio eradication provides two types of benefits: financial, to countries that are polio free (which have to pay for this national public good), and health, to countries that still have the disease.

As the vaccination effort encompasses more countries, the cumulative global cost of defending against polio increases but the global disease threat becomes limited to fewer people. As the cost increases, the financial benefits of eradication become more appealing, since eradication would render vaccination needless, eliminating the costs. And as vaccination expands, what is required to achieve eradication, in light of past investments, becomes less demanding. Thus the incentive structure is eventually tipped to make the prospect of eradication attractive. The benefits of stopping all control measures once polio eradication has been achieved are estimated at $1.5 billion a year (Aylward, Hennessey, and others 2000).[5]

Figure 1 illustrates this coevolution of the global disease burden from polio and the global financial effort for polio prevention. As the world moves toward the right along the horizontal axis (that is, as it advances in time), fewer and fewer countries have polio but more and more need to vaccinate. Thus as the cumulative global threat of polio decreases, the financial effort of vaccination increases. The financial payoff occurs only when all control measures are stopped.[6]

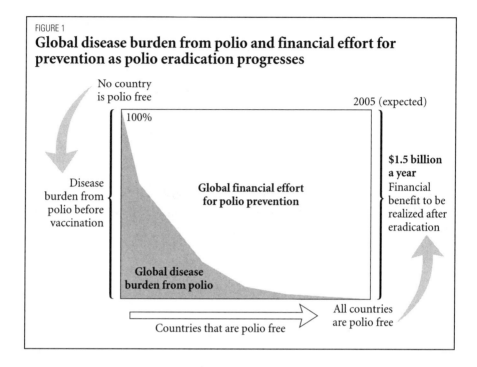

FIGURE 1
Global disease burden from polio and financial effort for prevention as polio eradication progresses

No country is polio free

2005 (expected)

100%

Disease burden from polio before vaccination

Global financial effort for polio prevention

$1.5 billion a year Financial benefit to be realized after eradication

Global disease burden from polio

Countries that are polio free

All countries are polio free

So, the case of polio shows how a fully public response developed, with the creation and deployment on a global scale of all the needed inputs for communicable disease control. Concern about polio in industrial countries led to investments in understanding the disease and in creating a vaccine (type 1 inputs). The vaccine was rapidly deployed in industrial countries, which had well-functioning public health systems. When the feasibility of eradication became clear and recognition of the health and financial benefits generated enough support, the global eradication campaign was launched, providing type 2 and 3 inputs to the developing countries that lacked them.

Policy response to HIV/AIDS: determined but partial
HIV attacks the immune system, exposing it to opportunistic infections and eventually causing AIDS. HIV has five major genetic subtypes. HIV-1B is the prevailing subtype in Europe and the United States. HIV-1C is the most common in Sub-Saharan Africa. Epidemiological studies suggest that HIV-1C is transmitted faster than the others because it is more transmissible through heterosexual intercourse and is inherently more pathogenic (Arhin-Tenkorang 2001). HIV/AIDS was initially regarded as a national public health problem. In Europe and the United States HIV/AIDS was made visible by politically active groups of homosexuals and intravenous drug users. These groups also influenced the design of control approaches and advocated for research and development on the disease.

As with polio, awareness increased as famous people became infected with the disease. Indeed, the pattern of the initial response to HIV/AIDS in the United States resembles that of the response to polio: acute public concern that mobilized society to respond to the threat.

As the epidemiology of HIV/AIDS became known, early responses in Europe and the United States focused on prevention. With the 1987 global AIDS program, the WHO took these responses to the international level. But by the early 1990s it was clear that prevention alone was not enough. A "risk and vulnerability" paradigm emerged, based on the idea that, beyond prevention, there would need to be measures to care for vulnerable populations so that they would have the economic and social capabilities to function. The resources mobilized for prevention and care in developing countries were never sufficient, but the limited publicness of the response has worsened because in recent years industrial countries have benefited from treatment. Antiretroviral therapy has added years of healthy, productive life for those infected with HIV. Lichtenberg (2001) estimates that each new HIV drug approved in the United States saves about 34,000 lives there. Developing countries have been largely excluded from this new dimension of the response to AIDS: type 1 inputs (though treatment drugs have been developed, their availability has been limited).

The reasons for the exclusion of developing countries result from the evolution of the response. New HIV/AIDS drugs are often protected by patents; in industrial countries concern about HIV/AIDS created markets for pharmaceuticals. In addition, most developing countries lack the infrastructure and human capacity needed for safe and effective antiretroviral therapy (type 2 inputs), though recent studies suggest that community-based alternatives can overcome a lack of fully functioning health systems as long as there is an uninterrupted supply of high-quality drugs (Farmer and others 2001). This suggests that community-based delivery can work, at least in the short run, overcoming the obstacles imposed by the lack of type 2 inputs.

The international community's focus on HIV prevention is being reconsidered. Scientific and empirical arguments for combining treatment with prevention have mounted. Antiretroviral therapy not only benefits those infected but also aids prevention (UNAIDS, International AIDS Society, and Bill and Melinda Gates Foundation Expert Group 2001). Reduced viral loads have been achieved in patients receiving antiretroviral treatment, lowering the probability of sexual transmission. The effectiveness of treatment in controlling the spread of HIV is reflected in the strategies recommended by the U.S. Centers for Disease Control and Prevention (USCDC 2001). Various scientific groups, including a team from Harvard University, have outlined modalities for the introduction of treatment that would minimize the risk of generating drug-resistant strains of HIV (Harvard University, Individual Members of the Faculty 2001).

The limited publicness of the response to HIV/AIDS, reflected in the lack of access to some key medical technologies, is impeding its control. By the end of 2001, 40 million people worldwide were infected with HIV/AIDS, up from 36.1 million in 2000. Since 1981 HIV/AIDS has been responsible for 24.8 million deaths. There were 5.3 million new infections in 2000 and another 5.0 million in 2001. In 2001 about three-quarters of AIDS deaths occurred in Sub-Saharan Africa (all figures from UNAIDS 2000, 2001). The incidence of HIV/AIDS is highly asymmetric, imposing an exceedingly high burden especially in Sub-Saharan countries. In Botswana, for example, life expectancy without HIV/AIDS would be 70 years; it is now 36. In Lesotho, Namibia, South Africa, Zambia, and Zimbabwe life expectancy without HIV/AIDS would be close to (in some cases more than) 20 years longer (UNDESA 2001, p. 59). It is now also recognized that the world may be witnessing the early stages of the global HIV/AIDS epidemic and that its long-term evolution is far from clear, with a high likelihood of explosive growth within the next few years (UNAIDS 2002).

In addition, medical technologies specific to the strain of HIV that most affects Sub-Saharan countries have not been developed. The scale and breadth of the efforts to treat HIV/AIDS in industrial countries often lead to results that, by chance, are also beneficial to developing countries. For example, antiretroviral drugs developed in industrial countries contribute to controlling the epidemic in Africa. But these spillovers are not always there. If vaccines are developed for the HIV strains prevalent in industrial countries, they are unlikely to work for the African strains.

Thus for HIV/AIDS the limited publicness of the response goes beyond restrictions on access to existing technologies: not even the incentives to invest in developing vaccines specific to African countries are in place. The limited publicness of the response to HIV/AIDS starts with lack of access to type 1 inputs (in the case of drugs in developing countries) and lack of availability of type 1 inputs (in the case of vaccines, not yet developed). Moreover, the lack of type 2 inputs (functioning public health care systems) adds even more to the exclusion, since it is used as a justification not to deploy existing interventions. After a long period of nationally centered responses (Tarantola 2001), HIV/AIDS is only now starting to receive an international response (Piot and Seck 2001).

Policy response to antimicrobial resistance: neglect
Antimicrobial resistance (AMR) is a natural biological process. Microorganisms evolve to develop resistance to the effects of antimicrobials. Resistant strains coexist with strains sensitive to antimicrobials, but over time the share of resistant microorganisms can reach 90 percent—rendering the antimicrobials ineffective. AMR has worsened recently as a result of the growing use and misuse of antimicrobials. About 10–15 years ago the share of resistant strains of *Staphylococcus*

aureus (the most common cause of blood infection and postsurgical infection) was close to 0 percent, but today it ranges from 28 percent in the United States to 70 percent in Japan and the Republic of Korea (Smith and Coast 2001). The costs of AMR-related infections are mounting: in the United States treating resistant infections cost more than $4 billion in 1995, more than $7 billion in 1997, and more than $10 billion in 2001 (Woodward, Smith, and others 2001).

AMR is neither new nor surprising. But the depth and burden of the problem have increased substantially in recent years. In industrial countries excessive prescription and use of antimicrobials contribute to AMR, while in developing countries underconsumption of antimicrobials contributes to AMR (Smith 1999). Underconsumption in developing countries is due to high prices, low incomes, limited access to quality health care, and minimal regulatory capacity. Since it is easier to constrain and regulate excessive supply than to ease the budget constraints of households and governments in developing countries, the problem may be tackled more easily in industrial countries (Woodward, Smith, and others 2001).

Findings from a recent study illustrate the scale of the problem in developing countries. In Tanzania 91 percent of antibiotics are prescribed with incorrect dosages. In India 90 percent of prescriptions did not have dosage specifications. Inappropriate prescriptions of antibiotics were reported for viral respiratory tract infections in 97 percent of cases in China and 81 percent in Ghana (Holloway 2000). Irregular supplies, unofficial supplies, and incorrect prescriptions result in infections that are more drug resistant in developing countries.

In addition, there has been a marked decline in antimicrobial research (Kettler 2000; WHO 2000). Pharmaceutical companies see higher rewards in developing drugs for the chronic diseases of the affluent that require long (even lifelong) treatment than in doing so for the infections that overwhelmingly affect the poor and require treatment only until the infection has been controlled. Moreover, new drugs are often reserved for "last line" interventions, precisely to contain AMR, further limiting the scope of the market. The end result is a lack of sorely needed pharmaceuticals, often for "old" diseases—such as malaria and tuberculosis—that are acquiring fierce multidrug resistance.

Awareness of AMR is increasing, with some industrial countries presenting strategies for its containment. The increase in awareness has resulted from the role played by the scientific community, which has often sounded the alarm on important public health issues. But AMR containment is a case where national action alone will be ineffective. The WHO (2001a) has taken steps toward a coordinated international effort, formulating international policy advice and guidelines. But the response has been timid and lacking in the development of new medical knowledge and technologies—once again, limited in publicness, since not even type 1 inputs are being developed.

New international concern about health: enhancing the publicness of the policy response

Health is a major concern of the international community. An abundance of recent policy statements have expressed this concern and called for urgent, force-ful action.[7] What explains the renewed interest in health? Why do past strategies apparently no longer work? This section addresses these questions and examines recent policy responses to global health concerns.

Why is health back at the top of the international agenda?

Two main forces are raising awareness and driving the renewed concern about health. The first is the crushing burden of disease (including noncommunicable diseases) in developing countries. The second is associated with new global risks generated by this excessive burden.

The crushing, unsustainable disease burden in developing countries. The asymme-try in the burden of disease between industrial and developing countries has increased (Evans and others 2001; Farmer 2001). Moreover, it is safe to assume that if communicable diseases receive only a partial policy response, the response to noncommunicable diseases is even more limited. Although the burden of com-municable diseases is much larger in Africa than in other regions, the burden of noncommunicable diseases is about the same in all regions (figure 2).

In some cases the burden of noncommunicable diseases results from the "dif-fusion of behaviors," leading to the global spread of health conditions that lack the epidemiological characteristics of communicable diseases. Chen, Evans, and Cash (1999) show that international trade and the globalization of advertising campaigns have contributed to the spread of health conditions associated with smoking. In addition, genetic disorders—which spread slowly and only when children inherit them from their parents—have become less geographically cir-cumscribed.

Consider sickle cell disease, a genetic disorder that spreads slowly and silently (see table 1). The disease is characterized by unusual red blood cells that are shaped like sickles and destroyed rapidly, causing a number of health conditions, includ-ing recurrent acute infections. Sickle cell disease was once confined to parts of Sub-Saharan Africa, northern Greece, southern Italy, southern Turkey, eastern Saudi Arabia, and central and southern India (Serjeant 1994). The slave trade introduced sickle cell disease to North and South America, but increased migration and interethnic relations have facilitated its global spread. An estimated 10 percent of the U.S. population is at risk for sickle cell disease (Arhin-Tenkorang 2001).

Poor people's large burden of communicable and noncommunicable diseases means that today's health challenges require more than monitoring and taking preventive action against infectious diseases. There is an important moral and

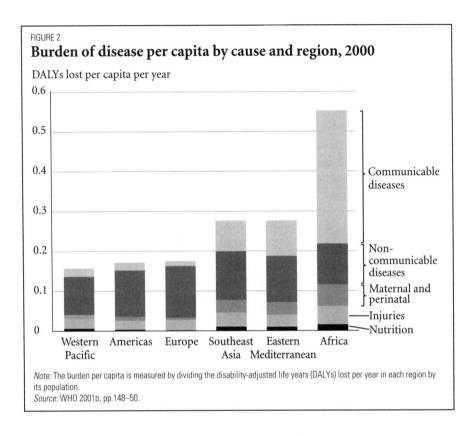

FIGURE 2
Burden of disease per capita by cause and region, 2000

DALYs lost per capita per year

Note: The burden per capita is measured by dividing the disability-adjusted life years (DALYs) lost per year in each region by its population.
Source: WHO 2001b, pp.148–50.

ethical challenge: too many people are suffering from avoidable illness and premature death. And as discussed in the next section, this burden is becoming unsustainable, because it generates serious cross-border spillovers and growing global risks.

New global risks from the disease burden in developing countries. The excessive disease burden in developing countries has adverse effects on countries other than those suffering the direct consequences of high rates of illness and premature death. These adverse effects create new forms of negative global externalities:

* *Infections spread to industrial countries from developing countries with large disease burdens.* One example is the possible increased prevalence in industrial countries of Africa's HIV strain. New HIV infections in Switzerland have characteristics similar to those fueling the epidemic in Africa: a predominance of heterosexual transmission and a high frequency of the African strain of the virus (Böni and others 1999). Another example is the increased share of tuberculosis cases among foreign-born residents; in the United States this share rose from 30 percent in 1992 to 46 percent in 2000. Tuberculosis is seven times as common among foreign-born as among U.S.-born residents. While the proportion of tuberculosis cases

exhibiting multidrug resistance fell from 3 percent in 1992 to 1 percent in 2000, the share of those cases occurring in foreign-born residents increased from 31 percent to 72 percent (USCDC 2002).

- *Large disease burdens harm economic growth and increase poverty.* Several studies have found a correlation between good health and other human development indicators, such as education, employment, and income.[8] The exceedingly large burden of disease in developing countries is crushing past development achievements and curtailing future development prospects. The disease burden exacerbates poverty, hinders economic performance, and augments population growth (Commission on Macroeconomics and Health 2001)—undermining the future of the countries affected as well as the international objective of global poverty reduction. These effects also limit investment and trade opportunities for firms in industrial countries. (About 42 percent of U.S. exports go to developing countries; Kassalow 2001.)

- *Large burdens of disease also threaten political stability and foster social unrest,* with possible global consequences. High infant mortality is strongly correlated with state collapse.[9] Indicators of disease-induced death are negatively correlated with state capacity (Price-Smith 2002). In industrial countries the rationale for public funding to control communicable diseases in developing countries is often associated with national and international peace and security (CIA 1999). Failure to control communicable diseases can heighten the perception of some countries' exclusion from growing economic integration, or at least exclusion from its benefits (UN Security Council 2000). Conceição (in this volume) presents preliminary estimates of the costs of the excessive disease burden.

- *Globalization risks losing its legitimacy,* because disease-stricken people in developing countries are likely to feel disenfranchised and abandoned. Directly or through their advocates, they may question why the asymmetries in addressing health challenges are so dramatic, especially now that politics and technology are bringing the world closer together.[10]

Recent policy responses: enhancing the publicness of the response

To address global health challenges, new responses are being designed and implemented that aim at moving toward "health for all," called for by the WHO in 1978 (WHO 1978). Achieving this goal requires acting to control communicable and noncommunicable diseases alike. The new responses are more public in the sense defined above: an effort is being made to develop and deploy all the inputs needed to improve the health conditions of all. Three main strategies are evident, with the first and second oriented toward the first type of disease control inputs and the third toward the second type:

- *Making health-related knowledge more public by design.* Lack of medical knowledge and technologies (drugs, vaccines) constrains the response to health challenges. As a result a number of initiatives, often taking the form of public-private partnerships (see appendix), have been established to conduct and support targeted research and development to create needed medical technologies. One example is the International AIDS Vaccine Initiative (http://www.iavi.org). The initiative has a dual objective: accelerating the development of HIV vaccines while ensuring that vaccines that receive support from the initiative will be made accessible worldwide. The Malaria Vaccine Initiative (http://www.malariavaccine.org) focuses on the same goals for malaria vaccines, while the Medicines for Malaria Venture (http://www.mmv.org) supports research and development for malaria drugs (see also http://www.emvi.org and http://www.amvtn.org). The Global Alliance for TB Drug Development (http://www.tballiance.org), similar to the Medicines for Malaria Venture, focuses on developing tuberculosis drugs that are more effective and easier to deploy.

- *Making medicines more affordable.* The response to diseases is often hindered not by the nonexistence of drugs and vaccines but by their cost. Protected by patents and priced according to the purchasing power of industrial countries, existing interventions may be beyond the reach of developing countries (Abbott 2002). Thus, at the urging of several developing countries[11] and civil society organizations,[12] the international community has reexamined rules for protecting intellectual property rights, notably the World Trade Organization (WTO) agreement on Trade-Related Aspects of Intellectual Property Rights (TRIPS). Oxfam's "cut the cost" campaign insistently urged the WTO to revise its intellectual property rules to make medicines more affordable (http://www.oxfam.org.uk/cutthecost), and the rules have been discussed in UN debates on human rights (UN Economic and Social Council 2000). At the 2001 WTO ministerial conference in Doha, Qatar, a declaration on TRIPS and public health recognized the scope and urgency of the public health problems posed by diseases such as HIV/AIDS, malaria, and tuberculosis. The declaration also recognized that the TRIPS agreement should not impede countries from declaring and dealing with public health emergencies, and acknowledged the possibility of allowing compulsory licensing. Correa (in this volume) explores mechanisms being considered to improve developing countries' access to medicines, including differential pricing, differential patenting, compulsory licensing, and parallel imports.

- *Strengthening capacity in developing countries.* Providing developing countries with needed interventions requires more than affordable medicines; it also requires type 2 inputs, that is, a national health infrastructure capable of delivering vaccines, administering treatments, and monitoring sickness and death. Some recent responses are trying to develop such infrastructure. For example, the Global Alliance for Vaccines and Immunization (http://www.vaccinealliance.org) is a public-private partnership that purchases and delivers vaccines in developing countries. The Global Fund to Fight AIDS, Tuberculosis, and Malaria (http://www.globalfundatm.org), created on the recommendation of the

UN Secretary-General (UN 2001), helps deliver interventions to control the three diseases. Both efforts work on the same principle of funding credible (externally and independently evaluated) country-based proposals. The aim is not only to deliver the urgently needed interventions, but also to build national health care capacity.[13]

POSSIBLE NEXT STEPS

This chapter has interpreted the health challenges facing the international community as resulting from the limited publicness of responses to communicable diseases and other health concerns. The ensuing—and exceedingly large—disease burden in developing countries is not only dashing their hopes for development; it is also generating negative externalities that affect, or will likely soon affect, industrial and developing countries alike.

The international community has started to address these challenges by enhancing the publicness of the responses: making medical knowledge more public by design and more affordable and accessible (type 1 inputs) and implementing programs to deliver existing interventions within countries (type 2 inputs). Although some recent responses to global health concerns have been more public, additional steps may be required to consolidate and strengthen the publicness of such efforts.

Recognizing mutual benefits and tapping new sources of funding

Developing countries receive considerable direct benefits when their disease burden is reduced, but other benefits are shared around the world. Beyond moral and ethical considerations, further easing the burden would attenuate or eliminate the global spillovers described above. Because the benefits are shared by all, the costs of global health interventions should also be shared by all.

This could mean, for example, that health programs in developing countries would be financed not just by those countries' domestic resources and aid allocations. Additional sources could include the health budgets of industrial countries. Resources could also come from industrial country tax credits or from defense or national security budgets.[14] In addition, international pooling of resources, as in the Global Alliance for Vaccines and Immunization and the Global Fund to Fight AIDS, Tuberculosis, and Malaria, is becoming an important instrument.

Current resources are insufficient, and there has been reluctance to commit long-term financing on the scale required. The Commission on Macroeconomics and Health (2001) estimates that substantially reducing the disease burden of developing countries—including controlling major diseases such as HIV/AIDS, malaria, and tuberculosis—would require about $27 billion a year from industrial countries by 2007. About $8 billion of this should be devoted to the Global Fund to Fight AIDS, Tuberculosis, and Malaria. In early 2002 the fund had

$700–800 million available for disbursements, but by March 2002 it had received 316 proposals requiring $1.15 billion (http://www.globalfundatm.org). Increasing resources is crucial, and aid alone may not be sufficient.[15]

Some new financing could come at no additional net cost—for example, from a domestic tax on cigarette sales. Such a tax would reduce tobacco consumption and generate revenues that could pay for interventions and for administration and enforcement of the tax. Public policy incentives should be reviewed to identify the scope for possible budget restructuring.

Increasing incentives for global health research

Without knowledge about health conditions and without technologies to prevent and treat them (type 1 inputs), little can be done to fight disease. Research and development to improve basic knowledge about diseases and to deliver products to fight them have long been encouraged and conducted by both the public and the private sector. Beyond biomedical research, knowledge about health conditions also requires better understanding of the social and economic determinants of health—which calls for investments in research on social behavior, economics, and health systems (Kettler 2002).

During the first half of the 20th century developing and industrial countries had similar priorities in drug and vaccine development. Finding vaccines and cures for diseases ranging from yellow fever to smallpox, from polio to tuberculosis, was in the interest of both groups of countries. But priorities in developing medical technologies have since diverged. Private industry has little incentive to address poor people's diseases. And basic research, supported largely by public entities in industrial countries, only incidentally relates to the health problems of poor people.

At the international level, incentives to develop medical technologies produce a gap in the generation of much-needed medical knowledge and create large asymmetries in the ability to use existing technologies. According to the Global Forum for Health Research (http://www.globalforumhealth.org), only 10 percent of world spending on health research and development is related to the health conditions that account for 90 percent of the global burden of ill health (the 10/90 gap). Of 1,223 new medicines commercialized between 1975 and 1997, only 13 were specifically oriented toward tropical diseases, with 2 resulting from military research and 5 from veterinary research. Only 4 (0.3 percent) resulted from purposeful research on tropical diseases (Pécoul and others 1999). Efforts are being made to correct this imbalance (see appendix), but even these fail to address some of the most neglected diseases affecting developing countries (Trouiller and others 2002). Much more needs to be done.

Michael Kremer suggests that the response may require both "pull" incentives (creating markets for drugs where they are absent) and "push" incentives (providing incentives to conduct research and development). Kremer indicates that a

particularly effective and efficient pull mechanism to encourage vaccine development would be the establishment by governments or private foundations of legally
binding commitments to purchase needed vaccines if and when they are developed (box 1).

According to estimates by the Commission on Macroeconomics and Health
(2001), about $3 billion a year would be required by 2007 to support research and
development oriented toward neglected diseases. Of this, half should go to a new
global health research fund devoted to supporting basic research and half to supporting targeted research and development for drugs, vaccines, diagnostics, and
other medical technologies, through the support of existing initiatives such as
those described in box 1. In addition, there should be a clear understanding that
if specified products were developed in the future, part of this $1.5 billion in
annual spending could be used to purchase them, as discussed in box 1.

BOX 1

A PURCHASE COMMITMENT FOR VACCINES
BY MICHAEL KREMER

Vaccines provide the best hope for a long-run sustainable solution for AIDS and
the other infectious diseases devastating poor countries: they are typically easier
to deliver than drugs, since they require no diagnosis and physicians are not
needed to administer them. But because pharmaceutical firms see little chance
of recouping their risk-adjusted research and development costs, little private
research is being conducted on vaccines for malaria, tuberculosis, and African
strains of HIV.

An extremely cost-effective way for international organizations, industrial
nations, or private foundations to stimulate research on such vaccines is to commit to purchasing effective vaccines once they have been developed. Such a purchase commitment not only would provide the incentive for vaccine
development, but also would ensure that price is not a barrier to people using
the vaccines.

Efforts to encourage vaccine development can be divided into two broad
categories: "push" programs subsidize research inputs—for example, through
research and development tax credits or grants to researchers—while "pull" programs reward the development of a vaccine. Both approaches have important
roles, but current policy underutilizes pull programs.

Push programs are well suited for financing basic research, while pull programs (such as a purchase commitment) have several attractive features for
encouraging more applied work, such as the later stages of vaccine development.
Importantly, the public pays nothing unless a viable vaccine emerges. Pull programs encourage researchers to select projects with a reasonable chance of yield-
ing a viable product rather than overselling their research prospects to research

BOX 1 CONTINUED

administrators and the public. They allow politicians and the public to be confident that they are paying for an actual product rather than supporting a development effort that might not be scientifically warranted. Pull programs also provide strong financial incentives for researchers to focus on developing a marketable product rather than pursuing other goals, such as publishing journal articles.

Finally, appropriately designed pull programs can help ensure that if new products are developed, they will reach those who need them. For example, industrial countries or private foundations could commit to purchasing a malaria vaccine for $5 per immunized person and making it available to developing countries for free or in return for a modest copayment.

For such pull programs to be effective, potential developers must believe that sponsors will not renege on their purchase commitments. In fact, courts have held that similar public commitments to reward contest winners or to purchase specified goods constitute legally binding contracts and that decisions made by independent parties to adjudicate such programs are binding. Clear eligibility and pricing rules can enhance a program's credibility. For example, it could be stipulated that candidate products must be cleared by a regulatory agency such as the U.S. Food and Drug Administration or European Medicines Evaluation Agency. This would ensure that funds are spent on bona fide vaccines.

A candidate product could also be subjected to a market test: nations wishing to purchase the product would need to provide a modest copayment in proportion to their per capita income. Such copayments would give countries an incentive to carefully investigate whether candidate products are appropriate for local conditions and provide a useful test of countries' commitment to a program. If a country is willing to pay, it is also more likely to be prepared to take the steps necessary to ensure that the vaccine is delivered to the people who need it.

The market promised by a program should be large enough to induce substantial effort by vaccine developers, but less than the social value of the vaccine. Several researchers have concluded that a real annual market of $250–500 million would be needed to motivate substantial research. Over 10 years a commitment at this level could save about 1.9 billion discounted disability-adjusted life years—equivalent to saving the lives of 63 million 30-year-olds. The average cost per year of life saved would be $4.

Any of several organizations—including national governments, the World Bank, and private foundations—have the ability to create a credible purchase commitment to stimulate vaccine research. If a commitment to purchase new vaccines fails to induce their development, it will have cost nothing. If it succeeds, it will save millions of lives at a few dollars each.

Note: For more information, see Kremer (2001a, 2001b).

The governance of health research has been debated for more than a decade (see Global Forum for Health Research 2002, especially chapter 3). One option to manage the new global research fund would be through a system of governance akin to the one used by the U.S. National Institutes of Health or the U.K. Medical Research Council (as also proposed by Kaul and Faust 2001), in which funding to research is based on a scientific peer-review process. An important objective of the fund would be to help build long-term scientific capacity in developing countries. So, funding could be made available for research groups in developing countries, which would submit proposals individually or together with other research groups from industrial or developing countries.

Another initiative that could enhance global incentives for research and development would be extending national orphan drug legislation to global diseases, a measure also proposed by the Commission on Macroeconomics and Health (2001). Orphan drug legislation provides pull and push incentives (for example, by easing terms for regulatory approval and providing public funds for research and development) to develop drugs for diseases that, in the current national context, affect a small number of people (and so a limited market) and thus fail to elicit a response from the private sector. Extending the scope to the international market could generate interest in neglected diseases.

Deploying rapid response task forces
Though important and relevant, the above suggestions are oriented toward long-term results. The current global health situation is a crisis—especially in the case of HIV/AIDS—calling for immediate action. Solutions are needed that allow more rapid action than is often possible with the slow pace of international health cooperation. Ill health means that people's security is at risk. Just as efforts are being made to upgrade the international community's capacity to respond to international military crises, consideration should be given to developing capacity for rapid responses to health emergencies. This could involve, for example, dispatching international health teams to help countries control spreading diseases as quickly as possible. Building national capacity is the only sustainable solution, but doing so is a long-term effort. Disease-stricken countries cannot wait for new vaccines and drugs to be developed or for national capacity to mature. The current crisis calls for an emergency response that supports the enhanced publicness of the other responses.

APPENDIX. BIOMEDICAL RESEARCH AND DEVELOPMENT
TO TREAT POOR PEOPLE'S DISEASES

Around the world about $70 billion a year is spent on biomedical research and development, but very little is devoted to the diseases of poor people. The oldest international initiative addressing the diseases of poor people is the Special

Programme for Research and Training in Tropical Diseases, a collaborative effort between the United Nations Development Programme (UNDP), World Health Organization (WHO), and World Bank. For more than 25 years this program has focused on orphan diseases. Malaria has long been among the diseases addressed by the program; tuberculosis was recently added.

The Global Forum for Health Research, a private foundation, was created in 1998 to help correct the 10/90 gap—the fact that just 10 percent of world spending on health research addresses 90 percent of the world's health problems. The forum works as a network of networks and as a catalyst to narrow the 10/90 gap.

An important new organizational arrangement has been the establishment of public-private partnerships. Such partnerships have been created in part because global health problems are so complex that no single agent (firm, government, or nonprofit) is likely to tackle them successfully. Some public-private partnerships are devoted to comprehensive responses to a disease, such as the Roll Back Malaria global partnership. But many have been created to support and conduct research and development for neglected diseases (see table).

The international initiatives listed in table have approximately $100 million in total annual funds, considerably less than the requirements suggested by the Commission on Macroeconomics and Health. But this amount excludes private and national spending on neglected diseases. While private spending is difficult to estimate, it is thought to be rather low. In terms of national spending, the U.S. National Institutes of Health is a particularly strong player. Its annual budget for AIDS research is about $2.5 billion (with proposed funding for 2002 of $357 million for research on an AIDS vaccine), while that for tuberculosis research is more than $80 million and for malaria research about $70 million (http://www. nih.gov).

Selected international initiatives supporting biomedical research and development for neglected diseases

Initiative	Funding year	Funding amount (millions of U.S. dollars)	Funders	Focus
Special Programme for Research and Training in Tropical Diseases A global program of scientific collaboration established in 1975 to coordinate, support, and influence global efforts to combat a portfolio of major diseases of the poor and disadvantaged. Supports R&D, training, and capacity building.	2002–03	95	UNDP, WHO, World Bank, private foundations, country contributions	Malaria (42%); TB (21%; added in 2000); others (each less than 6%); R&D, training, and capacity building
Global Forum for Health Research A private foundation that monitors the 10/90 gap, develops priority setting methodologies, and acts as a catalyst and as a "network of networks." Supports initiatives oriented toward reducing the gap, often providing seed money and administrative support.	2000 Endowment	2.3 1	Rockefeller Foundation, WHO, country contributions	Initiatives to reduce the 10/90 gap
International AIDS Vaccine Initiative A nonprofit scientific and charitable organization founded in 1996 to ensure the development of safe, effective, accessible HIV vaccines. Focuses on accelerating scientific progress, mobilizing public support through issue advocacy and education, encouraging industrial involvement in AIDS vaccine development, and working to ensure global access to a vaccine.	1999 2000 2001	3.9 11.5[a] 19.4[a]	Bill and Melinda Gates Foundation, Sloan Foundation, World Bank, country contributions, pharmaceutical industry	Development of an AIDS vaccine through support of R&D and enlargement of the number and scope of actors engaged in the effort

Initiative	Date	Amount	Funding sources	Purpose
Medicines for Malaria Venture A public-private partnership established in late 1999 to address the market failure reflected in the lack of incentives to develop medicines for malaria. Supports R&D projects with varying degrees of risk.	2001 2002	4.2 15[a]	Private foundations, country contributions, World Bank, WHO, Global Forum for Health Research, pharmaceutical industry	R&D on malaria medicines (6 R&D projects in 2001; 14 expected in 2002)
Malaria Vaccine Initiative A public-private partnership created in 1999 to accelerate the development of a malaria vaccine. Works with national and international agencies and organizations, supporting laboratories, the coordination and management of pilot production, and the release of products for clinical trials.	1999	50[b]	William H. Gates Foundation	Vaccine for malaria
Multilateral Initiative on Malaria Created in 1997 to strengthen and sustain, through collaborative research and training, the capacity of malaria-endemic countries in Africa to carry out research required to develop and improve tools for malaria control.	No data available		Country contributions, U.S. National Institutes of Health, Wellcome Trust and other foundations, pharmaceutical industry	Coordination and mobilization of resources for cooperative malaria research
Global Alliance for TB Drug Development A public-private partnership created in 2000 with the aim of accelerating the discovery and development of cost-effective drugs, by outsourcing drug R&D projects, and moving drug compounds along the development line to regulatory approval and the market at affordable prices for countries with the highest burden from TB.	2001–05	150[a]	Rockefeller Foundation, Bill and Melinda Gates Foundation, country contributions, pharmaceutical industry	TB drug development, from research to regulatory approval and market placement at affordable prices

Selected international initiatives supporting biomedical research and development for neglected diseases

Initiative	Funding year	Funding amount (millions of U.S. dollars)	Funders	Focus
Action TB				
An international coordinated research program set up by GlaxoSmithKline in 1993 with the aim of finding new targets for TB therapies, identifying novel vaccine candidates, and identifying surrogate markers for use in clinical trials. Involves more than 20 academic research groups in Canada, South Africa, the United Kingdom, and the United States and supports the work of more than 40 researchers.	1993–2003	30	GlaxoSmithKline	TB drug development

a. Projected or expected funding.
b. One-time grant.
Source: Authors compilation from relevant documentation.

NOTES

1. Franklin D. Roosevelt, the U.S. president from the early 1930s through most of World War II, was a victim of polio.

2. Salk also thought that the vaccine should be made available to all. When asked who would control the new vaccine, Salk replied, "I'd say it belongs to everyone. I mean, could you patent the sun?" (Seavey, Smith, and Wagner 1998, p. 175).

3. To accelerate the eradication effort, in 1999 the Bill and Melinda Gates Foundation (http://www.gatesfoundation.org) provided $50 million and the UN Foundation (http://www.unfoundation.org) provided $28 million. The U.S. Centers for Disease Control and Prevention provides technical support, including genetic fingerprinting to identify the strains of poliovirus in an outbreak.

4. Although the continuing support of the U.S. Centers for Disease Control and Prevention to the eradication effort, as mentioned above, should not be understated.

5. It is not yet clear when and how immunization efforts would stop once the world is declared free of polioviruses. For an analysis of possible risks, see Dowdle and others (2002).

6. According to Cornes and Sandler (1986), eradication of diseases that spread indiscriminately around the world such as polio is a weakest link global public good: eradication cannot be achieved if one country stays out, so the global public good is provided only when the last country with the disease is certified as being free of it.

7. See UN (2000, 2001); the G-8 Okinawa Summit Declaration, 23 July 2000; and the Abuja Declaration and Framework for Action for the fight against HIV/AIDS, tuberculosis, and other infectious diseases in Africa, 27 April 2001 (http://www.oau-oua.org/afrsummit/docs.htm). U.S. public health policy is increasingly concerned with global health (Bunyavanich and Walkup 2001; http://www.globalhealth.gov); the United Kingdom has also shown concern for global health (UKPIU 2001).

8. Preston (1975) notes a negative relationship between per capita income and mortality. Abel-Smith and Leiserson (1978) examine health and economic development. Fogel (1994) shows the relationship between improvements in health and improvements in living standards for Europeans and North Americans. Strauss and Thomas (1998) provide an overview centered on developing countries.

9. Esty and others (1998, p. vii), analyzing the characteristics of states more likely to collapse, find that among hundreds of variables, high infant mortality is one of only three that consistently separate states that fail from others. In a critical assessment of this work, King and Zeng (2001, p. 650) question the validity of these conclusions—except in the case of infant mortality: "The infant mortality result is fairly striking: only states with governments that are sufficiently competent to keep infant mortality below the global median have comparatively low probabilities of state failure; other countries, even when they are alike in all other measured respects to the G7, have substantial probabilities of failure (as high as 0.25)."

10. For the multiple relationships between globalization and health, see Garrett (2000) and Lee, Buse, and Fustukian (2002). See also Dollar (2001), Cornia (2001),

and Woodward, Drager, and others (2001). Differing views on globalization and health are offered in Feachem (2001) and Lee (2002). Lee and Collin (2001) comprehensively summarize empirical research on globalization and health.

11. Notably South Africa, where a march organized by the Treatment Action Campaign (http://www.tac.org.za) contributed to the Global Treatment Access Campaign (http://www.globaltreatmentaccess.org/).

12. For example, the campaign for access to essential medicines by Médecins Sans Frontières (http://www.accessmed-msf.org/index.asp).

13. In the case of HIV/AIDS the response to the pandemic may have to be multifaceted, going beyond strengthening the health sector (UNDP 2002).

14. The tax credits could include credits for research performed in industrial countries on diseases affecting mainly developing countries and credits on sales to developing countries. See Attaran and others (2000) on the second proposal. See also *Vaccines for the New Millennium Act* of 2001 (U.S. Senate bill 895; U.S. House of Representatives bill 895) and UKPIU (2001), aimed at encouraging research to prevent and treat diseases primarily affecting developing countries.

15. There is also an indirect argument for increasing health spending in developing countries: national health systems become more efficient after a threshold level of health spending per capita has been achieved (Evans and others 2001). Thus increasing health spending in developing countries could help achieve this threshold, which would mean that further resources would be used more effectively.

References

Abbott, Frederick M. 2002. "WTO TRIPS Agreement and Its Implications for Access to Medicines in Developing Countries." Study Paper 2a. Commission on Intellectual Property Rights, London.

Abel-Smith, Brian, and Alcira Leiserson. 1978. *Poverty, Development and Health Policy.* Geneva: World Health Organization.

Acharya, Arnab, Sarah England, Mary Agocs, Jennifer Linkins, and Bruce Aylward. 2001. "Producing a Global Public Good: Polio Eradication." Paper presented at the International Development Research Center Workshop on Global Public Goods for Health, 4–6 June, Ottawa, Canada.

Arhin-Tenkorang, Dyna. 2001. "The GPG Dimensions of Enhanced Health Care of the Poor: A Case Study of Sickle Cell Disease and HIV/AIDS." United Nations Development Programme, Office of Development Studies, New York, N.Y.

Attaran, Amir, Michael Kremer, Jeffrey Sachs, and Sara Sievers. 2000. *A Tax Credit for Sales of HIV, Tuberculosis, and Malaria Vaccines.* Cambridge, Mass.: Harvard University, Center for International Development.

Aylward, R. Bruce, Karen A. Hennessey, Nevio Zagaria, Jean-Marc Olivé, and Stephen L. Cochi. 2000. "When Is a Disease Eradicable? 100 Years of Lessons Learned." *American Journal of Public Health* 90 (10): 1515–20.

Aylward, R. Bruce, Harry F. Hull, Stephen L. Cochi, Roland W. Sutter, Jean-Marc Olivé, and Bjorn Melgaard. 2000. "Disease Eradication as a Public Health Strategy: A Case Study of Poliomyelitis Eradication." *Bulletin of the World Health Organization* 78 (3): 285–97.

Böni, Jürg, Halina Pyra, Martin Gebhardt, Luc Perrin, Philippe Bürgisser, Lukas Matter, Walter Fierz, Peter Erb, Jean-Claude Piffaretti, Elisabeth Minder, Peter Grob, Johann J. Burckhardt, Marcel Zwahlen, and Jörg Schüpbach. 1999. "High Frequency of Non-B Subtypes in Newly Diagnosed HIV-1 Infections in Switzerland." *Journal of Acquired Immune Deficiency Syndromes* 22 (2): 174–79.

Bunyavanich, Supinda, and Ruth B. Walkup. 2001. "US Public Health Leaders Shift toward a New Paradigm of 'Global Health'." *American Journal of Public Health* 91: 1556–58.

Chen, Lincoln C., Tim G. Evans, and Richard A. Cash. 1999. "Health as a Global Public Good." In Inge Kaul, Isabelle Grunberg, and Marc A. Stern, eds., *Global Public Goods: International Cooperation in the 21st Century*. New York: Oxford University Press.

CIA (U.S. Central Intelligence Agency). 1999. "The Global Infectious Disease Threat and Its Implications for the United States." [http://www.odci.gov/cia/publications/nie/report/nie99-17d.html]. January 2002.

Commission on Macroeconomics and Health. 2001. *Macroeconomics and Health: Investing in Health for Economic Development.* Geneva: World Health Organization.

Cooper, Richard N. 1989. "International Cooperation in Public Health as a Prologue to Macroeconomic Cooperation." In Richard N. Cooper, Barry Eichengreen, C. Randall Henning, Gerald Holtham, and Robert D. Putnam, eds., *Can Nations Agree? Issues in International Economic Cooperation.* Washington, D.C.: Brookings Institution.

Cornes, Richard, and Todd Sandler. 1986. *The Theory of Externalities, Public Goods and Club Goods.* Cambridge and New York: Cambridge University Press.

Cornia, Giovanni Andrea. 2001. "Globalization and Health: Results and Options." *Bulletin of the World Health Organization* 79 (9): 834–41.

Dodgson, Richard, Kelley Lee, and Nick Drager. 2002. "Global Health Governance: A Conceptual Review." Global Health Governance Discussion Paper 1. London School of Hygiene and Tropical Medicine, Center on Global Change and Health.

Dollar, David. 2001. "Is Globalization Good for Your Health?" *Bulletin of the World Health Organization* 79 (9): 827–33.

Dowdle, Walter R., Howard E. Gary, Raymond Sanders, and Anton M. van Loon. 2002. "Can Post-Eradication Laboratory Containment of Wild Polioviruses Be Achieved?" *Bulletin of the World Health Organization* 80 (4): 311–16.

Esty, Daniel C., Jack A. Goldstone, Ted Robert Gurr, Barbara Harff, Marc Levy, Geoffrey D. Dabelko, Pamela T. Surko, and Alan N. Unger. 1998. "State Failure

Task Force Report: Phase II Findings." Science Applications International Corporation, McLean, Va.

Evans, David B., Ajay Tandon, Christopher J. L. Murray, and Jeremy A. Lauer. 2001. "Comparative Efficiency of National Health Systems: Cross-National Econometric Analysis." *British Medical Journal* 323: 307–10.

Farmer, Paul. 2001. *Infections and Inequalities: The Modern Plagues.* Berkeley: University of California Press.

Farmer, Paul, Fernet Léandre, Joia Mukherjee, Rajesh Gupta, Laura Tarter, and Jim Young Kim. 2001. "Community-Based Treatment of Advanced HIV Disease: Introducing DOT-HAART (Directly Observed Therapy with Highly Active Antiretroviral Therapy)." *Bulletin of the World Health Organization* 79 (12): 1145–51.

Feachem, Richard A. G. 2001. "Globalisation Is Good for Your Health, Mostly." *British Medical Journal* 323: 504–06.

Fogel, Robert. 1994. "Economic Growth, Population Health and Physiology: The Bearing of Long-Term Prospects on the Making of Economic Policy." *American Economic Review* 84 (3): 369–95.

Garrett, Laurie. 2000. *Betrayal of Trust: The Collapse of Global Public Health.* New York: Hyperion.

Global Forum for Health Research. 2002. *The 10/90 Report on Health Research 2001–2002.* Geneva: Global Forum for Health Research.

Harvard University, Individual Members of the Faculty. 2001. "Consensus Statement on Antiretroviral Treatment for AIDS in Poor Countries." [http://www.cid.harvard.edu/cidinthenews/pr/consensus_aids_therapy.pdf]. June 2001.

Holloway, Kathleen. 2000. "Who Contributes to Misuse of Antimicrobials?" *Essential Drugs Monitor* 28/29: 9.

Kassalow, Jordan S. 2001. *Why Health Is Important to U.S. Foreign Policy.* New York: Council on Foreign Relations.

Kaul, Inge, and Michael Faust. 2001. "Global Public Goods and Health: Taking the Agenda Forward." *Bulletin of the World Health Organization* 79 (9): 869–74.

Kettler, Hannah E. 2000. *Narrowing the Gap between Provision and Need for Medicines in Developing Countries.* London: Office of Health Economics.

———. 2002. "Using Innovative Action to Meet Global Health Needs through Existing Intellectual Property Regimes." Study Paper 2b. Commission on Intellectual Property Rights, London.

King, Gary, and Langche Zeng. 2001. "Improving Forecasts of State Failure." *World Politics* 53 (July): 623–58.

Kremer, Michael. 2001a. "Creating Markets for New Vaccines: Part I—Rationale." In Adam B. Jaffe, Josh Lerner, and Scott Stern, eds., *Innovation Policy and the Economy.* Cambridge, Mass.: MIT Press.

————. 2001b. "Creating Markets for New Vaccines: Part II—Design Issues." In Adam B. Jaffe, Josh Lerner, and Scott Stern, eds., *Innovation Policy and the Economy*. Cambridge, Mass.: MIT Press.

Lee, Kelley. 2002. "Informed and Open Debate on Globalisation and Health Is Needed." *British Medical Journal* 324: 44.

Lee, Kelley, and Jeff Collin. 2001. "A Review of Existing Empirical Research on Globalization and Health." Background paper for the Annual Meeting of the World Health Organization–HSD Scientific Resource Group on Globalization and Health. London School of Hygiene and Tropical Medicine.

Lee, Kelley, Kent Buse, and Suzanne Fustukian. 2002. Health Policy in a Globalizing World. Cambridge and New York: Cambridge University Press.

Lichtenberg, Frank. 2001. "The Effect of New Drugs on Mortality from Rare Diseases and HIV." NBER Working Paper 8677. National Bureau for Economic Research, Cambridge, Mass.

Loughlin, Kelly, and Virginia Berridge. 2002. "Historical Dimensions of Global Health Governance." Global Health Governance Discussion Paper 2. London School of Hygiene and Tropical Medicine, Center on Global Change and Health.

Lyons, F. S. L. 1963. *Internationalism in Europe 1815–1914*. Leyden: A. W. Sythoff.

Mills, Anne. 2001. "Technology and Science as Global Public Goods: Tackling Priority Diseases of Poor Countries." Paper presented at the Annual Bank Conference on Development Economics–Europe, Paris, June 25–26.

PAHO (Pan-American Health Organization). 1992. *Pro Salute Novi Mundi: A History of the Pan American Health Organization*. Washington, D.C.

Pécoul, Benard, Pierre Chirac, Patrice Trouiller, and Jacques Pinel. 1999. "Access to Essential Drugs in Poor Countries: A Lost Battle?" *Journal of the American Medical Association* 281 (4): 361–67.

Philipson, Thomas. 1999. "Economic Epidemiology and Infectious Diseases." NBER Working Paper 7037. National Bureau for Economic Research, Cambridge, Mass.

Piot, Peter, and Awa Marie Coll Seck. 2001. "International Response to the HIV/AIDS Epidemic: Planning for Success." *Bulletin of the World Health Organization* 79 (12): 1106–12.

Preston, Samuel H. 1975. "The Changing Relation between Mortality and Level of Economic Development." *Population Studies* 29: 231–48.

Price-Smith, Andrew T. 2002. *The Health of Nations: Infectious Disease, Environmental Changes, and Their Effects on National Security and Development*. Cambridge, Mass.: MIT Press.

Sandler, Todd, and Daniel G. Arce M.. 2002. "A Conceptual Framework for Understanding Global and Transnational Goods for Health." *Fiscal Studies* 23(2): 195–222.

Seavey, Nina Gilden, Jane S. Smith, and Paul Wagner. 1998. *A Paralyzing Fear: The Triumph over Polio in America.* New York: TV Books.

Serjeant, Graham R. 1994. *Sickle Cell Disease.* 2nd ed. Oxford: Oxford Medical Publications.

Smith, Richard D. 1999. "Antimicrobial Resistance: The Importance of Developing Long-Term Policy." *Bulletin of the World Health Organization* 77 (10): 862.

Smith, Richard D., and Joanna Coast. 2001. "Global Resistance to the Growing Threat of Antimicrobial Resistance." CMH Working Paper WG2: 17. World Health Organization, Commission on Macroeconomics and Health, Geneva.

Steckel, Richard H. 2001. "Health and Nutrition in the Pre-Industrial Era." NBER Working Paper 8542. National Bureau for Economic Research, Cambridge, Mass.

Strauss, John, and Duncan Thomas. 1998. "Health, Nutrition and Economic Development." *Journal of Economic Literature* 36 (2): 766–817.

Tarantola, Daniel. 2001. "Facing the Reality of AIDS—A 15-Year Process?" *Bulletin of the World Health Organization* 79 (12): 1095.

Trouiller, Patrice, Piero Olliaro, Els Torreele, James Orbinski, Richard Laing and Nathan Ford. 2002. "Drug Development for Neglected Diseases: a Deficient Market and a Public-health Policy Failure." *The Lancet.* 359, June 22: 2188–94.

UKPIU (U.K. Performance and Innovation Unit). 2001. *Tackling the Diseases of Poverty.* London: Cabinet Office.

UN (United Nations). 2000. "Millennium Declaration." General Assembly Resolution 55/2. New York.

————. 2001. "Declaration of Commitment on HIV/AIDS." Adopted by the General Assembly special session on HIV/AIDS. New York.

UNAIDS (Joint United Nations Programme on HIV/AIDS). 2000. "Global Summary of the HIV/AIDS Epidemic (December)." [http://www.unaids.org/]. November 2001.

————. 2001. "AIDS Epidemic Update (December)." [http://www.unaids.org/]. December 2001.

————. 2002. *Report on the Global HIV/AIDS Epidemic.* Geneva: UNAIDS.

UNAIDS (Joint United Nations Programme on HIV/AIDS), International AIDS Society, and Bill and Melinda Gates Foundation Expert Group. 2001. "AIDS: The Time to Act." Statement issued after 6–8 May meeting in Mont Pèlerin, Switzerland.

UNDESA (United Nations Department of Economic and Social Affairs). 2001. *World Population Prospects: The 2000 Revision—Highlights.* ESA/P/WP.165. Population Division. New York.

UNDP (United Nations Development Programme). 2002. "A Multifaceted Response to the HIV/AIDS Pandemic." *Essentials* No. 6. New York.

UN Economic and Social Council. 2000. "Intellectual Property Rights and Human Rights: Sub-Commission on Human Rights Resolution 2000/7." E/CN.4/SUB.2/RES/2000/7. New York.

UN Security Council. 2000. "Resolution 1308." S/RES/1308 (2000). New York.

USCDC (U.S. Centers for Disease Control and Prevention). 2001. *HIV Prevention Strategic Plan through 2005.* Atlanta, GA: U.S. Centers for Disease Control.

———. 2002. "Tuberculosis Morbidity among US-Born and Foreign-Born Populations—United States, 2000." *Morbidity and Mortality Weekly Report* 51 (5): 101–04.

WHO (World Health Organization). 1978. *Declaration of Alma-Ata.* Adopted at the International Conference on Primary Health Care, Alma-Ata, USSR, 6–12 September 1978.

———. 2000. *Overcoming Antimicrobial Resistance.* WHO/CDS/2000.2. Geneva.

———. 2001a. *Global Strategy for the Containment of Antimicrobial Resistance.* WHO/CDS/CSR/DRS/2001.2. Geneva.

———. 2001b. *World Health Report 2001: Mental Health—New Understandings, New Hope.* Geneva.

———. 2002. *Weekly Epidemiological Record* 13 (77): 97–108.

Woodward, David, Nick Drager, Robert Beaglehole, and Debra Lipson. 2001. "Globalization and Health: A Framework for Analysis and Action." *Bulletin of the World Health Organization* 79 (9): 875–81.

Woodward, David, Richard Smith, Arnab Acharya, Robert Beaglehole, and Nick Drager. 2001. "Communicable Disease Control: A GPG for Health." World Health Organization, Geneva.

Zacher, Mark W. 1999. "Global Epidemiological Surveillance: International Cooperation to Monitor Infectious Diseases." In Inge Kaul, Isabelle Grunberg, and Marc A. Stern, eds., *Global Public Goods: International Cooperation in the 21st Century.* New York: Oxford University Press.

GLOBAL TRADE
FOR LOCAL BENEFIT:
FINANCING ENERGY
FOR ALL IN COSTA RICA

RENÉ CASTRO AND SARAH CORDERO

First movers often have an advantage. But when it comes to the environment, late-comers sometimes enjoy an advantage as well. To illustrate this counterintuitive proposition, this chapter examines one of Costa Rica's policy goals—clean, sustainable electricity for all its citizens—through the lens of global public goods.[1]

The global public goods perspective is logical for people and policymakers in Costa Rica. Like other Central American countries, Costa Rica is acutely aware of the risks that global warming would entail for the region. Many viewed recent experiences with El Niño as serious warning signs. Costa Rica is rich in natural resources, such as forests, that are sought-after commodities around the world. But Costa Rica, again like many other countries, does not want to pursue economic growth and development at the expense of the atmosphere. Thus economic growth and poverty reduction—and with them, electricity for all—must be achieved through a comprehensive strategy that relies on renewable, nonpolluting energy sources.

Climate stability is important for the lives of Costa Ricans and is a major national policy concern—but one with global dimensions. In a way Costa Rica's people and policymakers are fortunate to face the dual challenge of providing electricity for all in an environmentally sound way. The reason is that this challenge provides incentives to engage with other countries both to secure financing and to pursue an approach that is globally sustainable. Costa Rica also benefits from being a latecomer in fossil fuel consumption, because its "lagging" position will allow it to be among the first movers in carbon emissions trading. Carbon trading is not yet a reality, however, because global climate stability and a clean atmosphere are global public goods that follow a summation production process: all actors, public and private, will have to cooperate for these goods to emerge—creating demand for the natural resources and environmental services that Costa Rica has to offer.

THE DUAL CHALLENGE: PROVIDING CLEAN ELECTRICITY FOR ALL IN A GLOBALLY SUSTAINABLE WAY

Poverty and lack of electricity are often closely correlated. Access to energy increases and diversifies poor people's choices and economic opportunities (UNDP 2000; UNDP, UNDESA, and World Energy Council 2000). In Costa Rica, as in many other developing countries, providing electricity to every household is a policy priority. Policymakers usually have a choice of energy sources: traditional fossil fuels (oil, natural gas, coal) or renewable energy sources (biomass, geothermal, hydropower, solar, wind). Fossil fuels produce energy services with air pollutants that can damage the health of local communities and with greenhouse gases that affect global climate stability. Renewable sources produce energy services free of air pollutants and greenhouse gases. The choice between sources must reflect the area being served and depends on natural endowments, access to technology, and economic and political considerations.

Since the 1970s fossil fuels have generated less than 10 percent of Costa Rica's electricity, reflecting a preference for hydropower and a limited endowment of fossil fuels. Hydropower now generates 85 percent of the country's electricity (ECLAC 2001, p. 700).

About 6 percent of Costa Ricans—fewer than 50,000 households—lack access to the electricity grid. Most of these households have limited energy needs and live in isolated, dispersed rural settlements. Extending the grid in these areas is seven times more costly than in urban areas (World Bank 1996). Thus an appropriate solution would be to provide decentralized, clean power systems.

Renewable energy technologies have reached a stage where their application in developing countries is increasingly feasible, at least technically (UNDP, UNDESA, and World Energy Council 2001, pp. 219–72; World Bank 2000). For example, photovoltaic solar power systems, which convert sunlight into electricity, have been adapted for situations of low and varying demand. Moreover, for low and moderate energy loads in areas with good solar exposure—such as most of Costa Rica's rural areas—photovoltaic systems with short-term battery storage might even be cheaper than grid supplies (Anderson 1997).

Hence photovoltaic power seems like a promising energy option for Costa Rica. Moreover, Costa Rica has gained experience with solar energy through various pilot projects. These projects suggest that a 120-kilowatt photovoltaic panel can meet the basic needs of one rural family.[2] With each unit costing $1,200, about $60 million would need to be invested to provide solar electricity to Costa Rica's 50,000 off-grid households.

But how much are these households able and willing to pay for solar power? Surveys have found that off-grid rural residents could afford to pay $2–16 a month for photovoltaic equipment and installation costs.[3] But only 1 in 6 respondents was willing to pay up to $14, and just half were willing to pay $3 (Castro and Cordero 2002; figure 1). Though these findings are only rough indications, they indicate that few off-grid households could afford solar technology that cost $1,200.

So, what other financing mechanisms are possible? Complementary finance could include subsidizing capital costs nationally, extending credit to potential users, and mobilizing external financial and technical assistance. But Costa Rica has not had much success with indirect subsidies to industries generating power from renewable resources. In addition, rural Costa Ricans have limited access to sources of credit. External assistance is already being used, however, through support that the Global Environment Facility (GEF) provides for the Plantas Eólicas project in Tejona.

The Global Environment Facility was created to help developing countries cover the incremental costs of projects with global environmental benefits—that is, the costs of transforming a project with national benefits into one with global benefits.[4] This financing enables developing countries to afford the often considerable upfront investment costs involved in switching to more environmentally sound economic activities. But the Global Environment Facility is not appropriate for providing longer-term incentives such as the subsidies that would be required to bring photovoltaic energy to poor Costa Ricans. The facility works on an ad hoc, project-by-project basis with limited, unpredictable resources that depend on voluntary contributions. This is not a sound basis on which to build a long-term energy and electricity policy.

Selling environmental services as a contribution to climate stability

A more reliable financing option may emerge as a result of growing global concern about climate change. This concern has generated new demand for environmental services, which Costa Rica is well endowed to supply efficiently.

International efforts to curb global warming

For two decades scientists have been alerting the international community to the risk of global warming. The most recent findings of the Intergovernmental Panel on Climate Change confirm that emissions of greenhouse gases generated by human activities "continue to alter the atmosphere in ways that are expected to affect the climate" (IPCC 2001, p. 3). Three-quarters of emissions of carbon dioxide—the main greenhouse gas—are due to the burning of fossil fuels and one-quarter to deforestation (IPCC 2001, p. 4).

In 1992 the international community adopted the United Nations Framework Convention on Climate Change, which urges countries to cut their greenhouse gas emissions. This goal was turned into a binding commitment with the adoption of the Kyoto Protocol in 1997. The protocol requires annex 1 countries (defined as industrial countries and most transition economies) to cut greenhouse gas emissions by an average of 5.2 percent from their levels in 1990. These targets are to be reached by 2008–12 and sustained through 2012. Developing countries did not have to commit to specific reduction targets under the protocol; annex 1 countries took the lead because they were responsible for most past emissions.

Many annex 1 countries are heavy polluters but also achieve high levels of energy efficiency. Thus for many it will be costly to reduce emissions at home. Many developing countries, including Costa Rica, have lower energy consumption, lower energy efficiency, or both. The Kyoto Protocol provides an incentive to cut greenhouse gas emissions but also offers an advantage to some developing countries, as latecomers in energy consumption. By offering corrective, offsetting arrangements to industrial countries, developing countries can reap financial or development benefits.

The protocol foresees three "flexibility mechanisms" that will allow industrial countries to meet their abatement targets by using the lower emission limitation costs of other countries: joint implementation, international emissions trading, and the Clean Development Mechanism. Under joint implementation an industrial country can receive "emissions reduction units" when it helps finance projects that reduce net emissions in other industrial countries (including transition economies). International emissions trading allows industrial countries to trade their emission allowances with other countries. The Clean Development Mechanism is designed to help non-annex 1 countries achieve sustainable development and contribute to the protocol's ultimate objective— global climate stability—while helping annex 1 countries achieve their targeted emission reductions. The mechanism enables industrial countries to earn emission credits when they invest in emission reduction projects in developing countries.

To enter into force, the Kyoto Protocol must be ratified by 55 countries, including annex 1 countries representing at least 55 percent of global greenhouse gas emissions in 1990. By May 2002, 84 countries had signed the protocol and 54— including just one annex 1 country—had ratified it. Even though the protocol is not yet effective, mounting global concern about climate stability and the prospect of a treaty have led to many pilot initiatives for trading in carbon emissions. Costa Rica hosts one of them.

Costa Rica's carbon trading system
As noted, the Kyoto Protocol does not commit developing countries to cutting greenhouse gas emissions. But it does encourage them to limit the growth of their emissions. Such efforts to contain emissions reflect the summation process that drives the provision of the global public good at stake. In other words, every effort to cut greenhouse gas emissions is a step—even if a modest one—toward curbing global warming. Such efforts also reflect the equitable nature of the protocol. That

is, countries have common but differentiated responsibilities for the provision of the global public bad; thus there are not yet binding targets for developing countries.

In this context some developing countries have started to explore the value of their assets and the services they could offer. Three types of services matter for climate change: increasing energy efficiency (by using less fuel to produce the same amount of power), switching to less carbon-intensive fuels (by developing clean energy), and sequestrating carbon released in the atmosphere (by promoting forests and controlling land uses and changes). Costa Rica's pilot project was originally aimed at promoting reforestation.

Costa Rica was one of the first developing countries to create a carbon emissions trading program through bilateral contracts selling carbon sequestration services to industrial countries. The development of its emissions credit program has gone through three stages. In the first stage (1994–95) the government tried to facilitate trades between individual domestic landowners and foreign governments or corporations. This phase was intended to compensate farmers and landowners for any income loss resulting from the adoption of land use programs that cut greenhouse gas emissions or logging methods that better preserve the carbon sequestration potential of forest covers. The authorities soon realized that it would be more efficient to consolidate emission reduction initiatives: negotiating one deal for a small reforestation initiative cost almost as much—for translators, lawyers, airline tickets, and the like—as for several consolidated initiatives. The first stage revealed the need to cut transaction costs to make carbon emissions trading viable and profitable.

In the second stage (1995–97) the Ministry of Environment and Energy assumed responsibility for consolidating and selling small projects. This effort resulted in the first-ever sale of an emission credit based on reforestation. A total of 238 reforestation initiatives, many bordering wildlife conservation areas, were consolidated to offer a credit to sequester 200,000 tons of carbon equivalents[5] over 20 years (the usual timeframe for this type of contract in Costa Rica). This credit was sold to the Norwegian government in 1996 for $10 a ton. This price reflected expected payments to cattle ranchers to induce them to convert their ranches into plantation forests. Despite the success of the transaction, Costa Rica's inspector general (the head of a government watchdog agency) criticized the ministry for having sold the credit at cost rather than seeking a higher price. Thus the second phase raised the complex issue of how to determine the price of a commodity not yet valued in a proper market.

In the third phase (1997–98) the Ministry of Environment and Energy addressed the inspector general's concerns by auctioning credits. It assembled enough projects to sequester 1 million tons of carbon equivalents over 20 years and offered them at a floor price of $20 a ton. Although several governments and multinational firms expressed interest, in the end there were no bidders. When asked why, some bidders privately told the minister that the floor price was too high. In March 1998, to help address bidders' concerns about additionality,[6] the ministry hired a French technical certification firm to audit the project and attest that reforestation would take place as promised.[7] Nevertheless, the ministry delayed auctioning the credits again until after national elections scheduled for later that year. Hence the third phase generated another lesson: it highlighted buyers' concerns about sellers' post-sale compliance with pre-sale commitments.

After the elections the new president, Miguel Angel Rodriguez, identified emissions trading as one of the few of his predecessor's programs that he intended to retain. One reason may be that President Rodriguez holds a doctorate in economics, which may have made him sympathetic to the rationale for and potential of such a scheme. In addition, environmental protection has always been popular in Costa Rica, and the president had won partly by appealing to rural voters who stood to benefit from emissions trading.

Thus the pilot project generated several lessons typical of a new market. It pointed to the challenge of defining precisely the commodity being offered, clarifying and allocating property rights, and instituting mechanisms for monitoring and compliance. The next section shows how these issues have been addressed and could be dealt with even more systematically in the future.

CREATING A NEW MARKET FOR ENVIRONMENTAL AND DEVELOPMENT SERVICES

After the pilot emissions trading project, several bilateral agreements were developed for clean energy offsetting arrangements. In April 2001 Costa Rica sold 260,000 tons of carbon emission reductions for $20.80 a ton; the reductions were made possible by building a wind power plant to reduce the use of fossil fuels. Decentralized photovoltaic systems for poor rural residents could be financed by selling similar emission credits to industrial countries. But would carbon emissions trading be sufficient to finance the provision of electricity for the 6 percent of Costa Ricans who lack it? What rules of the game need to be defined at the local, national, and international levels to create a win-win situation where emissions are cut and poor people have access to electricity over the long run?

How much should carbon emission reductions cost?
In July 1999 the World Bank Prototype Carbon Fund announced that carbon emission reductions should cost $20–30 a ton. However, there is still a lack of consensus on pricing, which calls for additional research on the valuation of sequestration and other environmental services offered by developing countries.

To fill this gap, Castro (1999) analyzed the implications of different price scenarios for forest conservation and agriculture in Costa Rica. The study confirmed two things. First, higher carbon prices would encourage landowners to supply more land for sequestration services. Second, Costa Rica could supply these services more efficiently than industrial countries. Thus the study showed that Costa Rica has a comparative advantage in selling carbon sequestration services and that, if there is solvable demand, trading these services internationally would make all countries better off. The study also suggested that carbon emissions trading would benefit biodiversity and fragile ecosystem protection. For example, if emission reductions cost about $100 a ton of carbon, 25 percent of Costa Rica's national territory could be maintained as a protected area.

If Costa Rican landowners were adequately paid for carbon sequestration, many might switch from planting crops to forests. Forest projects would most likely replace traditional activities such as raising beef cattle and growing rice, which require a lot of land. Forests would be less likely to replace more profitable export crops such as coffee, bananas, and pineapples. Castro (1999) found that if the carbon price were $83 a ton, a farmer producing—or having the potential to produce—the average agricultural mix for Costa Rica might switch to forest plantations such as pine *(Pinus patula)*.

Carbon sequestration payments could also induce landowners to preserve natural forests outside protected areas. For example, preservation is more profitable than raising beef cattle or growing rice if emission reductions cost $20 a ton of carbon (table 1). But if a landowner had natural forest land suitable for export crops, the carbon price would have to exceed $100 a ton for preservation to be competitive.

Thus the Castro study suggests a need to reassess Costa Rica's natural endowments through the lens of climate stability—a global public good of growing concern—and against the backdrop of many heavy polluters' interest in emissions trading. Such a reassessment would have to objectively consider all benefits and drawbacks. If forest projects replace subsistence agriculture, there may be a trade-off between food security and environmental services such as climate change mitigation. In this case environmental considerations might interfere with poverty alleviation. The issue of balancing local and global benefits and public and private benefits, discussed by Perrings and Gadgil (in this volume), also applies here.

Sales of emission credits could subsidize poor people's access to photovoltaic systems. If the carbon dioxide emissions avoided by installing 1,900 photovoltaic systems were traded for $28 a ton of carbon, the revenue could finance about 20 percent ($3) of the systems' monthly cost (see figure 1).[8] As in the pilot forest project, these credits could be sold through bilateral arrangements with industrial countries or in an international market for carbon emissions.

Making the carbon market global
Previous sections have shown how creating new markets for environmental services—carbon sequestration and clean energy—could help pay for electricity

TABLE 1

Carbon indifference prices between forest protection and competing agricultural activities in various regions and private natural forests in Costa Rica

(U.S. dollars a ton)

Crop or activity	La Amistad	Rincón de la Vieja	Palo Verde	Piedras Blancas	Barra Honda	Guanacaste	Carara	Barbilla
Coffee	386	219	275	168	228	226	211	227
Pineapples	372	458	522	524	502	469	549	487
Watermelons	309	378	432	431	415	389	455	403
Yams	251	305	350	346	335	314	368	327
Avocados	245	298	342	338	327	307	360	320
Plantains	244	297	341	337	326	306	359	319
Tiquisque[a]	198	240	277	270	263	248	291	258
Passion fruit	189	228	263	256	250	235	276	245
Tomatoes	170	204	236	228	224	211	248	221
Forest plantations	124	35	71	14	51	50	54	62
Bananas	102	118	140	129	130	124	147	131
Palm hearts	98	114	135	124	125	119	142	126
Yucca[a]	91	106	126	114	116	111	132	118
Coconuts	73	82	99	87	91	87	104	93
Dairy cattle	66	74	90	77	81	79	94	84
African palms	63	70	85	72	77	74	89	80
Oranges	63	71	86	74	78	76	90	81

523

TABLE 1 CONTINUED

Carbon indifference prices between forest protection and competing agricultural activities in various regions and private natural forests in Costa Rica

(U.S. dollars a ton)

Crop or activity	La Amistad	Rincón de la Vieja	Palo Verde	Piedras Blancas	Barra Honda	Guanacaste	Carara	Barbilla
Sugar cane	61	68	83	70	75	73	87	78
Beef and dairy cattle	51	55	68	55	61	59	71	64
Lemons	35	35	46	32	39	39	48	44
Beans	27	25	35	20	28	29	36	33
Melons	23	20	30	15	23	24	31	28
Potatoes	22	19	29	14	22	23	30	27
Rice	12	6	14	<0	8	10	14	14
Beef cattle	11	6	13	<0	7	9	13	13
Mangoes	3	<0	1	<0	<0	<0	<0	1
Managed forestry	3	<0	2	<0	<0	<0	1	2

a. Tiquisque and yucca are root crops similar to cassava.

Note: The carbon indifference price is the price at which a producer is indifferent between selling carbon and selling an alternative product being produced using the same land.

Source: Castro 1999.

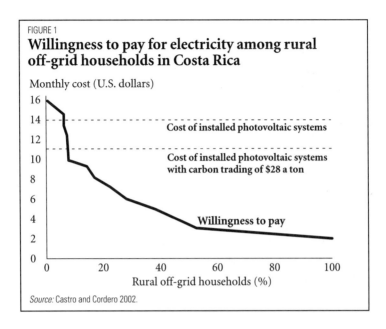

FIGURE 1

Willingness to pay for electricity among rural off-grid households in Costa Rica

Monthly cost (U.S. dollars)

Cost of installed photovoltaic systems

Cost of installed photovoltaic systems
with carbon trading of $28 a ton

Willingness to pay

Rural off-grid households (%)

Source: Castro and Cordero 2002.

access for poor, off-grid Costa Ricans. A variety of market-based instruments can be used to achieve this win-win situation. But how can the bilateral arrangements of the emissions trading pilot project be integrated with an international market?

As discussed, the Kyoto Protocol created three flexible, market-based mechanisms to reduce global greenhouse gas emissions. Estimates show that the larger is the global market, the cheaper it is to meet the protocol's objectives and so to pay for carbon emission reductions. If emissions abatement is undertaken domestically only for annex 1 countries, a ton of carbon costs an estimated $77. If emission reductions can be achieved through joint implementation or a tradable permit market among annex 1 countries, the price falls to $37 a ton. If developing countries participate in a global permit market, the average price falls to $30 a ton (Morozova and Stuart 2001, p. 39). These prices are higher than those in the bilateral offsetting arrangements between Costa Rica and industrial countries and higher than the $28 estimated by Castro (1999) to improve access to solar electricity in rural Costa Rica.

At the same time, the larger is the market, the lower are the costs of providing the final global public good, climate stability. Based on the "G-cubed" model cited by Baron (1999), without emissions trading the costs of abatement under the Kyoto Protocol would be 0.3 percent of GNP in the United States, 0.8 percent in Japan, and 1.4 percent in the other industrial countries that belong to the Organisation for Economic Co-operation and Development (OECD). With trading, emission controls would absorb just 0.2–0.5 percent of GNP in these countries.

But some researchers suspect that these estimates are optimistic, for two reasons (see Baron 1999). First, the models assume that every country would choose the most cost-effective strategy for controlling domestic emissions. But if policymakers protect politically sensitive industries and regions from adopting even low-cost measures, the costs of abatement without trading might be much higher.

Second, the models assume fully fluid markets for emissions trading with no significant barriers or transaction costs. But in practice, developing countries' lack of commitment to specific emission targets is a cause of concern for annex 1 countries. Annex 1 countries are especially concerned about leakage and slippage. The net benefits of a carbon sequestration project could be reduced if a landowner takes money earmarked for forest conservation and uses it to convert a forest to cropland in another area (leakage) or increases carbon emissions by, for example, buying more vehicles (slippage).

Such outcomes would be a major impediment to carbon emissions trading and at the very least would require some neutral party to ensure that the additionality requirement was met—that is, that the emissions reduction would not have occurred anyway under business as usual. Germany has emerged as the leader of a number of industrial countries opposed to significant emissions trading with developing countries until they commit to emission targets. Germany has argued that without emission commitments, additionality would be hard to determine and easily evaded.

Despite these theoretical concerns and without a clear definition of how the additionality test would be met for the Clean Development Mechanism, some countries and large multinational businesses with high emission control costs are interested in buying credits. For example, British Petroleum recently set up a system to trade emission credits among its plants in industrial and developing countries, and discovered that its marginal costs of abatement were likely to be almost $70 a ton of carbon. Thus it was interested in buying low-cost credits from other sources as a way to hedge its bets. Moreover, buying credits generated favorable publicity.

Most of the emission trades proposed at the global level are for electricity projects and so are compatible with Costa Rica's desire to develop clean electricity for poor people. There is also growing interest in including reforestation in the Clean Development Mechanism. Reforestation credits are usually offered for a limited period—say, 20 years—with the idea that at the end the forest will be logged and replanted. Some environmental groups oppose reforestation credits because the credits would have to be replaced if the forests were logged. Greenpeace, the international environmental group, has called reforestation credits a "time bomb" that will cause serious problems when they expire. But advocates of reforestation point out that other credits are also for limited periods—for example, a wind turbine can only be expected to last 20 years. Moreover, hopefully in 20 years technological progress will have cut the costs of emissions abatement.

Additional steps toward the global market
International negotiations on climate change proceed slowly. During negotiations between the parties to the United Nations Framework Convention on Climate Change in Bonn, Germany (July 2001) and Marrakech, Morocco (October –November 2001), the United States reaffirmed that it would not ratify the Kyoto Protocol. Nonparticipation in the global emissions trading system by the biggest emitter of greenhouse gases (24 percent of the world total) will have important economic consequences for all parties: it will lower compliance costs and the international price of carbon (to $25 a ton) and reduce the level of resources flowing through the protocol's flexibility mechanisms (Grubb, Hourcade, and Oberthur 2001).

Still, the Marrakech agreement moved forward on procedures for the Clean Development Mechanism by easing a prompt start of it (with $6.5 million in financial support in the 2002–03 budget) and by authorizing the mechanism's executive board to approve methodologies for baselines, accredit operational entities, and develop and maintain a registry for the mechanism.[9] The Marrakech agreement also authorizes unilateral use of the Clean Development Mechanism, meaning that a developing country can undertake a project under the mechanism without an annex 1 country and market the resulting emission credits. In addition, afforestation and reforestation are eligible under the mechanism but cannot be used to control more than 1 percent of the concerned party's base-year emissions.

One of the most important and complex future steps is to scientifically determine the precise amount of carbon saved from a Clean Development Mechanism project. Many models have been used to estimate sequestration and mitigation potential. Early models calculated that at the global level about 500 million hectares were needed (Sedjo and Solomon 1989) or available (Nordhaus 1991) for carbon sequestration. Early models indicated that Latin America and Africa could provide at least half the required land, with low preparation costs and high forest-growing rates. More recent studies—such as a Harvard University study for Central America (Panayotou 2001) and a University of Mexico study (Masera 2000)—have compared carbon and fossil fuel options. The study for Central America calculates 54 millions tons a year in carbon reductions from forests (through conservation, forest management, and reforestation), compared with 6 million tons from fossil fuel emission reductions. The Mexico study calculates that forests accounted for 87 percent of the 40 million tons in carbon reductions available in Mexico in 2000.

Economists agree that carbon sequestration through afforestation and reduced deforestation may be a cost-effective way to cut global atmospheric concentrations of greenhouse gases (Castro and Cordero 1999; Masera 2000; Stavins and Newel 2000). Now that afforestation and reforestation are included in the international regime, it is essential to gather scientific evidence to value the environmental services that developing countries can offer in the global market for emissions.

Plan B: reducing carbon emissions and debt

Because of the uncertainties surrounding the Kyoto Protocol, even developing countries such as Costa Rica—that is, pioneers in developing trade arrangements to market carbon credits—are considering alternative resource mobilization options for global emissions trading.

In 1995 the Costa Rican government promoted a mechanism that links debt reduction in developing countries to carbon reduction in industrial countries (*The Washington Times,* 1 August 2001). This "trees for debt" initiative is a variation of what Taylor (2001) calls a "world fund that would be financed with debt claims of the developed country parties upon developing country parties of the Kyoto Protocol." These claims would be used to generate instruments that would be sold to carbon-producing companies in industrial countries as part of their carbon reduction programs (Costa Rican Office of Joint Implementation 1997). Taylor (2001) adds, "The depositing country would participate in the proceeds of the sales to rescue part of the debt value and cancel the liabilities of the debtor countries. In exchange for the debt cancellations, the developing and debtor country parties, by entering into agreements with the fund, would commit domestic resources equivalent or proportional to the annual service alleviation, toward the development of national carbon fixation programs in their territories."

The "trees for debt" proposal, however, follows a different rationale than emissions trading. It looks at developing countries as aid recipients rather than as equal partners in a global bargain. The financial agreement proposed between the debtor and the developing country is based on poverty considerations. Creating adequate rules of the game for developing countries in new markets, in contrast, is based on recognizing the services that these countries offer to the international community—that is, their contribution to global welfare. This should be the criterion guiding their participation in the global production of a stable climate.

Conclusion

This case study has explored how developing countries' scarcity of resources can sometimes be exchanged for richer actors' scarcity of greenhouse gas emission rights. Local initiatives to enhance development by providing electricity or paying local farmers to protect forests can also contribute to the provision of global public goods such as climate stability. Indeed, over the long term combining the two objectives is probably the most efficient self-sustaining strategy.

Creating a market for carbon emissions trading will not be easy. It took 10 years to create another new market, the sulfur emissions market in the United States, just at the national level. But the challenge will be worthwhile.

At the same time, developing countries must be fully engaged in international negotiations on climate change. After 2012 these countries are expected to have differentiated binding commitments to cut their greenhouse gas emissions. As Blanchard and others (in this volume) stress, the rules of the game for the next stage should combine efficiency and equity. Whether and to what extent they do so depends, in no small measure, on developing countries' involvement in the debate.

NOTES

1. This chapter is based on Castro and Cordero (2002), which provides a more detailed examination of the issues raised here.

2. Each day this system supplies four hours of lighting (with two high-efficiency 15-watt bulbs), three hours of a 10-watt radio, and one hour of an 80-watt black and white television (World Bank 2000, p. 87). It produces an average of 0.35 kilowatt-hour a day, or 10.5 kilowatt-hours a month (with 3.5 hours of effective daily use).

3. The surveys were conducted between November 2000 and February 2001 by CID Gallup, a Costa Rican company that conducts public opinion surveys and market research. The surveyors interviewed a stratified random sample of 405 off-grid residents, with a standard error of ±4.8 percent.

4. See http://www.gefweb.org/Operational_Policies/Eligibility_Criteria/Incre mental_Costs/incremental_costs.html.

5. Tons of carbon equivalent are the present value of the annual flows of carbon dioxide.

6. Here additionality means that the emission reductions would not have occurred under business as usual—that is, the emission reductions produced by the project are additional to any that would have occurred in its absence.

7. The firm, Société Générale de Surveillance Group, had established a forestry offset carbon verification service.

8. The Costa Rican commission in charge of rural electrification estimates that 1,900 of the 50,000 off-grid households can be efficiently supplied solely by photo-voltaic systems.

9. For an advance, unedited version of the Marrakech accords and declaration, see http://unfccc.org/cop7/documents/accords_draft.pdf.

REFERENCES

Anderson, Dennis. 1997. "Renewable Energy Technology and Policy for Development." *Annual Review of Energy and the Environment* 22: 187–215.

Baron, Richard. 1999. "The Kyoto Mechanisms: How Much Flexibility Do They Provide?" In Richard Baron, Maratina Bosi, and Alessandro Lanza, eds., *Emis-*

sions Trading and the Clean Development Mechanism: Resource Transfers, Project Costs and Investment Incentives. Bonn: International Energy Agency.

Bartels, Carlton. 2001. "Carlton Bartels of CO2e.com Answers Questions Regarding the Greenhouse Gas (GHG) Emissions Trading Market Place." FOW Derivatives Intelligence for the Risk Professional 365: 42–43.

Castro, René S. 1999. "Valuing the Environmental Service of Permanent Forest Stands to the Global Climate: The Case of Costa Rica." Ph.D. diss. Harvard University, Cambridge, Mass.

Castro, René S., and Sarah Cordero. 2002. "The Supply of Clean Energy to the Rural Poor in Central America as a Response to Global Climate Change." ODS Working Paper 11. United Nations Development Programme, Office of Development Studies, New York.

Castro, René S., Sarah Cordero, and Jose A. Gómez-Ibañez. 2000. "Potential Impact of the Emerging CO2 Market: Building on the Costa Rican Experience." In Luis Gómez-Echeverri, ed., Climate Change and Development. United Nations Development Programme, Regional Bureau for Latin America and the Caribbean, and Yale School of Forestry and Environmental Studies. New Haven, Conn.: Yale School of Forestry and Environmental Studies.

Costa Rican Office of Joint Implementation. 1997. "Costa Rican Certifiable, Tradable Greenhouse Gas Offset." Ministry of Energy, San Jose.

ECLAC (Economic Commission for Latin America and the Caribbean). 2001. Statistical Yearbook for Latin America and the Caribbean 2000. New York: United Nations Publications.

Field, Martha A., and William W. Fisher III. 2001. Legal Reforms in Central America: Dispute Resolution and Property Systems. Cambridge, Mass.: Harvard University Press.

Grubb, Michael, Jean-Charles Hourcade, and Sebastian Oberthür. 2001. Keeping Kyoto. London: Climate Strategies.

IPCC (Intergovernmental Panel on Climate Change). 2001. Summary for Policy Makers: A Report of Working Group I. [http://www.ipcc.ch/pub/spm22-01.pdf]

Larraín B., Felipe . Economic Development in Central America. 2 vols. Cambridge, Mass.. Harvard University Press.

Masera, Omar. 2000. "Promotion of Reduction Strategies for Greenhouse Gas Emissions in Latin America: The Mexican Experience." Presented at the annual meeting of the board of governors of the Inter-American Development Bank, Tulane University, March, New Orleans, La.

Morozova, Svetlana, and Marc Stuart. 2001. "The Size of the Carbon Market Study." In United Nations Conference on Trade and Development, Greenhouse Gas Market Perspectives: Trade and Investment Implications of the Climate Change Regime. New York and Geneva: UNCTAD.

Nordhaus, William. 1991. "The Cost of Slowing Climate Change: A Survey." *Energy Journal* 12 (1): 37–65.

Panayotou, Theodore, ed. 2001. *Environment for Growth in Latin America: Environmental Management for Sustainability and Competitiveness.* Cambridge, Mass.: Harvard University Press.

Sedjo, Roger A., and Allen M. Solomon. 1989. "Climate and Forests." In Norman J. Rosenberg, William E. Easterling, Pierre Crosson, and Joel Darmstadter, eds., *Greenhouse Warming: Abatement and Adaptation.* Washington, D.C.: Resources for the Future.

Stavins, Robert N.1999. "The Costs of Carbon Sequestration: A Revealed Preference Approach." *American Economic Review* 89 (4): 994–1009.

Stavins, Robert N., and Richard Newell. 2000. "Climate Change and Forest Sinks: Factors Affecting the Costs of Carbon Sequestration." *Journal of Environmental Economics and Management* 40 (3): 211–35.

Taylor-Dormond, Marvin. 2001. Personal communication. Controller of the Central American Bank for Economic Integration. 24 August.

UNDP (United Nations Development Programme). 2000. *Human Development Report 2000.* New York: Oxford University Press.

UNDP, UNDESA (United Nations Department of Economic and Social Affairs), and World Energy Council. 2000. *World Energy Assessment.* New York: United Nations Development Programme.

World Bank. 1996. *Rural Energy and Development: Improving Energy Supplies for Two Billion People.* Washington, D.C.

———. 2000. *Energy Services for the World's Poor.* Washington, D.C.

CONSERVING BIODIVERSITY: RECONCILING LOCAL AND GLOBAL PUBLIC BENEFITS

CHARLES PERRINGS AND MADHAV GADGIL

Poverty and biodiversity are interlinked in many ways. A number of studies (Dasgupta 1993, 1995; Pearce and Warford 1993) have identified correlations between rural poverty, population growth, landlessness, and pressures on natural resources—including biodiversity. Moreover, the links between poverty and biodiversity run in both directions. Poverty can undermine biodiversity, and biodiversity loss and the resulting degradation of ecosystems can exacerbate poverty. Biodiversity sustains the productivity of ecosystems, enabling them to provide economically important local services such as the hydrological cycle—including flood control, water supply, waste assimilation, nutrient recycling, soil conservation and regeneration, and crop pollination (Daily 1997). Loss of biodiversity causes long-term damage to people's health and food security.

Yet poor people often ignore the long-term effects of biodiversity loss. A number of studies have found that income levels influence the rate at which people discount the future. Although poor people may be risk averse, they tend to heavily discount the future environmental impacts of their actions (see Holden, Shiferaw, and Wik 1998; Pender 1996; and Perrings and Stern 2000). That is, they place more weight on the short-term cash benefits of intensive agriculture and forestry than on the long-term benefits (economic and otherwise) of conservation.

This chapter argues that the apparent tradeoff between poverty reduction and biodiversity conservation is largely false. Moreover, it could be avoided—or at least significantly reduced—by introducing some rather basic policy reforms. These reforms could improve the well-being of all interested parties—rich and poor, public and private. Biodiversity conservation is a public good that offers benefits across a wide range of temporal and spatial scales. Current strategies for conserving it often focus on its global benefits, ignoring its local benefits. Yet by doing so, these strategies not only fail to deliver important local benefits, they also place at risk a global public good: maintenance of the global gene pool. An optimal pattern of protection should reflect both the global and local public benefits of biodiversity conservation. The policy reforms offered in this chapter are designed to achieve that goal.

Special attention is paid to the different public and private benefits from biodiversity as a public good and to their implications for its conservation. In particular, the chapter considers the different interests of national, regional, and global stakeholders in biodiversity conservation and draws conclusions for strategies to protect certain areas, for the financing of conservation efforts, and for institutional reforms at the national and international levels.

BIODIVERSITY AS A PUBLIC GOOD

To understand the problem of biodiversity loss and to identify efficient and effective conservation strategies, it is useful to disentangle the various dimensions of the complex good *biodiversity conservation*. According to the Convention on Biological Diversity, biodiversity means "the variability among living organisms from all sources including, *inter alia*, terrestrial, marine and other aquatic ecosystems and the ecological complexes of which they are part; this includes diversity within species, between species and of ecosystems" (UN 1992, art. 2, para. 1). Understanding biodiversity's various dimensions as a public and private good makes it easier to understand incentives to conserve it. This section considers two properties of biodiversity: its local and global public benefits and its private and public benefits (see also Sandler 1993).

Local and global public benefits
Biodiversity loss typically imposes two rather different costs. The first results from the loss of genetic information. The most obvious such loss is caused by the global extinction of species. But such losses also result from the fragmentation or demise of individual (local) populations. The genetic information contained in any species is spatially structured, and the extirpation of any genetic population involves a largely irreversible loss of information. Accordingly, biodiversity loss at any level diminishes the world's gene pool—an intergenerational global public good (Sandler 1999). This gene pool comprises the genetic information contained in the set of species on Earth as well as the information that may be provided in the future through the evolution of those species.

The second cost of biodiversity loss results from the reduction, fragmentation, exclusion, or deletion of a species from managed ecosystems. Such processes may or may not mean that the species is at risk of extinction. But again, a public good is at stake. The conservation of species in managed ecosystems protects the functioning of those systems and the ecological services they provide (table 1). Changes in the abundance of species in local systems may undermine those services—that is, biodiversity loss may generate multiple bads.

TABLE 1

Ecosystem functions and services

Regulation functions	Production functions	Carrier functions	Information functions
Ecosystems support economic activity and human welfare by: • Protecting against harmful cosmic influences • Regulating climate • Protecting watersheds and catchments • Preventing erosion and protecting soil • Storing and recycling industrial and human waste • Storing and recycling organic matter and mineral nutrients • Maintaining biological and genetic diversity • Exerting biological control • Providing migratory, nursery, and feeding habitats	Ecosystems provide basic resources such as: • Oxygen • Food and drinking water • Water for industry, households, and other users • Clothing and fabrics • Building, construction, and manufacturing materials • Energy and fuel • Minerals • Medicinal resources • Biochemical resources • Genetic resources • Ornamental resources	Ecosystems provide space and a suitable substrate for: • Habitation • Agriculture, forestry, fishery, and aquaculture • Industry • Engineering projects such as dams and roads • Recreation • Nature conservation	Ecosystems provide aesthetic, cultural, and scientific benefits through: • Aesthetic properties • Spiritual and religious significance • Cultural and artistic inspiration • Educational and scientific information • Potential information of value to future scientists

Source: Heywood 1995, p. 879.

534

Not all of nature's services are beneficial. They also include risks and threats such as malaria infection in tropical areas. Thus the benefits of biodiversity conservation need to be balanced against its costs. Moreover, not all community members may agree on the value of the benefits of conservation. Conflicts of interest need to be resolved through the political process.

The local and global benefits of biodiversity conservation involve public goods in the sense that the benefits are largely nonexclusive and nonrival. The global public good—the information contained in the gene pool—is a pure public good. But the local benefits of biodiversity conservation have a quasi-private character. They include benefits that can be privately captured, such as harvests from wild stocks. The quasi-private nature of such benefits explains why international conservation strategies tend to focus more on global than on local benefits—more on ex situ conservation and protection of biodiversity "hot spots" than on conservation of local ecosystems.

Private and public benefits
The local services provided by well-functioning ecosystems are often pure public goods: nonrival in consumption and nonexcludable, available for all people to enjoy. But the individual components of an ecosystem are often private goods. Biological resources such as animals and plants are rival in consumption and, if harvested in sufficient quantities, scarce. Worldwide, biological resources such as timber, fish, ivory, and medicinal plants are privately owned and routinely traded in international markets. Property rights matter because in the absence of coordinated conservation efforts, the level of conservation effort is determined by the value of conservation that can be captured privately. That is, biodiversity conservation is an impure public good. Some of its benefits may be captured privately, and some accrue to everyone.

As with other public goods, biodiversity conservation suffers from free riding. Without coordination, individuals and countries will not volunteer conservation efforts beyond the level in their own interest, and that level is determined by the value of conservation that can be captured privately. Every community member has an incentive to free ride on the conservation efforts of other community members and to neglect the benefits that his or her conservation efforts confer on other members (see appendix).

The same problem occurs at the global level. Every member of the global community has an incentive to free ride on the conservation efforts of others and to neglect the benefits that his or her conservation efforts confer on other members of the global community. The extent of the free-rider problem depends on the production technology used to supply public goods (Sandler 1997).[1]

Biodiversity conservation is a complex good that supports multiple, often contradictory services. Conservation may involve tradeoffs between private and public benefits and between local and global public goods. Effective conservation requires cooperation within and between local and global communities. Where compliance is difficult to monitor and enforce, concerned stakeholders must provide their full participation and support. But optimal participation and cooperation require well-informed decisionmaking. The value of biodiversity provides an important guide for decisionmaking.

THE VALUE OF BIODIVERSITY

The values of most environmental public goods are unknown. Few reliable estimates are available for the costs of underproviding such goods and the benefits of corrective action. Biodiversity is no exception, because valuing it poses many conceptual and methodological challenges. Although such efforts have generated a large literature, the results remain rudimentary. Existing estimates of the benefits of global conservation are hardly adequate for decisionmaking (see Costanza and others 1997 for an implicit valuation). And while the value of the private benefits of biological resources is a useful proxy for the value of local biodiversity conservation, it is no more than a lower bound.

Valuing local benefits
Markets for foods and fibers are the main drivers of resource allocations in agriculture, forestry, and fisheries. But the market prices of products from these sectors typically do not reflect the costs to society of private agricultural specialization, land conversion, or marine exploitation. Market prices do not capture the value of global public benefits such as carbon sequestration or of local public benefits such as watershed protection, habitat provision, and nutrient recycling. Thus estimates of biodiversity values based on the market prices of outputs are poor reflections of social opportunity costs.

For example, the value of tropical forestland harvested for timber and nontimber products is the privately capturable value of land that is common property or subject to open access use. This value is typically lower than the value of the same land were it converted to other uses such as tourism. For example, a World Bank study of Mantadia National Park in Madagascar found that opening the park to tourism would generate more than three times the benefits of its use by local populations (Munasinghe 1993; Kramer and others 1994).

A similar problem exists in production systems. Market forces encourage farmers to choose crops with narrow genetic bases but high mean yields. As a result farmers often ignore the benefits to the farming community of greater genetic diversity in terms of averting the risk of crop failure. In ecological terms, biodiversity ensures that ecosystems are resilient, with resilience defined as a system's capacity to retain productivity following disturbance (Holling 1973; Common and Perrings 1992; Levin and others 1998). Lower diversity increases mean yields (at least in the short run) but also increases risk. Conversely, greater diversity reduces risk, but at the potential cost of lower mean yields. The farming community's attitude toward risk will determine its concern about the effect of diversity on the variance of yields.

Estimates of the value of biodiversity that can be captured privately, such as the value of harvested products, are poor proxies for the value of biodiversity conservation as a local public good. Most ecological services requiring a mix of species are not valued in the market. Prices do not reflect the implications of changes in land use for the provision of ecological services. In principle, valuing conservation efforts in terms of local public benefits requires specifying a production function that describes the relationship between the conserved species and the relevant ecological services (Mäler 1974; Smith 1991).[2] In practice, few studies specify this functional relationship.[3]

Valuing global benefits

Few studies have assessed the value of maintaining the global gene pool, the global public good secured by biodiversity conservation. (The exception are studies on carbon sequestration, which is largely independent of the diversity of species; see Pearce and Moran 1994; Brown and Pearce 1994; Fankhauser 1995; and Pearce 1998.) There are no credible estimates of the impact that local or global species extinctions have on the value of this global public good.

One very crude indicator is provided by the grants given by the Global Environment Facility (GEF) for global biodiversity conservation. The GEF finances conservation in developing countries if the efforts meet two criteria: they are additional to (that is, over and above) what the countries would do if they had only local or national benefits in mind, and they contribute to agreed global environmental goals. In principle, grants are based on the net incremental costs of biodiversity conservation (see also the financing chapter by Kaul and Le Goulven in this volume). The funds disbursed during the first eight years of GEF operations (1990–98) indicate ecosystem and conservation priorities (table 2).

The largest portion of GEF funding for biodiversity went to forest systems (40 percent), followed by coastal, marine, and freshwater systems (17 percent) and mountain systems (6 percent). Thus the bulk of GEF funds were targeted at conserving biodiversity in "natural" rather than "managed" ecosystems—particularly in ecosystems with high levels of endemism. Less attention was paid to biodiversity in agroecosystems. This pattern reflected the fact that the global public benefits of biodiversity conservation lie in the emergency prevention of species extinctions in so-called hot spots.

But in recent years GEF's approach has changed, and it now has a program that promotes the conservation and sustainable use of genetic resources of actual or potential importance to agriculture and food production. Specifically, the program supports projects that protect or enhance the ecological goods and services provided by biodiversity in agroecosystems.

TABLE 2

Global Environment Facility allocations for biodiversity conservation, 1990–98

(millions of U.S. dollars)

Type of disbursement	Pilot phase, 1990–93	GEF 1, 1994–98	Total (percent)
Ecosystem specific	212.3	356.4	74.1
Arid and semiarid systems	29.6	51.8	10.6
Coastal, marine, and freshwater systems	57.1	72.1	16.8
Forest systems	107.3	202.6	40.4
Mountain systems	18.3	29.9	6.3
General and institutional	121.9	76.5	25.9
Enabling grants	14.0	25.2	5.1
Short-term responses	107.9	51.3	20.8
Total	334.2	432.9	100.0

Source: Pearce, Moran, and Krug 1999.

CURRENT TRENDS IN BIODIVERSITY LOSS— AND CONSERVATION RESPONSES

Ecosystems face many pressures. The ways that local communities, countries, and the international community respond to those pressures reflect the various dimensions of the publicness of biodiversity conservation—of linked collective action problems as well as the costs of biodiversity loss and benefits of conservation. Current trends in biodiversity loss indicate that conservation is underprovided. This section reviews these trends and the conservation strategies adopted to counter them.

Estimates and costs of biodiversity loss

Underinvestment in biodiversity conservation has led to what scientists agree is a global mass extinction event (Wilson 1992; Leakey and Lewin 1997). The World Wildlife Fund estimates that in the past 30 years the world has lost a third of its natural wealth (WWF 2000). But scientists disagree on the number of species going extinct and on the economic and biological consequences of these extinctions (Ehrlich 1998). Because habitat destruction is often cited as the main cause of species extinctions, natural forest loss is the measure most often used to estimate species extinctions. Extinction rates are highest in low-income countries, although biodiversity loss was also significant during earlier stages of development in today's industrial countries (WWF 2000). Still, current global extinctions largely reflect local land use decisions in developing countries.

Changes in land use affect biodiversity in both managed systems and their ecological hinterlands. Consider agroecosystems. Market-induced specialization, animal and plant selection, and modern plant and animal breeding have narrowed the genetic base of agriculture to the point where most of the global food supply derives from a handful of species: wheat, rice, corn, oats, sorghum, plantains, tomatoes, potatoes, cattle, sheep, pigs, chickens, and ducks. Moreover, within each of these species there has been a substantial loss of genetic diversity. For example, the adoption in recent decades of high-yielding rice varieties has led to the abandonment of traditional varieties bred over thousands of years. In India 10 rice varieties account for about three-quarters of production. Before the green revolution about 30,000 varieties were cultivated, with no dominant varieties. Bangladesh, Indonesia, and Sri Lanka exhibit similar concentrations of production in a small number of varieties (Cervigni 2001).

The global cost of the local loss of land races and wild relatives is the forgone opportunity to use their genetic material to breed or engineer desirable traits in crops that could be cultivated worldwide. All cultivated crop varieties and livestock strains contain genetic material from land races, wild relatives, and traditional livestock strains. At least half of the increase in agricultural productivity during the 20th century was due to artificial selection, recombination, and intraspecific gene transfers. For example, Mexican beans have been used to improve resistance to the Mexican bean weevil, which destroys or damages up to 25 percent of stored beans in Africa and 15 percent in South America. Thus the loss of land races and traditional varieties has potentially high global costs.

A further consequence at the local level is that agroecosystems have become more susceptible to shocks and changes in environmental conditions. Adopting crops with a narrow genetic base increases average yields, but it also increases the variance of yields (Conway 1993). The public good at stake in the simplification of agroecosystems is their capacity to maintain productivity over a range of conditions. Preliminary estimates confirm that the loss of crop genetic diversity increases the variance of farm incomes in both industrial countries (Gatto 2001) and developing countries (Prakash and Pearce 2001).

Conservation strategies

Historically, the scale of biodiversity conservation efforts has been related to the resource catchment of the society involved (Gadgil 1996). For example, conservation in hunter-gatherer, shifting cultivator, and horticultural societies was location-specific and often embedded in nature worship. Conservation efforts included protection of sacred groves, ponds, and river stretches. These protected areas provided a range of benefits. For example, the sacred groves (called *orans*) in the Indian state of Rajasthan supported the fuel and fodder needs of local communities while safeguarding tree growth (box 1; see also Gokhale and others 1998; Gadgil, Berkes, and Folke 1993; and, for examples from a range of indigenous societies, Posey 1999).

In addition to their amenity, cultural, and spiritual significance, protected areas have been important sources of foods, fuels, fibers, seeds and other plant regeneration material, and habitat for important species such as pollinators. Many such areas offered reserve supplies of foods, fuels, and fibers that were exploited only in extreme conditions. That is, they represented community savings, though in the form of real rather than financial assets. Such protected areas were typically small, often between 1 and 10 hectares and seldom more than 100 hectares.

As societies' resource catchments have grown, so have protected areas. Agrarian societies protected aristocratic hunting preserves that sometimes extended over thousands of hectares. These areas also provided fodder, fuelwood, and small game for the common people. In addition, industrial (and some developing) countries have created national parks that cover hundreds and sometimes thousands of square kilometers—initially to provide recreation and more recently to conserve biodiversity.

The international community has developed two ways to conserve biodiversity. In situ conservation involves protecting ecosystems and natural habitats and maintaining viable populations of species in their natural surroundings (UN 1992, art. 8). Ex situ conservation refers to conservation in zoos, botanical gardens, breeding programs, germplasm laboratories, and gene and seed banks (UN

BOX 1

TRADITIONAL PROTECTED AREAS—THE *ORAN* OF DOLI KALAN

Orans are a traditional, extensive system of sacred forests and pasture lands in the semiarid and arid tracts of the Indian state of Rajasthan. Until 1954 orans were under the control of local landlords, and all villagers observed a taboo on the felling of green trees and used deadwood and fodder in a regulated fashion. These lands were brought under government control in 1954, but in the absence of an alternative system of regulation, orans have been overused and encroached on for agriculture and habitation.

The 34-hectare oran of Doli Kalan (Barmer district) is an exception due to the Bishnoi farmers in the village. Bishnois are a religious sect committed to protecting *Prosopis cinerarea* trees, peafowl, and antelope. They are the dominant community in Doli Kalan and, despite no legal backing, they keep all outsiders away from their oran. They also enforce a strict taboo on lopping any green parts from the oran, including leaves of *Prosopis cinerarea* trees. As a result this oran has well-maintained tree cover and a good population of peafowl and antelope.

Source: Gadgil 1998.

1992, art. 9). Ex situ conservation is aimed at protecting the gene pool. In situ conservation protects both genetic information and the ecological services supported by the conserved species.

As noted, in many countries in situ conservation involves large parks or protected areas in biodiversity hot spots and other high-endemism areas. Large protected areas offer important scale economies. By reducing the ratio of boundary length to protected area, for example, they lower the cost of protection per hectare. And by concentrating on species-rich areas, they lower the cost per species saved. Still, the creation of large conservation areas ignores the fact that biodiversity conservation offers two quite different sets of benefits—that is, it is a joint public good. In addition to preserving genetic information, biodiversity conservation supports the kind of ecological services that motivated historical conservation efforts. These services tend to increase with the ratio of boundary length to protected area. They also depend on the proximity of the protected area to the activities that benefit from the services.

The local public goods offered by biodiversity conservation imply a different scale and pattern of protected areas. They are less sensitive to species richness or endemism. They are also more closely connected to the productivity and resilience of managed, productive agriculture, forestry, and fisheries. The provision of distinct public goods generally requires conservation of distinct sets of species. The set of pollinators is not the same as the set of nutrient recyclers, the set of soil stabilizers, and so on.

From the perspective of these ecological services, one society has a limited interest in the conservation efforts of other societies, because the benefits of conservation in other societies do not accrue to it. Indeed, different societies may have conflicting interests in the diversity of species. Eco-tourists, recreational hunters, and wildlife ecologists in industrial countries are typically interested in different species and different protection regimes than are crop and livestock farmers in developing countries. The first group generally prefers larger protected areas. The second group prefers smaller areas, with overlapping zones for conservation and productive use. If conservation efforts are intended only to maintain the global gene pool, focusing on hot spots is probably the most efficient and effective strategy. But if poverty reduction is also a goal, current conservation strategies need to be rethought to capture the value of biodiversity for local communities.

MOVING TOWARD MORE SUSTAINABLE AND EQUITABLE USE OF BIODIVERSITY

At current deforestation rates, tropical forest habitats will nearly disappear within 50 years. The main reason, as noted, is that the private benefits of conservation are less than the private opportunity costs of conversion (Panayotou 1995). So, in the absence of coordination, what is the best way to enhance the private benefits of conservation? And what is the best way to coordinate national and international conservation efforts?

As a first step, more detailed studies are needed on the costs of a business as usual approach and the benefits of alternative conservation options—including the likely distribution of those benefits. In addition, given the plethora of international, regional, and bilateral agreements on biotic and abiotic resources (Brown Weiss 1993), the interactive effects of such agreements need to be better understood. Many multilateral negotiations aim to induce countries to adopt national conservation policies that provide global benefits. The Convention on Biological Diversity and its financial instrument, the Global Environment Facility, and the International Treaty on Plant Genetic Resources for Food and Agriculture (developed by the UN Food and Agriculture Organization) both emphasize the benefits to nation-states of acting in the global interest.[4] But neither of these international agreements nor the principles guiding Global Environment Facility operations address local interests in protecting important ecosystem services.[5]

Because most local conservation efforts are limited by the private returns to conservation, countries must reassess their national incentive structures. Biodiversity loss is the result of two sets of failures: market failures and public policy failures. Adjusting national incentives has, in turn, two elements. One is generating incentives for biodiversity conservation. The other is discouraging perverse incentives against conservation.

But incentives are also needed to protect public goods at the local level, where millions of foresters, farmers, hunters, harvesters, herders, and fishers use environmental resources every day. Local incentives imply a mix of direct incentives (taxes, subsidies, grants, compensation payments, user fees and charges), indirect incentives (through fiscal, social, and environmental policies), and disincentives (prosecution leading to fines and other penalties).

Thus a dual-track approach is needed. International agreements are important for the international coordination of conservation efforts and for the provision of national incentives to protect the global gene pool. National policies are essential to link countries to international frameworks and to foster national cooperation and fairness. But international and national frameworks will achieve little unless biodiversity conservation makes sense locally—in the context of local ecosystems and local people's lives. Local communities must be fairly rewarded for conservation efforts they make in the national, regional, and global interest, and those conservation efforts must be consistent with the protection of local public goods. A locally rooted conservation strategy calls for some or all of the following policy measures.

Co-locating production and conservation areas

Creating and maintaining large protected reserves in areas with high biodiversity will undoubtedly remain part of the international strategy for biodiversity conservation. But large protected areas alone will not solve biodiversity loss at the local or the global level. A strong case can be made for a complementary system of many small protected areas.

For many environmental gradients, smaller protected areas can capture variation more effectively than can larger areas. In addition, smaller areas can better meet local conservation needs in agriculture, forestry, and fisheries. This decentralized approach matches the conservation practices of traditional societies. Reports from the northeastern hill states of India, for example, suggest that at least 10 percent of the land area is conserved as sacred groves or ponds—meeting the goal proposed at the Fourth World Congress on National Parks and Protected Areas. But the protected area is extremely dispersed (Gadgil, Hemam, and Reddy 1997).

Protecting a few large islands of globally significant diversity surrounded by oceans of low-diversity landscapes does not ensure sustainable, equitable use of biodiversity. What is needed is a two-pronged approach. The global public good, the world's gene pool, can be partly protected by creating special refuges. But protecting the local public good requires achieving an optimal—not necessarily maximal—level of biodiversity in production forests, aquatic bodies, and pastoral and arable ecosystems. This goal is best achieved by co-locating production and conservation areas.

A practical guide to the appropriate scale of governance for local environmental public goods may be provided by the spatial spread of traditional access rights. The formal recognition of those rights would be a good starting point for the (re)institution of local authorities empowered to manage access to those goods and to have a say in determining the local-private balance in the use of local ecosystems. India's joint forest management committees offer an example of this approach (box 2). Similar indigenous management systems have emerged in other parts of the world (Ostrom 1990; World Resources Institute and others 1993).

The global public benefits of biodiversity conservation would also gain from a greater emphasis on complementary local efforts because such a dual-track approach would facilitate species innovation. This approach would add dynamic efficiency to the static efficiency provided by maintenance of the gene pool, with significant potential benefits for humankind's future well-being.

Although the most important goal of this strategy is to develop conservation efforts that increase direct local benefits, there are potential global benefits from local conservation efforts. For example, and as noted, the global cost of the local loss of land races and wild relatives is the forgone opportunity to use their genetic material to breed desirable traits in crops cultivated worldwide. According to the incremental cost argument, those responsible for local conservation efforts should be compensated for such global benefits. A decentralized approach to local conservation is indispensable. But its success will critically depend on whether it "pays"—and hence, whether it offers a fair deal and becomes self-sustaining.

BOX 2

INDIGENOUS MANAGEMENT SYSTEMS—THE DHANI VILLAGE FOREST COMMITTEE

All community-based forest resource management institutions that existed in India prior to British rule were dismantled when the state took over forestlands. More productive lands were converted into "reserve" forests, dedicated to production of commercial timber. Less productive lands were assigned as "revenue" forests for meeting local biomass needs. But because communities had no control over revenue forests, they were treated as open access resources. Reserve forests were depleted of valuable timber but retained better vegetative cover during British rule. Revenue forests, devoid of all regulation, were far more degraded. At independence in 1947 the demand for commercial timber rose rapidly as a result of promotion of forest-based industries, and reserve forests too were soon depleted.

More recently, the system of joint forest management was introduced. Local communities were given some authority to protect patches of forests and assigned a share of the timber as a reward (Gadgil and Guha 1995). This approach has been successful despite the reluctance of forest managers to share authority with villagers, their refusal to assign good forestland for this purpose, and the lack of cohesion in many village communities. Although there is a limited number of formal village forest committees, the legal recognition accorded to them has triggered the establishment of thousands of informal such committees entirely managing their own affairs without any involvement by the forest authorities in tribal villages in the state of Orissa.

The Dhani forest committee is one such committee. It brings together five villages and has promoted the regeneration of 840 hectares of forest tract since 1987. Among the committee's notable features are its flexible regulations, implemented in an adaptive fashion. The general body of the committee oversees the management of the forest as well as issues such as framing rules, resolving conflicts, taking action against offenders, and distributing benefits. The general body has a regular meeting once a year. But in an emergency-such as a forest offense or amendment of existing rules, a meeting of the general body can be called at any time.

Over the years the committee has changed its rules in response to changing conditions. In the first year of operations, for instance, no people or cattle were permitted to enter the forest. After that the area was opened for grazing outside the rainy season from October to June. At the same time, people were permitted to enter the forest to collect dry and fallen wood and leaf litter between July and February. Subsequently, poor members of the community were permitted to extract a limited quantity of fuelwood.

continued overleaf

BOX 2 CONTINUED

Restoration of the vegetation has led to the return of wildlife to the area. The Dhani Village Forest Committee considered a proposal to declare the forest a wildlife sanctuary. But the proposal was rejected on the grounds that it would lead to a takeover by the government and denial of villager access to forest resources that had been replenished by their voluntary efforts (Gadgil 1998).

Through the Convention on Biological Diversity, some of these issues are being addressed in international negotiations. For example, the International Treaty on Plant Genetic Resources for Food and Agriculture recognizes the roles and rights of local farmers. In fact, Africa has developed a model law for protecting the rights of local communities, farmers, and breeders and for regulating access to biological resources (Egziabher 2001, p. 11). But the success of such decentralized management systems depends on the willingness of the international community to support a bottom-up perspective—one in which local ecosystem conservation is the foundation of the global institutional architecture for biodiversity conservation.

Adjusting incentives

As noted, better ways are needed to compensate individuals and communities for local conservation efforts. This implies establishing property rights and incentives that confront people with the full costs of their actions and providing compensation for those who confer local or global public benefits on others.

Take watershed protection. Although communities derive considerable benefits from local watershed protection, the main beneficiaries are often downstream users who are protected from floods and who receive larger flows of higher-quality water than would be the case without protection. The watershed value of forests should be reflected in water and irrigation prices, perhaps through a fee for watershed protection. These fees should then accrue to the community authorities responsible for forest protection.[6] In countries that rely on hydropower, such as Costa Rica, El Salvador, Lao People's Democratic Republic, Sri Lanka, and Vietnam, watershed protection costs could be recouped through electricity tariffs.

Conservation could also generate income through levies on activities such as eco-tourism and the recreational and commercial harvest of wild-living resources. The co-location of many wildlife reserves, wildlife management areas, and hunting concessions in terrestrial systems, and of marine protected areas and fisheries in aquatic systems, reflects the dual role of protected areas. The areas are both conservation mechanisms and reservoirs for the harvested species. Co-location strategies are attractive because the complementarity of conservation and exploitation increases revenue—for example, wildlife reserves support eco-tourism while adjacent hunting concessions support recreational hunting. Indeed, the potential benefits from the commercial harvest of protected species are the expressed motivation for creating marine protected areas (Roberts 2000).

Such co-location strategies are typically far more profitable than better-known arrangements for bio-prospecting. Bio-prospecting contracts between pharmaceutical companies and developing countries, such as between Merck and Costa Rica's Institute Nacional de Biodiversidad, have received a lot of publicity. The contracts seek to mobilize investment in biodiversity conservation by offering the companies access to genetic resources, protected by the assignment of intellectual property rights to genetic "discoveries" (Schulz and Barbier 1997). In addition, bio-prospecting offers local people a fair share of the deal to make conservation worthwhile for them. But such contracts are not widespread, and they generally have not yielded competitive returns (Barbier and Aylward 1996; Simpson, Sedjo, and Reid 1996; Pearce, Moran, and Krug 1999).

Similarly, there is potential for local conservation benefits through emissions trading, especially when it involves forest conservation for carbon sequestration (see Castro and Cordero in this volume). But emissions trading involving reforestation for carbon sequestration is less obviously linked to biodiversity conservation and should probably be discounted (Barbier and Perrings 2001).

The financing of local conservation efforts is complex. Communities seeking to relate their conservation efforts to the global public good may need considerable support. They will find themselves linked to international markets and actors with far more power, information, and skills in determining costs and benefits. Certainly, international agreements and national policies can do more to ensure that emerging markets and trade in environmental goods and services work as well as possible. But markets are primarily intended to achieve allocative efficiency. Additional instruments may be needed to ensure that the benefits of conservation are fairly distributed. That said, the local benefits of local conservation efforts, if properly recognized and compensated, are often sufficient to warrant action regardless of any global benefits. Indeed, this should be the primary focus of reform.

Extending the Global Environment Facility
The equitable sharing of international benefits faces powerful obstacles. The Global Environment Facility's incremental cost principle implies that countries should be compensated for contributing to global public goods. But the structure of international markets and the rules governing international trade and investment mean that transactions falling outside the facility's projects carry no guarantee of equitably shared benefits.

The solution is not to restrict those markets. Indeed, there is considerable scope for markets to be further developed to deliver external benefits to local biodiversity conservation. But if local communities are to be compensated for agroecosystem conservation efforts that yield global benefits, the Global Environment Facility's focus and resources need to be extended. Developing countries have a strong interest in and an even stronger argument for such an extension.

The Global Environment Facility's long-standing emphasis on creating protected areas has started to be relaxed in recognition of the fact that many off-reserve conservation and development projects increase biodiversity protection in reserves as a side benefit. A financially strengthened Global Environment Facility might serve both the Convention on Biological Diversity and the International Treaty on Plant Genetic Resources for Food and Agriculture by addressing the incremental costs of biodiversity conservation in agroecosystems. The main beneficiaries would be small farmers, as custodians of agricultural biodiversity—consistent with the reference to equitable benefit sharing in the convention and the recognition of farmers' rights in the treaty. More important, the new approach would reflect the concerns of developing countries, which argue that the loss of species in local production systems—and especially the loss of intraspecific crop genetic diversity—has been undervalued in global conservation strategies.

International institutional reforms

At the international level, legislative and operational responsibility for the conservation of genetic diversity rests with a range of UN and other agencies: the Food and Agriculture Organization, United Nations Environment Programme, United Nations Educational, Scientific, and Cultural Organization, World Intellectual Property Organization, World Trade Organization, and through the Global Environment Facility, the World Bank and United Nations Development Programme. Given this fractured architecture, some analysts have called for the creation of a World Environment Organization (Whalley and Zissimos 2000) or Global Environment Organization (Runge 2001). These suggestions have also been prompted by the view that the World Trade Organization is not the place to discuss the environmental effects of trade (Bhagwati 2000; Barrett 2000). In addition, as this chapter has shown, no institution systematically addresses trade in global environment services, such as the global public benefits of biodiversity conservation.[7]

As a first interim step pending the formation of a World Environment Organization or Global Environment Organization, it is worth considering the World Heritage Action Trust (2000) recommendation to establish a UN consultative council on biodiversity and food security. This council could promote initiatives by UN agencies and other organizations and reconcile conflicting approaches to the issues. More important, it could explore the institutional requirements of a strategy for protecting the global public interest in off-reserve biodiversity conservation, particularly in sustainably managed agroecosystems.

A second proposal could be to support the extension of the Consultative Group on International Agricultural Research (CGIAR). The CGIAR was established in 1971 to help developing countries meet their food security needs. During its first 20 years the CGIAR, through its 16 international centers, conducted research for developing countries and established the world's largest collection of germplasms. Thus the CGIAR has contributed significantly to the provision of such global public goods as the global gene pool and knowledge for all (Dalrymple 2001). But the subglobal public benefits of conservation have traditionally not been considered in conservation strategies. In the mid-1990s the CGIAR underwent a reorientation (Waters-Bayer 2001). It seems that it is now well positioned to pursue the dual-track approach to conservation suggested here, complementing its tradition of providing global benefits with a decentralized conservation strategy such as its proposed participatory plant breeding program.

CONCLUSION

Biodiversity conservation offers both local and global public benefits. But these benefits tend to be undervalued, and conservation efforts tend to be motivated more by their private benefits than by any public benefits. The little coordinated international conservation that does occur is focused on the global public benefit of biodiversity—maintenance of the gene pool. Conservation policy should consider four reforms:

- Complementing current large-scale conservation efforts with a decentralized strategy that co-locates production and conservation areas, and puts area management rights and responsibilities in the hands of local authorities.
- Adjusting incentives to reward local communities for their conservation efforts—and to hold accountable actors who produce negative externalities.
- Extending the Global Environment Facility's portfolio and resources to support local conservation efforts that yield global public benefits.
- Consolidating the international institutional architecture to allow more systematic trade in global environmental services.

If these reforms were implemented, the tradeoffs between poverty reduction and biodiversity conservation would be less sharp. Biodiversity conservation and poverty reduction could not only go hand in hand, but would be mutually reinforcing.

APPENDIX

Formally, suppose that V^i denotes the welfare of the ith of n communities. This welfare is assumed to depend on consumption of a bundle of market goods, x^i, and a global public good, biodiversity conservation, $Y = y^1, y^2, \dots, y^n$. If there are m members of the ith community, this implies that $V^i = V^i(U_1^i, \dots, U_m^i)$ and $U_j^i = U_j^i(x, y_j^i, y_1^i, \dots, y_m^i)$ for all $j = 1, \dots, m$. The problem faced by the ith community is of the general form:

$$\text{Max}_{xi, yi} \; V^i = V^i(x^i, y^i, Y).$$

That is, the ith community obtains benefits directly from its conservation efforts, y^i, and from the global benefits generated by its contribution to global conservation efforts, Y. Barbier and Perrings (2001) pose the problem for the ith community in the following way:

$$\text{Max}_{xi, ui} \; V^i(.) = V^i(x^i, y^i, C(Y, Z) \mid x^i + py^i = I^i)$$

where $C(Y, Z)$ is a conservation function that increases with the size of the global public good (the level of biodiversity), Y, $C_Y > 0$, and the resources committed to conservation, Z, $C_Z > 0$. If all communities do not cooperate, the welfare of the ith community is maximized where:

$$\frac{V_{y^i}^i}{V_{x^i}^i} = p - \frac{V_c^i}{V_{x^i}^i} C_{y^i}$$

whereas the welfare of the global community requires that:

$$\frac{V_{y^i}^i}{V_{x^i}^i} = p - \Sigma \frac{V_c^i}{V_{x^i}^i} C_y$$

The extra terms reflect the conservation benefits that the ith community confers on others. If the "cost" of conservation is denoted as w, the globally optimal level of conservation will satisfy:

$$\frac{V_{y^i}^i}{V_{x^i}^i} = p - w \frac{C_Y}{Y_Z}$$

NOTES

1. The supply technology, in turn, depends on the nature of the public good. Consider the control of biological invasions, a "weakest link" public good. A national quarantine policy to protect against invasive pathogens reduces the risk to all people in the country concerned. The benefits of quarantine are neither rival nor exclusive: if one person benefits from the protection offered by a quarantine policy, it does not affect the cost of quarantine or reduce the benefits of quarantine to others. But the level of protection offered to the entire community depends on the level of protection supplied by the least effective quarantine facility. If one quarantine facility fails to

identify and exclude an invasive pathogen, all are at risk. That all other quarantine facilities may do so is irrelevant. Ex situ genetic conservation measures, by contrast, are "best shot" public goods. In this case free riding imposes no costs on society.

2. Specifically, if Q is the marketed output of an economic activity and it depends on both a range of marketed inputs, $\mathbf{x} = x_1,\ldots,x_n$ (capital, labor, materials, and so on) and on a natural resource, R, that depends on the set of species, $s = s_1,\ldots,s_m$, then the production function can be written as:

$$Q = Q[x_1,\ldots,x_n, R(s_1,\ldots,s_m)].$$

If P denotes the value of Q, then the value of the ith species, s_i, is the value of the marginal impact of that species: $(PdQ/dR)(dR/ds_i)$. If a change in the abundance of the ith species also affects the abundance of other species in the community, then the value of the ith species, s_i, is $PdQ/dR[dR/ds_i + (dR/ds)(ds/ds_i)]$. That is, it includes both the direct and indirect impacts of a change in the abundance of s_i.

3. An early exception is the valuation by Hodgson and Dixon (1988) of watershed functions in Bacuit Bay, Palawan, the Philippines. This study considered the offsite effects of forest depletion—specifically, the impact of logging activities on sedimentation that in turn affected coral cover, coral diversity, marine tourism, and fish production in Bacuit Bay. The study found that annual sediment deposits of 100 million metric tons per square kilometer led to the extinction of one coral species a year. This extinction was correlated with a 0.8 percent decrease in fish biomass. The negative impact on coral cover of annual sediment deposits of 400 million metric tons per square kilometer was calculated to cause a 2.4 percent decrease in fish biomass.

4. The International Undertaking on Plant Genetic Resources for Food and Agriculture, adopted by the Food and Agriculture Organization (FAO) in 1983, was the first international agreement on the management of food and agricultural plant genetic resources. After the Convention on Biological Diversity was adopted in 1992, the specificity of agricultural biodiversity was acknowledged by the parties to the convention, and the FAO's undertaking was revised to harmonize with the convention. In November 2001 the FAO adopted the undertaking as the International Treaty on Plant Genetic Resources for Food and Agriculture. The treaty will go into effect once 40 countries have ratified it.

5. Barrett (1994) concludes that, at best, an agreement like the Convention on Biological Diversity could achieve an outcome only slightly better than the noncooperative Nash equilibrium. For biodiversity conservation to increase, locally capturable returns to investment in it will have to improve.

6. The Dunoga Bone Combined Irrigation and National Park System in Sulawaesi, Indonesia, shows how water fees can be used to finance biodiversity conservation.

7. The Convention on International Trade in Endangered Species deals with international markets for individual species or products of species. This is different from the trade in global environmental services, such as carbon sequestration or biodiversity conservation, discussed in this chapter.

REFERENCES

Barbier, Edward B., and R. Bruce Aylward. 1996. "Capturing the Pharmaceutical Value of Biodiversity in a Developing Country." *Environmental and Resource Economics* 8 (2): 157–81.

Barbier, Edward B., and Charles Perrings. 2001. "The Economics of Biodiversity Conservation in Agroecosystems." University of York, Centre for Environment and Development Economics, York.

Barrett, Scott. 1994. "The Biodiversity Supergame." *Environmental and Resource Economics* 4 (1): 111–22.

———. 2000. "Trade and the Environment: Local Versus Multilateral Reforms." *Environment and Development Economics* 5 (4): 349–60.

Bhagwati, Jagdish. 2000. "On Thinking Clearly About the Linkage Between Trade and the Environment." *Environment and Development Economics* 5 (4): 485–96.

Brown, Katrina, and David W. Pearce. 1994. "The Economic Value of Non-marketed Benefits of Tropical Forests: Carbon Storage." In John Weiss, ed., *The Economics of Project Appraisal and the Environment.* London: Edward Elgar.

Brown Weiss, Edith. 1993. "International Environmental Law: Contemporary Issues and the Emergence of a New World Order." *Georgetown Law Journal* 81: 675–710.

Cervigni, Raffaello. 2001. *Biodiversity in the Balance: Land Use, National Development and Global Welfare.* Cheltenham, U.K.: Edward Elgar.

Cole, Matthew A., Anthony J. Rayner, and John M. Bates. 1997. "The Environmental Kuznets Curve: An Empirical Analysis." *Environment and Development Economics* 2 (4): 401–16.

Common, Michael S., and Charles Perrings. 1992. "Towards an Ecological Economics of Sustainability." *Ecological Economics* 6: 7–34.

Conway, Gordon R. 1993. "Sustainable Agriculture: The Trade-offs with Productivity, Stability and Equitability." In Edward B. Barbier, ed., *Economics and Ecology: New Frontiers and Sustainable Development.* London: Chapman and Hall.

Costanza, Robert, Ralph d'Arge, Rudolf de Groot, Stephen Farber, Monica Grasso, Bruce Hannon, Karin Limburg, Shahid Naeem, Robert V. O'Neill, Jose Paruelo, Robert G. Raskin, Paul Sutton, and Marjan van den Belt. 1997. "The Value of the World's Ecosystem Services and Natural Capital." *Nature* 387: 253–60.

Daily, Gretchen. ed. 1997. *Nature's Services: Societal Dependence on Natural Systems.* Washington, D.C.: Island Press.

Dalrymple, Dana G. 2001. "International Agricultural Research as a Global Public Good." U.S. Agency for International Development, Bureau for Economic Growth, Agriculture, and Trade, Washington, D.C.

Dasgupta, Partha. 1993 *An Inquiry into Wellbeing and Destitution*. Oxford: Clarendon Press.

―――. 1995. "The Population Problem: Theory and Evidence." *Journal of Economic Literature* 33: 1897–902.

Ehrlich, Paul R. 1998. "The Loss of Diversity: Causes and Consequences." In Edward O. Wilson, ed., *Biodiversity*. Washington, D.C.: National Academy Press.

Ehrlich, Paul R., and Edward O. Wilson. 1991. "Biodiversity Studies: Science and Policy." *Science* 253: 758–62.

Egziabher, Tewolde Berhan Gebre. 2001. "Enhancing the Sustainable Use of Agrobiodiversity." *Bridges between Trade and Sustainable Development* (July–August): 9–10 and 14.

Fankhauser, Samuel. 1995. *Valuing Climate Change: The Economics of the Greenhouse*. London: Earthscan.

Gadgil, Madhav. 1996. "Managing Biodiversity." In Kevin J. Gaston, ed., *Biodiversity: A Biology of Numbers and Difference*. Oxford: Blackwell Science.

―――. 1998. "Conservation: Where Are the People?" *The Hindu Survey of the Environment* 98: 107–37.

Gadgil, Madhav., Fikret Berkes, and Carl Folke. 1993. "Indigenous Knowledge for Biodiversity Conservation." *Ambio* 22 (2–3): 151–55.

Gadgil, Madhav, and Ramachandra Guha. 1995. *Ecology and Equity: Use and Abuse of Nature in Contemporary India*. London: Routledge.

Gadgil, Madhav, Natab S. Hemam, and B. Mohan Reddy. 1997. "People, Refugia and Resilience", In Carl Folke and Fikret Berkes, eds., *Linking Social and Ecological Systems*. Cambridge: Cambridge University Press.

Gatto, Elisa. 2001. "Biological Diversity, Stability and Productivity of Agroecosystems: A Panel Data Analysis." University of York, Environment Department, York.

Gokhale, Yogesh, Ramachandra Velankar, M. D. Subash Chandran, and Madhav Gadgil. 1998. "Sacred Woods, Grasslands and Waterbodies as Self-organized Systems of Conservation." In Ramakrishnan, Palayanoor Sivaswamy, K. G. Saxena, and U. M. Chandrashekara, eds., *Conserving the Sacred for Biodiversity Management*. New Delhi: Oxford and IBH Publishing.

Heywood, Vernon, ed. 1995. *Global Biodiversity Assessment*. Cambridge: Cambridge University Press.

Hodgson, Gregor, and John A. Dixon. 1988. "Logging Versus Fisheries and Tourism in Palawan." East-West Environment and Policy Institute Occasional Paper 7. East-West Center, Honolulu, Hawaii.

Holden, Stein T., Bekele Shiferaw, and Mette Wik. 1998. "Poverty, Market Imperfections and Time Preferences: Of Relevance for Environmental Policy?" *Environment and Development Economics* 3 (1): 105–30.

Holling, Crawford S. 1973. "Resilience and Stability of Ecological Systems." *Annual Review of Ecology and Systematics* 4: 1–23.

Kramer, Randall A., Narendra Sharma, Priya Shyamsundar, and Mohan Munasinghe. 1994. "Cost and Compensation Issues in Protecting Tropical Rainforests: Case Study of Madagascar." Working Paper. World Bank, Environment Department, Washington, D.C.

Leakey, Richard, and Roger Lewin. 1997. La Sixième Extinction. Paris: Flammarion.

Levin, Simon A., Scott Barrett, Sara Aniyar, William Baumol, Christopher Bliss, Bert Bolin, Partha Dasgupta, Paul Ehrlich, Carl Folke, Inge-Marie Gren, Crawford S. Holling, Ann-Marie Jansson, Bengt-Owe Jansson, Karl-Göran Mäler, Dan Martin, Charles Perrings, and Eytan Sheshinski. 1998. "Resilience in Natural and Socioeconomic Systems." Environment and Development Economics 3 (2): 222–35.

Lovejoy, Thomas E. 1980. "A Projection of Species Extinction." In Gerald O. Barney, ed., The Global 2000 Report to the President: Entering the Twenty-first Century. Vol. 2. Council on Environmental Quality. Washington, D.C.: U.S. Government Printing Office.

Mäler, Karl-Göran. 1974. Environmental Economics: A Theoretical Enquiry. Oxford: Blackwell.

May, Robert M. 1972. "Will a Large Complex System Be Stable?" Nature 238: 413–14.

Munasinghe, Mohan. 1993. "Environmental Economics and Biodiversity Management in Developing Countries." Ambio 22 (2–3): 126–35.

Myers, Norman. 1979. The Sinking Ark: A New Look at the Problem of Disappearing Species. Oxford: Pergamon Press.

Ostrom, Elinor. 1990. Governing the Commons: The Evolution of Institutions for Collective Action. New York: Cambridge University Press.

Panayotou, Theo 1995. "Environmental Degradation at Different Stages of Economic Development." In Ahmed Iftikhar and Jan A. Doelman, eds., Beyond Rio: The Environmental Crisis and Sustainable Livelihoods in the Third World. London: Macmillan.

Pearce, David W. 1998. Economics and Environment: Essays on Ecological Economics and Sustainable Development. Cheltenham: Edward Elgar.

Pearce, David W., and Dominic Moran. 1994. The Economic Value of Biodiversity. London: Earthscan.

Pearce, David W., and Jeremy Warford. 1993. World Without End: Economics, Environment, and Sustainable Development. Oxford: Oxford University Press.

Pearce, David W., Dominic Moran, and Wolf Krug. 1999. "The Global Value of Biological Diversity: A Report to UNEP." University College London, Centre for Social and Economic Research on the Global Environment.

Pender, John L. 1996. "Discount Rates and Credit Markets: Theory and Evidence from Rural India." Journal of Development Economics 50 (2): 257–96.

Perrings, Charles. 1995. "Biodiversity Conservation as Insurance." In: Tim Swanson, ed., Economics and Ecology of Biodiversity Decline. Cambridge: Cambridge University Press.

Perrings, Charles, and David Stern. 2000. "Modelling Loss of Resilience in Agroecosystems." *Environment and Resource Economics* 16 (2): 185–210.

Perrings, Charles, Carl Folke, and Karl-Göran Mäler. 1992. "The Ecology and Economics of Biodiversity Loss: The Research Agenda." *Ambio* 21 (3): 201–11.

Posey, Darrell, ed. 1999. *Cultural and Spiritual Values of Biodiversity.* London: Intermediate Technology Publications for United Nations Environment Programme.

Prakash, T. N., and David W. Pearce. 2001. "Resilience as a Measure of Environmental Sustainability: The Case of Karnataka Agriculture, India." University College London, Department of Economics.

Raven, Peter H. 1988. "On Diminishing Tropical Forests." In Edward O. Wilson, ed., *Biodiversity.* Washington, D.C.: National Academy Press.

Reid, Walter V., and Kenton R. Miller. 1989. "Keeping Options Alive: The Scientific Basis for Conserving Biodiversity." World Resources Institute, Washington, D.C.

Roberts, Callum. 2000. "Selecting Marine Reserve Locations: Optimality Versus Opportunism." *Bulletin of Marine Science* 66 (3): 581–92.

Runge, C. Ford. 2001 "A Global Environment Organization (GEO) and the World Trading System: Prospects and Problems." Working Paper 01-1. University of Minnesota, Center for International Food and Agricultural Policy, St. Paul.

Sandler, Todd. 1993. "Tropical Deforestation: Markets and Market Failures." *Land Economics* 69 (3): 225–33.

———. 1997. *Global Challenges.* Cambridge: Cambridge University Press.

———. 1999. "Intergenerational Public Goods: Strategies, Efficiency, and Institutions." In Inge Kaul, Isabelle Grunberg, and Marc A. Stern, eds., *Global Public Goods: International Cooperation in the 21st Century.* New York: Oxford University Press.

Schulz, Carl-Erik, and Edward B. Barbier. 1997. "Trade for Nature." Working Paper ENV80.97. Fondazione Eni Enrico Mattei, Milan, Italy.

Simberloff, Daniel. 1986. "Are We on the Verge of a Mass Extinction in Tropical Rain Forests?" In David K. Elliott, ed., *Dynamics of Extinction.* New York: John Wiley.

Simpson, R. David, Roger Sedjo, and John Reid. 1996. "Valuing Biodiversity for Use in Pharmaceutical Research." *Journal of Political Economy* 104 (1): 163–85.

Smith, V. Kerry. 1991. "Household Production Functions and Environmental Benefit Estimation." In John B. Braden and Charles D. Kolstad, eds., *Measuring the Demand for Environmental Quality.* Amsterdam: North Holland.

Swanson, Timothy. 1992. "Economics of a Biodiversity Convention." *Ambio* 21 (3): 250–57.

UN. 1992. "Framework Convention on Biological Diversity." *International Legal Materials* 31: 818–41.

Waters-Bayer, Ann. 2001. "The Process of Change in International Agricultural Research for Development and the Role of NGOs." [www.ngoc-cgiar.org/].

Whalley, John, and Ben Zissimos. 2000. "Trade and Environment Linkage and a Possible World Environment Organization." *Environment and Development Economics* 5 (4): 510–16.

Wilson, Edward O. 1992. *The Diversity of Life.* Cambridge, Mass.: Belknap Press of Harvard University Press.

World Conservation Monitoring Centre. 1992. *Global Biodiversity: Status of the Earth's Living Resources.* London: Chapman and Hall.

World Heritage Action Trust. 2000. *Governance for a Sustainable Future.* London.

World Resources Institute, National Biodiversity Institute of Costa Rica, Rainforest Alliance, and African Centre for Technology Studies. 1993. "Biodiversity Prospecting Using Genetic Resources for Sustainable Development." World Resources Institute, Washington, D.C.

WWF (World Wildlife Fund). 2000. *The Living Planet Report.* [www.panda.org/livingplanet/lpr00/index.cfm].

PROBLEMS OF PUBLICNESS AND ACCESS RIGHTS: PERSPECTIVES FROM THE WATER DOMAIN

LYLA MEHTA

Since the publication of Kaul, Grunberg, and Stern (1999) a growing number of issues have been examined from the viewpoint of global public goods—from climate change to financial stability and HIV/AIDS control. Some of these analyses have been textbook-like cases describing idealized situations divorced from the sociopolitical and cultural realities in which public goods (and bads) are embedded. Rather than add another issue—water—to this literature, this chapter evaluates the concept of global public goods in terms of its usefulness for guiding debates on people's access to water.

The chapter argues that more attention must be paid to two issues:

- Diverging perceptions of the nature of the good and of how it should be accessed and delivered.
- The power of different actors in determining its distribution.

Neglecting these issues can impede local, regional, and international efforts to enhance the equitable distribution of public goods, a point often overlooked in the rather idealized literature on global public goods.

Water is a contested resource: though it is often considered a common pool resource, it is rival in consumption. In many parts of the world people no longer perceive water as a common good. As a result it divides communities. Access to water reflects power asymmetries, socioeconomic inequalities, and other distribution factors such as land ownership. Moreover, the scope of water's benefits and the reach of its externalities—which struggles over its use may generate—are mostly local or national. In some cases they may have regional repercussions. But the notion of "global water wars" may be exaggerated. Thus water is far from having the properties of a global public good.

Parts of this chapter draw on Mehta (2000). The author is grateful to Arnab Acharya, Keith Bezanson, Peter Davis, Birgit Brixen Jacobsen, and Celestine Nyamu for valuable suggestions and comments.

Still, it is important to evoke the notion of water's publicness—especially given the current globalisation of water and recent moves to turn water, essentially an impure and highly localized public good, into a globalized private good. Many analysts argue that because water is increasingly scarce, it is increasingly valuable—and that this value should be made evident by pricing water and allowing markets to establish the "right" price for it.

But these developments and debates sometimes overlook the needs of poor people. Their needs should be considered by emphasizing water's central role for life in general and human well-being in particular. It can be argued that policies should make water a global public good by design. But given the contested nature of water, evoking its publicness may not be enough. Making goods public by design is only a means. The desired end of making water a public good is ensuring all people's access to it. Thus it is imperative to institutionalize access to water as a human right.[1]

This chapter begins by examining situations that shape people's access to water and hence its public availability. It then explores the extent to which water has local, national, regional, or global dimensions—or even all of them in some measure. The discussion then turns to current debates on the notion of water as an economic good that would best be managed by markets or, at least, market-based mechanisms. This perspective is contrasted with the view that access to water is a human right. Finally, the chapter explores how the notion of global public goods can be used to promote people's access to water as a human right.

IS WATER A COMMON OR CONTESTED GOOD?

Water is essential for all aspects of life. It is the lifeblood of ecosystems, vital for many eco-hydrological functions. In addition, rivers, wells, and seas are crucial to many people's livelihoods. For poor people, access to clean and affordable water is a prerequisite to achieving a minimum standard of health and to undertaking productive activities—particularly in rural areas, where poor people often depend on agricultural activities on both rainfed and irrigated lands. People around the world value water for both its noneconomic and economic characteristics. Water also has deep symbolic and spiritual significance in many cultures, ranging from the holy significance of the Ganga and Narmada rivers in India to the role of Balinese water temples in irrigation management in Indonesia (see Mehta and Punja forthcoming and Lansing 1987 for a discussion of the symbolic and cultural value of water.).

In recent years much prominence has been accorded to water issues at the national, regional, and international levels. Water is a key area for social and public policy and is acquiring growing importance in international development. But does that mean that water is a public good? Public goods provide benefits not confined to a single individual and, once provided, can be enjoyed by many people for free. In other words, pure public goods are nonrival and nonexcludable in consumption. A good example is national defense.

Water generally does not exhibit such features. For example, oceans provide benefits to aquatic and human life, usually for free. But the overuse or abuse of an ocean by one group through, say, the release of effluents in location X will lead to pollution and the depletion of fish stocks in location Y, undermining people's capacity to benefit from the ocean. Thus in this case the ocean is rival in consumption. Rivers and waterways are also rival in consumption in that overuse and pollution undermine their potential benefits.

Following the conventional notion of public goods, water is usually seen as an impure public good—as a common pool resource that is nonexcludable but rival in consumption. Indeed, a vast body of work has documented how people collectively act and use various institutional arrangements in managing their water supplies, often under conditions of water scarcity. For example, pioneering work on irrigation by Coward (1985) and Uphoff (1992) analyzes the strengths of indigenous systems in managing common pool resources. Wade (1988) and Ostrom (1990) analyze the factors enhancing collective action in irrigation systems and the conditions under which local institutions are used to manage local water resources.

Many empirical studies have shown how people cooperate in times of resource pressure and scarcity (Berkes 1989; Bromley and Cernea 1989; Ostrom 1990). In addition, common property scholars have shown how Hobbesian notions of anarchy—where states, regions, and people engage in noncooperative strategies and fight over scarce resources—may not be accurate or predictable. For example, research has shown that local people and global stakeholders have deep understanding of water in their immediate environments and tend to cooperate in times of adversity to avoid the high transaction costs that would result from a failure to comply (Ostrom 1990; Ostrom and Keohane 1995). All these studies explicitly or implicitly draw on the notion of water as a common property resource. But what constitutes the commons?

A growing body of work points to the limitations of some of these collective action approaches in water (see Mosse 1997; Mehta 2001; Cleaver 2000; and Potanski and Adams 1998). Anthropological and sociological studies have highlighted the flaws of valorizing indigenous institutional arrangements without understanding their complexity. Criticism is also levied on ahistorical and apolitical understandings of local communities and collective action arrangements. Moreover, conventional community-based management approaches have based their analyses on simplistic notions of the community and community management. These notions tend to obscure questions about social differentiation in water management and about the power relations that shape water use even at the community level.

Thus local management of natural resources can be conflict-ridden, exclusive, and characterized by competing knowledge claims (Mehta, Leach, and Scoones 2001). Members of the same society can have very different access to and control over land and water resources. For example, detailed research on water scarcity in the Indian village of Merka found that common property resources are highly contested. Their use is determined by factors such as feudal legacies, gender, class, caste, and power relations (Mehta 2001).

In such situations it is impossible to speak of water as a common good because there is no common or collective community. People see water as an issue over which they compete and are divided. Thus there is an urgent need to broaden the notion of water users. In most cases users are disparate groups with diverse institutional and social positions.

These issues suggest that the standard definition of public goods is too abstract and formal to capture real-life ambiguities in the diverse water worlds that people draw on to survive and to sustain their livelihoods. The factors that mediate or hinder access to public goods tend to be glossed over. For example, Sandler (1999) refers to groundwater pollution cleanup as a pure public good. But access to groundwater is usually inalienably linked to land rights. Thus the landless may benefit significantly less than the landed in terms of access to drinking water and irrigation.

Power relations and knowledge asymmetries are only beginning to gain currency in public goods discussions that address the role of preferences (see ODS 2001 and Sweden Ministry for Foreign Affairs 2001a). But they are often key factors in determining how public goods are delivered and accessed. Thus it is important to distinguish between the theoretical or abstract notion of water as a common pool resource and water as a real-life resource beset with problems of access. Goods may be public in theory but not in practice.

IS WATER GLOBAL OR LOCAL?

How global is water? Since the Mar del Plata Conference in 1977, there have been several international declarations on water. In addition, many supranational organizations (often referred to as global public policy partnerships; see Kaul and Ryu 2001; Reinicke 1998; and Reinicke and Deng 2000)—such as the World Commission on Dams (http://www.dams.org/), World Water Council (http://www.walrus.com/~abe/wwc/background/organization.htm), and Water Supply and Sanitation Collaborative Council (http://www.wsscc.org/)—are addressing global water problems and issues. But do these efforts make water a global public good?

To qualify as a global public good, a good's benefits or costs must be quasi-universal. Examples include communicable disease control and the global cultural heritage. Water, by contrast, tends to be highly localized and at best regional in scope. Its availability varies over time and space and depends on such factors as climate, season, and temperature. Rainfall, vegetation, and grass cover vary from place to place, making it difficult to provide blanket statements on the global state of water.

Furthermore, most people experience and perceive water differently. In rural Kutch in western India, villagers refer to water in seven ways (sweet, saline, bland, surface, subterranean, ripe, and raw), and each type has different costs and benefits for different groups (Mehta 2002). Villagers have locally rooted notions about how water should be shared, distributed, and consumed. Thus water is rooted in and defined by its locality (Mehta 2002; Robert 1993). Even river management across basins and borders is rarely global is scope (Sweden Ministry for Foreign Affairs 2001b). Successful transboundary river management (as on the Nile) will likely facilitate dialogue in a certain region (the Middle East) but will probably not do much to enhance or undermine global peace. In such cases water is at best a regional public good.

What about notions of global water crises and global water wars? Could these be considered global public bads, universally affecting people's well-being and health? The figures are well known. An estimated 1.1 billion people lack access to safe water and almost 2.5 billion people—40 percent of the world's population—lack access to adequate sanitation (Neto and Tropp 2000, p. 227). Moreover, it has been argued that increasing global consumption of water coupled with population growth will lead to severe water shortages, with profound effects on food security, health, and human well-being (Postel 1992, 1996).

But these negative impacts will not be uniform around the world. Access to water between countries, within regions and countries, and between women and men is highly unequal. Apart from obvious geographic differences between water-rich and water-poor areas, water shortages have different effects on different social groups (Mehta 2002). The analogy of parched throats amid lush green irrigated fields is well known. Issues of power and control over water become more acute as its scarcity increases.

The speculated water wars could be global. Ismail Serageldin has asserted that many of the wars of the 21st century will be about water, not oil (Cooper 1995, p. 1115). But as Wolf (1997) argues, no major war has been fought over water in recent millenniums. By contrast, 145 water treaties were signed in the 20th century to enhance cooperation between states on water issues. Of course, water can be used as a weapon of war. If the Indus Water Treaty were violated by India or Pakistan, there would be massive destruction to lives and property—but here too the destruction would largely be regional, not global. Similarly, conflicts over the River Jordan are unlikely to affect large segments of the world population, as would a global public bad.

But even if one avoids populist statements about global water crises and water wars, there is no reason to be sanguine. Flawed management has led to polluted and overexploited freshwater sources—including rivers, streams, lakes, wetlands, and groundwater aquifers—undermining water quality and making it unfit for human use. Moreover, freshwater withdrawals have doubled in the past 50 years (WCD 2000). Rising and competing demands have increased pressure on water resources, resulting in higher vulnerability, food insecurity, poverty, and ill health for people as well as negative impacts on the environment.

Thus the notion of global public goods is not entirely applicable to water. Water is best seen as an impure public good with local, national, or regional benefits and costs. Moreover, because access to water is mediated by power relations, it is highly unequal. Water is also a highly contested resource that is engendering active political and economic debates.

POLITICAL STRUGGLES OVER WATER

Current debates on water are guided by two opposing views. One is that water is an economic good that should be priced and would best be managed through markets or at least through market-based mechanisms, such as user fees and charges. The other view is that access to water is a human right.

The changing nature of water: from common pool resource to private good

Many water debates and policies seek to shift its position on the public-private continuum. One step in this direction is being taken by those who argue that water is an economic good that should be priced in the interest of its efficient management. Another is being taken by those who believe that water services should be privatized.

Water as an economic good. Since the Dublin Declaration of 1992 (http://www.wmo.ch/web/homs/icwedece.html), water is increasingly seen as having economic value in all its competing uses. By implication it is being argued that the basic human need for safe drinking water is no longer a sufficient criterion for providing an engineered supply free of charge (Black 1998, p. 55). Because water is scarce, goes the logic, it must be used judiciously and its demand managed. Free water is considered wasted.

Accordingly, efficient resource management is equated with water having a price.[2] The price signal is thus evoked as a way to solve water scarcity problems. The underlying assumption in most discourses—especially those originating in donor countries—is that there is congruity between viewing water as a right and as an economic good. For example, the United Nations Children's Fund (UNICEF) and the World Water Council mention economic efficiency arguments and rights-based arguments in the same breath (see Nigam and Rasheed 1998, pp. 3–7). It is argued that even if something is a right, there is no denying the need to pay for it, as with food.

Public policy at the international level has focused on the neglect of demand management in water supply and sanitation, particularly in developing countries. By contrast, in countries such as India water supply has traditionally been considered a social welfare measure (Reddy 1999, p. 80), though many Indian households pay for public water services. But due to liberalization there has been a push to recover costs in the water sector, especially for service delivery.

Much has been made in the literature of households' willingness to pay for water (Altaf, Jamal, and Whittington 1992; Whittington and Choe 1992). Willingness to pay is usually estimated to be 1–10 percent of household spending and about 5 percent of household consumption. But recent studies are challenging these assumptions, and speak of linking willingness to pay to ability to pay (Reddy and Vandemoortele 1996; Ghosh and Nigam 1995). For example, in the water-scarce Indian state of Rajasthan, Reddy (1999) finds that willingness to pay is much less than 5 percent of consumption. Yet willingness to pay proponents usually treat households as black boxes, ignoring the power dynamics within them, the naturalization of women's water-related tasks, and the low opportunity costs attached to women's time.[3]

This is not to say that poor households do not pay for water. In some parts of the world poor households spend a staggering 25 percent of their income on water (Barlow 1999).[4] In rural India private water markets exist alongside public provision. Some poor people are more willing to buy water from neighbors or water vendors than to pay fixed rates for communal water supplies. In other contexts poor people may not want to pay for communal water when they can get it for free from a local water hole. For them, free water is desirable water.

This discussion points to the tremendous variation in people's decisions about their water supplies—both within and between rural and urban areas and among men and women. In some cases water can simultaneously be a free good, an economic good, and a social good. Public and private water supplies often exist side by side, and the choices that people make about providers depend on a variety of reasons that might not seem entirely rational to outsiders. Thus there is a continuum of public and private goods in the water domain.

Uniform, nondiscriminatory water pricing may not capture all these institutional dynamics and may be unfair to poor people, particularly women. Furthermore, uniform pricing does not take into account externalities such as health issues. When people cannot afford clean water and sanitation, it can lead to the spread of diseases—with children, women, and the elderly being the most vulnerable.

In addition, the low opportunity costs attached to women's time in many parts of the world, combined with their limited decisionmaking power in households, may not lead to a pressing desire among household heads to support better water supply systems for which they would be willing to pay. Thus cultural practices and social and gender relations also influence water pricing. Market forces do not operate in a vacuum: they are influenced by social practices, cultural norms, and local institutional settings.

Could merely declaring water an economic good lead to its more prudent use? Some kind of demand management is required to curb excess water consumption by powerful actors—such as swimming pool owners in the deserts of Arizona (United States) or irrigation water lords in western India who are responsible for a declining water table. Demand-based approaches should not unduly tax poor people and should prevent rich people from being exonerated from water thefts. The polluter pays principle has proven effective in reducing industrial water pollution and water use. It could also be applied to other types of water consumption (such as irrigation use and agricultural runoff).

But it would be flawed to think that the acceptance of water as an economic good is the only way to solve water shortages or generate more efficient water use. There is a danger that pricing mechanisms might tax poor rather than rich people. To avoid that, water prices should be structured progressively, with cross-subsidies that charge rich people more for higher consumption and better services. Without such redistributive mechanisms as well as demand-based measures, skewed access to and control over water resources will continue—worsening water shortages.

Privatization of water services. In recent years water has moved away from being viewed as a common good (however impure) and public service to a commodity being managed according to economic principles (Finger and Allouche 2002, p. xiii). This change is partly due to the growing influence of powerful players—such as the World Bank and transnational corporations—that are paving the way for the privatization of water services. At the World Water Forum in The Hague (Netherlands) in 2000 and to a lesser extent at the International Conference on Freshwater in Bonn (Germany) in 2001, there were heated debates about the private sector's role in delivering water. One of the main arguments for privatizing water services is that the public sector lacks finances for all the massive investments entailed (World Bank 1994). Moreover, the public sector is made out to be too bureaucratic, inefficient, and corrupt.

By contrast, the private sector is invoked as being flexible, efficient, and essential. According to Ismail Serageldin, chair of the World Commission on Water for the 21st Century (http://www.worldwatercommission.org/), turning over water services to private corporations is one of the best ways to provide good services to poor people at suitable prices (Petrella 2001, p. 72). Private sector involvement in basic services has also been thrust on many African countries as part of the conditionalities imposed by the World Bank in the course of economic restructurings.

The polarized state-market opposition in global water debates seems to be missing a crucial point. If it is agreed that enhancing poor people's water security is a basic goal of water interventions, then increasing access and addressing equity concerns emerge as high priorities. The driving question thus needs to be: does privatization promote increased, more equitable access to water?

Poor people often pay much more for water than do rich people. In South Africa some poor rural residents pay 10 times more for water than do rich yet consume just one-tenth as much. Would private involvement redress this inequity? Experiences with water privatization have not always been poor-friendly. One reason involves the nature of water markets. Because water companies are usually monopolies and so face little competition, they tend not to be very responsive to user needs. Thus there has been a marked lack of incentives to service non-profit-making sectors (such as rural residents and the urban poor) or to invest in unprofitable sectors (such as wastewater and sanitation; see Finger and Allouche 2002 and Ugaz 2001).

In many cases water prices have been raised beyond agreed levels within a few years of privatization, and people who could not pay have been cut off (Bayliss 2001; Petrella 2001).[5] But privatization has often also enhanced efficiency—reducing leakages and improving billing and collections (Nickson 2001). In Manila (the Philippines), however, the private operator failed to protect water from environmental degradation (Finger and Allouche 2002, p. 167). And a three-country study in Africa found that although privatization lowered tariffs and improved billing and collections, high prices and disconnections hit the poorest groups in society the hardest (Bayliss 2001).

Moreover, overlapping institutional arrangements have led to confusion about responsibilities for maintenance and investment.[6] Private companies have often ignored existing regulation. In addition, the regulatory framework so key to water privatization in, say, the United Kingdom, is badly flawed in many developing countries. Privatization also does not eliminate government's key role in capital investment, especially in short-term concessions. For the most part the global market for private water services is dominated by a few French multinational corporations. Research on French water companies has revealed a marked lack of transparency and several corruption scandals (Petrella 2001, p. 99).

Privatization of water services appears to have worked best in areas that benefited from earlier state subsidies. In countries lacking strong state investments, it remains to be seen how private corporations will ensure water provision to poor people, particularly during periods of economic insecurity and recession. In addition, privatization models focus on drinking water provision and tend to have a strong urban bias. It is not yet clear how they can be applied in rural areas where people sustain their livelihoods in a diverse and holistic manner, and where reliance on the state, donors, and nongovernmental organizations (NGOs) is greater. Moreover, it is doubtful whether the private sector will invest in sewerage and sanitation, which are less profitable than water supply.

Another dimension involves water's potential to become a tradable commodity. It is not inconceivable that in the near future, treaties on trade—such as the North American Free Trade Agreement or agreements under the World Trade Organization—will allow corporations to mine the water of water-rich areas and transport it to water-poor areas (for example, water exported from water-rich Canada to California or from Austria to southern Europe). Corporations such as Monsanto are moving into the water sector and establishing water businesses in India and Mexico, capitalizing on these countries' acute water shortages (Shiva 1999).

The amount of public money in the water sector is staggering. For example, between 1992 and 1997 the Indian government spent more than $1.2 billion on water projects—while the World Bank spent $900 million (Shiva 1999). If this public money were diverted to the private sector, control over this crucial resource would be a guarantor of profits in an age of grave water scarcity (both manufactured and real). Theoretically, the mass transportation of water from water-rich to water-poor areas could have humanitarian motives. But it is unlikely that corporations will be in the water business and encourage the mass transportation of water out of concern for poor people's human rights to water and sanitation. Thus, from being the last bastion of state intervention, water is increasingly emerging as the "last infrastructure" or "blue gold" for private investors (Barlow 1999).

The commodification of water could erode people's informal rights to free water. For example, in many poor rural communities in Bangladesh, people have access to free water from wells on private land. The sale of such water in some parts of water-abundant Bangladesh is unthinkable. How would the promotion of saleable water affect local norms of informal rights to water for all? It is hard to imagine an outcome that is anything other than detrimental for most people, especially the poorest. Far more nuanced research is required on the nexus between livelihoods, rights, and environmental integrity in issues involving the privatization of water services, at the local level and globally—for example, under the General Agreement on Trade in Services. Until the potential consequences of trade in water are fully assessed, water should not be turned into a tradable commodity.

Is access to water a human right?

In the 1970s international debates stressed the importance of water in meeting basic needs such as health and sanitation. Health care was considered a responsibility of national government, and experience—particularly from the United Kingdom in the 19th century—showed that better water supplies and sanitation were a key driver in this area. The debates highlighted the roles of the state, government, and donors in providing basic water services.

More recently, a growing number of analysts have argued eloquently that access to safe and adequate water is a human right.[7] Advocacy for positive rights—such as access to water, food, and shelter—marks a sharp change from the negative or liberal understanding of rights that underpins notions of liberal democracy. (For example, the right to free speech is construed as freedom from interference in expressing one's opinions rather than the right to have the information and education needed to develop opinions.) Neoliberal traditions have traditionally viewed negative civil and political rights as essential to understanding what, for example, constitutes citizenship.

But these traditions have been reluctant to award the same widespread attention to social and economic rights, because such rights have strong links to social justice and imply moving away from the neoliberal notion that people's socioeconomic status is determined by the market (Plant 1998, pp. 57–58). Over the past century, however, citizenship has increasingly been seen as encompassing social and economic rights. In fact, the distinction between negative and positive rights is highly problematic because both involve state intervention and commitments for their protection.

Supporters argue that water and sanitation are not just basic needs but fundamental human rights based on the criteria established in the 1948 Universal Declaration of Human Rights (which, incidentally, does not distinguish between negative and positive rights) and made explicit in the 1986 Convention on the Rights of the Child. Recognizing water as a human right would require creating national and international legal obligations and responsibilities, making water a focus of world attention, and stipulating a minimum allocation of water per person.

Various donors have suggested basic per capita water requirements ranging from 20–50 liters a day regardless of culture, climate, or technology. For example, South Africa's White Paper on Water Policy, considered the state of the art in water resource literature, sets the per capita allocation at 25 liters a day (http://www.polity.org.za/govdocs/white_papers/water.html). In its Vision 21 the Water Supply and Sanitation Collaborative Council defines an absolute per capita minimum of 20 liters a day (WSSCC 2000). But the council also recognizes that any estimated minimum should be qualified by considerations of culture, service levels, and distances between water sources and users. The council notes the additional health benefits that come with household connections, which usually result in minimum per capita consumption of 40 liters a day. Vision 21 also recommends that every country promote several basic hygiene practices (WSSCC 2000, p. 35). And it links the right to water with a broader vision of human development, poverty reduction, and empowerment of poor people, particularly women (WSSCC 2000, pp. 5–6, 13).

Gleick (1999) and other analysts call for a fixed allocation of water resources. But it seems more useful to insist that people all over the world have access to safe and adequate water that ensures a basic level of healthy functioning and well-being—as in the capabilities approach developed by Sen (1992) and more recently by Nussbaum (2000). In this approach the focus is not on the quantity of entitlements but on the principle of equality and capability to do and to be.

The absolute quantity of water that people require differs based on age, gender, religion, occupation, and so on. But the principle of ensuring sufficient water to achieve a minimum capability remains the same. This minimum requirement may be extended to water for production in some cases (as recent debates in South Africa, for example, suggest). Indeed, seeing water within the capability framework would require strong state intervention and responsibility in providing access to it as a human right and as a key element of citizenship.

There are compelling arguments for viewing access to water as a human right. Significantly improving water and sanitation can reduce the spread of disease and improve people's health and well-being. It can enhance poor households' dignity and independence and free up the one to four hours a day poor women and children spend collecting water. Declaring access to water as a human right could also limit the commodification and commercialization of water, because market mechanisms are unlikely to guarantee its provision to all people—and certainly not on a fair basis.

How could the human right to water be financed? The responsibility of national governments for ensuring the minimum supply required for people's well-being and survival—that is, to achieve a minimum capability—cannot be underestimated. This could be in the form of a free lifeline of water that meets people's basic requirements based on local conditions. The 20/20 Initiative proposed at the 1995 World Summit for Social Development, aimed at achieving universal access to basic social services, suggests taxing rich people and allocating 20 percent of official development assistance and 20 percent of developing country budgets to these services (UNICEF 1994). Vision 21 recommends creating cross-subsidies, swapping debt relief for basic service delivery, and reallocating resources away from high-cost high-technology projects. Other possible financing measures include increasing donor commitments to public services and urging donors to avoid requiring private investment in public services as a condition of aid.

The notion of water as a human right lacks widespread support from the powerful actors that shape global water debates, most of whom prefer to see water security for all as a goal rather than as a universal right. There are several reasons for their lack of support. Rights usually go hand in hand with responsibilities. And if the responsibility for providing water is slowly being shifted to a variety of actors with strong market leanings, ensuring the human rights of poor people might not be a top priority relative to increasing efficiency and maximizing profits. In addition, the United States has always been resistant to advancing social and economic rights, which even today weakens the political feasibility of water as a human right. Furthermore, accepting water as a universal right would require suggesting that, at least theoretically, water is a global public good by design—public in consumption, there for all to consume, and requiring strong government commitments combined with international cooperation and resource transfers.[8]

Hence there is an unresolved struggle between efforts aimed at making water more private, in the interest of efficiency; and making water public by design, in the interest of equity. This struggle often stems from the fact that people do not distinguish between water as a resource that may be free and the services involved in it delivery—which, at least in urban areas, entail costs. More important, the struggle persists because of reluctance among powerful players to acknowledge that principles of social and economic justice must not be sacrificed for reasons related to wider political economy.

Conclusion

This chapter began by arguing that it is difficult to view water as a global public good because its costs and benefits differ widely across the globe. Water is not a pure public good. Instead it is best seen as an impure public good or common good, bearing in mind that technical definitions of global public goods have tended to ignore users' competing claims and interests in the benefits and losses of commons.

Thus water provision needs to be organized according to the scope of the water system in question. At times it will have to be managed locally, at other times nationally, and other times regionally. In addition, constant attention must be paid to power asymmetries and inequalities in water distribution and delivery at the local, national, and regional levels. Central governments could ensure that all voices are heard.

Safeguarding water as a public good, however impure, also depends on the range and scope of the resource base. At the local level, water harvesting and microcatchment treatment, if done sensitively, can lead to both social equity and ecological regeneration. On a regional scale, river basin management can enhance both regional cooperation and ecosystem needs. In recent years integrated water management has been promoted as the best way to integrate socioeconomic and natural resource systems, with the catchment as the unit of management. Integrated management requires developing governance structures and institutions that reflect the physical and social complexities of planning, decisionmaking, and implementation and that balance the needs of people, industry, and agriculture (GWP 2000). Although integrated management is worthwhile, there is a need to ensure that it is not implemented in a top-down manner—failing to incorporate the perspectives of the disempowered—and without provisions for negotiation, conflict resolution, and deliberation.

Water rights are embedded in wider legal instruments and tenure arrangements that can be competing and conflicting, calling into question water's publicness. But water can be made more public through institutional mechanisms that protect it from overuse and misuse and that devise equitable distribution processes. These mechanisms need to be rooted in local and regional dynamics,

avoiding top-down global blueprints—and with decisionmaking based on negotiated outcomes.

The poorly defined nature of water rights can lead to conflicts over access. For
example, if rich farmers' land rights allow them to overexploit communal tanks,
it can undermine their poor neighbors' right to water. Similarly, if a transnational
corporation acquires rights to provide water in a certain area, it can affect a poor
community's right to access safe and adequate water. Thus the contested nature
of water rights requires an explicit acknowledgement of the human right to water
in UN and international water declarations.[9]

At the 2001 Bonn Freshwater Conference many stakeholders—including representatives of governments and business—made verbal endorsements of the
human right to water, but the final conference document failed to explicitly
acknowledge it. Legal protection is required to ensure commitment, to provide
grounds for redress in cases of accountability failures, and to mobilize resources
at local and international levels. One approach to legal protection would be to
institute a universal human right on access to safe and adequate water.

Even though water is rarely global in scope, there is considerable scope for
international action and cooperation. As the Bonn Freshwater Conference
showed, stakeholders ranging from NGOs to businesses and governments can
reach consensus on key issues and recommendations for action. Moreover, international cooperation has become increasingly important given the global nature
of water debates and of social movements calling for equity in the ownership and
management of water resources.

Some analysts have argued that creation of a world water parliament and several regional water parliaments could formalize social and economic rights to
water. These rights could be evoked in cases of competing claims over the same
resource base—for example, people's right to water should take priority over economic development and national interests. There is also a need to provide mechanisms to redress grievances. For example, people could turn to an international
body such as a world water court if their right to water was violated. Such a court
could also help resolve interbasin disputes within regions.

These principles should also inform decisions on the provision of water. All
players—NGOs, businesses, public institutions—need to work toward water justice. Empirical research is lacking on how the private sector has performed in
terms of promoting poor people's access to water. Until more data exist, the international community must ensure that private participation is not imposed on
developing countries as part of aid programs. In addition, national governments
need to develop inclusive regulations that protect the interests of poor people (see
Finger and Allouche 2002 and Ugaz 2001).

Similarly, public-private partnerships require the consent of local communities. The voices of local actors, especially women, need to be sought given that public-private partnerships rarely take place on level playing fields. National and

international civil society organizations should continue to monitor public and private agencies to ensure transparency and accountability. In addition, the international community must ensure that water is not allowed to become a global commodity, tradable on the open market, because this could seriously undermine people's right to it.

Supranational organizations such as the World Commission on Dams and the Global Water Partnership (http://www.gwpforum.org/servlet/PSP) will continue to play an important role in global water governance. Donors and the international community should build on and institutionalize the recommendations made by the World Commission on Dams for decisionmaking in developing water resources. These recommendations include thoroughly investigating all options and alternatives, obtaining the free, informed, and prior consent of indigenous people, securing public acceptance of binding formal agreements among all stakeholders, and implementing arrangements for monitoring and addressing grievances from future projects (WCD 2000). The challenge in governing water resources is striking a balance between the principles of subsidiarity and global governance, bearing in mind the messy middle of institutional overlaps, power, and politics. Because water is so crucial for human survival and for the integrity of nature, efforts to make water more public and ensure everyone's access to safe and adequate supplies need to be embedded in local realities combined with global action and concern.[10]

NOTES

1. This statement is made with full awareness of the contested, political nature of human rights declarations, of critiques of sweeping universalism, and of the need to locate rights-based discourses in local contexts (see Baxi 2002). But access to safe and adequate water is fundamental and requires unequivocal official endorsement as a human right—though notions of what this right constitutes must be subjected to discursive contest

2. One argument could be that water for production (industry and large-scale agriculture) is an economic good has investment costs, capital costs, operations and maintenance costs, and opportunity and environmental costs. See also Winpenny (1994).

3. There are several similar, perhaps more sophisticated debates about user fees in primary health care and primary education—and the two sectors offer many lessons for water.

4. In Indian slums people also pay for "free" water provided by municipal authorities through bribes to truck drivers and tap operators.

5. For example, in Manila (the Philippines), even though winning tenders had specified price levels, International Water (a U.K.-U.S. consortium) doubled prices within two years. In the highly controversial plan to privatize water services in Cochabamba, Bolivia, prices would have increased 35 percent (Hall 2000).

6. In many cases the private company provides services in an arena that had been dominated by informal vendors and local entrepreneurs. This increases people's choice but also competition and confusion. The role of informal and unregistered service providers in the delivery of water and the relationship between informal and formal providers are underresearched and unresolved.

7. See, for example, the NGO statement at the Bonn Conference on Freshwater (NGO Major Group 2001); Vision 21 of the Water Supply and Sanitation Collaborative Council (WSSCC 2000); Petrella (2001); Gleick (2000); Jolly (1998), and right-to-water@iatp.org.

8. Practically, this would not be possible given all the constraints outlined in the first two sections of this chapter.

9. It is problematic that several major references on human rights have no specific citations related to water (see Gleick 1999). Whether water is implied, as suggested by Gleick (1999), is open to question.

10. This is in keeping with contemporary human rights debates that accept the complicated, historical nature of these rights and argue for cultural variation and contextualization without changing the definition of the rights (see Cowan, Dembour, and Wilson 2001).

References

Altaf, Mira Anjum, Haroon Jamal, and Dale Whittington. 1992. "Willingness to Pay for Water in Rural Punjab, Pakistan." Water and Sanitation Report 4. United Nations Development Programme–World Bank Water and Sanitation Programme, Washington, D.C.

Barlow, Maude. 1999. "Blue Gold: The Global Water Crisis and the Commodification of the World's Water Supply." International Forum on Globalization, San Francisco, Calif.

Baxi, Upendra. 2002. *The Future of Human Rights.* New Delhi: Oxford University Press.

Bayliss, Kate. 2001. "Water Privatisation in Africa: Lessons from Three Case Studies." University of Greenwich, Public Services International Research Unit.

Berkes, Firket. 1989. *Common Property Resources: Ecology and Community-Based Sustainable Development.* London: Belhaven Press.

Black, Maggie. 1998. "Learning What Works: A 20 Year Retrospective View on International Water and Sanitation Cooperation." United Nations Development Programme–World Bank Water and Sanitation Programme, Washington, D.C.

Bromley, Daniel, and Michael Cernea. 1989. "The Management of Common Property Natural Resources: Some Conceptual and Operational Fallacies." Discussion Paper 57. World Bank, Washington, D.C.

Cleaver, Frances. 2000. "Moral Ecological Rationality, Institutions and the Management of Common Property Resources." *Development and Change* 31 (2): 361–83.

Cooper, Mary H. 1995. "Global Water Shortages." *Congressional Quarterly Researcher* 5 (47): 1113–34.

Cowan, Jane, Marie-Bénédicte Dembour, and Richard A. Wilson. 2001. *Culture and Rights: Anthropological Perspectives.* Cambridge: Cambridge University Press.

Coward, E. Walter Jr.. 1985. "Technical and Social Change in Currently Irrigated Regions: Rules, Roles and Rehabilitation." In Michael M. Cernea, ed., *Putting People First: Sociological Variables in Rural Development.* Oxford: Oxford University Press.

Finger, Matthias, and Jeremy Allouche. 2002. *Water Privatisation: Trans-national Corporations and the Re-regulation of the Water Industry.* London: Spon Press.

Ghosh, Ghourishankar, and Ashok Nigam. 1995. "Comments on 'Financing Water Supply and Sanitation under Agenda 21' by John Briscoe and Mike Garn." *Natural Resources Forum* 19 (1): 161–65.

Gleick, Peter H. 1999. "The Human Right to Water." *Water Policy* 1 (5): 487–53.

———. 2000. *The World's Water 2000–2001: The Biennial Report on Freshwater Resources.* Washington, D.C.: Island Press.

GWP (Global Water Partnership). 2000. "Integrated Water Resources Management." Technical Advisory Committee Background Paper 4. Stockholm.

Hall, David. 2000. "Water Privatisation—Global Domination by a Few." Corporate Watch 12 (autumn). [http://www.corporatewatch.org.uk/magazine/issue12/cw12w1.html].

Jolly, Richard. 1998. "Water and Human Rights: Challenges for the Twenty-First Century." Address at the Conference of the Belgian Royal Academy of Overseas Sciences, 23 March, Brussels.

Kaul, Inge, and Grace Ryu. 2001. "Global Public Policy Partnerships: Seen through the Lens of Global Public Goods." In *Global Public Goods: Taking the Concept Forward.* Office of Development Studies Discussion Paper 17. United Nations Development Programme, New York.

Kaul, Inge, Isabelle Grunberg, and Marc A. Stern, eds. 1999. *Global Public Goods: International Cooperation in the 21st Century.* New York: Oxford University Press.

Lansing, Stephen. 1987. "Balinese 'Water Temples' and the Management of Irrigation." *American Anthropologist* 89 (2): 326–41.

Mehta, Lyla. 2000. "Water for the Twenty-First Century: Challenges and Misconceptions." IDS Working Paper 111. Institute of Development Studies, Brighton, U.K.

———. 2001. "Water, Difference and Power: Unpacking Notions of Water 'Users' in Kutch, India." *International Journal of Water* 1 (3–4).

———. 2002. "The Naturalisation of Scarcity: The Politics and Poetics of Water in Kutch, India." Brighton: Institute of Development Studies.

Mehta, Lyla, and Anand Punja. Forthcoming. "Changing Water Worlds: Official and Resettlers' Perceptions of the Water/Wellbeing Nexus in Gujarat." In Amita Baviskar, ed., *The Cultural Politics of Water*. New Delhi: Oxford University Press.

Mehta, Lyla, Melissa Leach, and Ian Scoones. 2001. "Editorial: Environmental Governance in an Uncertain World." *IDS Bulletin* 32 (4).

Mosse, David. 1997. "The Symbolic Making of a Common Property Resource: History, Ecology, and Locality in a Tank-irrigated Landscape in South India." *Development and Change* 28 (3): 467–504.

Neto, Frederico, and Hakan Tropp. 2000. "Water Supply and Sanitation Services for All: Global Progress during the 1990s." *Natural Resources Forum* 24 (3): 225–35.

NGO Major Group. 2001. "NGO Statement at the Bonn Conference on Freshwater." Email communication from the International Rivers Network, 7 December.

Nickson, Andrew. 2001. "Tapping the Market. Can Private Enterprise Supply Water to the Poor?" *Insights* 37.

Nigam, Ashok, and Sadig Rasheed. 1998. "Financing of Freshwater for All: A Rights Based Approach." UNICEF Staff Working Paper EPP-EVL-98_003. United Nations Children's Fund, New York.

Nussbaum, Martha. 2000. *Women and Human Development: The Capabilities Approach*. New Delhi: Kali for Women.

ODS (Office of Development Studies). 2001. "Global Public Goods: Taking the Concept Forward." Discussion Paper 17. United Nations Development Programme, New York.

Ostrom, Elinor. 1990. *Governing the Commons: The Evolution of Institutions for Collective Action*. New York: Cambridge University Press.

Ostrom, Elinor, and Robert O. Keohane, eds. 1995. *Local Commons and Global Interdependence: Heterogeneity and Co-operation in Two Domains*. Cambridge, Mass.: Harvard University, Center for International Affairs.

Petrella, Riccardo. 2001. *The Water Manifesto: Arguments for a World Water Contract*. London: Zed.

Plant, Raymond. 1998. "Citizenship, Rights, Welfare." In Jane Franklin, ed., *Social Policy and Social Justice*. Cambridge: Polity Press.

Postel, Sandra. 1992. *The Last Oasis: Facing Water Scarcity*. London: Earthscan and Worldwatch Institute.

————. 1996. *Dividing the Waters: Food Security, Ecosystem Health, and the New Politics of Scarcity*. Washington, D.C.: Worldwatch Institute.

Potanski, Tomasz, and William M. Adams. 1998. "Water Scarcity, Property Regimes and Irrigation Management in Sonjo, Tanzania." *Journal of Development Studies* 34 (4): 86–116.

Reddy, Ratna V. 1999. "Quenching the Thirst: The Cost of Water in Fragile Environments." *Development and Change* 30 (1): 79–113.

Reddy, Sanjay, and Jan Vandemoortele. 1996. "User Financing of Basic Social Services: A Review of Theoretical Arguments and Empirical Evidence." UNICEF Staff Working Papers, Evaluation, Policy, and Planning Series. United Nations Children's Fund, New York.

Reinicke, Wolfgang H. 1998. *Global Public Policy: Governing Without Government?* Washington, D.C.: Brookings Institution Press.

Reinicke, Wolfgang H., and Francis Deng. 2000. *Critical Choices: The United Nations Networks and the Future of Global Governance.* Ottawa: IDRC Publishers.

Robert, Jean. 1993. "Water for All: Common Right, Public Service or Commodity?" Habitat International Coalition, New York.

Sandler, Todd. 1999. "Intergenerational Public Goods: Strategies, Efficiency and Institutions." In Inge Kaul, Isabelle Grunberg, and Marc A. Stern, eds., *Global Public Goods: International Cooperation in the 21st Century.* New York: Oxford University Press.

Sen, Amartya. 1992. *Inequality Re-examined.* Oxford: Clarendon Press.

Shiva. Vandana. 1999. "Monsanto's Expanding Monopolies." Email communication from the International Rivers Network, October.

Sweden Ministry for Foreign Affairs. 2001a. *Financing and Providing Global Public Goods: Expectations and Prospects.* Report prepared by Francisco Sagasti and Keith Bezanson on behalf of the Institute of Development Studies. Stockholm.

————. 2001b. *Transboundary Water Management as an International Public Good.* Report prepared by the Overseas Development Institute and Arcadis Euroconsult. Stockholm.

Ugaz, Cecilia . 2001. "A Public Goods Approach to Regulation of Utilities." WIDER Discussion Paper. World Institute for Development Economics Research, Helsinki, Finland.

UNICEF (United Nations Children's Fund). 1994. *Implementing the 20/20 Initiative.* New York.

Uphoff, Norman. 1992. *Learning from Gal-Oya: Possibilities for Participatory Development and Post-Newtonian Social Science.* Ithaca, N.Y.: Cornell University Press.

Wade, Robert. 1988. *Village Republics: Economic Conditions for Collective Action in South Africa.* Cambridge: Cambridge University Press.

Whittington, Dale, and Minja Kim Choe. 1992. "Economic Benefits Available from the Provision of Improved Potable Water Supplies." WASH Technical Report 77. Washington, D.C.

Winpenny, James. 1994. *Managing Water as an Economic Resource.* London and New York: Routledge

Wolf, Aaron. 1997. "'Water Wars' and Water Reality: Conflict and Cooperation along International Waterways." Paper presented at the High Level Group on International Water Management in the 21st Century, 18–20 December, Valencia, Spain.

World Bank. 1994. *World Development Report 1994: Infrastructure for Development.* New York: Oxford University Press.

WCD (World Commission on Dams). 2000. *Dams and Development: A New Framework for Decision-Making.* London: Earthscan. [www.dams.org/report/].

WSSCC (Water Supply and Sanitation Collaborative Council). 2000. "Vision 21: A Shared Vision for Hygiene, Sanitation and Water Supply and A Framework for Action. Also Forming the Water for People Component of the World Water Vision." Geneva. [http://www.wsscc.org/].

CORRUPTION AND GLOBAL PUBLIC GOODS

PETER EIGEN AND CHRISTIAN EIGEN-ZUCCHI

Attitudes toward corruption changed dramatically in the 1990s, shifting from broad acceptance—and even a perception that corruption can promote economic growth by "greasing the wheels of commerce"—to almost universal abhorrence. A growing body of literature suggests that high levels of corruption are associated with poverty, inequality, reduced investment, low foreign direct investment, and weak economic performance (Lambsdorff 1999). Moreover, many who once thought that corruption could not be controlled now believe that it can be attenuated and that it deserves urgent attention.

This chapter explores the intersection between corruption and public goods. Corruption is an important part of public goods analysis, and the public goods framework helps in understanding some of the difficulties in controlling corruption. The relationship between corruption and public goods arises directly from the definition of corruption as "the misuse of entrusted power for private benefit" (Transparency International 2000, p. 2). The provision of public goods generally requires the exercise of entrusted power by the state, creating the potential for corruption.

The standard methods used to provide public goods at the national level do not apply in the international arena. Governments use coercion to raise the resources needed to provide chosen public goods and eliminate free riding. But at the international level there is little supranational authority that can effectively translate preferences into the provision of global public goods. Instead, global public goods are typically provided as a result of negotiated voluntary contributions by a group of nations sharing an encompassing interest.[1]

Martin (1999, p. 52) emphasizes that theories of international cooperation rely heavily on the assumption that nation-states primarily act in their self-interest, casting many interactions as prisoner's dilemmas. Cooperation among states will last only if it is somewhat self-enforcing—through repeated games, for example. Overcoming the prisoner's dilemma and limiting free riding is even more difficult in the international arena than in the national context, and the likelihood of underprovision that much greater. Moreover, as Kaul, Grunberg, and Stern (1999, p. 8) note, "public goods often face a double jeopardy: market failure compounded by government failure." Corruption is a major source of government failure.

Although corruption control is insufficient for the effective provision of global public goods, it is crucial—affecting both the political economy of global public goods and their production and delivery. The reason is that corruption distorts decisionmaking on which global public goods to produce and at what level, raising the cost of providing them. Thus corruption control is an important input into the production of other critical public goods, including sound economic management, well-functioning markets, and reliable human security. But corruption control is itself a public good, because its benefits—lowering transaction costs and facilitating more effective decisionmaking by economic agents—are largely nonrival and nonexcludable. The chapter explores the difficult incentives surrounding the production of the global public good of corruption control. It also provides a case study showing how an international civil society organization, Transparency International, has helped build coalitions between governments and private corporations to control corruption in the international arena.

CORRUPTION AS A HINDRANCE TO THE PROVISION OF GLOBAL PUBLIC GOODS

The production of global public goods involves local, national, regional, and international inputs and participation by governments, civil society, and private actors. The consumption of public goods is to varying degrees nonrival and nonexcludable at the national, regional, and global levels (Kaul, Grunberg, and Stern 1999; Sandler 1999). Despite this wide range of inputs, actors, and consumption attributes, the provision of global public goods generally involves the following steps:

- Recognizing a need.
- Identifying stakeholders.
- Negotiating levels of provision and burden sharing.
- Taking action.
- Monitoring activity.

This process obtains whether the global public good is provided by a private individual, a firm, a civil society organization, a government, a group of governments through a multilateral agreement, or an international organization.

Each of these steps is vulnerable to corruption. For example, in international organizations and national governments, where most global public goods are produced, corruption gums the mechanism for aggregating individual preferences into collective action. If policymakers have managed to identify both the appropriate type and amount of public goods to be provided, corruption raises the cost of provision and undermines delivery. If policymakers have made an error in judgment, corruption offers incentives to continue along the same path rather than make adjustments. And if policymakers are pursuing their private interests at the expense of the public interest, corruption again induces bad policies and leads to bad outcomes.

Thus controlling corruption is essential for the effective provision of global public goods of the right sort at the right level. Closer examination of corruption in international organizations and national governments shows how it undermines the provision of global public goods.

The impact of corruption in international organizations

Global public goods are often organized or provided through international organizations. This approach is used because when national governments are acting alone in their self-interest, they often cannot internalize the full benefits—nor share the costs—of contributing to the goods' provision. But while corruption appears to be a bigger problem in national governments, it has also been discovered in international organizations—directly impairing their ability to provide and deliver global public goods.

A widely publicized case of apparent corruption in setting an international agenda and shaping global public goods involves the International Whaling Commission. Established to provide the global public good of sustainable management and conservation of whales (and other cetaceans), the commission is responsible for generating data on whale stocks and population trends and for coordinating national whaling policies. On 19 July 2001, in an article titled "Bribery on Whaling Admitted by Japan," the *Daily Telegraph* (London) reported that:

> *Japan has admitted for the first time that it bribed poor nations to support its pro-whaling stance. Anti-whalers have alleged for years that Japan uses its aid budget to persuade other nations to vote for a return to commercial whaling. In an interview with the Australian Broadcasting Corporation, Maseyuki Komatsu, the head of Japan's fishery agency, confirmed the suspicions. "Japan does not have military powers. Our means are diplomatic communication and overseas development aid," he said. "To get appreciation of Japan's position it is natural we resort to those two major tools. I think there is nothing wrong with that."*

At the 2000 International Whaling Commission conference in Adelaide, Australia, six Caribbean nations voted with Japan on almost every issue, including blocking an Australian proposal for a whale sanctuary in the South Pacific. Dominica's environment minister, Atherton Martin, subsequently resigned "in protest of what he called Japan's 'extortion' of his country's support for whaling, with threats to withdraw aid" (*Daily Telegraph*, 19 July 2001). On 23 July 2001, in an article titled "Japan Loses Face with Whales-for-Aid Stance," the *Evening Post* (Wellington, New Zealand) reported that:

> *Client nations such as St. Kitts and Nevis, Grenada and the Grena-dines...were wooed to IWC [International Whaling Commission] mem-bership at Japan's behest. All are recipients of Japanese aid; to suggest they've any genuine interest in whales, whaling and the Southern Ocean sanctuary promoted by New Zealand and Australia stretches credulity.*

This pressure on the International Whaling Commission's policymaking undermines the provision of global public goods by increasing the likelihood that a global commons—the world's whale population—will be overexploited, possibly to the point of extinction. More broadly, this example illustrates that the process of establishing property rights is vulnerable to corruption as actors jockey for advantage during the movement of a good along the private-public continuum. In this case institutional and technological innovations, combined with greater scarcity of whales, encourage the good (whales) to move from being an open access resource to one for which actors obtain limited rights of use. Many other global commons are also reaching critical levels of overexploitation, and corruption threatens to undermine a determined and impartial international response.

Efforts to garner undue influence through corruption are also evident in other international organizations. One is the International Olympic Committee, an international nongovernmental, nonprofit organization responsible for organizing perhaps the world's most important and internationally unifying sporting event. The Olympics are meant to set an example of peaceful competition among nations—and by doing so, to foster important global public goods such as international peace, security, and understanding.

Because of the political prestige and economic activity that the Olympics bring, the selection of host countries and cities is one of the most closely watched aspects of the International Olympic Committee's work. (The Olympics occur every two years, alternating between summer and winter games.) Thus the Olympics are a good with mixed properties: besides the global public goods mentioned, they also generate important private benefits for host countries and cities—increased tourism, international visibility, and possibly greater attractiveness to investors. As a result national governments and local organizing committees go to great lengths to have their sites selected for the games—and attempt to sway the International Olympic Committee in their favor.

The selection of Salt Lake City, Utah (United States), for the most recent Winter Olympics generated enormous corruption-related controversy. On 28 January 1999, in an article titled "City of Latter-Day Scandal," *The Economist* reported that:

The Salt Lake City boosters handed out cash and benefits worth about $780,000 to secure the 2002 Winter Olympics for their city. The gifts included scholarships, free medical care, expensive firearms, [and] help with a lucrative property deal.

Corruption might have impaired the International Olympic Committee's ability to provide a global public good, because other cities might have contributed more to the Olympics' stated objectives than did Salt Lake City.

Another example of corruption in an international organization involves the World Bank, the world's largest development institution. The Bank contributes to global public goods through its efforts to promote development, reduce poverty, fight disease, eliminate hunger, attenuate global inequality, and protect the environment. In December 2000 an internal investigation revealed that three "staff members were paid or agreed to receive kickbacks by two separate groups of Swedish companies in exchange for steering certain Bank contracts to those firms" (World Bank 2000a). The contracts affected by the kickbacks, which included contracts for activities deemed ineligible for Bank support, were worth less than $900,000.[2]

Moderate levels of corruption—or even perceptions of it—would compromise the World Bank's ability to help provide global public goods. Moreover, if just one international organization were found wanting in proper business practices, general support for international cooperation could suffer, undermining the provision of global public goods across the board.

The impact of corruption in national governments

Most corruption appears to occur in national governments, probably because they enjoy coercive powers as well as monopolies over various services and administrative functions. International organizations do not enjoy such powers: if a government is unhappy with an international organization's efforts, it can in principle withdraw its membership. Such exit is more difficult for individuals dissatisfied with a national government's provision of public goods.

Corruption at the national level undermines global public goods by perverting governments' participation in their provision. For example, in an environment of pervasive corruption a government will be unable to make the credible commitments required for international agreements to work. Reaching an accord on, say, managing ocean fisheries or limiting carbon dioxide emissions will be more difficult if some signatories are suspected of accepting bribes to allow additional fishing or to avoid the cost of installing scrubbers on the smokestacks of coal-burning plants. And even if an agreement is reached on the appropriate size of the fish catch, bribes made in exchange for treaty-busting fishing will cause fishery protection to fall below the agreed level—causing global public goods to suffer.

Corruption may also affect the types of global public goods provided, by distorting the decisionmaking process in which individual preferences are aggregated and translated into collective action. Because national governments contribute voluntarily to the provision of global public goods, corruption at this level again directly impairs many such goods.

Money laundering shows how weak governance at the national level directly hinders the provision of global public goods. Money laundering is linked to many global public bads, including international terrorism and drug trafficking. To combat it, the Financial Action Task Force on Money Laundering—established by the Organisation for Economic Co-operation and Development (OECD)—requires financial institutions in its 29 member countries to report suspect transactions (FATF 1996). In October 2001 the task force suggested additional measures to staunch the flow of financing for terrorism, including a requirement that financial institutions inform regulators if there are reasonable grounds to suspect that funds will be used for that purpose. The measures also strengthened government powers to freeze assets, require more extensive reporting of suspect transactions, and created a blacklist of countries that handle terrorists' money (FATF 2001).

Corruption hampers the implementation of such international agreements because it encourages the establishment of tax havens and undermines the enforcement of anti–money laundering measures. As Transparency International (2001, p. 206) notes: "Unfortunately, laundering only needs to be good enough to defeat the capacity of financial investigation skills and the burden of proof in any of the jurisdictions along its economic path." Legal and regulatory shortcomings in countries providing tax havens as well as in other countries allow criminals to misuse trusts, foundations, and professional partnerships to bypass regulatory measures.

Moreover, while the Financial Action Task Force on Money Laundering has blacklisted 19 "noncooperative countries and territories"—including Egypt, Hungary, Israel, and the Russian Federation—it also acknowledges that almost two-thirds of its 29 member nations fail to fully comply with its anti–money laundering recommendations.[3] Differences in national legislation allow corruption to flourish in international banking, enabling illegal funds to be transferred wherever there are easily abused loopholes. Thus corruption in national governments directly undermines international efforts to provide the important global public good of preventing money laundering.

Controlling the flow of diamonds out of conflict areas is another example of how corruption at the national level directly impedes the provision of a global public good, in this case international peace and security. In recent years the scramble for "blood diamonds" has fueled conflicts in the Democratic Republic of Congo and Liberia, while rebel armies in Angola and Sierra Leone have used such diamonds to buy arms and enrich elites. Foreign armies, including

Zimbabwe's, have provided military support in exchange for diamond mining concessions, while international companies have sent dealers to war zones to buy illegal stones.

But action by civil society has had a big impact on the international diamond industry, largely through the work of Global Witness (http://www.global witness.org/indexhome.html). Global Witness (2000) proposes an international certification system that could be applied to the trade in conflict diamonds in Angola and elsewhere. When De Beers announced in February 2000 that it would no longer sell African gems originating in zones controlled by forces rebelling against legitimate governments, an attempt was born to forge a new regulatory architecture for the international diamond trade. South Africa's government took the lead in launching the Kimberley Process, a global tracking system of export certification and import verification. Controls using a "chain of warranties" are intended to close the loopholes opened when national laws make no distinction between the country of origin and the country from which diamonds are shipped.

But until a critical mass of countries signs up—Angola, Belgium, the Democratic Republic of Congo, and Sierra Leone were among the first—national indifference to the corruption behind blood diamonds will continue to distort international trade and impede effective sanctions against regimes with little respect for human rights. For example, senior government officials of Burkina Faso, Liberia, and Togo have benefited from illicit diamonds by providing cover for exports from troubled areas (Transparency International 2001, pp. 215–16).

An extensive literature sheds light on the high costs of corruption at the national level—and its global ramifications. Kaufmann, Kraay, and Zoido-Lobaton (1999) find a strong causal link between governance and development outcomes, including GDP per capita, infant mortality, and adult literacy. Gupta, Davoodi, and Tiongson (2000) show that widespread corruption adversely affects key social indicators such as child mortality rates, income inequality, education levels, and poverty rates. Mauro (1995) and Knack and Keefer (1995), among others, confirm the importance of sound institutions and good governance for strong GDP growth and show that corruption inhibits the emergence of strong institutions. Wei (1997) finds that corruption discourages foreign direct investment and plays a big part in "aid fatigue," undermining donor contributions to development assistance. And all these effects of corruption fall disproportionately on poor people, because wealthier groups are better able to find suitable substitutes when public goods are underprovided.[4]

Corruption prevents markets from functioning properly, reduces private investment, attracts talented people to unproductive activities, and distorts optimal management of natural resources. Corruption also undermines national efforts to control disease, confront the drug trade, and protect rain forests. The global implications of all this include denuded forests; fewer trading opportunities; increased disease, drug trafficking, and political instability; and contagion from financial crises such as the one in East Asia in the late 1990s.

CORRUPTION CONTROL AS A GLOBAL PUBLIC GOOD

The previous section suggests that corruption control is an important intermediate input into the production of public goods because of its central role in the effective functioning of government. This section argues that corruption control is itself a public good that is often nationally and internationally nonexcludable and nonrival. Corruption control is nonexcludable because in many cases those contributing to the effort will be unable to exclude noncontributors from enjoying some of the benefits. It is nonrival because one actor's benefiting from good governance does not impinge on another's ability to do so.

As with other global public goods, the international nature of the corruption problem complicates effective intervention because there is little supranational authority. Moreover, not only would beneficiaries prefer not to contribute to the provision of good governance if others are contributing, but the incentive to defect and engage in corrupt practices is stronger when other actors curb their own illicit activities. These difficulties are well described by the classic prisoner's dilemma, where all would be better off if the cooperative solution obtained but individual players face a strong incentive to defect, undermining cooperation.

In general, each company or country would prefer to see corruption controlled by others without having to constrain its own behavior and shoulder monitoring and enforcement costs. But some parties who want to contribute to controlling corruption may be unable to participate. For example, a trader or entrepreneur in a highly corrupt developing country may want to reduce corruption to attract credit or foreign direct investment, but confronting a corrupt autocrat or entrenched interests (possibly with external allies) may entail extremely high costs.

How might governance in such a country be improved? Domestic pressures might grow until the regime collapses under the burden of corruption, or the outside world might become increasingly intolerant of corruption. International organizations, such as the World Bank or International Monetary Fund, and civil society organizations, such as Transparency International, could support the domestic elements working to improve governance. In addition, outside organizations seeking to avoid the negative externalities of political and economic instability might have an encompassing interest in providing the public good regardless of the contributions of other beneficiaries. Nonetheless, the global public good of good governance is likely to be underprovided.

Another feature of corruption control that makes its provision difficult is a problem akin to the tragedy of the commons: the absence of corruption provides an additional incentive for corruption. The issue is similar to efforts to provide the public good of fisheries protection. If fishing fleets avoid an area to protect fisheries, for example, the returns from fishing that area will rise, increasing incentives to fish the area. If a corruption-free playing field is the commons, nations will have a greater incentive to permit their commercial interests to (over)exploit the commons and engage in corruption, especially if detection is unlikely. Similarly, in the absence of corruption, a bribe-paying firm faces less competition along this margin, raising the returns from corrupt practices.

These incentive problems are quite similar to the classic prisoner's dilemma scenario. The game is presented at the level of the firm in figure 1, but it is equally applicable at the level of the nation (to undertake or not to undertake an effort to prevent international corruption). The payoffs from a course of action—to pay a bribe or not to pay a bribe—are shown in the figure, with the first variable accruing to firm 1 and the second to firm 2. If a is greater than b and c is greater than d, the symmetric game yields a dominant strategy in which both firms pay a bribe, regardless of whether the other firm pays a bribe or not. Given the payoff structure, if firm 2 pays a bribe, firm 1 will be better off also paying a bribe ($a > b$). If firm 2 does not pay a bribe, firm 1 will again be better off paying a bribe ($c > d$). Thus the result will be the top left quadrant, with each receiving a payoff of a.

If d is greater than a, the cooperative solution—in which neither firm pays a bribe—offers a greater benefit to both firms. The higher payoffs from cooperating are the inducement to cooperate and defeat corruption. However, since the benefit from bribing by any one firm is still higher ($c > d$) if the other firm does

FIGURE 1

The prisoner's dilemma applied to corruption

		Firm 2	
		Pay bribe	Do not pay bribe
Firm 1	Pay bribe	a , a	c , b
	Do not pay bribe	b , c	d , d

not bribe, the incentive to defect from the cooperative solution remains strong. Hence, the conditions for a prisoner's dilemma scenario obtain ($c > d > a$).

The bribery game is not as cozy as it may appear. In a globalizing world—with market integration, transnationalization of production, and greater trade and foreign investment—corrupt practices increasingly constitute an incalculable risk that market players do not like. Corruption involves a range of behaviors that undermine business and complicate monitoring. In addition, the payoffs are not fixed. With globalization and integration, the benefits of being able to operate in a corruption-free environment increase (because of lower transaction costs), and corruption is more likely to have transnational ramifications (Eigen-Zucchi 2001).

Moreover, the costs of moving from the noncooperative top left quadrant, where both players receive a payoff of a, to the cooperative bottom right quadrant, where both players receive a reward of d, may be falling as better commitment technologies emerge. These technologies include freer information flows and stronger accounting standards. Third-party monitoring by civil society is another technology for strengthening commitment to corruption control. As elaborated below, facilitating such monitoring is an important part of the global public good of corruption control provided by civil society.

Some of these aspects of corruption control are apparent in the U.S Foreign Corrupt Practices Act of 1977, which prohibited the payment of bribes by U.S. citizens and U.S. companies and their subsidiaries. To the extent that U.S. firms were competing with one another on the basis of bribery, they were in a noncooperative equilibrium.

The main driver behind the Foreign Corrupt Practices Act was the Watergate scandal and the subsequent Congressional hearings into questionable corporate donations to U.S. President Richard Nixon's reelection campaign (Geo-JaJa and Mangsum 1999). These hearings led to revelations of corporate donations to regimes abroad, such as Lockheed's payments to the Tanaka government in Japan. The drive for anticorruption legislation began under Gerald Ford's administration as firms disclosed more bribery to the Securities and Exchange Commission and the cost of corruption was perceived to be growing. As the U.S. House of Representatives (1977, p. 2) conference report on the Foreign Corrupt Practices Act noted:

> *The payment of bribes to influence the acts or decisions of foreign officials, foreign political parties or candidates for foreign political office is unethical. It is counter to the moral expectations and values of the American public. But not only is it unethical, it is bad business as well. It erodes public confidence in the integrity of the free market system. It short-circuits the marketplace by directing business to those companies too inefficient to compete in terms of price, quality or service, or too lazy to engage in honest sales-*

manship, or too intent upon unloading marginal products. In short, it rewards corruption instead of efficiency and puts pressure on ethical enterprises to lower their standards or risk losing business.

Bribery of foreign officials by some American companies casts a shadow on all U.S. companies. The exposure of such activity can damage a company's image, lead to costly lawsuits, cause the cancellation of contracts, and result in the appropriation of valuable assets overseas.

Thus lawmakers perceived corruption control as in the interests of the United States regardless of the contributions of other countries. That suggests that in the wake of the Watergate scandal, the costs of corruption within the United States were large. Indeed, by the early 1980s the bribery scandal involved 450 firms and more than $1 billion (Clinard 1990, p. 121). The shadow cast on all U.S. companies, regardless of whether they participated in bribery or not, indicates that some companies were in the bottom left or top right quadrants of the prisoner's dilemma game. These considerations prompted the move to the government-enforced cooperative solution.

The experience with the Foreign Corrupt Practices Act points to another prisoner's dilemma game—this one in international competition in trade and investments. Remarkably, when the act went into force in the United States, no other nation followed suit with similar legislation. Other nations did not want to incur the cost of providing the global public good of corruption control, including the costs of monitoring and enforcement. Indeed, in many industrial countries bribes remained tax deductible as legitimate business expenses. Moreover, corporate interests in other countries benefited from the constrained behavior of U.S. firms. Although figures remain disputed, the U.S. Department of Commerce estimates that U.S. companies lost out on 100 contracts worth about $45 billion in 1994 and 1995 because of their inability to pay bribes, and the U.S. Treasury estimates lost business at about $30 billion a year (cited in Galtung 2000).

Lambsdorff (1998) argues that this effect is also evident in his study of trade patterns and bribery. Controlling for a variety of factors, Lambsdorff shows that firms in Malaysia and Sweden are at a disadvantage relative to corrupt counterparts, while the export performance of firms in such countries as Belgium, Italy, and the Republic of Korea is positively related to corruption in importing countries. From this, Lambsdorff concludes that the differences stem from exporters' varying propensities to pay bribes.

Still, some authors have questioned the size of the losses to U.S. business interests. Much of the competition that U.S. firms face is from other U.S. firms and is determined by the technological uniqueness and quality of the goods and services offered (Parker 1976 and Romeneski 1982, cited in Geo-JaJa and Magnum 1999). Some U.S. firms surely lost business as a result of the Foreign

Corrupt Practices Act, both to other U.S. firms and to international competition that was not encumbered by the restrictions on bribery that an international accord would bring. Still, the cost of corruption within the United States was acutely perceived and had risen to a point compelling unilateral action.

In sum, when some firms refrain from paying bribes, other firms have a greater incentive to win business through such corrupt practices. Similarly, when some nations constrain their exporters, other nations face a stronger incentive to allow their companies to use corruption to their competitive advantage. As Richardson (2001, p. 101) notes, "assuming that increased business integrity and corporate unwillingness to bribe are a public good, those businesses that continue to offer bribes (and find takers) become free riders with an advantage over their competitors." If others are controlling corruption, payoffs from defection (bribery) are likely to be even higher than gains from cooperation. It is also plausible that if others are not controlling corruption, it still pays to engage in bribery. In the prisoner's dilemma that emerges, each nation or company perceives a dominant strategy to defect and not contribute to the control of corruption.

Thus providing the global public good of corruption control is difficult. But globalization and heightened publicity are contributing to increasing awareness among the public and policymakers of the costs of corruption, spurring efforts to reduce it. In addition, a new commitment technology has arisen in the form of participation by civil society organizations, lowering the costs of controlling corruption and facilitating such steps as the signing in 1997 of the OECD convention against bribery.

THE ROLE OF TRANSPARENCY INTERNATIONAL IN FIGHTING CORRUPTION

Many civil society organizations have played an important role in controlling corruption. Among the leaders is Transparency International, which was founded in 1993 by 10 people from industrial and developing countries who were deeply concerned about corruption and believed that the end of the cold war offered an opportunity to combat it. Transparency International has increased understanding of corruption and nurtured growing consensus about its harm, raising public awareness. Together with lobbying organizations in a position to confront powerful and concentrated interests, Transparency International has also facilitated an exit from the prisoner's dilemma by forging coalitions, mobilizing domestic support through a network of national chapters, and monitoring agreements so that signatories feel assured that others are in compliance.

In the early 1990s, before Transparency International was founded, little progress had been made against corruption. In 1977 the International Chamber of Commerce developed Rules of Conduct to Combat Extortion and Bribery, but these were widely regarded as unenforceable and so proved ineffective. As noted, the United States was alone in criminalizing bribery of foreign officials, and in many OECD countries bribes were tax deductible, treated as legitimate business expenses.

In the research literature social scientists equivocated about the effects of corruption. Some drew distinctions between good and bad corruption, arguing that bribes paid to reduce bureaucratic delays and remove other obstacles, for example, might be good corruption because they promote economic efficiency (Galtung 2000, p. 20).

In the development community there was little enthusiasm for addressing corruption, mainly because of concerns about maintaining development assistance levels and worries about overreaching legal mandates on an issue still largely regarded as a domestic political problem. For example, many experienced development professionals in the World Bank were well aware of the deleterious effect of corruption on development efforts. But the Bank's legal department maintained that involvement in this issue would run counter to its charter requiring that loan decisions be made without regard for political considerations (Galtung 2000, p. 23).

But with the end of the cold war, international priorities shifted, and aid effectiveness became a central focus of domestic political debates on foreign aid budgets. As a growing body of research pointed to corruption as a major factor undermining development, Transparency International found support among governments, international organizations, and multinational corporations.

Transparency International's basic approach centers on a nonconfrontational effort to build "national, regional, and global coalitions that embrace the state, civil society, and the private sector to fight domestic and international corruption" (Galtung 2000, p. 26). It pursues this objective by building public awareness, lobbying governments, and facilitating agreements to reduce corruption. One of its most important and enduring contributions has been to help place corruption firmly on the agenda in national politics, academic research, and policies of international financial institutions. It has done so by emphasizing the adverse effects of corruption (which fall disproportionately on poor people) and by generating publicity.

Transparency International's most effective tool in raising public awareness has been the Corruption Perceptions Index, published annually since 1995. The 2001 index is based on 14 surveys, at least 3 of which are required for a country to be included in the index.[5] Among the 91 countries included in the 2001 index, Finland is perceived to be the least corrupt and Bangladesh the most.

Transparency International's approach is exemplified by its development of "integrity pacts" and by its role in the adoption of the OECD antibribery convention. And it is based on the evolving research literature about the nature of corruption and the key components of successful anticorruption initiatives.

Some features of corruption and components of effective control
Transparency International's efforts have been greatly aided by in-depth analyses of corruption's characteristics. Applying a transaction costs approach, Lambsdorff (2002) studies specific instances of corruption found in the general media. He identifies three main actions that participants in a corrupt transaction must take:

- They must find counterparts and specify a contract.
- They must develop some mechanism to enforce the contract and prevent opportunism, since the exchange typically is not simultaneous.
- They must find ways of dealing with an ongoing relationship after the transaction, because each now holds incriminating information about the other (Lambsdorff 2002, pp. 3–4).

Lambsdorff suggests that an effective strategy for combating corruption is to find ways of disrupting these actions.

Richardson (2001) lists several criteria for an effective anticorruption campaign. Although many sophisticated programs have been developed, at their most basic level they must "(1) reduce the incentives and opportunities to extort and bribe; (2) greatly increase the risks of detection to future bribers and bribe-takers; and (3) increase the likelihood and severity of penalties when bribery is detected" (p. 91). As elaborated below, anticorruption efforts, including those of Transparency International, have operated on all these levels and have also sought to address the prisoner's dilemma.

Integrity pacts
The latest edition of Transparency International's *Source Book* (2000) describes global best practice in confronting corruption and provides case studies on the laws, institutions, and procedures that seem effective. Developed to root out corruption in large government projects, integrity pacts between governments and companies bidding for projects are agreements that authorities will not demand or accept, and firms will not offer "—directly or through intermediaries—any bribe gift, favor or other advantage ... in exchange for an advantage in the bidding, bid evaluation, contracting and implementation process related to the contract" (Transparency International 2001b, p. 2). These pacts are forging coalitions among bidders, government agencies, and civil society organizations in about 50 competitive situations around the world.

Integrity pacts address the prisoner's dilemma by generating a credible commitment so that participants do not fear being disadvantaged by competitors continuing to pay bribes. The pacts provide independent third-party oversight by credible civil society organizations and transparency in the bidding and implementation of projects. In addition, participants commit to disclosing the family assets of all senior personnel at the level of project manager and above. This approach raises the transaction costs of finding counterparts and specifying a contract and increases the risk of detection.

Integrity pacts also specify sanctions for noncompliance, including cancellation of the contract, liability for damages to both the government and other parties, forfeiture of any deposit, and disqualification from future government contracts for some time. The procedural rules increase the likelihood of detection, and the sanctions, especially the liability for damages and future disbarment, increase the penalty. This raises the stakes considerably, complicating the post-bribery relationship.

By developing the integrity pact, Transparency International has identified concrete steps that stakeholders can take in reducing corruption. Through the pact, Transparency International helps build coalitions that provide an exit strategy from a prisoner's dilemma game, where each bidding company fears that refraining from bribery would place it at a competitive disadvantage. Such commitments are credible only if the procedures are transparent and monitored. So, Transparency International has outlined measures to make the procedures transparent and involved civil society organizations to provide third-party oversight. These build credibility where government and business working alone would probably fail. Finally, ex ante agreements on substantial sanctions raise the risk and cost of engaging in bribery.

The OECD antibribery convention

Integrity pacts operate mainly at the national level, involving governments, national civil society organizations, and domestic and international businesses. Transparency International has also sought to confront the "supply side" of bribery through international agreements, most significantly the OECD Convention on Combating Bribery of Foreign Public Officials in International Business Transactions. The aim in these international agreements is to help national governments make a coordinated escape from the corruption trap.

When Transparency International began advocating reforms to control the systematic, large-scale corruption of decisionmakers—mainly officials and politicians in developing countries—most OECD countries had legal systems that tolerated foreign bribery by their exporters. Not only were bribes treated as tax-deductible business expenses, but government subsidies, through export financing and insurance, accommodated foreign bribery as an unpleasant but necessary part of doing business in emerging markets.

Efforts to change this state of affairs were met with pronouncements from cabinet members and high officials of OECD countries about their exporters' need to bribe abroad. In Germany, for example, the governing coalition of Helmut Kohl defeated several attempts by opposition parties to introduce reforms outlawing foreign bribes by German export companies, arguing that they would destroy German jobs. Lord Young, a former minister of trade and industry in the

United Kingdom, said of bribery abroad that if "you want to be in business, you have to do [it]" (cited in Galtung 2000, p. 20).

Until 1993 the tax deductibility of bribes paid by French firms in international business transactions was facilitated by an office in the Ministry of Finance called the "confessional" (Pujas 2000, p. 11). Even after this office was closed, a prepayment declaration continued to allow tax deductibility of bribes paid abroad. Moreover, the French government supported a version of enabling legislation for the 1997 OECD antibribery convention that would have prevented the prosecution of bribery of foreign public officials if the corrupt agreements were concluded before the passage of the new law. That would have allowed corrupt practices reflected in long-term contracts to be sustained even after the new restrictions on foreign bribery were implemented. The measure, however, was defeated in parliament (Pujas 2000, p. 11).

Corruption in the international arena seemed so widespread, so much the norm, that it appeared impossible to stop without inflicting irreparable harm on national commercial interests. A classic prisoner's dilemma: widespread disgust with the bribery of foreign officials, increasing fear about the risks and devastation caused by corruption, but no exit route without losing business. In a competitive environment where governments seek to promote the commercial interests of national corporations and where monitoring and enforcement are more difficult, making a coordinated escape seemed an insurmountable challenge.

Yet the tide was beginning to turn. In 1994 a U.S.-led diplomatic initiative resulted in the adoption of the first OECD recommendation on corruption (Galtung 2000, p. 32). In confidential meetings of business leaders arranged by Transparency International at the Aspen Institute in Berlin and in other communications, it became apparent that many firms opposed corruption. Typically, firms that do not bribe perceive a competitive disadvantage, while those that do:

> *often have to hire dishonest agents; keep two sets of books to preserve secrecy; bypass corporate controls; incur the unpredictable risks of discovery, unenforceable performance, and blackmail; and condone dishonest behavior or the tolerance of it by their own executives. (Richardson 2001, p. 84)*

Transparency International, through its network of chapters in OECD countries, lobbied for an anticorruption agreement at the OECD, promoting a coordinated and simultaneous termination of corrupt practices. A breakthrough came when some of the largest European multinational corporations—including all the participants in the meetings at the Aspen Institute—signed an open letter to their government ministries urging them to support the OECD convention.

Signed at the end of 1997, the OECD Convention on Combating Bribery of Foreign Public Officials in International Business Transactions entered into force in February 1999, when it had been ratified by 12 of the signatories. By the end of

2001 the convention had been ratified by 34 of 35 signatory states, including several non-OECD members.[6]

> *The convention defines* bribery *and* foreign official *broadly and stipulates that the bribery of a foreign public official shall be punishable by effective, proportionate and dissuasive criminal penalties. The range of penalties shall be comparable to that applicable to the bribery of the Party's own public officials. (Article 3)*

This wording commits signatories to prosecuting corruption committed abroad and, like the integrity pacts, raises the transaction costs of engaging in corrupt practices and increases the risk of detection. Although the convention has no formal mechanism for punishing signatories who fail to enforce antibribery laws, publicity and national and international condemnation are expected to ensure good faith efforts.

The convention does, however, stipulate an elaborate system "to monitor and promote the full implementation of this Convention . . . [through] the framework of the OECD Working Group on Bribery in International Business Transactions" (Article 12). The working group prepares detailed reports on the domestic legislation of participating countries and engages in extensive consultations where civil society organizations such as Transparency International are able to make their views known. To further reassure signatories that other participants are complying with the convention, Transparency International has created its own working group to monitor compliance and a checklist that its national chapters can use to review national enabling legislation.[7]

The global public good and prisoner's dilemma features of international corruption control are evident in the text of the convention. The preamble states that "all countries share a responsibility to combat bribery in international business transactions," a call on national governments not to free ride in the provision of this global public good. The preamble also calls for "the prompt criminalization of such bribery in an effective and coordinated manner," suggesting the need for a coordinated and simultaneous escape from a prisoner's dilemma. Finally, Article 5 stipulates that enforcement "shall not be influenced by considerations of national economic interest, the potential effect upon relations with another State or the identity of the natural or legal persons involved," again emphasizing the need for signatories to look beyond immediate national interest and commit to strict enforcement.

As a result of the convention, legal systems have become dramatically more inhospitable to global corruption and international financial institutions have integrated governance issues into the core of their operations. Transparency International played a substantial role in facilitating this coordinated exit from the corruption trap.

Conclusion

Providing global public goods is a major challenge, and controlling the international scourge of corruption is no exception. Two features of corruption increase its importance from a global public goods perspective and make confronting the problem especially difficult. First, controlling corruption is an intermediate input into the production of other public goods, including global public goods. Corruption distorts decisions about which public goods to provide and at what level, and can undermine international agreements to prevent global public bads such as money laundering or fisheries depletion.

Second, controlling corruption is itself a global public good, being largely nonrival and nonexcludable. If one nation or corporation desists from corrupt practices, benefits accrue to both those who contribute to this global public good and those who do not, strengthening the incentive to defect. Thus efforts to control international corruption are well described by the classic prisoner's dilemma: each nation or company would prefer that bribery stop but would face high costs of doing so if others continued to engage in corrupt practices. A coordinated exit from the corruption trap involves substantial commitment, monitoring, and enforcement problems.

Ultimately, the global public good of corruption control will be provided and durable only if the public demands it and is vigilant and empowered. Central to the process are attractive measures that are difficult to reverse, such as improving education, deepening democracy, and increasing transparency and access to information. Civil society has emerged as an effective partner of government and private actors in helping to overcome commitment problems and channeling dispersed interests. Through the commitment and support of members, governments, and institutions, Transparency International has contributed strongly to the global public good of corruption control—generating information about the deleterious effects of corruption, raising public awareness, and helping to place the issue firmly on domestic and international agendas.

Successfully confronting corruption requires both national and international initiatives, because in some countries national efforts on their own would be too weak and because international efforts would be poorly received without domestic grassroots support. This dual need is reflected in Transparency International's structure, which includes more than 80 national chapters that mobilize public support for anticorruption measures, including integrity pacts, and provide monitoring and vigilance.

Several other civil society organizations also work at the national grassroots level. For example, using information provision as its main tool, Global Witness emphasizes the link between the exploitation of natural resources—such as diamonds or forests—and conflicts or human rights violations. The National

Democratic Institute fights corruption by promoting democracy and government accountability (http://www.ndi.org). The Anti-corruption Gateway is a repository of information about combating corruption (http://www.nobribes.org). Similarly, the Uganda Debt Network endeavors to raise awareness among the general public of the need to call authorities to account for the allocation of funds from international loans or financial support (http://www.udn.or.ug). The network monitors schools and hospitals where official funds have been allocated, to see whether they are really receiving textbooks or medicines. The network enlists musicians and artists to promote its work with the public. Such initiatives are critical for continued improvement in governance.

At the international level Transparency International has helped actors make a coordinated exit from the prisoner's dilemma game by promoting the OECD antibribery convention and similar initiatives. By providing third-party oversight, credible civil society organizations can help overcome commitment problems and reassure participants that they are not alone in constraining corrupt practices. Only through a partnership among governments, private actors, and civil society organizations can government accountability be strengthened and corruption effectively curtailed. Such partnerships provide a tangible example of the crucial role civil society organizations might play in providing global public goods.

NOTES

1. McGuire and Olson (1996) show that a group or individual has an encompassing interest in providing public goods when the private returns exceed the cost of providing the goods, regardless of contributions by other beneficiaries.

2. World Bank (2000a) reports that "investigators from the Bank's Corruption and Fraud Investigations Unit as well as the Office of Business Ethics and Integrity were alerted to the activity through a call placed to the Bank's hotline for reporting fraud and corruption."

3. For the list of noncooperative countries and territories, see http://www1.oecd.org/fatf/NCCT_en.htm.

4. For a discussion of how corruption disproportionately affects poor people, see World Bank (2000b, p. 102).

5. For more on the Corruption Perceptions Index for 2001, see http://www.transparency.org/documents/cpi/2001/cpi2001.html.

6. For information on the signatories, see http://www.oecd.org/pdf/M00017000/M00017037.pdf.

7. For an update on implementation of the OECD antibribery convention, see Quinones (2001).

REFERENCES

Clinard, Marshall Barron. 1990. *Corporate Corruption: The Abuse of Power.* New York: Praeger.

Eigen-Zucchi, Christian. 2001. "The Measurement of Transactions Costs." Ph.D. diss. George Mason University, Department of Economics, Fairfax, Va. [http://eigen1. tripod.com/tpi.pdf].

FATF (Financial Action Task Force on Money Laundering). 1996. "The Forty Recommendations." Organisation for Economic Co-operation and Development, Paris. [http://www1.oecd.org/fatf/pdf/40Rec_en.pdf].

————. 2001. "Special Recommendations on Terrorist Financing," Organisation for Economic Co-operation and Development, Paris. [http://www1.oecd.org/fatf/ SRecsTF_en.htm].

Galtung, Fredrik. 2000. "A Global Network to Curb Corruption: The Experience of Transparency International." In Ann M. Florini, ed., *The Third Force: The Rise of Transnational Civil Society.* Washington, D.C.: Carnegie Endowment for International Peace.

Geo-JaJa, Macleans A., and Garth L. Mangum. 1999. "The Foreign Corrupt Practices Act's Consequences for U.S. Trade: The Nigerian Example." *Africa Economic Analysis* 27 (March). [http://www.afbis.com/analysis/corruption.htm].

Global Witness. 2000. "Conflict Diamonds: Possibilities for the Identification and Certification and Control of Diamonds." Briefing Document. London. [http:// www.globalwitness.org/campaigns/diamonds/downloads/conflict.pdf].

Gupta, Sanjeev, Hamid Davoodi, and Erwin Tiongson. 2000. "Corruption and the Provision of Health Care and Education Services." IMF Working Paper 00/116. International Monetary Fund, Washington, D.C.

Kaufmann, Daniel, Aart Kraay, and Pablo Zoido-Lobaton. 1999. "Governance Matters." Policy Research Working Paper 2196. World Bank, Development Research Group and World Bank Institute, Washington, D.C.

Kaul, Inge, Isabelle Grunberg, and Marc A. Stern, eds. 1999. *Global Public Goods: International Cooperation in the 21st Century.* New York: Oxford University Press.

Knack, Stephen, and Philip Keefer. 1995. "Institutions and Economic Performance: Cross-Country Tests Using Alternative Institutional Measures." *Economics and Politics* 7 (3): 207–27.

Lambsdorff, Johann Graf. 1998. "An Empirical Investigation of Bribery in International Trade." *European Journal of Development Research* 10 (1): 40–59.

————. 1999. "Corruption in Empirical Research: A Review." Working paper. Transparency International, Berlin.

————. 2002. "Making Corrupt Deals: Contracting in the Shadow of the Law." *Journal of Economic Behavior and Organization* 48 (3): 221–41.

Martin, Lisa. 1999. "The Political Economy of International Cooperation." In Inge Kaul, Isabelle Grunberg, and Marc A. Stern, eds., *Global Public Goods: International Cooperation in the 21st Century.* New York: Oxford University Press.

Mauro, Paolo. 1995. "Corruption and Growth." *Quarterly Journal of Economics* 110 (3): 681–712.

McGuire, Martin, and Mancur Olson. 1996. "The Economics of Autocracy and Majority Rule: The Invisible Hand and the Use of Force." *Journal of Economic Literature* 34 (March): 72–96.

Parker, Welcott. 1976. "Bribery in Foreign Lands: The Difference between Expedite and Suborn." *Vital Speeches,* 15 February, pp. 281–84.

Pujas, Veronique. 2000. "Corruption via Party Financing in France." Working paper prepared for a Transparency International workshop on corruption and political party funding, October, La Pietra, Italy. [http://www.transparency.org/working_papers/country/france_paper.html].

Quinones, Enery. 2001. "Implementing the Anti-Bribery Convention: An Update from the OECD." In Transparency International, *Global Corruption Report 2001.* Berlin. [http://www.globalcorruptionreport.org].

Richardson, Peter. 2001. "Corruption." In P. J. Simmons and Chantal de Jonge Oudraat, eds., *Managing Global Issues: Lessons Learned.* Washington, D.C.: Carnegie Endowment for International Peace.

Romeneski, Mark. 1982. "The FCPA of 1977: An Analysis of Its Impact and Future." *Boston College International and Comparative Law Review* 5 (2): 405–30.

Sandler, Todd. 1999. "Intergenerational Public Goods: Strategies, Efficiency and Institutions." In Inge Kaul, Isabelle Grunberg, and Marc A. Stern, eds., *Global Public Goods: International Cooperation in the 21st Century.* New York: Oxford University Press.

Transparency International. 2000. *Source Book 2000: Confronting Corruption—The Elements of a National Integrity System.* Berlin. [http://www.transparency.org/sourcebook].

———. 2001a. *Global Corruption Report 2001.* Berlin. [http://www.globalcorruptionreport.org].

———. 2001b. "The Integrity Pact (TI-IP): The Concept, the Model and the Present Applications: A Status Report." Berlin. [http://www.transparency.org/building_coalitions/integrity_pact/i_pact.pdf].

U.S. House of Representatives. 1977. *Unlawful Corporate Payments Act of 1977.* Conference Report. Washington, D.C. [http://www.usdoj.gov/criminal/fraud/fcpa/1977hse.htm].

Wei, Shang-Jin. 1997. "How Taxing Is Corruption on International Investors?" NBER Working Paper 6030. National Bureau of Economic Research, Cambridge, Mass.

World Bank. 2000a. "World Bank Investigation Reveals Three Staff Members and Swedish Firms Engaged in Corruption; Staff Members Fired, Funds to Be Reimbursed." Press release, 6 December. Media Division, Washington, D.C.

———. 2000b. *World Development Report 2000/2001: Attacking Poverty.* New York: Oxford University Press.

FURTHER READING

COMPILED BY MASHA BELIAEVA

Acocella, Nicola. 1998. "The Foundations of Economic Policy: Values and Techniques." Cambridge: Cambridge University Press.

Anderson, Jock. R. 1998. "Selected Policy Issues in International Agricultural Research: On Striving for International Public Goods in an Era of Donor Fatigue." *World Development* 26 (6): 1149–1161.

Arce M., Daniel G., and Todd Sandler. 2002. *Regional Public Goods: Typologies, Provision, Financing, and Development Assistance.* Stockholm: Almqvist & Wicksell International for the Expert Group on Development Issues, Swedish Ministry for Foreign Affairs.

Auerbach, Alan J., and Martin S. Feldstein. 1987. *Handbook of Public Economics.* Vol. 2. Amsterdam: North-Holland Publishing Company.

Barrett, Scott. 2001. "International Cooperation for Sale." *European Economic Review* 45: 1835–50.

Breton, Albert. 1965. "A Theory of Government Grants." *Canadian Journal of Economics and Political Science* 31 (2): 175–87.

———. 1996. *Competitive Governments: An Economic Theory of Politics and Public Finance.* Cambridge: Cambridge University Press.

Buchanan, James M., and Richard A. Musgrave. 1999. *Public Finance and Public Choice: Two Contrasting Visions of the State.* Cambridge, Mass.: MIT Press.

Carbone, Maurizio. 2002. "Global Public Goods: A New Frontier in Development Policy?" *ACP-EU Courier* 191: 38–40.

Cerny, Philip G. 1995. "Globalization and the Changing Logic of Collective Action." *International Organization* 49 (4): 595–625.

Chichilnisky, Graciela. 1997. "Development and Global Finance: The Case for an International Bank for Environmental Settlements." ODS Discussion Paper 10. United Nations Development Programme, Office of Development Studies, New York.

Cooper, Richard N. 1989. "International Cooperation in Public Health as a Prologue to Macroeconomic Cooperation." In Richard N. Cooper, Barry Eichengreen, C. Randall Henning, Gerald Holthan, and Robert D. Putnam, eds., *Can Nations Agree? Issues in International Economic Cooperation.* Washington, D.C.: Brookings Institution Press.

Cornes, Richard, and Todd Sandler. 1996. *The Theory of Externalities, Public Goods and Club Goods.* Cambridge: Cambridge University Press.

Cullis, John, and Philip Jones. 1998. *Public Finance and Public Choice: Alternative Perspectives.* New York: Oxford University Press.

Dalrymple, Dana G. 2001. "International Agricultural Research as a Global Public Good." Paper presented at the Warren E. Kronstad Commemorative Symposium, CIMMYT (International Maize and Wheat Improvement Center) Wheat Programme, 15–17 March, Ciudad Obregon, Sonara, Mexico.

Dasgupta, Partha, Karl-Goran Maler, and Alessandra Vercelli, eds. 1997. *The Economics of Transnational Commons.* New York: Oxford University Press.

Demsetz, Harold. 1970. "The Private Production of Public Goods." *Journal of Law and Economics* 13: 293–306.

———. 1993. "The Private Production of Public Goods, Once Again." *Critical Review* 7: 559–66.

Dixit, Avinash K. 1996. *The Making of Economic Policy: A Transaction-Cost Politics Perspectives.* Cambridge, Mass.: MIT Press.

Dodgson, Richard, Kelley Lee, and Nick Drager. 2002. "Global Health Governance: A Conceptual Review." Global Health Governance Discussion Paper 1. London School of Hygiene and Tropical Medicine, Centre on Global Change and Health, London.

Drache, Daniel, ed. 2001. *The Market vs. the Public Domain: After the Triumph (Governance and Change in the Global Era).* New York: Routledge.

Ferroni, Marco, and Ashoka Mody, eds. 2002. *International Public Goods: Incentives, Measurement, and Financing.* Washington, D.C.: Kluwer Academic Publishers and World Bank.

France Ministry of Foreign Affairs and Ministry of the Economy, Finance, and Industry. 2002. *Global Public Goods.* Paris.

Freeman, Phyllis, and Mark Miller. 2001. "Scientific Capacity Building to Improve Population Health: Knowledge as a Global Public Good." Prepared for the World Health Organization Commission on Macroeconomics and Health, Working Group 2: Global Public Goods for Health, Geneva. [http://www3.who.int/whosis/cmh/cmh_papers/e/pdf/wg2_paper03.pdf]

Graham, Carol. 1998. *Private Markets for Public Goods: Raising the Stakes in Economic Reform.* Washington, D.C: Brookings Institution Press.

Held, David, Anthony McGrew, David Goldblatt, and Jonathan Perraton. 1999. *Global Transformations: Politics, Economics and Culture.* Stanford, Calif.: Stanford University Press.

Hettne, Bjorn, Andras Inotai, and Osvaldo Sunkel. 1999. *Globalism and the New Regionalism.* Basingstoke, U.K.: Macmillan.

Hirshleifer, Jack. 1983. "From Weakest-Link to Best-Shot: The Voluntary Provision of Public Goods." *Public Choice* 41: 371–86.

IDRC (International Development Research Center). 2001. *Global Public Goods for Health: Making Globalization Work to Improve the Health of the Poor.* Report on the IDRC, Canadian International Development Agency, Health Canada, and World Health Organization Workshop on Global Public Goods for Health, 4–6 June, Ottawa, Canada.

Jha, Raghbendra. 1998. *Modern Public Economics.* London: Routledge.

Kanbur, Ravi. 2001. "Cross-Border Externalities, International Public Goods and Their Implications for Aid Agencies." Department of Economics, Cornell University, Ithaca, N.Y. [http://www.people.cornell.edu/pages/sk145/]

Kanbur, Ravi, Todd Sandler, and Kevin Morrison. 1999. "The Future of Development Assistance: Common Pools and International Public Goods." Policy Essay 25. Overseas Development Council, Washington, D.C.

Kapur, Devesh. 2002. "The Common Pool Dilemma of Global Public Goods: Lessons from the World Bank's Net Income and Reserves." *World Development* 30 (3): 337–54.

Kaul, Inge, Isabelle Grunberg, and Marc A. Stern. 1999. *Global Public Goods: International Cooperation in the 21st Century.* New York: Oxford University Press.

Kaul, Inge, Katell Le Goulven, and Mirjam Schnupf. 2002. "Global Public Goods Financing: New Tools for New Challenges." United Nations Development Programme, Office of Development Studies, New York.

Kindleberger, Charles P. 1986. "International Public Goods without International Government." *American Economic Review* 76 (1): 1–13.

Markowska, Agnieszka, and Tomasz Zylicz. 1999. "Costing an International Public Good: The Case of the Baltic Sea." *Ecological Economics* 30: 301–16.

Mendez, Ruben. 1992. *International Public Finance.* New York: Oxford University Press.

———. 1993. *The Provision and Financing of Universal Public Goods.* London: London School of Economics and Political Science, Centre for the Study of Global Governance.

Mills, Anne. 2001. "Technology and Science as Global Public Goods: Tackling Priority Diseases of Poor Countries." Paper presented at the Annual Bank Conference on Development Economics–Europe, Paris, June 25–26.

Mueller, Dennis C. 1989. *Public Choice II.* Cambridge: Cambridge University Press.

Musgrave, Richard A., and Peggy B. Musgrave. 1989. *Public Finance in Theory and Practice.* 5th ed. New York: McGraw-Hill.

Nordhaus, William D. 1994. *Managing the Global Commons.* Cambridge, Mass.: MIT Press.

North, Douglass C. 1981. *Structure and Change in Economic History.* New York: W. W. Norton.

————. 1990. *Institutions, Institutional Change, and Economic Performance.* Cambridge: Cambridge University Press.

Nye, Joseph S. Jr. 2002. *The Paradox of American Power: Why the World's Only Superpower Can't Go It Alone.* New York: Oxford University Press.

Nye, Joseph S. Jr., and John Donahue, eds. 2000. *Governance in a Globalizing World.* Washington, D.C.: Brookings Institution Press.

Oates, Wallace E. 1972. *Fiscal Federalism.* New York: Harcourt Brace Jovanovich.

————. 1999. "An Essay on Fiscal Federalism." *Journal of Economic Literature* 37 (September): 1120–49.

Office of Development Studies. 2001. *Global Public Goods: Taking the Concept Forward.* Discussion Paper 17. New York: United Nations Development Programme.

Olson, Mancur. 1965. *The Logic of Collective Action: Public Goods and the Theory of Groups.* Cambridge, Mass.: Harvard University Press.

Ostrom, Elinor. 1990. *Governing the Commons: The Evolution of Institutions for Collective Action.* Cambridge: Cambridge University Press.

Overseas Development Institute. 2001. "Transboundary Water Management as an International Public Good." Produced for the Sweden Ministry of Foreign Affairs, Stockholm, Sweden.

Papandreou, Andreas A. 1998. *Externality and Institutions.* Oxford: Clarendon Press.

Pearce, David, and Edward B. Barbier. 2000. *Blueprint for a Sustainable Economy.* London: Earthscan.

Reinicke, Wolfgang. 1998. *Global Public Policy: Governing without Government?* Washington, D.C.: Brookings Institution Press.

Reinicke, Wolfgang, and Francis Deng. 2000. *Critical Choices: The United Nations Networks and the Future of Global Governance.* Ottawa: International Development Research Center.

Rodrik, Dani. 1999. "The New Global Economy and Developing Countries: Making Openness Work." Policy Essay 24. Overseas Development Council, Washington, D.C.

————. 2001. "The Global Governance of Trade: As If Development Really Mattered." Background paper to the United Nations Development Programme Project on Trade and Sustainable Human Development, New York.

Rosen, Harvey. 1999. *Public Finance.* 5th ed. Boston: Irwin/McGraw-Hill.

Sachs, Jeffrey D. 2000. "A New Framework for Globalization." In Roger B. Porter, Pierre Suavé, Arvind Subramanian, and Americo Beviglia Zampetti, eds., *Efficiency, Equity, Legitimacy: The Multilateral Trading System at the Millennium.* Washington, D.C.: Brookings Institution Press.

Samuelson, Paul A. 1954. "The Pure Theory of Public Expenditure." *Review of Economics and Statistics* 36 (November): 387–89.

Samuelson Paul A., and William D. Nordhaus. 2001. *Economics*. 17th ed. New York: McGraw-Hill.

Sandler, Todd. 1982. "A Theory of Intergenerational Clubs." *Economic Inquiry* 20 (2): 191–208.

———. 1998. "Global and Regional Public Goods: A Prognosis for Collective Action." *Fiscal Studies* 19 (3): 221–47.

Sandmo, Agnar. 2000. *The Public Economics of the Environment*. Oxford: Oxford University Press.

Simmons, P. J., and Chantal de Jonge Oudraat, eds. 2001. *Managing Global Issues: Lessons Learned*. Washington, D.C.: Carnegie Endowment for International Peace.

Stålgren, Patrik. 2000. "Regional Public Goods and the Future of International Development Co-operation: A Review of the Literature on Regional Public Goods." Working Paper 2000:2. Sweden Ministry for Foreign Affairs, Stockholm.

Stiglitz, Joseph E. 1995. "The Theory of International Public Goods and the Architecture of International Organizations." Background Paper 7. United Nations, Department of Economics and Social Information and Policy Analysis, New York.

———. 2000. *Economics of the Public Sector*. New York: W. W. Norton.

Sweden Ministry for Foreign Affairs. 2001. "Financing and Providing Global Public Goods: Expectations and Prospects." Prepared by Keith Bezanson and Francisco Sagasti on behalf of the Sussex University Institute of Development Studies. Stockholm.

Sweden Parliamentary Commission on Swedish Policy for Global Development. 2002. *Towards a More Equitable World Free from Poverty*. Swedish Government Official Report SOU 2001:96. Stockholm. Executive summary available in English at http://www.globkom.net/betankande/summary.pdf.

Tiebout, Charles M. 1956. "A Pure Theory of Local Expenditures." *Journal of Political Economy* 64 (October): 416–24.

Tubiana, Laurence. 2000. *Environnement et développement: L'enjeu pour la France*. Rapport au Premier Ministre. Paris: La Documentation Française.

Tubiana, Laurence, and Charles Perrings. 2000. "Global Governance for Environment: Equity and Efficiency." In Joseph E. Stiglitz and Pierre-Alain Muet, eds., *Governance, Equity, and Global Markets: The Annual Bank Conference on Development Economics, Europe*. Oxford: Oxford University Press.

Underdal, Arild, and Oran R. Young. Forthcoming. *Regime Consequences: Methodological Challenges and Research Strategies*. Dordrecht, the Netherlands: Kluwer Academic Publishers.

UN (United Nations). 2001. *Report of the High-level Panel on Financing for Development* [also known as the "Zedillo Report"]. Document A/55/1000. New York.

Woodward, David, Nick Drager, Robert Beaglehole, and Debra Lipson. 2001. "Globalization and Health: A Framework for Analysis and Action." *Bulletin of the World Health Organization* 79 (9): 875–81.

World Bank. 2001a. *Global Development Finance: Building Coalitions for Effective Development Finance.* Washington, D.C.

———. 2001b. *The World Bank and Global Public Policies and Programs: An Evaluation Strategy.* Washington, D.C.

Young, Oran. 1999. *Governance in World Affairs.* Ithaca, N.Y.: Cornell University Press.

GLOSSARY

club good: an intermediate case between a pure public good and a pure private good. With a club good exclusion is feasible, but the optimal size of the club is generally larger than one person. An example is a film shown in a theater, where it is possible for the good to be priced (exclusion can be practiced) and for a number of people to share the good without diminishing each other's consumption of it. The optimal size of a club is that which maximizes the group's joint utility.

economies of scale: when increased output lowers a product's average cost.

economies of scope: when producing two products together is cheaper than producing them separately.

externality: when an individual, firm, country, or other entity takes an action but does not bear all its costs (negative externalities) or receive all its benefits (positive externalities).

final public good: like private goods, public goods can be differentiated by the stages of their production process. Final public goods are those desired for consumption, such as clean air, efficient markets, and peace and security. Producing final public goods often requires inputs of many private goods, public goods, or both. Public goods that contribute to the production of a final public good are called intermediate public goods. For example, achieving clean air or a stable climate requires international agreements (such as the Kyoto Protocol) and national regimes (such as for sustainable energy or forest management). Sometimes a public good can be final from one perspective and intermediate from another. Consider knowledge. People desire some elements of knowledge for their own sake. Other elements (such as medical knowledge) may be used in the production of vaccines (which are private goods), with the goal of producing a final public good—say, disease control or, more generally, enhanced healthy living conditions.

Definitions are adapted from Joseph E. Stiglitz's *Economics,* second edition (New York: W. W. Norton, 1997); from *The MIT Dictionary of Modern Economics,* fourth edition (Cambridge, Mass.: MIT Press, 1992); and from Richard Cornes and Todd Sandler's *The Theory of Externalities, Public Goods and Club Goods,* second edition (New York: Cambridge University Press, 1996). The definition of *public good* reflects the ideas presented in Kaul and Mendoza (in this volume).

free rider: someone who enjoys the benefits of a good without paying for it. Because it is difficult to keep people from using pure public goods, those who benefit from them have an incentive to avoid paying for them.

global public good: a public good with benefits that are strongly universal in terms of countries (covering more than one group of countries), people (accruing to several, preferably all, population groups), and generations (extending to both current and future generations, or at least meeting the needs of current generations without foreclosing development options for future generations).

intermediate public good: see final public good.

market failure: when a market fails to achieve economic efficiency.

moral hazard: the tendency for people who purchase or are provided with insurance to be less cautious because they have less reason to avoid what they are insured against.

nonexcludable: describes benefits that are available to all people once a good is provided. By contrast, a good's benefits are excludable if they can be withheld by the owner or provider. Firework displays, pollution control devices, and street lighting yield nonexcludable benefits because once they are provided, it is difficult if not impossible to exclude people from enjoying their benefits.

nonrival: when a good can be consumed by one person without detracting from the consumption opportunities available to others. Sunsets are nonrival (or indivisible) when views are unobstructed.

Pareto efficient: when no rearrangement of a resource allocation can make anyone better off without making someone else worse off.

prisoner's dilemma: when the independent pursuit of self-interest by two parties makes both worse off.

provision of public goods: typically consists of two separate but intertwined processes. The first is the political process, which involves making decisions about which public goods to produce, how much of them to produce, how to shape them, and at what net cost and benefit to whom. The second is the production process, which involves bringing together contributions from all concerned actor groups, sectors, and countries. Financing issues should be considered in both parts of the provision process because they may critically influence actors' incentives to cooperate.

public good: goods with nonrival consumption and nonexcludable benefits have a strong potential for publicness. For example, it generally costs little or nothing to give an additional person access to statistical data. Yet only some data are in the public domain—available for all people to use free of charge. Other data are private and must be purchased. Thus it is important to distinguish between a good's potential and de facto publicness. Only de facto public goods are actually available for all people to consume.

transaction costs: the extra costs (beyond the price of the purchase) of conducting a transaction, whether in terms of money, time, or inconvenience.

ABOUT THE CONTRIBUTORS

CECILIA ALBIN
Cecilia Albin is a lecturer at the University of Reading and director of the Centre for International Security and Non-Proliferation at the same university, in the United Kingdom. Previously she was deputy director of the Global Security Programme at the University of Cambridge. A specialist on international negotiation, conflict resolution, and equity issues, Albin's latest book is *Justice and Fairness in International Negotiation* (Cambridge University Press, 2001).

DYNA ARHIN-TENKORANG
Dyna Arhin-Tenkorang is at the London School of Hygiene and Tropical Medicine, in the United Kingdom, and recently served as senior economist for the World Health Organization's Commission on Macroeconomics and Health. Her research focuses on equity in the health sectors of developing countries, including insurance financing. Arhin-Tenkorang holds a Ph.D. from the London School of Economics and Political Science.

SCOTT BARRETT
Scott Barrett is professor in the Paul H. Nitze School of Advanced International Studies at Johns Hopkins University, in the United States. Previously he served on the faculty of the London School of Economics. Barrett is the author of *Environment and Statecraft* (Oxford University Press, 2002), and was educated in Canada, the United Kingdom, and the United States.

ODILE BLANCHARD
Odile Blanchard is assistant professor at the University of Grenoble, in France, as well as researcher in the Institute of Energy Policy and Economics at the same university. Until the mid-1990s her research centered on energy demand and modeling in developing countries; it now focuses on economic issues related to climate change. Her current research analyzes climate change mitigation policies and their effects on international equity and economic efficiency. Blanchard holds a Ph.D. from the University of Grenoble.

ARIEL BUIRA
Ariel Buira is a senior member of Saint Antony's College at Oxford University, in the United Kingdom. Previously he held various positions at the Inter-

national Monetary Fund, including economist (1970–75), executive director representing Mexico (1978–82), and international director (1982–93). During 1994–97 he was a member of the board of governors of the Bank of Mexico, and during 1998–2001 he was Mexico's ambassador to Greece. In 2002 he served as general coordinator and special envoy of the Mexican government for the UN Conference on Financing for Development. Buira has written extensively on macroeconomics and international monetary issues.

RENÉ CASTRO

René Castro is visiting professor at INCAE (Central-American Business Administration Institute) and a consultant for the United Nations Development Programme, working in Latin America. During 1994–98 he was Costa Rica's minister of mining, environment, and energy, heading the country's delegations to the UN conventions on climate change, biodiversity, and protection of the ozone layer. Before that he was vice minister of the interior, national director of transportation, and president of the municipal city council of San José. Previously he worked for the private sector in Central America and various development organizations. Castro holds a Ph.D. from Harvard University.

PAMELA CHASEK

Pamela Chasek is visiting assistant professor and director of international studies at Manhattan College, in New York City. She is also cofounder and editor of the International Institute for Sustainable Development's *Earth Negotiations Bulletin,* which reports on UN environment and development negotiations. Chasek holds a Ph.D. from the Paul H. Nitze School of Advanced International Studies at Johns Hopkins University.

PEDRO CONCEIÇÃO

Pedro Conceição is senior policy analyst and deputy director, Office of Development Studies at the United Nations Development Programme. Previously he was professor at the Technical University of Lisbon, in Portugal, and a researcher at the Center for Innovation, Technology, and Policy Research at the same university. Conceição holds a Ph.D. from the Lyndon B. Johnson School of Public Affairs at the University of Texas at Austin.

SARAH CORDERO

Sarah Cordero was academic director of the International Program on Project Evaluation at INCAE (Central-American Business Administration Institute) and is currently a Ph.D. candidate at the Massachusetts Institute of Technology. She is also the coauthor of, most recently, *Project Evaluation and Environmental Impact Assessment* (1995) and *Environmental Impact Evaluation and Sustainability of Development* (1998).

CARLOS M. CORREA
Carlos M. Correa is director of the Center for Interdisciplinary Studies on Industrial Property and Economics Law, of the Master Program on Science and Technology Policy and Management, and of the Post-graduate Program on Intellectual Property at the University of Buenos Aires, in Argentina. He is also a member of the Commission on Intellectual Property Rights, established by the U.K. Department for International Development, and has consulted for several regional and international organizations. In addition, Correa has written several books and articles on technology and intellectual property. He holds a Ph.D. from the University of Buenos Aires.

PATRICK CRIQUI
Patrick Criqui is a senior researcher in the Institute of Energy Policy and Economics at the University of Grenoble, in France, and teaches at the Université Pierre Mendès-France, in Grenoble, and at the École Polytechnique Fédérale de Lausanne, in Switzerland. He has more than 20 years of experience in research on international energy economics and modeling and is responsible for the Energy-Environment Group at the Institute of Energy Policy and Economics. Criqui has also consulted for the TOTAL oil company (1992–93) and was rapporteur of the French Planning Agency's *Energy 2010–2020* Study Group. He holds a doctorate from the University of Grenoble.

MEGHNAD DESAI
Meghnad Desai, named Lord Desai of St Clement Danes in 1991, is professor of economics at the London School of Economics and Political Science, where he is also director of the Centre for the Study of Global Governance. His recent publications include "Globalisation: Neither Ideology Nor Utopia" (*Cambridge Review of International Affairs,* autumn/winter 2000) and *Marx's Revenge: The Resurgence of Capitalism and the Death of Statist Socialism* (Verso, 2002). Desai holds a Ph.D. from the University of Pennsylvania.

MICHAEL EDWARDS
Michael Edwards is director of governance and civil society for the Ford Foundation, in New York City. Previously he was senior civil society specialist at the World Bank, and before that spent 15 years working for nongovernmental organizations focused on international relief and development, including Oxfam U.K. (as regional director for Southern Africa) and Save the Children U.K. (as director of research, evaluation, and advocacy). Recent publications by Edwards include *Global Citizen Action* (Lynne Rienner, 2001) and *Future Positive* (Earthscan, 2000).

PETER EIGEN

Peter Eigen is founder and chair of Transparency International, an international nongovernmental organization fighting corruption. He previously worked at the World Bank, focusing on Africa and Latin America. He has undertaken research and taught at Frankfurt University, Harvard University, Johns Hopkins University, and Berlin University, is a visiting scholar at the Carnegie Endowment for Democracy, and has written numerous publications on global governance issues—especially corruption. Eigen holds an honorary doctorate from the Open University, in the United Kingdom, and is a member of advisory groups to the World Movement for Democracy, World Trade Organization, and Harvard University Center for International Development. He holds a doctorate from Frankfurt University.

CHRISTIAN EIGEN-ZUCCHI

Christian Eigen-Zucchi is a consultant in the Development Economics Research Group at the World Bank, working on *World Development Report 2003: Sustainable Development in a Dynamic Economy*. He has taught at George Mason University, in the United States, and published several papers on public choice, growth, and globalization. Eigen holds a Ph.D. from George Mason University.

MADHAV GADGIL

Madhav Gadgil is at the Indian Institute of Science, where he established an interdisciplinary school of ecological research. Previously he was distinguished visiting lecturer at the University of California at Berkeley and visiting professor at Stanford University, in the United States. In addition, he is a fellow of the Indian National Science Academy and a foreign associate of the U.S. National Academy of Sciences, and has served as a member of the Science Advisory Council to the prime minister of India and as chair of the Science and Technology Advisory Panel of the Global Environment Facility. Gadgil also works with environmental nongovernmental organizations and writes a column on natural history for a popular Indian newspaper. He holds a Ph.D. from Harvard University.

STEPHANY GRIFFITH-JONES

Stephany Griffith-Jones is a professorial fellow in the Institute of Development Studies at the University of Sussex, in the United Kingdom. She has been a senior consultant to numerous international organizations and national governments, including the World Bank, European Commission, Inter-American Development Bank, president of Brazil, and Czech Central Bank. In 2000 she served as deputy director of international finance at the

Commonwealth Secretariat. Griffith-Jones holds a Ph.D. from the University of Cambridge and has written extensively on finance and macroeconomic policy issues.

DAVID HELD

David Held is Graham Wallas Professor of Political Science at the London School of Economics and Political Science. He is the author of many books, including *Democracy and the Global Order: From the Modern State to Cosmopolitan Governance* (Polity Press, 1995), *Models of Democracy,* second edition (Polity Press, 1996), and, as coauthor, *Global Transformations: Politics, Economics and Culture* (Polity Press, 1999). Held is currently writing *Cosmopolitanism: Globalization Tamed* (scheduled for release in 2003).

INGE KAUL

Inge Kaul is director of the Office of Development Studies at the United Nations Development Programme (UNDP). During 1990–95 she was director of UNDP's Human Development Report Office, where she coordinated teams of authors producing the annual *Human Development Report.* Before that she held other senior policy positions at the UNDP. Kaul has extensive research experience in developing countries and has written numerous publications and reports on development finance and aid.

ALBAN KITOUS

Alban Kitous is a researcher in the Institute of Energy Policy and Economics at the University of Grenoble, in France. His work focuses on modeling trading schemes for international emission permits. Previously he worked for the European Commission (Directorate-General Environment) and for the Belgium Federal Planning Agency, helping to prepare for the sixth and seventh sessions of the conference of the parties to the UN Framework Convention on Climate Change. Kitous has also helped develop systems for reducing international emissions based on the targets set in the Kyoto Protocol.

MICHAEL KREMER

Michael Kremer is professor of economics at Harvard University and a senior fellow at the Brookings Institution. He is a recipient of a MacArthur "genius" fellowship and a Presidential Early Career Award for Scientists and Engineers. His recent research includes evaluations of sovereign debt, of health and education programs in developing countries, and of incentives for research and development on malaria, tuberculosis, HIV/AIDS, and other diseases that hit developing countries especially hard. Kremer holds a Ph.D. from Harvard University.

KATELL LE GOULVEN

Katell Le Goulven is a policy analyst in the Office of Development Studies at the United Nations Development Programme. Previously she was a research fellow in the Economics Department at the Ecole Nationale Supérieure Agronomique de Montpellier, in France, and consultant for Solagral, a French nongovernmental organization. She has researched and published articles on microeconomics, institutional economics, agricultural economics, and international political economy. Le Goulven holds a Ph.D. from the Ecole Nationale Supérieure Agronomique de Montpellier and the University of Montpellier.

ANTHONY MCGREW

Anthony McGrew is professor of international relations at the University of Southampton, in the United Kingdom. His research interests include globalization and global governance, with a focus on their implications for state capacity, democracy, international relations theory, and U.S. foreign policy. McGrew's recent publications include *Global Transformations* (Polity Press, 1999), *Governing the Global Polity: From Government to Global Governance* (Polity Press, scheduled for release in 2002), and *Globalization/Anti-Globalization* (scheduled for release in 2002).

LYLA MEHTA

Lyla Mehta is a sociologist and research fellow in the Institute of Development Studies at the University of Sussex, in the United Kingdom. She has written extensively on dams and on water, gender, and environmental issues. Mehta holds a doctorate from the University of Sussex.

RONALD U. MENDOZA

Ronald U. Mendoza is the policy analyst for international trade and finance in the Office of Development Studies at the United Nations Development Programme. Previously he performed research for and served as a consultant to, among others, the Federal Reserve Bank of Boston, state of New Hampshire, Economist Intelligence Unit, and several nongovernmental organizations in Manila, the Philippines. Mendoza holds graduate degrees from Fordham University and Harvard University.

CHARLES PERRINGS

Charles Perrings is professor of environmental economics and environmental management at the University of York, in the United Kingdom; president-elect of the International Society for Ecological Economics; and editor of the journal *Environment and Development Economics* (Cambridge University Press). In the past he has been a professor at the University of California at

Riverside and at the University of Botswana, director of the Beijer Institute's Biodiversity Programme at the Royal Swedish Academy of Science, and a members of the Royal Society's environment committee. Perrings' research interests include biodiversity, modeling of dynamical ecological-economic systems, management of environmental public goods under uncertain conditions, and environmental implications of economic development.

LAVANYA RAJAMANI

Lavanya Rajamani is a junior research fellow in public international law at Worcester College, at Oxford University, and a freelance project director for the Global Environment and Trade Study, sponsored by the Yale University Center for Environmental Law and Policy. She also teaches international law and conducts research on international environmental law, focusing on interactions between trade and the environment and on laws related to international climate change. Until recently Rajamani worked at the Foundation for International Environmental Law and Development, in London, and among other activities provided legal support services to the Alliance of Small Island States.

TODD SANDLER

Todd Sandler is Robert R. and Katheryn A. Dockson Chair of International Relations and Economics at the University of Southern California at Los Angeles. He is the author of *Economic Concepts for the Social Sciences, Global Challenges: An Approach to Environmental, Political, and Economic Problems,* and *Collective Action: Theory and Applications;* and the co-author of *The Theory of Externalities, Public Goods, and Club Goods,* second edition. His articles have appeared in the *Journal of Economic Literature, American Economic Review, American Political Science Review, Quarterly Journal of Economics, Journal of Economic Theory,* and elsewhere. In addition, Sandler has worked for a variety of national and international entities, including the Overseas Development Council in Washington D.C., Swedish Ministry for Foreign Affairs, U.S. Department of Defense, and World Bank.

AGNAR SANDMO

Agnar Sandmo is professor of economics at the Norwegian School of Economics and Business Administration. He is former president of the European Economic Association and has held a number of visiting appointments at foreign universities. His main fields of research have been public economics and the economics of uncertainty. Within public economics he has written on theories of taxation and public goods as well as on the use of theory to understand the economics of the welfare state. Much of Sandmo's recent work has involved the intersection between public and environmental economics.

LAURENT VIGUIER

Laurent Viguier is a research fellow in the Department of Management Studies at the University of Geneva, in Switzerland. Previously he was a researcher in the Institute of Energy Policy and Economics at the University of Grenoble, in France, and a visiting fellow in the Joint Program on the Science and Policy of Global Change at the Massachusetts Institute of Technology. Viguier holds a Ph.D. from the University of Grenoble.

SIMON ZADEK

Simon Zadek is chief executive of the Institute of Social and Ethical AccountAbility, an international professional institute promoting social and ethical accountability within organizations. He has worked as an adviser, mentor, and external assuror for corporations in Africa, North and South America, and Europe, as well as for national and international public institutions and civil society organizations. He has written many publications on corporate accountability, most recently *The Civil Corporation: The New Economy of Corporate Citizenship* (Earthscan, 2001).

INDEX

Aaronson, Susan, 208

Abatement costs: and emission allowances, 284–85; and enforcement, 323; under no-trading scenario, 293, 294t–295t; with trading allowed, 293–98

Abbott, Frederick M., 499

Abel-Smith, Brian, 509n8

Ability to contribute argument, 242n12

Abuja Declaration, 509n7

Access: to communications network, 205, 348; to energy, 517; to environmental goods, 543; to medicines, 203, 423n3, 499; to political communities, 194; and publicness, 88–89; to technologies, 474; types of, 100t; to venue, 272; to water, 556–75

Accountability, 30–32; and democracy, 192, 194; desire for, 78; of global public policy partnerships, 51; IMF and, 225–26, 232, 235; nonstate actors and, 205, 209, 211–14; reconsideration of, 185

Acharya, Arnab, 490, 495

Acocella, Nicola, 105n5

Action, 13–15

Action TB, 508

Active metabolites, 418, 425n18

Actors: groups of, spanning, 6, 47–52

Adams, William M., 558

Addison, John, 414

Africa: antimicrobial resistance in, 495; and CDM, 254; HIV/AIDS in, 492, 494; IMF and, 233; regionalism in, 188; sub-Saharan, TRIPS agreement and, 465t, 466

African Centre for Technology Studies, 543

Agarwal, Anil, 300n2

Agencies: aid, 378; enmeshment of public and private, 189; multilateral, characteristics of, 388–89; and provision of global public goods, 63; single-issue, 389

Agenda 21, 217, 363n28

Agendas: active involvement with, 264; for aid versus financing, 358–59; fairness and, 270; for financial reform, 446–48; on health care, 496–98; nonstate actors and, 206

Agénor, Pierre-Richard, 436

Aggregation technologies, 134–36, 359n1; refining concept of, 92–93; transnational public goods by, supply prognoses for, 140–42, 141t

Agreements: for biodiversity conservation, 542; fostering, 44–45; and global politics, 188; governments and, 29; legally binding, trend toward, 351; nonstate actors and, 206; and second generation partnerships, 394; strengthening of, 247t, 249–50

Agreement to Promote Compliance with International Conservation and Management Measures by Fishing Vessels on the High Seas, 325

Aharonian, Greg, 424n8

Aid, 333t; agencies, 378; cancellation of, 345–46; and club goods, 148; versus financing for global public goods, 5, 36, 39, 329–30, 336–37, 337t, 356; for health care, 486–87; versus lump-sum transfers, 126; rationale for, 330, 358; recommendations for disentangling from financing, 357–59

Aid fatigue, 39, 582

Albin, Cecilia, 263–79, 607

Algiers, Charter of, 55n10

Allen, Mark, 353

Alliance building, 257; for financial reform, 447–48; new realities and, 259–60

Alliance of Small Island States (AOSIS), 254–55

Allocation: definition of, 330; versus distribution, 38–39; financing as, 36; international component of, 40–41, 344–56; model of, assumptions for, 114–16; new body for, 331; policy princi-